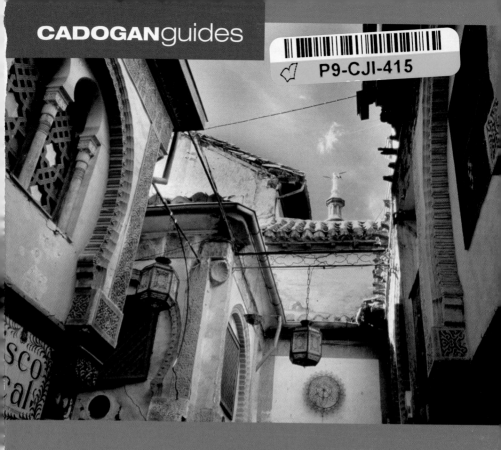

ANDALUCÍA

*'There are a few spots around the Mediterranean
where the presence of past glories becomes almost tangible,
a mixture of mythic antiquity, lost power and dissipated energy
that broods over a place like a ghost.'*

Dana Facaros & Michael Pauls

About the Guide

The **full-colour introduction** gives the authors' overview of the country, together with suggested **itineraries** and a regional **'where to go' map** and **feature** to help you plan your trip.

Illuminating and entertaining **cultural chapters** on local history, art, architecture, food, wine, nature and everyday life give you a rich flavour of the country.

Planning Your Trip starts with the basics of when to go, getting there and getting around, coupled with other useful information, including a section for disabled travellers. The **Practical A–Z** deals with all the **essential information** and **contact details** that you may need while you are away.

The **regional chapters** are arranged in a loose touring order, with plenty of public transport and driving information. The author's top **'Don't Miss'** ✪ **sights** are highlighted at the start of each chapter.

A **language and pronunciation guide**, a **glossary** of cultural terms, ideas for **further reading** and a comprehensive **index** can be found at the end of the book.

Although everything we list in this guide is **personally recommended**, our authors inevitably have their own favourite places to eat and stay. Whenever you see this **Author's Choice** ★ icon beside a listing, you will know that it is a little bit out of the ordinary.

Hotel Price Guide (*see also* p.84)

Luxury	€€€€€	€180 and above
Very Expensive	€€€€	€130–180
Expensive	€€€	€80–130
Moderate	€€	€50–80
Inexpensive	€	under €50

Restaurant Price Guide (*see also* p.91)

Expensive	€€€	€40 and above
Moderate	€€	€20–40
Inexpensive	€	under €20

About the Authors

Dana Facaros and Michael Pauls have written over 30 books for Cadogan Guides. They have lived all over Europe with their son and daughter, and are currently ensconced in a old farmhouse in southwestern France with a large collection of tame and wild animals.

8th Edition published 2008

01 INTRODUCING ANDALUCÍA

There is a story about haughty Queen Isabel, so proud of her conquest of the godless Moors of Andalucía, that sums up this region's sad history. The Moors, known as being lovers of art and poetry, were also the great architects of water, making the dry hills of the south into lush fields and gardens; Spanish folk tales often speak of them almost as sorcerers. During the campaigns against Granada, Isabel found herself lodging at the Alcázar of Córdoba, where an old Moorish water wheel in the Guadalquivir churned up water for the pools and fountains of the Alcázar gardens. After a few nights Isabel ordered that it be dismantled – it disturbed her sleep.

The ghost of Islamic al-Andalus still haunts the south, and a more graceful and delicate spirit could not be desired. In the gardens and palaces, and in the white villages, this great, lost civilization is a separate reality that shines through centuries of Spanish veneer. And what of the new Andalucía, after its centuries of trouble, of oppression and inquisitions, expulsions, poverty and emigration? It's looking pretty well, thank you, with its exuberant life and culture, and a delightful, fun-loving population of generally sane and friendly people, as much of an attraction as the land itself. Andalucía is a minefield of unexploded stereotypes: sequined matadors and strumming guitars, torrid flamenco and hot-blooded Gypsies, orange blossom and jasmine. They may be hard to avoid, but then again, why try? Few regions of Europe have been blessed with such stereotypes. Visitors never weary of them, and the Andalucíans certainly don't either; they cultivate and polish them with the greatest of care.

Previous page: Granada

Opposite page: Seville oranges; wall tiles, Alhambra, Granada, pp.289–96

Above, from top: Bridge, Ronda, p.263; church, El Rocío, p.190

*Opposite page:
Alhambra, Granada,
pp.289–96*

*Above: Window, white
village, Las Alpujarras,
pp.306–309*

Today, with its green and white flag flying proudly on every public building, autonomous, democratic Andalucía may have the chance to rediscover itself. With a fifth of Spain's population, its biggest tourist industry and potentially its richest agriculture, it holds great promise for the future. And as the part of Spain with the longest and most brilliant artistic heritage – not only from the Moors, but from the troubled, creative, post-Reconquista Andalucía that has given Spain Velázquez, García Lorca, de Falla and Picasso – the region may find it still has the resources once more to become the leader in Spain's cultural life.

For its size, the region contains a remarkable diversity of land-scapes – from Spain's highest mountains to endless rolling hills covered with olive trees, Europe's biggest marshland reserve and even some patches of desert. And no other part of Spain can offer so many interesting large cities. Andalucía is a world unto itself; it has as many delights to offer as you have time to spend.

*Above: Castillo de
Sotomayor,
Belalcázar, p.154*

*Below: Jerezano horses,
Jerez de la Frontera,
p.206; Arabic script
decoration, Alhambra,
Granada, pp.289–96*

Where to Go

The whimsical charms of Andalucía's capital city, **Sevilla**, with its colourful *barrios* and great monuments, are the primary subject of the first chapter, with side-steps into nearby Roman Itálica, Moorish Carmona, and Estepa with its Baroque showpieces.

From Sevilla we head up the long valley of the Río Guadalquivir into the heart of Andalucía and the provinces of **Córdoba and Jaén**. Flanked by the broad spine of the Sierra Morena to the north (famous for good hunting and cured hams), and a sea of sunflowers and olive groves to the south, the river is dotted with fine *andaluz* towns, from the citadel of Córdoba itself (and its remarkable Mezquita) to neatly clipped Baeza and Úbeda, with their unrivalled ensembles of Renaissance architecture.

For the next chapter, **Huelva, Cádiz and Gibraltar**, we move to the Costa de la Luz, the less-developed western flank of Andalucía's famous coastline. Inland, through forests of holm oak and cork, lie hidden the little-visited villages of the Sierra de Aracena – an easy day out from Huelva by car. Heading on down the coast past Las Marismas, Europe's greatest marshland wildlife reserve, we come to the hundred shades of Cádiz, Europe's oldest city (or so it claims). The province is packed with diversions, from the *bodegas* of Jerez – synonymous with sherry – to the moist microclimate of the Sierra de Grazalema, home to golden eagles and species of pre-Ice Age flora. We also offer a taste of North Africa proper, with an excursion across the Straits from Algeciras. Finally, from the smoky souks of Tangier we hop back across eight miles of water for the ultimate culture shock: pie and mash and red phone boxes in Gibraltar, that peculiar British enclave at the southern tip of Europe.

The Mediterranean's biggest playground, **Málaga and the Costa del Sol** is the one part of Andalucía that needs little introduction. But as well as conveying the true excitement (or horror, depending on your temperament) of this adrenaline-charged multinational coastline, we seek to dig up the hidden delights of Málaga province, including the towns and villages of the Serranía de Ronda.

Anyone with more than a few days to spare in Andalucía comes to **Granada**, drawn by the Moorish excess of the Alhambra. After a tour of this great fortified palace, our final chapter guides you through the gardens and whitewashed neighbourhoods of the city, with the backdrop of Spain's tallest mountain, Mulhacén, to the north, and the delightful villages of Las Alpujarras to the south. Beyond the mountains of the Sierra Nevada lie the arid and lonely eastern reaches of Granada province and **Almería**, a landscape immortalized in countless spaghetti westerns. Finally, we hit Almería itself, the crystal waters of the Costa de Almería and trendy Mojácar, set on a hill 'like a pile of sugar cubes'.

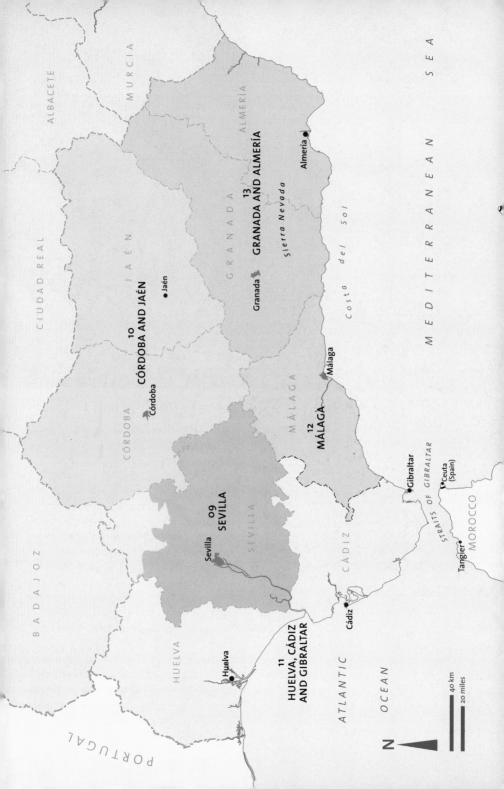

A Lost Civilization

Most people are completely bowled over by their first sight of Moorish Spain: the courtyards and gardens of Granada's Alhambra, Córdoba's Great Mosque, the elegant tower of La Giralda in Sevilla. There's a different beauty in the works of al-Andalus, a beauty unique in the world. Something uncanny happened when the Arabs blundered into Spain in the year 711. A brilliant civilization inexplicably materialized, and a province that had been mired in the Dark Ages suddenly turned into a wealthy, sophisticated, slightly otherworldly nation that spent perhaps too much of its time writing poems, planting gardens and crafting astrolabes.

Above, from top: La Mezquita, Córdoba, pp.142–5; decorative tiles, Alhambra, Granada, pp.289–96

It was all too delicate to last, but the best of al-Andalus was never entirely lost. You can see it in the art of the Moors' *mudéjar* disciples, in modern *azulejo* tile designs, and even in the patterns in which the Andalucíans plant their olive groves and gardens. The memory of al-Andalus shines best in intricate geometry; the patterns woven into its tiles, brickwork, textiles and metalwork have become part of the region's DNA.

A Mania for *Manzanilla*

It starts with a glass of sherry and a plate of olives, both of which at their finest are labelled '*manzanilla*'. Andalucia's classic *apéritif* makes the perfect introduction not only to the evening, but also to a way of living that has style and panache. The Spaniards do not dine so much as graze continuously, and emulating them provides much of the fun in visiting.

Above, clockwise from top: Market, Cádiz, p.196; ripening olives; sherry casks, Jerez de la Frontera, p.204

The tapas will be there all day, diverting you from virtue when you're supposed to be in the museum. When it's finally time to stop snacking and start the serious eating, you'll find a refined cuisine with roots that go back to the Arabs and even the Romans. Seafood is the star, and few peoples take it more seriously. Beyond that, the region is famous for ham, refined desserts laced with almonds, bulls' tails, those unbelievable *manzanilla* olives, and a few hundred different versions of gazpacho.

Sol y Sombra

For all its colour and teeming cities, Andalucía is also a land of vast brown spaces. The contrast between intense animation and empty silences has always defined life here. It mirrors the eternally blue sky overhead, and the starkly demarcated play of light and shadow, as we see it in the bullring for the ritual drama of the *corrida*. Every time you look at it, Andalucía is either turned completely on or completely off, with nothing in between. The spectacular contrasts occur in the landscape itself, like a sudden glimpse of almond blossoms on a dusty plain. The artists have always copied it – in their habit of decorating a plain building with a small panel of utter sculpted madness, as in Vicente Acero's rococo façade for Guadix cathedral, or the way Andalucíans brighten up a bar, a flat or a church dome with a splash of brilliantly coloured tiles.

Above: The Axarquía, pp.274–5

Below: Columbus and the Catholic Kings, Alcázar de los Reyes Cristianos, p.146

Opposite page: Campanile and tiled dome, by Bridge of Triana, Sevilla, p.111

Almond Blossoms and Rose Gardens

The picture of the Andalucía most people carry around in their minds can be one-dimensional: endless sandy beaches, and behind them mostly empty spaces, with all the delights concentrated in the cities. But the spaces in between aren't so empty after all, if you know where to look.

The coast, for starters, has other attractions besides flat expanses of sand, from the wetland paradise of the Guadalquivir delta to windsurfing at trendy Tarifa. Landscapes blanketed in silver olive groves or glossy-leafed orange or lemon trees, or neatly striped with vines, come straight out of the picture book of Mediterranean charms. And a haunting beauty pervades the region's many small mountain chains, each concealing green and memorable hideaways of ancient forests and hovering eagles. Not far from sun-soaked Málaga is one of the country's natural wonders, the spectacular El Chorro gorge, its sheer walls of limestone tossed about at crazy angles; and Spain's highest mountains, the snowbound Sierra Nevada, overlook the coast, so close that you can ski and swim on the same day.

Above: Parque Nacional del Coto Doñana, p.191

Below: Olive groves

Opposite page: El Chorro gorge, near Málaga, p.271

Larger than Life

Andalucía is best known for its tremendous stereotypes: thundering guitars and charging bulls and lace mantillas and on and on... So it should come as no surprise that this region also has a fine taste for the outlandish. More than a few visitors see the bizarre costumes and wailing music of a Holy Week parade, or the twisted and garish art of a Valdés Leal, and head right back home.

It's not all quite so dark. Offbeat Andalucía also means visiting Pontius Pilate's house in Sevilla, or the genuine Wild West landscapes around Almeria with their spaghetti western film sets, or the Cartuja in Granada, where you can reflect on the Aztec influence on Spanish art. Scholars call it Mexican Baroque.

And then there's the truly profound strangeness of the Costa del Sol, the multicultural European village where everyone is always happy. Here also you'll find a tiny enclave where a distant northern people has imposed its eccentric manners and customs – the most peculiar corner of the whole Mediterranean that is Gibraltar.

Above: Church, Arcos de la Frontera, p.209

Below: Casa de Pilatos, pp.118–19

Opposite page, from top: Baths, Alcázar, Sevilla, pp.106–108; Torre del Oro, Sevilla, p.110; Arcos de la Frontera, pp.208–209

Itineraries

The Best of Andalucia in Just a Little Over Two Weeks

Days 1–3 You'll probably be starting in **Sevilla**. The Andalucían capital is worth at least three whole days (if you're not starting from Sevilla, you can still do this circuit from any point and end up where you started).

Day 4 Head eastwards, for a look at the attractions of two typically Andalucían towns, **Carmona** and **Écija**, on your way to Córdoba.

Days 5 and 6 Besides the Great Mosque and the other attractions, **Córdoba** is an agreeable place to spend an extra day.

Day 7 Continue eastwards for a genuine surprise, the lovely Renaissance towns of **Baeza** and **Úbeda**.

Day 8 After so many towns, here's a chance to enjoy some of Andalucía's natural wonders. Tour the back roads around **Cazorla** and its national park and then head south, through some startlingly empty spaces, and end up in the equally startling cave-city of **Guadix**.

Days 9–11 Now we come to **Granada**. Take the night tour of the Alhambra if you can; see the gardens and the Albaicín, and three days will have passed before you know it.

Day 12 Leave Granada towards the sea, and detour for a while behind the **Sierra Nevada** into the villages of the **Alpujarras** before ending the day on the coast at **Salobreña** or **Almuñecar**.

Day 13 This is the day for cruising the coast, through **Málaga** and westwards, with a stop at any beach that catches your fancy.

Day 14 Head inland at **San Pedro de Alcántara**, and spend the rest of the day in the lovely town of **Ronda**.

Day 15 Using Ronda as a base, you can easily explore the mountain villages and the **Sierra de Grazalema** national park, ending up in **Arcos de la Frontera**.

Day 16 Today, you are rewarded for all that exploring with a little sherry and flamenco at **Jerez de la Frontera** and **Sanlúcar de Barrameda**.

Day 17 The last day is reserved for a trip through the wetlands of the **Coto Doñana** park, before heading back to Sevilla.

A Week of Wild Andalucía

Day 1 Start in Sevilla and head straight for the coast, to explore Europe's Everglades at the **Coto Doñana** national park (you might want to skip this day in high summer, when the wetlands are largely dried out)

Day 2 From here, head north into the **Sierra de Aracena**, where there is another small national park and a beautiful stalactite cave, the **Gruta de las Maravillas**.

Days 3 and 4 Now, head back towards Sevilla, and continue on to **Ronda** and the **Sierra de Grazalema**. Amid some of the region's most gorgeous settings, there are scenic roads, walking paths, caves and forests, all in a relatively small area.

Day 5 Not far to the east, around **Antequera**, you can spy on the flamingos at the **Laguna de Fuente de Piedra** or walk the dramatic **El Chorro gorge**.

Days 6 and 7 Continue eastwards, through Granada and into Spain's highest mountains, the **Sierra Nevada**, and the delightful valley of the **Alpujarras**.

Above: Alájar, Sierra de Aracena, p.186

Below: Chimneys, Las Alpujarras, pp.306–309

CONTENTS

Contents

History

02

Prehistory

Southern Spain has been inhabited since remotest antiquity. The area around Huelva is only one of the places in Spain where remains from the early Pleistocene have been found, and some finds on the peninsula suggest somebody was poking about here as far back as one million years ago. Only 250,000 years ago, they were making tools out of elephant tusks, when they were lucky enough to catch one. A site near the centre of Marbella, of all places, was recently excavated in search of its Middle Palaeolithic remains.

Neanderthal man wandered all over Spain some 50,000 years ago, and Gibraltar seems to have been one of his favourite locations. Later people, the devious and quarrelsome *homo sapiens*, contributed the simple cave paintings in the Cueva de la Pileta and some other sites near Ronda *c.* 25,000 BC – nothing as elaborate as the famous paintings at Altamira and other sites in northern Spain, though they date from about the same time.

The great revolution in human affairs known as the **Neolithic Revolution**, including the beginnings of agriculture and husbandry, began to appear around the Iberian coasts *c.* 6000 BC. By the 4th millennium BC, the Neolithic people had developed an advanced culture, building dolmens, stone circles and burial mounds all along the fringes of western Europe – Newgrange, Avebury, Stonehenge, Carnac. In southern Spain, they left the huge tumuli at Antequera called the Cueva de Romeral and the Cueva de Menga.

By *c.* 3200 BC they had learned to make use of copper, and a metalworking nation created the great complex at Los Millares near Almería, a veritable Neolithic city with fortifications, outer citadels and a huge tumulus surrounded by circles of standing stones. Los Millares and sites associated with it began to decline about 2500 BC, and most of them were abandoned by 2000 BC, replaced by different, bronze-working peoples who often founded their settlements on the same old sites.

1100–201 BC

The native Iberians learn that if you've got a silver mine in your back yard, you'll never be lonely

In the 2nd millennium BC, while early civilizations rose and fell in the Middle East and eastern Mediterranean, the west remained a backwater – southern Spain in particular found nothing to disturb its dreams until the arrival of the **Phoenicians**, who 'discovered' Spain perhaps as early as 1100 BC (that is the traditional date; many archaeologists suspect they did not appear until 900 or 800 BC). As a base for trading, they founded Gades (Cádiz), claimed to be the oldest city in western Europe, and from there they slowly expanded into a string of colonies along the coast. The Phoenicians were after Spain's mineral resources – copper, tin, gold, silver and mercury, all in short supply in the Middle East at this time – and their trade with the native Iberians made the Phoenicians the economic masters of the Mediterranean (the flood of Andalucian silver from the Río Tinto mines into the Middle East caused one of history's first recorded spells of inflation, in the Assyrian Empire). Such wealth eventually attracted the Phoenicians' bitter rivals, the **Greeks**, who arrived in 636 BC and founded a trading post at Mainake near Málaga, though they were never to be a real force in the region.

The great mystery of this era is the fabled kingdom of **Tartessos**, which covered all or part of Andalucía. The name seems to come from Tertis, an ancient name of the Guadalquivir River. Phoenician records mention it, as does Herodotus, and it may be the legendary 'Tarshish' mentioned in the Book of Kings, its great navy bringing wares of Spain and Africa to trade with King Solomon. With great wealth from the mines of the Río Tinto and the Sierra Morena, Tartessos may have appeared about 800–700 BC. Very little is known of the real story behind the legends of Tartessos, but they reflect the fact that Iberian communities throughout the peninsula were rapidly gaining in wealth and sophistication. Archaeologists refer to the 7th and 6th centuries as the 'orientalizing period' of Iberian culture, when the people of Spain were adopting wholesale elements of life and art from the Phoenicians and Greeks. Iberians imported Greek and Phoenician art, and learned to copy it for themselves. They developed an adaptation of the Phoenician alphabet, and began an agricultural revolution that has shaped the land up to this day with two new crops brought to them by their eastern visitors – the grape and the olive.

By the 6th century, the Phoenicians of the Levant were under Babylonian rule, and **Carthage**, their western branch office, was building an empire out of their occupied coasts in Spain, Sicily and North Africa. About 500 BC the Carthaginians gobbled up the last remains of Tartessos and other coastal areas, and stopped the Greek infiltration. The Carthaginians maintained the status quo until 264–241 BC, when Rome drubbed them in the **First Punic War**.

Before that, Carthage had been largely a sea power. After Rome built itself a navy and beat them, the Carthaginians changed tack and rebuilt their empire as a land power, based on the resources and manpower of Spain. Beginning in 237, they established military control throughout most of the peninsula, under **Hamilcar Barca**. This, along with other factors, alarmed Rome enough to reopen hostilities. In the rematch, the **Second Punic War** (218–201 BC), Hamilcar's son **Hannibal** marched off to Italy with his elephants and a largely Spanish army; meanwhile, the Romans under **Scipio Africanus** entered Spain by sea. Scipio's first intention was merely to cut off Hannibal's supply routes to Italy. It was a brilliant stroke and the Romans eventually gained control of all Iberia, winning important battles at Bailén in 208 and Alcalá del Río, near Sevilla, the following year. After that, Scipio was able to use Spain as a base to attack Carthage itself, forcing Hannibal to evacuate Italy and leading to total victory for Rome.

201 BC–AD 409

The Romans muscle in, and do to the Spaniards what the Spaniards will one day do to the Mexicans

Unlike their predecessors, the Romans were never content to hold just a part of Spain. Relentlessly, they slogged over the peninsula, subjugating one Celtic or

Iberian tribe after another, a job that was not entirely completed in northern Spain until AD 220. Even then, rebellions against Rome were frequent and bloody, including a major one in Andalucía in 195. Rome had to send its best – Cato, Pompey, Julius Caesar and Octavian (Augustus) were all commanders in the Spanish conquest. Caesar, in fact, was briefly governor in Andalucía, the most prosperous part of the peninsula, and the one that adapted most easily to Roman rule and culture.

Not that Roman rule was much of a blessing. Iberia, caught in the middle of a huge geopolitical struggle between two powerful neighbours, had simply exchanged one colonial overlord for another. Both were efficiently rapacious in the exploitation of the all-important mines, keeping the profits for themselves alone. As in every land conquered by the legions, most of the best land was collected together into huge estates owned by the Roman élite, on which the former inhabitants were enslaved or reduced to the status of tenant farmers. The Iberians had reasons to resist as strongly as they did.

At first the Romans called Andalucía simply 'Further Spain', but eventually it settled in as **Baetica**, from the Bætis, another ancient name for the Guadalquivir river. During the first three centuries AD, when the empire was at its height, Baetica became a prosperous, contented place; thanks to its great mineral and agricultural wealth, the richest part of the empire west of Italy and Tunisia. Baetica poured out oceans of plonk for the empire; the Romans sniffed at its quality but they were never shy about ordering more. In Rome today you can see a 160ft (48m) hill called Monte Testaccio, made entirely of broken amphorae – most of them from Spain.

Besides wine, oil and metals, another export was dancing girls; Baetica's girls were reputed to be the hottest in the empire. And for the choicer Roman banquets, there was *garum*, a highly prized condiment made of fish guts. Modern gourmets have been trying to guess the recipe for centuries.

New cities grew up to join Cádiz, Itálica and Málaga. Of these, the most important were **Hispalis** (Sevilla) and **Corduba** (Córdoba), which became Baetica's capital. Other towns owe their beginnings to the common Roman policy of establishing colonies populated by army veterans, such as Colonia Genetiva Iulia Ursa – modern Osuna. Among the cosmopolitan population were Iberians, Celts, Phoenicians, Italians and a sizeable minority of **Jews**. During the Diaspora, Rome settled them here in great numbers, as far from home as they could possibly put them; they would play an important and constructive role in Spanish life for the next 1,500 years.

The province also had a talent for keeping in the mainstream of imperial politics and culture. Vespasian had been governor here, and Baetica gave birth to three of Rome's best emperors: Trajan, Hadrian and Theodosius. It also contributed almost all the great figures of the 'silver age' of Latin literature – Lucan, both Senecas, Martial and Quintilian. None of these, of course, were really 'Andalucians' except by birth; all were part of the thin veneer of élite Roman families that owned nearly everything, and monopolized colonial Spain's political and cultural life. Concerning the other 99 per cent of the population, we know very little.

409–711
Finally rid of its Roman bosses, Spain hasn't a minute before some malodorous, blue-eyed Teutons come to take their place

By the 4th century, the crushing burden of maintaining the defence budget and the government bureaucracy sent Spain's economy, along with the rest of the empire's, into a permanent depression. Cities declined and, in the countryside, the landowners gradually squeezed the majority of the population into serfdom or outright slavery. Thus when the bloody, anarchic **Vandals** arrived in Spain in 409, they found bands of rural guerrillas, or *bagaudae*, to help them in smashing up the remnants of the Roman system. The Vandals moved on to Africa in 428, leaving nothing behind but, maybe, the name Andalucía – some believe it was originally Vandalusia.

The next uninvited guests were the **Visigoths**, a ne'er-do-well Germanic folk who had caused little trouble for anyone until they were pushed westwards by the Huns. After making a name for themselves by sacking Rome under their chief Alaric in 410, they found their way into Spain four years later, looking for food. By 478 they had conquered most of it, including Andalucía, and they established an independent kingdom stretching from the Atlantic to the Rhône. The Visigoths were illiterate, selfish and bloody-minded, but persistent enough to endure, despite endless dynastic and religious quarrels; like most Germans, they were Arian heretics. There weren't many of them; estimates of the original invading horde range up to some 200,000, and for the next three centuries they would remain a warrior élite that never formed more than a small fraction of the population. For support they depended on the landowners, who were making the slow but logical transition from Roman *senatores* to feudal lords. An interruption to their rule, at least in the south, came in 553; Justinian's reviving eastern empire, having already reclaimed Italy and Africa, tried for Spain too.

Byzantine resources proved just enough to wrest Andalucía from the Visigoths, but the overextended empire was hardly able to hold all its far-flung conquests for very long. Over the following decades the Visigoths gradually pushed them back, though some coastal bases remained in Byzantine hands as late as the Arab invasion.

Despite all the troubles, Andalucía at least seems to have been doing well – probably better than anywhere else in western Europe – and there was even a modest revival of learning in the 7th century, the age of St Isidore (*c.* 560–636), famous scholar of Sevilla. King Leovigild (573–86) was an able leader; his son Reccared converted to orthodox Catholicism in 589. Both helped bring their state to the height of its power as much by internal reform as military victories. Allowing the grasping Church a share of power, however, proved fatal to the Visigoths. The Church's depredations against the populace and its persecutions of Jews and heretics made the Visigothic state as many enemies within as it ever had beyond its borders. By the time of King Roderick, a duke of Baetica who had usurped the throne in one of the kingdom's periods of political turbulence, Visigothic Spain was in serious disarray.

711–56

The Spaniards are conquered by a people they have never before heard of

The great wave of Muslim Arab expansion that began in Mohammed's lifetime was bound to wash up on Spain's shores sooner or later. A small Arab force arrived in Spain in 710, led by **Tarif**, who gave his name to today's Tarifa on the Straits. The following year brought a larger army – still only about 7,000 men – under **Tariq ibn-Ziyad**, with the assistance of dissident Visigoths opposed to Roderick, and a certain Count Julian, Byzantine ruler of Ceuta, who supplied the ships to ferry over the Arab-Berber army. Tariq quickly defeated the Visigoths near Barbate, a battle in which Roderick was killed. Toledo, the Visigothic capital, fell soon after, and a collection of Visigothic nobles were on their way to Baghdad in chains as presents to the caliph. Within five years, the Arabs had conquered most of the peninsula, and they were crossing the Pyrenees into France.

The ease of the conquest is not difficult to explain. The majority of the population was delighted to welcome the Arabs and their Berber allies. The overtaxed peasants and persecuted Jews supported them from the first. Religious tolerance was guaranteed under the new rule; since the largest share of taxes fell on non-believers, the Arabs were happy to refrain from forced conversions. The conquest, however, was never completed. A small Christian enclave in the northwest, the kingdom of Asturias, survived following an obscure but symbolic victory over the Moors at Covadonga in 718. At the time, the Arabs would barely have noticed; Muslim control of most of Spain was solid, but hampered almost from the start by dissension between the Arabs, the neglected Berbers, the large numbers of Syrians who arrived later, in another army sent from the east, and among the various tribes of the Arabs themselves. The Berbers had the biggest grudge. Not only did the Arabs look down on them, but in the distribution of confiscated lands they were not given their promised fair share. The result was a massive **Berber revolt** in 740. This was put down with some difficulty, but it was only one of a number of troubles, as fighting between the various Arab princes kept Spain in an almost continuous state of civil war. Between the feuding invaders, Spain passed through one of the darkest centuries in its history.

756–929

Spain becomes al-Andalus, and things are looking up

Far away in Damascus, the political struggles of the caliphate were being resolved by a general massacre of the princes of the Umayyad dynasty, successors of Mohammed; a new dynasty, the Abbasids, replaced them. One young Umayyad, **Abd ar-Rahman**, escaped; he fled to Córdoba, and took power there with the support of Umayyad loyalists. After a victory in May 756, he proclaimed himself emir, the first leader of an independent emirate of al-Andalus. At first, Abd ar-Rahman was only one of the contending petty princes fighting over a ruined, exhausted country. Eventually he prevailed over them all, though the chronicles of the time are too thin to tell us whether he owed his ascendancy to military talent, good fortune or just simple tenacity. It took him over 30 years of fighting to do the job and, besides rival Arabs, he had to contend with invading Christian armies sent by Charlemagne in the 770s – a campaign that, though unsuccessful, left us the legend of Roland at Roncesvalles, source of the medieval epic *Chanson de Roland*.

Under this new government, Muslim Spain gradually recovered its strength and prosperity. Political unity was maintained only with great difficulty, but trade, urban life and culture flourished. Though their domains stretched as far as the Pyrenees, the Umayyad emirs referred to it all as **al-Andalus**. Andalucía was its heartland and Córdoba, Sevilla and Málaga its greatest cities, unmatched by any others in western Europe. Abd ar-Rahman kept his capital at Córdoba and began the Great Mosque there, a brilliant and unexpected start to the culture of the new state.

After Abd ar-Rahman, the succession passed without difficulty through Hisham I (788–96), al-Hakim I (796–822), and Abd ar-Rahman II (822–52), all of them sound military men, defenders of the faith and patrons of musicians and poets. Abd ar-Rahman I's innovations, the creation of a professional army and palace secretariat, helped considerably in maintaining stability. The latter, called the *Saqaliba*, a civil service of imported slaves, was made up largely of Slavs and black Africans. The new dynasty seems also to have worked sincerely to establish justice and balance among the various contentious ethnic groups. In the days of Abd ar-Rahman I, only a fifth of al-Andalus's population was Muslim. This figure would rise steadily throughout the existence of al-Andalus, finally reaching 90 per cent in the 1100s, but emirs would always have to deal with the concerns of a very cosmopolitan population that included haughty Arab aristocrats prone to factionalism, leftover Roman and Visigothic barons, who might be Christians or *muwallads* (converts to Islam), Iraqis, Syrians, Yemeni and various other peoples from the eastern Muslim world, Berbers (who made up the bulk of the army), Jews, slaves from the farthest corners of three continents, and all the old native Iberian population.

One weakness, shared with most early Islamic states, was the personal, non-institutional nature of rule. Individuals and groups could address their grievances only to the emir, while governors in distant towns had so much authority that they often began to think of themselves as independent potentates – a cause of frequent rebellions in the reigns of Mohammed I (852–86) and Abd Allah (888–912). Closer to home, discontented *muwallads* in the heart of Andalucía coalesced around the rather mysterious figure of **Umar ibn-Hafsun**. After his rebel army was defeated in 891, he and his followers took refuge in the impregnable fortress of Bobastro, in the mountains near Antequera, carrying on a kind of guerrilla war against the emirs. Later Christian propagandists claimed ibn-Hafsun as a Christian. Though this is unlikely, a church can still be seen among the ruins of Bobastro. After ibn-Hafsun's death, his sons held out until Bobastro was finally taken in 928.

A less serious problem, though a bothersome one, was the **Vikings**, who raided Spain's coasts just as they did all others within the reach of their longboats. Even though their raids took them as far as Sevilla, al-Andalus was better able to fight off the Northmen than any of the Christian states of Europe; under the reign of **Abd ar-Rahman II**, al-Andalus made itself into a sea power, with bases on both the Mediterranean and the Atlantic. In those days, interestingly enough, al-Andalus held on to two key port towns in North Africa – Ceuta and Melilla, to guard its southern flank – just as Spain does today. The pirates of Fraxinetum, La Garde-Freinet in southern France, made life miserable for the Provençals and helped keep the western Mediterranean a Muslim lake; they too acknowledged the sovereignty of Abd ar-Rahman.

929–1008
A caliph rises in the west, and a great civilization reaches its noonday

In the tenth century, al-Andalus enjoyed its golden age. **Abd ar-Rahman III** (912–61) and **al-Hakim II** (961–76) collected tribute from the Christian kingdoms of the north and from North African states as far as Algiers. In 929, Abd ar-Rahman III assumed the title of caliph, declaring al-Andalus entirely independent of any higher political or religious authority. Umayyad Al-Andalus was in fact cooperating closely with the Abbasid caliphate in Baghdad, but Shiite heretics in North Africa had declared their own caliph at Tunis, and Abd ar-Rahman who, like all the emirs, was orthodox in religion, was not about to let himself be outranked by an upstart neighbour. After the peaceful reign of al-Hakim II, a boy caliph, Hisham II, came to the throne in 976. In a fateful turn of events, effective power was seized by his minister Abu Amir al-Ma'afiri, better known by the title he assumed, **al-Mansur** ('the Victorious', known to the Christians as 'Almanzor'). Though an iron-willed dictator with a penchant for bloody slaughter of anyone suspected of opposing him, al-Mansur was also a brilliant military leader, one who resumed the offensive against the growing Christian kingdoms of the north. He recaptured León, Pamplona and Barcelona, sacked almost every Christian city at least once, and even raided the great pilgrimage shrine at Santiago de Compostela in Galicia, stealing its bells to hang up as trophies in the Great Mosque of Córdoba.

A more resounding al-Andalus accomplishment was keeping in balance its diverse and increasingly sophisticated population, all the while accommodating three religions and ensuring mutual tolerance. At the same time, they made it pay. Al-Andalus' cities thrived far more than any of their neighbours, Muslim or Christian, and the countryside was more prosperous than it has been before or since. The Arabs introduced cotton, rice, dates, sugar, oranges, artichokes and much else. Irrigation, begun under the Romans, was perfected; contemporary observers counted over 200 *nurias*, or water wheels, along the length of the Guadalquivir, and even parched Almería became a garden. It was this 'agricultural revolution', the application of eastern crops and techniques to a land perfectly adapted for them, that made all the rest possible. It meant greater wealth and an increased population, and permitted the growth of manufacturers and commerce far in advance of anything else in western Europe.

At the height of its fortunes, al-Andalus was one of the world's great civilizations. Its wealth and stability sustained an impressive artistic flowering – obvious today, even from the relatively few monuments that survived the Reconquista. Córdoba, with al-Hakim's great library, became a centre of learning; Málaga was renowned for its singers, and Sevilla for the making of musical instruments. Art and life were also growing closer. About 822, the famous **Ziryab** had arrived in Córdoba from Baghdad. A great musician and poet, mentioned often in the tales of the *Thousand and One Nights*, Ziryab also revolutionized the manners of the Arabs, introducing eastern fashions, poetic courtesies, and the proper way to arrange the courses of a meal. It wasn't long before the élite of al-Andalus became more interested in the latest graft of Shiraz roses than in riding across La Mancha to cross swords with the barbaric Asturians.

When Christian Europe was just beginning to blossom, al-Andalus and Byzantium were its exemplars and schoolmasters. Religious partisanship and western pride have always obscured the relationship; how much we really owe al-Andalus in scholarship – especially the transmission of Greek and Arab science – in art and architecture, in technology, and in poetry and the other delights of civilization, has never been completely explored. Contacts were more common than is generally assumed. Christian students often found their way to Toledo or Córdoba – like the French monk, one of the most learned Christians of his day, who became Pope Sylvester II in 999.

Throughout the 10th century, the military superiority of al-Andalus was great enough to have finally erased the Christian kingdoms, had the caliphs cared to do so; it may have been a simple lack of aggressiveness and determination that held them back, or perhaps simply a constitutional inability of the Arab leaders to deal with the green, chilly, rainy world of the northern mountains. The Muslim–Christian wars of this period cannot be understood as a prelude to the Crusades, or to the bigotry of Fernando and Isabel. Pious fanaticism, in fact, was conspicuously lacking on both sides, and if the chronicles detail endless wars and raids, they were always about booty, not religion. Al-Andalus had its ambassadors among the Franks, the Italians, the Byzantines and the Ottonian Holy Roman Empire, and it usually found no problem reaching understandings with any of them. In Spain itself, dynastic marriages between Muslims and Christians were common, and frontier chiefs could switch sides more than once without switching religions. The famous **El Cid** would spend more time working for Muslim rulers than Christians, and all the kings of León had some Moorish blood. Abd ar-Rahman III himself had blue eyes and red hair (which he dyed black to keep in fashion); his mother was a Basque princess from Navarre.

1008–85
Disaster, disarray; al-Andalus breaks into pieces

It is said that the great astronomer Maslama of Madrid, who was also court astrologer at Córdoba, foretold the end of the caliphate just before his death in 1007. A little political sense, more than knowledge of the stars, would have sufficed to demonstrate that al-Andalus was approaching a crisis. After the death of al-Mansur in 1002, the political situation began to change dramatically. His son, Abd al-Malik al-Muzaffar, inherited his position as vizier and de facto ruler and held the state together until his death in 1008, despite increasing tensions. All the while, Hisham II remained a pampered prisoner in the sumptuous palace-city of **Medinat**

al-Zahra, outside Córdoba. The lack of political legitimacy in this ministerial dictatorship, and the increasing distance between government and people symbolized by Medinat al-Zahra, contributed to the troubles that began in 1008. Historians suggest that the great wealth of al-Andalus had made the nation a bit jaded and selfish, that the rich and powerful were scarcely inclined to compromise or sacrifice for the good of the whole. The old Arab aristocracy, in fact, was the most disaffected group of all. Al-Mansur's conquests had been delivered by a kind of new model army, manned by Berber mercenaries. With their military function gone, the nobles saw their status and privilege steadily eroding.

Whatever the reason, the caliphate disintegrated with startling suddenness after 1008. Nine caliphs ruled between that year and 1031, most of them puppets of the Berbers, the Saqaliba or other factions. Civil wars and city riots became endemic. Al-Mansur's own Berber troops, who felt no loyalty to any caliph, caused the worst of the troubles. They destroyed Medinat al-Zahra, and sacked Córdoba itself in 1013.

By 1031, when the caliphate was abolished, an exhausted al-Andalus had split into at least 30 squabbling states, run by Arab princes, Berber officers or even former slaves. Almost overnight, the balance of power between Muslim and Christian had reversed itself. In 999, al-Mansur had been sacking the towns of the north as far as Pamplona. Only a decade later, the counts of Castile and Barcelona were sending armies deep into al-Andalus, intervening by request of one party or the other.

The years after 1031 are known as the **age of the** *taifas*, or of the 'Party Kings' (*muluk al tawa'if*), so-called because most of them owed their position to one of the political factions. Few of these self-made rulers slept easily in an era of constant intrigues and revolts, shifting alliances and pointless wars. The only relatively strong state was that of Sevilla, founded by former governor **Mohammed ibn-Abbad**, who was also the richest landowner in the area. For political legitimacy he claimed to rule in the name of the last caliph, who had disappeared in the sack of Medinat al-Zahra, and miraculously reappeared (ibn-Abbad's enemies claimed the 'caliph' was really a lookalike mat weaver from Calatrava). Ibn-Abbad was unscrupulous, but effective; his successes were continued by his sons, who managed to annexe Córdoba and several other towns. Under their rule Sevilla replaced stricken Córdoba as the largest and most important city of al-Andalus.

1085–1212
Moroccan zealots come to Spain's defence, if only for a while

The total inability of the 'Party Kings' to work together made the 11th century a party for the Christians. Nearly all the little states were forced to pay heavy tribute to Christian kings. That, and the expenses of their lavish courts and wars against each other, led to sharply higher taxes and helped put an end to a 200-year run of economic expansion. **Alfonso VI**, King of Castile and León, collected tribute from most of the *taifas*, including even Sevilla. In 1085, with the help of the legendary warrior El Cid, he captured Toledo. The loss of this key fortress-city alarmed the *taifas* enough for them to request assistance from the **Almoravids** (*al-Murabitun*, the 'warrior monks') of North Africa, a fanatical fundamendalist movement of the Berbers that had recently established an empire stretching from Morocco to Senegal, with its capital at the newly founded city of Marrakech.

The Almoravid leader, **Yusuf ibn-Tashufin**, crossed the Straits and defeated Alfonso in 1086. Yusuf liked al-Andalus so much that he decided to keep it; by 1110 the Almoravids had gobbled up the last of the surviving *taifas* and had reimposed Muslim rule as far as Saragossa (Zaragoza). Under their rule, al-Andalus became more of a consciously Islamic state than it had ever been before, uncomfortable for the Christians and even for the cultured Arab aristocrats, with their gardens and their poetry (and their long-established custom of dropping in on Christian monasteries for a forbidden glass of wine). The chronicles give some evidence of Almoravid oppression directed against Christian communities, and even deportations. Religious prejudices were hardening on both sides, especially since the Christians evolved their crusading ethos in the 1100s, but the Almoravids did their best to help bigotry along.

Popular rebellions against the Almoravids in the Andalucian cities were a problem from the start, and a series of big ones put an end to their rule in 1145. Al-Andalus rapidly dissolved into confusion and a second era of 'Party Kings'. Two years later, Almoravid power in Africa was defeated and replaced by that of the **Almohads**, a nearly identical military-religious state. The Almohads (*al-Muwahhidun*, 'upholders of divine unity') began with a Sufi preacher named ibn-Tumart, proselytizing and proclaiming *jihad* among the tribes of the Atlas mountains of Morocco. By 1172 the Almohads had control of most of southern Spain. Somewhat more tolerant and civilized than the Almoravids, their rule coincided with a cultural reawakening in al-Andalus, a period that saw the building of La Giralda in Sevilla. Literature and art flourished, and in Córdoba lived two of the greatest philosophers of the Middle Ages: the Arab, Ibn Rushd (Averroës), and the Jew, Moses Maimónides. The Almohads nevertheless shared many of the Almoravids' limitations. Essentially a military regime, with no deep support from any part of the population, they could win victories over the Christians (as at Alarcos in 1195) but were never able to take advantage of them.

1212–1492
Al-Andalus falls to the eaters of pork; one small corner remains to the faithful

At the same time, the Christian Spaniards were growing stronger and gaining a new sense of unity and national consciousness. The end for the Almohads, and for al-Andalus, came with the **Battle of Las Navas de Tolosa** in 1212, fought near the traditional site for climactic battles in Spain – the Despeñaperros pass, gateway to Andalucía. Here, an army from all the states of Christian Spain under Alfonso VII (1126–57) destroyed Almohad power for ever. Alfonso's son, **Fernando III** (1217–52), captured Córdoba (1236) and Sevilla (1248), and was made a saint for his trouble.

The people of Sevilla would have found it ironic; breaking with the more humane practices of the past, Fernando determined to make al-Andalus's capital a Christian city once and for all and, after starving the population into submission by siege, he expelled every one of them, allowing them to take only the goods they could carry. **Alfonso X** (the Wise, 1252–84), noted for his poetry and the brilliance of his court, completed the conquest of western Andalucía in the 1270s and 1280s.

In the conquest of Sevilla, important assistance had been rendered by one of Fernando's new vassals, **Mohammed ibn-Yusuf ibn-Nasr**, an Arab adventurer who had conquered Granada in 1235. The **Nasrid Kingdom of Qarnatah** (Granada) survived partly from its co-operation with Castile, and partly from its mountainous, easily defensible terrain. For the next 250 years it would be the only remaining Muslim territory on the peninsula. Two other factors helped keep Granada afloat. One was a small but very competent army, which made good use of a chain of strong border fortresses in the mountains to make Castile think twice about any serious invasion. Granada was also able to count on help from the Marenid emirs of Morocco, who succeeded to power in North Africa after the collapse of the Almohad state. The Marenids half-heartedly invaded Spain twice, in 1264 in support of a Muslim revolt, and again in 1275; for a long time afterwards they were able to hold on to such coastal bases as Algeciras, Tarifa and Gibraltar.

As a refuge for Muslims from the rest of Spain, Granada became al-Andalus in miniature, a sophisticated and generally peaceful state, stretching from Gibraltar to Almería. It produced the last brilliant age of Moorish culture in the 14th century, expressed in its poetry and in the art of the Alhambra. It was not, however, always a happy land. When they were not raiding Granada's borders, the Castilians enforced heavy tributes on it, as they had with the Party Kings of the 11th century. It wasn't easy to prosper under such conditions, and things were made worse by the monopoly over trade and shipping forced on the Granadans by the predatory Genoese, who in those days were an affliction to Christian and Muslim Spaniards alike. Affected by a permanent siege mentality, and filled with refugees from the lands that had been lost, Granada seems to have acquired the air of melancholy that still clings to the city today.

In the rest of Andalucía, the Reconquista meant a profound cultural dislocation, as the majority of the Muslim population chose to flee the rough northerners and their priests. The Muslims who stayed behind (the *mudéjares*, meaning those 'permitted to remain') did not fare badly at first. Their economy remained intact, and many Spaniards remained fascinated by the extravagant culture they had inherited. In the 1360s, King Pedro of Castile (1350–69) was signing his correspondence 'Pedro ben Xancho' in a flowing Arabic script, and spending most of his time in Sevilla's Alcázar, built by artists from Granada. There was even a considerable return of Muslim populations, to Sevilla and a few other towns from which they had been forced out; this took place with the approval of the Castilian kings, who needed their labour and skills to rebuild the devastated land. Throughout the period, though, the culture and the society that built al-Andalus were becoming increasingly diluted, as Muslims either left or converted, while the Castilians imported large numbers of Christian settlers from the north. Religious intolerance, fostered as always by the Church, was a growing problem.

1492–1516
A rotten queen and a rotten king send the Andalucians down a road of misery

The final disaster, for Andalucía and for Spain, came with the marriage in 1469 of **King Fernando II of Aragón** and **Queen Isabel I of Castile**, opening the way, 10 years later, for the union of the two most powerful states on the peninsula. The glory of the occasion has tended to obscure the historical realities, and writers too often give a free ride to two of the most vicious and bigoted figures in Spanish history. If Fernando and Isabel did not invent genocide, they did their hypocritical best to sanctify it, forcing a maximalist solution to a cultural diversity they found intolerable. As state-sponsored harassment of the *mudéjares* increased across Spain, the 'Catholic Kings' also found the time was right for the extinction of Granada. Fernando, a tireless campaigner, constantly nibbled away at the Nasrid borders for a decade, until little more than the capital itself remained. It had not been easy, but Fernando was fortunate enough to have one of the greatest soldiers of his day running the show – Gonzalo de Córdoba, El Gran Capitán, who would later use the tactics developed on the Granada campaign to conquer southern Italy for Spain.

Granada fell in 1492, completing the Reconquista. Fernando and Isabel ('Los Reyes Católicos') expelled all the Jews from Spain the same year; their **Inquisition** – founded by Fernando and Isabel, not by the Church, and entirely devoted to their purposes – was in full swing, terrorizing 'heretical' Christians and converted Jews and Muslims and effectively putting an end to all differences of opinion, religious or political. In the same year, **Columbus** (who had been present at the fall of Granada) sailed from Andalucía to the New World, initiating the Age of Discovery.

Under the conditions of Granada's surrender in 1492, the *mudéjares* were to be allowed to continue their religion and customs unmolested. Under the influence of the Church, in the person of the famous Archbishop of Toledo, Cardinal Cisneros, Spain soon reneged on its promises and attempted forced conversion, a policy cleverly designed to justify itself by causing a revolt. The **First Revolt of the Alpujarras**, the string of villages near Granada in the Sierra Nevada, in 1500, resulted in the expulsion of all Muslims who failed to convert – the majority of the population had already fled – as well as decrees prohibiting Moorish dress and un-Christian institutions such as public bathhouses.

Beyond that, the Spanish purposely impoverished the Granada territories, ruining their agriculture and bankrupting the important silk industry with punitive taxes and a ban on exports. The Inquisition enriched the Church's coffers, confiscating the entire property of any converted Muslims who could be found guilty of backsliding in the faith. A second revolt in the Alpujarras occurred in 1568, after which Philip II ordered the prohibition of the Arabic language and the dispersal of the remaining Muslim population throughout the towns and cities of Castile. By this time, paranoia had a partial justification. Spain was locked in a bitter struggle against the Ottoman Empire, and the Turks had established bases as close as the Maghreb coast; the threat of a Muslim revival was looking very real. But paranoia was not directed at Muslims alone. In the same year, the Inquisition began incinerating suspected Protestants in Sevilla, and the systematic persecution of the *conversos* – Jews who had converted to Christianity, in some cases generations before – was well under way. Intolerance had become a way of life.

1516–1700
The new Spain chokes on its riches and power, and Andalucía suffers the most

In the 16th century, the new nation's boundless wealth, energy and talent were squandered by two rulers even more vile than Los Reyes Católicos. Carlos I, a Habsburg who gained the throne by marriage when Fernando and Isabel's first two heirs died, emptied the treasury to purchase his election as Holy Roman Emperor. Outside Spain he is better known by his imperial title, **Charles V** (1516–56), a sanctimonious tyrant who had half of Europe in his pocket and dearly wanted the other half. His megalomaniac ambitions bled Spain dry, a policy continued by his son **Philip II** (1556–98), under whom Spain went bankrupt three times.

Throughout the century, Andalucía's ports were the base for the exploration and exploitation of the New World. Trade and settlement were planned from Sevilla, and gold and silver poured in each year from the Indies' treasure fleet. In the 16th century the city's population increased fivefold, to over 100,000. Unfortunately, what money did not immediately go to finance the wars of Charles and Philip was gobbled up by the nobility, the Genoese and German bankers, or by inflation – the 16th-century 'price revolution' caused by the riches from America. The colonies needed vast amounts of manufactured goods and had solid bullion to pay for them, but despite Sevilla's monopoly on the colonial trade, Andalucía found itself too badly misgoverned and economically primitive to supply any of them.

The historical ironies are profound. Awash in money, and presented with the kind of opportunity that few regions ever see through their entire history, Andalucía instead declined rapidly from one of the richest and most cultured provinces of Europe to one of the poorest and most backward. Fernando and Isabel had begun the process, distributing the vast confiscated lands of the Moors to their friends, or to the Church and military orders. From its birth the new Andalucía was a land of huge estates, exploited by absentee landlords and worked by sharecroppers – the remnants of the original population as well as the hopeful colonists from the north, most of whom were reduced in a generation or two to virtual serfdom. It was the story of Roman Spain all over again, and in the end Andalucía found that it had become just as much a colony as Mexico or Peru.

By the 17th century, the destruction of Andalucía was complete. The Inquisition's terror had done its work, eliminating any possibility of intellectual freedom and reducing the population to the lowest depths of superstition and subservience. Their trade and manufactures ruined, the cities stagnated; agriculture suffered as well, as the complex irrigation systems of the Moors fell into disrepair and were gradually abandoned. The only opportunity for the average man lay with emigration, and Andalucía contributed more than its share to the American colonies.

The shipments of American bullion peaked about 1610–20, and after that the decline was precipitous. As for the last surviving Muslims, the *moriscos*, they were expelled from Spain in 1609. The greatest concentration of them, surprisingly, was not in Andalucía, but in the fertile plains around Valencia. The king's minister, the Duke of Lerma, was a Valencian, and apparently he came up with the plan in hope of snatching some of their confiscated land. The leaders of the Inquisition opposed the expulsions, since they made most of their profits shaking down *moriscos*, but the land-grabbers won out, and by 1614 some 275,000 Spanish Muslims had been forced from their homes.

1700–1931
Bourbon reformers, Napoleonic hoodlums, and a long parade of despots cross the stage; the Andalucians start to fight back

For almost the next two centuries, Andalucía has no history at all. The perversity of Spain's rulers had exhausted the nation. Scorned for its backwardness, Spain was no longer even taken seriously as a military power. The **War of the Spanish Succession**, during which the English seized Gibraltar (1704), replaced the Habsburgs with the Bourbons, though their rule brought little improvement. Bourbon policies, beginning with **Philip V** (1700–46), followed the lead of their cousins in France, and a more centralized, rationalized state did attempt to bring improvements in roads and other public works, as well as state-sponsored industries in the French style, such as the great royal tobacco factory in Sevilla. The high point of reform in the 18th century was the reign of **Carlos III** (1759–88), who expelled the Jesuits, attempted to revive trade and resettled the most desolate parts of Andalucía. New towns were founded – the *Nuevas Poblaciones* – such as La Carolina and Olavide, though in such a depressed setting that the foreign settlers Carlos brought in could not adapt, and the new towns never really thrived. One bright spot was an ancient city, long in the shadows, which now found a new prominence. Cádiz succeeded Sevilla as the major port for the colonial trade, and in these years became one of the most prosperous and progressive cities in Spain.

Despite three centuries of decay, Andalucians responded with surprising energy to the French occupation during the **Napoleonic Wars**. The French gave them good reason to, stealing as much gold and art as they could carry, and blowing up castles and historical buildings just for sport. As elsewhere in Spain, irregulars and loyal army detachments assisted the British under Wellington. In 1808, a force made up mostly of Andalucians defeated the French at the **Battle of Bailén**. In 1812, a group of Spanish liberals met in Cádiz to declare a constitution, and under this the Spanish fitfully conducted what they call their **War of Independence**.

With victory, however, came not reforms and a constitution, but reaction and the return of the Bourbons. For most Andalucians, times may have been worse than ever, but Romantic-era Europe was about to discover the region in a big way. The trend had already started with Mozart's operas set in Sevilla, and now the habit resumed with Washington Irving's *Tales of the Alhambra* in 1832, and Richard Ford's equally popular *Handbook for Travellers in Spain* in 1845. Between the lost civilization of the Moors, which Europeans were coming to value for the first time, and the natural colour of its daily life, backward, exotic Andalucía proved to be just what a jaded continent was looking for. The region provided some of the world's favourite stereotypes, from Gypsies and flamenco to *toreadores* and Don Juans. Bizet's *Carmen* had its debut in 1873.

The real Andalucians, meanwhile, were staggering through a confusing century that would see the loss of Spain's American colonies, coups, counter-coups, civil wars on behalf of pretenders to the throne (the two Carlist Wars of the 1830s and 1870s), a short-lived First Republic in 1874 and several de facto dictatorships. Andalucía, disappointed and impoverished as ever, contributed many liberal leaders. It also knew a mining boom, especially at the famous Río Tinto mines in Huelva province, the same that had been worked in Phoenician times. Typically, in what had become a thoroughly colonial economy, all the mines were in the hands of foreign, mostly British owners, and none of the profits stayed in Andalucía. The desperate peasantry, living at rock bottom in an archaic feudal structure, became one of the most radicalized rural populations in Europe.

At first, this manifested itself as simple outlawry, especially in the Sierra Morena (and in northern Spain, Corsica, Sardinia, southern Italy, north Africa – the 19th century was a great age for bandits all over the Mediterranean). In 1870, an Italian agitator and associate of Bakunin named Giuseppe Fanelli brought **Anarchism** to Andalucía. In a land where government had never been anything more than institutionalized oppression, the idea was a hit; Anarchist ideas and institutions found a firmer foothold in Spain than anywhere else in Europe, oddly concentrated in two very different milieux: the backward Andalucian peasantry and the modern industrial workers of Barcelona. Anarchist-inspired guerrilla warfare and terrorism increased steadily in Andalucía, reaching its climax in the years 1882–6, directed by a secret society called the **Mano Negra**. Violence continued for decades, met with fierce repression by the hated but effective national police, the Guardia Civil. In 1910 the national Anarchist trade union, the CNT, was founded at a congress in Sevilla.

Despite their poverty and troubles, Andalucians could occasionally make a game attempt to show they were at least trying to keep up with the modern world – most spectacularly at the 1929 *Exposición Iberoamericana*, Sevilla's first World Fair, which left the city a lovely park and some impressive monuments. The Fair project had been pushed along by Spain's dictator of the 1920s, General **Miguel Primo de Rivera**. Though a native Andalucian, from Jerez, Primo de Rivera did little else for the region. Rising discontent forced his resignation in 1929, and two years later municipal elections turned out huge majorities all over Spain for Republicans. King Alfonso XIII abdicated, and Spain was about to become a very interesting place.

1931–9
Civil War – the second Reconquista

The coming of the democratic **Second Republic** in 1931 brought little improvement to the lives of Andalucians, but it opened the gates to a flood of political agitation from extremists of every faction. Andalucía often found itself in the middle, as in

1932 when General Sanjurjo attempted unsuccessfully to mount a coup from Sevilla. Peasant rebellions intensified, especially under the radical right-wing government of 1934–6, when attempted land seizures led to such incidents as the massacre at Casas Viejas in 1934. Spain's alarmed Left formed a Popular Front to regain power in 1936, but street fighting and assassinations were becoming daily occurrences, and the new government seemed powerless to halt the country's slide into anarchy. In July 1936, the army uprising, orchestrated by Generals **Francisco Franco** and **Emilio Mola**, led to the **Civil War**. The Army of Africa, under Franco's command, quickly captured eastern Andalucía, and most of the key cities in the province soon fell under Nationalist control. Battle-hardened from campaigns against the Rif in the mountains of Spanish Morocco in the 1920s, the Army of Africa was the most effective force in the Spanish Army. Many of its battalions were made up of native Moroccans, who brought with them another bitter Spanish irony: generals fighting in the name of old Christian, monarchist Spain, bringing mercenary Muslim troops into the country for the first time in 500 years.

In Sevilla, a flamboyant officer named Gonzalo Queipo de Llano (later famous as the Nationalists' radio propaganda voice) single-handedly bluffed and bullied the city into submission, then led an armoured column to destroy the working-class district of Triana. In arch-reactionary Granada, the authorities and local fascists massacred thousands of workers and Republican loyalists, including the poet Federico García Lorca. Málaga, the last big town under Republican control, fell to Mussolini's Italian 'volunteers' in February 1937. Four thousand more loyalists were slaughtered there, and Franco's men bombed and strafed civilian refugees fleeing the city.

Thereafter, Andalucía saw little fighting, though its people shared fully in Nationalist reprisals and oppression. Franco, who had spent most of his career in the colonial service, had no problem using the same terror tactics on fellow Spaniards that the army had habitually practised on Africans. A Nationalist officer estimated that some 150,000 people were murdered in Andalucía by 1938, and in Sevilla alone at that time, the Nationalists were still shooting up to 80 people a day.

1939 to the Present
Forty years of Francisco Franco and, finally, a happy ending

After the war, in the dark days of the 1940s, Andalucía knew widespread destitution and, at times, conditions close to famine. Emigration, which had been significant ever since the discovery of America, now became a mass exodus, creating huge Andalucian colonies in Madrid and Barcelona, and smaller ones in nearly every city of northern Europe.

Economic conditions improved marginally in the 1950s, with American loans to help get the economy back on its feet and the birth of the Costa del Sol on the empty coast west of Málaga. A third factor, often overlooked, was the quietly brilliant planning of Franco's economists, setting the stage for Spain's industrial takeoff of the 1960s and '70s. In Andalucía, their major contributions were industrial programmes around Sevilla and Cádiz and a score of dams, providing cheap electricity and ending the endemic, terrible floods.

When **King Juan Carlos** ushered in the return of democracy, Andalucians were more than ready. **Felipe González**, the socialist charmer from Sevilla, ran Spain from 1982 to 1996, and other Andalucians are well represented in every sector of government and society. They took full advantage of the revolutionary regional autonomy laws of the late 1970s, building one of the most active regional governments and giving Andalucía some control over its destiny for the first time since the Reconquista. And in other ways history seems to be repeating itself over the last 20 years: the Arabs have returned in force, building a mosque in the Albaicín in Granada, making a home from home along the western Costa del Sol, and bringing economic if not exactly cultural wealth to the area. Jews once more are free to worship, and do so in small communities in Málaga, Marbella and Sevilla. In 1978 the first synagogue to be built since the Inquisition was consecrated at El Real in Málaga province.

Economically, Andalucía has steadily progressed, a trend reflected by the unemployment rate, which has dropped from a whopping 40 per cent in the 1990s to 14 per cent in 2007. On the downside, the unbridled construction that has taken place in the Costa del Sol has detracted from its appeal as a destination for foreign residents or second-home owners, while bureaucratic corruption led to the imprisonment in 2006 of several town hall officials on the Costa, including the former mayors of Marbella and Estepona resorts.

Some things never change, however; throughout the region, Andalucians maintain their ebullient, extrovert culture, living as if they were at the top of the world, especially during the numerous celebratory fiestas and *ferias*.

Art and
Architecture

03

Until the coming of the Moors, southern Spain produced little of note, or at least little that has survived. To begin at the beginning, there are the 25,000-year-old cave drawings at the Cueva de la Pileta, near Ronda, and Neolithic dolmens near Antequera and Almería. No significant buildings have been found from the Tartessians or the Phoenicians, though remains of a 7th-century BC temple have been dug up at Cádiz. Not surprisingly, with their great treasury of metals, the Iberians were skilled at making jewellery and figurines in silver and bronze (also ivory, traded up from North Africa, where elephants were still common). They built walled towns on defensible sites, and their most significant religious buildings (besides the eastern-style temples built by the Phoenicians and Carthaginians) were great storehouses where archaeologists have discovered caches containing thousands of simple *ex-voto* statuettes.

Real art begins with the arrival of the Greeks in the 7th century BC. The famous Lady of Elche in the Madrid museum, though found in the region of Murcia, may have been typical of the Greek-influenced art of all the southern Iberians; their pottery, originally decorated in geometrical patterns, began to imitate the figurative Greek work in the 5th century BC. The best collections of early work are in the Archaeological Museum at Sevilla – though everything really exceptional ends up in Madrid.

During the long period of Roman rule, Spanish art continued to follow trends from the more civilized east (ruins and amphitheatres at Itálica, Carmona, Ronda; a reconstructed temple at Córdoba; museums in Sevilla, Córdoba and Cádiz). Justinian's invasion in the middle of the 6th century BC brought new influences from the Greek world, though the exhausted region by that time had little money or leisure for art. Neither was Visigothic rule ever conducive to new advances. The Visigoths were mostly interested in gaudy jewellery and gold trinkets (best seen not in Andalucía, but in the museums of Madrid and Toledo). Almost no building work survives; the Moors purchased and demolished all of the important churches, but made good use of one architectural innovation of the Visigothic era, the more-than-semicircular 'horseshoe' arch.

Moorish

The greatest age for art in Andalucía began not immediately with the Arab conquest, but a century and a half later, with the arrival of Abd ar-Rahman and the establishment of the Umayyad emirate. The new emir and his followers had come from Damascus, the old capital of Islam, and they brought with them the best traditions of emerging Islamic art from Syria. 'Moorish art', like 'Gothic', is a term of convenience that can be misleading. Along with the enlightened patronage of the Umayyads, this new art catalysed the dormant culture of Roman Spain, creating a brilliant synthesis; of this, the first and finest example is **La Mezquita**, the Great Mosque of Córdoba.

La Mezquita was recognized in its own time as one of the wonders of the world. We are fortunate it survived, and it is chilling to think of the (literally) thousands of mosques, palaces, public buildings, gates, cemeteries and towers destroyed by the

Christians; the methodical effacement of a great culture. We can discuss Moorish architecture from its finest production, and from little else. As architecture, La Mezquita is full of subtleties and surprises (*see* pp.142–5). Some Westerners have tended to dismiss the Moorish approach as 'decorative art', without considering the philosophical background, or the expression of ideas inherent in the decoration. Figurative art was prohibited in Islam, and though lions, fantastical animals and human faces peek out frequently from painted ceramics and carvings, for more serious matters artists had to find other forms. One of them was Arabic calligraphy, which soon became an Andalucian speciality. In architecture and the decorative arts, the emphasis was on repetitive geometric patterns, mirroring a Pythagorean strain that had always been present in Islam; these made the pattern for an aesthetic based on a meticulously clever arrangement of forms, shapes and spaces, meant to elicit surprise and delight. The infinite elements of this decorative universe, and the mathematics that underlie them (*see* **Snapshots of Andalucía**, pp.53–5) come together in the most unexpected of conclusions – a reminder that unity is the basic principle of Islam.

The 'decorative' sources are wonderfully eclectic, and easy enough to discern. From Umayyad Syria came the general plan of the rectangular, many-columned mosques, along with the striped arches; from Visigothic Spain, the distinctive horseshoe arch. The floral arabesques and intricate, flowing detail, whether on a mosque window, a majolica dish or a delicately carved ivory, are the heritage of late-Roman art, as can be clearly seen on the recycled Roman capitals of La Mezquita itself. The Umayyads in Syria had been greatly impressed by Byzantine mosaics, and had copied them in their early mosques. This continued in Spain, often with artists borrowed from Constantinople. Besides architectural decoration, the same patterns and motifs appear in the minor arts of al-Andalus, in painted ceramics, textiles and in metalwork, a Spanish speciality since prehistoric times – an English baron of the time might have traded an entire village for a fine Andalucian dagger or brooch.

Such an art does not seek progress and development in our sense; it shifts slowly, like a kaleidoscope, and carefully, occasionally finding new and subtler patterns to captivate the eye and declare the unity of creation. It carried on, without decadence or revolutions, until the end of al-Andalus and beyond. The end of the caliphate and the rise of the Party Kings, ironically enough, was an impetus for art. Now, instead of one great patron there were 30, with 30 courts to embellish. Under the Almoravids and Almohads, a reforming religious fundamentalism did not mean an end to art, though it did cut down some of its decorative excesses. The Almohads, who made their capital at Sevilla, created the **Torre del Oro** and the tower called **La Giralda**, model for the great minarets of Morocco.

The Christian conquest of Córdoba, Sevilla and most of the rest of al-Andalus (1212–80) did not finish Moorish art. The tradition continued intact, with its Islamic foundations, for another two centuries in the kingdom of Granada. In the rest of Spain, Muslim artists and artisans found ready employment for nearly as long; their *mudéjar* art briefly contended with imported styles from northern Europe to become the national art of Spain. Most of its finest productions are not in

Andalucía at all; you can see them in the churches and synagogues of Toledo, the towers of Teruel and many other towns of Aragón. The trademarks of *mudéjar* building are geometrical decoration in *azulejo* tiles and brickwork, and elaborately carved wooden *artesonado* ceilings. *Mudéjar* styles and techniques would also provide a strong influence in Spain, for centuries to come, in all the minor arts, from the *taracea* inlaid woodcraft of Granada to fabrics, ceramics and metalwork. And the Moorish love of intricate decoration would resurface again and again in architecture, most notably in the Isabelline Gothic and the Churrigueresque.

Granada, isolated from the rest of the Muslim world and constantly on the defensive, produced no great advances, but this golden autumn of Moorish culture brought the decorative arts to a state of serene perfection. In the **Alhambra** (built in stages throughout the 14th century, during the height of the Nasrid kingdom), where the architecture incorporates gardens and flowing water, the emphasis is on panels of ornate plaster work, combining floral and geometric patterns with calligraphy – not only Koranic inscriptions, but the deeds of Granada's kings and contemporary lyrical poetry. Another feature is the stucco *muqarnas* ceilings (sometimes called 'stalactite ceilings'), translating the Moorish passion for geometry into three dimensions.

Granada's art and that of the *mudéjares* cross paths at Sevilla's **Alcázar**, expanded by Pedro the Cruel in the 1360s; artists from Granada did much of the work. Post-1492 *mudéjar* work can also be seen in some Sevilla palaces, such as the **Palacio de las Dueñas** or the **Casa de Pilatos**. The smaller delights of late Moorish decorative arts include painted majolica ware, inlaid wooden chests and tables (the *taracea* work, still a speciality of Granada), and exquisite silver and bronze work in everything from armour to astronomical instruments; the best collection is in the Alhambra's **Museo Nacional de Arte Hispano-Musulmán**.

Gothic and Renaissance

For art, the Reconquista and the emergence of a united Spain was a mixed blessing. The importation of foreign styles gave a new impetus to painting and architecture, but it also gradually swept away the nation's Moorish and *mudéjar* tradition, especially in the south, where it put an end to 800 years of artistic continuity. In the 13th and 14th centuries, churches in the reconquered areas were usually built in straightforward, unambitious Gothic, as with **Santa Ana** in Sevilla, built under Pedro the Cruel, and the simple and elegant parish churches of Córdoba. In the 1400s, Gothic lingered on without noticeable inspiration; Sevilla's squat and ponderous cathedral, the largest Gothic building anywhere, was probably the work of a German or Frenchman.

The Renaissance was a latecomer to Andalucía, as to the rest of Spain. In 1506, when the High Renaissance had already hit Rome, the Spaniards were building a Gothic chapel in Granada for the tombs of Fernando and Isabel. This time, though, they had an architect of distinction: **Enrique de Egas** (*c.* 1445–1534), who had already created important works in Toledo and Santiago de Compostela, made the Capilla Real Spain's finest late-Gothic building, in the lively style called 'Isabelline Gothic', which roughly corresponds to the contemporary French Flamboyant or English Perpendicular. Isabelline Gothic is only one part of the general tendency of Spanish art in these times, which has come to be called the **Plateresque**. A *platero* is a silversmith or a jeweller, and the style takes its name from the elaborate decoration applied to any building, whether Gothic or Renaissance.

The Plateresque in the decorative arts had already been established in Sevilla (with the huge cathedral retable, begun in 1482), and would continue into the next century, with the cathedral's Capilla Real and sacristy, and the 1527 Ayuntamiento (town hall), by Diego de Riaño. Other noteworthy figures of this period are the Siloés: **Gil de Siloé**, a talented sculptor, and his son **Diego**, who came to Andalucía after creating the famous Golden Staircase in Burgos cathedral, and began the cathedrals at Granada (1526) and Úbeda. The Granada cathedral provided a precursor for High Renaissance architecture in Spain; Diego de Siloé was responsible for most of the interior, taking over the original Gothic plan and making it into a lofty, classical space in a distinctive, personal style. He is also responsible for the cathedral of Guadix, and contributed to the Capilla del Salvador at Úbeda.

Charles V took a personal interest in Granada, and de Siloé had a hard time convincing the king that his new architecture was really an advance over the more obvious charms of Isabelline Gothic. Charles eventually came round, while at the same time mainstream Renaissance architecture arrived with **Pedro Machuca** (1485–1550), who had studied in Italy. Strongly influenced by the monumental classicism of Bramante, his imposing Palacio de Carlos V (1527–8), built for the king in the Alhambra at Granada, was the most famous and influential work of the Spanish Renaissance; it actually predates the celebrated High Renaissance Roman palaces it so closely resembles. Andalucía's Renaissance city is Úbeda, with an ensemble of exceptional churches and palaces. Its above-mentioned Sacra Capilla del Salvador contains some of the finest Renaissance reliefs and sculpture in Spain.

In the stern climate of the Counter-Reformation, architecture turned towards a disciplined austerity, the *estilo desornamentado* introduced by **Juan de Herrera** at Philip II's palace-monastery of El Escorial, near Madrid. Herrera gave Sevilla a textbook example in his Lonja, a business exchange for the city's merchants (1582). His most accomplished follower, **Andrés de Vandelvira**, brought the 'unornamented style' to a striking conclusion with his Hospital de Santiago in Úbeda, and other works in Úbeda and Baeza; he also began the ambitious cathedral at Jaén.

Baroque and Beyond

This style, like the Renaissance, was slow in reaching southern Spain. One of the most important projects of the 17th century, the façade for the unfinished Granada cathedral, wound up entrusted to a painter from Granada, **Alonso Cano** (1601–67), called in his time the 'Spanish Michelangelo' for his talents at painting, sculpture and architecture. The idiosyncratic and memorable result (1664), with its three gigantic arches, shows some appreciation for the new Roman style, though it is firmly planted in the Renaissance. Real Baroque arrived three years later, with Eufrasio López de Rojas's façade for Jaén Cathedral (1667).

The most accomplished southern architect in the decades that followed was **Leonardo de Figueroa** (1650–1730), who combined Italian styles with a native Spanish delight in colour and patterns in brickwork; he worked almost entirely in Sevilla (El Salvador and San Luís, both begun 1699, Colegio San Telmo, 1724, and the Convento de la Merced, now the Museo de Bellas Artes). His son Ambrosio Figueroa continued in the same style. Spanish sculpture was largely a matter of gory realism done in wood, as in the work of **Juan Martínez Montañés** (Sevilla cathedral). **Pedro de Mena** (1628–88), an artist from Granada known for wood sculpture, started out as Alonso Cano's assistant, and later did the relief panels in the choir of Málaga cathedral.

The 17th century has often been described as a golden age of painting in Andalucía. It begins with **Francisco Pacheco** of Sanlúcar de Barrameda (1564–1664). Not much of a painter himself, Pacheco is still a key figure in the beginning of this Andalucian school: founder of an academy, teacher and father-in-law of Velázquez, author of an influential treatise, the *Arte de la Pintura* – and official censor to the Sevilla Inquisition. Giving ample room for exaggeration, this 'golden age' does include **Velázquez** (1599–1660), a native *sevillano* who left the region for ever in 1623 when he became painter to the king. Almost none of his work can be seen in the south. Of those who stayed behind, the most important was Alonso Cano. Cano studied sculpture under Montañés, and painting under Pacheco alongside Velázquez. His work often has a careful architectonic composition that betrays his side career as an architect, but seldom ranges above the pedestrian and devotional. Cano's sculpture, often in polychromed wood, can be seen in Granada cathedral, including the *Immaculate Conception* (1655) that many consider his masterpiece.

Francisco Herrera of Sevilla (1576–1656) shows more backbone, in keeping with the dark and stormy trends of contemporary Italian painting, under the influence of Caravaggio. His son, Francisco Herrera the younger (1627–85) was a follower of Murillo who spent little time in Sevilla. One of the most intriguing painters of the time is **Juan Sánchez Cotán** (1561–1627), the 'father of Baroque realism' in Spain, noted for his strange, intense still lifes. Sánchez Cotán, whose work had a great influence on Zurbarán, spent the last years of his life as a monk in Granada.

Best of all is an emigrant from Extremadura, **Francisco de Zurbarán** (1598–1664), who arrived in Sevilla in 1628. He is often called the 'Spanish Caravaggio', and though his contrasts of light and shadow are equally distinctive, this is as much a disservice as a compliment. Set in stark, bright colours, Zurbarán's world is an unearthly vision of monks and saints, with portraits of heavenly celebrities that seem painted from life, and uncanny, almost abstract scenes of monastic life like the *Miracle of Saint Hugo* in Sevilla's Museo de Bellas Artes. Later in life, Zurbarán went a bit soft, coming increasingly under the influence of his younger contemporary Murillo. Seeing the rest of his work would require a long trip across two continents; Napoleon's armies under Maréchal Soult stole hundreds of his paintings, and there are more than 80 in the Louvre alone.

In the next generation of southern artists the worst qualities of a decaying Spain are often painfully evident. Sculpture declined precipitously, with artists adding glass eyes and real human hair in an attempt to heighten even more the gruesome realism of their religious subjects. Among the painters, **Bartolomé Esteban Murillo**

(1617–82), another *sevillano*, is the best of the lot; two centuries ago he was widely considered among the greatest painters of all time. Modern eyes are often distracted by the maudlin, missal-illustration religiosity of his saints and Madonnas, neglecting to notice the exceptional talent and total sincerity that created them. Spaniards call his manner the *estilo vaporoso*. Zurbarán's and Murillo's reputations suffered a lot in the 19th century from the large number of lesser works by other painters who copied their subjects and styles, and whose works were later attributed to the two masters. Murillo founded the Academy of Painting at Sevilla and was its first leader; he died after a fall from the scaffolding in 1682.

Somewhat harder to digest is **Juan de Valdés Leal** (1622–90), who helped Murillo organize the Sevilla Academy. His work is considerably more intense and dramatic than Murillo's, and he is best known for the ghoulish, death-obsessed allegories he painted for the reformed Don Juan, Miguel de Mañara, at the Hospital de la Caridad in Sevilla (these two artists can be compared in Sevilla's museum and at the Caridad). After 1664, the head of sculpture at the Academy was **Pedro Roldán** (1624–99). Born in Antequera, Roldán was a fellow student of Pedro de Mena at Granada. Roldán was perhaps the most notable exponent of the Spanish desire to combine painting, sculpture and architecture in unified works of art. He is best known for his altarpiece at Sevilla's Caridad, which Valdés Leal polychromed, and he also contributed works for the façade of Jaén Cathedral. Roldán's daughter Luisa became a sculptor too – the only Spanish woman ever to become a king's court sculptor (for Charles II).

If any style could find a natural home in Spain, it would be the **rococo**. Eventually it did, though a lack of energy and funds often delayed it. Spain's most important architecture in this time, the elaborately decorated work of the Churriguera family and their followers, is mostly in the north, in Salamanca and Madrid. In Andalucía, **Vicente Acero** introduced the tendency early on, with a striking façade for the cathedral at Guadix. He had a chance to repeat it on a really important building project, the new Cádiz cathedral, but the money ran out, and the result was a stripped-down Baroque shell – ambition without the decoration. The great Fábrica de Tabacos in Sevilla (1725–65), the largest project of the century in Andalucía, met a similar end, leaving an austere work, an unintentional precursor of the neoclassical. Whenever the resources were there, Andalucian architects responded with a tidal wave of eccentric embellishment worthy of the Moors – or the Aztecs. Pre-Columbian architecture may have been a bigger influence on Spain than is generally credited; judge for yourself at the chapel and sacristy of the Cartuja in Granada (1747–62), the most blatant interior in Spain.

Elsewhere, the decorative freedom of the rococo led to some unique and delightful buildings, essentially Spanish and often incorporating eclectic references to the styles of centuries past. José de Bada's church of San Juan de Dios (1737–59) in Granada is a fine example. In Córdoba, there is the elegant Convento de la Merced (1745), and the *Coro* of the cathedral, inside La Mezquita, a 16th-century Gothic work redecorated (1748–57) with elaborate stucco decoration by **Juan de Oliva** and stalls and overall design by **Pedro Duque Cornejo**. Sevilla, in its decline, was still building palaces, blending the new style with the traditional requirements of a patio and grand staircase; the best of the century's palaces, however, is in Écija, the Palacio de Peñaflor (1728). Many smaller towns, responding to the improved economic conditions under Philip V and Charles III, built impressive churches, notably in Priego de Córdoba, Lucena, Utrera, Estepa and Écija.

In view of all Andalucía's troubles, it should not be surprising that little has been produced in the last two centuries. **Pablo Picasso**, born in Málaga, was the outstanding example of the artist who had to find his inspiration and his livelihood elsewhere. Despite the lack of significant recent architecture, Andalucians hold on to the glories of their past with tenacity; splashes of *azulejo* tiles and Moorish decoration turn up in everything from bus stations and market-houses to simple suburban cottages. For some 500 years now, Andalucians have most often been constrained by their sorry history to follow styles and inspirations from outside. Few regions of Europe, however, can show such a remarkable heritage of locally nurtured arts and crafts, styles and motifs, the heritage of both Moor and Christian. Now that prosperity and confidence are slowly coming back, we might hope that Andalucía can find something in its old glories that fits a modern age, and amaze and delight the world once again.

Snapshots of Andalucía

04

Bullfights

In Spanish newspapers, you will not find accounts of the bullfights (*corridas*) on the sports pages. Look in the 'arts and culture' section, for that is how Spain has always thought of this singular spectacle. Bullfighting combines elements of ballet with the primal finality of Greek tragedy. To Spaniards, it is a ritual sacrifice without a religion, and it divides the nation irreconcilably between those who find it brutal and demeaning, an echo of the old Spain best forgotten, and those who couldn't live without it. Its origins are obscure. Some claim it derives from Roman circus games, others that it started with the Moors, or in the Middle Ages, when the bull faced a mounted knight with a lance.

There are bullrings all over Spain, and as far afield as Arles in France and Guadalajara, Mexico, but modern bullfighting is quintessentially Andalucían. The present form had its beginnings around the year 1800 in Ronda, when Francisco Romero developed the basic pattern of the modern *corrida*; some of his moves and passes, and those of his celebrated successor, Pedro Romero, are still in use today.

The first royal *aficionado* was Fernando VII, the reactionary post-Napoleonic monarch who also brought back the Inquisition. He founded the Royal School of Bullfighting in Sevilla, and promoted the spectacle across the land as a circus for the discontented populace. Since the Civil War, bullfighting has gone through a period of troubles similar to those of boxing in the USA. Scandals of weak bulls, doped-up bulls, and bulls with the points of their horns shaved have been frequent. Attempts at reform have been made, and all the problems seem to have decreased bullfighting's popularity only slightly.

In keeping with its ritualistic aura, the *corrida* is one of the few things in Andalucía that begins strictly on time. The show commences with the colourful entry of the *cuadrillas* (teams of bullfighters or *toreros*) and the *alguaciles*, officials dressed in 17th-century costume, who salute the 'president' of the fight. Usually three teams fight two bulls each, the whole taking only about two hours. Each of the six fights, however, is a self-contained drama performed in four acts. First, upon the entry of the bull, the members of the *cuadrilla* tease him a bit, and the *matador*, the team leader, plays him with the cape to test his qualities. Next comes the turn of the *picadores*, on padded horses, whose task is to slightly wound the bull in the neck with a short lance or *pica*, and the *banderilleros*, who agilely plant sharp darts in the bull's back while avoiding the sweep of its horns. The effect of these wounds is to weaken the bull physically without diminishing any of its fighting spirit, and to force it to keep its head lower for the third and most artistic stage of the fight, when the lone *matador* conducts his pas de deux with the deadly, if doomed, animal. Ideally, this is the transcendent moment, the *matador* leading the bull in deft passes and finally crushing its spirit with a tiny cape called a *muleta*. Now the defeated bull is ready for 'the moment of truth'. The kill must be clean and quick, a sword thrust to the heart. The corpse is dragged out to the waiting butchers.

More often than not the job is botched. Most bullfights, in fact, are a disappoint-ment, especially if the *matadores* are *novilleros* or beginners, but to the *aficionado* the chance to see one or all of the stages performed to perfection makes it all worthwhile. When a *matador* is good, the band plays and the hats and handkerchiefs fly. A truly excellent performance earns as a reward from the president one, or both, of the bull's ears; or rarely, for an exceptionally brilliant performance, both ears and the tail.

You'll be lucky to see a bullfight at all; there are only about 500 each year in Spain, mostly coinciding with holidays or a town's fiesta. During Sevilla's *feria* there is a bullfight every afternoon at the famous Maestranza ring, while the rings in Málaga and Puerto de Santa María near Cádiz are other major venues. Tickets can be astronomically expensive and hard to come by, especially for a well-known *matador*; sometimes touts buy out the lot. Get them in advance, if you can, and directly from the office in the *plaza de toros* to avoid the hefty commission charges. Prices vary according to the sun – the most expensive seats are entirely in the shade.

City Slickers

You're on the train for Córdoba, passing the hours through some of the loneliest landscapes in Europe. For a long time, there's been nothing to see but olive trees – gnarled veterans, some of them planted in the time of Fernando and Isabel. You may see a donkey pulling a cart. At twilight, you pull in at the central station, and walk four blocks down to the Avenida del Gran Capitán, an utterly Parisian boulevard of chic boutiques and pompous banks, booming with traffic.

You don't often see Andalucians going off on picnics in the country. The ground is dry, vegetation usually sparse, and the sun can seem like a death ray even in winter. Climate has always forced people here to seek their pleasure elsewhere; it is the impetus behind their exquisite gardens, and it has made them the most resolutely urban people in Europe. In city centres the air is electric, a cocktail of motion, colour, and fragrances that goes to your head like the best *manzanilla*. It has probably had much the same ambience for over 2,000 years; the atmosphere may be hard to recapture, but we can learn a lot by looking at decoration and design.

We know little about city life in Roman times – only that for relatively small populations, towns such as Itálica had amphitheatres and other amenities comparable to any in the empire. The cities of Moorish Spain were a revelation, with libraries, public gardens and street lighting at a time when feudal Europe was scratching its carrot rows with a short stick. Their design, similar to that of North African and Middle Eastern cities, can be discerned (with some difficulty) in parts of Granada, Córdoba and Sevilla today. It is difficult to say what aspects of the design of Andalucía's Moorish cities are legacies from Roman Baetica, and what was introduced by the Moors themselves. Enclosure was the key idea in Moorish architecture: a great mosque and its walled courtyard occupied the centre, near the fortified palace (*alcázar* or *alcazaba*) and its walled gardens. Along with the markets and baths, these were located in the *medina*, and locked up behind its walls each night. The residential quarters that surrounded the *medina* were islands in themselves, a maze of narrow streets where the houses, rich or poor, looked inwards to open patios while turning blank walls to the street. Some of these survive, with their original decoration, as private homes in Granada's Albaicín.

In Roman times, the patio was called a peristyle. The gracious habit of building a house around a colonnaded central court was perfected by the Greeks, and became common across the Roman Mediterranean. Today, while most of us enjoy the charms of our cramped flats and dull, squarish houses, the Andalucians have never given up their love of the old-fashioned way. In Córdoba especially, the patios of the old quarters spill over with roses, wisteria and jasmine; each year there is a competition for the prettiest. Besides the houses, some of the cellular quality of Moorish cities survived the Reconquista. In 16th-century Sevilla, thick with artful bandits, the silversmiths had their own walled quarter (and their own cops to guard it). The Moorish urban aesthetic evolved gracefully into the modern Andalucían: the simple, unforgettable panorama of almost any town – an oasis of brilliant white rectangularity, punctuated sharply by upright cypresses and the warm sandstone of churches, palaces and towers.

One Spanish invention, combining Italian Renaissance planning with native tradition, was the arcaded, rectangular square usually called the *Plaza Mayor*. The best are in Madrid and Salamanca, but many Andalucían towns have one, and there is a huge dilapidated specimen in Córdoba. Architecturally unified – the four walls often seem like a building turned inside-out – the *Plaza Mayor* translated the essence of the patio into public space. Such a square made a perfect stage for the colourful life of a Spanish city. Spanish theatres in the great age of Lope de Vega and Calderón took the same form, with three sides of balconies, the fourth for the stage, on the narrow end, and a Shakespearean 'pit' at ground level. In the last two centuries, while the rest of Spain continued to create innovations in urban design and everyday pageantry, impoverished Andalucía contributed little – some elegant bullrings, certain exquisite redesigns of the old Moorish gardens, a few grand boulevards like the Alameda of Málaga and the *paseos* of Granada, and some eccentric decorations, such as the gigantic, sinister stone birds of prey that loom over most city centres – symbols of an insurance company.

Since the 1970s and the end of Francoism, one can sense a slickness gathering momentum: a touch of anonymous good design in a shop sign, new pavements and lighting, ambitious new architecture with a splash of colour and surprise. The *El Corte Inglés* department store in Málaga has been known to be entirely covered in computer-controlled electric lights at Christmas, nearly a vertical acre of permanent fireworks, flashing peacock tails and other patterns in constantly changing, brilliant colours – as spectacular and futuristic a decoration as any city has ever had. Watch out for these sharp Andalucíans – and for Spaniards in general. While we fog-bound northerners are nodding off with Auntie at twelve o'clock, they may well be plotting the delights of the future.

Dust in the Wind

The poets of al-Andalus devoted most of their attention to sensuous songs of love, nature, wine, women and boys, but amid all the lavish beauty there would linger, like a *basso continuo*, a note of refined detachment, of melancholy and futility. Instead of forgetting death in their man-made paradises, the poets made a point of reminding their listeners of how useless it was to become attached to these worldly delights. After all, only God is forever, and why express love to something that would one day turn to dust? Why even attempt to build something perfect and eternal – the main ingredients of the lovely, delicate Alhambra are plaster and wood. The Nasrid kings, were they to return, might be appalled to find it still standing.

The Christians who led the Reconquista had no time for futility. In their architecture and art they built for eternity, plonking a soaring church right in the middle of the Great Mosque and an imperial palace on the Alhambra – literal, lapidarian, emanating the power and total control of the temporal Church and State. Their oppression reduced the sophisticated songs of the Moorish courts to a baser fatalism. The harsh realities of everyday life encouraged people to live for the moment, to grab what happiness they could in an uncertain world. This uncertainty was best expressed by the 17th-century Spanish playwright Pedro Calderón de la Barca, especially in his great *La Vida es Sueño* (Life is a Dream), known as the Catholic answer to *Hamlet*.

There wasn't much poetry in Granada between 1492 and the advent of Federico García Lorca, born in 1898 in the Vega just outside town. Lorca, a fine musician as well as a poet and playwright, found much of his inspiration in what would be called nowadays Granada's 'alternative' traditions, especially those of the Gypsies. In 1922, Lorca was a chief organizer of Granada's first *cante jondo* festival, designed to bring flamenco singing to international attention and prevent it from sliding into a hackneyed Andalucían joke. In 1927 he published the book of poems that made him the most popular poet in Spain, the *Romancero Gitano* (Gypsy Ballads). His plays, like *Bodas de Sangre* (Blood Wedding) and *Yerma* (The Barren One), have the lyrical, disturbing force of the deepest *cante jondo*. But of post-Reconquista Granada he was sharply critical, accusing Fernando and Isabel of destroying a much more sophisticated civilization than their own – and as for the modern inhabitants of Granada, they were an imported reactionary bourgeois contingent from the north, not 'real' Andalucíans. Lorca criticized, but he kept coming back, and had dreams of bringing the city's once great culture back to life.

In Granada, a commemorative park at Víznar marks the spot where, on 18 August 1936, local police or rebel soldiers took Lorca and shot him dead. No one knows who gave the orders, or the reason why; the poet had supported the Republic but was not actively political. When news of his secret execution leaked out, it was an embarrassment to Franco, who managed to hush up the affair until his own death. But most historians agree that the killing was a local vendetta for Lorca's outspoken views of his home town, a blood sacrifice to the stone god of Fernando and Isabel and Charles V who fears all change, closing (one can only hope) once and for all the circle of bittersweet futility, frustration and death.

Flamenco

For many people, flamenco is the soul of Spain, like bullfighting, and an essential part of the culture that sets it apart from the rest of the world. Good flamenco, with that ineffable quality of *duende*, has a primitive, ecstatic allure that draws in its listeners until they feel as if their very hearts were pounding in time with its relentless rhythms, their guts seared by its ululating Moorish wails and the sheer drama of the dance. Few modern experiences are more cathartic.

As folklore goes, however, flamenco is newborn. It began in the 18th century in Andalucía, where its originators, the Gypsies, called one another '*flamencos*' – a derogatory term believed to date back to the days when Charles V's Flemish (*flamenco*) courtiers bled Spain dry. These Gypsies, especially in the Guadalquivir delta cities of Sevilla, Cádiz and Jerez, sang songs of oppression, lament and bitter romance, a kind of blues that by the 19th century began to catch on among all the other downtrodden inhabitants of Andalucía.

Yet despite flamenco's recent origins, the Andalucían intelligentsia, especially Lorca and Manuel de Falla, found (or invented) much to root it deeply in the south's soil and soul. Its rhythms and Doric mode are as old as Andalucía's ancient Greek settlers; its spirit of improvisation and spontaneity date from the famous Córdoba school of music and poetry, founded in 820 by Abu al-Hassan Ali ibn Nafi, better known as Ziryab, the 'Blackbird'; the half-tonal notes and lyrics of futility of the *cante jondo*, or deep song, the purest flamenco, seem to go straight back to the Arab troubadours of al-Andalus. But just how faithfully the music of al-Andalus was preserved among the Gypsies and others to be reincarnated as flamenco will never be known; the Arabs knew of musical notation, but disdained it in their preference for improvisation.

By the late 19th century, flamenco had gone semi-public, performed in the back rooms of cafés in Sevilla and Málaga. Its very popularity in Spain, and the enthusiasm set off by Bizet's *Carmen* abroad, began seriously to undermine its harsh, true quality. At the same time, flamenco's influence spread into the popular and folk repertories to create a happier, less intense genre called the *sevillana* (often songs in praise of you know where). When schoolchildren at a bus stop in Cádiz burst into an impromptu dance and hand-clapping session, or when some old cronies in Málaga's train-station bar start singing and reeling, you can bet they're doing a *sevillana*. In the 1920s attempts were made to establish some kind of standards for the real thing, especially *cante jondo*, though without lasting results; the 'real, original flamenco' was never meant to be performed as such, and will only be as good as its 'audience'. This should ideally be made up of other musicians and flamenco aficionados, whose participation is essential in the spontaneous, invariably late-night combustion of raw emotion, alcohol, drugs and music, to create *duende*.

Flamenco not only remains popular in Spain, but is undergoing something of a renaissance. It all started in the 1970s and 1980s when Paco de Lucía, a native of Algeciras, took his art to the international stage, fusing it with jazz. Paco's music is a must for any lover of flamenco guitar; he continues to produce traditional records as well as recording crossover with other musicians like John McLaughlin and Al Di Meola. Within Spain, Chambao, from Málaga, have fused flamenco with electronic sounds, and singers like Niña Pastori are following in their wake. On a pop level, flamenco has achieved an international audience thanks to the Gypsy Kings (who are French) and the Michael Flatley-style dance spectaculars of Joaquín Cortés.

The Founding Father

Andalucía for itself, for Spain and for Humanity.

So reads the proud device on the regional escutcheon, hurriedly cooked up by the Andalucíans after the regional autonomy laws of the 1970s made them masters in their own house once again. Above the motto we see a strong fellow, mythological-ly underdressed and accompanied by two lions. Though perhaps more familiar to us for his career among the Hellenes, he is also the first Andalucían – HERCULES DOMINATOR FUNDATOR.

The Greeks themselves admit that Hercules found time for two extended journeys to the distant and little-known West. In the eleventh of his Twelve Labours, the Apples of the Hesperides caper, he made it as far as the environs of Tangier, where he dispatched the giant Antaeus. The tenth Labour brought Hercules into Spain, sailing in the golden goblet of Helios and using his lion skin for a sail. In the fabled land of Tartessos, on the 'red island' of Erytheia, he slew the three-headed titan Geryon and stole his cattle. Before heading back to Greece, he founded the city of Gades, or Cádiz, on the island (Cádiz, surrounded by marshes, is almost an island). He also erected his well-known Pillars, Gibraltar and Mount Abyle, across the way in Africa. His return was one of the all-time bad trips; whenever you're crazed and dying on some five-hour 'semi-direct' Andalucían bus ride (say, Granada to Córdoba via Rute), think of Hercules, marching Geryon's cows through Spain and over the Pyrenees, then making a wrong turn that took him halfway down the Italian peninsula before he noticed the mistake. After mortal combats with several other giants and monsters, he finally made it to Greece – but then his nemesis, Hera, sent a stinging blue-tail fly to stampede the cattle. They didn't stop until they reached the Scythian Desert.

To most people, Hercules is little more than mythology's most redoubtable Dog Warden, rounding up not only Cerberus, the Hound of Hell, but most of the other stray monsters that dug up the roses and soiled the footpaths of the Heroic Age. But there is infinitely more than this to the character of the most-travelled, hardest-working hero of them all. In antiquity, wherever Hercules had set foot the people credited him with founding nations and cities, building roads and canals, excavating lakes and draining swamps. And there is the intellectual Hercules, the master of astronomy and lord of the zodiac, the god of prophecy and eloquence who taught both the Latins and the Spaniards their letters. One version has it that the original Pillars of Hercules were not mountains at all, but columns, like those of the Temple of Jerusalem, and connected with some alphabetical mysticism.

Ancient mythographers had their hands full, sorting out the endless number of deities and heroes known to the peoples of Europe, Africa and the Middle East, trying to decide whether the same figure was hiding behind different names and rites. Varro recorded no fewer than 44 Hercules, and modern scholars have found the essential Herculean form in myths from Celtic Ireland to Mesopotamia. Melkarth, the Phoenician Hercules, would have had his temples in southern Spain long before the first Greek ever saw Gibraltar. Not a bad fellow to have for a founding father – and a reminder that in Andalucía the roots of culture are as strong and as deep as in any corner of Europe.

Getting Them Back

In the 1970s Robert Graves recalled overhearing two Londoners talking about their vacations: 'I went to Majorca this year,' says one. Her friend asks, 'Where's that?' and receives the answer, 'I don't know, I flew.' But the boom years of the Spanish package tour are definitely over. The drop in visitors is ringing alarm bells in Spain, and Europe's most intelligent and capable tourism bureaucracy is making a determined effort to put the country back in its former position by means of a far-sighted and extensive change of image.

The downmarket profile of resorts like Torremolinos will take a long time to change in the minds of the foreign public, who understandably but somewhat mistakenly connect it with tattooed lager louts, late-night punch-ups and raucous discos belting out music until dawn. There's a fair degree of snobbery involved in these attitudes; who in Britain, for example, boasts of having just spent a holiday on the Costa del Sol, with destinations such as Turkey, Florida and the Caribbean beckoning at affordable prices? The principal obstacle to attracting and sustaining mass tourism is the quality of holiday and destination on offer. Although the independent traveller is happy to pack guidebook, camera and sensible shoes, and head off on a cultural pilgrimage to Granada's Alhambra, Córdoba's Mezquita, Sevilla's Giralda or the Cádiz Carnival, and along the way experience and indulge in the *real* Andalucía, the majority of visitors are interested in less ethereal pursuits, and the ingredients for their fun are beaches, hotels, food and entertainment at a reasonable price.

Spain can meet these criteria; too well, some malcontent Hispanophiles would say – those who think that the country has sacrificed its integrity to provide monstrous concrete resort playgrounds, paint them white and pass them off as Andalucian *pueblos*. So what can be done? It's too late to tear down what already exists, but it's time the government pushed the stop button on the coastal developments, on the Costa del Sol particularly, but no less so on the Costa de la Luz, where full-scale construction would mean, and in some places has already meant, the ruination of an untamed stretch of coast. Control future development, improve the existing infrastructure and abolish Spain's reputation as solely a paradise for sun-seeking tipplers, and maybe more visitors will come for the most genuine of motives – to get a balanced view of a country rich in history, culture and fun.

Hot-blooded Andalucian Women

Andalucía is home to roughly a fifth of Spain's people, which means that more than one-tenth of the population consists of the most sultry, sensuous women in all of Europe. Ah, *señores*, how they arch their supple torsos in an improvised *sevillana*, clicking their magic castanets! *Dios*, how provocative they are behind the iron grilles of their windows, with their come-hither, burning black eyes blinking over flickering fans at their handsome *caballero*, throwing him a red rose symbolizing promise and desire!

Ever since the first boatload of dancing girls from Cádiz docked at the slave-markets of ancient Rome, the women of Andalucía have had to put up with this – an extraordinary reputation for grace, beauty and amorous dispositions. Travellers' accounts and novels elaborate on their exotic charms, spiced by the languor of the Moorish harem odalisque and the supposed promiscuity of the passionate Gypsy. After all, when Leporello counts off his master's conquests in Mozart's *Don Giovanni*, which country comes out on top? Spain, of course, with 1,003 victims to the arch-libertine's art of persuasion.

Nothing kept this fond male fancy afloat as much as the fact that nubile Andalucían women were tantalizingly inaccessible, thanks to a rigid Latin code of honour second to none. It took the Industrial Revolution, the Sevilla tobacco factory and a French visitor, Prosper Mérimée, to bring this creature of the imagination out into the open, in the form of the beautiful Gypsy temptress *Carmen* (1845), rendered immortally saucy in Bizet's opera of 1873. Step aside, Don Juan, or be stepped on! This new stereotype was as quick to light up a cheroot as to kick aside her sweetheart for a strutting matador in tight trousers. Not surprisingly, it wasn't long before the tobacco factory and its steamy, scantily clad examples of feminine pulchritude (labouring for a handful of pesetas each day) attracted as many tourists as the Giralda tower.

Alas, where is the kitsch of yesteryear? Modern young Andalucían women are, like modern Andalucian men, among the most normal, mentally well-balanced people in the world. Ask them about the cloistered *señoritas* of the past and they'll laugh. Ask them about the unbridled Carmen, and they'll laugh. Ask them about the bizarre wind called the *solano* that troubles Cádiz in the springtime, a wind that in the old days drove the entire female population en masse to the beach, where they would fling off their clothes and dive into the sea to seek relief while the local cavalry regiment stood guard. Ask them about it, and they'll just laugh.

Roses of the Secret Garden

Western art and Islamic art are two worlds that will never agree. Even today, the sort of folk who believe in the divinity of Michelangelo or the essential greatness of the Baroque can be found in print, sniffing at the art of the Alhambra as merely 'decorative'. On the other side, you will discover a state of mind that can dismiss our familiar painting and sculpture as frivolous, an impious obsession with the appearances of the moment that ignores the transcendent realities beneath the surface. A powerful idea was in the air in the 7th–8th centuries, perhaps a reaction against the worldliness and incoherence that drowned classical civilization. It was not limited to Islam alone; the 'iconoclastic' controversy in Byzantium, following the attempt of Emperor Leo III to end the idolatrous veneration of icons, was about the same issue.

However this argument started, Islam grew up with an aversion to figurative art. At the same time, Islam was gaining access to the scientific and mathematical heritage of Greece and Rome, and finding it entirely to its liking. A new approach to art gradually took form, based on the sacred geometry of Byzantine architecture and on a trend of mathematical mysticism that goes back to Pythagoras. Number, proportion and symmetry were the tools God used to create the world. The same rule could be found in every aspect of creation, and could be reproduced in art by the simple methods of Euclidean geometry. This geometry now found its place not only in the structure of a building, but also in its decoration.

Once the habit of thinking this way was established, it profoundly affected life and art in all the Islamic world, including Spain. The land itself became a careful mosaic, with neat rows of olive trees draped over the hills and the very beans and carrots in the gardens laid out in intricate patterns. (Andalucían farmers still do it: you can see a remarkable example of such a landscape from the *mirador* in Úbeda, *see* p.171.) While nature was being made to imitate art, Muslim artists, consciously or not, often imitated the hidden processes of nature – the Córdoba mosque grew like a crystal with the columns and aisles of each new addition. Often, they created novelties by changing scales, reducing and replicating old forms to make new, more complex ones. One example of this is the Visigothic horseshoe arch. You can see it in its simplest form at Córdoba or Medinat al-Zahra; later, as in Sevilla's Alcázar, the same arch is made of smaller versions of itself. And in the Alhambra you'll see arches made of arches made of arches, seeming to grow organically down from the patterns on the walls. A tree or a snowflake finds its form in much the same way. (Fans of chaos theory, take note – the Moors had anticipated fractals and Koch curves 600 years ago.)

Three dimensions is the domain of the mundane shell, the worldly illusion. The archetypes, the underlying reality, can be more fittingly expressed in two. With their straightedge and compass, Islamic artists developed a tradition of elaborate geometrical decoration, in painted tiles, stucco, or wooden grilles and ceilings. The highest levels of subtlety reached by this art were in Isfahan, Persia, in Egypt, and in Granada. The foundation, as in all constructive geometry, was the circle ('Man's heart is the centre, heaven the circumference', as a medieval Christian mystic put it). From this, they wove the exquisite patterns that embellish the Alhambra, exotic blooms interlaced in rhythms of 3, 5, 6, 8 or 12. This, however, is not the shabby, second-hand symbolism of our times. A 12-pointed flower does not *symbolize* the firmament and the 12 signs of the zodiac, for example; it *recalls* this, and many other things as well. For philosophers, these patterns could provide a meditation on the numerical harmony of creation; for the rest of us, they stand by themselves, lovely, measured creations, whispering a sweet invitation to look a bit more closely at the wonders around us. The patterns of the Alhambra haunt Andalucía to this day. In Granada especially, these geometric flowers are endlessly reproduced on *azulejo* tiles in bars and restaurants, and in the *taracea* (marquetry) boxes and tables sold in the Alcaicería.

One of the favourite games of the Islamic artists was filling up space elegantly, in the sense that a mathematician understands that word. In geometry, only three regular polygons, when repeated, can entirely fill a flat plane: the hexagon (as in a honeycomb); the square (as on a chessboard); and the equilateral triangle. Some not-so-regular polygons (any triangle or parallelogram, for example) can do it too. Try and find some more complex forms; it isn't easy. One modern artist fascinated

1

2

3

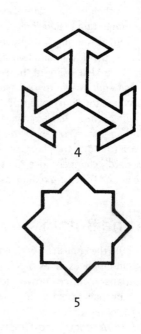

4

5

by these problems was Maurits Cornelis Escher, whose tricks of two-dimensional space are beloved of computer programmers and other Pythagoreans of our own age. Figures 1, 2 and 4 above can fill a plane. The second, with a little imagination and geometrical know-how, could be made into one of Escher's space-filling birds or fishes. Figure 3 doesn't quite do the job, but properly arranged it creates a secondary pattern of eight-pointed stars (figure 5) in between. For a puzzle, try and multiply each of the first four on paper to fill a plane. Answers can be found on the walls of the Alhambra.

By now, you may suspect that these shapes were not employed without reason. In fact, according to the leading authority on such matters, Keith Critchlow (in his book *Islamic Patterns*), the patterns formed by figures 1 and 3 mirror the symmetrical arrangement of numbers in a magic square. Triangular figures 2 and 4 are based on the *tetractys*, a favourite study of the Pythagoreans.

But a Spanish Muslim did not need to be a mathematician to appreciate the lesson of this kind of geometry. Everyone understood the basic tenet of Islam – that creation is One: harmonious and complete. Imagine some cultured minister of a Granadan king, musing under the arcades of the Court of the Lions, reflecting perhaps on the nature that shaped the roses in the court, and how the same laws are proclaimed by the ceramic blossoms within.

Castra

In laying out their military camps, as in anything else, the Romans liked to go by the book. From Britain to Babylonia, they established hundreds of permanent forts (*castra* in Latin) all seemingly stamped out of the same press, with a neatly rectangular circuit of walls and two straight streets, the *cardo* and *decumanus*, crossing in the middle. Many of these grew into towns (any place in Britain, for example, that ends in *-chester* or *-caster*).

In Spain, where the Roman wars of conquest went on for 200 years, there are perhaps more of these than anywhere else, and it's interesting to try and trace out the outlines of the Roman *castrum* while you're exploring a Spanish city. In Barcelona's Barri Gòtic, the plan is obvious, and in Ávila and Cáceres the streets and walls have hardly changed since Roman times. But with a little practice and a good map you can find the *castra* hiding inside Córdoba and a score of other towns.

Spain and Britain

Where would the English be without Spain? Where would they get their Brussels sprouts in January, or canaries, or Seville oranges for marmalade? Long ago the ancient Iberians colonized Cornwall (of course historians can be found who say they arrived in Spain from Britain), and ever since, these two lands have been bound by the oldest of crossed destinies, either as the closest of allies, as in the Hundred Years' War, or the most implacable of enemies.

Strange little connections would fill a book. Morris dancing, or Moorish dancing if you like, is said to have travelled back to Britain with John of Gaunt after his unsuccessful campaign to snatch the throne of Castile. One of Elizabeth II's biggest crown jewels was a gift from Pedro the Cruel to the Black Prince; Pedro had murdered an ambassador from Muslim Granada to get it off his turban. In politics we can thank Spain for words like propaganda, Fifth Column (both from the Civil War) and liberal (from the 1820s). Among the Jews expelled by Fernando and Isabel in 1492 were the ancestors of Disraeli.

In Spain, the Welsh may feel right at home in the green mining country of Asturias, and the Irish can honour the memory of the 19th-century prime minister O'Donnell, the famous governor of Cádiz, Conde O'Reilly or the thousands of their countrymen who escaped persecution to settle in Galicia in the 16th century. The true Scotsman will make a pilgrimage to the Vega of Granada to look for the heart of Robert the Bruce, hero of the battle of Bannockburn. In 1330 Sir James Douglas was taking Bruce's heart to be buried in the Holy Land, when crusading zeal sidetracked him to Spain. In battle against the Moors of Granada, Douglas and his knights became surrounded beyond hope of rescue. Spurring his horse for a last attack, Douglas flung the Bruce's heart into the enemy ranks, crying, 'Go ye first, as always!'

Natural Andalucía

05

The Andalucian Landscape

Andalucía covers the southern fifth of the Iberian peninsula, occupying an expanse equivalent to slightly more than half the area of Portugal. Its natural border to the north is the rugged Sierra Morena range; the wild Atlantic batters its western shores and the timid Mediterranean laps its southern coast.

The **Sierra Morena** range, although reaching barely 1,200m (4,000ft), was for a long time a deterrent to northern invaders. The only natural interruption is the **Pass of Despeñaperros**, the 'gateway to Andalucía'. Numerous early travellers spoke with awe of the first time they traversed this pine-clad gorge; the frontier that separated 'the land of men from the land of gods'. Arriving in Andalucía at this point provides a strong contrast indeed from the barren plains of **La Mancha** to the north. These peaks, rich in minerals, sweep down to the fertile **Guadalquivir plain**, widening towards the western coast to form broad salt marshes and mud flats – including the **Coto Doñana National Park**, one of the largest bird sanctuaries in Europe. From here, the coast as far as the Portuguese border is virtually one long sandy beach, with a hinterland of undulating farming terrain and the gentle mountains of **Huelva** province.

South of the Guadalquivir valley the land rises again to form the craggy **Serranía de Ronda** mountain range, home to bandits and smugglers for centuries; the terrain then descends sharply to meet the balmy palm-lined shores of the Mediterranean, with Tarifa, the furthest south you can go on mainland Europe, and a mere 12km (7½ miles) from the African coast, and Gibraltar, that geological oddity of a rock, whose outline resembles one of the sentinel lions on guard at the foot of Nelson's column in London.

From the Serranía de Ronda the land dips and rises eastwards till it joins the snowcapped **Sierra Nevada**, the highest peaks on mainland Spain, below which lie long beaches, tiny coves and crystal-clear water.

Andalucian Wildlife and Flora

Andalucía, where the continents once met, is one of western Europe's last important havens for a wide variety of wildlife. The land ranges from the long sandy beaches and marshy wetlands of the western coast through the craggy shores of the east, with altitudes rising to over 11,500ft (3,500m) in the Sierra Nevada. A few pristine areas hinting at an older Europe remain hidden in the land's pockets and, aside from the botched cleanup after the tragic pollution of the Doñana wetlands in 1998, the government seems keen to ensure that they remain untouched. Wolves and lynx still prowl, raptors circle overhead and in spring and autumn millions of migrating birds flock to fuel up en route to Africa.

Although the seas are now too polluted to teem with life, passengers heading for Morocco on the ferry will be unlucky not to see whales and dolphins passing through the straits, and there have even been reports of the occasional great white shark.

Agriculture in Southern Spain

Dry as it is, Andalucía when properly tended has been the garden of Spain. The soil in most areas, *argiles de montmorillonite*, holds water like a sponge. The Romans first discovered how to irrigate it; the Moors perfected the system, and also introduced the palm and such crops as cotton, rice, oranges and sugar. Today most of the inhabitants of the region live in cities – it's traditionally one of the most urbanized regions in Europe – but its farmers have discovered the modern delights of tractors and of owning their own land. Unless the Habsburgs or the Francoists come back, the region will have no excuse for not making a good living. Between the towns, spaces seem vast and empty, with endless hillsides of olives, vineyards, wheat and sunflowers. Come in the spring, when the almond trees are in blossom, the oranges turn orange and wild flowers surge along the roadsides – providing the unforgettable splash of colour that characterizes Andalucía and its warm, vibrant people.

Plant Life

Among the 5,000 species of flowering plant in Andalucía are 150 that are unique to the region. In spring the meadows of the Cádiz coast fill the air with scent and the countryside with colour. Wild lupins, convolvulus and orchids vie with irises, mallows and a hundred dancing butterflies in an area that has never known pesticides. Aromatic herbs and alpine flowers bloom a few months later on the higher ground, when the snow is at its thinnest, and on the lower slopes of the Serranía de Ronda there is still a small isolated forest of the rare pinsapo fir.

Mammals

Although wolves, lynx and wild boar roam in Andalucía there is little reason to shudder if you walk alone in the hills – you'll be very lucky to see one, and even if you do, it's likely to be a rear view. There are fewer than 1,200 pardel lynx and only 75 wolves hunting in the Doñana and the Sierra Morena. Smaller mammals are more numerous – rabbits and hares abound, garden dormice hang around in trees, often close to houses. These are prey to martens, mongooses, wildcats, badgers and weasels. Otters are still plentiful, although rarely seen, while the pale Algerian hedgehog has evolved longer legs and larger ears than its European counterpart, presumably to help it escape from under the wheels of the increasing number of cars that speed along Andalucía's roads.

Little pipistrelle bats flutter by day and larger noctules flap by night. A fine country for bats, is Spain. Almost everywhere in the country (but especially around Granada) you'll see clouds of them cavorting at twilight, zooming noiselessly past your ears and doing their best to ensure you get a good night's sleep by gobbling up all the mosquitoes they can. Spaniards don't mind them a bit, and the medieval kings of Aragón even went so far as to make them a dynastic emblem, derived from a Muslim Sufi symbol. Lots of bats, of course, presumes lots of caves, and Spain has more than its share. The famous grottoes of Nerja and Aracena are only a couple of the places where you can see colossal displays of tinted, aesthetically draped stalactites. Hundreds were decorated in one way or another by Palaeolithic man;

even though the most famous, at Altamira, are closed to the public, you can still see some cave art by asking around for a guide in Vélez Rubio west of Murcia. This last area, from Vélez as far west as Granada, actually has a huge population still living in caves – quite cosily fitted out these days – and in Granada itself you can visit the 'Gypsy caves' for a little histrionic flamenco and diluted sherry.

Finally, there are Spanish ibex, red and fallow deer (as well as *emigré* Corsican mouflon) in the hills of the Sierra Nevada, Cazorla and the Serranía de Ronda.

Reptiles and Amphibians

The most unusual of Andalucía's reptiles is the *Amphibisbaenia*, which looks, at first glance, like a giant pork sausage. Closer inspection reveals it to be a caecilian – a subterranean reptile that slips in somewhere between snake and lizard on the reptile family tree. Caecilians spend much of their time underground chasing worms, surfacing for a breather only during the night or after heavy rain. You're more likely to see a snake or a lizard. Chameleons stick to the coast, wall lizards are everywhere and little chirruping geckos hunt for small insects near outside lights or in hotel rooms. Of the eight species of snake, only the Lataste's viper, ugly, with a horn on the end of its nose, is venomous. Other reptiles with protuberances include the very rare spur-thighed tortoises whose habitats in northeastern Almería and Doñana are under threat from development and pollution.

Marsh frogs are the most vocal of the amphibians and green tree frogs the most beautiful. These share Andalucía with 15 other species including the sharp-ribbed salamander and a variety of toads and newts.

Birds

Andalucía's most numerous wildlife enthusiasts are ornithologists who descend on the region in spring and autumn to follow the flocks of migrating birds on their way to or from Africa. Hundreds of binoculars trace the movements of storks and huge raptors as they soar ever higher over the Rock of Gibraltar catching thermals to prepare for the crossing.

Winter and summer visitors like little bitterns, purple herons, bee-eaters and golden orioles find safe haven in Andalucía's growing number of protected areas. This is the only place in Europe where you will find the Spanish imperial eagle, black-shouldered kite, red-necked nightjar, azure-winged magpie, marbled duck and numerous others. And it's the only place in the world (aside from the Maghreb) where you'll find white-headed duck, rescued from the brink of extinction by a conservation effort that began a few decades ago. Other rarities include the shy purple gallinule, betrayed by its bright red legs and the collared pratincole that breeds in the Guadalquivir marshes. Europe's largest colony of greater flamingos crowd the salt lake of Fuente de Piedra near Málaga and hordes of shrieking swallows and swifts swoop around church towers and blocks of flats everywhere.

Insects

Ornithologists rub shoulders with lepidopterists in Andalucía – there are 30 different species of blues alone here, along with clouded yellows, swallowtails, Spanish fritillaries and marbled whites and the spectacular two-tailed pasha, which is as large as a small bird. There are even sporadic visitors from across the Atlantic including the milkweed and the American painted lady. Moths include the hummingbird hawk moth and the great peacock moth, both of which fly in daytime. Among the other insects are bright green praying mantis, who compete with geckos in the hunt for southern Spain's ubiquitous flies, industrious dung beetles and a variety of invisible but omnipresent cicadas and crickets.

Wildlife Reserves

There are over 20 important wildlife reserves in Andalucía – the coast, the wetlands behind it, the scrub deserts of Almería and the mountain slopes of the Sierra Nevada. They are given different names, depending on their importance. **Reservas Naturales** are usually small sites of specific scientific interest such as lagoons or copses. **Parques Naturales** are larger and permit traditional land use within their borders. **Parques Nacionales** are of international importance with restricted access and close control of human activities.

The Coast

Most famous and most spectacular of all is the **Coto Doñana**, on the Cádiz coast, one of only two *parques nacionales* in southern Spain. Though the terrain may appear flat and monotonous at first, it consists of a range of different and distinct habitats including cork oak forest, scrubland, swamp, raised flooded areas and reedy channels filled by the Guadalquivir as it reaches the coast. These are a haven for hundreds of species of native and migratory birds including the largest population of Spanish imperial eagles in the world. These share the wetlands with pardel lynx, wild boar and 50 other species of mammals, reptiles and amphibians.

Andalucía's other important wetland areas are both close to cities. The **Marismas de Odiel** near Huelva is home to 30 per cent of the European spoonbill population and in the winter, flocks of up to 2,000 flamingos. The **Bahía de Cádiz** also has abundant birdlife, important for breeding little terns, avocets and Kentish plovers.

Other significant wildlife sites along the coast include the clifftop forests of the **Acantilado y Pinar de Barbate**, the beaches and flower-filled marshlands of **Los Lances** near Tarifa and the semi-desert of the **Cabo de Gata** peninsula east of Almería.

Inland

Inland from Tarifa lies **Los Alcornocales**, one of the largest cork oak forests in the world. Some of the Lusitanian and cork oaks here are over a thousand years old, and

National Parks

Among the most important parks and reserves in the Andalucian area are:

- Parque Nacional Coto Doñana
- Reserva Nacional de Sierra de Tejeda
- Reserva Nacional de Cortes de la Frontera
- Coto Nacional de la Pata del Caballo
- Parque de Cabo de Gata-Níjar
- Parque de la Bahía de Cádiz
- Parque Natural de los Alcornocales
- Parque Natural de Acantilado y Pinar de Barbate
- Parque Natural de las Sierras Subbéticas de Córdoba
- Parque Natural de Sierra Nevada
- Laguna de la Fuente de Piedra

they form a tangle with wild olives and laurels. Golden eagles nest here, as do griffon vultures and eagle owls.

Los Alcornocales borders on the **Parque Natural de la Sierra de Grazalema**, part of the Serranía de Ronda, the wettest place on the Iberian peninsula, proving that the rain in Spain definitely does not fall mainly in the plain. The plants and animals seem to love it. More than 1,300 species of vascular plant thrive here, including the *pinsapo*, a fir found only here, the endangered *Narcissus baeticus* daffodil, irises and 27 species of wild orchid.

The **Desierto de Las Tabernas**, made famous by Sergio Mendes, Clint Eastwood and Lee Van Cleef, is a little less lush but equally full of endemic rare plant life including the toadflax, the sea lavender, the crucifer and a variety of aromatic thymes. Reptiles love it here and if you are lucky you may see an ocellated lizard, Europe's largest, at up to a metre long.

The Sierras

Wolves still live in the eastern **Sierra Morena**, which is punctuated by a series of wildlife sites and *parques naturales*, from its beginnings on the Portuguese border right through to the Sierra de Cazorla in the east. The **Despeñaperros**, a kilometre-deep gorge that bisects it in northern Jaén, was once the only crossing point between Andalucía and the Spanish *meseta*.

The higher **Sierra Nevada** *parque nacional*, which peaks at 3,482m (11,420ft), is famous for its alpine flowers, which include 70 endemic species and its butterflies. Spanish ibex, rescued from the brink of extinction in the 1940s, also live here. They are seen most easily in the evening on the lower peaks. The lower slopes, known locally as *'zona erizo'* (hedgehog zone) are shrouded in prickly scrub, and below them the valleys of the **Alpujarras** are filled with birdsong, butterflies and semi-tropical fruits – even custard apples grow here.

Food
and Drink

06

Read an old guidebook to Spain and, when the author gets around to the local cooking, expressions like 'eggs in a sea of rancid oil' and 'mysterious pork parts' or 'suffered palpitations through garlic excess' pop up with alarming frequency. One traveller in the 18th century fell ill from a local concoction and was given a purge, 'known on the comic stage as "Angelic Water". On top of that followed four hundred catholic pills, and a few days later... they gave me *escordero* water, whose efficacy or devilry is of such double effect that the doctors call it ambidexter. From this I suffered agony.'

You'll fare much better than 18th-century travellers; in fact, the chances are you'll eat some of the tastiest food you've ever had at almost half the price you would have paid for it at home. The massive influx of tourists has had its effect on Spanish kitchens, but so has the Spaniards' own increased prosperity and, perhaps most significantly, the new federalism. Each region, each town even, has come to feel a new interest and pride in the things that set it apart, and food is definitely one of those; the best restaurants are almost always those that specialize in regional cooking.

Regional Specialities

Food

The greatest attraction of *andaluz* cuisine is the use of simple, fresh ingredients. Seafood plays a big role, and marinated or fried fish (*pescados fritos*, also known in Sevilla as *pescaíto frito*) is a speciality. (The traditional marinade, or *adobo*, is a mixture of water, vinegar, salt, garlic, paprika, cumin and marjoram.) Other specialities include the wholesome broth made with fish, tomato, pepper and paprika, and the famous cured hams of Jabugo and Trevélez. Almost everybody has heard of gazpacho; there are dozens of varieties, ranging from the *porra* of Antequera made with red peppers, to the thick, tasty Córdoban version, *salmorejo*, topped with finely chopped ham and boiled egg. Olives, preserved in cumin, wild marjoram, rosemary, thyme, bay leaves, garlic, fennel and vinegar, are a particular treat, and so especially are the plump, green manzanilla olives from Sevilla.

In Granada, an unappetizing mixture of brains, bulls' testicles, potatoes, peas and red peppers results in a very palatable *tortilla Sacromonte*, and many restaurants in the city work wonders with slices of beef *filete* or loin larded with pork fat and roasted with the juice from the meat and sherry. However, watch out for odd little dishes like *revoltillos*, whose name gives you a fair warning of what flavours to expect in this subtle dish of tripe, rolled and secured with the animal's intestines, mercifully lined with ham and mint.

The province of Cádiz takes the place of honour in *andaluz* cuisine; its specialities to look out for in restaurants are *cañaillas* (sea snails), *pastel de pichón* (pigeon pâté), *calamares con habas* (squid with beans), *archoba* (a highly seasoned fish dish) or *bocas* (small crab). Córdoba, too, has a fine culinary tradition, including dishes with a strong Arab and Jewish influence, like *calderetas*, lamb stew with almonds. But Córdoba is also the home of one of the most famous *andaluz* dishes, *rabo de*

Olive Oil from Jaén

Olive oil is an important part of the cuisine of Jaén (*see* p.175) and contributes to dishes such as *espinacas jiennenses* (spinach Jaén-style) and *ajilimojili* (potatoes, red peppers, oil and vinegar). There's even a dessert called *ochío* – oil cakes covered by a layer of salt and paprika. *Pipirrana* is considered a local speciality with peppers, tomatoes, onions, hard-boiled egg and tuna fish. It's especially popular in the summer. During the winter try *migas de pan* or breadcrumbs, usually served with pieces of pork, though also as a sweet dish eaten like popcorn. Wherever you eat, look out for Jaén black pudding, a concoction of pork, beef, garlic, paprika, nutmeg and sherry, *cabrito asado* (roast baby kid with garlic) and *chorizo*. The clay *cazuela* bowl gives its name to a savoury cake made from chickpeas (garbanzo beans), aubergine (eggplant), marrow and sausage, topped with sesame seeds.

As you might expect, olive oil is extremely inexpensive all over the province of Jaén; in the country you might stumble across a local co-operative which sells it even more cheaply than do the shops. Look out for really superior extra virgin oils, such as Oro Mágina, with its virtually nought per cent acidity. But there's more in the olive than just the oil in these parts. Increasingly, Andalucía, the 'Saudi Arabia of olive oil', is finding ways to use the rest of the squeezed-out fruit. It's a good thing they have, since a single co-operative can pile up over 10,000 tons of it a year. In the old days farmers used to dry them out in cakes and use them for fuel, and now they're running a 12-megawatt power station near the village of Benameji, south of Córdoba. It's worked so well that two more have been built, including one near Jaén, and the company that designed them is exporting the process to other countries around the Mediterranean. It's just another example of the new Spain at work – with over a thousand big windmills, and half of Europe's solar power, they're the EU leader in renewable energy.

toro, a spicy concoction of oxtail, onions and tomatoes. Also try the *buchón* (rolled fish filled with ham, dipped in breadcrumbs, then fried). As one might expect, the Sierras offer dishes based on the game and wild herbs found in the mountains. Here, freshwater lakes teem with trout, and wild asparagus grows on the slopes. The town of Jaén is particularly well known for its high-quality oil and vinegar, and delectable salads are a feature of most menus (try the *pipirrana*). All over Andalucía you will find *pinchitos*, a spicier version of its Greek cousin the *souvlaki*, a mini-kebab of lamb or pork marinated in spices.

Fish and seafood, fresh from the coast, dominate cuisine in Málaga but there are plenty of gazpachos, particularly *ajo blanco* – a creamy white garlic and almond soup served with grapes. Prawns and mussels are plump and, served simply with lemon, are divine. The Costa del Sol's traditional beachside delicacy is sardines, speared on a stick and cooked over a wood fire – best when eaten with a good salad and washed down with chilled white wine. *Boquerones* (often mistaken for the peculiarly English whitebait but in fact a variety of anchovy) feature widely in restaurants and tapas bars, along with *pijotas*, small hake that suffer the indignity of being sizzled with tail in mouth. Forget British fried fish; in Málaga *fritura mixta* is one of Spain's culinary art forms.

To finish off your meal, there are any number of desserts (*postres*) based on almonds and custards, and the Arab influence shows through in, for example, the excellent sweetmeats from Granada and the *alfajores* (puff pastry) from Huércal, Almería. Nearly every village in the province has its own dessert, usually influenced once again by the Moors. Try the almond tarts in Ardales, the honey-coated pancakes in Archidona and the mixture of syrup of white roses, oil and eggs called *tocino de cielo* in Vélez. There again, you can always substitute a sweet Málaga dessert wine for pudding – delicious sipped with dry biscuits.

The presence of 1.5 million foreign residents, mainly clustered along the southern coast, has had an effect on the Costa del Sol culinary scene, although Spanish restaurants still manage to hold their own. A bewildering choice of Indonesian, Belgian, Swedish, Chinese, French, Italian and numerous other nationalities' cuisines confront the tourist. The standard is in fact quite high in most 'ethnic' restaurants, and prices are reasonable because of the fierce competition. A host of British establishments (mostly pubs) offer the whole shebang: roast beef, Yorkshire pudding and three veg, and apple pie and custard, and all for bargain prices.

Drink

No matter how much other costs have risen in Spain, **wine** (*vino*) has remained awesomely inexpensive by northern European or American standards. What's more, it's mostly very good and there's enough variety from the regions for you to try something different every day. If you take an empty bottle into a *bodega*, you can usually bring it out filled with the wine that suits your palate. (A *bodega* can be a bar, wine cellar or warehouse, and is worth a visit whatever its guise.)

When dining out, a restaurant's *vino del lugar* or *vino de la casa* is always your least expensive option; it usually comes out of a barrel or glass jug and may be a surprise either way. Some 20 Spanish wine regions bottle their products under strict controls imposed by the Instituto Nacional de Denominaciones de Origen (these almost always have the little maps of their various regions pasted on the back of the bottle). In many parts of Andalucía you may have difficulty ordering a simple bottle of white wine, as, on requesting *una botella de vino blanco de la casa*, you will often be served something resembling diluted sherry. To make things clear, specify a wine by name or by region – for example *una botella de Rioja blanco* – or ask for *un vino seco*, and the problem should be solved. Spain also produces its own champagne – *cava* – which seldom has the depth of the French, nor the lightness of an Italian *prosecco*, but is refined enough to drink alone. The principal house, Cordoniú, is always a safe bet.

Some *andaluz* wines have achieved an international reputation for high quality. Best known is the *jerez*, or what we in English call **sherry**. If you want to learn how to discern a *fino* from an *amontillado*, go to one of the warehouse *bodegas* of Jerez where you can taste the sherry as you tour the site. When a Spaniard invites you to have a *copita* (glass) it will nearly always be filled with this Andalucian sunshine. It comes in a wide range of varieties: *manzanillas* are very dry; *fino* is dry, light and young (the famous Tío Pepe); *amontillados* are a bit sweeter and rich and originate from the slopes around Montilla in Córdoba province; *olorosos* are very sweet dessert sherries, and can be either brown, cream, or the fruity *amoroso*.

The white wines of Córdoba grown in the Villaviciosa region are again making a name for themselves, after being all but wiped out by phylloxera in the early 20th century. In Sevilla, wine is produced in three regions: Lebrija; Los Palacios (white table wines); and Aljarafe, where full-bodied wines are particular favourites. Jaén also has three wine-producing regions.

Torreperogíl, east of Úbeda, produces wine little known outside the area, but extremely classy. Take your bottle along to the local *bodega* when you are here, as many wines are on tap only. In Bailén, the white, rosé and red table wines resemble those of the more famous La Mancha vineyards. In the west of the province, Lopera white wines are also sold from the barrel. Málaga and Almería do not produce much wine, although the sweet, aromatic wines of Málaga are famous (and famously undrinkable to most English palates, but persevere). Two grapes, muscatel and Pedro Ximénez, define Málaga province wines and sherries. All are sweet and enjoyed with gusto in bars; the best known is the Málaga Virgen.

Many Spaniards prefer **beer** (*cerveza*), which is also good, though not quite the bargain wine is. The most popular brands are Cruzcampo and San Miguel, and most bars sell it cold in bottles or on tap – Mahou produce a black beer, similar to Guinness; if you see it, try it.

Imported whisky and other **spirits** are pretty inexpensive, though even cheaper are the versions Spain bottles itself, which may come close to your familiar home favourites. Gin, believe it or not, is often drunk with Coke. Bacardi and Coke is a popular thirst-quencher but beware, a Cuba Libre is not necessarily a rum and Coke, but Coke with anything, such as gin or vodka – you have to specify – then, with a flourish worthy of a matador, the barman will zap an ice-filled tumbler in front of you, and heave in a quadruple measure. No wonder the Costa del Sol has a staggering six chapters of Alcoholics Anonymous.

Coffee, tea, all the international soft-drink brands and *Kas*, the locally made orange drink, round out the average café fare. If you want tea with milk, say so when you order, otherwise it may arrive with a piece of lemon. Coffee comes with milk (*café con leche*) or without (*café solo*). Spanish coffee is good and strong, and if you want a lot of it order a *doble* or a *solo grande*; one of those will keep you awake through the guided tour of any museum.

Food and Drink in Gibraltar

In the past, to say that eating out in Gibraltar could be a depressing experience was a compliment. Sausage, beans and chips have long been the zenith of Gibraltar's culinary achievement, with only a handful of exceptions. However, food here is no longer solely restricted to authentic pub grub and fish 'n' chips (although both are still widely available). For the best restaurants on the Rock, get out of the environs of Main Street and head for Queensway Quay, or the more established Marina Quay, where you will find a reasonable selection of seafood, Italian dishes and even tapas treats. Away from the quays, olive oil, the sun-dried tomato or anything grilled (as opposed to fried) is almost unheard of. The least dangerous dining in the centre of town is probably Indian cuisine, where standards do rise a little. Chinese is largely inedible.

You can drink to your heart's content in Gibraltar (wend your way to one of the 360 or so pubs on the Rock), but your liver may be happy to know that costs are about double the Spanish equivalent. Pubs are generally open all day till 11pm. Wines and spirits are cheap in the supermarkets and off-licences, but no bargain in restaurants or pubs.

Restaurant Basics

Sticklers for absurd bureaucracy, the Spanish government rates **restaurants** by forks. (This has become a bit of a joke – a car repair shop in Granada has rated itself two wrenches.) The forks have nothing to do with the quality of the food, though they hint somewhat at the prices. Unless it's explicitly written on the bill (*la cuenta*), service is not included in the total, so tip accordingly. Be careful, though: eating out in southern Spain – especially away from the Costa and big towns – is still a hit-and-miss affair. You will need luck as well as judgement. Spain has plenty of bad restaurants; the worst offenders are often those with the little flags and 10-language menus in the most touristy areas. But common sense should warn you off these. On the other hand, kitsch 'Little Chef' type cutouts are rampant along country roads, beckoning you inside – and, unlike in the UK, they're not necessarily indicative of a second-class establishment. If you dine where the locals do, you'll be assured of a good deal, if not necessarily a good meal.

Almost every restaurant offers a *menú del día*, or a *menú turístico*, featuring an appetizer, a main course, dessert, bread and drink at a set price, always cheaper than if you had ordered the items à la carte. These are always posted outside the restaurant, in the window or on the plywood chef at the door; decide what you want before going in if it's a set-price menu, because these bargains are hardly ever listed on the menu the waiter gives you at the table.

One step down from a restaurant are **comedores** (literally, dining rooms), often tacked on to the backs of bars, where the food and décor are usually drab but cheap, and **cafeterías**, usually those places that feature photographs of their offerings of *platos combinados* (combined plates) to eliminate any language problem. **Asadores** specialize in roast meat or fish; **marisqueras** serve only fish and shellfish – you'll usually see the sign for '*pescados y mariscos*' on the awning. Keep an eye out for **ventas**, usually modest family-run establishments in the countryside, offering excellent *menús del día*. They specialize in typical *andaluz* dishes of roast kid or lamb, rabbit, paella, game (partridge crops up often) and many pork dishes, chorizo sausage and varieties of ham. Visit one at Sunday lunch time, when all Spanish families go out – with a bit of luck things may get out of hand, and guitars and castanets could appear from nowhere, in which case abandon all plans for the rest of the day.

If you're travelling on a budget, you may want to eat one of your meals a day at a **tapas bar** or *tasca*. Tapas means 'lids', since they started out as little saucers of goodies served on top of a drink. They have evolved over the years to become the basis of the world's greatest snack culture. Bars that specialize in them have platter after platter of delectable titbits – shellfish, mushrooms baked in garlic, chicken croquettes, *albóndigas*, the ubiquitous Spanish meatball, quails' eggs and stews. (*Tortilla* is seldom as good as it looks, unless you like eating re-heated shoe-leather.) All you have to do is pick out what looks best and point to it. At about €2 a go, it doesn't really matter if you pick a couple of duds. Order a *tapa* (hors d'œuvre), or a *ración* (big helping) if it looks really good. It's hard to generalize about prices, but on average, €6 of tapas and wine or beer should fill you up. Sitting down at a table rather than eating at the bar attracts a token surcharge. Another advantage of tapas is that they're available at what most Americans or Britons would consider normal dining hours. Spaniards are notoriously late diners; 2pm is the earliest they would consider sitting down to their huge 'midday' meal – at Jerez's premier restaurant, no self-respecting local would be seen dead in the place before 4pm. Then, after work at 8pm, a few tapas at the bar hold them over until supper at 10 or 11pm. After living in Spain for a few months this makes perfect sense, but it's exasperating to the average visitor. On the coasts, restaurants tend to open earlier to accommodate foreigners (some as early as 5pm) but you may as well do as the Spaniards do. *See* 'Eating Out', p.91, in **Practical A–Z**, for restaurant price categories.

Spanish Menu Reader

Entremeses (Hors d'œuvres)
aceitunas olives
alcachofas con mahonesa artichokes with mayonnaise
caldo broth
entremeses variados assorted *hors d'œuvres*
huevos de flamenco baked eggs in tomato sauce
gambas pil pil prawns (shrimps) in spicy garlic sauce
gazpacho cold soup
huevos al plato fried eggs
huevos revueltos scrambled eggs
pimientos fritos fried green peppers
sopa de ajo garlic soup
sopa de espárragos asparagus soup
sopa de fideos noodle soup
sopa de garbanzos chickpea soup
sopa de lentejas lentil soup
sopa de verduras vegetable soup
tortilla Spanish omelette, with potatoes
tortilla a la francesa French omelette

Pescados (Fish)
acedías small plaice
adobo fish marinated in white wine
almejas clams
anchoas anchovies
anguilas eels
angulas baby eels (elvers)
ástaco crayfish
atún tuna fish
bacalao codfish (usually dried)
besugo sea bream
bogavante lobster
bonito tunny
boquerones anchovies
caballa mackerel
calamares squid
cangrejo crab
centollo spider crab
chanquetes whitebait
chipirones baby squid
  ...en su tinta ...in its own ink

chirlas baby clams
escabeche pickled or marinated fish
gambas prawns (shrimps)
langosta lobster
langostinos giant prawns
lenguado sole
lubina sea bass
mariscos shellfish
mejillones mussels
merluza hake
mero grouper
navajas razor-shell clams
ostras oysters
pejesapo monkfish
percebes barnacles
pescadilla whiting
pez espada swordfish
platija plaice
pulpo octopus
rape monkfish
raya skate
rodaballo turbot
salmón salmon
salmonete red mullet
sardinas sardines
trucha trout
veneras scallops
zarzuela fish stew

Carnes y Aves (Meat and Fowl)
albóndigas meatballs
asado roast
bistec beefsteak
buey ox
callos tripe
cerdo pork
chorizo spiced sausage
chuletas chops
cochinillo sucking pig
conejo rabbit
corazón heart
cordero lamb
faisán pheasant
fiambres cold meats
filete fillet
hígado liver

jabalí wild boar
jamón de York cooked ham (for sandwiches)
jamón Iberico cured ham
jamón serrano baked ham
lengua tongue
lomo pork loin
morcilla blood sausage
paloma pigeon
pato duck
pavo turkey
perdiz partridge
pinchitos spicy mini-kebabs
pollo chicken
rabo de toro bull's tail with onion and tomato
riñones kidneys
salchicha sausage
salchichón salami
sesos brains
solomillo sirloin steak
ternera veal
Note: *potajes, cocidos, guisados, estofados, fabadas* and *cazuelas* are all different kinds of stew.

Verduras y Legumbres (Vegetables)
ajo garlic
alcachofa artichoke
apio celery
arroz rice
arroz a la marinera rice, saffron and seafood
berenjena aubergine (eggplant)
cebolla onion
champiñones mushrooms
col, repollo cabbage
coliflor cauliflower
endibia endive (chicory)
ensalada salad
espárragos asparagus
espinacas spinach
garbanzos chickpeas (garbanzo beans)
judías (verdes) French beans
lechuga lettuce
lentejas lentils
patatas potatoes
    ...fritas/salteadas ...fried/sautéed
    ...al horno ...baked
pepino cucumber
pimiento pepper
puerro leek
remolacha beetroot (beet)
setas Spanish mushrooms
zanahoria carrot

Frutas (Fruit)
albaricoque apricot
almendras almonds
cerezas cherries
ciruela plum
ciruela pasa prune

frambuesas raspberries
fresas strawberries
    ...con nata ...with cream
higos figs
limón lemon
manzana apple
melocotón peach
melón melon
naranja orange
pera pear
piña pineapple
plátano banana
pomelo grapefruit
sandía watermelon
uvas grapes

Postres (Desserts)
arroz con leche rice pudding
bizcocho/pastel/torta cake
blanco y negro ice cream and coffee float
flan crème caramel
galletas biscuits (cookies)
helado ice cream
pajama flan (*see* above) with ice cream
pasteles pastries
queso cheese
requesón cottage cheese
tarta de frutas fruit pie
turrón nougat

Bebidas (Drinks)
agua con hielo water with ice
agua mineral mineral water
    ...sin/con gas ...without/with fizz
batido de leche milkshake
café (con leche) coffee (with milk)
cava Spanish champagne
cerveza beer
chocolate hecho hot chocolate
granizado slush, iced squash
leche milk
té (con limón) tea (with lemon)
vino (tinto, rosado, blanco) wine (red, rosé, white)
zumo de manzana/naranja apple/orange juice

Useful Phrases
menu *carta*
fixed price lunch menu, set meal *menú del día*
change *cambio*
waiter/waitress *camarero/a*
Do you have a table? *¿Tiene una mesa?*
    ...for one/two? ¿... para uno/dos?
The menu, please *Déme el menú, por favor*
Do you have a wine list? *¿Hay una lista de vinos?*
The bill (check), please *La cuenta, por favor*
Can I pay by credit card? *¿Puedo pagar con tarjeta de crédito?*

Planning Your Trip

07

72

07

Planning Your Trip | When to Go

When to Go

Climate

Andalucía is hot and sunny in the summer, and generally mild and sunny by day in the winter – in fact, with an average 320 days of sunshine in the region, you can count on more sun here than anywhere else in Europe. Autumn weather is normally warm and comfortable, but can pack a few surprises, from torrential rains to droughts. The mild winters in coastal regions give way to warm springs with minimal rainfall. Temperatures inland can be considerably lower, especially in the mountainous regions, and the *Levante* wind can make life uncomfortable, even in summer, when it will not only blow your beach umbrella away but might even make you a bit kooky.

For comfort, spring and autumn are the best times to visit; winter is generally pleasant on the Mediterranean coast, but can be damp and chilly inland. Spanish homes (and hotel rooms) are not made for winter; you'll probably be more comfortable outside.

Gibraltar's climate is Mediterranean, of course, but it also manifests the cloud and rain characteristic of British weather. The moisture-laden *Levante* batters Gibraltar's shores and is forced up the sheer face of the rock, to condense in the lower temperatures at the top, forming a dense cloud that can be seen for miles; during winter the cloud may deposit a relentless shower.

Festivals

Fiestas or *ferias* are incredibly important to Andalucians, no matter what the cost in money and lost sleep; they are a celebration of being alive in a society constantly aware of the inevitability of death. One of the most spiritually deadening aspects of Francoism was the banning of many local and regional fiestas. These are now celebrated with gusto, and if you can arrange your itinerary to include one or two you'll be guaranteed an unforgettable holiday. Besides those listed opposite, there are literally thousands of others, and new ones spring up all the time.

Many village patronal fiestas feature *romerías* (pilgrimages) to a venerated shrine. Getting there is half the fun, with everyone in local costume, riding on horseback or driving covered wagons full of picnic supplies. Music, dancing, food, wine and fireworks are all necessary ingredients of a proper fiesta, while the bigger ones often include bull-fights, funfairs, circuses and competitions. *Semana Santa* (Holy Week) is a major tourist event, especially in Sevilla. The processions of *pasos* (ornate floats depicting scenes from the Passion) carried in a slow march to lugubrious tuba music, and accompanied by children and men decked out in costumes later copied by the Ku Klux Klan, are worth fighting the crowds to see. And while a certain amount of merrymaking goes on after dark, the real revelry takes place after Easter, in the unmissable April *feria*.

Dates for most festivals tend to be fluid, flowing towards the nearest weekend; if the actual date falls on a Thursday or a Tuesday, Spaniards 'bridge' the fiesta with the weekend to create a four-day whoopee. Check dates at the tourist office in advance.

For a guide to Andalucía's *ferias*, festivals, pageants, carnivals and cultural events, get the free booklet *52 and a half weeks*, available from most local tourist offices.

For a list of **Spanish national holidays**, see p.92.

Average Temperatures in °C (°F)

	Jan		April		July		Oct	
	max	min	max	min	max	min	max	min
Sevilla	15 (59)	6 (43)	23 (74)	11 (52)	35 (95)	21 (70)	26 (79)	14 (58)
Málaga	17 (63)	9 (49)	21 (70)	13 (56)	29 (84)	21 (70)	23 (74)	16 (61)
Cádiz	15 (59)	8 (47)	21 (70)	12 (54)	29 (84)	20 (68)	23 (74)	15 (59)

Average Monthly Rainfall in mm (inches)

	Jan	April	July	Oct
Sevilla	99 (4)	80 (3)	0 (0)	37 (1.5)

Calendar of Events

January

First week Granada: commemoration of the city's capture by the Catholic Kings.

Málaga: Epiphany parade of *Los Reyes Magos* (Three Wise Men).

February

Third week Isla Cristina: winter carnival in coastal town. Festivities include *Entierro de las Sardina* – the burial of the sardine.

Last week Cádiz: perhaps the best carnival in Spain and certainly the oldest, with parades, masquerades, music and fireworks in abundance.

March/April

Easter week Sevilla: the most important *Semana Santa* celebrations, with over 100 processions, broken by the singing of *saetas* (sacred laments).

Córdoba: the city's 26 processions are perhaps the most emotionally charged of all, moving along the streets around the Great Mosque.

Málaga, Granada, Úbeda: also put on major celebrations.

April

Last week Sevilla: the capital's *Feria*, originally a horse fair, has now grown into the greatest festival of Andalucía. Costumed parades of the gentry in fine carriages, lots of flamenco, bullfights and drinking.

Last week Andújar (Jaén): hosts the *Romería de la Virgen de la Cabeza*, a pilgrimage from all over Andalucía that culminates in the procession to the sanctuary in the nearby Sierra Morena.

End of month Jerez: Horse Fair with equestrian events and sherry-tasting.

May

First week Almería: *Peña de Taranto* Cultural Week. The foremost flamenco singers meet for this prestigious annual contest.

Navas de San Juan (north of Úbeda): in honour of *Nuestra Señora de la Estrella*, one of the most important pilgrimages in Jaén.

Everywhere: *Cruces de Mayo*. The arrival of spring is celebrated with the placing of crosses made of flowers in the streets and square. Especially popular in Córdoba.

Granada: *El Día de la Cruz*, where large crosses made of flowers are set up throughout the city.

First Friday Jaca: re-enacts the victory over the Moors by local women.

First week Jerez de la Frontera: much like the *Feria* in Sevilla.

Second week Córdoba: every third year (next in 2010), the *Concurso Nacional de Arte Flamenco*, with over 100 singers, guitarists and dancers.

Mid-May Marbella: if you thought this town was just for tourists, come and take part in the Marbella *Feria de San Bernabé*, a five-day extravaganza.

Pentecost (May or June) El Rocío (Huelva): the biggest *romería* in all Spain. Pilgrims converge on this tiny spot in Las Marismas, south of Sevilla, in gaily decorated wagons for a week of wild carrying-on.

Last week Sanlúcar de Barrameda: the *Manzanilla* wine fair, where vast quantities of fried fish and shellfish are consumed, helped down by equally copious amounts of *Manzanilla*; dancing, singing and sporting events are also held.

End May or early June Zahara de la Sierra (Cádiz): sees four days of spectacular festivities begin on the Thursday after Trinity Sunday, celebrating Corpus Christi.

June

Second week Mojácar: Moorish and Christian troops re-enact the surrender of the town to the Christian army at Mojácar's annual two-day fiesta.

Mid-month Granada: start of the month-long *Festival Internacional de Música y Danza*, which attracts big international names and includes classical music, jazz and ballet; flamenco competitions are held in odd-numbered years.

Third week Alhaurín de la Torre (Málaga): fair and festival in honour of the patron San Juan; entertainment includes a parade of giant figures and the *torre del cante*, one of the best flamenco gatherings in the region.

July

Middle two weeks Córdoba: International Guitar Festival – classical, flamenco and Latino.

16 Málaga and coastal resorts: *Virgen del Carmen* – decorated boats with firework displays.

Last two weeks Lebrija: flamenco festival. La Línea: summer fair.

End of month Almería: festival, including numerous jazz concerts.

August

Three days at the beginning of Aug and three days in mid-Aug Horse races along the beaches of Sanlúcar de Barrameda.

3 Huelva: *Colombinas* – bullfights and other sporting events.

5 Trevélez (Granada): has a midnight pilgrimage up Mulhacén, Spain's highest mountain, so that pilgrims arrive exhausted but in time for prayers at midday.

First two weeks Ronda: Pedro Romero festival – bullfights, equestrian parades, folk groups.

15 Competa: wine festival.

15–16 Vejer (Cádiz): Assumption of the Virgin and San Roque festivities, with flamenco.

Mid-month Málaga: its *feria* is gaining a reputation as one of the best, with a week of concerts, bullfights, dancing and singing.

Last week Sanlúcar de Barrameda (Cádiz): exaltation of the Río Guadalquivir and major flamenco events.

Toro: *Fiesta de San Agustín*, with bulls and a 'fountain of wine'.

September

First week Jerez: has a *Vendimia* wine festival.

Second week Chipiona: flamenco, bull-running, bullfights.

Ronda: puts on an 18th-century-style bullfight in its ring.

Alájar (Huelva): As well as many other places in the region, Alájar celebrates the Nativity of the Virgin.

End of month Úbeda: fair with stalls and bullfights.

October

6–12 Fuengirola: *Feria del Rosario*.

Third week Jaén: festival of San Lucás, bullfights, cultural and sporting events.

December

First week Martos (Jaén): *Fiesta de la Aceituna*. Annual four-day olive festival celebrating the olive in all its glory.

Gibraltar Calendar

5 Jan Three Kings Cavalcade.
April–June Gibraltar Festival.
21 Oct Trafalgar Day.
Nov–Dec Drama Festival.

Tourist Information

After receiving millions of tourists each year for the last three decades, no country has more helpful information offices, or more intelligent brochures and detailed maps. Every city has an office, and about two-thirds of the time you'll find someone who speaks English. At times they'll be less helpful in the big cities in the summer. Often, though, you'll be surprised at how well they know details about accommodation and transport. Many large cities also maintain **municipal tourist offices**, though they're not usually as well equipped as those run by the Ministry of Tourism, better known as **Turismo**. The official tourist website for Andalucía is *www.andalucia.org*.

Opening hours for most offices are Mon–Fri 9.30–1.30 and 4–7, and Saturday mornings. In the larger cities, they stay open all day.

Spanish National Tourist Offices Abroad

UK: 22–23 Manchester Square, London W1M 5AP, **t** (020) 7486 8070.

USA: Water Tower Place, Suite 915, East 845 North Michigan Ave, Chicago, IL 60611, **t** (312) 642 1992; Wilshire Boulevard, Suite 960, Beverly Hills, CA 90211, **t** (213) 658 7188; Fifth Avenue, New York, NY 10022, **t** (212) 759 8822.

Canada: 2 Bloor Street West, Toronto, Ontario M4W 3E2, **t** (416) 961 3131.

Australia: 203 Castlereagh Street, PO Box A-685, Sydney, **t** (02) 264 7966.

Gibraltar Information Bureau

UK: 179 The Strand, London WC2R 1EH, **t** (020) 7836 0777.

Consulates and Embassies

Foreign Embassies, etc. in Spain

UK: C/Fernando el Santo 16, Madrid, **t** 91 700 82 00; Málaga, **t** 95 235 23 00; Gibraltar: (Vice Consulate) 65 Irish Town, **t** 78 305, *www.ukinspain.com*.

Ireland: Paseo de la Castellana 46, 28001 Madrid, **t** 91 436 40 93; Sevilla, **t** 952 21 63 61.

USA: C/Serrano 75, Madrid, **t** 91 587 22 00; consular office for passports, around the corner at Pso de la Castellana; 52 Pso de las Delicias 7, Sevilla, **t** 95 423 18 85; Avda Juan Gómez, Edificio Lucía, Málaga, **t** 95 247 48 91, *www.spainemb.org*.

Canada: C/Núñez de Balboa 35, Madrid
t 91 423 3250, *www.canada-es.org.*

Australia: Plaza del Descubridor Diego de
Ordas 3, Madrid, t 91 353 66 00; Barcelona
t 93 490 90 13, *www.spain-embassy.gov.au.*

New Zealand: Plaza de la Lealtad 2, Madrid,
t 91 523 02 26, *www.nzembassy.com.*

Spanish Embassies, etc. Abroad

UK: 20 Draycott Place, London SW3 2RZ,
t (020) 7589 8989; 1a Brook House, 70 Spring
Gardens, Manchester M2 2BQ, t (0161) 236
1262; 63 North Castle Street, Edinburgh
EH2 3LJ, t (0131) 220 1843.

Ireland: 17a Merlyn Park, Ballsbridge, Dublin 4,
t (01) 269 1640.

USA: 545 Boylston Street, Boston, MA 02116,
t (617) 536 2506; 180 North Michigan Avenue,
Chicago, IL 60601, t (312) 782 4588; 2655
Le Jeune Road, 203 Coral Gables, Florida,
t (305) 446 5511; 5055 Wilshire Blvd, Suite 960
Los Angeles, CA 90036, t (323) 938 0158; 150
East 58th Street, New York, NY 10155, t (212)
355 4080; 2375 Pennyslvania Avenue NW,
Washington, DC 20009, t (202) 728 2330.

Canada: 1 West Mount Square, Montreal H3Z
2P9, t (514) 935 5235; 200 Front Street, Toronto,
Ontario, t (416) 977 1661.

Australia: Level 24, St Martin's Tower, 31
Market St, Sydney NSW 2000, t (02) 61 24 33.

New Zealand: 345 Great South Rd, Takanini,
Auckland, t (09) 299 6019.

Entry Formalities

Passports and Visas

There are no formal entry requirements for
EU passport holders. Nationals of EU countries that are signatories to the Schengen
agreement no longer require even a passport; however, the UK is *not* a signatory and
passengers arriving at Spanish airports from
the UK must still present a valid passport.

Holders of US, Canadian, Australian and
New Zealand passports can enter Spain for
up to 90 days without a visa; visitors from
other countries will need a visa, available
from any Spanish consulate.

For Gibraltar there are no extra visa requirements for US citizens, and EU nationals have
the same rights and status as in the UK.

Note that you *must* present your passport at
the border in Gibraltar.

For the most up-to-date information, check
with the Spanish embassy or consulate in
your home country.

Customs

Customs are usually easy to get through –
unless you come in via Morocco, when they'll
search everything. Duty-free allowances have
been abolished within the EU for goods for
personal use; in practice, Customs will be
more likely to ask questions if you buy in
bulk, e.g. more than 3,200 cigarettes or 400
cigarillos, 200 cigars or 3kg of tobacco; plus
10 litres of spirits, 90 litres of wine and 110
litres of beer.

For travellers coming from outside the EU,
the duty-free limits are 1 litre of spirits or 2
litres of liquors (port, sherry or champagne),
plus 2 litres of wine and 200 cigarettes.

If you are travelling from the UK or the USA,
don't bother taking any alcohol – it's cheaper
to buy drink off the supermarket shelves.

Travellers from the USA are allowed to take
home, duty-free, goods to the value of $400,
including 200 cigarettes or 100 cigars; plus
one litre of alcohol. For more information, call
the US Customs Service. You're not allowed
to bring back absinthe or Cuban cigars.
Canadians can bring home $300 worth of
goods in a year, plus their tobacco and
alcohol allowances.

UK Customs, t 0845 010 9000,
www.hmce.gov.uk.

US Customs, t (202) 354 1000,
www.customs.gov.

Disabled Travellers

Facilities for disabled travellers are limited
within Spain and public transport is not
particularly wheelchair-friendly, though
RENFE usually provides wheelchairs at main
city stations. You are advised to contact the
Spanish Tourist Office, which has compiled a
factsheet and can give general information
on accessible accommodation, or any of the
organizations that specifically provide services for people with disabilities.

For international organizations that
provide travel information and advice, *see*
box, overleaf.

Disability Organizations

In Spain

Coordinadora Estatal de Minusvalidos Fisicos, Rio Rosas 54, Madrid, t 91 535 06 19, *www. cocemfe.es*. General services and advice.

Mobility Abroad, Urb. Los Porches, Avda Antonio Machado, Benalmádena, 29630, t 95 244 77 64, *www.mobilityabroad.com*. Arranges the hire of wheelchairs, scooters, bath lifts and walkers. Branches in the Costa Blanca, Mallorca and the Algarve.

ONCE (Organización Nacional de Ciegos de España), C/José Ortega y Gasset 22–24, t 91 577 37 56, *www.once.es*. The Spanish association for blind people, offering a number of services to blind travellers (such as Braille maps).

In the UK

RADAR (Royal Association for Disability and Rehabilitation), Unit 12, City Forum, 250 City Rd, London EC1V 8AF, t (020) 7250 3222, *www.radar.org.uk* (*open Mon–Fri 10–4*). Information and books on travel.

RNIB (Royal National Institute of the Blind), 105 Judd St, London WC1H 9NE, t (020) 7388 1266, *www.rnib.org.uk*.

Holiday Care Service, The Hawkins Suite, Enham Palace, Enham Alamein, Andover SP11 6JS, t 0845 124 9971, *www.holidaycare.org.uk*. Accessible hotels and attractions.

In the USA

American Foundation for the Blind, 11 Penn Plaza, Suite 300, New York, NY 10001, t (212) 502 7600, t 800 232 5463, *www.afb.org*. This is the best source of information in the US for visually impaired travellers.

Mobility International USA, PO Box 10767, Eugene, OR 97440, t (541) 343 1284, *www. miusa.org*. Provides information on international educational exchange programmes and volunteer service overseas for the disabled.

SATH (Society for Accessible Travel and Hospitality), 347 5th Ave, Suite 610, New York, NY 10016, t (212) 447 7284, *www.sath.org*. Travel and access information; also has details of other access resources on the web.

Insurance and EHICs

There is a standard agreement for citizens of EU countries, entitling them to a certain amount of free medical care, but it's not straightforward. You must complete all the necessary paperwork before you go to Spain, and allow a couple of months to make sure it comes through in time. You will need to get a free **European Health Insurance Card**, or EHIC (available online at *www.dh.gov.uk/travellers*, or *www.ehic.org.uk*, or by calling t 0845 606 2030, or by post using the forms available from post offices). Note that the EHIC has replaced the old E111.

No **inoculations** are required to enter Spain, though it never hurts – in a manner of speaking – to check that your tetanus jab is up to date, as well as some of the more exotic inoculations (typhoid, cholera and gamma globulin) if you want to venture on into Morocco.

You should consider **travel insurance**, available through most travel agents, banks and the Post Office. For a small monthly or one-off charge, not only is your health insured, but your bags and money too. Some policies will even refund a missed charter flight if you're too ill to catch it. (Not least, it's a small price to pay for avoiding the minefield of bureaucratic regulations surrounding the EHIC). Many English and English-speaking doctors now have arrangements with European insurance companies and send their account directly to the company without you, the patient, having to fork out. But, whether you pay on the spot or not, be sure to save all doctors' bills, pharmacy receipts and police documents (if you're reporting a theft).

Money and Banks

Spain's official currency is the **euro**. Euros come in denominations of €500, €200, €100, €50, €20, €10 and €5 (banknotes) and €2, €1, 50 cents, 20 cents, 10 cents, 5 cents, 2 cents and 1 cent (coins). For the latest **exchange rates**, see *www.xe.com/ucc*.

Spain's city centres seem to have a bank on every street corner, and most of them will exchange money; look for the *cambio* or exchange signs and the little flags. There is a slight difference in the rates, though usually not enough to make shopping around worthwhile. Beware exchange offices, as they can charge a hefty commission on all transactions. You can often change money at travel agencies, hotels, restaurants or the big department stores, but these usually charge whopping commissions. Most big supermarkets have *telebancos* or **ATMs**.

Travellers' cheques, if they are from one of the major companies, will pass at most bank exchanges.

Wiring money from overseas entails no special difficulties; just give yourself two weeks to be on the safe side, and work through one of the larger institutions (Banco Central, Banco de Bilbao, Banco Español de Crédito, Banco Hispano Americano, Banco de Santander, Banco de Vizcaya). All transactions have to go through Madrid.

Credit cards will always be helpful in towns, rarely in the country. Note that you must show identification, such as your passport, when you are shopping using a credit card. Few museums or monuments accept credit cards. Direct **debit cards** are also useful ways of obtaining money, though you should check with your bank before leaving to ensure your card can be used in Spain. But do not rely on a hole-in-the-wall machine as your only source of cash; if, for whatever reason, the machine swallows your card, it usually takes 10 days to retrieve it.

Note that for credit cards and debit cards, you pay a flat fee for each cash withdrawal.

Money in Gibraltar

In Gibraltar you can use Gibraltar pounds, UK sterling or euros, though you'll lose a bit on the exchange rate with euros. Spanish banks in Gibraltar tend to give a better rate of exchange from sterling to euros.

Getting There

By Air

From the UK

British Airways flies up to 10 times a day to Andalucía, with flights from London Gatwick and Heathrow to Málaga, Gatwick to Sevilla and Gatwick to Gibraltar (flights to Gibraltar are operated by GB Airways). The Spanish airline **Iberia** operates on many of the same routes, and also offers direct services from the UK to Alicante, Jerez de la Frontera and Sevilla. **Monarch Airlines** operates scheduled and chartered services from Aberdeen,

Birmingham, Gatwick, Luton and Manchester to Málaga, although some of these are available in summer only.

Málaga is a main destination for low-cost carriers, although services are much reduced in winter: British Midland's budget airline, **bmiBaby**, flies from East Midlands, Manchester, Birmingham and Cardiff; **Jet2** flies from Leeds, Newcastle, Blackpool and Manchester, and **Thomsonfly** from Birmingham, Bournmouth, Cardiff, East Midlands, Glasgow and Gatwick; **easyJet** operates services from Belfast, Bristol, East Midlands, Gatwick, Glasgow, London Luton, Stansted and Liverpool to Málaga. There are flights from Exeter, Southampton and Norwich with **Flybe**; from Dublin with **Ryanair** and from Dublin and Belfast with the Irish national carrier **Aer Lingus**.

Several charters serve **Almería**, but there are also low-cost flights with Ryanair and easyJet. British Airways, Monarch and Iberia also offer direct flights to Almería.

The small airport at **Jerez de la Frontera** has flights with Ryanair from London Stansted.

Ryanair flies from London Stansted, and Monarch from London Gatwick, to **Granada** and **Sevilla**.

The best deals are almost always found on the Internet. For the cheapest deals with the budget airlines, book well in advance: nearer your departure date you may find that the standard carriers offer a better deal. Most companies offer promotional fares from time to time outside the peak seasons of midsummer, Christmas and Easter, although a degree of flexibility over travel dates may be necessary to secure them.

Charter flights can be very cheap, and offer the added advantage of departing from local airports. Companies such as **Thomson**, **Airtours** and **Unijet** offer return flights from as little as £60. Some of the best deals have return dates limited strictly to one week or two and sometimes four, the maximum allowed under the regulations. In many cases a return charter ticket is a big saving over a one-way regular fare, even if your itinerary means you have to let the return half lapse. Check your local economy travel agent, or in your local paper, or the Sunday papers. In London, look in the *Evening Standard* and *Time Out*. TV Teletext and the Internet are

Airline Carriers

UK and Ireland

Aer Lingus, t 0870 876 5000, *www.aerlingus.com.*

Air France, t 0870 142 4343, *www.airfrance.com.*

Air Scotland, t (0141) 222 2363, *www.air-scotland.com.*

bmiBaby, t 0871 224 0224 (10p/min), *www.bmibaby.com.*

British Airways, t 0870 850 9850, *www.ba.com.*

British Midland, t 0870 607 0555, *www.flybmi.com.*

easyJet, t 0871 224 2366, *www.easyjet.com.*

FlyBe, t 0871 700 0535, *www.flybe.com.*

GB Airways, t 0845 77 333 77 (UK), *www.gbairways.com.*

Iberia, t 0870 609 0500, *www.iberia.com.*

Jet2, t 0871 226 1737, *www.jet2.com.*

Monarch Airlines, t 08700 40 50 40, *www.monarch-airlines.com.*

Ryanair, (UK) **t** 0871 246 0000 (10p/min), (Ireland) **t** 0818 30 30 30, *www.ryanair.com.*

Thomsonfly, t 0870 190 0737, *www.thomsonfly.com.*

USA and Canada

Air Canada, toll free **t** 1-888 2712 7786, *www.aircanada.ca.*

American Airlines, toll free **t** 800 523 3273, *www.aa.com.*

Continental Airlines, toll free **t** 800 231 0856, *www.continental.com.*

Iberia, toll free **t** 902 400 500, *www.iberia.com.*

United Airlines, toll free **t** 1-800 864 8331, *www.united.com.*

Other Airlines with Routes via Europe

British Airways, toll free **t** 1 800 AIRWAYS (1 800 247 9297), *www.britishairways.com.*

KLM (partners with NWA), toll free **t** 800 692 2345, *www.nwa.com.*

Lufthansa, toll free **t** 800 645 3880, *www.lufthansa.com.*

Virgin Atlantic, toll free **t** 800 821 5438, *www.virgin-atlantic.com.*

Charters, Discounts, Students and Special Deals

UK and Ireland

Budget Travel, 134 Lower Baggot St, Dublin 2, **t** (01) 631 1111, *www.budgettravel.ie.*

STA Travel, *www.statravel.co.uk.* Has over 400 branches all over the world, including more than 50 in the UK. Check the website for more information, or call **t** 0871 2300 040.

Trailfinders, 194 Kensington High St, London W8, **t** 0845 050 5945, *www.trailfinders.com.*

USIT, Aston Quay, Dublin 2, **t** (01) 602 1904, www.usitnow.ie. Also: Cork, **t** (021) 427 0900; Galway, **t** (091) 565 177; Limerick, **t** (061) 332 079; Waterford, **t** (051) 351 762.

Websites (UK and Ireland)

www.aboutflights.co.uk (**t** *0870 330 7311)*
www.cheapflights.co.uk
www.ebookers.com
www.expedia.co.uk
www.flyaow.com
www.justcities.com
www.lastminute.com
www.majortravel.co.uk
www.online-travellers.co.uk
www.opodo.co.uk
www.orbitz.com
www.packyourbags.com
www.sky-tours.co.uk
www.traveljungle.co.uk
www.travellersweb.com
www.travelocity.com
www.travelselect.com
www.whichbudget.com

USA and Canada

If you're resilient, flexible and/or youthful and prepared to shop around for budget deals on stand-bys or even courier flights (you can usually only take hand luggage on the latter), you should be able to get yourself some rock-bottom prices. Check the *Yellow Pages* for courier companies. For discounted flights, try the small ads in newspaper travel pages. Numerous travel clubs and agencies also specialize in discount fares, but they may require you to pay an annual membership fee. See *www.travel discounts.com* and *www.smartertravel.com.*

Airhitch, *www.airhitch.org.* Last-minute discount tickets to Europe.

Last Minute Travel Club, (USA/Canada) **t** 800 442 0568, *www.lastminutetravel.com.* Annual membership entitles you to cheap stand-by deals, special car rental rates in Europe and deals on train passes.

STA, *www.statravel.com,* with branches at most universities and at 2871 Broadway, New York, NY, **t** (212) 865 2700, and ASUC Building, 1st Floor, Berkeley, CA 94720, **t** (510) 642 3000.

Travel Cuts, 187 College St, Toronto, Ontario ON M5T 1P7, **t** (888) FLY CUTS (toll free) or **t** (416)

979 2406 from the USA, *www.travelcuts.com*. Canada's largest student travel specialists, with six offices plus one in New York.

Websites (USA and Canada)
www.eurovacations.com
www.expedia.com
www.flights.com
www.lastminute.com
www.orbitz.com
www.priceline.com (bid for tickets)
www.smartertravel.com
www.traveldiscounts.com
www.travelocity.com

also good sources of information on cheap charter flights to Spain, with some remarkable last-minute deals.

Get your ticket as early as possible, but try to be sure of your plans, as there are no refunds for missed flights – most travel agencies sell insurance, and indeed, most charter companies now insist upon it so that you don't lose all your money if you become ill and have to cancel.

Students and those under 26 have the additional option of special discount charters, departing from the UK, but make sure you have proof of student status. An official **ISIC card** (available from STA travel) costs £7; for more information see *www.isiccard.com*.

From the USA and Canada
There are numerous carriers that serve Spain. Most regular flights from the USA or Canada are to Madrid or Barcelona. **Iberia**, the national airline, offers fly-drive deals and discounts.

Remember that some of the best transatlantic deals are to London, from where you should be able to get a low-cost flight to Spain departing within a day or two of your arrival. This is an especially inexpensive way to go in the off season. The Sunday *New York Times* has the most listings, but, as always, the best deals are to be found on the web.

By Sea and Car
By sea is a good way to go if you mean to bring your car, motorbike, caravan or bicycle, but book well in advance – prices rise dramatically as the ferries fill up.

From the **UK via France**, the shortest ferry/catamaran crossing from the UK is currently **Dover–Calais** with P&O Ferries or SeaFrance. **Speed Ferries** operates a Dover–Bologne crossing, **Norfolkline** travels Dover–Dunkirk, **Transmanche** Newhaven–Dieppe, Newhaven–Le Havre and Portsmouth–Le Havre, and **Brittany Ferries** operates between Cork and Plymouth to Roscoff in Brittany, Portsmouth to Caen, Cherbourg and St-Malo, and Poole to Cherbourg. **Condor Ferries** sails between Poole and St-Malo, via Jersey or Guernsey, mid-May–Sept, and between Weymouth and St-Malo year-round, with a change of ferry in the Channel Islands. **Irish Ferries** sails from Rosslare to Cherbourg and Roscoff.

Prices vary considerably according to season and demand so shop around for the best deal.

From any of these ports the most direct route takes you to Bordeaux, down the western coast to the border at Irún, and on to San Sebastián, Burgos and Madrid, from where you can head south and choose your entry point into Andalucía.

An alternative route is from Paris to Perpignan, crossing the border at the Mediterranean side of the Pyrenees, then along the coast to Barcelona, where the E15 will take you south. Both routes take an average of two days' steady driving.

Ferry Operators
Brittany Ferries, t 08709 076 103/**t** 08705 360 360, *www.brittanyferries.com*. In Santander the address is the Estación Marítima, **t** 94 221 4500.

Condor Ferries, t 0845 243 5140, *www.condorferries.co.uk*.

Irish Ferries, (UK) **t** 08705 17 17 17, (Ireland) **t** 0818 300 400, *www.irishferries.com*.

Norfolkline, t 08708 70 10 20, *www.norfolklineferries.co.uk*.

P&O Ferries, t 08705 980 333 (UK), **t** 902 02 04 61 (Spain), *www.poferries.com*. In Bilbao, Cosme Echevarrieta 1, 48009 Bilbao, **t** 94 423 4477.

Sea France, t 08705 711 711, *www.seafrance.com*.

Speed Ferries, t 08702 200 570, *www.speedferries.com*.

Transmanche, t 0800 917 1201, *www.transmancheferries.com*.

See also ***www.ferrybooker.com*** for both ferry and Eurotunnel bookings.

You may find it more convenient and less tiring to try the ferry from Portsmouth to Bilbao or Plymouth to Santander, which cuts out driving through France and saves expensive *autoroute* tolls. These sea links between the **UK and Spain** are operated by Brittany Ferries and P&O Ferries.

For the scenery, opt for one of the routes over the Pyrenees, through Puigcerdá, Somport-Canfranc or Andorra, but expect heavy traffic; if you're not in a hurry, take the classic route through Roncesvalles and Vall d'Arán, or through Tarbes and Aragnouet through the tunnel to Parzán.

Brittany Ferries operates between Plymouth and Santander twice weekly, and prices for foot passengers are roughly equivalent to a return flight; children of 4–15 go for slightly over half-price, under-4s free. Prices for vehicles vary according to size and season: high season is from late June until early September, when the return fare for two people plus car is up to £800 with a reclining seat on board. Fares drop in low season. On-board accommodation is mandatory in high season; this costs from £150 per person based upon four people sharing a four-berth cabin, to £220 or more for a deluxe twin-berth cabin. There are also cheaper 5- and 10-day returns. The 24–27hr crossing can be rough.

P&O Ferries runs the Portsmouth–Bilbao route, with crossings twice weekly throughout the year except for a three-week break in January, and during February when there is just one weekly crossing. Peak season runs from mid-July to mid-August when the return fare for an average-length car and four adults is around £900, including accommodation in a four-berth cabin. This drops to around £600 in the winter months. Return fare for an adult foot passenger in peak season is around £300, and about half that out of season, including accommodation in a two-berth cabin. P&O fares include accommodation on all crossings, and prices vary dramatically according to the date and time of sailing. Children aged 4–15 travel just over half-price and under-4s go free. Good value 5- and 8-day mini-breaks are also available.

To **drive in Spain** you'll need **registration** and **insurance** documents, and a **driving licence**. Drivers with a valid licence from an EU country, the USA, Canada or Australia no

Drivers' Clubs

For more information on driving in France, contact the AA, RAC or, in the USA, the AAA:
AA, general enquiries, **t** 0870 600 0371, *www.theaa.com*.
RAC, general enquiries, **t** 0870 572 2722, *www.rac.co.uk*.
AAA (USA), **t** 800 222 4357, *www.aaa.com*.

longer need an international licence. If you're coming from Ireland or the UK, adjust the dip of your **headlights** to the right.

By Rail

From London to Andalucía takes at least a day and a half and requires a change of trains in Paris and Madrid or Barcelona. A two-month return, London–Madrid, costs from £145; for London–Sevilla you will need to change in Madrid anyway. Students, those under 26 and holders of a Senior Citizen's Railcard can get reductions. Time can be saved by taking the Eurostar, which runs very frequently and takes under 2½ hours from London (St Pancras) to Paris (Gare du Nord). Fares are lower if booked at least 14 days in advance. A useful online journey planner for all European journeys is the German Railways' website, *www.bahn.de*.

If you plan to take some long train journeys, it may be worth investing in a **rail pass** (see *www.raileurope.co.uk/inter-rail*). The Eurodomino pass for European citizens has now been cancelled and become part of **InterRail**; you can get a single country pass, or a one-month **InterRail Global Pass** which allows you to explore multiple countries over a longer period of time. Check the *www.interrailnet.com* or the Rail Europe website for current prices and special offers. These cards are not valid on trains in the UK, and supplements are charged for some trains.

Visitors from North America have a wide choice of passes, including **Eurailpass, Europass**, and **France 'n' Spain pass**, which can all be purchased in the USA. The Eurailpass allows unlimited first-class travel through 18 European countries for 15, 21, 30, 60 or 90 days; it saves the hassle of buying numerous tickets but will only pay for itself if you use it a lot; a 15-day (second-class) Eurailpass Youth costs $440; 26-year-olds and over can get a 15-day Eurailpass for $675, a 21-day pass for $877, 30 days for $1,088, or 3 months for $1,895; all fares include discounted fares on Eurostar plus free or discounted travel on selected ferries, lake steamers, boats and buses. Passes are not valid in the UK. There are also Senior Passes for the over-60s.

Rail tickets to Spain from the UK, or vice versa, and couchette and sleeper reservations in France, can be obtained from **Rail Europe**, which is also a good source of information on the different passes available.

Within Spain, contact Spanish railways (**RENFE**) on t 902 24 02 02, or *www.renfe.es*. Timetables are available online (also in English) and you can book tickets over the phone or online.

Rail Europe (UK), 178 Piccadilly, London W1, t 08708 371 371, *www.raileurope.co.uk*.

Rail Europe (USA and Canada), t 877 257 2887 (US), or t 800 361 RAIL (Canada), *www.raileurope.com*.

Eurostar, t 08705 186 186, *www.eurostar.com*.

www.seat61.com. An informative, reliable independent train travel website.

By Bus or Coach

One major company, **Eurolines**, offers departures several times a week in the summer (twice a week out of season, but you may have to change) from London to Spain, along the east coast as far as Alicante, or to Algeciras via San Sebastián, Burgos, Madrid, Córdoba, Granada and Málaga. Journey time is 37 hours from London to Málaga, and 40 hours to Algeciras – longer if you have to change (usually in Paris). Fares from London to Málaga start from around £150 return for under-25s, £170 for over-26s. Peak season fares between 1 July and 31 August are slightly higher. There are discounts for anyone under 26, senior citizens and children under 12. The national coach companies operate services that connect with the continental bus system. In the summer, the coach is the best bargain for anyone under 26; off-season you'll probably find a cheaper charter flight.

Eurolines, t 08705 143 219, *www.eurolines.co.uk* or *www.nationalexpress.com*.

Getting Around

By Air

Internal flights in Spain are primarily on Iberia and Air Europa. However, there are some other carriers on national routes including the budget airline **Vueling** (*www.vueling.com*), with flights between Málaga and Barcelona or Bilbao, and between Sevilla and Barcelona.

In Andalucía you'll find airports in Almería, Córdoba, Granada, Jerez (Cádiz), Málaga, Sevilla, and Melilla in North Africa. Prices are less of a bargain than they used to be, although if you shop around and are willing to travel at night, and avoid buying tickets at the last moment, you can pick up some cheap deals, especially if you're going on a round trip. Also, check out the national charters in Spanish travel agencies.

By Sea

The *Acciona-Trasmediterránea* line, t 902 45 46 45, *www.trasmediterranea.com*, operates services from Málaga to Melilla; Algeciras to Ceuta and Tangiers; and Almería to Ghazaouet, Melilla and Nador.

Ferrimaroc, t 950 27 48 00, *www.ferrimaroc.com*, offers frequent ferry services from Almería to Nado (Morocco).

Ferrys Rápidos del Sur, t 956 68 18 30, *www.frs.es*, runs frequent fast ferry services from Algeciras, Tarifa and Gibraltar to Tangiers (Morocco).

By Rail

Mister Traveller, take the Spanish Train!
RENFE brochure

Democracy in Spain has made the trains run on time, but Western Europe's most eccentric railway company, **RENFE**, still has a way to go. The problem isn't the trains themselves – they're almost always clean and comfortable, and do their best to keep to the schedules – but the new efficient RENFE remains so complex that it will foul up your plans at least once. There are no fewer than 13 varieties of train, from the luxury *Trenhotel* (night express train) to the excruciating *semi-directo* and *ferrobús*, which stop at every hamlet to deliver mail.

The best are the **Talgo** trains, speedy and stylish beasts in gleaming stainless steel; the Spaniards are very proud of them. **TER** trains are almost as good. There has been one great leap forward in Spanish rail transport in the last few years, and that is the introduction of **AVE services** – high-speed rail links – originally developed for the Sevilla Expo in 1992. A new AVE line from Málaga to Madrid is scheduled to open in 2008, reducing the journey time to just 2½ hours.

For **information and tickets**, call the RENFE information line, **t** 902 24 02 02, or book online at *www.renfe.es* (the website is available in English). Always buy tickets in advance if you can – one of RENFE's little tricks is to close station ticket-windows 10 minutes before your train arrives – and do allow a few minutes to check in. Other stations don't open the ticket-windows until the train is a couple of minutes away, causing panic and confusion. Don't rely on the list of trains posted; always ask at the station or travel office.

Fares are generally considerably lower than in the UK, but there are supplements on the faster trains that can put another 80 per cent on top of the basic price. If you plan to do a lot of riding on the rails, buy the *Guía RENFE*, an indispensable government publication with all the times and tariffs, available from any station newsagent. Every variety of train has different services and a different price. RENFE ticket people and conductors can't always get them straight, and, as in the UK, confusion is rampant, except again on Talgo and AVE routes where the published prices are straightforward. There are discounts for children (under-4s free; 4–12 half-price), large families, senior citizens (half-price) and regular travellers, and 25 per cent discounts on *Días Azules* ('blue days') for round-trip tickets only. 'Blue days' are posted in the RENFE calendars in every station. There is a pass for people under 26, the *tarjeta joven*, and youth fares are available from **TIVE** **offices** in large cities.

Rail Excursions

Andalucía's answer to the **Transcantábrica**, which operates in northwest Spain, is the **Al-Andalus Expreso**, a luxury tour taking passengers from Sevilla to Córdoba, Granada, Málaga and Jerez. Although expensive, the carriages are done out in period décor and the cuisine is superb. The trip takes 4–5 days, but a common complaint is that the train spends an excessive amount of time in a railway siding while passengers are bussed to the sights.

Al Andalus Expreso, C/Capitán Haya, Madrid 28020, **t** 91 570 1621, *www. alandalus-expreso.com*.

By Car

This is certainly the most convenient way of getting about, and often the most pleasurable. However, bear in mind that only a few hotels – the more expensive ones – have garages or any sort of parking, and in cities parking is always difficult. A useful tip to remember is that spaces which appear to be private – e.g. the underground car parks of apartment blocks and offices – are often public, and rates are usually modest. Spain's highway network is adequate, usually in good repair, and sometimes impressive. The system of *autopistas* (motorways) is constantly expanding. Spanish road building is remarkable for its speed if not always its durability.

Once you venture off the beaten track, be prepared for a few surprises; some roads in Andalucía wind tortuously up mountain-sides, with steep drops into gorges below. The old N340 along the coast is much safer with the addition of frequent lane-changing slip roads, bridges and underpasses, while the new bypasses around Fuengirola and Marbella have been built to genuine motorway standards. Travelling between Málaga and Gibraltar, which used to be known as 'mortuary mile', is undoubtedly much safer than it was thanks to a new motorway, which bypasses the towns between Estepona and Algeciras.

Americans should not be intimidated by driving in Europe. Learn the international road-sign system (charts available to members from most auto clubs; *see* p.80), brush up on your gear-changing technique, and get used to the idea of few signals and traffic constantly converging from all directions. **Seat belts** are mandatory. The **speed limit** is 100kph (62 mph) on national highways, unless marked, and 120kph (75mph) on motorways. Drive with the utmost care at all times – having an accident will bring you untold headaches, and, to make matters worse, many Spaniards drive without insurance.

Hitchhiking can be dangerous, and drivers in Andalucía rarely give lifts.

Car Hire

This costs roughly the same as elsewhere in Europe. The big international companies are the most expensive, and seldom the most service-orientated. Smaller companies will, for example, deliver a car to your hotel when you want it, and collect it again when you no longer require it. On the *costas*, prices for the smallest cars begin at about €130 per week, which includes unlimited mileage and full insurance (CDW), according to season. An all-in weekly rate for a two-door Opel Corsa in mid-season picked up from and returned to Málaga airport should be about €180. If your rental begins at Málaga airport, try booking it locally in advance. One of the cheapest and most reliable local operators is **Crown**, *www.crowncarhire.com*, the largest car-hire company in Andalucia, which regularly offers great deals. All the major international car rental firms have offices throughout Andalucia, including **Avis**, *www.avis.com*; **Hertz**, *www.hertz.com*; **Europcar**, *www.europcar.com*; and **National** (linked to the Spanish car hire firm **Atesa**), *www.national.com*. An online rental agency, **Pepe Car**, *www.pepecar.com*, has offices in Seville, Málaga, Almería, Cádiz, Granada and Huelva.

Check if your airline offers any car deals when you book your ticket. However, pre-booked car rentals offer no refunds should your plans change.

Taxis

The average **fare** within a city will be €5–10. Taxis are metered, and drivers are entitled to certain surcharges (for luggage, night or holiday trips, to the train or airport, etc.), and if you cross the city limits they can usually charge double the fare shown.

It's easy to hail a cab from the street, from the numerous taxi ranks (with easy-to-spot **TAXI** signs) and there will always be a few around the stations.

By Bus

With literally dozens of companies providing services over Andalucía, expect choice at the price of confusion. Not all cities have bus stations; in some there may be a dozen little offices spread around town for each firm. Buses, like the trains, are cheap by northern European standards, but still no bargain; if you're travelling on the cheap, you'll find that getting around is your biggest expense. Usually, whether you go by train or bus will depend on simple convenience; in some places the train station is far from the centre, in others the bus station is. As is the custom at RENFE stations, tickets on the inter-city bus routes are sometimes sold at the last minute.

Small towns and villages can normally be reached by bus only through their provincial capitals. Buses are usually clean, dependable and comfortable, and there's plenty of room for baggage in the compartment underneath. On the more luxurious buses that link the main cities of Andalucía, as well as the services along the coast, you get air-conditioning and even a movie (*Rambo*, *Kung Fu*, sappy Spanish flicks from the Franco era or locally produced rock videos). Tourist information offices are the best sources for bus information.

City Buses

Every Spanish city has a perfectly adequate system of public transportation. You won't need to make much use of it, though, for in almost every city all attractions are within walking distance of each other. City bus journeys usually cost around €1, and if you intend to use buses often there are books of tickets called *abonamientos* or *bono-bus*, or *tarjeta* cards to punch on entry, available at reduced rates from tobacco shops. Bus drivers will give change but often don't accept notes of more than €10. In many cities, the bus's entire route will be displayed on the signs at each stop (*parada*). And don't take it for granted that the bus will stop just because you are waiting – nearly every stop apart from the terminus seems to be a request stop. Flamboyant signals and throwing yourself across its path are the only ways of ensuring the bus will stop for you.

Where to Stay

Hotels in Spain are still bargains – though, as with prices for other facilities, Spain is gradually catching up with the rest of western Europe. One thing you can still count on is a consistent level of quality and service; the Spanish government regulates hotels intelligently and closely. Room prices must be posted in the hotel lobbies and in the rooms, and if there's any problem you can ask for the complaints book or *Libro de Reclamaciones*. No one ever writes anything in these; any written complaint must be passed on to the authorities immediately. Hotel-keepers will usually prefer to correct the problem for you.

The prices given in this guide are for double rooms with bath (unless stated otherwise) – see box, above right, for a guide to the **hotel price categories** we use. Prices for single rooms will average about 60 per cent of a double, while triples or an extra bed are around 35 per cent more. Within the price ranges shown, the most expensive are likely to be in the big cities, while the cheapest places are always in provincial towns. On the whole, prices throughout Andalucía are surprisingly consistent. But no government could resist the chance to insert a little bureaucratic confusion: accommodation in Spain is classified in a complex system. Look out for the **blue plaques** next to the doors of all *hoteles, hostales*, etc., which identify the classification.

If you're travelling around a lot, a good investment would be the guide to *Hotels and Apartments* (€5) published annually by the tourist board. Unfortunately, it usually sells out quickly. The government publication *Guía de Hoteles* is also useful, a great fat book with every classified hotel and *hostal* in Spain (except the very cheap one-star *pensiones*), available in many bookshops, €10. The government also publishes similar guides to holiday flats (*apartamentos turísticos*), campsites and *casas rurales* (rural accommodation). Another useful guide is the big, fat *Guía de Hoteles y Restaurantes de España*, one of a series of guides published annually by El País Aguilar, available from almost all bookshops. Local tourist information offices will have a complete accommodation list for their province, and

Hotel Price Categories

The prices given in this guide are for double rooms with bathrooms but do not include **VAT** (IVA), which is charged at 7 per cent on all hotel rooms.

luxury	€€€€€	over €180
very expensive	€€€€	€130–180
expensive	€€€	€80–130
moderate	€€	€50–80
inexpensive	€	under €50

some can be very helpful with finding a room when things are tight. The official tourist information websites, particularly *www.andalucia.org*, have full details of all accommodation options.

Paradores

The government, in its plan to develop tourism in the 1950s, started this nationwide chain of classy hotels to draw some attention to little-visited areas. They restored old palaces, castles and monasteries, furnished them with antiques and installed fine restaurants featuring local specialities.

Paradores for many people are one of the best reasons for visiting Spain. Not all are historical landmarks; in resort areas, they are as likely to be cleanly designed modern buildings, usually in a great location with a pool and sports facilities. As their popularity has increased, so have their prices; in most cases the rooms and the restaurant will be the most expensive in town. They are classed as three- or four-star hotels, and their prices per night range from €70 in provincial towns to €150 and upwards for the most luxurious. Many offer out-of-season or weekend promotional rates, including fantastic 'youth rates' (which can make a *parador* cheaper than a one-star hotel). They also have a

Parador Advance Booking

Spain: Head office, C/Requena 3, 28013 Madrid, **t** 91 516 66 66.

UK: Keytel International, 402 Edgware Road, London W2 1ED, **t** (020) 7616 0300, *www.keytel.co.uk*.

USA: Marketing Ahead Inc., 381 Park Ave South, Suite 718, New York, NY 10016, **t** 800 223 1356, *www.marketingahead.com*.

useful five-night pass, which currently offers accommodation for just €90 a night (with supplements at the most luxurious places).

If you can afford a *parador*, there is no better place to stay. We've mentioned most of them in this book. *See www.parador.es.*

Hoteles

Hoteles (H) are rated with from one to five stars according to the services they offer. These are the most expensive places, and even a one-star hotel will be a comfortable, middle-range establishment. *Hotel residencias* (HR) are the same, only without a restaurant. Many of the more expensive hotels have some rooms available at prices lower than those listed. They won't tell you this, though; you'll have to ask. You can often get discounts in the off season but will be charged more during festivals; these are supposedly regulated, but in practice hoteliers charge whatever they can get. If you want to attend these events, book as far in advance as possible.

Hostales and Pensiones

Hostales (Hs) and *pensiones* (P) are rated with one to three stars. These are more modest places, often a floor in an apartment block. A three-star *hostal* is usually roughly equivalent to a one-star hotel. *Pensiones* may require full- or half-board (there aren't many of these establishments, only a few in resort areas). *Hostal Residencias* (HsR), like *hotel residencias*, do not offer meals except breakfast, and not always that. Of course, *hostales* and *pensiones* with one or two stars will often have rooms without private baths at considerable savings.

Be warned: cheap *hostales* in ports (such as Málaga, Cádiz and Algeciras) can be crummy and noisy beyond belief – as you lie unable to sleep, you can only marvel at the human body's ability to produce such a wealth of unidentifiable sounds, coming through the paper-thin walls of the next room.

Fondas, Casas de Huéspedes and Camas

The bottom of the scale is occupied by the *fonda* (F) and *casa de huéspedes* (CH), little

different from a one-star *hostal*, though generally cheaper. Off the scale completely are hundreds of unclassified cheap places, usually rooms in an apartment or over a bar and identified only by a little sign reading *camas* (beds) or *habitaciones* (rooms). You can also ask in bars or at the tourist office for unidentified *casas particulares*, private houses with a room or two; in many villages these will be the best you can do, but they're usually clean – Spanish women are manic housekeepers. The best will be in small towns and villages, and around universities.

Occasionally you'll find a room over a bar run by somebody's grandmother that is nicer than a four-star hotel, complete with frilly pillows, lovely old furnishings and a shrine to the Virgin Mary. It always helps to see the room first. In cities, the best places to look are right in the centre, not around the bus and train stations. Most inexpensive establishments will ask you to pay a day in advance.

Alternative Accommodation

Youth hostels exist in Spain, but they're usually not worth the trouble. Most are open only in the summer; there are the usual inconveniences and silly rules, and they're often in out-of-the-way locations. You'll be better off with the inexpensive *hostales* and *fondas* – sometimes these are even cheaper than youth hostels – or ask at the local tourist office for rooms available in **university halls of residence**.

If you fancy some peace and tranquillity, the national tourist office has a list of **monasteries** and **convents** that welcome guests. Accommodation starts at about €20 a night, meals are simple and guests may usually take part in the religious ceremonies.

Camping

Campsites are rated with from one to three stars, depending on their facilities, and in addition to the ones listed in the official government handbook there are always others, rather primitive, that are unlisted. On the whole camping is a good deal, and facilities in most first-class sites include shops, restaurants, bars, laundries, hot showers, first aid, swimming pools, telephones and, occasionally, tennis courts.

Caravans and camper vans converge on the more developed sites, but if you just want to pitch your little tent or sleep out in some quiet field, ask around in the bars or at likely farms. Camping is forbidden in many forest areas because of fears of fire, as well as on the beaches (though you can often get close to some quieter shores if you're discreet). If you're doing some hiking, bring a sleeping bag and stay in the free *refugios* along the major trails.

The government handbook *Guía de Campings* can be found in most bookstores and at the Spanish tourist office; further details can be obtained from the **Camping and Caravanning Club**, Greenfields House, Westwood Way, Coventry CV4 8JH, t 024 7669 4995, *www.campingandcaravanningclub. co.uk*. Reservations for sites can be made through **Federación Española de Empresarios de Camping**, C/Valderribas 48, Esq 3, 1C, 28007 Madrid, t 91 448 12 34, *www.fedcamping.com*.

Resort Accommodation

Almost everything along the coasts of Andalucía has been built in the last 30 years, and anonymous high-rise buildings abound. Lately the trend has turned towards low-rise 'villages' or *urbanizaciones* built around a pool, usually on or near the beach. We've tried to include only the places that stand out in some way, or which are good bargains for their rating. Resorts offer a choice of hotels in every price range, though the best bargains tend to be in the places where foreigners fear to tread, or at any rate tread less – the Costa de la Luz west of Cádiz, or the small resorts close to Almería.

If you intend to spend a couple of weeks on the Costa del Sol, your best bet is to book an all-inclusive package deal from the UK or USA. Most hotels in the big resorts cater for package tours, and may not even answer a request for an individual reservation during the peak season. The coast has some stylish hotels, particularly around Marbella and the upmarket areas of the western Costa del Sol. However, all sorts of bargains are to be had, especially if you plan a long-term stay in winter, a practice often followed by cold pensioners from the north. Incidentally, all beaches in Spain are public, which sounds extremely politically correct but in fact is a mixed blessing.

Where to Stay in Gibraltar

Gibraltar doesn't have the same range of accommodation, and there are no official categories; the only guide to quality is price – unfortunately not an accurate guarantee of standards anywhere. Based on Spanish categories, most hotels would fall into the two- or three-star bracket, with one or two exceptions, but don't expect any bargains – £75 is about average for a double room with bath, and there's little cheaper than that unless you go on a package deal.

There are no camping facilities in Gibraltar, but plenty on the Spanish side of the border, from where you can make a day trip.

Note that if you are travelling in a caravan (camper), you will not be allowed to take it in, as the streets are narrow and congested at the best of times. You can, of course, leave it on the Spanish side, but mind where you park – you could return to find it displaying a ticket, or clamped, or simply towed away.

Tour Operators and Special-interest Holidays

Golf

The south coast of Spain is teeming with golf courses – there are more than 50 of them on the Costa del Sol. Most hotels nearby cater specifically for the golfer and there are numerous specialist golf operators. There is a list of courses and fees at *www.andalucian-golf-booking.com*, and the official website, *www. andalucia.org*, has a complete list of every course in the region.

Longshot, 75 King St, South Shields, Tyne & Wear NE33 1DP, t 0808 1565 927, *www. longshotgolf.co.uk*. Golfing holidays. Also *see* **Cadogan Travel**, opposite.

Language-learning

Spanish language courses generally last 2–12 weeks. Course fees average €300 for two weeks; private tuition costs around €12–20 per hour. Accommodation can be arranged, whether boarding with families or in an apartment. There are countless language schools in Andalucía: among the largest and best known are **Don Quijote**, *www.donquijote.org* and

Academia SLC (Spanish Language Center), C/Ricardo Soriano 36 s/n, Edif. Maria III, 29600 Marbella, t 952 90 15 76, *www. spanishlanguagec.com*.

Carmen de las Cuevas, Cuesta de los Chinos 15, Albaicín, t 958 22 10 62, *www.carmencuevas. com*. Language and Spanish culture courses, including flamenco.

Centro de Idiomas Quorum, C/San Miguel 25, Nerja, t 95 252 37 88, *www.quorumspain.com*.

Instituto de Español Picasso, Pza de la Merced 20, 29080 Málaga, t 95 221 39 32, *www. instituto-picasso.com*.

Eurolingua, *www.eurolingua.com*. There are also excellent 'Spanish for Foreigners' courses offered at **Málaga University**, *http://malaga-university.org*.

Exit, C/Alameda 5, Marbella, t 952 779 223, *www.exitgate2.com*. A company based in Andalucía which organizes Spanish courses, part-time work and internships for students seeking to study or work in the country.

Lingua Service Worldwide Ltd, 42 Artillery Road, Woodbury, CT 0798, t 203 263 6346, *www. linguaserviceworldwide.com*. US operator offering short-term residential Spanish courses in Málaga, Granada and Sevilla.

Spas (Balnearios)

In Andalucía there's a spa to cater for every complaint, from allergies to rheumatism.

Balneario del Alhama de Granada, Alhama de Granada, t 958 35 00 11, *www.balneario alhamadegranada.com*. The Romans and Arabs once bathed here.

Balneario de Carratraca, Carratraca, t 952 45 80 71. Near Ardales, in the hills behind Málaga. *Open 15 June–15 Oct*.

Balneario de Chiclana, Chiclana da la Frontera, t 956 40 05 20, *www.balneariodechiclana. com*. People have been taking the waters here for 200 years.

Balneario Fuente Amargosa, Tolox, t 95 248 70 91. A 19th-century spa in a hilltop village overlooking the coast.

Balneario de Lanjarón, Lanjarón, t 958 77 01 37, *www.balneariodelanjaron.com*. On the lower slopes of the Sierra Nevada.

Tour Operators and Self-catering (in the UK)

Abercrombie & Kent, St George's House, Ambrose St, Cheltenham GL50 3LG, t 0845 070 0610, *www.abercrombiekent.co.uk*. Upmarket holidays and villas.

ACE Study Tours, Sawston Road, Babraham, Cambridge CB2 4AP, t (01223) 835 055,

www.acestudytours.co.uk. Art, architecture, archaeology and natural history tours.

Al-Andalus Expreso (*see* p.82). Luxury train tours across Andalucía.

Alternative Travel Group, 69–71 Banbury Road, Oxford OX2 6PE, t (01865) 315 678, *www. atg-oxford.co.uk*. Arranges walking tours around Andalucía.

Andalucian Adventures, Washpool, Horsley, Glos GL6 0PP, t (01453) 834 137, *www. andalucian-adventures.co.uk*. Walking, wellness, yoga, activity and painting tours in southern Spain.

Andante Travels, The Old Barn, Old Road, Alderbury, Salisbury, SP5 3AR, Wilts, t (01722) 713 800, *www.andantetravels.co.uk*. Arranges archaeological and historical study tours of Roman Spain. Also walking holidays.

Andrew Brock Travel, 29a Main St, Lyddington, Oakham, Rutland LE15 9LR, t (01572) 821 330, *www.andrewbrocktravel.co.uk*. Walking holidays in southern Andalucía.

Bird Holidays, 10 Ivegate, Yeadon, Leeds LS19 7RE, t (0113) 391 0510, *www.birdholidays.co.uk*. Bird-watching holidays in the Coto Doñana National Park (Huelva), and around Tarifa.

Cadogan Travel, 37 Commercial Road, Southampton SO15 1 GG, t 0845 615 4390, *www.cadoganholidays.com*. Upmarket holidays (including golfing holidays) in Gibraltar, southern Spain and Morocco.

Cortijo Romero, 22 Cottage Offices, Latimer Park, Latimer, Chesham HP5 1TU, t (01494) 765 775, *www.cortijo-romero.co.uk*. Alternative holidays (personal development, yoga, Tai Chi, etc.) in a rural farmhouse.

Cox & King's Travel Ltd, Gordon House, 10 Green Coat Place, London SW1P 1PH, t (020) 7873 5000, *www.coxandking.com*. Luxury city breaks and tours of Andalucía and Morocco.

CV Travel, 43 Cadogan Street, London SW3 2PR, t (020) 7384 5894, *www.cvtravel.net*. Small luxury hotels and upmarket villas on the coast and inland.

Equitour, t 0871 720 0183, *www.equitour.co.uk*. Riding holidays throughout Spain, including several locations in Andalucía.

Exodus, Grange Mills, Weir Road, London SW12 0NE, t (020) 8675 5550, *www.exodus. co.uk*. Offers walking and activity tours throughout Spain.

Naturetrek, Cheriton Mill, Cheriton, Alresford, Hampshire SO24 0NG, t (01962) 733 051, *www.naturetrek.co.uk*. Runs birdwatching and botanical tours in Andalucía and the Coto Doñana.

Page & Moy Ltd, 136–140 London Road, Leicester LE2 1EN, t 0870 833 4012, *www. page-moy.com*. Cultural guided tours throughout Spain.

Plantagenet Tours, 85 The Grove, Moordown, Bournemouth BH9 2TY, t (01202) 521 895, *www.plantagenettours.com*. A changing programme of cultural tours in Andalucía and Catalunya run by a passionate, learned and entertaining ex-college professor.

Prospect Music & Art Tours, PO Box 4972, London W1A 7FL, t (020) 7486 5704, *www.prospecttours.com*. Tours led by art and music historians.

Ramblers Holidays, Box 43, Welwyn Garden City, Herts AL8 6PQ, t (01707) 331 133, *www.ramblersholidays.co.uk*. Walking tours in the Sierra Nevada.

Tall Stories, Brassey House, New Zealand Avenue, Walton on Thames, Surrey KT12 1QD, t (01932) 252 002, *www.tallstories.co.uk*. Adventure holidays.

Unicorn Holidays, 2–10 Cross Road, Tadworth, Surrey KT20 5UJ, t (01737) 812 255. Specializes in tailor-made holidays, with high-quality character hotels and *parador* accommodation.

The Walking Safari Company, 29a Main St, Lyddington, Oakham, Rutland LE15 9LR, t (01572) 821 330, *www.walkeurope.com*. Walking and painting holidays in Andalucía.

Tour Operators (in the USA and Canada)

Abercrombie & Kent International, 1520 Kensington Road, Oak Brook, IL 60521, t 1 630 954 2944, *www.abercrombiekent.com*. Upmarket holidays and villas.

Alta Tours, 1801 Skycrest Drive No.7, Walnut Creek, CA 94102, t (toll-free) 800 338 4191, *www.altatours.com*. Escorted tours and customized travel, including cruises around Sevilla and Cadiz and hiking trips in Andalucía.

Escapade Vacations, Isramworld, 223 Park Avenue South, New York, NY 10003, t 800 223 7460, *www.escapadevacations.com*. Package and themed tours including 'Seville by Night' and 'Historic Spain'.

Heritage Tours, 121 West 27 Street, Suite 1201, New York, NY 10001, t (toll free) 800 378 4555, *www.heritagetoursonline.com*. Customized cultural and historical tours in and around Andalucía, Granada and Sevilla.

Marketing Ahead Inc., 381 Park Ave South, Suite 718, New York, NY 10016, t 800 223 1356, *www.marketingahead.com*. Leading *parador* agents in the USA.

Saranjan Tours, PO Box 292, Kirkland WA 98083-0292, t 1 800 858 9594, *www. saranjan.com*. US-based holiday operator offering private cooking classes and gourmet tours in both Sevilla and the region around.

Trafalgar Tours, 801 E Katella Avenue, Anaheim, CA 92805 t (toll free) 1-866 544 4434, *www. trafalgartours.com*. All-inclusive 9–10-day tours of Spain, many starting in Madrid before heading south to Granada and Cordoba.

Tour Operators (in Spain and Gibraltar)

Cabalgar-Rutas Alternativas, 18412 Bubión (Granada), t 95 876 3135, *www.riding andalucia.com*. Offers horse riding and hiking trips in the *sierras* of Granada and to the coast of Almería.

Dolphin Safari, Marina Bay, Gibraltar, PO80, t 95 677 19 14, *www.dolphinsafari.gi*. Arranges dolphin-spotting trips from May to October.

Nevadensis, Plaza de la Libertad s/n, 18411 Pampaneira (Granada), t 95 876 31 27, *www.nevadensis.com*. Organizes walking tours, mountaineering, cross-country skiing.

Rancho Los Lobos, 11339 Jimena de la Frontera (Cádiz), t 95 664 04 29, *www.rancholoslobos. com*. Riding holidays.

The Spirit of Andalucía, c/o Sally von Meister, Apartado 20, El Nobo, 29480 Gaucín (Málaga), t 95 215 13 03, *www.elnobo.co.uk*. Courses in cooking and painting.

Practical A–Z

08

Imperial–Metric Conversions

Length (multiply by)
Inches to centimetres: 2.54
Centimetres to inches: 0.39
Feet to metres: 0.3
Metres to feet: 3.28
Yards to metres: 0.91
Metres to yards: 1.1
Miles to kilometres: 1.61
Kilometres to miles: 0.62

Area (multiply by)
Inches square to centimetres square: 6.45
Centimetres square to inches square: 0.15
Feet square to metres square: 0.09
Metres square to feet square: 10.76
Miles square to kilometres square: 2.59
Kilometres square to miles square: 0.39
Acres to hectares: 0.40
Hectares to acres: 2.47

Weight (multiply by)
Ounces to grams: 28.35
Grammes to ounces: 0.035
Pounds to kilograms: 0.45
Kilograms to pounds: 2.2
Stones to kilograms: 6.35
Kilograms to stones: 0.16
Tons (UK) to kilograms: 1,016
Kilograms to tons (UK): 0.0009
1 UK ton (2,240lbs) = 1.12 US tonnes (2,000lbs)

°C	°F
40	104
35	95
30	86
25	77
20	68
15	59
10	50
5	41
-0	32
-5	23
-10	14
-15	5

Volume (multiply by)
Pints (UK) to litres: 0.57
Litres to pints (UK): 1.76
Quarts (UK) to litres: 1.13
Litres to quarts (UK): 0.88
Gallons (UK) to litres: 4.55
Litres to gallons (UK): 0.22
1 UK pint/quart/gallon =
1.2 US pints/quarts/
gallons

Temperature
Celsius to Fahrenheit:
multiply by 1.8 then
add 32

Fahrenheit to Celsius:
subtract 32 then multiply
by 0.55

Spain Information

Time Differences
Country: + 1hr GMT; + 6hrs EST
Daylight saving from last weekend in March
to end of October

Dialling Codes
*Note: to dial within Spain and within a province,
include the area code (Andalucía 95).*

Spain country code 34 (Gibraltar 350)

To Spain from: UK, Ireland, New Zealand 00 /
USA, Canada 011 / Australia 0011 then dial 34
and the full number

From Spain or Gibraltar to: UK 00 44; Ireland
00 353; USA, Canada 001; Australia 00 61; New
Zealand 00 64 then the number without the
initial zero

From Spain to Gibraltar: 00 350 then the local
five-digit number

Directory enquiries: 11811

International directory enquiries: 176

Emergency Numbers
General emergency number: 112

Embassy Numbers in Spain
UK: 95 35 23 00 (Málaga); **Ireland** 95 221 63 61
(Sevilla); **USA**: 95 423 1885 (Sevilla); **Canada** 91
423 32 50 (Madrid); **Australia** 91 353 66 00
(Madrid); **New Zealand** 91 523 02 26 (Madrid)

Shoe Sizes

Europe	UK	USA
35	2½ / 3	4
36	3 / 3½	4½ / 5
37	4	5½ / 6
38	5	6½
39	5½ / 6	7 / 7½
40	6 / 6½	8 / 8½
41	7	9 / 9½
42	8	9½ / 10
43	9	10½
44	9½ / 10	11
45	10½	12

Women's Clothing

Europe	UK	USA
34	6	2
36	8	4
38	10	6
40	12	8
42	14	10
44	16	12

Crime and the Police

General emergency number **t** 112

Crime is not really a big problem in Spain, and Spaniards talk about it perhaps more than is warranted. Pickpocketing and robbing parked cars are the specialities; in Sevilla they like to take the whole car. The big cities are the places where you should be careful. Crime is also spreading to the tourist areas, particularly the Costa del Sol. Even on the Costa, though, the crime rate is roughly a quarter of that in Britain. Note that in Spain possessing less than 8 grams of cannabis is legal; buying and selling it, however, is not. And anything else may easily earn you the traditional 'six years and a day'.

There are several species of **police**, and their authority varies with the area. Franco's old goon squads, the *Policía Armada*, have been reformed and relatively demilitarized into the *Policía Nacional*, once known as 'chocolate drops' for their brown uniforms, but now they wear blue and white. The *Policía Municipal* in some towns do crime control, while in others they simply direct traffic.

Mostly in rural areas, there's the *Guardia Civil*, with green uniforms, but no longer do they don the black patent-leather tricorn hats. Laurie Lee called them the 'poison dwarfs of Spain', but they too have been reformed; now they're most conspicuous as a highway patrol, assisting motorists and handing out tickets. Most traffic violations are payable on the spot; the traffic cops have a reputation for upright honesty.

Gibraltar has no serious crime to speak of, and, given its albeit diminishing military status, security is tight.

Eating Out

Price categories quoted in the 'Eating Out' sections throughout this book are prices for the set menu or for a three-course meal with drinks, per person.

See also **Food and Drink**, pp.63–70, for typical restaurant hours.

Restaurant Price Categories

expensive	€€€	over €40
moderate	€€	€20–40
inexpensive	€	under €20

Unless it's explicitly written on the bill (*la cuenta*), service in most restaurants is not included in the total, so tip accordingly. If you dine where the locals do, you'll be assured of a good deal, if not necessarily a good meal.

Almost every restaurant offers a *menú del día* or *menú turístico*, featuring an appetizer, a main course, dessert, bread and drink at a set price, always cheaper than if you had ordered the items *à la carte*.

Since a 2006 extension to the ban on smoking in public spaces, many restaurants are also now largely no-smoking.

Bars and **cafés** collect much of the Spaniards' leisure time. They are wonderful institutions, where you can eat breakfast or linger over a glass of beer until four in the morning; in any of them you could see an old sailor delicately sipping his camomile tea next to a young mother, baby under her arm, stopping by for a beer break during her shopping. Some have music – jazz, rock or flamenco; some have great snacks, or *tapas*, some have games or pinball machines.

Electricity

The current is 225 AC or 220 V, the same as most of Europe. Americans will need converters, and the British will need two-pin adapters for the different plugs. Adapters and converters are sold in department stores such as El Corté Ingles and electrical shops.

Health and Emergencies

General emergency number **t** 112

There is a standard agreement for citizens of EU countries, entitling them to a certain amount of free medical care, with an EHIC; *see* **Planning Your Trip**, p.76. If you need medical treatment while in Spain, you must visit a state surgery (*consultorio*), health centre (*centro sanitario*) or hospital clinic (*ambulatorio*) and show your card. If you are asked to pay, you are being treated privately and your bills will not be refunded. Note that not all medical treatment is covered: dentistry, for example, is excluded. The Department of Health website has comprehensive information on *www.dh.gov.uk/travellers*, or you can call the EHIC line on **t** + 44 191 203 5555 from outside the UK.

The newspaper *Sur* lists *farmacias* in large cities that stay open all night, and every pharmacy displays a duty roster outside so you can locate one nearby which is open.

The **tap water** is safe to drink in Spain, but it generally doesn't taste very nice.

Maps

Cartography has been an art in Spain since the 12th-century Catalans charted their Mediterranean empire in Europe's first great school of map-making. The tourist offices hand out beautifully detailed maps of every town, and have an excellent visitors map for Andalucía (free).

The best large-scale maps are produced by Almax Editores. Topographical maps for hikers and mountaineers can be obtained from CNIG (Centro Nacional de Información Geográfica), part of the Instituto Geográfico Nacional (IGN). They have shops in all the provincial capitals including Avda Divina Pastora, Granada, **t** 958 90 93 20 and C/Ramos Carrión 48, Málaga, **t** 952 21 20 18.

Media

The left-leaning *El País* is Spain's biggest national newspaper, closely followed in the circulation stakes by *El Mundo*, a centre-right broadsheet. Circulation for both is painfully low; Spaniards just don't read newspapers. Both papers include weekly arts and entertainment supplements. *El País* has the best regional film listings, indicating where you can see some great films subtitled instead of dubbed (look out for *versión original* or its abbreviation '*vo*'). Major British papers are available in all tourist areas and big cities and the *New York Herald Tribune* (which has a small English-language supplement from *El País*), the *Wall Street Journal* and *USA Today* are readily available wherever Americans go. Most hit the news-stands a day late.

There are also publications in English on the Costa del Sol, notably *Sur* in English, a surprisingly high-quality English-language round-up of the Málaga paper with news, good features and a riveting classified ads section (also available online at *www.surin english.com*); *Costa del Sol News*, with more of the same, *http://costadelsolnews.es*; and

Absolute Marbella and *Essential Marbella*, two free glossy monthly magazines. Most British papers are flown daily to Gibraltar, while the *Daily Mail* is printed daily in Madrid.

National and Public Holidays

The Spaniards, like the Italians, try to have as many public holidays as possible. And everything closes. And, if the holiday falls on a Thursday, for example, they'll make a 'bridge' (*puente*) and stay closed on the Friday too. The big holidays, celebrated throughout Spain, are Corpus Christi in late May or early June, *Semana Santa* during the week before Easter, *Asunción* on 15 August and *Día de Santiago* on 25 July, celebrating Spain's patron, St James. *See* pp.72–4.

Public Holidays in Spain

1 Jan *Año Nuevo* (New Year's Day)
6 Jan *Epifanía* (Epiphany)
Mar/April *Viernes Santo* (Good Friday), *Domingo de la Resurrección* (Easter Sunday)
1 May *Día del Trabajo* (Labour Day)
May/June Corpus Christi
25 July *Día de Santiago* (St James's Day)
15 Aug *Asunción* (Assumption)
12 Oct *Día de la Hispanidad* (National Day)
1 Nov *Todos los Santos* (All Saints' Day)
6 Dec *Día de la Constitución* (Constitution Day)
8 Dec *Inmaculada Concepción* (Immaculate Conception)
25 Dec *Navidad* (Christmas Day)

Public Holidays in Gibraltar

1 Jan New Year's Day
Mid-March Commonwealth Day
Mar/April Good Friday and Easter Monday
1 May May Day
May Spring Bank Holiday (last Monday of month)
Mid-June The Queen's Birthday
Aug August Bank Holiday (last Monday of month)
12 Sept Gibraltar Day
25 Dec Christmas Day
26 Dec Boxing Day

Opening Hours

Most **banks** are open Mon–Thurs 8.30–2.30, Fri 8.30–2 and Sat in winter 8.30–1.

The less important **churches** are often closed. Some cities probably have more churches than faithful communicants, and many are unused. If you're determined to see one, it will never be hard to find the *sacristán* or caretaker. Don't be surprised when cathedrals and big churches charge for admission – just consider the costs of upkeep.

Shops usually open from 10am. Spaniards take their main meal at 2pm and, except in the larger cities, most shops shut down for 2–3 hours in the afternoon, usually from 1pm or 2pm. In the south, where it's hotter, the siesta can last from 1pm to 5pm. In the evening most establishments stay open until 7pm or 8pm, or later still in tourist resorts.

Although their opening times have become more chaotic lately, major **museums** and **historical sites** tend to follow shop hours, but are shorter in the winter months; nearly all close on Mondays. We have tried to list the hours for the important sights. Seldom-visited ones have a raffish disregard for their official hours. Don't be discouraged; bang on doors and ask around.

We haven't bothered to list **admission prices** for all museums and sites. Usually the sum is trivial and often fluctuating – hardly anything will cost more than €5, usually much less; EU nationals are admitted free to many monuments, and several are free to everyone at least one day a month. The Alhambra in Granada, La Mezquita in Córdoba and La Giralda in Sevilla are the most notable exceptions.

Opening Hours in Gibraltar

Shops in Gibraltar are generally open 9–6 on weekdays, and 9–1 on Saturdays; **banks** are open 9–3.30 weekdays only. Most **sights** remain open on Saturday afternoons, which can be a quiet time to visit.

Photography

Serious photographers should give some consideration to the strong sunlight and high reflectivity of surfaces (pavements and buildings) in towns.

Post Offices

Every city, regardless of size, seems to have one **post office** (*correos*) and no more. It will always be crowded, but unless you have packages to mail, you may not ever need to visit one. Don't confuse post offices with the **Caja Postal**, the postal savings banks, which look just like them. Post offices also handle telegrams, which normally take 4hrs to arrive within Europe but are very expensive. There is also, of course, the *poste restante* (general delivery). In Spain this is called *lista de correos*, and it is as chancy as anywhere else.

Most tobacconists sell **stamps** (*sellos*) and they'll usually know the correct postage for whatever you're sending. The standard charge for sending a letter is €0.58 (EU) and €0.78 (North America, up to 20 grammes). Send everything air mail (*por avión*).

Mailboxes are bright yellow and scarce.

More information is available from *www.correos.es* (in Spanish only).

Post Offices in Gibraltar

Post offices in Gibraltar are open 9.30–6; mail sent from here in theory arrives much faster than from Spain, but don't rely on it.

Shopping

There are some delightful tacky tourist wares – Toledo 'daggers', plastic bulls and flamenco dolls *ad nauseam*. There are also some good buys to be had, for instance the high-quality **leather goods** from Córdoba and the town of Ubrique, which has been producing leatherwork since Roman times. Moorish craftsmen later had a major influence on the method of treating the cured skin for export. But, though the quality is good, the design seldom compares with its Italian counterpart. While Córdoba is better known for its ornate embossed leather for furniture decoration and **filigree jewellery**, Ubrique specializes in handmade items such as diaries, suitcases, bags and wallets. If you want an everlasting memory of Andalucía, have your **boots** made to measure in Valverde del Camino, Huelva province.

Ceramic plates, pottery and colourful *azulejo* tiles are made all over Andalucía; the quality varies enormously, from the shoddy factory-made products adorning tourist shop shelves to the sophisticated ceramic ware you will find in the Triana district of Sevilla.

Granada is well known for its **inlaid wood** *taracea* work (chests, chessboards and music boxes), although these can be rather crudely produced. Spanish **woven goods** are reasonably priced; Sevilla produces exquisite *mantillas* and embroidered shawls, and is the centre for the extraordinary designs that adorn the bullfighter's costume. In the Alpujarras a concentrated effort is being made to revive old skills, using the wooden loom particularly, to produce the typical **woollen blankets and rugs** for which this area has long been known – a fascinating mixture of ancient Christian and Arab designs. Brightly coloured handwoven blankets are the claim to fame of Grazalema, a village less than 20km (12 miles) to the west of Ronda. In the province of Almería, the village of Níjar produces colourful *jarapas* – woven blankets and mats.

Smoking

Introduced in 2006, the ban on smoking in public spaces extends to offices, sporting arenas and other public venues; many restaurants, bars and hotels are also now largely no smoking.

Sports and Activities

Many Spaniards **gamble**; there seem to be an infinite number of lotteries run by the State (the *Lotería Deportiva*), for the blind (ONCE), the Red Cross or the Church; there's at least one bingo-hall in every town and there are casinos in all major resorts.

Watch out for posters for **concerts**, **ballets** and especially for **circuses**. The little travelling Spanish troupes with their family acts, tents, tinsel and names like 'The National Circus of Japan' will charm you; they often gravitate to the major fiestas throughout the summer.

Football has pride of place in the Spanish heart, while **bullfighting** (*see* **Snapshots**, pp.46–7) and **cycling** vie for second place; all are shown regularly on television.

Gibraltar has a number of sports clubs and associations, many of them private. For further information, ask at the tourist office.

Cycling

If you do want to bring your own bicycle to Spain, you can make arrangements by ferry or train; by air, you'll almost always have to dismantle it to some extent and pack it in some kind of crate. Each airline seems to have its own policy. The south of Spain would be suicide to bike through in summer.

Cycling Federation of Andalucía, C/Ferraz 16, 28008 Madrid, **t** 91 542 04 21.

Fishing and Hunting

Fishing and hunting are long-standing Spanish obsessions, and you'll need to get a licence for both. Freshwater fishing permits (*permisos de pesca*) are issued from the **Consejería de Agricultura y Pesca** (Agriculture and Fishing Council), which has an office in each of the the provincial capital cities. A maritime recreational fishing licence (1st and 3rd class) is required for fishing from the shore or from a boat near the coast; get it from the **Delegación Provincial de la Consejería de Agricultura y Pesca**, which also has an office in each provincial capital city (you'll find all the details on the official tourist website, *www.andalucia.org*).

Spanish Fishing Federation (Federación Española de Pesca y Casting), C/Navas de Tolosa 3, 28013 Madrid, **t** 91 532 83 52, *www.fepyc.es*.

Consejero de Agricultura y Pesca, C/Tabladilla, Sevilla, **t** 95 503 20 00.

You may bring sporting guns to Spain, but you must declare them on arrival and present a valid firearms certificate with a Spanish translation bearing a consulate stamp. Hunters (boar and deer are the big game, with quail, hare, partridges and pigeons, and ducks and geese along the coasts in the winter) are obliged to get a licence as well (*permiso de caza*) from the local autonomous community, presenting their passports and record of insurance coverage.

Spanish Hunting Federation (Federación Española de Caza), C/Francos Rodríguez 70, 28039 Madrid, **t** 91 311 14 11, *www.fedecaza.com*.

Football

Soccer is Spain's most popular sport, and the Spanish Primera is possibly the best football league in the world. Barcelona, Real

Madrid and Valencia are the best teams to watch; fans of Málaga, Sevilla and Real Betis will argue over whose team is the best in Andalucía. The season lasts from September to June, and matches are usually trouble-free.

Spanish Football Federation (Real Federación Española de Futbol), C/Ramón y Cajal s/n, Madrid, **t** 91 495 98 00, *www.rfef.es*.

Golf

English settlers built Spain's first golf course at the Río Tinto mines in the 19th century, and since the advent of Severiano Ballesteros Spaniards, too, have gone nuts for the game. The warm, sunny winters, combined with greens of international tournament standard, attract golfing enthusiasts from all over the world throughout the year. At the last count, there were 60 courses along the Costa del Sol, over a third of all golf courses in Spain. The Marbella area alone boasts over two dozen fine courses, some so 'exclusive' that if you manage to get in you could find yourself teeing off next to Sean Connery. On the other hand, there is an abundance of humbler clubs where a few euros will get you a round. Most places hire out clubs. Inland you'll find courses around the big cities.

Many hotels cater specifically for the golfer and there are many tour operators (*see* p.86).

Royal Spanish Golf Federation, C/Capitán Haya 9–5, 28020 Madrid, **t** 91 555 26 82, *www.golfspainfederacion.com*.

Hiking and Mountaineering

Thousands of hikers and mountaineers are attracted to the paths in the Sierra Nevada above Granada and the Serranía de Ronda. The tourist office or the Spanish Mountaineering Federation provide a list of *refugios*, which offer mountain shelter in many places. Some are well equipped and can supply food. Most, however, do not, so take your own sleeping bags, cooking equipment and food with you. Hiking boots, windproof and waterproof clothing are essential, as is a detailed map of the area, issued by the Instituto Geográfico Nacional (*see* p.92), or the Servicio Geográfico Ejército.

Spanish Mountaineering Federation (Federación Andaluza de Montañismo),

Camino de Ronda 101, Edificio Atalaya, Granada, **t** 95 829 13 40. The website *www.fedamon.com* has a full list of *refugios*.

Horse Racing

Horse racing is centred in Madrid, but there is a winter season at the Pineda racecourse in Sevilla, and a summer season at the Hipodromo Costa de Sol near Mijas. One of the most dramatic events is the annual beach race in Sanlúcar de Barrameda, *see* p.73.

Spanish Horse Racing Federation, Plaza Marqués de Salamanca 2, 28006 Madrid, **t** 91 577 78 92, *www.rfhe.com*.

Horse Riding

Andalucía has some perfect terrain for riding, whether exploring the Serranía de Ronda, the smugglers' trails around Cádiz, or following in the hoofprints of Sir John Betjeman's wife, Penelope Chetwode, who boldly trekked through the Sierra Nevada in the 1960s, a journey fascinatingly recorded in her journal *Two Middle Aged Ladies in Andalucía*. There are a number of stables offering organized treks.

Pelota

Pelota, although a Basque game by origin, has a following in Andalucía. This is a thrilling game, where contestants wearing basket-like gloves propel a hard ball with great force at high walls, rather like squash. The fast action on the *jai-alai* court is matched by the wagering frenzy of the spectators.

Spanish Pelota Federation (Federación Española de Pelota), Los Madrazos 11, 28014 Madrid, **t** 91 521 42 99, *www.fepelota.com*.

Skiing

Many of the mountains popular with hikers at other times of the year attract ski crowds in the winter. An hour from Granada you can be among the Iberian Peninsula's highest peaks and Europe's southernmost ski resorts, whose après-ski life is steadily improving.

In Spain, it's easy to arrange all-inclusive ski packages through a travel agent. A typical deal would include six nights' accommodation in a three- or four-star hotel with half board and unlimited use of ski lift for the week, at a cost of around €600. With instruction fees, count on €60–80 extra per week.

An offical website, *www.cetursa.es*, has complete information on accommodation, ski passes, snow reports and instruction. There's also an information line, **t** 958 24 91 00.

Tennis

There is just as much fervour for tennis as for golf, inspired by international champion Rafael Nadal. Again, the best clubs are to be found on the coast, and every resort hotel has its own courts. The most famous tennis school in Andalucía lies just behind Fuengirola on the Mijas road. If you're looking for a game in Marbella, call **Los Monteros Tennis Club, t** 95 277 17 00, *www.monteros.com*.

Royal Spanish Tennis Federation, Avda Diagonal 618, 08021 Barcelona, **t** 93 201 08 44.

Water Sports

Water sports are the most popular activities in the summer. You can rent a surfboard and learn how to use it at almost any resort; aficionados head for Tarifa, Europe's windsurfing centre and the continent's southernmost tip.

If you bring your own boat, get the tourist office's literature on marinas before setting out. You have a choice of 30 along the coasts of Andalucía. There's a full calendar of sailing events and races, as well as sailing schools and rentals. A number of reservoirs have also become quite popular for water sports.

Royal Spanish Sailing Federation, C/Luis de Salazar 12, 28002 Madrid, **t** 91 519 50 08, *www.rfev.es*.

Underwater activists flock to the Almería coast in particular for its sparkling water and abundant marine life.

Spanish Subaqua Federation (Federación Española de Actividades Subacuáticas), C/Santaló 15, 08021 Barcelona, **t** 93 200 67 69, *www.fedas.es*.

Spanish Waterski Federation (Federación Española de Esquí Náutico), Sabino de Arana 30, 08028 Barcelona, **t** 93 330 89 03, *www.feen.es*.

Telephones

Spain has one of the best and cheapest telephone systems in Europe, although it can be rather confusing to use. All **local numbers** in Spain contain seven digits plus a code, which now must be dialled even from within a province. In Andalucía, this code is 95.

Some **phone boxes** accept cards and coins, although coin-operated booths are getting harder to find and it's much more usual to use pre-paid Telefónica phonecards (available from tobacconists for €5, €10, €15 and €20). Instructions for use are given in English.

Overseas calls from Spain are among the most expensive in Europe; calls to the UK can cost €1.50 a minute and to the USA substantially more. The cheapest way to call abroad is to find a *locutorio*, a phone centre (there are usually several around bus and train stations). Otherwise, you can buy cheap pre-paid international calling cards with a scratch-off PIN number, which are cheaper.

Expect to pay a big surcharge if you telephone from your hotel or any public place that does not have a coin slot. **Cheap rate** is from 10pm to 8am Mon–Sat and all day Sun and public holidays.

For calls **to Spain from the UK**, dial 00 followed by the country code (34), the area code and the number. For **international calls from Spain**, dial 00, wait for the higher tone and then dial the country code (44 for the UK; 1 for the USA and Canada). To call **Gibraltar from Spain or the UK**, dial 00 then 350 followed by the local five-digit number. (The country code for Gibraltar if you are calling from elsewhere is 350.) To **phone abroad from Gibraltar**, dial 00 followed by the country and area codes.

Time

Spain is 1 hour ahead of GMT, 6 hours ahead of US Eastern Standard Time, 9 hours ahead of Pacific Coast Time.

Spanish summertime (daylight-saving), as in the UK, runs from the last Sunday in March to the last Sunday in October.

Toilets

Outside bus and train stations, public facilities are rare in Spain. On the other hand, every bar on every corner has a toilet. Don't feel uncomfortable using it without buying something – the Spaniards do it all the time. Just ask for *los servicios* (on signs they are sometimes referred to as *aseos*).

Sevilla

Apart from in the Alhambra of Granada, the place where the lushness and sensuality of al-Andalus survives best is in Sevilla, Andalucía's capital. Sevilla may be Spain's fourth-largest city, but it is a place where you can pick oranges from the trees and see open countryside from the centre of town.

09

Don't miss

1 A Gothic giant
Sevilla Cathedral **p.102**

2 Uplifting *mudéjar* style
Alcázar **p.106**

3 Superfine Spanish art
Museo de Bellas Artes **p.113**

4 Charming narrow streets
Santa Cruz **pp.118–20**

5 *Azulejo* tiles galore
Plaza de España **p.121**

See map overleaf

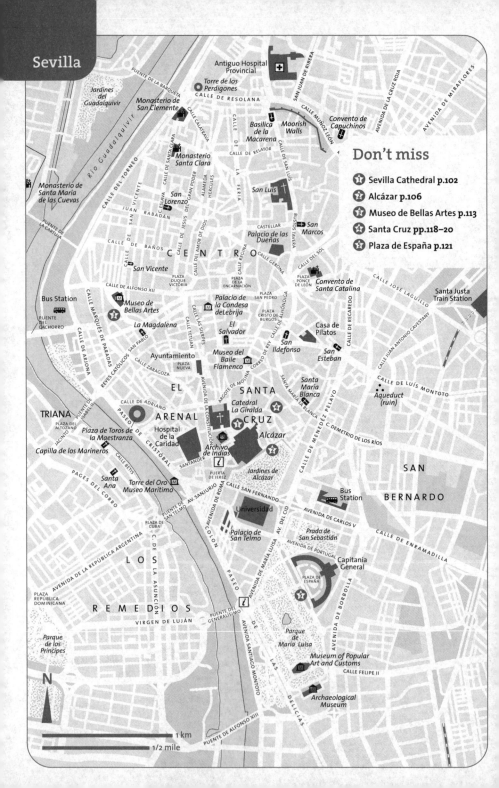

The City

Come in spring if you can, when the gardens are filled with birdsong and the air is heavy with the scent of jasmine and a hundred other blooms. If you come in summer, you may melt: the lower valley of the Guadalquivir is one of the hottest places in Europe. The pageant of Sevilla unfolds in the shadow of La Giralda, still the loftiest tower in Spain. Its size and the ostentatious play of its arches and arabesques make it the perfect symbol for this city, full of delightful excess and the romance of the south.

At times Sevilla has been a capital, and it remains Spain's eternal city; neither past reverses nor modern industry have been able to shake it from its dreams. That its past glories should return and place it alongside Venice and Florence as one of the jewels in the crown of Europe, a true metropolis with full international recognition, is the first dream of every *sevillano*. Sevilla is still a city very much in love with itself. Even the big celebrations of *Semana Santa* and *Feria* – although enjoyable for the foreigner (anyone from outside the city), with revelry in every café and on every street corner – are essentially private; the *sevillanos* celebrate in their own *casitas* with friends, all the time aware that they are being observed by the general public, who can peek but may not enter, at least not without an *enchufe* ('the right connection'). Sevilla is much like a beautiful, flirtatious woman: she'll tempt you to her doorstep and allow you a peck on the cheek – whether you get over the threshold depends entirely on your charm.

History: from Hispalis to Isbiliya to Sevilla

One of Sevilla's distinctions is its long historical continuity. Few cities in western Europe can claim never to have suffered a dark age, but Sevilla flourished after the fall of Rome – and even after the coming of the Castilians.

Roman Hispalis was founded on an Iberian settlement, perhaps one of the cities of Tartessos, and it soon became one of the leading cities of the province of Baetica, as well as its capital. Itálica, the now ruined city, lies just to the northwest; it is difficult to say which was the more important. During the Roman twilight, Sevilla seems to have been a thriving town. Its first famous citizen, San Isidore, was one of the Doctors of the Church and the most learned man of the age, famous for his great *Encyclopedia* and his *Seven Books Against the Pagans*, an attempt to prove that the coming of Christianity was not the cause of Rome's fall.

Sevilla was an important town under the Visigoths, and after the Moorish conquest it was second only to Córdoba as a political power and a centre of learning. For a while after the demise of the western caliphate in 1023 it became an independent kingdom,

Getting to Sevilla

By Air

Sevilla has regular flights from Madrid and Barcelona, and Ryanair flies from London Stansted. **San Pablo airport** is 12km east of the city, and the **airport bus** is run by Amarillos Tour and leaves from the Puerta de Jerez, with a stop at the Santa Justa station. Departures are every 30mins between 6.45am and 11.30pm, less frequently at weekends. For airport information call **t** 95 444 90 00, *www.aena.es.*

By Train

Estación de Santa Justa, in Avenida Kansas City in the northeast of town, is the modern Expo showpiece. There are several trains daily to Madrid by **AVE** in 2hrs 15mins, and a daily Talgo to Barcelona. A new direct line has also been introduced from Málaga to Seville which takes just over two hours; approximately the same as the driving time. The central **RENFE** office is at C/Zaragoza 29, **t** 95 441 41 11. Information and reservations, **t** 90 224 02 02, *www.renfe.es.*

By Bus

There are two bus stations in Sevilla, one at **Plaza de Armas**, information **t** 95 490 80 40, and one at **Prado de San Sebastián**, information **t** 95 441 71 11. All buses for Andalucía except those for Huelva leave from the Plaza de Armas near the river; buses for Huelva and the rest of Spain leave from Prado de San Sebastián. Information is available from the tourist office and at bus stations.

---

paying tribute to the kings of Castile. Sevilla suffered under the Almoravids after 1091, but enjoyed a revival under their successors, the Almohads, who made it their capital and built the Giralda as the minaret for their new mosque.

The disaster came for Muslim Isbiliya in 1248, 18 years after the union of Castile and León. Fernando III's conquest of the city is not a well-documented event, but it seems that more than half the population found exile in Granada or Africa preferable to Castilian rule; their property was divided among settlers from the north. Despite the dislocation, the city survived, and found a new prosperity as Castile's window on the Mediterranean and South Atlantic trade routes (the River Guadalquivir is navigable as far as Sevilla). Everywhere in the city you will see its emblem, the word NODO (knot) with a double knot between the O and D. The word recalls the civil wars of the 1270s, when Sevilla was one of the few cities in Spain to remain loyal to Alfonso the Wise. Alfonso is recorded as saying '*No m'a dejado*' ('She has not forsaken me'); *madeja* is another word for knot, and placed between the syllables NO and DO it makes a clever rebus, besides being a tribute to Sevilla's loyalty to medieval Castile's greatest king.

From 1503 to 1680, Sevilla enjoyed a legal monopoly of trade with the Americas, and it soon became the biggest city in Spain, with a population of over 150,000. The giddy prosperity this brought, in the years when the silver fleet ran full, contributed much to the festive, incautious atmosphere that is often revealed in Sevilla's character. Sevilla never found a way to hold on to much of the American wealth, and what little it managed to grab was soon dissipated in showy excess. There was enough to attract great

Getting around Sevilla

The narrow, twisting streets of old Sevilla are a delight to stroll around, and most of the main sights are bunched within walking distance of each other.

By Bus

There is a good city bus service; among the most useful lines are buses **C3** and **C4**, which circle the perimeter of the old city, and lines **C1** and **C2**, which make a larger circle and encompass Triana, La Cartuja, the main train station (Estación de Santa Justa) and the bus station on Plaza de Armas. **Night bus** routes are prefaced with the letter A. The tourist information office has free bus maps with explanations in English, including a table called '**How to Get There**'. For information, call **t** 90 071 01 71; for lost property call **t** 95 455 72 22.

Buy single **tickets** (€1) on the bus; 3- or 7-day tourist passes which offer unlimited travel for a set period, and the *bonobús* (good for 10 journeys, €5.34) are available at the Prado de San Sebastián, Plaza Nueva and Plaza Encarnación, and at some *estancos* (newsagents). More information from **TUSSAM, t** 90 245 99 54, *www.tussam.es*.

By Taxi

Taxis are everywhere and fairly inexpensive; if you do need to call one, try **Radio Taxis, t** 95 458 00 00/95 467 55 55, or **Tele Taxi, t** 95 462 22 22/95 462 14 61.

By Bicycle or Moped

Bicycles can be rented at **Cyclotour**, Parque de María Luisa, **t** 95 427 45 66. Rent mopeds from **Rentamoto**, C/Padre Méndez Casariego 17, **t** 95 441 75 00, *www.rentamoto.net*.

By Tour

Sightseeing buses and river cruises depart from the **Tower of Gold** (*Torre del Oro*). Bus tours are offered by **Sevilla Tour, t** 90 210 10 81, *www.sevillatour.com*, and **Sevirama, t** 95 456 06 93, *www.busturistico.com*. For river cruises see **Cruceros Turísticos Torre del Oro, t** 95 456 16 92, *www.crucerostorredeloro.com*; **Cruceros del Sur, t** 95 456 16 72; and **Buque El Patio**, Paseo de Colón 11, **t** 95 421 38 36.

---

artists such as Velázquez, Zurbarán and Murillo, and the city participated fully in the culture of Spain's golden age – even Don Quixote was born here, conceived by Cervantes while he was doing time in a Sevilla prison for debt.

It was in this period, of course, that Sevilla was perfecting its charm. Poets and composers have always favoured it as a setting. The prototypes of Bizet's *Carmen* rolled their cigars in the Royal Tobacco Factory, and for her male counterpart Sevilla contributed Don Juan Tenorio, who evolved through Spanish theatre in plays by Tirso de Molina and Zorrilla to become Mozart's *Don Giovanni*; the same composer also used the city as a setting for *The Marriage of Figaro*. The historical ironies are profound: amid all this opulence, Andalucía was rapidly declining from one of the richest and most cultured provinces of Europe to one of the poorest and most backward. Over the 17th and 18th centuries the city stagnated.

In 1936 the Army of Africa, under Franco's command, quickly took control of Andalucía. In Sevilla, a flamboyant officer named Gonzalo Queipo de Llano single-handedly bluffed and bullied the city into submission. As soon as the Moroccan troops arrived he turned them loose to butcher and terrorize the working-class district of Triana. Queipo de Llano was soon to be famous as the

Nationalists' radio propaganda voice, with shrill, grotesque nightly broadcasts full of sexual innuendoes about the Republic's politicians, and explicit threats of what his soldiers would do to the Loyalists' women once they were conquered.

Various industrial programmes, including a new shipbuilding industry, were started up by Franco's economists in the 1950s, stemming the flow of mass emigration and doing something to reduce the poverty of the region. But when King Juan Carlos ushered in the return of democracy the city was more than ready. In the late 1970s, Andalucíans took advantage of revolutionary regional autonomy laws, building one of the most active regional governments in the country. Felipe González, a socialist from Sevilla, ran Spain from 1982 up to 1996, when the many political scandals of 1995 and economic discontent finally discouraged the electorate from returning him to office.

In 1992, crimped and prinked, Sevilla opened her doors to the world for Expo '92. Fresh romance and excess mingled with the old. New roads, new bridges and a new opera house combined with Moorish palaces and monuments in a vainglorious display that attracted 16 million visitors. But despite the massive investment, some 15 years later it is clear that the hoped-for regeneration of the region is taking its time. That said, more recently, the city's economy and level of unemployment has witnessed a marked improvement due, in part, to the considerable increase in tourism, as well as a healthy surge in local industry and commerce.

The Cathedral and Around

The Biggest Gothic Cathedral in the World

 Sevilla Cathedral
t 95 421 49 71, www. catedraldesevilla.es; open July–Aug Mon–Sat 9.30–3.30, Sun and hols 2.30–6; Sept–June Mon–Sat 11–5, Sun 2.30–6; adm, free on Sun; opening hours are subject to change, so check

For a while after the Reconquista, the Castilians who repopulated Sevilla were content to use the great Almohad mosque, built at the same time as La Giralda (*see* p.105), the flamboyant bell tower which is the city's symbol. But at the turn of the 1400s, in a fit of pious excess, it was decided to build a new cathedral so grand that 'future ages shall call us mad for attempting it'. If they were mad, at least they were good organizers – they got it up in slightly over a century. The architects are unknown, but the original master is thought to have been either French or German.

The exterior, with its great rose window and double buttresses, is as fine as any of the Gothic cathedrals of northern Spain – if we could only see it. On the western front especially, facing the Avenida de la Constitución, the buildings close in; walking around its vast bulk, past the fence of Roman columns joined by thick chains, is like passing under a steep, ragged cliff. Some of the best original sculptural work is on the two portals flanking the main door: the **Door of Baptism** (left) and **Door of Birth** (right), covered with elaborate late 15th-century terracotta figures by Frenchman Lorenzo Mercadante de Bretaña and his follower Pedro Millán.

The ground plan of this monster, roughly 125m by 185m (400ft by 600ft), probably covers the same area as did the mosque. On the northern side, the **Court of the Orange Trees** (Patio de los Naranjos), planted with the trees for which it is named, preserves the outline of the mosque courtyard. The Muslim fountain survives, along with some walls and arches. On the left, the Moorish 'Gate of the Lizard' has hanging from it a stuffed crocodile, said to have been a present from an Egyptian emir asking for the hand of a Spanish infanta.

Along the eastern wall is the entrance of the **Biblioteca Colombina**, a library of ancient manuscripts and an archive of Columbus's life and letters, founded by his son, who obviously inherited his father's itchy feet. He travelled with his father to the Indies, took expeditions to Africa and Asia, and was part of Charles V's entourage in Flanders, Germany and Italy. He collected over 20,000 volumes on his travels, and bequeathed them to the city when he died in 1539.

Enter the cathedral through the newly built **visitor's centre** on the southern side. From here, visitors are ushered through a bright new museum of religious art, where works by Zurbarán, Murillo and Van Dyck stand out among the otherwise rather dull collection of paintings, sculptures, vestments and ornaments.

The cathedral's cavernous interior overpowers the faithful with its size more than its grace or beauty. The main altarpiece is the world's biggest retable, almost 37om (120ft) high and entirely covered with carved figures and golden Gothic ornaments; it took 82 years to make, and takes about a minute to look at. Just behind the Main Chapel (Capilla Mayor) and the main altar, the **Royal Chapel** (Capilla Real) contains the tombs of San Fernando, conqueror of Sevilla, and of Alfonso the Wise; Pedro the Cruel and his mistress, María de Padilla, are relegated to the crypt underneath. (The Capilla Real is used for daily worship and is not part of the cultural visit: to see it, you'll need to slip in between masses via the entrance on the square behind the cathedral.) Above the iron grille at the entrance to the Royal Chapel, the Moor Axataf hands over the keys of the city to a triumphant Fernando III. The art of the various chapels around the cathedral is lost in the gloom, but Murillo's masterpiece *La Visión de San Antonio* (1656) hangs in the Chapel of San Antonio (in the northern aisle), and a luminous, stark retable depicting the life of St Paul by Zurbarán is fixed in the Chapel of San Pedro (to the left of the Royal Chapel). At the rear of the cathedral, glass cases contain the largest and most lavish of the cathedral's religous ornaments, including elaborate

Semana Santa and Feria

The penitential rituals of the medieval *cofradías*, or fraternities, form the basis of the solemn processions at the heart of Sevilla's *Semana Santa* (Holy Week), although they owe their current theatrical pizzazz to the Baroque era. Every year between Palm Sunday and Easter Saturday, 57 *cofradías* hoist up their *pasos* (floats) and process through the crowds along the sinuous streets from their church to the great cathedral and back, taking, as decreed by a humane cardinal in the 17th century, the shortest possible route. Even this can take between four and twelve hours, with the occasional pit stop at a bar or local convenience. The musical accompaniment is a solemn and sonorous *marcha*, and occasionally a single voice will break in with a *saeta*, a soaring mournful song sung a capella, and closely related to flamenco.

Most of the *cofradías* carry two *pasos*: the first, the **Paso de Cristo**, depicts a scene between the Last Supper and the Resurrection, and the second, called the **Paso Palio**, carries the Virgin, weeping at the death of her son. Both are ornately carved and gilded, but it is the second *paso* that draws all eyes as each *cofradía* vies to produce the most beautiful Virgin, resplendent in a richly embroidered cape and covered by a swaying canopy. There are two main contenders in this beauty contest: **La Macarena** (*see* p.117) and her rival from across the river in Triana, **La Esperanza de Triana** (*see* p.112). But, in Sevilla, everyone has a Virgin, and the crowds will wait for hours to see 'their' Virgin pass.

The most important *cofradías* – El Silencio, El Gran Poder, La Macarena, El Calvario, La Esperanza de Triana and Los Gitanos – are given top billing and process on Good Friday morning, the high point of *Semana Santa*. The heavy floats are carried by 20 to 30 *costaleros*, for whom it is a great honour to be chosen and who practise for weeks ahead of time. It's hard, hot and claustrophobic work hidden beneath the *paso*, and it's essential that their moves are synchronized and guided by the black-suited *capataz* (overseer). Around the floats are the *Nazarenos* in their macabre pointed hats and masks, carrying candles and banners. The Penitents, who follow the Paso de Cristo and bear wooden crosses, are often performing authentic acts of penitence and process barefoot (many others just want to dress up and be in the show). They also wear the long flowing robes and masks of the *Nazarenos*, but their hoods are not supported by the conical *antifaz* and so hang down at the back. The official procession route, scented with thick clouds of incense, runs along C/Sierpes to Plaza El Salvador and Plaza de San Francisco, and then to the enormous cathedral itself. Boxes are set up for important figures, while the streets and balconies are crammed with up to a million spectators, most men in blue suits and the ladies in black *mantilla* veils. Easter Sunday sees the first bullfight of the year.

After all the gloom and solemnity of *Semana Santa*, Sevilla erupts a week or two later in a week-long party – the April *Feria*. Another medieval institution, it was re-introduced to the city by a Basque and a Catalan in the mid-19th century. Originally a cattle market, nothing remains of its original purpose other than the circus-style striped tents, or *casetas*, which have become increasingly ornate through the years (prizes are awarded for the most beautiful) and are divided into two sections: the front has stalls for food and drink and the back is used for dancing. The drink, of course, is sherry, and calculations suggest that as much is drunk in this one week in Sevilla as the rest of Spain drinks in a year. Having the right connections, or *enchufe*, is supremely important: to be denied entrance to the most élite tents is to lose considerable face (it helps if you've made some local friends). The *Feria* now takes place in the *barrio* of Los Remedios, but the council is besieged by so many applications for *casetas* that it may have to move again. The streets are decorated with thousands of lanterns; horses and carriages push through dense, jubilant crowds, many people wearing traditional costume (the women's flamenco costumes are especially dazzling); and the nearby funfair reverberates with screams of laughter. The festivities begin with a ceremonial lighting of the lanterns at midnight on Monday and culminate in a firework extravaganza the following Sunday, which also marks the official opening of the bullfighting season at La Maestranza.

silver reliquaries with silk-wrapped bones. Nearby in the southern aisle, four stern pallbearers on a high pedestal support the **tomb of Christopher Columbus**, although his bones were shifted, lost and rediscovered with such regularity that it is impossible to know with any certainty whose remains are borne so ceremoniously aloft. The pallbearers represent the kingdoms of Castile, León, Navarra and Aragón. Columbus has been something of a refugee since his death. In the 16th century his remains were moved from Valladolid to the island of Santo Domingo, and after Dominican Independence from there to Havana cathedral. In 1899, after Cuba became independent, he was brought to Sevilla, and this idio-syncratic monument was put up to honour him. In the Dominican Republic, they'll tell you Columbus is still buried in Santo Domingo. Of course, most Spaniards are convinced that Columbus was born in Spain, not in Genoa, so it is appropriate that the life of this most elusive character should have mysteries at both ends.

In the **Chapter House**, which has an Immaculate Conception by Murillo, Sevilla's bishop can sit on his throne and pontificate under the unusual acoustics of an elliptical Baroque ceiling. The adjacent **Sacristy** contains a few largely undistinguished paintings, but in the adjoining **Tesoro** (treasury) spare a moment for the reliquaries. Juan de Arfe, maker of the world's biggest silver monstrances, is represented here with one that is almost a small palace, made with 410kg (900lbs) of silver and complete with marble columns. Spain's most famous and possibly most bizarre reliquary is the **Alfonsine Tables**, filled with over 200 tiny bits of tooth and bone. Said to have belonged to Alfonso the Wise, they were made to provide extra-powerful juju for him to carry into battle. (Interestingly, the term 'Alfonsine tables' also refers to the famous astronomical tables made for the same king by Jewish scholars of Toledo, used all over Europe until the 1600s to calculate eclipses and the movements of the planets.)

La Giralda

La Giralda
same opening hours as the cathedral – both are visited with one ticket

You can catch the 100m (319ft) tower of La Giralda peeking over the rooftops from almost anywhere in Sevilla; it will be your best friend when you get lost in the city's labyrinthine streets. This great minaret, with its *ajimeces* and brickwork arabesques, was built under the **Almohads**, from 1172 to 1195, just 50 years before the Christian conquest. (Two similar minarets, built in the same period, still survive in Marrakech and Rabat in Morocco, and the trio are known as the **Three Sisters**.) The surprisingly harmonious spire stuck on top is a Christian addition. Whatever sort of turret origin-ally existed was surmounted by four golden balls stacked up at the very top, designed to catch the sun and be visible to a traveller one day's ride from the city; all came down in a 13th-century earth-quake. On the top of their spire, the Christians added a huge, revolving statue of Faith as a weather vane (many writers have noted the curious fancy of having a supposedly constant Faith turning with the four winds). It is **El Giraldillo** – the weather vane –

that gives its name to the tower as a whole. The climb to the top is fairly easy, with shallow ramps instead of stairs – wide enough for Fernando III to have ridden his horse up after the conquest in 1248. He was probably not the first to ride up – it is likely that the *muezzin* used a donkey to help him to the top to call the faithful to prayer. There are plenty of viewing ledges on the way up, and a handful of glassy chambers exhibiting fragments of La Giralda's past, such as the robust 14th-century door which combines Gothic motifs and verses from the Koran, and the memorial stone of Petrus de la Cera, one of the knights who seized the city in November 1248 and couldn't bear to leave. There are also the remains of the monstrous hooks and pulleys which hoisted the stones into place.

Archivo de Indias (The Archive of the Indies)

Archivo de Indias
t 95 421 12 34;
open Mon–Sat 10–4,
Sun 10–2

In common with most of its contemporaries, parts of Sevilla's cathedral were public ground, used to transact all sorts of business. A 16th-century bishop put an end to this practice, but prevailed upon Philip II to construct next to the cathedral an **Exchange** (*Lonja*), for the merchants. Philip sent his favourite architect, Juan de Herrera, then still busy with El Escorial, to design it. The severe, elegant façades are typical of Herrera's work, and the stone balls and pyramids on top are practically his signature.

By the 1780s, little commerce was still going on in Sevilla, and what was left of the American trade passed through Cádiz. Also, two foreigners, a Scot and a Frenchman, had had the gumption to publish histories of the Indies unflattering to the Spanish, so Charles III converted the lonely old building to hold the **Archive of the Indies**, the repository of all the reports, maps and documents that the Crown had collected during the age of exploration. Inside, a glorious staircase of rosy jasper marble leads handsomely to the upper floors, where the artefacts and treasures are stored in almost six miles of 18th-century Cuban mahogany and cedarwood shelves.

The Alcázar

Alcázar
*www.patronato-
alcazarsevilla.es; open
April–Sept Tues–Sat
9.30–7, Sun and hols
9.30–5; Oct–Mar
Tues–Sat 9.30–5, Sun
and hols 9.30–1.30;
closed Mon; adm*

It's easy to be fooled into thinking this is simply a Moorish palace; some of its rooms and courtyards seem to come straight from the Alhambra (*see* pp.289–94). Most of them, however, were built by Moorish workmen for **King Pedro the Cruel** of Castile in the 1360s. The Alcázar and its king represent a fascinating cul-de-sac in Spanish history and culture, and allow the possibility that al-Andalus might have assimilated its conquerors rather than been destroyed by them.

Pedro was an interesting character. In Froissart's *Chronicle*, we have him described as 'full of marveylous opinyons...rude and rebell agaynst the commandements of holy churche'. Certainly he didn't mind having his Moorish artists, lent by the kings of Granada, adorn his palace with sayings from the Koran in Kufic calligraphy. Pedro preferred Sevilla, still half-Moorish and more than half-decadent, to Old Castile, and he filled his court here with Moorish poets, dancers and bodyguards – the only ones he trusted. But he was not the man for the job of cultural synthesis. The evidence, in so far as it is reliable, suggests he richly deserved his honorific 'the Cruel', although to many underdog *sevillanos* he was Pedro the Just.

Long before Pedro, the Alcázar was the palace of the Moorish governors. Work on the Moorish features began in 712 after the capture of Sevilla. In the 9th century it was transformed into a palace for Abd ar-Rahman II. Important additions were made under the Almohads, since the Alcázar was their capital in al-Andalus. Almost all the decorative work you see now was done under Pedro, some by the Granadans and the rest by Muslim artists from Toledo. It is the outstanding production of *mudéjar* art in Spain.

The Alcázar is entered through the little gate on the Plaza del Triunfo, on the southern side of the cathedral. The first courtyard, the **Patio de León**, has beautiful arabesques overlooking a small ornamental garden, and is separated by delicate arches from the wide expanse of the **Patio de la Montería**. At the far end of the courtyard is the lovely façade of the interior palace, decorated with inscriptions in Gothic and Arabic script.

Much of the best *mudéjar* work can be seen in the adjacent halls and courts; their seemingly haphazard arrangement was in fact a principle of the art, to increase the surprise and delight in passing from one to the next. Off the Court of León is the **Sala de la Justicia**, with a stunning star-shaped coffered ceiling. This is where Pedro I passed the sentence of death on his brother, who'd had had the temerity to have an affair with Pedro's wife (*see* 'Convent of Santa Clara', pp.116–17). Behind it, the lovely secluded **Patio del Yeso,** with its delicate lacy plasterwork, is largely a survival of the Almoravid palace of the 1170s, itself built on the site of a Roman *praetorium*. The largest and most beautiful of the courtyards is the **Patio de las Doncellas** (the 'Court of the Maidens'), entered through the gate of the palace façade, which is named after the young Christian brides who were given as peace offerings to the Moors. The Islamic motto 'None but Allah conquers' is entwined with the heraldic devices of the Kingdom of Castile and León. The gallery was added during the reign of Charles V. The courtyard leads to the **Salón de Embajadores**, a small domed chamber that is the finest in the Alcázar despite the jarring addition of heavily carved balconies from the time of Philip II. In Moorish times this was the throne room. Another courtyard, the **Patio de las Muñecas** ('courtyard of the dolls'), once the hub of the palace's domestic life, takes its name from two tiny faces on medallions at the base of one of the horseshoe arches – a little joke on the part of the Muslim stone-carvers; to find them will bring you luck (look on the right-hand arch of the northern gallery). The columns come from the ruins of Medinat al-Zahra.

Spanish kings couldn't leave the Alcázar alone. Fernando and Isabel spoiled a large corner of it for their **Casa de la Contratación**, a planning centre for the colonization of the Indies. There's little to see in it: a big conference table, a model of the *Santa María* in wood, and a model of the royal family (Isabel's) in silver.

Charles V, who was married here in 1526 to Isabelle of Portugal, added a **palace** of his own, as he did in the Alhambra. This contains a spectacular set of **Flemish tapestries** showing finely detailed scenes of Charles' campaigns in Tunisia. Upstairs, you can take a guided tour of the **royal apartments** (an extra €3) if the royal family are not at home – the Alcázar is the oldest palace in use in Europe. Most of the furnishings are 19th-century, but there are some remarkable 15th- and 16th-century *artesonado* ceilings, as well as Isabel La Católica's chapel and Pedro the Cruel's bedroom.

Within its walls, the Alcázar has extensive **gardens**, with pools, avenues of clipped hedges, and lemon and orange trees. Concerts are held here on summer nights. The park is deceptively large, but you can't get lost unless you find the little **labyrinth** near the pavilion built for Charles V in the lower gardens. Outside the walls, there is a formal promenade called the **Plaza Catalina de Ribera** with two monuments to Columbus, and the extensive **Jardines de Murillo**, bordering the northern wall of the Alcázar.

From the Cathedral to the River: El Arenal

Avenida de la Constitución, passing the façade of the cathedral, is Sevilla's main street and, in the spring of 2007, was thankfully pedestrianized. Between it and the Guadalquivir is the neighbour-hood of **El Arenal**, once the city's bustling port district, thronged with sailors, shopkeepers, idlers and prostitutes. Those colourful days have long gone – even its old name, 'Baratillo' meaning 'shambles', was changed in the 18th century by writers in search of a more romantic past. El Arenal means, poetically, 'expanse of sand', referring to its isolation outside the old Arabic city perimeter, when only a slim stretch of wall along the river protected it from invaders. Now it is a quiet, tranquil district with small shops and cafés, without the distinction of the Santa Cruz quarter, but with an earthy charm all of its own.

Heading down to the river, you will pass through one of the few surviving rampart gates leading to the old port area, the **Gate of Olive Oil** (Postigo del Aceite), a 16th-century remodelling of an old Moorish gate, with vertical grooves for slotting in flood barriers when the river sporadically burst its banks. The city's coat of arms was added during the refurbishment, along with a little chapel.

Hospital de la Caridad

Hospital de la Caridad
t 95 422 32 32,
www.santa-caridad.org;
open Mon–Sat 9–1.30
and 3.30–6.30,
Sun 9–1; adm

Behind a colourful façade on C/Temprado is the **Charity Hospital**, built in 1647 in the old warehouse area which used to back on to the port. This piece of ground was used for hanging criminals until the 15th century, when the Cofradía de la Caridad sought permission to give the dead a Christian burial and provide shelter for the poor. The original hospital was established in the docklands Chapel of San Jorge, before its reconstruction in infinitely grander style during the 17th century. The new, improved hospital's benefactor was a certain Miguel de Mañara (*see* box, below), a

The Worst Man in the World

Life does imitate art, sometimes, and it seems that, rather than serving as a model for Tirso de Molina, Miguel de Mañara (*see* above) saw the play *El Burlador de Sevilla* in 1641 when he was fourteen years old, and decided that he himself would become Don Juan. His story is as *sevillano* as anyone could ask, but this Mañara was in fact a Corsican, the son of a wealthy landowner living in Spain. The Corsicans are almost as proud of him as they are of Napoleon.

Like Napoleon, he wasn't the most amazing of physical specimens, with unprepossessing features arranged around a big Corsican nose, but his intensity and force of character were always enough to get him in the door, and usually well beyond it. The first notorious scandal he caused in Sevilla was taken right out of the play. He seduced a woman named Doña Teresita Sánchez, who was renowned for her chastity and virtue, and then, when her father caught them together in her bedroom, Mañara killed him. With the police on his heels, he managed to escape and joined the Spanish army fighting in the Netherlands, where he performed with such conspicuous bravery that eventually the charges against him were dropped, and he returned to Sevilla.

There were bigger escapades to come. Mañara travelled to Corsica, where he was not known, and seduced his own cousin. Then he went back to Sevilla and had another go at Doña Teresita, who after her father's murder had become a nun. God, apparently, had had enough of Miguel de Mañara, and He sent him a vision of his own death and funeral, late at night on the corner of Sevilla's C/del Ataúd and C/de la Muerte (Street of the Coffin and Street of Death). The old rake – he had reached the ripe old age of 21 – was frightened sufficiently to send a letter to Doña Teresita explaining his designs, and how he had planned to abandon her. The shock of learning that he had never really loved her was too much, and she died that night.

Mañara resolved to reform himself – and, because this is Sevilla, his redemption took a form as extreme as his former life of evil. At first he married and behaved himself; but the visions of his own funeral kept recurring and he eventually joined the fraternity of the Santa Caridad, and took it over as prior. Here, Mañara became a local legend. He spent his entire fortune on this hospital, and was known for personally caring for the sick during a plague, feeding the poor and comforting the afflicted. He even extended his pity to Sevilla's dogs, building the low trough in the convent wall to give them a drink. His confessions are still kept at the hospital's archive and he is buried near the chapel entrance in a tomb, where he himself ordered the inscription: 'Here lie the ashes of the worst man the world has ever known.' There was a movement to make Mañara a saint, but so far he has only reached the title of Venerable.

reformed rake who has been claimed (erroneously, as the dates just won't add up) as the prototype for Tirso de Molina's Don Juan.

Though it still serves its intended purpose as a charity home for the aged, visitors come to see the art in the hospital chapel. The entrance is through a shadowy magenta and ochre courtyard with a double gallery, palms, fountains and panels of 17th-century Dutch Delft tiles brought from a convent in Cádiz. Much of the chapel's art has gone, unfortunately – in the lobby they'll show you photographs of the four Murillos stolen by Napoleon. The remaining eight in the series still hang here, a cosy group of saints and miracles, among them St Isabel of Hungary tending the poor, and a wild-eyed Moses drawing water from the rock. Murillo, a close friend of Mañara, and a prominent lay brother, was also responsible for the *azulejo* panels on the chapel façade depicting St George astride a rearing horse, St James, and three overwrought virtues, Faith, Hope and Charity. Among what remains inside are three works of art, ghoulish even by Spanish standards, that reflect the funereal obsessions of Miguel de Mañara, who commissioned them. Juan de Valdés Leal (1622–90) was a competent enough painter, but warmed to the task only with such subjects as you see here: a bishop in full regalia decomposing in his coffin, and Death snuffing out your candle. Even better than these is the anonymous, polychrome, bloody Jesus, surrounded by smiling Baroque *putti*, who carry whips and scourges instead of harps. Murillo's reported judgement on these pictures was that 'one has to hold one's nose to look at them'.

The Casa de la Moneda (Mint) and Torre del Oro (Tower of Gold)

On Calle Santander stands the renovated **Torre de la Plata** (Tower of Silver), and, along from it on Calle Habana, the **Mint**, rebuilt in the 16th century from a 13th-century Muslim watchtower, to cope with the flood of precious metals pouring in from the Indies. Here, the gold and silver marks of the Spanish empire were minted in dizzying quantities. Picture the scene when the annual silver fleet came in – for over a century the fleet's arrival was the event of the year, the turning point of an annual feast-or-famine cycle when debts would be repaid, and long-deferred indulgences enjoyed.

The Moorish **Torre del Oro**, which takes its name from the gold and *azulejo* tiles that covered its 12-sided exterior in the days of the Moors, stands on the banks of the Guadalquivir. The tower, built by the Almohads in 1220, was the southernmost point of the city's fortifications. In times of trouble, a chain would be stretched from the tower and across the Guadalquivir. In 1248 the chain was broken by an attacking fleet led by Admiral Ramón de Bonifaz; the supply route with Triana was cut off and Sevilla fell. The interior

Museo Marítimo
*t 95 422 24 19;
open Tues–Fri 10–2, Sat
and Sun 11–2; closed
Aug; adm, free Tues*

now houses the small **Museo Marítimo**, with plans, models, documents, weapons and maps of the golden age of the explorers.

The Cathedral of Bullfighting

On the river, just north of the tower, is another citadel of *sevillano* charm. **La Maestranza** bullring, with its blazing white and ochre arches, is not as big as Madrid's, but it is still a lovely building and perhaps the most prestigious of all *plazas de toros*. It was begun in 1760 under the auspices of the aristocratic equestrian society of the Real Maestranza de Caballería (which still owns it) in order to practise equestrian displays, including bullfights, and it was largely responsible for raising the profile of an otherwise dying and insalubrious neighbourhood. The Carlist Wars got in the way and the bullring was, amazingly, not finished until 1880, which is why it took on its characteristic oval shape – to squeeze itself in among the surrounding buildings. Today it is known as the 'cathedral of bullfighting' and is particularly celebrated for its extraordinary acoustics; it is said that every rustle of the matador's cape can be heard. From April until September, it carries a packed schedule; if you like to watch as your *rabo de toro* (oxtail) is prepared, you may be fortunate enough to see a *corrida* while in town (*see* pp.46–7

Museo Taurino
*t 95 422 45 77, www.
realmaestranza.com;
open daily 9.30–7, or
9.30–3 when a
bullfight is on; adm*

and p.129). Inside is the **Museo Taurino**, with a small shop, and displays of antique posters, portraits of celebrated bullfighters, the mounted heads of famous bulls, elaborate costumes and other memorabilia. Carmen stands haughtily outside, hand on hip, surveying the bullring that saw her tragic end in Bizet's opera.

**Teatro
Maestranza**
*t 95 422 33 44, www.
teatromaestranza.com*

The large, modern, circular building on the Paseo de Cristóbal Colón which echoes the shape of La Maestranza is the **Teatro Maestranza**, a grand opera house built for Expo '92.

Triana

Across the Guadalquivir from the bullring is the neighbourhood of Triana, an ancient suburb that takes its name from the Emperor Trajan. Until the mid-19th century it was joined to the city centre by a pontoon, a flimsy string of boats that would get washed away by the frequent floods; finally, in 1852, the first fixed bridge was constructed, officially named the Bridge of Isabel II, but known to all as the **Bridge of Triana**. Even now, people glance at the carved lion's head at the Triana end of the bridge: an old superstition warns that, if the water rises to the lion's mouth, Sevilla will be flooded again. The bridge culminates in Plaza del Altozano, with a statue of the famous bullfighter Juan Belmonte (1892–1962), whose motto was purportedly 'stop, pacify and control'. He looks as if he could manage it still. The neighbourhood has a reputation for being the 'cradle of flamenco'. Queipo de Llano's troops wrecked a lot of it at the beginning of the Civil War, but there are still picturesque white streets overlooking the Guadalquivir.

On the riverbank on the right-hand side of the Bridge of Triana (with the bridge at your back) is the Paseo Nuestra Senora de la O, a charming avenue where a colourful and cheap produce market is now held. On the same spot, five centuries ago, the Castle of San Jorge, originally built by the Moors, became the infamous **Castle of the Inquisition**, a prison for those accused of Judaism, heresy and witchcraft. Sevilla's first *auto-da-fé* was held here in 1481 and the castle was destroyed only in 1820, when the Inquisition was finally abolished. The air used to be thick with fumes from the kilns which clustered around this part of town, and the streets around C/Castilla and C/San Jorge are still some of the best for finding Triana ceramics. The area's workmen make all Sevilla's *azulejo* tiles.

C/Betis, right on the river on the left-hand side of the Bridge of Triana, is one of the liveliest streets, with a string of bars and restaurants with wonderful views. The Feria de la Velá is held here in July, in honour of Triana's patron saint, Santa Ana, with dancing, buskers and street vendors. A gunpowder factory once stood here, until it exploded, catapulting dozens of people into the river.

The C/Pureza, behind it, leads to the Plaza de Santa Ana and one of the oldest Christian churches in the city. Towards the end of the 13th century, Alfonso X was miraculously cured of a strange disease of the eye and ordered the construction of a church in thanks. Built around 1276, the simple, Gothic church of **Santa Ana** holds a 16th-century retable by Pedro de Campaña, and a fabulous *azulejo*-tiled tomb by Nicoloso Pisano. The most famous treasure is the enormous silver monstrance which forms part of Triana's Corpus Chico procession. The square around the church becomes especially animated during big festivals, particularly around Corpus Christi and Christmas, when it erects a huge nativity scene.

Capilla de la Virgen de la Esperanza
C/Pureza; open Mon–Sat 9–1 and 5.30–9, Sun 9–1

Back on C/Pureza, there stands the lovely **Capilla de la Virgen de la Esperanza**, home to Triana's celebrated weeping figure of the Virgin of Hope, main rival to the equally famous figure in the *barrio* of La Macarena (*see* pp.116–17) during the *Semana Santa* processions and celebrations. The chapel is also known as the Chapel of Sailors (Capilla de los Marineros), who would come here to pray for a safe return from their voyages, and from where Mass used to be bellowed, so that all the sailors in the galleons moored along the river could hear.

Triana was traditionally a rich recruitment area for the ships setting out to discover new lands and fabulous treasures. C/Rodrigo de Triana is named after a local sailor who voyaged to the Indies with Columbus and first spied the New World. Another chapel popular with seafarers is that of the **Convento de Los Remedios** in the Plaza de Cuba; sailors would blast their cannons in homage to the Virgen de Los Remedios (Virgin of Redemption) as they passed in their galleons, and pray for her protection on their Atlantic voyages. The convent later became the Hispano-Cuban Institute for the History of America, but Franco closed it down after a tiff with Fidel Castro.

The street leading off the Plaza de Cuba into the relatively new, and now rather upmarket suburban quarter of Los Remedios is named after **Juan Sebastián Elcano**, who sailed with Magellan on his fateful voyage round the world. Two hundred and sixty-five sailors left Sevilla in 1519 and, after they had battled their way around the Cape of Good Hope, Magellan was killed in the Philippines. Elcano took command of the last remaining ship and limped home with just 18 sailors three years later. Also near the Plaza de Cuba is **Calle Salado**, undistinguished by day but the best place for dancing *sevillanas* by night.

Northwest of the Cathedral: Art and the Auto-da-fé

Back across the river, over the Bridge of Triana, you'll approach the **San Eloy** district, full of raucous bars and hotels. On C/San Pablo is **La Magdalena** (1704), rebuilt by Leonardo de Figueroa on the ruins of the Dominican Convent of San Pablo, itself fused with an even older mosque. The eccentric Baroque façade is decorated with sundials, and the colourful dome is supported by long-suffering South American Indians. Among the art inside are two paintings of the *Life of St Dominic* by Zurbarán, and gilded reliefs by Leonardo de Figueroa. Above the door is a hint of the church's nefarious past: the shield of the Inquisition. Heresy trials took place in this church and the condemned were led through the Door of the Jews, since closed up and hidden behind a chapel. Heretics were then burned in the Prado de San Sebastián or in the Plaza de San Francisco, remodelled for the purpose. Many of the paintings and frescoes celebrate the triumph of the Catholic faith and the suppression of heresy, including a mural by Lucas Valdés, son of Valdés Leal, depicting an auto-da-fé. The face of the accused was scratched out by his outraged descendants, and restorers had to fill in the blank.

Museo de Bellas Artes (Fine Arts Museum)

⭐ **Museo de Bellas Artes**
Convent of Merced, C/San Roque; open Tues 2.30–8.30, Wed–Sun 9.30–5; adm, free to EU citizens

This excellent collection is housed in the **Convento de Merced** (1612), on C/San Roque, expropriated for the state in 1835. It is set around three courtyards, the first of which is handsomely decorated with lustrous tiled panels taken from Sevilla's convents. There are some fine medieval works: some naïve-looking virgins, and an especially expressive triptych by the Master of Burgos from the 13th century. **Pedro Millán**, one of the most influential sculptors of the period, is well represented; the *Burial of Christ* is haunting and, in another sculpture, a mournful Christ stares in disbelief at the gash in his side. The Italian sculptor **Pietro Torrigiano** (the fellow who broke Michelangelo's nose, and who died here, in the Inquisition's prisons) has left an uncanny, barbaric wooden *St Jerome*. This saint, Jerónimo in Spanish, is a favourite in Sevilla, where he is pictured with a rock and a rugged cross instead of his usual lion. Torrigiano's *Virgen de Belén* (c. 1525) has a luminous clarity and stillness. There is a comprehensive collection of altar-pieces and retables from this period, with fiery scenes of hell and damnation, set off by the decapitated head of John the Baptist leering through a glass case. Through another of the lovely courtyards planted with orange trees, the main staircase, known as the Imperial Staircase, and richly decorated in the Mannerist style with angels swarming across the dome, leads to a room full of the works of the most mannered of them all, **Murillo** (a *sevillano*, buried in Santa Cruz). Among the paintings is an *Immaculate Conception* and many other artful missal-pictures, accompanied by a number of pieces by the prolific painter Valdés Leal. Much more interesting are the works of **Zurbarán**, who could express spirituality without the simpering of Murillo or the hysteria of the others. His series of female saints is especially good, and the *Miracle of St Hugo* is perhaps his most acclaimed work. A series of paintings executed for the main altarpiece for the Monasterio Cartujo de Santa María de las Cuevas (*see* pp.121–2) has also found its way here. Occasionally even Zurbarán slips up; you may enjoy the *Eternal Father* with great fat toes and a triangle on his head, a *St Gregory* who looks like the scheming Church executive he really was, and the wonderful *Apotheosis of St Thomas Aquinas*, in which the great scholastic philosopher rises to his feet as if to say 'I've got it!' The room is dominated by an astounding *Cristo Crucificado* (c. 1630–40). Don't miss El Greco's portrait of his son Jorge, or the wonderful stark portraits by Ribera. There are also works by Jan Brueghel, Caravaggio and Mattia Preti, and a less interesting section of 19th- and 20th-century works, mainly portraits of coy *sevillanas*, fluttering their fans or dandling pooches, and dashing dandies, swaggering in their finery.

North of the Cathedral: The Heart of the City

Since Moorish times, Sevilla's business and shopping area has been the patch of narrow streets north of La Giralda. **Calle Las Sierpes** ('Serpent Street') is its heart, a sinuous pedestrian lane

El Salvador remains
For tours of the remains, check the website, www. colegialsalvador.org, or call t 95 459 54 05

lined with every sort of old shop, named after an ancient inn sign which depicted the jaws of a snake – or perhaps just because it is so winding. Just to the north, El Salvador is the city's second-biggest religious building after the cathedral, a fine Baroque church by Leonardo de Figueroa. Its once-vibrant 'bull's blood' plasterwork has faded to a dusky rose but major restoration is finally under way. On the left is a door leading to the **Patio de los Naranjos**; its dilapidated Roman columns and arches are almost all that remain of what was once the city's principal mosque (and before that a Visigothic cathedral, and before that a Roman basilica) in a neat patchwork of pragmatic expropriation across two millennia – and at least four sets of religious beliefs. The old minaret was turned into the belfry. Restoration work has uncovered more remains, which can usually be explored by guided tour, although at present all visits are temporarily suspended. The square in front of the church is one of Sevilla's liveliest, with hip young kids sprawling on the church steps, and throngs of people sipping chilled sherry from the tiny *bodeguitas* opposite.

East of the Plaza del Salvador is little **Plaza Alfalfa**, now another vibrant nightspot, along with **Plaza de la Encarnación** a couple of streets to the north. The Plaza Alfalfa, once the site of the Roman forum and medieval markets selling meat and alfalfa, is at the heart of the city's oldest merchant district, with narrow half-timbered houses jostling for space on the tiny streets. Many of the narrow streets and squares in this district are named after the trades that were once carried out here, like the C/de la Pescadería, once the scene of a busy fishmarket, and tiny Plaza del Pan, where the bakers plied their trade.

Palacio de la Condesa de Lebrija
t 95 421 81 83, www. palaciodelebrija.com; open May–Sept Sun–Fri 10.30–1 and 5–8, Sat 10–2; Oct–April Mon–Fri 10–1 and 4.30–7, Sat 10–1, closed Sun; adm, guided visits of apartments extra

Not far from the Plaza de la Encarnación, on bustling C/Cuna, is the **Palacio de la Condesa de Lebrija**. The Countess of Lebrija was one of Spain's first female archaeologists and an inveterate hoarder: she transformed her family home (a 16th-century palace) with thousands of archaeological odds and ends discovered at the excavations in Itálica (*see* pp.129–30) and around Sevilla. Fine Roman mosaics cover the entire first floor, and other original pieces hang, framed, on the walls. The vestibule glows with thousands of brightly coloured *azulejo* tiles, painted in Triana in the 18th century. A collection of tiny artefacts, also gleaned from Itálica, includes a handful of engraved signet rings made from cornelian, agate and glass, and shards of pottery (the prettiest are from Arabic pots which gleam like mother-of-pearl). The private apartments are open to visitors, and offer a glimpse into the world of an unconventional *sevillana* aristocrat. Back out on C/Cuna are a number of Sevilla's fanciest flamenco shops, with all kinds of dresses and accessories.

On the **Plaza Nueva**, Sevilla's modern centre, you can see the frothy **City Hall** (Ayuntamiento), with a fine, elaborate Plateresque façade, built as the brand-new home for the town councillors in 1564 after Charles V complained about the shabbiness of their existing one. The **Plaza de San Francisco**, which spreads out on the other side of the City Hall, was remodelled at the same time in order to serve as a suitably grand backdrop for the city's processions and its executions. From here, Avenida de la Constitución changes its name to C/Tetuán. Sevilla has found a hundred ways to use its *azulejos*, but the best has to be in the **billboard** on this street for 1932 Studebaker cars – so pretty that no one's had the heart to take it down.

La Macarena and Around

The northern end of Sevilla contains few monuments, though most of its solid, working-class neighbourhoods are clustered around Baroque parish churches. The **Alameda de Hércules** has been adorned since the 16th century with statues of Hercules, the mythical founder of the city, and Julius Caesar, credited with building the city's walls. This is the centre of one of the shabbier yet most appealing parts of the city, with a growing number of boho-chic bars, music shops and cafés now paving the way for a wave of gentrification. A fashionable promenade until the late 19th century, it nose-dived into disrepute when the bordellos and gambling dens took over at the end of the 19th century, and then had another brief flicker of glory as one of the foremost flamenco venues in Andalucía in the early 1900s. Statues of two of flamenco's finest performers, Aurora Pavón and Manolo Caracol, stand at either end of the avenue. It can still be seedy and occasionally slightly threatening at night, but the neighbourhood bars are very popular with Sevilla's hip, arty crowd.

The earthy *barrio* of **La Feria**, next to El Arenal, is a delightfully old-fashioned mercantile quarter, once the district of artisans and wool craftsmen, and is made up of a patchwork of crooked streets around the wide boulevard of C/de la Feria itself. Thursday mornings are particularly lively, animated by **El Jueves**, the celebrated antiques and bric-a-brac market that has been going strong since the 13th century.

Santa Clara and **San Clemente** are two interesting 13th-century monasteries in this area, both established soon after Fernando III's victory over the Muslims in 1289; the former includes one of Sevilla's best *artesonado* ceilings and a Gothic tower built by Don Fadrique. There were two Don Fadriques, both of whom came to sticky ends, and both of whom are responsible for the tower, according to separate legends. The first was Fernando III's son, who built his palace on this spot and carried on an affair with his widowed stepmother – to the disgust of his brother, who had him executed. The second was Pedro the Cruel's brother, who began an affair with Doña Blanca, Pedro's abandoned wife, for which he too lost his head. And these aren't the only dramatic tales to cling to the convent: Pedro I, an infamous womanizer, pursued a terrified gentlewoman named Doña María, stripped her husband of his lands and property and executed him. Doña María took refuge in the convent and disfigured herself by throwing burning oil on her face. This story doesn't have an entirely sad ending: eventually her lands were returned to her and she founded the convent of Santa Iñés in 1374. Her tomb is opened annually on 2 December and her body is said to have never decomposed.

The convent of **San Clemente** is the city's oldest, built on the remains of a Moorish palace; once a rich convent which enjoyed royal patronage, it was stripped of its lands during the Napoleonic occupation, when the nuns were ousted and the buildings were seconded for use as a warehouse and prison. A beautiful 16th-century *mudéjar* coffered ceiling and handsome frescoes by Valdés Leal and his son managed to survive the sacking.

Also near the Alameda de Hércules, in C/de Jesús de la Grand Poder, is the imposing **Basilica de Jesús de la Grand Poder**, a favourite spot for *sevillano* weddings. The basilica contains a much-revered 17th-century statue of the same name by Juan de Mesa. It is solemnly paraded through the streets on Good Friday morning.

North of C/San Luís, some of the city's **Moorish walls** survive, near the Basilica de La Macarena, which gives the quarter its name. The basilica, a garish 1940s neo-Baroque construction luridly frescoed with puffs of fluorescent angels, is home to the most worshipped of Sevilla's idols, a delicate Virgin with glass tears on her cheeks who always steals the show in the *Semana Santa* parades. Like a film star she makes her admirers gasp and swarm around her, crying '¡O la hermosa! ¡O la guapa!' ('O beautiful Virgin! O lovely Virgin!'). Fleets of veiled old ladies jostle for the closest position to her feet, and twitter over the thousands of photographs laid out in the shop. The small adjacent **museum** (*entrance inside the chapel*) is devoted to her costumes, a breathtaking giant-sized Barbie wardrobe of superbly embroidered robes encrusted with gold and jewels, and solid gold crowns and ceremonial paraphernalia. Also here are the elaborately carved and gilded floats which take part in the *Semana Santa* parades; the first depicts the moment when Pontius Pilate passed the sentence of death on Christ, and the second carries the Virgin herself, weeping for the death of her son.

South from here, along C/San Luis, you'll pass another Baroque extravaganza, Leonardo de Figueroa's **San Luís**, built for the Jesuits (1699–1731), with twisted columns and tons of encrusted

Basilica de La Macarena
www.hermandaddela macarena.org; open Mon–Sat 9–2 and 5–9, Sun 9.30–2 and 5–9; adm for museum

ornament. Lovely **San Marcos**, down the street, has an elaborate façade with a graceful combination of Gothic and Moorish elements, and one of Sevilla's last surviving *mudéjar* towers. The austere interior, with its soaring wooden roof supported by beautifully carved and decorated beams, is adorned with elegant, white, Moorish horseshoe-shaped arches.

Convento de Santa Paula
guided tours, Tues–Sun 10–1; adm

Just east is the Convento de Santa Paula, with a finely detailed doorway with pink and blue inlaid tiles by Francisco Pisano and Pedro Millán (1504), and a pretty, much-embellished openwork bell tower. You can take an excellent guided tour of the interior or just stop off at the little shop selling the jams and confectionery made by the nuns. Nearer the river, on the grand avenue of Resolana, seek

Torre de los Perdigones
open daily 10–7; adm

out one of the city's latest attractions, the Torre de los Perdigones, a former munitions factory which includes a giant periscope that presents a sweeping image of the city projected onto a giant three-dimensional concave disc.

Santa Cruz and Beyond

⭐ **Santa Cruz**

If Spain envies Sevilla, Sevilla envies Santa Cruz, a tiny, exceptionally lovely quarter of narrow streets and whitewashed houses. It appears to be the true homeland of everything *sevillano*, with flower-bedecked courtyards and iron-bound windows, though there is something unnervingly pristine about it. This is hardly surprising given that it was calculatedly primped up between 1912 and 1920 by the Ministry of Tourism in order to give visitors something to gawp at. Before 1492 this was the Jewish quarter of Sevilla; today it's the most aristocratic corner of town, and the most touristy. In the old days there was a wall around the *barrio*; today you may enter through the Murillo Gardens, from the C/Mateos Gago behind the cathedral apse, or from the **Patio de las Banderas**, a pretty Plaza Mayor-style square next to the Alcázar. In

Hospital de los Venerables
t 95 456 26 96; open daily 10–2 and 4–8; adm

the heart of this area lies the Hospital de los Venerables, a former home for the elderly and now an art gallery set around a delightful courtyard. On the eastern edge of the *barrio*, **Santa María la Blanca** (on the street of the same name) was a pre-Reconquista church; some details remain, but the whole was rebuilt in the 1660s, with spectacular rococo ornamentation inside and paintings by Murillo.

On the eastern fringes of the old town, Santa Cruz fades gently into other peaceful, pretty areas – less ritzy, though their old streets contain more palaces. One of these, built by the Dukes of

Casa de Pilatos
t 95 422 52 98; open daily Oct–Feb 9–6; Mar–Sept 9–7; adm

Medinaceli (1480–1571), is the Casa de Pilatos (House of Pilate) on Plaza de Pilatos, one of Sevilla's loveliest hidden corners. The site once belonged to a judge who was condemned to death for heresy and had his lands confiscated by the Inquisition. They were snapped up by Don Pedro Enrique, the governor of Andalucía, who began construction of a palace in 1481, of which only the dauntingly named Chapel of Flagellation remains. His son, yet another Don Fadrique, was responsible for the present pleasing jumble of *mudéjar* and Renaissance work, with a lovely courtyard. It was constructed just after his return from a pilgrimage to Jerusalem, where, so the story goes, he was so struck by the Praetorium, Pontius Pilate's official residence, that he decided to model his palace at home on it. The entrance, a mock-Roman triumphal arch done in Carrara marble by sculptors from Genoa, is studded with Crusaders' crosses in commemoration of the pilgrimage. Each year in March, a *Vía Crucis*, following the Stations of the Cross, takes place between the House of Pilate and the Cruz del Campo, apparently the same distance as that between Pontius Pilate's house in Jerusalem and Mount Calvary. The entrance arch leads through a small courtyard into the **Patio Principal**, with 13th-century Granadan decoration, beautiful coloured tiles, and rows of Roman statues and portrait busts. These form a perfect introduction to the dukes' excellent collections of antique sculpture in the surrounding rooms (many of which have splendid coffered ceilings), including a Roman copy of a Greek herm (a boundary marker with the head of the god Hermes on it), imperial portraits, and a bust of Hadrian's boyfriend, Antinous. There is a series of delightful **gardens and courtyards** cooled with trickling fountains and bowers; the rose garden is especially lovely, particularly in spring, when the walls erupt in a blaze of bougainvillea. There is an optional tour (*in Spanish*) of the **private apartments**. You can see 18th-century furniture (particularly impressive in the dining hall), paper-thin porcelain from England and Limoges, fanciful Japanese vases and a rather humdrum collection of paintings, from portraits of stolid dukes and duchesses to a bullfight (set in Madrid) by Goya.

Behind the House of Pilate, **San Esteban**, rebuilt from a former mosque, has an altarpiece by Zurbarán. Farther up on noisy, traffic-filled Avenida de Luís Montoto are the forlorn remains of an Almoravid **aqueduct**. Nudging up against the House of Pilate is the convent of **San Leandro**, founded in 1295, although this building dates from 1369 and has been considerably embellished and refurbished since. Only the entrance courtyard can be viewed most of the year, but the richly endowed church, with two beautiful retables by Juan Martínez Montañés, opens on the 22nd of each month, when hordes of supplicants descend to petition Santa Rita de Casia, the enormously popular patron saint of lost causes. On C/Águilas, **San Ildefonso** has a pretty polychrome 18th-century façade and two perky towers.

Museo del Baile Flamenco
t 95 424 03 11; open daily 9–6; adm

Nearby, the **Museo del Baile Flamenco** (Flamenco Museum) at C/Manuel Rojas Marcos 3 was opened in 2007 by the legendary flamenco dancer Cristina Hoyos and includes fabulous audio-visual and multimedia displays explaining the history, culture and soul of Spanish flamenco.

South of the Cathedral

Sevilla has a building even larger than its cathedral – twice as large, in fact, and probably better known to the outside world. Since the 1950s it has housed parts of the city's **university** and it does have the presence of a college building, but it began its life in the 1750s as the state **Tobacco Factory** (Fábrica de Tabacos). In the 19th century it employed as many as 12,000 women to roll cigars. (One of its workers, of course, was Bizet's Carmen.) These sturdy women, with 'carnations in their hair and daggers in their garters', hung their capes on the altars of the factory chapels each morning, rocked their babies in cradles while they rolled cigars, and took no nonsense from anybody. Next to the factory, the **Hotel Alfonso XIII**, built in 1929, is believed to be the only hotel ever commissioned by a reigning monarch – Alfonso literally used it as an annexe to the Alcázar when friends and relations came to stay. This landmark is well worth a visit, if you're not put off by an icy doorman. To the west of the hotel lies the Baroque **Palacio de San Telmo**, originally a naval academy, which became the court of an offshoot of the royal family in the mid-19th century. The dowager duchess María Luisa Fernanda de la Bourbon donated the elegant 19th-century ornamental gardens, the Delicias Gardens, to the city in 1893, and they formed the basis of the lovely city park which would bear her name.

María Luisa Park

For all its old-fashioned grace, Sevilla has in recent decades become one of the most forward-looking and progressive cities in Spain. In the 1920s, while they were redirecting the Guadalquivir and building the new port and factories that are the foundation of the city's growth today, the *sevillanos* decided to put on an exhibition. In a tremendous burst of energy, they turned the entire southern end of the city into an expanse of gardens and grand boulevards. The centre of it is the **Parque de María Luisa**, a paradisiacal half-mile of palms and orange trees, covered with flowerbeds and dotted with hidden bowers and pavilions, one of the loveliest parks in Europe. Two of the largest pavilions, built by Aníbal González, on the **Plaza de América** have been turned into museums. The Museo Arqueológico (Archaeological Museum), with an impressively dour neo-Plateresque façade, has an excellent collection of pre-Roman jewellery and icons, and some tantalizing artefacts from mysterious Tartessos. The Romans are represented,

Museo Arqueológico
t 95 423 24 01; open Tues 2.30–8.30, Wed–Sat 9.30–8, Sun and hols 9–2.30, closed Mon; adm, free to EU citizens

as in every other Mediterranean archaeology museum, with copies of Greek sculpture and oversized statues of emperors, but also with a mosaic of the Triumph of Bacchus, another of Hercules, architectural fragments, some fine glass, and finds of all sorts from Itálica and other nearby towns. Across the plaza, the **Museo de Artes y Costumbres Populares** (Museum of Popular Art and Customs), in the Mudéjar Pavilion, with a gleeful motif of tiny unicorns and griffons dancing across blue tiles, is Andalucía's attic, with everything from ploughs and saucepans to flamenco dresses and exhibits from the city's two famous celebrations, *Semana Santa* and the April *Feria*.

Museo de Artes y Costumbres Populares
t 95 423 25 76; open Tues 2.30–8.30, Wed–Sat 9.30–8, Sun and hols 9–2.30; adm

Plaza de España

⭐ Plaza de España

In the 1920s at least, excess was still a way of life in Sevilla, and to call attention to the *Exposición Iberoamericana* they put up a building even bigger than the Tobacco Factory. With its grand Baroque towers (stolen gracefully from Santiago de Compostela), fancy bridges, staircases and immense colonnade, the Plaza de España is World's Fair architecture at its grandest and most outrageous. Much of the fanciful neo-Spanish architecture of 1930s Florida and California may well have been inspired by this building. The Fair, as it turned out, was a flop: attendance proved disappointing, and when it was over Sevilla was left nearly bankrupt. The dictator, Primo de Rivera, who was himself from Jerez, and who had put a lot of money and effort into this fair to show off his native region, died while it was still running, at the lowest depths of unpopularity. For all that, the *sevillanos* are glad they at least have this building and its park to show for the effort. They gravitate naturally to it at weekends, to photograph each other and nibble curious pastries. One of the things Sevilla is famous for is its painted *azulejo* tiles; they adorn nearly every building in town, but here on the colonnade a few million of them are devoted to maps and historical scenes from every province in Spain, while in front of them a series of ceramic-encrusted footbridges span a canal.

La Cartuja and Contemporary Art

The Isle of La Cartuja was part of the Expo '92 site, and up until fairly recently was a fairly desolate area. More recently, a university faculty has opened here, together with a business technology park comprising around 200 companies, plus concert and performance venues. Some of the original Expo pavilions are now also devoted to holding business fairs and conferences, and another section has become the Isla Mágica funfair.

Infinitely more interesting is the monastery of **Santa María de las Cuevas y la Cartuja** (St Mary of the Caves), the partially restored

09

Sevilla | La Cartuja and Contemporary Art

Carthusian monastery where Columbus once stayed while he mulled over his ambitions and geographical theories. Pottery kilns proliferated here from the 12th century, and the Virgin is said to have appeared in one of the workshops. A Franciscan hermitage was established in honour of the vision and in 1399 Gonzalo de Mena, the archbishop of Sevilla, founded the Cartuja monastery. It grew to become a virtually self-sufficient walled city, giving refuge to spiritual figures such as Teresa de Jesús as well as all the Spanish monarchs who passed through Sevilla. At the peak of its affluence, the monastery was richly endowed with masterpieces by great artists from Zurbarán to Murillo. Since then, sadly, the building has suffered numerous indignities; the monks were driven out by Marshal Soult, who used it as a garrison during the Napoleonic occupation of 1810–12 and is responsible for the damage to the extraordinary *artesonado* ceiling in the refectory – his troops used the gable for target practice. As if this wasn't enough, the city sold it off in the 1830s to Liverpudlian Charles Pickman, who turned it into a ceramics factory. The brick kilns still soar above the monastery garden, which is full of orange trees. Now the monastery is home to the **Centro Andaluz de Arte Contemporáneo** (Andalucían Centre of Contemporary Art, aka CAAC), one of the most singular and absorbing contemporary arts centres in Spain. The atmospheric ruins of the monastery itself serve as a palimpsest of the waves of invaders who have stripped it bare of most of its treasures, and yet, despite them, it retains a hushed and reverent stillness. Among the art now displayed on the ruined walls is a series of eight blazing paintings by José Manuel Bioto, in hazy, dreamy ochres and indigos, in the main chapel, and a limpid collection of Japanese-inspired panels in St Anne's Chapel, where Columbus was once laid to rest. Attached to the monastery complex are the main exhibition galleries, in an unobtrusive, light-filled, modern building entered through a courtyard draped in a forest of vines. These are devoted to temporary exhibitions which focus on both emerging and established Andalucían artists and international artists who develop projects designed specifically for the space. This is one of the most engaging and vibrant places in Spain to see contemporary art, and it shouldn't be missed.

Centro Andaluz de Arte Contemporáneo y la Cartuja
t 95 503 70 83; open Oct–Mar Tues–Fri 10–8, Sat 11–8, Sun 10–3; April–June and Sept Tues–Fri 10–9, Sat 11–9, Sun 10–3; July–Aug Tues–Fri 10–8 (CAAC closes 3pm), Sat 11–3, Sun 10–3, plus Nocturama, evening concerts, cinema and art exhibitions; adm

(i) **Sevilla >**
municipal offices: Plaza de San Francisco 19, t 95 459 52 88; C/Arjona 28, t 95 422 17 14; Paseo de las Delicias 9, t 95 423 44 65;

provincial offices: Avenida de la Constitución 21, t 95 422 14 04; airport, t 95 444 91 28; Santa Justa station, t 95 453 76 26

Tourist Information and Services in Sevilla

There are three **municipal** tourist offices and three **provincial** information offices. All have information on the **Sevilla Card** (*www.sevillacard.es*), valid for 1, 2 or 3 days, with unlimited use of public transport, free or discounted entrance to monuments and museums, free or discounted rides on the tourist buses and boats, plus a raft of other discounts.

Internet, Telephones and Post

Internet cafés arrive and disappear with alarming frequency; ask the tourist information office for an up-to-date list. They also have several free terminals in the office on Plaza San

Francisco. You'll find public telephones on every street corner, but for international calls head to a *locutorio*. There are several along C/Trajano (near the Plaza Duque de la Victoria).

Alfalfa 10, Plaza de la Alfalfa 10, **t** 95 421 38 41.

Seville Internet Centre, C/Almirantazgo 2, **t** 95 450 02 75.

The main **post office** is at Avenida de la Constitución 32, **t** 90 219 71 97.

Shopping in Sevilla

All the paraphernalia associated with Spanish fantasy, such as *mantillas*, castanets, wrought iron, *azulejo* tiles and embroidery, is available in Sevilla. **C/Cuna** is the best place to find flamenco wear and accessories, and several of the convents sell jams and confectionery. **Triana**, of course, is the place to find *azulejo* tiles and perfumed soaps.

If you want to pick up a First Communion outfit or any kind of religious kitsch there is an astonishing number of shops devoted to it around the **Plaza El Salvador**. If you want to look the part at *Feria*, deck yourself out at one of several equestrian shops, including Jara y Sedal, C/Adriano 16.

For fashion, there is a branch of the luxurious leather store Loewe on the **Plaza Nueva**, as well as other up-market designer shops. The most famous *sevillano* designers are Victorio and Lucchino, which have an outlet on Plaza Nueva. **C/O'Donnell** has a number of more affordable boutiques.

There are two branches of **El Corte Inglés**, where the well-heeled *sevillanos* shop, and, on **Plaza Duque de la Victoria**, a branch of Zara (also to be found at C/Velázquez) and one of Mango, both perennial Spanish fashion favourites.

Vértice is an international bookshop, **C/San Fernando** 33, **t** 95 421 16 54, near the cathedral, with a small selection of English-language literature and local guides. For a pleasant wander, head for the pedestrianized **C/Sierpes**, which is packed with all the international fashion chains (Zara, Mango, H&M).

(★) **Hotel Taberna de Alabardero** >>

Where to Stay in Sevilla

Sevilla ✉ 41000

Hotels are more expensive in Sevilla than in most of Spain. High season is March and April; during *Semana Santa* and the April *Feria* you should book even for *hostales*, preferably a year ahead. Low season is July and August, when the inhabitants flee from the heat, and January to early March. See *www.hotelesdesevilla.com*, which offers online booking.

Luxury (€€€€€)

★★★★★Alfonso XIII, C/San Fernando 2, **t** 95 491 70 00. Built by King Alfonso for the Exposición Iberoamericana in 1929, this is the grandest hotel in Andalucía, giving a unique experience, albeit at a price. Sevilla society still meets around its lobby fountain and somewhat dreary bar. Its restaurant, **San Fernando**, is good if pricey.

★★★★Las Casas del Rey de Baeza, Plaza Jesús de la Redención 2, **t** 95 456 14 96, *www.hospes.es*. Also in Santa Cruz, with an elegant white and ochre façade and stylish rooms with wi-fi and CD/DVD players.

Very Expensive (€€€€)

★★★★Hotel Doña María, C/Don Remondo 19, **t** 95 422 49 90, *www.hdmaria.com*. Charming, and superbly located by the cathedral. Among the mostly antique furniture are four-poster beds and beautifully painted headboards; there is also a tiny rooftop pool with stunning views.

★★★★Hotel Taberna de Alabardero, C/Zaragoza 20, **t** 95 456 06 37, *www.tabernadealabardero.com*. The former home of a Romantic poet, with an outstanding restaurant and culinary school. Seven charming and intimate rooms, all with Jacuzzi, are set around the courtyard. The service is discreet and the cuisine sublime. Prices include breakfast in the award-winning restaurant (*see* overleaf).

★★★Las Casas de la Judería, Plaza Santa María la Blanca, Callejón de Dos Hermanos 7, **t** 95 441 51 50, *www.casasypalacios.com*. A row of charming and perfectly restored town houses in the Santa Cruz quarter, with airy rooms around a patio and a lovely Arab-style pool in the gardens.

***Las Casas de los Mercaderes, C/Álvarez Quintero 9/13, **t** 95 422 58 58, *www.casasypalacios.com*. In the Arenal district, the stylish rooms have been sympathetically restored and are arranged around an 18th-century arcaded courtyard.

★ **Casa Numero 7 >**

Casa Numero 7, C/Virgenes 7, **t** 95 422 15 81, *www.casanumero7.com*. An utterly delightful place in the heart of Santa Cruz, like staying in an elegant private home. There are just six rooms, with antiques and paintings from the owner's private collection. The style is relaxed but aristocratic and the staff couldn't be nicer.

Expensive (€€€)

***Hotel Alminar, C/Álvarez Quintero 52, **t** 95 429 39 13, *www.hotelalminar. com*. Opened in 2006, with 12 superb rooms decorated in earth colours with parquet floors and lashings of cream linen; a couple have private terraces and cathedral views.

***Hotel Puerta de Seville, C/Puerta de la Carne 2, **t** 95 498 72 70, *www. hotelpuertadesevilla.com*. Rooms are set around a small inner courtyard at this excellent-value hotel on the edge of Santa Cruz. The décor includes Regency-style striped fabrics, antiques and old-fashioned oil paintings.

★ **La Casa del Maestro >**

La Casa del Maestro, C/Almudena 5, **t 95 450 00 07, *www.lacasadelmaestro. com*. In the former home of flamenco guitarist Niño Ricardo, with pretty if rather small rooms and a delightful roof terrace. In a short street just south of Plaza Ponce de León.

Hotel Alcántara, C/Xímenez de Enciso 28, **t 95 450 05 95, *www.hotel alcantara.net*. In a converted old mansion in the centre of the Barrio Santa Cruz, with quiet, spacious, simply decorated rooms. There are rooms for three and four, also.

Hostería del Laurel, Plaza de los Venerables 5, **t 95 422 02 95, *www. hosteriadellaurel.com*. Overlooking a slightly touristy square, this engagingly quirky hotel, with layered turrets and terraces, once attracted several Romantic poets.

Hotel Maestranza, C/Gamazo 12, **t 95 422 67 66, *www.hotelmaestranza.*

com. A traditional little hotel with a tiled lobby, slightly fussy rooms and very helpful staff. Prices drop a category or two in low season.

Amadeus, C/Farnesio 6, **t 95 450 14 43, *www.hotelamadeussevilla.com*. An atmospheric, historic hotel filled with antiques with a background of soothing classical music. The rooms have oriental rugs and dark wood furniture and there's a roof terrace for enjoying breakfast with Giralda views.

Moderate (€€)

Hostal Atenas, C/Caballerizas 1, **t 95 421 80 47, *www.hostal-atenas. com*. Quiet and pleasant, in a good location between the Plaza Pilatos and the cathedral. Take a cab – it's hard to find.

San Francisco, C/Mariana Pineda 9, **t 95 450 15 41, *www.sanfranciscoh.com*. Virtually across from the cathedral, this fairly new hotel has pleasant modern rooms, a central patio and a terrace with views.

Córdoba, C/Farnesio 12, **t 95 422 74 98. Offers a dozen clean, bright rooms, all with a/c and en-suite bathrooms, set around a typical *sevillano* patio. Booking essential.

Hostería de Doña Lina, C/Gloria 7, **t 95 421 09 56, *www.hlina.com*. In the Santa Cruz area, a charmingly kitsch place with whitewashed rooms.

Hotel Murillo, C/Lope de Rueda 9, **t 95 421 60 95, *www.hotelmurillo.com*. Old-fashioned, family-run; the prices are very reasonable for this hotel's central location in Santa Cruz, with grand salons but simple rooms. It also offers apartments.

Hostal Naranjo, C/San Roque 11, **t 95 422 58 40, *www.bandbsevilla.com*. By the Fine Arts Museum, on a quiet street in a tiled old building.

Hostal Londres, C/San Pedro Mártir 1, **t 95 421 28 96. Also near the Fine Arts Museum, in a fine old building, this is a quiet place to stay.

*Hotel Simón, C/García de Vinuesa 19, **t** 95 422 66 60, *www.hotelsimon sevilla.com*. A restored 18th-century mansion in a fine position just off the Avenida de la Constitución by the cathedral. This good-value option gets booked up quickly. Pick your room carefully – they vary considerably.

Inexpensive (€)

For inexpensive *hostales*, the Santa Cruz quarter is, surprisingly, the best place to look, particularly on the quiet side streets off C/Mateos Gago.

*Argüelles, C/Alhóndiga 58, **t** 95 421 44 55. Small rooms, with a garden and terrace.

*Hostal Bailén, C/Bailén 75, **t** 95 422 16 35. A delightful old building with a garden and courtyard in the Santa Cruz quarter. There's also a tiny two-room apartment available in summer.

*Hostal Doña Feli, C/Jesús del Gran Poder 130, **t** 95 490 10 48, *www.hostal dfeli.com*. Simple but comfortable rooms, set around a pretty tiled patio filled with flowers.

*Fabiola, C/Fabiola 16, **t** 95 421 83 46. Quiet and cool, with a little courtyard full of plants; near Santa María Blanca.

Apartments

If you are travelling on a budget, or with a family, renting an apartment can be a good option.

Apartamentos Murillo, **t** 95 421 09 59, *www.hotelmurillo.com* (€€€). One- and two-bedroom apartments in the heart of the Barrio Santa Cruz.

Sevilla Apartamentos, **t** (mobile) 667 511 348, *www.sevillapartamentos.com* (€€). A friendly, family-run business offering immaculate studios and one- and two-bedroom apartments.

Eating Out in Sevilla

Restaurants in Sevilla are more expensive than in most of Spain, but even around the cathedral and the Santa Cruz quarter there are a few places that can simply be dismissed as tourist traps. Remember that in the evening the *sevillanos*, even more than most Andalucíans, enjoy bar-hopping for tapas.

Expensive (€€€)

Salvador Rojo, C/San Fernando 23, **t** 95 422 97 25. Near Hotel Alfonso XIII but virtually hidden. The décor is almost spartan, which is all the more reason to concentrate on the food, a selection of creative *andaluz* dishes that are deftly prepared by Salvador Rojo himself. *Closed Sun.*

Taberna del Alabardero, C/Zaragoza 20, **t** 95 456 06 37. One of Sevilla's best-known restaurants, also home to an illustrious school for chefs. Head up the grand marble staircase to a series of wood-panelled dining rooms set around the central courtyard, each with a different ambience. There are elegant guest rooms available (*see* 'Where to Stay'), a café-bistro for lighter (and cheaper) fare, and a sumptuous, tile-lined bar with an adventurous range of tapas.

Moderate (€€)

La Albahaca, Plaza Santa Cruz 12, **t** 95 422 07 14. On a delightful small square northeast of the Alcázar; there is a Basque twist to many of the classic dishes and the menu changes with the season. *Closed Sun.*

Casa Robles, C/Álvarez Quintero 58, **t** 95 456 32 72. In a wonderful setting, with dishes combining traditional cooking and the best of new cuisine. It specializes in pastries.

Egaña-Oriza, C/San Fernando 41, **t** 95 422 72 11. Splendidly situated on the corner of the Jardines Alcázar, opposite the university, with an excellent adjacent tapas bar. Among its delights are clams on the half-shell and a kind of *sevillano* jugged hare. *Closed Sat lunch, Sun and Aug.*

Marea Grande, C/Diego Angulo Íñiguez 16, **t** 95 453 80 00. Fish-lovers should head slightly out of the centre for this plush establishment, one of the city's finest seafood restaurants. *Closed end of Aug and Sun.*

Poncio, C/Victoria 15, **t** 950 34 00 10. This elegant, colourful restaurant in Triana (west of Santa Ana church) has won awards for its creative *andaluz* cuisine prepared with the freshest seasonal ingredients.

Becerrita, C/Recaredo 9, **t** 95 441 20 57. Run by the affable Jesús Becerra, who serves traditional *andaluz* dishes in intimate surroundings. *Closed Sun eve.*

Enrique Becerra, C/Gamazo 2, **t** 95 421 30 49. Enrique followed in his father's footsteps (he is the fifth generation of this family of celebrated *sevillano* restaurateurs), with this prettily tiled restaurant. The menu is based on regional dishes like lamb stuffed with spinach and pine nuts. For dessert, try the house speciality, *pudding de naranjas Santa Paula*, made with *sevillano* marmalade from the

Convent of St Paula. There is also a lively tapas bar. *Closed Sun and Aug.*

Thebussem, C/Matheos Gago 9, **t** 95 421 40 30. The striking décor here is thanks to owner/painter Gonzalo Ferrer, whose canvases cover the walls. The innovative menu includes dishes like Moroccan *suyat* and cheese mousse with a black liquorice froth.

El Corral del Agua, Callejón del Agua 6, **t** 95 422 48 41. Seasoned travellers usually steer clear of cutesy wishing wells, but the garden in which this one stands is a haven of peace. Next to Washington Irving's garden. *Closed Sun, and Jan and Feb.*

El Bacalao, Plaza Ponce de León 15, **t** 95 421 66 70. For infinite varieties of *bacalao* (dried salted cod), this delightful restaurant and tapas bar is the only place to go; some meat and game is also served. *Closed Sun eve.*

El Faro de Triana, Puente Triana, **t** 95 433 61 92. Enjoys a peerless position with a vast terrace overlooking the Guadalquivir in Triana. Fresh fish and seafood are the speciality, including *gambas pil pil* (prawns in spicy sauce).

Mesón Don Raimundo, C/Argote de Molina 26, **t** 95 422 33 55. By the cathedral and set in a 17th-century convent, with an eclectic décor of religious artefacts and suits of armour. No enforced abstinence here, though: a large selection of traditional *andaluz* dishes based on fish, shellfish and game; there is also a fine wine list. *Closed Sun eve.*

La Judería, C/Cano y Cueto, **t** 95 442 64 56. In the old Jewish quarter, with brick arches and terracotta tiles. It has an almost bewildering range of richly flavoured regional dishes, game in season, dozens of fish dishes and, to finish up, delicious home-made desserts. Great tapas in the bar, too. *Closed Tues and two weeks in Aug.*

Restaurante San Marco, C/Cuna 6, **t** 95 421 24 40. One of six in town; in an 18th-century palace with an enormous Moorish carved wooden door. The cuisine is Franco-Italian and the desserts are particularly good. *Closed Mon lunch and Sun.*

Rincón de Casana, C/Santo Domingo de la Calzada 13, **t** 95 453 17 10. Fine traditional cuisine served in rustic surroundings. *Closed Sun June–Aug.*

Río Grande, C/Betis 70, **t** 95 427 39 56. On the Triana side of the Guadalquivir, you can dine here with a tremendous view of the Tower of Gold and La Giralda. Specializes in regional cuisine.

Egoísta, C/Calatrava s/n, **t** 95 490 87 32. A funky restaurant that opened in 2007, where you can eat, drink, buy clothes, visit an art gallery and enjoy jazz at weekends. The cuisine is creative and international, with dishes from China, Japan and India.

La Isla, C/Arfe 25, **t** 95 421 53 76. An excellent fish restaurant specializing in *zarzuela* (Catalan seafood stew) and fish and seafood grills. The brightly tiled dining room is a delight.

Inexpensive (€)

Bodegón Torre del Oro, C/Santander 15, **t** 95 422 08 80. The rafters are hung with hams and the dining room shares the space with the bar. There's a three-course set meal with wine and the *raciones* are excellent.

La Illustre Víctima, C/Dr Letamendi 35 (not far from the Plaza de Alameda de Hércules). A friendly, laid-back and pleasingly chaotic café-bar.

Pizzeria San Marco, Mesón del Moro 6–10, **t** 95 421 43 90. Run by the same family as the Restaurante San Marco (*see* above), with pizzas and pasta in an old Arab bathhouse.

El Rincón de Anita, Plaza del Christo de Burgos 23, **t** 95 421 74 61. A pretty tile-lined restaurant and tapas bar on a charming square with a terrace. Classic *andaluz* home cooking. *Closed Sat lunch in Aug.*

Vegetarian

Habanita, C/Golfo 3 (just off Plaza Alfalfa), **t** 60 671 64 56 (€). Relaxed, colourful veggie restaurant with Caribbean and Cuban specialities, plus great *caipirinhas* and *mojitos*.

La Mandrágora, C/Albuera 11, **t** 95 422 01 84 (€). In a country where meat and fish reign supreme, it's a nice surprise to find this friendly vegetarian restaurant with an excellent menu. Everything is home-cooked – even the piquant salsas. *Closed Sun.*

Ice Cream and *Pastelerías*

La Campana, C/Sierpes 1. Delicious cakes, coffee or ice cream at this historic café.

 ⭐ Habanita >>

Alfalfa 10, Plaza de Alfalfa 1. One of the nicest café-bars on trendy Plaza de Alfalfa, with very untypical but delicious cappuccino and strudel.

Horno Santa Cruz, C/Guzmán el Bueno 12. Blue and white tiles and a plant-filled courtyard – the perfect place to buy bread and pastries.

⭐ La Eslava >>

Ochoa, on C/Sierpes. Another of the city's prettiest old *pastelerías*.

Tapas Bars

Tapas bars are an intrinsic part of daily life in Sevilla, and even the smartest restaurants often have excellent tapas bars attached.

Alcoy 10, C/Teodosio 66, t 95 490 57 02. An innovative new tapas bar with original treats like mini kebabs of prawns or honey-drenched pork. The outside tables get filled up fast.

Bar España, C/San Fernando 41. Attached to the Egaña-Oriza, this place is chic, bright, cosmopolitan – and the Basque tapas are sensational.

Bar Europa, C/Siete Revueltas 35, t 95 433 13 54. A much-loved local classic on a pretty square, which has been going since 1925.

Bar Giralda, C/Mateo Gago 1, t 95 422 74 35. Located in an old Moorish bathhouse, with a great range to choose from. Popular with tourists and locals alike.

Bar Manolo, on buzzing Plaza de Alfalfa, t 95 421 41 76. The best of several tapas bars on the square. It's lively at breakfast as well as evening.

Bar Modesto, C/Cano y Cueto 5, t 95 441 68 11. Another well-established favourite with wonderful seafood tapas offerings, and a dining room for full meals.

Bodega La Albariza, C/Betis 6A, t 95 433 20 16. Serves its astonishing range of tapas on empty sherry casks in the bar. There is a little dining area at the back with a very reasonably priced menu.

⭐ Patio San Eloy >>

Bodega Santa Cruz, C/Mateo Gago (on the corner of C/Rodrigo Caro). Attracts a university crowd and serves an excellent selection of tapas, which will be chalked up at your place at the bar.

⭐ Bodega Santa Cruz >

Casa Morales, C/García de Vinuesa 11, t 95 422 12 42. Just a skip away from the cathedral, this is purportedly

Sevilla's second-oldest bar, with sawdust scattered across the tiled floor and a range of simple tapas.

Casa Plácido, C/Mesón del Moro. Serves excellent and reasonably priced tapas in an old-style tiled bar.

La Eslava, C/Eslava 3, t 95 490 65 68. Many of Sevilla's best tapas bars also have dining rooms at the back; this is one of the nicest. The restaurant has a more extensive menu. *Closed Sun, Mon eve and 1–21 Aug.*

Las Golondrinas, C/Antillano Campos 26, t 95 433 16 26. Great *alcachofas* (artichokes) and *tortilla* in a charming tiled two-floor bar.

Hostería del Laurel, Plaza de los Venerables 5, t 95 422 02 95. Serves superb tapas in a room filled with hanging *jamón* and beautiful Triana tiles. The restaurant is also excellent.

Las Infantas, C/Arfe 36, t 95 422 96 89. Heading down towards the river, this is a very stylish bar popular with young professionals.

Kiosko de las Flores, Plaza del Altozano, t 95 433 38 98. A pretty and informal café-bar partly overlooking the river, justly celebrated for its *pescaítos fritos*.

Mesón de la Infanta, C/Dos de Mayo 26, t 95 456 15 54. This restaurant in El Arenal has a popular tapas bar which attracts well-heeled locals. Good hams and fine wines.

El Rinconcillo, C/Gerona 40, t 95 422 31 83 (north of the cathedral, between the Church of San Pedro and the Convent of Espíritu Santo). Sevilla's oldest bar, dating from 1670 and decorated in moody brown *azulejos* – and reputedly where the custom of topping a glass with a slice of sausage or a piece of bread and ham (the first tapas) began.

Patio San Eloy, C/San Eloy 9, t 95 450 10 64. One of the most atmospheric bars in town, where the customer overspills sit on the broad tiled steps. There's a small corner counter for enjoying *fino* from the barrel and stacked sandwich tapas.

Bar Santa Ana, C/Pureza 82, t 95 427 21 02. Always packed with locals, this bar is for bullfighting fans and dishes up tasty traditional tapas like crumbly Manchego cheese and tortilla.

⭐ **Sol y Sombra >**

Sol y Sombra, C/Castilla 149–51, t 95 433 39 35. Over in Triana, this is a very atmospheric place with sawdust on the floor and *taurino* memorabilia. The superb tapas change daily, and there's a restaurant next door.

Las Teresas, C/Sta Teresa. A traditional café in the heart of the Barrio Santa Cruz, with walls lined with old photos.

Entertainment and Nightlife in Sevilla

Bars and Clubs

The **Plaza del Salvador** fills up quickly in the evenings, so start your night with a chilled sherry at the tiny **Antigua Bodeguita** or one of its neighbours, opposite the church. Sip the sherry with the locals out in the square or lounging on the church steps, and ponder your next move. One particular pleasure is to set out on a bar crawl, trying different sherries and tapas.

Many of the liveliest bars are around the **Plaza de Alfalfa**; head down **C/Boteros** for some of the buzziest. **C/Pérez Galdós** is another good street for popular bars, with hordes of youthful *sevillanos* and *sevillanas* spilling out on to the pavement. The **Santa Cruz** quarter is equally vibrant, although you'll find more young foreigners here.

Antigüedes, C/Argote de Molina 40. Has books suspended, pages flapping, from the ceiling and a bizarre assortment of plastic limbs. Close to the cathedral, it gets packed out with a mix of young foreigners and locals.

Bar Berlín, C/Boteros 4. Loud, crammed and great fun.

Bilindo, Pso de las Delicias s/n, t 95 462 61 51; **Alfonso**, Avda de la Palmera s/n, t 95 423 37 35; **El Chile**, Pso de las Delicias s/n, t 95 423 56 59. All enormously popular in summer: drink and dance outdoors until dawn.

Café de la Prensa, C/Betis 8, t 95 433 34 20. A great place for a coffee or a cocktail, with a terrace overlooking the river. This is Triana's busiest street, with lots of bars and cafés.

Habanilla Café, Alameda de Hércules 63, t 95 490 27 16. Tiled bar and café full of arty, boho-chic *sevillanos*.

El Mundo o Otro Bar, C/Siete Revueltas 5, t 95 422 96 95. Trendy gay-friendly bar with tongue-in-cheek retro décor.

Utopia, C/Barco 1. Opened in 2006, with lots of slouching space attracting a mainly student crowd; music covering mainly rock and electronica.

Flamenco

If you've been longing to experience flamenco, Sevilla is a good place to do it. The most touristy flamenco factories will hit you for €10 and upwards per drink. Bars in Triana and other areas do it better for less; try C/Salado and environs in Triana, or across the river in the Santa Cruz quarter. The tourist office on Avenida de la Constitución has a noticeboard with details of shows.

Flamenco *Tablaos* (Shows)

These cost around €22–30 for the show plus a drink. Dinner will set you back around €55.

El Arenal, C/Rodo 7, t 95 421 64 92, *www.tablaoarenal.com*. Touristy, but the dancers and musicians are very accomplished. Shows at 8 and 10.30.

Los Gallos, Plaza de Santa Cruz s/n, *www.tablaolosgallos.com*. *Sevillanas* and flamenco dancing lit by the flashes of tourist cameras. Shows at 8 and 10.30pm.

El Palacio Andaluz, C/María Auxiliadora 18B, t 95 453 47 20, *www.elpalacioandaluz.com*. More formal, with a 1½hr show staged for tourists in an expensive restaurant. Shows at 7.30 and 10pm.

Flamenco Bars with Live Performances

La Carbonería, C/Levíes 18, t 95 422 99 45. Still one of the best venues in the city for extemporaneous performances of all styles. Live shows are Thursdays and some Sundays.

Lola de los Reyes, Avda Blas de Infante 6, t 95 427 75 76. Well off the beaten track, this is under an apartment block on the edge of Sevilla. Packed with locals who know all the words to the songs; Lola dances and belts out some spine-tingling flamenco.

El Simpecao, C/Castilla 82, t 95 446 22 07. A lively Triana bar; live flamenco at weekends.

El Tamboril, Plaza Santa Cruz s/n, t 95 456 15 90. Come here for *sevillanas* dancing – similar to flamenco but slightly less tortured and frenetic.

Music, Theatre and Opera

They do play other kinds of music in Sevilla, and the publications *El Giraldillo* and *Ocio*, available free in bars, cafés and hotels, have listings. The tourist office's free *Welcome Olé* also contains event listings.

For mainstream drama, the best-known theatre is the **Lope de Vega**

Theatre, found on Avenida María Luisa, t 95 459 08 67. The **Maestranza Theatre**, Paseo de Cristóbal Colón 22, t 95 422 33 44, *www.teatromaestranza. com*, is one of the top opera houses in Europe.

Bullfighting

See a bullfight in the famous **Maestranza** if you can, but don't just turn up! Get tickets far ahead. Prices at the box office, C/Adriano 37, t 95 422 35 06, will be cheaper than at the little stands on C/Sierpes.

Sevilla Province

Heading South

If you're travelling south on your way to Jerez or Cádiz, stops at a few towns on the way will make an interesting alternative to the big four-lane highway. **Alcalá de Guadaira**, off the N334, is jocularly known in Sevilla as Alcalá de los Panaderos ('of the bakers'), as it used to supply the city with its daily bread. Its **castle** is the best-preserved Almohad fortress in Andalucía.

Just outside Utrera, the tiny village of **Palmar de Troya** received a visit in 1968 from the Virgin Mary (to little girls, as usual), which led to the founding of a new church, the **Orden de la Santa Faz**, a vast complex of towers and pillars which can be seen for miles around. They have their own 'pope' in Palmar and include among their saints Franco, José Antonio and Ramón Llull.

Lebrija, near the Guadalquivir off the main road to Jerez, goes back to the civilization of Tartessos; some important finds from here now grace the museums of Sevilla and Madrid. The church of **Santa María de la Oliva** is really a 12th-century Almohad mosque, with a typical Middle Eastern roof of domes and a tower that is a miniature version of La Giralda, built in the 19th century. The main altarpiece is a work of Alonso Cano – but Lebrija is better known for its wine and ceramics, and as a lively centre of flamenco, with an annual festival called the Caracol.

Take care before you start any rambles in the countryside; this area south of Sevilla contains some of the best-known ranches where fighting bulls are bred, and the bulls run free.

Itálica
t 95 599 65 83; open Oct–Mar Tues–Sat 9–5.30, Sun 10–4; April–Sept Tues–Sat 8.30–8.30, Sun 10–4; adm, free to EU citizens

Itálica

Eight kilometres north of Sevilla, in the direction of Mérida, the only significant Roman ruins in Andalucía are at Itálica. The first Roman colony in Spain, this city was founded in the 3rd century BC by Scipio Africanus as a home for his veterans after their victory in the Punic Wars; a Tartessian town may have originally occupied the site. Itálica thrived in the imperial age. Three great emperors, Trajan, Hadrian and Theodosius, were born here, as were the poet Lucan and the moralist Seneca. The biggest ruins are an **amphitheatre**, with seating for 40,000, some remains of temples, and a street of villa foundations. The village of **Santiponce**, near the ruins, has a fine Gothic-*mudéjar* monastery built for the Cistercians in 1301, using surviving columns and other materials from the ruins. **San Isidoro del Campo** has a gruesome St Jerome on the altarpiece, carved in the 1600s by Juan Martínez Montañés (1566–1649), and has recently incorporated a gallery that includes several exceptional medieval frescoes.

From Sevilla to Córdoba

Carmona

The first town along the A4/E5, Carmona, seems like a miniature Sevilla. It may well be much older. Remains of a Neolithic settlement have been found around town; the Phoenician colony that replaced it grew into a city and prospered throughout Roman and Moorish times. Pedro the Cruel favoured it and rebuilt most of its Alcázar. Sitting proudly with views over the valley, this fortress is now a magnificent *parador*.

Getting around Sevilla Province

There are several **buses** daily from the Plaza de Armas bus station in Sevilla to **Santiponce** and the Roman ruins at **Itálica**. **Carmona**, **Écija** and **Marchena** are not on a train line, but they are all linked by regular **buses** from Sevilla (which depart from the Plaza de Armas bus station, *see* p.100). There are bus links between Carmona and Écija and two bus services a day from Carmona to Córdoba.

Osuna is on the **train** line between Sevilla and Málaga, with several services daily. It is also well connected by bus to Sevilla, Córdoba and Málaga.

If you are **driving**, the A4/E5 heads east to **Carmona** and **Écija**, while the A92 runs southeast to **Marchena** (turn left on to the A364), Osuna and **Estepa**.

Alcázar
t 95 414 08 11; open Tues–Sat 10–6, Sun 10–3; adm, free to EU citizens

Ayuntamiento
t 95 414 00 11; open Mon–Fri 8–3

Museo de la Ciudad
t 95 414 01 28, www. museociudad-carmona. org; open mid-June–Aug Mon–Fri 10–2 and 4.30–8.30pm, Sat–Sun 9.30–2; Sept–mid-June Mon 11–7, Wed–Sun 11–7; adm, free Tues in summer

Santa María
open April–mid-Aug Mon–Fri 9–2 and 5.30–7.30, Sat 9–2; mid-Sept–Mar Mon–Fri 9–2 and 5–7, Sat 9–2; closed mid-Aug–mid-Sept; adm

San Pedro
open Thurs–Mon 11–2; adm

Necropolis
t 95 414 08 11; open mid-June–mid-Sept Tues–Fri 9–2, Sat 10–2; mid-Sept–mid-June Tues–Fri 9–5, Sat 10–2; adm

Zoo
t 95 419 16 96, www.zoocarmona.com; open daily 11–9; adm

Carmona is well worth a day's exploration. Its walls, mostly Moorish fortifications built over Roman foundations, are still standing, including a grand gateway on the road from Sevilla, the **Puerta de Sevilla**, which now houses the tourist office. The upper levels form the remnants of the Almohad **Alcázar**, built upon Carthaginian and Roman ruins, and you can climb to the top of the **Torre del Oro** next to the Puerta de Sevilla (entrance through the tourist information office) for fantastic views. Continue through the arch and up to the palm-decked **Plaza de San Fernando**, where the under-16s and over-60s gather; the old **Ayuntamiento** here has a Roman mosaic of Medusa in its courtyard.

Nearby, the **Museo de la Ciudad** is the town's excellent and engaging history museum, housed in a 16th-century mansion. Set around a pair of pretty patios linked with winding staircases, the galleries are stacked full of thoughtful and well laid-out exhibits on the town's history over the last few thousand years. There's plenty for kids, with interactive exhibits clearly labelled in English and Spanish. Head up Calle Martín López to the lofty 15th-century church of **Santa María**, built on the site of an old mosque.

The old quarters of town have an ensemble of fine palaces, and *mudéjar* and Renaissance churches. On one of these, **San Pedro** (1466) (just outside the city walls by the Puerta de Sevilla), you'll see another imitation of La Giralda, La Giraldilla – though she has a cleaner exterior and is not as fussily ornate.

Carmona's prime attraction is the Roman **necropolis**, a series of rock-cut tombs off the Avenida Jorge Bonsor, a good 10-minute walk from the centre. Some, like the 'Tomb of Servilia', are elaborate creations with subterranean chambers and vestibules, pillars, domed ceilings and carved reliefs. Near the entrance to the site are the remains of the Roman **amphitheatre**, forlorn and unexcavated. There's a small **zoo** and conservation centre to the west of the town centre, which promotes the reintroduction of endangered species to their natural habitat.

Marchena and El Arahal

Twenty-eight kilometres south of Carmona, on the C339, the town of **Marchena** still retains many of its wall defences dating from Roman times, with later Moorish and Christian additions. Of its gates, the arch of **La Rosa** is best, and in the Torre del Oro there is an **archaeological museum**. The Gothic church of **San Juan Bautista** has a retable by Alejo Fernández and a sculpture by Pedro Roldán. There's also a small **museum** with a collection of paintings by Zurbarán. Nearby **El Arahal** is a bleached white town well worth visiting for its Baroque monuments, notably the church of **La Victoria**, of *mudéjar* origin.

Osuna and Estepa

From here, you can continue on the N333 back towards Écija and Córdoba, or take a detour eastwards on the N334 to **Osuna**. Founded by a busy, go-ahead governor named Julius Caesar, this was an important Roman military centre for the south of Spain, and survives as an attractive little city of white houses with characteristic *rejas* over every window. Osuna was an aristocratic town after the Reconquista, home of the objectionable Dukes of Osuna who lorded it over much of Andalucía. Their 'pantheon' of tombs may be seen in the fine Renaissance **Colegiata** church in Plaza de la Encarnación, on a hill on the west side of town. Inside is a memorable *Crucifixion* by José Ribera, and four other works of his in the high altar retable. Behind the church is the old university building, founded in 1548 and now serving as a school.

Several decorative façades of 16th-century mansions can be seen along the Calle San Pedro. Osuna has a little **archaeology museum** on Plaza de la Duquesa Invierno, in the Torre del Agua, part of the old fortifications, and a museum of dubious art in **La Encarnación** convent, a Baroque work of the late 18th century; the cloister is done out in ceramic tiles.

Back on the N334 you'll come to **Estepa**, a smaller version of Osuna known for its Christmas biscuits made with almonds (*polverones* and *mantecados*), and for the mass suicide of its inhabitants, who preferred not to surrender to the Roman enemy in 208 BC. Above the town are the remains of a **castle** with a well-preserved Almohad keep. The two Baroque showpieces are the churches of **El Carmen**, in the main square, with a spectacular façade, and the 18th-century **Virgen de los Remedios**.

Colegiata
t 95 181 04 44, open Oct–April 10.30–1.30 and 3.30–6.30; May–Sept 10–1.30 and 4–7, closed Sun afternoons in July and Aug; adm

Museo Arqueológico
t 95 481 12 07, open Tues–Sun Oct–April 11.30–1.30 and 4.30–6.30; May and Sept 11.30–13.30 and 5–7; June–Aug 10–2; adm

La Encarnación
open Oct–April 10.30–1.30 and 3.30–6.30; May–Sept 10–1.30 and 4–7, closed Sun afternoons in July and Aug; adm

Écija

Écija makes much of one of its nicknames, the 'city of towers', and tries to play down the other – the 'frying pan of Andalucía', which isn't exactly fair; any Andalucian town can overheat you thoroughly on a typical summer's day, and only a born Andalucian could tell the difference.

Nowadays you'll be put off by the clinical outskirts of the town and by the ill-concealed gasholders; all was once forgiven when you reached the **Plaza de España**, which was one of the loveliest in Andalucía, charmingly framed by tall palms with an exquisite fountain at its centre (now in safe-keeping). However, the local council decided to dig it all up in order to construct an underground car park beneath – only to discover an extensive Muslim burial ground dating from the 12th century, and impressive Roman baths complete with sculptures. At the time of research, the rebuilding of the *plaza* was near completion with some parking incorporated and much of the excavated site on display to the public. Many of the artefacts discovered have been moved to the nearby Museo Histórico Municipal (*see* below).

The **Ayuntamiento** stands at one end of the square and, if you ask politely, you may be able to look at a Roman mosaic in the council chamber, lovingly described by Laurie Lee in *A Rose For Winter*. On the top floor, a **camera obscura** offers a wonderful 360-degree view of Écija's lovely, tower-spiked skyline.

Camera Obscura
open daily 10.30–1.30; adm

The façade of the 18th-century **Santa María** wouldn't look out of place in a Sergio Leone movie. Most of the towers are sumptuously ornate, rebuilt after the great earthquake of 1755 – the one that flattened Lisbon. Santa María has one, along with **San Juan Bautista**, gaily decorated in coloured tiles, and **San Gil**. This last is the highest of the towers, and within are paintings by Alejo Fernández and Villegas Marmolejo.

Santa María/San Juan Bautista/ San Gil
open 10–1; free

Écija also has a set of Renaissance and Baroque palaces second in Andalucía only to those in Úbeda; most of these showy façades can be seen on or near the Calle Emilio Castellar. Worth visiting is the **Palacio de Benamejí**, dating from the 18th century, which houses the tourist office and the **Museo Histórico Municipal**, where you can find some interesting archaeological remains, part *mudéjar*, part Baroque, plus some Roman mosaics, and various reliefs, coins and glass. The **Peñaflor Palace** (1728) in Calle de Castellar – currently being converted into a four-star hotel – is one of the outstanding works of Andalucían Baroque, with its grandiose façade and lovely patio. In the evening the town buzzes. After the big-city crush of Sevilla, you might find that this is the perfect place to spend a couple of days – busy enough to be interesting, but not too frantic.

Museo Histórico Municipal
open June–Sept Tues–Sun 9–2; Oct–May Tues–Fri 9.30–1.30 and 4.30–6.30, Sat–Sun 9–2

Where to Stay and Eat in Sevilla Province

ⓘ **Carmona ›**
Oficina Municipal de Turismo, Alcázar de la Puerta de Sevilla s/n, t 95 419 09 55, www. turismo.carmona.org; open Mon–Sat 10–6, Sun 10–3

Carmona ✉ 39554

There are several *casas rurales* near Carmona; ask at the tourist office.

*****Casa de Carmona**, Plaza de Lasso 1, t 95 419 10 00, *www.casadecarmona. com* (€€€€). Lovingly restored by Marta Medina and her artist son Felipe, this 16th-century palace is the last word in refined good taste.

****Hotel Alcázar de la Reina**, Plaza de Lasso 2, t 95 419 62 00, *www. alcazar-reina.es* (€€€). A modern hotel built behind a beautiful old façade, with one of the best restaurants in town, **La Ferrara** (*see* overleaf). Great facilities including a pool.

⊛ **Parador Alcázar del Rey Don** ⟩

ⓘ **Osuna** ⟩⟩
*Casa de la Cultura,
Plaza Mayor s/n,
t 95 481 57 32,
www.ayto-osuna.org;
open 10–2 and 5–7*

ⓘ **Estepa** ⟩⟩
*Plaza del Carmen 1,
t 95 591 27 71, www.
estepa.com; open
Mon–Fri 9–2 and 3–10*

ⓘ **Écija** ⟩⟩
*Ayuntamiento, Plaza
de España 1, t 95 590 29
33, www.ecija.es; open
July–Aug Mon–Fri
9.30–2, Sat–Sun
10.30–1.30; May–June
and Sept–Oct Mon–Fri
9.30–3, Sat–Sun
10.30–1.30*

ⓘ **Marchena** ⟩
*C/Las Torres 48, t 95
484 61 67, www.
ayto-marchena.com*

****Parador Alcázar del Rey Don
Pedro**, Argollón s/n, **t** 95 414 10 10,
www.parador.es (€€€). In a section of
Cruel Pete's summer palace, the finest
in Andalucía for style and comfort. It
has superlative views, a garden, pool
and luxurious furnishings; good value.

***Pensión Comercio**, C/Torre del Oro,
t 95 414 00 18 (€€). One of the few
pensiones in town; a typical whitewashed house with a tiled patio.

La Ferrara, Plaza de Lasso 2, **t** 95 419 62
00, *www.alcazar-reina.es* (€€). In the
Alcázar de la Reina, with an unusual
combination of Italian trattoria food
and fine traditional Andaluz cuisine.

Molino de la Romera, C/Sor Angelá de
la Cruz, **t** 95 414 20 00 (€€). Just down
from the *parador* and set in a historic
15th-century former oil mill, which can
be visited separately. Offers superb
food and some of the best views in
town. Specializes in local meats.

San Fernando, Plaza San Fernando,
t 95 414 35 56 (€€). This elegant
restaurant has the best reputation in
town, and is set in a handsome 16th-
century palace. Try the seasonal game
dishes, which are outstanding. *Closed
Sun eve, Mon and Aug.*

Mesón La Cueva, Barbacana Baja 2,
t 95 419 18 11 (€). Situated just below
the city walls, these whitewashed
caves have a heavy emphasis on pork
and an extensive vegetable menu.

Bar Plaza, Plaza San Fernando, **t** 95 419
00 67 (€). A popular restaurant with
locals, serving solid traditional dishes
and a reasonably priced *menu del día*
(€9). *Closed Mon eve and Aug.*

Marchena ✉ 39554

****Hostal Los Ángeles**, on the Ctra
Sevilla–Málaga, Km 67, **t** 95 484 70 88
(€). Basic roadside hotel with a
popular restaurant.

****Ponce**, Plaza Alvarado 2, **t** 95 484 31
80 (€). The only central accommodation, this simple *pensión* has basic
rooms with or without bathrooms.

Casa Carrillo, C/Las Torres 39, **t** 95 481
31 98, *www.casacarrillo.com* (€). A
classic eating place in Marchena, with
excellent tapas and creative local
dishes in the *comedor*.

Los Muleros, Travesía de San Ignacio,
t 95 484 31 99 (€). Try local specialities.

Osuna and Estepa ✉ 41640

****Palacio Marqués de la Gomera**,
C/San Pedro 20, Osuna, **t** 95 481 22 23,
www.hotelpalaciodelmarques.com
(€€€). A beautiful conversion of one of
the town's more impressive Baroque
mansions, with an arcaded central
courtyard. There is a good restaurant:
traditional Mediterranean cooking.

***Hotel Manantial de Roya**, Paseo
Manantial de Roya s/n, Estepa, **t** 95 591
57 80, *www.complejomanantialderoya.
com* (€€). This modern hotel has
excellent facilities (including a
swimming pool); good value.

Caballo Blanco, C/Granada 1, Osuna,
t 95 481 01 84 (€€). Centrally located
former coaching inn, with a
restaurant and garage.

****El Balcón de Andalucía**, Avda
Andalucía 11, Estepa, **t** 95 591 26 80 (€).
The best of a handful of *hostales* in
Estepa, with a pool and garden.

Doña Guadalupe, C/Plaza Guadalupe,
Osuna, **t** 95 481 05 58 (€€). A very good
reputation and great home-made
desserts. *Closed Tues and 1–15 Aug.*

Écija ✉ 41400

****Palacio de los Granados**, C/Emilio
Castelar 42, **t** 95 590 53 44, *www.
palaciogranados.com* (€€€). A lovely
boutique hotel in a restored Baroque
palace; patios, a pool, and the Condé
Nast 'excellent service' award in 2007.

****Hotel Platería**, C/Platería 4, **t** 95 590
27 54, *www.hotelplateria.com* (€€).
Just off the main square, with a lovely
marble courtyard and restaurant.

****Hotel Sol Pirula**, Avda Miguel de
Cervantes 50, **t** 95 483 03 00, *www.
hotelpirula.com* (€€). A friendly hotel
with air-conditioned rooms, a garage
and a decent restaurant, **Casa Pirula**.

Las Ninfas, Palacio de Benamejí,
C/Cánovas del Castillo 4, **t** 95 590 45
92 (€€). The setting is stylish and
subtle, the food light.

Bodegón del Gallego, C/Arcipreste
Aparicio 3, **t** 95 483 26 18 (€€). Stylish
andaluz dishes.

El Bisturí, Plaza de España 23, **t** 95 483
10 66 (€). On the main *plaza* and
specializing in food from across Spain.

Bar La Reja, C/Garcilópez 1, **t** 95 483 30
12. A friendly local bar with a cosy
atmosphere and excellent tapas.

Córdoba
and Jaén

The Río Guadalquivir was al-Andalus's great highway, lined with tall water wheels and prosperous farms, while its barges carried the luxuries of the East up to the caliphs and their court.

For all the noise on the costas, this valley remains the heart of the real Andalucía. Right in the centre of it lies a marvel, Córdoba, a citadel of pure Andalucian duende that guards at its heart one of the most fascinating buildings on the planet.

10

Don't miss

See map overleaf

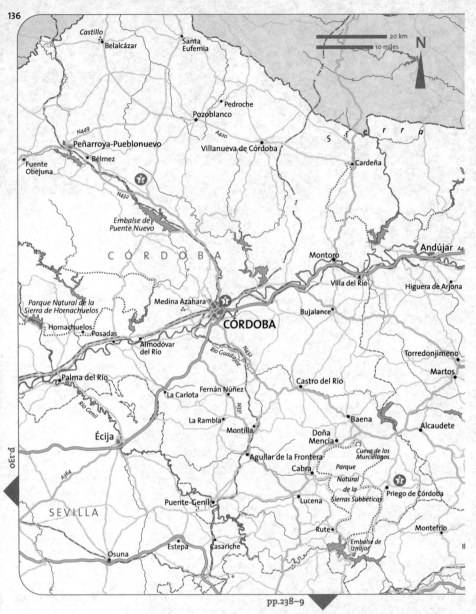

North of Córdoba is the Sierra Morena, famous for good hunting and cured hams, as well as Belalcázar with its remarkable castle. To the south it's mostly endless rows of olive trees. To the east, it's a slow, leisurely journey up the valley of the slow, leisurely Río Guadalquivir, passing a few million more olive trees and, in places, endless miles of sunflowers, a grand sight in the early summer. The main attractions are two lovely, out-of-the-way towns with exceptional ensembles of Renaissance architecture: Baeza and

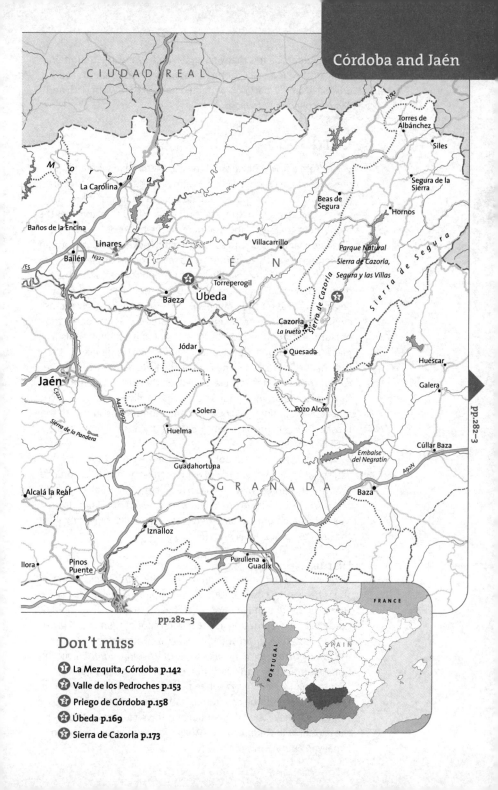

CIUDAD REAL

Torres de
Albánchez

Siles

M o r e n a

La Carolina

Segura de la
Sierra

Beas de
Segura

Baños de la Encina

Hornos

Linares

Villacarrillo

Parque Natural
Sierra de Cazorla,
Segura y las Villas

J A É N

Bailén N322

Torreperogil

Baeza   Úbeda

Sierra de Cazorla

Sierra de Segura

Cazorla
La Irueta

Jódar

Quesada

Huéscar

Jaén

Galera

Solera

Pozo Alcón

Sierra de la Pandera

Huelma

Embalse
del Negratín

Cúllar Baza

Guadahortuna

G R A N A D A

Baza

Alcalá la Real

A92N

Iznalloz

Purullena
Guadix

llora   Pinos
Puente

pp.282–3

pp.282–3

FRANCE

PORTUGAL   SPAIN

Don't miss

Úbeda. Andalucía has many natural wonders, but the mountain range of the Sierra de Cazorla is among the most beautiful and unspoiled, and is part of a protected natural park with a rich and diverse collection of wildlife.

Córdoba

There are a few spots around the Mediterranean where the presence of past glories becomes almost tangible, a mixture of mythic antiquity, lost power and dissipated energy that broods over a place like a ghost. In Istanbul you can find it, in Rome, or the monuments of Egypt, and also here on the banks of the Guadalquivir at Córdoba's southern gate. Looking around, you can see reminders of three defunct empires: a Roman bridge, a triumphal arch built for Philip II, and Córdoba's Great Mosque, more than a thousand years old. The first reminds us of the city's beginnings, the second of its decline; the last one scarcely seems credible, as it speaks of an age when Córdoba was one of the most brilliant metropolises of all Europe, city of half a million souls, a place faraway storytellers would use to enthral audiences in the rude halls of the Saxons and Franks. The little plaza by the bridge concentrates melancholy like a magnet; there isn't much left for the rest of the town. Córdoba's growth has allowed it a chance to renovate its sparkling old quarters and monuments, and with the prosperity has come a contentment the city hasn't known since the Reconquista.

Everyone who visits Córdoba comes for the Great Mosque, but you should spare some time to explore the city itself. Old Córdoba is one of the largest medieval quarters of any European city, and certainly the biggest in Spain. More than Sevilla, it retains its Moorish character, in a maze of whitewashed alleys opening into the loveliest patios in all Andalucía.

History

Roman Corduba, built on a prehistoric site, was almost from the start the leading city of interior Spain, capital of the province of Hispania Ulterior and later of the reorganized province of Baetica. Córdoba had a reputation as the garden spot of Hispania; it gave Roman literature Lucan and both Senecas, among others, testimony to its prominence as a city of learning. Córdoba became Christianized at an early date. Ironically, the True Faith got its come-uppance here in 572, when the Arian Visigoths under Leovigild captured the city from Byzantine rule. When the Arabs conquered, they found it an important town still, and it became the capital of al-Andalus when Abd ar-Rahman established the Umayyad emirate in 756.

Getting to and around Córdoba

By Train

Córdoba is on the major Madrid–Sevilla **railway** line, so there are about 12 trains a day in both directions run by AVE, with a journey time of 45mins from Sevilla and 1hr 40mins from Madrid. Slower regional trains take twice as long from Sevilla, but cost about a third of the price of the plush AVE. There are also frequent Talgo services to Málaga (about 2hrs 15mins), Cádiz, Valencia and Barcelona, and regular trains to Huelva, Algeciras and Alicante. There are no direct trains for Granada: buses are more convenient.

Córdoba's **train station** is on the Glorieta Tres Culturas, off Avenida de América, 1.6km north of La Mezquita. Numerous buses link the station with the city centre, and there is also a taxi rank.

By Bus

The main **bus station** is just behind the train station, on the Glorieta Tres Culturas. There are regular services with **Alsina Graells** (t 90 233 04 00, *www.continental-auto.es*) to Sevilla (at least three daily), Granada, Cádiz and Málaga and most nearby towns. Buses also go long-distance, to Madrid (one daily), Valencia (three daily) and Barcelona (two daily): for general **bus information** call t 95 740 40 40. The train is probably a better bet for Sevilla and Málaga.

The Córdoba **city bus** network is complicated, so it's best to check with the tourist information office about times and departure points. Otherwise, call the bus information line (*see* above).

If you want to go to **Medina Azahara** and don't have your own transport, it's best to take a **guided tour** (information at the tourist office), as local buses will leave you a good 2km from the site.

For 300 years, Córdoba enjoyed the position of unqualified leader of al-Andalus. It is impossible to take the chronicles at face value – 3,000 mosques, 80,000 shops and a library of 400,000 volumes in a city stretching for 16km along the banks of the Guadalquivir. We could settle for half these totals and still be impressed. Beyond doubt, Córdoba was a city without equal in the West as a centre of learning. It would be enough to mention two 12th-century contemporaries: Averroës, the Muslim scientist and Aristotelian philosopher who contributed so much to the rebirth of classical learning in Europe, and Moses Maimónides, the Jewish philosopher (and later personal physician to Saladin in Palestine) whose reconciliation of faith and reason were assumed into Christianity by St Thomas Aquinas. Medieval Córdoba was a great trading centre, and its luxury goods were coveted throughout western Europe (the old word *cordwainer* is a memory of Córdoba's skill in leatherwork). At its height, Córdoba would be pictured as a city of bustling international markets, great palaces, schools, baths and mosques, with 28 suburbs and the first street lighting in Europe. Its population, largely Spanish, Moorish and Arab, included students and merchants from all over Europe, Africa and Asia, and an army and palace secretariat made up largely of slaves and black Africans. We can sense a certain decadence; in it Muslims, Christians and Jews lived in harmony, at least until the coming of the fanatical Almoravids and Almohads. Riots in Córdoba were an immediate cause of the break-up of the caliphate in 1031, but here, as in Sevilla, the coming of the Reconquista was an unparalleled catastrophe.

When Fernando III ('the Saint') captured the city in 1236, much of the population chose flight over putting themselves at the mercy

Córdoba

GLORIETA
PRETORIO

SANTA MARIA DE TRASIERRA

GTA.
MARGARITAS

Bus Station

RENFE
Train
Station

AVENIDA DE AMÉRICA

Convento
de Merced/
Diputación
de Córdoba

AVDA GRAN CAPITÁN

AV. RONDA TEJARES

Jardines
de La
Agricultura

AV. CERVANTES

C. JOSÉ CRUZ CONDE

To Medina
Azahara

AVENIDA MEDINA AZAHARA

AV. GRAN CAPITÁN

AVENIDA REPÚBLICA ARGENTINA

C. CONCEPCIÓN

C. DE GONDOMAR

PZA LAS
TENDILLAS

San Nicolás

PÉREZ DE CASTRO

C. DE SEVILLA

C. JESÚS MARIA

AV. GRAN

Plaza de
Toros

PZA COSTA
DEL SOL

CALLE DE ANTONIO MAURA

PASEO DE LA VICTORIA

LOPE DE HOCES

C. BARROSA

VIA PARQUE

Almodóvar
Gate

F. RUANO

C. ALMANZOR

Casa del
Indiano

C. BUEN ASTOR

B. BÉLMONTE

Casa
Museo
Arte Sobre
Piel

PLAZA
BENAVENTE

Synagogue

Casa de
Sefarad

Museo
Taurino

AV. DOCTOR FLEMING

PLAZA
JUDÁ LEVÍ

La
Mezquita

C. DE TORRIJOS

C. CORRE

AVENIDA DEL AEROPUERTO

AV. CONDE DE VALLELLANO

AMADOR DE LOS RÍOS

Triunfo

Water wheel

Alcázar de los
Reyes Cristianos

AVENIDA DEL ALCÁZAR

N

AV. CORREGIOR

Moorish
Walls
(ruins)

500 metres
500 yards

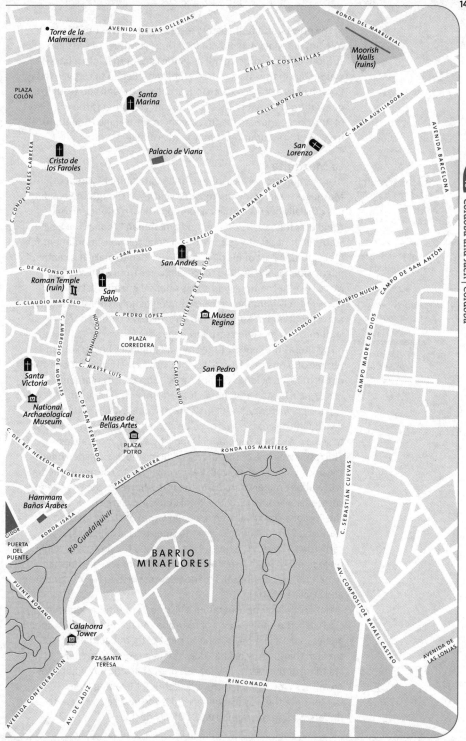

of the priests, although history records that he was unusually tolerant of the Jews. It did not last. Three centuries of Castilian rule sufficed to rob Córdoba of all its glories and turn it into a backwater. Only in the last hundred years has it begun to recover; today, Córdoba has also become an industrial city, though you wouldn't guess it from its sympathetically restored centre. It is the third city of Andalucía, and was the first big town since Franco's death to have elected a Communist mayor and council.

La Mezquita

La Mezquita
ticket booth on the Patio de los Naranjos, t 95 747 05 12; open Mar–Oct Mon–Sat 10–7, Sun 2–7; Feb and Nov Mon–Sat 10–6.30, Sun 2–6.30; Jan and Dec Mon–Sat 10–5.30, Sun 2–5.30; adm; you can enter free between 8.30 and 10am, but must remain silent;
Museo Diocesano
open Mon–Sat 9.30–3; free with adm to Mezquita

La Mezquita is the local name for Abd ar-Rahman's **Great Mosque**. Mezquita means 'mosque' and, even though the building has officially been a cathedral for more than 750 years, no one could ever mistake its origins. **Abd ar-Rahman I**, founder of a new state, felt it necessary to construct a great religious monument for his capital. As part of his plan, he also wished to make it a centre of pilgrimage to increase the sense of divorce from eastern Islam; Mecca was at the time held by his Abbasid enemies. Islam was never entirely immune to the exaltation of holy relics, and there is a story that Abd ar-Rahman had an arm of Mohammed to legitimize his mosque as a pilgrimage site.

The site, at the centre of the city, had originally held a Roman temple of Janus, and later a Visigothic church. Only about one-third of the mosque belongs to the original. Successive enlargements were made by Abd ar-Rahman II, al-Hakim and al-Mansur. Expansion was easy: the plan of the mosque is a simple rectangle, divided into aisles by rows of columns, and its size was increased to serve a growing population simply by adding more aisles. The result was one of the largest of all mosques, exceeded only by the one in Mecca. After 1236 it was converted to use as a cathedral without any major changes. In the 1520s, however, the city's clerics succeeded in convincing the Royal Council, over the opposition of the Córdoba city government, to allow the construction of a choir and high altar, enclosed structures typical of Spanish cathedrals. Charles V, who had also opposed the project, strongly reproached them for the desecration when he saw the finished work – though he himself had done even worse to the Alhambra and Sevilla's Alcázar.

Most people come away from a visit to La Mezquita somewhat confused. The endless rows of columns and red-and-white striped arches make a picture familiar to most of us, but actually, to see them in this gloomy old hall does not increase one's understanding of the work. They make a pretty pattern, but what does it mean? It's worth going into some detail, for learning to see La Mezquita the way its builders did is the best key we have to understanding the refined world of al-Andalus.

Before entering, take a few minutes to circumnavigate this massive, somewhat forbidding pile of bricks. Spaced around its 685 metres (2,050ft) of wall are the original entrances and windows, excellent examples of Moorish art. Those on the western side are the best, from the time of al-Mansur: interlaced Visigothic horseshoe arches, floral decorations in the Roman tradition, and Islamic calligraphy and patterns, a lesson in the varied sources of this art. The only entrance to the mosque today is the **Puerta del Perdón**, a fine *mudéjar* gateway added in 1377, opening on to the **Patio de los Naranjos**, the original mosque courtyard, planted with orange trees, where the old Moorish fountain can still be seen. Built into the wall of the courtyard, over the gate, the original minaret – a legendary tower said to be the model for all the others in al-Andalus – has been replaced by an ill-proportioned 16th-century bell tower. From the courtyard, the mosque is entered through a little door, the **Puerta de las Palmas**. Inside, it's as chilly as Sevilla cathedral.

Now here is the first surprise. The building is gloomy only because the Spanish clerics wanted it that way. Originally there was no wall separating the mosque from the courtyard, and that side of the mosque was entirely open. In the **courtyard**, trees were planted to continue the rows of columns, translating inside to outside in a remarkable *tour de force* that has rarely been equalled in architecture. To add to the effect, the entrances along the other three walls would have been open to the surrounding busy markets and streets. It isn't just a trick of architecture, but a way of relating a holy building to the life of the city around it. In the Middle East, there are many medieval mosques built on the same plan as this one; the pattern originated with the first Arabian mosques, and later in the Umayyad Mosque of Damascus, one of the first great shrines of Islam. In Turkey they call them 'forest' mosques, and the townspeople use them like indoor parks, places to sit and reflect or talk over everyday affairs. In medieval Christian cathedrals, whose doors were always open, it was much the same. The sacred and the secular become blurred, or rather, the latter is elevated to a higher plane. In Córdoba, this principle is perfected.

In the aesthetics of this mosque, too, there is more than meets the eye. Many European writers have seen it as devoid of spirituality, a plain prayer-hall with pretty arches. To the Christian mind it is difficult to comprehend. Christian churches are modelled after the Roman basilica, a government hall, a seat of authority with a long central aisle designed to humble the suppliant as he approaches the praetor's throne (altar). Mosques are designed with great care to free the mind from such behaviour patterns. In this one, the guiding principle is a rarefied abstraction – the same kind of abstraction that governs Islamic geometric decoration. The repetition of columns is like a meditation in stone, a mirror of Creation where unity and harmony radiate from innumerable centres. Another contrast with Christian churches can be found in an obscure matter – the distribution of weight. The Gothic masters of the Middle Ages learned to pile stone up from great piers and buttresses to amazing heights, to build an edifice that aspires towards heaven. Córdoba's architects amplified the height of their mosque only modestly by a daring invention – adding a second tier of arches on top of the first. They had to, constrained as they were by the short columns they were recycling from Roman buildings, but the result was to make an 'upside-down' building, where weight increases the higher it goes, a play of equilibrium that adds to the mosque's effect. There are about 580 of these columns, mostly from Roman ruins and Visigothic churches the Muslims pulled down. Originally, legend credits La Mezquita with a thousand. Some came from as far as Constantinople, a present from the emperors. The same variety can be seen in the capitals – Roman, Visigothic, Moorish and a few mysteries.

The *Mihrab* and Later Additions

The surviving jewel of the mosque is its *mihrab*, an octagonal chamber set into the wall and covered by a beautiful dome of interlocking arches, added in the 10th century under al-Hakim II. A Byzantine emperor, Nikephoros Phokas, sent artists to help with its mosaic decoration, and a few tons of enamel chips and coloured glass cubes for them to work with. That these two states should have had such warm relations isn't that surprising; in those days, any enemy of the pope and the western Christian states was a friend of Constantinople. Though the *mihrab* is no longer at the centre of La Mezquita, it was at the time of al-Hakim II; the aisle extending from it was the axis of the original mosque.

Treasury
adm included in entrance ticket

Next to the *mihrab* is the Treasury, a fanciful Baroque chamber with a lofty dome which contains some of the cathedral's treasures, including a vast 16th-century silver monstrance, some gaudy Baroque ecclesiastical plate, and a pair of elaborate reliquaries. On the other side of the *mihrab*, the tiny **Museo Visigodo de San Vicente** is tucked away in the corner of the Mezquita and displays a small collection of 6th- and 7th-century capitals and inscriptions from the Visigothic basilica that formerly occupied the site. Near the main entrance by the Puerta de las Palmas, an opening in the floor looks down on to **Roman ruins** which predate the Visiogothic church and include fragments of a mosaic.

Looking back from the *mihrab*, you will see what once was the exterior wall, built in Abd ar-Rahman II's extension, from the year 848. Its gates, protected indoors, are as good as those on the west façade and better preserved. Near the *mihrab* is the **Capilla de**

Villaviciosa, a Christian addition of 1377 with fancy convoluted *mudéjar* arches that almost succeed in upstaging the Moorish work. Behind it is a small chapel, the **Capilla Real**, usually closed off. Fortunately, you can see most of it above the barriers; its exuberant stucco and *azulejo* decoration are among the greatest works of *mudéjar* art. Built in the 14th century as a funeral chapel for Fernando IV and Alfonso XI of Castile, it is contemporary with the Alhambra and shows some influence of the styles developing in Granada. Far more serious intrusions are the 16th-century **Coro** (choir) and **Capilla Mayor** (high altar). Not unlovely in themselves, they would not offend anywhere but here. Luckily, La Mezquita is so large that from many parts of it you won't even notice them. Begun in 1523, the Plateresque Coro was substantially altered in the 18th century, with additional stucco decoration, as well as a set of Baroque choir stalls by Pedro Duque Cornejo. Between the Coro and Capilla Mayor is the **tomb of Leopold of Austria**, Bishop of Córdoba at the time the works were completed (and, interestingly, Charles V's uncle). For the rest of the Christian contribution, dozens of locked, mouldering chapels line the outer walls of the mosque. Never comfortable as a Christian building, today the cathedral seems to be hardly used at all, and regular Sunday masses are generally relegated to a small corner of the building.

Around La Mezquita

The masses of tatty souvenir stands and third-rate cafés that surround La Mezquita on its busiest days unwittingly recreate the atmosphere of the Moorish souks that once thrived here, but walk a block in any direction and you'll enter the essential Córdoba – brilliant whitewashed lanes with glimpses into dreamily beautiful patios, each one a floral extravaganza. One of the best is a famous little alley called **Calle de las Flores** ('Street of the Flowers'), just a block northeast of La Mezquita, although sadly its charms are diminished by the hordes of visitors who flock to see it.

Below La Mezquita, along the Guadalquivir, the melancholic plaza called **Puerta del Puente** marks the site of Córdoba's southern gate with a decorative **arch** put up in 1571, celebrating the reign of Philip II. The very curious Churrigueresque monument next to it, with a statue of San Rafael (the Archangel Raphael), is called the **Triunfo** (1651). Wild Baroque confections such as this are common in Naples and southern Italy (under Spanish rule at the time); there they are called *guglie*. Behind the plaza, standing across from La Mezquita, is the **Archbishop's Palace**, built on the site of the original Alcázar, the palace of Abd ar-Rahman.

The **Roman bridge** over the Guadalquivir probably isn't Roman at all any more; it has been patched and repaired so often that practically nothing remains of the Roman work. Another statue of

Calahorra Tower
*www.torrelacalahorra.
com; open May–Sept
daily 10–2 and 4.30–
8.30; Oct–April daily
10–6; virtual reality tours
summer 10.30, 11.30,
12.30, 5, 6, and 7; winter
11, 12, 3 and 4; adm*

**Alcázar de los
Reyes Cristianos**
*open Tues–Sat 10–2
and 5.30–7.30, Sun and
hols 9.30–3; summer
10–2 only; adm*

Baños Califales
*open Tues–Sat 10–2
and 5.30–7.30, Sun
9.30–2.30; adm*

Parque Zoológico
open daily 9–7; adm

Synagogue
*t 95 720 29 28; open
Tues–Sat 10–2 and
3.30–5.30; Sun
9.30–1.30; adm, free to
EU citizens*

Raphael can be seen in the middle – probably replacing an old Roman image of Jupiter or Mercury. The stern-looking **Calahorra Tower** (Torre de la Calahorra), built in 1369 over Moorish foundations, once guarded the southern approaches of the bridge and has been in its time a girls' school and a prison; now it contains a gimmicky museum, with a hi-tech multivision spectacle where you are asked to strap on infra-red headphones for a virtual reality tour through the city's history.

Just to the west, along the river, Córdoba's **Alcázar de los Reyes Cristianos** was rebuilt in the 14th century and used for 300 years by the officers of the Inquisition. There's little to see as it's now mainly used for official functions, but you can potter about the remnants of the Baños Reales (Royal Baths) with their star-shaped roof openings and admire a series of Roman mosaics in the Salón de los Mosaicos. There are wonderful views of La Mezquita and the town from the belvedere atop the walls. The scented gardens are peaceful and lovely, an Andalucian amenity much like those in Sevilla's Alcázar. The gigantic stone figures of Columbus and the Catholic Kings are impressive. On the river's edge you'll see an ancient water wheel; at least some of the Moors' talent for putting water to good use was retained for a while after the Reconquista. This is the mill that disturbed Isabel's dreams when she stayed at the Alcázar; it was rebuilt only in the early 1900s.

Just around the corner from the Alcázar, on Avenida Doctor Fleming, are the **Baños Califales**. This vast, elaborately decorated bath complex was probably built in the 10th century. The finest surviving decoration is to be found in the marble-columned Sala Templada, where the caliph would soak under stellar skylights.

If you continue walking along the Guadalquivir, after about a kilometre you'll come to **Parque Cruz Conde** and the **Parque Zoológico**, a small zoo set in gardens with about 200 species including elephants, tigers, llamas and reptiles.

The Judería

As in Sevilla, Córdoba's ancient Jewish quarter has recently become a fashionable area, a nest of tiny streets between La Mezquita and Avenida Dr Fleming. Part of the Moorish walls can be seen along this street, and the northern entrance of the Judería is the old **Almodóvar gate**. The streets are tricky, and it will take some effort to find Calle Maimónides and the 14th-century **synagogue**, after which you will find yourself repeatedly back at this spot, whether or not you want to be there. The diminutive Córdoban synagogue is one of the two oldest and most interesting Jewish monuments in Spain (the other is the Tránsito in Toledo). Set back from the street in a tiny courtyard, it was built in the Granadine style of the early 14th century and, according to Amador de los Ríos,

How lovely is Thy dwelling-place O Lord of Hosts! My soul grows weak and longs for Thy courtyards.

Hebrew inscription on synagogue wall

dates from 1315. After the expulsion, it was used as a hospital for hydrophobes, and later became the headquarters of the cobblers' guild. There is an interesting plaster-work frieze of Alhambra-style arabesques and Hebrew inscriptions. The recess for the Ark (which contained the holy scrolls) is clearly visible, and the ladies' gallery still intact. Despite few obvious signs of the synagogue's original function, its atmosphere is still charged; it is somehow easy to imagine this small sanctum as a focus of medieval Jewry's Golden Age, a centre of prayer and scholarship spreading religious and moral enlightenment. While modern Córdoba has no active Jewish community, several *marrano* families live in the city and can trace their ancestry to the pre-expulsion age. Some have opened shops in the Judería selling 'Judaica', which ranges from tacky trinkets and tapes of Israeli folk songs to beautiful Jewish artefacts worked from Córdoban silver. You'll find several in the **Zoco**, a little souk-style courtyard opposite the synagogue.

Casa de Sefarad
t 95 742 14 04, www. casadesefarad.com; open Mon–Sat 11–7, Sun 11–2; adm

Casa Museo Arte Sobre Piel
t 95 705 01 31, www. artesobrepiel.com; open Tues–Sun 10.30–2 and 4–8

Museo Municipal de Arte Cordobés y Taurino
t 95 720 10 56; open Sept–June Tues–Sat 10–2 and 4.30–6.30 (5.30–7.30 winter), Sun 9.30–2.30; July–Aug Mon–Sat 8.30–2.30, Sun 9.30–2.30; adm

A couple of streets east from the synagogue, the **Casa de Sefarad** on C/Averroes opened in 2007 and has a permanent exhibition about the Sephardic community in Córdoba, spread over five thematic rooms. A second new museum to open in this area is the **Casa Museo Arte Sobre Piel**, on Plaza de Agrupación de Cofradías, which exhibits intricate and quite beautiful leather-decorated and embossed wall hangings and *objets d'art*.

In Calle Ruano, the 15th-century **Casa del Indiano** is a palace with an eccentric façade. On Plaza Maimónides is the **Museo Municipal de Arte Cordobés y Taurino** with its beautiful courtyard – not surprisingly, it's a museum dedicated to the bullfights. Manolete and El Cordobés are the city's two recent contributions to Spanish culture; here you can see a replica of Manolete's sarcophagus, the furniture from his home and the hide of Islero, the bull that did him in, along with more bullfight memorabilia than you ever thought existed. The Art Nouveau posters are beautiful, and among the old prints you can pay homage to the memory of the taurine malcontent Moñudo, who ignored the *toreros* and went up into the stands after the audience.

White Neighbourhoods

From the mosque you can walk eastwards through well over a mile of twisting white alleys, a place where the best map in the world wouldn't keep you from getting lost and staying lost. Though it all looks much the same, it's never monotonous. Every little square, fountain or church stands out boldly, and forces you to look at it in a different way from how you would look at a modern city – another lesson in the Moorish aesthetic. These streets have probably changed little since 1236, but their best buildings are a series of **Gothic churches** built soon after the

Reconquista. Though small and plain, most are exquisite in a quiet way. Few have any of the usual Gothic sculptural work on their façades, to avoid offending a people accustomed to Islam's prohibition of images. The lack of decoration somehow adds to their charm. There are a score of these around Córdoba, and nothing like them elsewhere in the south of Spain. **San Lorenzo**, on C/María Auxiliadora, is perhaps the best, with a rose window designed in a Moorish motif of interlocking circles. Some 15th-century frescoes survive around the altar and on the apse. **San Pablo** (1241), on the street of the same name, is early Gothic (five years after the Christian conquest) but contains a fine *mudéjar* dome and ceiling. Others include **San Andrés**, on C/Varela, two streets east of San Pablo, **Santa Marina** on C/Morales, and the **Cristo de los Faroles** on the Plaza Capuchinos, with a strange and much-venerated statue of Christ of the Lanterns outside. Have a look inside any you find open; most have some Moorish decoration or sculptural work in their interiors, and many of their towers (like San Lorenzo's) were originally minarets. **San Pedro**, off Calle Alfonso XII, was the Christian cathedral under Moorish rule, largely rebuilt in the 1500s. Just east of San Pedro you can duck into the Museo Regina, Plaza D. Luis Venegas, an impressive jewellery museum plus a workshop and gift store where you can pick up a trinket or two.

Museo Regina
t 95 749 68 89, www.
museoregina.com; adm

The neighbourhoods have other surprises, if you have the persistence to find them. **Santa Victoria** is a huge austere Baroque church on Calle Juan Valera, modelled after the Roman Pantheon.

Nearby, on Plaza Jerónimo Páez, a fine 16th-century palace houses the National Archaeological Museum, the largest in Andalucía, with Roman mosaics, a two-faced idol of Janus that probably came from the temple under La Mezquita, and an unusual icon of the Persian *torero*-god Mithras; the museum also holds some Moorish-looking early Christian art, and early funeral steles with odd hieroglyphs. The large collection of Moorish art includes some of the best work from the age of the caliphate, including finds from Medina Azahara. At the entrance is a small gallery with a plaque to 'Franco Caudillo de España' but it's generally closed.

National Archaeological Museum
t 95 747 40 11, open
Tues 2.30–8.30,
Wed–Sat 9–8.30, Sun
9–2.30; adm, free to EU
citizens

East of the Calle San Fernando, the wide street that bisects the old quarter, the houses are not as pristinely whitewashed as those around La Mezquita. Many parts are a bit run down, which does not detract from their charm. In the approximate centre of the city is the **Plaza de la Corredera**, which is an enclosed 'Plaza Mayor', like the famous ones in Madrid and Salamanca. This ambitious project, surrounded by uniform blank façades (an echo of the *estilo desornamentado*) was never completed, and despite renovation it still feels neglected, except during the morning produce market which closes in one side, or during outdoor concerts on summer evenings (the tourist office has details).

Wiggle though the crooked streets north of here to the lovely
Palacio de Viana, Plaza de Don Gómez 2, a Renaissance palace set
around a dozen beautiful patios filled with trailing plants. You can
amble around the patios and the pretty 18th-century garden, or be
guided around the elegant restored interior, with its tapestries,
paintings, archaeological fragments, ancient weapons and
exquisite *artesonado* ceilings.

Palacio de Viana
*t 95 749 67 41; open
June–Sept Mon–Sat
9–2, Oct–May Mon–Fri
10–1 and 4–6, Sat 10–1;
interior: guided
tours only; adm*

Heading south from the Plaza de la Corredera, the **Museo de
Bellas Artes** is on the lovely Plaza del Potro (mentioned by
Cervantes, along with the little *posada* that still survives on it).
Its collections include works of Valdés Leal, Ribera, Murillo and
Zurbarán, two royal portraits by Goya, and works by Córdoban
artists of the 15th and 16th centuries. Beware the 'museum' across
its courtyard, dedicated exclusively to the works of a local named
Julio Romero de Torres, the Spanish Bouguereau. Much prized by
the Córdobans, this turn-of-the-last-century artist's *œuvre* consists
almost entirely of naked ladies. East from here, the crooked alleys
continue for a mile, as far as the surviving stretch of **Moorish walls**
along Ronda del Marrubial. On the way, consider dipping into the
Hammam Baños Árabes, a wonderful traditional Moorish-style
bathhouse with hot and cold water and massages. There is also a
tetería (tea room) where you can relax with a glass of mint tea.

**Museo de
Bellas Artes**
*t 95 747 13 14;
open Tues 2.30–8.30,
Wed–Sat 9–8.30, Sun
9–2.30; adm, free to
EU citizens*

**Hammam
Baños Árabes**
*t 95 748 47 46, www.
hammamspain.com/
cordoba; adm*

Plaza de las Tendillas

The centre of Roman Corduba has, by chance, become the centre
of the modern city. Córdoba is probably the slickest and most up-
to-date city in Andalucía (though Sevilla would beg to differ), and it
shows in this busy district of crowded pavements, modern shops,
cafés and wayward youth. The contrast with the old neighbourhoods is startling, but just a block off the Plaza, on Calle
Gondomar, the beautiful 15th-century church of **San Nicolás** will
remind you that you're still in Córdoba.

In the other direction, well-preserved remains of a collapsed
Roman temple, one of the most complete Roman monuments in
Spain, have been discovered on the Calle Nueva near the *ayuntamiento*. The city has been at work reassembling the walls and
columns and already the front pediment is partially complete,
though its setting, in the middle of what looks like an abandoned
building site, makes it far from a captivating experience.

Next to the **Plaza de Colón**, a park a few blocks north of the Plaza
de las Tendillas, the **Torre de Malmuerta** ('Bad Death') takes its
name from a commander of this part of the old fortifications who
murdered his wife in a fit of passion; it became the subject of a
well-known play by Lope de Vega, *Los Comendadores de Córdoba*.

Across the Plaza de Colón is a real surprise: the rococo **Convento
de la Merced** (1745), an enormous building that has been restored

to house the provincial government and often hosts cultural exhibitions on various subjects. Don't miss it. The façade has been redone in its original painted *esgrafiado*, almost decadently colourful in pink and green, and the courtyards and grand staircases inside are incredible – more a palace than a monastery.

Medina Azahara (Medinat al-Zahra)

Medina Azahara
t 95 732 91 30; open May–mid-Sept Tues–Sat 10–8.30; mid-Sept–April Tues–Sat 10–6.30; adm, free to EU citizens

Eight kilometres west of the centre of Córdoba, Caliph Abd ar-Rahman III began to build a palace in the year 936. The undertaking soon got out of hand and, with the almost infinite resources of the caliphate to play with, he and his successors turned Medina Azahara ('City of the Flower', named after one of Abd ar-Rahman's wives) into a city in itself, with a market, mosques, schools and gardens, a place where the last caliphs could live in isolation from the world, safe from the turbulent street politics of their capital. Hisham II was kept a virtual prisoner here by his vizier, al-Mansur.

The scale of it is pure *Arabian Nights*. One chronicler records an ambassador, being taken from Córdoba to the palace, finding his path carpeted the entire 8km (5-mile) route and lined with maidens to hold parasols and refreshments for him. Stories were told of the palace's African menageries, its interior pillars and domes of crystal, and curtains of falling water for walls; another fountain was filled with flowing mercury. Such carrying-on must have aroused a good deal of resentment; in the disturbances that put an end to the caliphate, Medina Azahara was sacked and razed by Berber troops in 1013. After having served as a quarry for 900 years it's surprising anything is left at all; even under Muslim rule, columns from the palace were being carted away as far as Marrakech. But in 1944 the royal apartments were discovered, with enough fragments to permit a restoration of a few arches with floral decorations. One hall has a roof on, and more work is under way, but as yet the rest is only foundations.

Tourist Information in Córdoba

ⓘ **Córdoba >**
regional office: C/Torrijos 10, t 95 747 12 35; open summer 9.30–8; winter 9.30–6 municipal office: Plaza Tendillas, s/n, t 90 220 17 74, www. turiscordoba.es

It's worth visiting the *turismo* to get a map – Córdoba has the biggest and most labyrinthine old quarter in Spain. The tourist office has a list of approved multilingual guides who can arrange tours of the mosque and other sights.

Shopping in Córdoba

Córdoba is famous for its silverwork – try the shops in **C/José Cruz Conde**, where you'll get better quality than in the old quarter round the mosque. Handmade crafts are made on the premises at **Meryan**, Calleja de las Flores 2, where they specialize in embossed wood and leather furniture. For antiques, there's one shop with a very good selection of Spanish art and furniture in **Plaza San Nicolás**, and they'll arrange packing and shipment. High-quality ladies' and gents' suede and leather goods are sold at **Sera**, on the corner of Ronda de los Tejares and Cruz Conde. The mainstream shopping areas are along **C/Conde de Gondomar** and **C/Claudio Marcelo**, on either side of Plaza de las Tendillas.

Where to Stay in Córdoba

Córdoba ✉ 14000

Luxury (€€€€€)

*****Palacio del Bailío**, C/Ramírez de las Casas Deza 10–12, **t** 95 749 89 93, *www.hospes.es*. Córdoba's first five-star hotel, housed in a stunning 16th-century mansion with several courtyards planted with citrus trees and stylish, modern rooms with hi-tech features, including wi-fi.

Very Expensive (€€€€)

****NH Amistad Córdoba**, Plaza de Maimónides 3, **t** 95 742 03 10. Sensitively converted from an old *palacio*, built into the original city walls with a large cobbled courtyard, carved wood ceilings and spacious, comfortable rooms. The breakfast buffet will set you up for the day.

⭐ Casa de los Azulejos >>

****Conquistador**, Magistral González Francés 17, **t** 95 748 11 02, *www.hotel conquistadorcordoba.com*. Across from the Mezquita, this classic Andalucian hotel has dazzling tiles and carved marquetry in the public spaces and elegant guest rooms with marble floors, some with balconies.

⭐ La Hospedería de Churrasco >

***La Hospedería de Churrasco**, C/Romero 38, **t** 95 729 48 08, *www. elchurrasco.com*. Each of the splendid guest rooms here is named after a celebrated 19th-century artist, and all are decorated with antiques and plush fabrics. It is linked to the celebrated **El Churrasco** restaurant (€€).

Expensive (€€€)

***Casa de los Naranjos**, C/Isabel Losa 8, **t** 95 747 05 87, *www.casadelos naranjos.com*. In an elegant town house with 20 rooms with wrought-iron bedheads and traditional dark furniture. There are two courtyards, one complete with bubbling fountain.

Lola, C/Romero 3, **t** 95 720 03 05, *www.hotelconencantolola.com*. In the heart of the old Jewish quarter in a restored 19th-century palace with many original fittings and furniture. All eight rooms are doubles, but they vary in size and style; the roof terrace has a view of the Mezquita tower.

⭐ Santa Ana >>

Posada de Vallina, C/Corregidor Luís de Cerda 83, **t** 95 749 87 50, *www.*

hotelvallina.com. One of the nicest hotels to have sprung up in the past few years, opposite La Mezquita. An old inn dating from Roman times, there are just 15 rooms, all sparkling and tastefully designed, some with mosque views, others facing the patio.

Hotel González, C/Manríques 3, **t** 95 747 98 19, *www.hotelgonzalez. com*. On the edge of the Judería. Some rooms contain family antiques, and the arabesque patio has a restaurant.

Hotel Mezquita, Plaza Santa Catalina 1, **t** 95 747 55 85, *hotel mezquita@wanadoo.es*. A 16th-century mansion sympathetically restored and with many of the original paintings and sculptures.

Casa de los Azulejos, C/Fernando Colón 5, **t** 95 747 00 00, *www. casadelosazulejos.com*. One of the prettiest options in Córdoba, with stylish rooms set around a delightful tiled patio spilling over with flowers, banana trees and palms.

Moderate (€€)

Albucasis, C/Buen Pastor 11, **t** 95 747 86 25. In the Judería, near La Mezquita, this former silversmith's is an attractive, affordable and immaculate place with a flower-filled courtyard and welcome parking facilities. *Closed Jan–mid-Feb.*

Hostal El Triunfo, C/Corregidor Luís de Cerda 79, **t** 95 749 84 84, *www. htriunfo.com*. Right by the mosque, in a 19th-century town house with tiled patio, this is a perfectly decent no-frills option with a nice restaurant.

Marisa, C/Cardenal Herrero 6, **t** 95 747 31 42, *www.hotelmarisa cordoba.com*. A simple establishment opposite the Patio de los Naranjos. The rooms are plainly furnished, yet comfortable, and there is a pleasant modern bar, plus private garage.

*Hotel Mirador de Córdoba, Avda del Brillante, km 5, **t** 95 727 21 80. Situated 5km from the centre of town, this Modernista-style hotel is full of neo-*mudéjar* decoration. It offers peace and a view of the Sierra Morena.

*Santa Ana, C/Cardenal Gonzalez 25, **t** 95 748 58 37. Opened in 2005 near the Mezquita; the rooms are dazzling white with dark wood fittings and snazzy modern artwork.

⭐ **Maestre** >

⭐ **El Barril** >>

⭐ **Casa Pepe de la Judería** >>

Maestre, C/Romero Barros 16, **t** 95 747 24 10, *www.hotelmaestre.com*. Two establishments on the same street, offering a range of bright rooms from doubles to small apartments; all have pretty tiled bathrooms and those in the hotel have air conditioning. Popular with backpackers, so book early.

Inexpensive (€)

***El Reposo de Bagdad**, C/Fernández Ruano 11, **t** 95 720 28 54. Small family-run *hostal* in the centre of the Jewish quarter; cosy rooms with a Moorish feel, plus a downstairs traditional tea room complete with cushions. Lots of atmosphere for the price.

***Hostal El Portillo**, C/Cabezas 2, **t** 95 747 20 91, *www.hostalelportillo.com*. Near the mosque, this pretty *hostal* offers simple rooms around a patio.

***Hostal Rey Heredia**, C/Rey Heredia 26, **t** 95 747 41 82. A good-value *hostal* set around a shady patio: the nicest rooms have tiny balconies. The shared bathrooms are all spotlessly clean.

***Hostal Seneca**, C/Conde y Luque 5 (just north of La Mezquita), **t** 95 747 32 34. A real find among the cheap *hostales*, with a beautiful patio full of flowers, nice rooms and sympathetic management. It tends to get booked up some way in advance.

Plenty of other inexpensive *fondas* can be found on and around Calle Rey Heredia – also known as the street with five names, so don't be thrown by all the different signs.

Eating Out in Córdoba

Córdoba is the heart of a wine-growing region; a few *bodegas* in town allow visitors, including the **Bodega Campos**, C/Lineros 32, **t** 95 747 41 42, and the **Bodega Guzmán**, C/Judíos 7, which both have restaurants serving their own wines.

Almudaina, Jardines de los Santos Mártires 1, **t** 95 747 43 42 (€€€). Set in an attractive old house dating from the 16th century. Its menu varies from day to day, depending on market availability, and special attention is paid to local produce. Look out for *ensalada de pimientos*, *alcachofas a la Cordobés*, and *lomo relleno a la Pedrocheña*, all above average. Closed

Sun June–Sept, and Sun eve the rest of the year.

El Caballo Rojo, C/Cardenal Herrero 28, **t** 95 747 53 75, *www.elcaballorojo.com* (€€€). Another of Córdoba's best-known restaurants: its menu is based on traditional *andaluz* cooking and old Arab recipes – *salmorejo* with cured ham, artichokes in Montilla wine, and white bean stew. The dining room is leafy and elegant.

Bodega Campos, C/Lineros 32, **t** 95 749 75 00 (€€€–€€). This handsome old *bodega* also offers fine *Cordobesa* cuisine: try the salt cod salad with orange or the steak with *setas* (oyster mushroom) sauce. *Closed Sun eve*.

El Barril, C/Concepción 16, **t** 95 748 58 08 (€€). A classic, crammed with old barrels and photos; try local wines and great tapas, or go straight for the *rabo de toro* or excellent seafood.

Casa Pepe de la Judería, C/Romero 1, **t** 95 720 07 44 (€€). Pretty tile decoration and a flowery patio, a beautiful, friendly spot. Tasty, unusual tapas at the bar (washed down with a glass of manzanilla from the barrel) or a fine restaurant serving regional cuisine.

El Churrasco, C/Romero 16, **t** 95 729 08 19 (€€). Situated in the heart of the Judería, specializing in meaty dishes including its namesake *churrasco* (grilled meat in a spicy sauce), as well as fish. There's a pretty interior patio and several dining rooms with beams and exposed brick. *Closed Aug*.

Rincón de Carmen, C/Romero 4, **t** 95 729 10 55 (€). Family-run, noisy and full of atmosphere. The local dishes are prepared well, and the prices are low. It also has a pleasant adjacent café with wicker chairs.

Bar Sociedad de Plateros, C/San Francisco 6, **t** 95 747 00 42 (€). Good tapas and cheap wine. It started out in the mid-19th century as a society to help struggling silversmiths and has since branched into the *bodega* business, with several around the city.

Bodega Guzmán, C/Judíos 7 (€). Another good *bodega* worth seeking out; it's a shrine to bullfighting with much memorabilia inside.

Bodegón Rafael, C/Deanes, **t** 95 747 13 20 (€). True *bodega* food and atmosphere. Sausages drape from barrels, religious figurines hang next to fake bulls' heads, radio and TV are on simultaneously. *Rabo de toro* with a glass of wine at a vinyl-topped table will cost next to nothing.

Bar Santos, C/Magistral González Francés 3. Despite being surrounded by souvenir shops, this traditional bar is a great place for tapas like *morcillo* (blood sausage) and sandwiches.

El Pisto, Plaza San Miguel 1, **t** 95 747 01 66. With bullfighting memorabilia, this bar attracts crusty locals, here for the ice-cold *fino* (sherry) and superb home-made tapas. *Closed Aug.*

El Tablón, C/Corregidor Luís de la Cerda, **t** 95 747 60 61 (€). Just around the corner from La Mezquita, this characterful place offers one of the best bargains in the city, with a choice of *menús del día* or *platos combinados* at less than €10, with glass of wine.

Entertainment and Nightlife in Córdoba

Córdoba is the birthplace of Paco Peña – one of Spain's most famous modern **flamenco** maestros. Peña is part of a long tradition of Córdoban flamenco, and the city is a good place to catch some great players and dancers in more authentic venues than, say, Sevilla. If you love flamenco, July is the best time to visit the city, during the **guitar festival**, when trills and flourishes drift out of every other room in Córdoba's White Neighbourhood and there are concerts nightly. At other times, wait until midnight and then head for one of the flamenco bars or shows tucked away throughout the city. These include:

Mesón La Bulería, Pedro López 3, **t** 95 748 38 38 (in the Judería).

Peña Flamenca Las Orejas Negras, Avda Carlos III 18, in Barrio Fátima.

Tablao Cardenal, C/Torrijos 10, **t** 95 748 33 20, next to the tourist office.

Though flamenco may be more authentic in Córdoba than in Seville, the **bar nightlife** is less lively. The most popular bars with locals are the street bars (*terrazas*) in **Barrio Jardín**, northwest of the Jardines de la Victoria, on the Avenida de la República end of **Camino de los Sastrés**.

The **Café Málaga**, C/Málaga 3, is good for a mellow drink, and **Velvet**, C/Alfaros 29, is relaxed during the week but livens up at weekends. **Barrio El Brillante**, northwest of the Plaza Colón, is full of upper-middle-class Spanish people in summer, particularly the nightclubs and bars found around Plaza El Tablero.

North of Córdoba: The Sierra Morena

 Valle de los Pedroches

The N432 out of Córdoba leads north to the Sierra Morena, the string of hills that curtain the western part of Andalucía from Extremadura, Castilla and La Mancha. This area is the Valle de los Pedroches, fertile grazing land for pigs, sheep and goats and an important hunting area for deer and wild boar – though it's a sad fact that most Spaniards are still irresponsible sportsmen, and the Andalucian hunter, a mild-mannered plumber or tobacconist during the week, will take a gun in his hand on Sunday and kill anything that moves. Thousands of these animals are stalked and shot in the numerous annual hunts, or *monterías*. The Valle de los Pedroches is also healthy hiking territory, but keep yourself visible at all times – you don't want to be mistaken for someone's supper.

The N432 winds 73km up to **Bélmez**, with its Moorish castle perilously perched on a rock, from which there are panoramic views over the surrounding arid countryside. **Peñarroya-Pueblonuevo** is a dull industrial town that has fallen into decline,

Getting to and around the Sierra Morena

but is useful here as a reference point. Sixteen kilometres west on the N432, the rather dismal village of **Fuente Obejuna** is best remembered for the 1476 uprising of its villagers, who dragged their tyrannical lord from his palace and treated him to a spectacularly brutal and bloody end. His sacked palace was replaced by a church, which still has its original polychromed wooden altar and painted altarpiece. The event is the subject of the drama *Fuente Ovejuna* by Lope de Vega. The village also has an Art Nouveau mansion, **Casa Cardona**, which would be more at home in Barcelona. Now sadly in a bad state of disrepair, its flourishes and cornices and multicoloured windows hint at a more prosperous time. Near the village are some excavations of Roman silver mines.

It's well worth making the trip 40km north of Peñarroya to **Belalcázar** and one of the most extraordinary castles in Andalucía. **El Castillo de Sotomayor** stands just outside the village and bears down on it like some malevolent force. In any other part of Europe this would be a high point on the tourist trail, but here, in one of the least visited corners of the province, it stands decayed and forlorn. Situated on an outcrop of rock and built on the ruins of an old Moorish fortress, the castle was begun early in the 15th century on the orders of Gutierre de Sotomayor, who controlled the whole of this area. A palace was added in the 16th century, but its dominant feature is the 46m- (150ft-) high **Torre del Homenaje**, and its wonderfully ornate carvings. The castle remained in the family until the Peninsular War when it was badly damaged. Sadly, it is not open to the public, but can be tramped around to get an idea of its size; all around lie remnants of the earlier fortress. The present owner has declined various offers to sell to an Arab buyer or to turn it into a *parador*, a shame really as it would surely be one of the most spectacular in Spain. The village itself has a pretty main square dominated by 15th-century **Iglesia de Santiago el Mayor**, with its late Gothic façade. Just outside the village is the convent of **Santa Clara de Columna**, founded in 1476 and still in use, though it is open for visits and you can buy biscuits made by the nuns; the fabulous *artesonado* ceilings and murals have currently undergone a much-needed renovation. The ruins of an old monastery, San Francisco, are nearby.

The CP236 heads east across an unremarkable landscape to the tiny village of **Santa Eufemia**, some 26km away. The ruins of a medieval castle stand just outside the village, nestling in a cleft in the rocks which rise spectacularly above it. There's a 15th-century

Gothic-*mudéjar* church, **La Encarnación**, and a well-preserved gate in the main square, as well as some good walking routes available from the *ayuntamiento*, in Plaza Mayor.

From here you could head down to **Pozoblanco** (take the N502 then the A420), famous for the last *corrida* of the renowned bullfighter Francisco Rivera, better known as Paquirri. Gored, he died in the ambulance on the way to Córdoba. Paquirri's widow, the singer Isabel Pantoja, soared to even greater heights of popularity on his death, with the Spanish public obsessed as ever by the drama of life and mortality.

Pedroche, 10km away, is a sleepy little village with a fine 16th-century Gothic church and a Roman bridge. This place too has had its fair share of drama – in 1936, Communist forces shot nearly a hundred of the menfolk; their deaths are commemorated by a plaque outside. Just outside the village lies the **Ermita de Piedras Santas**, a nondescript 16th-century building with some pretty atrocious art inside; it becomes the scene of a pilgrimage on 8 September. As many as 50,000 people from the villages around come to pay their respects to their *patronada*. Beyond the villages of **Villanueva de Córdoba** and **Cardeña** to the east is the **Parque Natural de la Sierra de Cardeña** – rolling hills forested in oak, more stag-hunting grounds and ideal rambling terrain.

Where to Stay in the Sierra Morena

North of Córdoba there's nothing in the way of de luxe accommodation, but the area has a reasonably wide selection of one- and two-star hotels. Tourist offices (including the provincial office in Córdoba, *see* p.150) have lists of *casas rurales* offering rooms or self-catering accommodation in rural parts of the region.

***Cortijo Palomar de la Morra, Avda Argentina 6, km 3, Pozoblanco, t 95 777 15 85, *www.palomardelamorra.com* (€€€). Just outside Pozoblanco, this traditional *cortijo* offers rustic-style accommodation with open fireplaces, beams and terracotta tiles, plus discounts for groups and activities, including cycling tours.

**Husa San Francisco, Ctra. Alcaracejos, km 2, Pozoblanco, t 95 777 14 35, *www.husa.es* (€€). Located in the Cardeña Natural Park and part of the prestigious Husa chain. Facilities include tennis courts, restaurant, private balconies and gardens.

**El Alamo, Ctra Comarcal 141, t 95 764 04 76 (€€). West of Córdoba, just outside pretty Horachuelos, this hotel with just 20 rooms offers comfortable accommodation at a very reasonable price with a good adjacent restaurant.

**Siena, C/Negrillos 1, Bélmez, t 95 758 00 34 (€). Modest hotel with air-conditioned rooms and a café-bar.

**Hostal Javi, C/Córdoba 31, Bélmez, t 95 757 30 99 (€). An excellent-value *hostal* with plushly decorated rooms of hotel quality with TV, minibar and large bathrooms, set round a delightful vine-covered staircase. Also has street parking and a pretty patio.

*Sevilla, C/Miguel Vigara 15, Peñarroya-Pueblonuevo, t 95 756 01 00 (€€). This is a comfortable place to stay, offering rooms with *en-suite* bathroom. Pets allowed.

*El Comendador, C/Luis Rodríguez 25, Fuente Obejuna, t 95 758 52 22, *hotel comendador@hotmail.com* (€). An adequate place to stay in Fuente Obejuna. The rooms are pretty basic, but the building itself, with a pretty patio, is lovely. Decent adjacent café.

*Volao, C/Perralejo 2, Villanueva de Córdoba, **t** 95 712 01 57 (€). Offers no frills for its very cheap rooms in the *hostal*; there is a more expensive hotel next door, as well.

Eating Out in the Sierra Morena

This area is famed throughout Andalucía for its supreme quality *jamón ibérico* (locally cured ham) and suckling pig; the excellent *salchichón* from Pozoblanco; and the strong, spicy cheese made from ewes' milk. Sadly it is often difficult for visitors to the region to sample them. There are no outstanding restaurants around, and even indifferent ones are pretty thin on the ground.

Driving off into the countryside in search of gastronomic delight can be a risky business; and, though you might strike lucky, to be sure of eating really well you should head for the village tapas bars or, better still, grab some goodies from a supermarket and have a picnic out.

La Bolera, C/Pedro Torrero 17, Belalcázar, **t** 95 714 63 00 (€€). The best-choice place to eat in town, with contemporary *andaluz* cuisine prepared with the freshest seasonal ingredients. *Closed Mon*.

Gran Bar, C/Córdoba 8, Bélmez, **t** 95 758 01 99 (€€). The best restaurant in Bélmez. *Closed Mon*.

Mesón Azahara, Plaza de la Independencia, Cardeña, **t** 95 717 45 27 (€). Offers reasonable home cooking, including freshly roasted meats.

La Paula, C/Castillo 3, Pedroche, **t** 95 713 70 23 (€). The lunch *menú* is just €7, but expect quantity rather than quality.

South of Córdoba

This is the heart of Andalucía, a vast tract of bountiful hills covered in olive groves and vines. The area is more densely populated and a bit more prosperous than most of the region's rural districts. The towns are closer together, all white, and all punctuated by the warm sandstone of their palaces and towers. Some did well even in Andalucía's grim 18th century (Osuna under its haughty dukes, and Priego de Córdoba with its once-famous textiles); others haven't enjoyed good fortune since the passing of the Moors. Some towns inspired poets and novelists, others are famous for leather or barrels. Along the way, on what we hope will be a properly Spanish picaresque journey through a region few tourists enter, there will be flamingos, dolmens, rococo frippery, memorabilia of Julius Caesar, a cask of *amontillado*, a pretty fair canyon, and 139 gargoyles.

The Cordobés Subbética and La Campiña

Here in the heartland of Andalucía lies the **Parque Natural de las Sierras Subbéticas de Córdoba** – a succession of wooded hills that dip into the valleys of the rivers Zagrillo, Salado and Caicena. The landscape of oak trees, olive groves and much shrubland is home to eagles, falcons and vultures, rabbit and partridge, adders, field mice, bats and badgers; the rivers and small lakes brim with bass, perch and trout. Most tourists miss these untouched corners of Andalucía, where the people are God-fearing and industrious, and where the visitor is welcomed but watched carefully.

Twenty kilometres north of Estepa at **Puente Genil**, an old Moorish-style mill still turns in a pretty setting along the Río Genil. In the town is the 15th-century church of **La Concepción**, but the town's latter-day claim to fame is as a food-manufacturing centre. *Semana Santa* here is a big affair, and people come from all over the province to see the very colourful procession in Roman costume and Biblical dress. An old railway line connecting Puente Genil with Linares has been turned into a walking route with each of its old stations refurbished into restaurants and cafés, one of which, La Cantina, can be found just outside the small village of **Doña Mencia**.

Further east of Puente Genil, **Lucena** is one of the centres of a great wine-growing region. The town is not known for its beauty, but for making the biggest wine barrels in Andalucía, and as the birthplace of the Baroque architect Hurtado Izquierdo. He produced the incredible La Cartuja chapel in Granada, though he is not responsible for Lucena's wonderful Baroque *sagrario* chapel in the church of **San Mateo**. Before the Reconquista, Lucena seems to have been an autonomous Jewish republic, and many families claim Jewish ancestry: a quick flick through the phone book reveals numerous Isaacs, Israels and Aarons. The town makes much of its Jewish and Moorish past; its tourist logo uses both the crescent moon of Islam and the Star of David, and the Festival of Three Cultures, at the end of May, has become an annual event. Other festivals worth timing your visit for are the jazz festival, also held at the end of May, and an international piano festival in the last week of August, but the biggest of all are the *Fiestas Aracelitanas*, held in early May, which culminate with a huge fireworks display.

San Mateo
open during services only

Lucena was also a major trading centre and its small industries still thrive today, notably the production of olive oil, furniture-making, and the manufacture of brass, copperware and barrels. All this has made the town one of the most prosperous in Andalucía, and crime and unemployment stand at virtually nil while property prices in the centre soar. On the Plaza de España is a battered castle; it was here in the **Tower of Moral** that Granada's last king, Boabdil el Chico, was imprisoned by Fernando in 1483. Now it's home to the tourist office and a small archaeological museum.

Museo Arqueológico
t 95 751 32 82; open as tourist office

Twenty kilometres south of here, the town of **Rute** produces the potent spirit *anís*, and has a museum which charts its history, at Paseo del Fresno 2. It also has a donkey sanctuary (follow signs for ADEBO, Asociación para la Defensa del Burro) above the town, endorsed by Queen Sofía, no less.

Rute museum
t 95 753 81 43; open Mon–Fri 9–2 and 5–7, Sat 10–2, but confirm hours with tourist office

The road from the sanctuary wends its way round one of Spain's largest and finest-set reservoirs, **Embalse de Iznájar**, which takes meltwater from the Sierra Nevada. It is named after the town tumbling down one of its shores. **Iznájar** itself is topped by a

Donkey sanctuary
visits 9–noon only

magnificent **Alcazaba** complex dating from the 8th century, with the **Iglesia de Santiago** added some 800 years later. Both can be visited; ask for the keys at the *ayuntamiento*, and leave your transport below – the road up is torturously steep and narrow.

Right at the centre of Andalucía, fittingly set in olive groves and vineyards, and with view of the Sierra Nevada to the southeast and the Guadalquivir valley to the north, is **Cabra**, 10km north of Lucena on the C340. As you enter the town, turn left towards the buildings above it, which include a **castle** that once belonged to the dukes of Cabra; opposite is the 16th-century **Iglesia de la Asunción**, a former mosque and a good example of the local Baroque architecture. Inside are 44 red marble pillars and an impressive 18th-century retable. On the way out of town on the A340 towards Priego de Córdoba you'll pass a series of swimming pools; they mark a natural spring, **La Fuente del Río**, source of the River Cabra. A few kilometres further is the turn-off for the hilltop shrine of the **Virgen de la Sierra**, from where you'll get extraordinary views across the mountains. The Virgin is celebrated in the town on 3–8 September, and there's an even wilder Gypsy Pilgrimage to the shrine in mid-June.

Priego de Córdoba

Priego de Córdoba

Asunción
open summer Tues–Sun 11–2 and 5.30–8; winter 10.30–1.30 and 4–7

Priego de Córdoba lies at the foot of the highest mountain in the province, **La Tiñosa**, and has a famous ensemble of Baroque churches, monasteries and fountains; the best is the **Asunción** church with a sumptuous stucco interior and, in its *sagrario* chapel (designed by Francisco Javier Pedrejas), perhaps the finest example of Baroque frippery in all Andalucía: cherubs and angels look down beatifically from an outrageously frothy ceiling, a golden balcony lines the dome and light pours in from the high windows. The other churches can't quite live up to this, but if you are in a Baroque mood look out for the **Aurora**, Carrera de Álvarez, where every available bit of ceiling space is decked out in flourishes; and **Iglesia de las Mercedes**, Carrera de las Monjas, whose interior is another brilliant white Pedrejas creation. In the church of **San Pedro**, on the square of the same name, is an image of the *Immaculada*, a work attributed to Alonso Cano, and an ornate Baroque altar by the *sevillano* master Hurtado Izquierdo.

Aurora/Iglesia de las Mercedes/ San Pedro
churches open 11–1.30

Castle
open Tues–Sat 11–1 and 4–6, Sun 11–1; adm

The Asunción sits just off the Plaza Abad Palomino, which is flanked along one side by an austere Moorish **castle**, remodelled in the 13th and 14th centuries. Behind the church lies the prettiest part of town, **Barrio de la Villa**, a maze of tiny winding streets bedecked with pot plants and little squares. The *barrio* gives on to the edge of town with views across the olive groves. Follow this road round and you will end up in the **Puerta del Sol** and Priego's pretty gardens.

The town's other pride is the Baroque **Fuente del Rey**, at the end of Calle Río: three connecting fountain pools lined with 139 gargoyles, and a centrepiece of Neptune and Aphrodite on a horse-drawn carriage. The town has fancy grillework around its windows and ornate front doors, as displayed along Calle Río. No.33, as well as housing the town's *turismo*, is also the birthplace of Niceto Alcalá Zamora, the president of the Spanish Republic in 1931–6. The building has been preserved and recreated with much of the president's original furniture and documents lining the walls.

President's rooms at No.33
open Tues–Sat 10–1.30 and 5–7.30; adm

Zuheros to Montilla

From Cabra the A316 heads northeast towards Baena, through the heart of the Subbética. You can make a number of detours on the way, the most rewarding of which would be to **Zuheros**, about 2km along the CO241. The village clings to an escarpment, topped by the ruins of a Moorish castle, and is set against a backdrop of jagged cliffs. As with so many of these tiny villages, there is not a great deal to do but gawp at the views and perhaps stop for a quick drink. There is a pretty church, **La Virgen de los Remedios**, a museum of local arts and customs in the **Casa Grande**, and another small museum displaying some of the finds from a cave 4km above the town: La Cueva de los Murciélagos, 'the Cave of the Bats'. It has a few faint cave paintings, the odd bit of bone, some stalagmite and stalactite formations, and a distinct lack of bats. If you've seen the caves at Nerja, Aracena or Gibraltar, this is a poor relation. The winding road up to the caves has a series of *miradors*, with spectacular views over the town and the rugged hills.

La Cueva de los Murciélagos
t 95 769 45 45, www.cuevadelosmurcielagos.com; guided tours in Spanish April–Sept Mon–Fri 12.30 and 5.30, Sat and Sun 11, 12.30, 2, 5 and 6.30; Oct–Mar Mon–Fri 12.30 and 4.30, Sat and Sun 11, 12.30, 2, 4 and 5.30; adm; ring ahead to confirm hours,

Some 5km northwest of Zuheros is another pretty village, **Doña Mencía**, where the novelist Juan Valera lived for several years. His former home has been turned into a small museum. The town is named after the wife of Alvar Pérez de Castro, a captain under Fernando III, who also rebuilt the castle. From here the road wends its scenic way out of the Subbética to **Baena**, a town of major importance in Moorish times, now squeezing out olive oil in quantity. The town has an official *denominación de origen* (DO), which grades its olive oils from the basic stuff we use for cooking to the top-notch oils, used for tapas or in gazpacho. Serious aficionados should check out the Museo del Olivar y el Aceite on C/Cañada 7 with its detailed history displays about oil production, as well as information on its use in cosmetics, food and health. There is tasting available, and a shop where you can stock up on loads of goodies that hopefully won't leak in your hand luggage.

Museo del Olivar y el Aceite
t 95 769 16 41, www.museoaceite.com; open April–Sept Tues–Sat 11–2 and 4–6, Sun 11–2; Oct–Mar Tues–Sat 11–2 and 6–8, Sun 11–2; adm

A clean, tightly packed town with narrow, whitewashed streets, Baena has little more to detain you but the ruins of a Moorish **castle** and a fine 18th-century arcaded building, once a warehouse and now a cultural centre and tapas bar (the **Mesón Casa del**

Monte) on the Plaza de la Constitución. C/Juan Rabadan connects this with the Plaza de España, supposedly the town centre but little more than a road junction. Baena sees most of its visitors arrive for the Holy Week celebrations, when a deafening drum-rolling competition is held to see who can play the longest and the loudest; it lasts two days.

Twenty-two kilometres northwest from Cabra is **Aguilar de la Frontera**, another attractive wine town (producing *solera fina*, mostly) perched on a hill. It has an unusual octagonal *plaza* (a copy of the one in Antequera), and the Renaissance church of Santa María del Soterraño. It also has a number of *bodegas* which can be visited, including Toro Albalá, just off the main road to Málaga, on the turn-off to Puente Genil. On the outskirts of the town, on the way to Puente Genil, are a number of permanent and seasonal semi-saline lakes, the largest of which is the **Laguna de Zónar**. During the winter months, the lakes are home to a large number of migrating birds, including white-headed ducks, marsh and Montagu harriers and flamingos. About 3km along this road is a helpful visitor centre; two trails around the reserve start here.

From Aguilar it's a short hop up the road to the prince of the wine-producing towns, **Montilla**, sitting on a rise amid endless acres of vines. Although *amontillado*, a pale sherry, takes its name from this town, the wine produced here is not a sherry, in that no extra alcohol is added to fortify it, unlike in Jerez. The town is refreshingly short of Baroque churches, but its *bodegas* can be visited to sample the good stuff. A small **museum** is dedicated to Garcilaso de la Vega, Hispano-Inca son of a *conquistador* and chronicler of the Inca civilization in the 16th century. The 1512 Gothic convent of **Santa Clara** is worth a visit for its *mudéjar* roof and Baroque altarpiece. The town is believed to be the site of the Battle of Munda, where former governor Caesar's men finally put paid to the Spanish followers of Pompey.

Toro Albalá
t 95 766 00 46,
www.toroalbala.com

Laguna de Zónar visitor centre
t 95 733 52 52;
open Fri 4–6, Sat and Sun 10–1 and 4–6

Where to Stay and Eat South of Córdoba

ⓘ **Lucena** >
Castillo Moral, Plaza Nueva 1, t 95 751 32 82, www.turlucena.com; open Mon–Fri 9–2 and 6–9, Sat, Sun and hols 11–2 and 7–9

ⓘ **Priego de Córdoba** >>
C/Río 33, t 95 770 06 25, www.turismo depriego.com; open Tues–Sat 10–1.30 and 5–7.30, Sun 10–1

Lucena ✉ 14900

****Santo Domingo**, C/El Agua 12, t 95 751 11 00, *www.husa.es* (€€€). Part of the Husa chain and set in a former convent, this is the best hotel in the area. It has all the four-star amenities, except a pool, at very good prices.

***Los Bronces**, on the Córdoba-Málaga road, t 95 751 62 80, *www. hotellosbronces.com* (€€). Your next best bet, with pool, TVs and a very good restaurant.

Xenil, C/García Lorca 3 (in Puente Genil), t 95 760 02 00 (€). The only hotel in the centre of Puente Genil, with clean and comfortable rooms.

Pensión Sara, C/Cabrillana 47, t 95 751 61 51 (€). The best budget option, with perfectly good rooms, all en suite and clean, and plenty of restaurants nearby.

Priego de Córdoba ✉ 14800

***Villa Turística de Priego**, 7km beyond Priego de Córdoba towards Zagrilla, t 95 770 35 03, *www.villa turisticadepriego.com* (€€). In its own very pretty grounds with a pool,

ⓘ **Puente Genil**
*Parque de los Pinos s/n,
t 95 760 90 61, www.
turismopuentegenil.org*

ⓘ **Baena >>**
*Calle Domingo de
Henares s/n, **t** 95 767 19
46, www.ayto-baena.es;
open Tues–Fri 9–2 and
5–8, Sat–Sun 10–2*

ⓘ **Cabra >>**
*C/Santa Rosalía 2, **t** 95
752 01 10, www.cabra.
net; open Mon–Fri
10–1.30 and 6–8, Sat
and Sun 10–1.30*

ⓘ **Montilla >**
*Casa del Inca, C/Capitán
Alonso de Vargas 3, **t** 95
765 24 62, www.
emontilla.com; open
Mon–Fri 10–2, Sat and
Sun 11–2*

tennis and numerous other activities; self-catering chalets also.

Río Piscina, Ctra Monturque–Alcalá la Real, km 44, **t 95 770 01 86, *www.hotelriopiscina.com* (€€). A modern hotel 1.5km outside town with a pool and tennis court, at reasonable rates.

*Pensión Rafi, C/Isabel la Catolica 4, **t** 95 754 07 49, *www.hostalrafi.net* (€). A good budget option in Priego de Córdoba itself, with satellite TV and phone; there's a good little restaurant.

Posada La Niña Margarita, in Los Villares (5km from Carcabuey on the road towards Rute), **t** 95 770 40 54 (€€). A real rural retreat in a small valley of streams and olive groves; rent the *posada* (sleeps 8) or one of five apartments. Pool and bike rental. Minimum two-night stay.

El Aljibe, Plaza del Llano del Castillo, **t** 95 770 18 56 (€€). Built over an Arab cistern (*aljibe*) with tapas and meals at reasonable prices. *Closed Mon.*

Balcón del Adarve, Paseo de Columbia 36, **t** 95 754 70 75 (€€). Delicious home-cooked regional cuisine in a traditional *mesón* overlooking the valley. *Closed Mon.*

Aguilar de la Frontera
✉ 14920

Aguilar has a number of places, but none offering any luxury.

Hostal Queen, C/Pescaderías 6, **t** 95 766 02 22 (€). The best place to stay, with a café and TVs in the rooms.

La Casona, Avda de Puente Genil, **t** 95 766 04 39 (€). A reliable restaurant that specializes in *churrascos*.

Montilla ✉ 14550

***Don Gonzalo, Ctra Madrid–Málaga, km 447, **t** 95 765 06 58, *www.hoteldon gonzalo.com* (€€). Part of the Husa chain, on the main road outside Montilla, with gardens, swimming pool, tennis court and nightclub.

*Hotel Los Felipes, C/San Franciso Solano 27, **t** 95 765 04 96 (€€). Looks pretty grim from the outside but in fact has a lovely old-fashioned dining room (€) and a piano bar.

Finca Buytrón, C/Gran Capitán 24, **t** 95 765 01 52, *www.fincabuytron.com* (€€). A *casa rural* (sleeps 12–16), this dates

from the 16th century; has a pool, library and an open fire.

Cortijo El Pinar, Ctra Montilla–Cabra, km 7, **t** 95 747 22 60, *www.cortijo elpinar.com* (€€). A refurbished farmhouse with three separate houses (each sleeps 2–4); has a patio, barbecue area, kitchen and pool.

Las Camachas, Ctra Madrid–Málaga, **t** 95 765 00 04 (€). A typical old *bodega*, where you can taste and buy the local wines along with delicious regional dishes including *cordero a la miel* (lamb with honey). The lunch *menú* is a reasonable €9.

Baena ✉ 14850, Cabra ✉ 14940

****Hotel Fuente de las Piedras, Avda Fuente de las Piedras s/n, Cabra, **t** 95 752 97 40, *www.mshoteles.com* (€€€). A large modern hotel built in traditional style, with all the amenities including a pool and sports facilities.

***La Casa Grande, Avda de Cervantes 35, Baena, **t** 95 767 19 05, *www.lacasa grande.es* (€€€). The best place to stay in Baena; in a restored old mansion, with the original chandelier in the lobby and a fine restaurant.

Guerrero, C/Pepita Jiménez 7, Cabra, **t** 95 752 05 07 (€€). A pleasant *pensión* in the centre; air-conditioned rooms with TVs, and English spoken.

Iponuba, C/Nicolás Alcalá 7, Baena, **t 95 767 00 75, *iponuba@interbook.es* (€). Comfortable, central and with a café attached.

Hostal Rincón, Llano Rincón 13, Baena, **t 95 767 02 23 (€). The budget option in Baena, near the centre, with a tapas bar and restaurant.

Casa del Monte, Plaza de la Constitución, Baena (in the *almacén*), **t** 95 767 16 75 (€€). Probably your best bet to eat out in Baena; delicious tapas.

Mesón del Vizconde, C/Martín Belda 16, Cabra, **t** 95 752 17 02 (€€–€). A charming, family-run restaurant serving tasty local specialities including lamb cooked with artichokes. *Closed Tues and July.*

Huerta de San Rafael, Ctra Badajoz–Granada (in Luque), **t** 95 766 74 97 (€). Finding a good roadside *venta* such as this (serving regional specialities at giveaway prices) is a real boon in this area.

★ **Cortijo La Haza >**

ⓘ **Rute**
Parque de Nuestra Señora del Carmen s/n,
t *957 53 29 29,*
www.rute.org

ⓘ **Zuheros >**
Crtra. Zuheros-Baena,
t *95 769 47 75,*
www.zuheros.com

Iznájar ✉ **14970**
Cortijo La Haza, Adelantado 119, Iznájar, t 95 733 40 51, *www.cortijo lahaza.com* (€€). An utterly charming whitewashed *finca* offering B&B and evening meals, close to the Iznájar reservoir. Original beams and wrought-iron beds. Caters for vegetarians.

Zuheros ✉ **14870**
Hotel Zuhaira, C/Mirador 10, t 95 769 46 93 (€€). On a narrow street in the centre, this charming small hotel has large rooms with rooftop views to the

valley beyond. There's a rustic bar and dining room. Popular with art groups.
Señorios de Zuheros, Horno 3, t 95 769 45 27, *www.zuherosapartamentos.com* (€). Modern apartments in the centre.

Nightlife South of Córdoba

Lucena has quite a lively nightlife with bars, pubs and Moorish tea rooms, many of them around the main square. The *turismo* even supplies a *Ruta de la Tapa*, a bit like a pub crawl but with food.

From Córdoba to Úbeda
The Gateway to Andalucía

In this section of the Guadalquivir valley, the river rises into the heights of the Sierra Morena; endless rolling hills covered with neat rows of olive trees and small farms make a memorable Andalucian landscape. Three large towns along the way, Andújar, Bailén and Linares, are much alike, amiable industrial towns still painted a gleaming white. This area is Andalucía's front door. The roads and railways from Madrid branch off here for Sevilla and Granada. Many big battles were fought nearby, including Las Navas de Tolosa near La Carolina, in 1212, which opened the way for the conquest of al-Andalus; and Bailén, in 1808, where a Spanish-English force gave Napoleon's boys a sound thrashing and built up Spanish morale for what they call their War of Independence.

Montoro

The A4 snakes along the Guadalquivir valley, and 42km east of Córdoba it brings you to the delightfully placed town of **Montoro**, sitting on a cliff overlooking a bend in the river. The facetious-looking tower that rises above the whitewashed houses belongs to the Gothic church of **San Bartolomé** in Plaza de España. Also in the square is the 16th-century **Ducal Palace**, now the *ayuntamiento* and tourist office, with a Plateresque façade. The beautiful 15th-century bridge that connects Montoro to its suburb, Retamar, is known as the **Puente de Las Donadas**, a tribute to the women of the village who sacrificed their jewellery to help finance its construction. Seek out the kitsch **Casa de las Conchas**, C/Criado 17 (signposted from the Plaza de España), a house and courtyard done out in hundreds of thousands of seashells gathered from the beaches of Spain by Francisco del Río over the past 50 or so years. He will show you round for a small fee and flog you a postcard.

Andújar

Approaching **Andújar**, a further 35km down the A4, you'll find the countryside dominated by huge, blue sunflower-oil refineries like fallen space stations. Sunflowers, like olives, are a big crop in the region and much in evidence in late summer. Nothing remains of Andújar's Moorish castle, but there are a couple of surprises in this town which might tempt you to linger a while. The 13th-century church of **Santa María**, in the *plaza* of the same name, has in one chapel the *Immaculate Conception* by Pacheco, Velázquez's teacher, and in another the magnificent *Christ in the Garden of Olives*, by El Greco. You may wonder how on earth an El Greco got here? One reason given is that the Río Guadalquivir, upon which the town stands, was once navigable as far as Andújar, and so the town grew rich through trade with the Americas. Many merchants and nobility settled here, one of whom, so legend has it, donated the painting to the church in lieu of a cash gift. This also accounts for the large number of palaces and mansions – though, due to shortage of funds, many are falling into disrepair and are not open.

The **Casa de Albarracín**, which dates from the 16th century and used to be the town hall, stands opposite the church of Santa María. The coat of arms has long since disappeared – pulled down by a departing nobleman or ordered off by an angry king. Nearby stands the **Torre del Reloj**, where the minaret of the Moorish mosque once stood. It was finished in 1534 and sports a fabulous imperial coat of arms symbolizing the town's loyalty to the then king, Charles V. The *torre* now houses the *turismo* (*see* p.166)

From here it's a short walk to the Plaza de España, which is dominated by the current *ayuntamiento*, housed in what was the town's playhouse. Beside it is **San Miguel**, the oldest church in

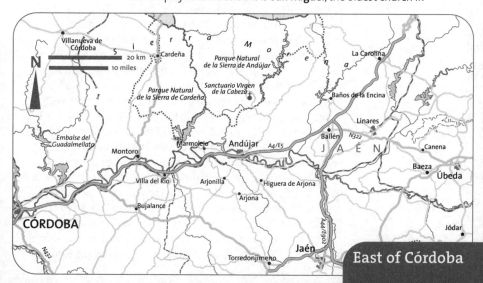

East of Córdoba

town, dating from Visigothic times. Inside is a beautiful choir with wrought-iron balustrades, the front carved in walnut. The tower outside the church leans slightly, a result of the Lisbon earthquake of 1755. The pink building on the other side of the square is the post office, with an arch leading through to the Plaza de la Constitución. Andújar also has a small **archaeological museum** housed in another fine building, the Palacio de los Niños de Gomez, which stands just behind a part of the Moorish city wall. Inside are a number of local ceramics and artefacts dating from Roman times. The exterior of the palace is decorated with two incongruous, and rather camp, figures, which are supposed to represent South American Indians.

Museo Arqueológico
t 95 351 31 78; open summer Tues–Fri 11–1; winter Tues–Fri 6–8

Around Andújar

Just before Andújar, just off the A4, lies the tiny spa village of **Marmolejo**, where the mineral water of the same name is bottled. There is little there to detain you, but a good hotel (*see* 'Where to Stay', p.166) and the spa itself, which lies 2km into the mountains and is open from May to the end of October. From Marmolejo you could rejoin the A4 or take a detour through endless olive groves to two pretty villages: **Arjonilla**, a production centre of olive oil, which you can smell on the way into town, and **Arjona** a few kilometres on. This village was once topped by a Moorish castle, but all that remains is the heavily restored church of Santa María, and the 17th-century chapel opposite. The walk up is worth it, however, for the wonderful views. Below is a pretty square, Plaza de la Constitución.

Another possible diversion, 30km north of Andújar on the J501, is the **Santuario de la Virgen de la Cabeza**. It's worth packing a picnic and enjoying the drive; when you get there you'll be rewarded with panoramic views, though there is very little left of the 13th-century sanctuary, which was blown to bits by Republicans after being seized by pro-Franco guards near the start of the Civil War. The present building and surroundings are a grotesque mishmash of Fascistic architecture, similar in style to El Valle de Los Caídos, Franco's tomb outside Madrid. In the crypt below there is a collection of photos and walking aids hanging from the walls, representing those who the Virgin has cured. One of Andalucía's biggest fiestas is the annual *romería* to the sanctuary on the last Sunday in April, when half a million pilgrims trek up on foot, horseback, carts and donkeys. The celebrations begin the week before with various competitions held in the centre of Andújar. On the Thursday, thousands of Andújarans dress up in traditional dress and layer the ground outside the Capilla del Virgen de la Cabeza, in C/Ollerías, with a blanket of flowers. The next day the streets, resonant with music, fill with people parading in costume on horseback. The pilgrimage proper begins early on the Saturday morning. The halfway point is **Lugar Nuevo**, near an old Roman bridge, where pilgrims stop for a giant picnic, before arriving at the sanctuary that night where an hourly mass begins. Finally, on Sunday morning the Virgin is brought out of the sanctuary and paraded down the hill. Of course all this means big business, and the sanctuary is spawning a village at its feet, with restaurants, bars and hotels to cater for the pilgrims.

Bailén

Back on the A4, 27 km farther east is the unprepossessing modern town of Bailén. The tomb of the Spanish general Francisco Javier Castaños (1756–1852), who so cleverly whipped the French troops and sent Napoleon back to the drawing board, is in the Gothic parish church of the **Encarnación**, which also has a sculpture by Alonso Cano. But don't dally here – the real treat is to be found 11km to the north on the A4 at **Baños de la Encina**, where the 10th-century oval Moorish **Castillo de Burgalimar** is one of the best preserved in all Andalucía. Dominating the town, the castle has 14 sturdy, square towers and a double-horseshoe gateway, scarcely touched by time, and from the walls you get a sweeping vista of the olive groves and distant peaks beyond Úbeda.

Castillo de Burgalimar
t 95 361 30 04; open 9–8

A hilly hour's trek from Baños, through arduous terrain, lies the natural refuge of **Canforos de Peñarrubia**, with its remarkable Bronze Age paintings of deer and scenes of animal-taming. Serious hikers should ask for a guide at the *ayuntamiento*.

Twenty kilometres north of here on the A4 is **La Carolina**, a model of 18th-century grid planning. The village owes its existence to forward-thinking Carlos III, who imported a few thousand German artisans in the late 1700s and set them to work excavating the lead and copper mines, tilling the fields and herding sheep. A side effect of this colonization was supposed to be the decline of banditry in the then wild and unpopulated hills. But within two generations almost all the Germans had died off or fled. The town and surrounding area are best known now as a large game-hunting reserve, particularly for partridge.

From Bailén the N322 heads east to the mining town of **Linares**, birthplace of the guitarist Andrés Segovia, who later moved on; others weren't so lucky – in 1947 the great bullfighter Manolete had an off day and met his end on the horns of a bull here. If things had gone well for him, he might have gone to view the finds from the Roman settlement of nearby Castulo, housed in the town's **archaeology museum** on C/Cánovas del Castillo, but unfortunately the last thing he saw was probably the ornate Baroque portal of the hospital San Juan de Dios. From Linares it's 27km to Úbeda; a little more than halfway you'll pass an elegant castle at **Canena**.

Linares archaeology museum
t 95 369 24 63; open daily 10–2, plus 4–6 on Sat and Sun

(i) **Andújar** >
Torre del Reloj, Plaza Santa María s/n, **t** *95 350 49 59, www. turismoandujar.com; open Tues–Sat 10–2 and 5–8*

(i) **Sierra de Andújar** >
on the J501, heading towards the Santuario de la Virgen de la Cabeza (see p.164), **t** *95 354 90 30*

(i) **Montoro**
Plaza de España 8, **t** *95 716 00 89, www. montoro.es; open Mon, Wed, Fri 8.30–3; Tues, Thurs 10–2 and 5–6.30; Sat 10–1*

Tourist Information East of Córdoba

The tourist office in **Andújar** has lots of information about the town, and offers free walking tours if you call ahead. It also has info on **footpaths** in the **Sierra de Andújar**, a natural park that forms part of the Sierra Morena.

Where to Stay and Eat East of Córdoba

Andújar ✉ 23740

La Colorá, Ctra Montoro–Adamuz, km 9, **t** 95 733 60 77 (€€€). A beautifully restored 18th-century *finca* set in olive groves, with elegant rooms, self-catering apartments and a lovely outdoor pool. *Closed Aug.*

***Gran Hotel & Spa, Calvario 101 (10km outside Andújar at Marmolejo), **t** 95 354 09 75, *www.granhotelspa.com* (€€€). Probably the area's best hotel, with a pool, health and beauty treatments, gardens and a restaurant.

***Hotel del Val, C/Hnos del Val 1, **t** 95 350 09 50, *www.hoteldelval.es* (€€). Just outside town, on the corner of the road up to the sanctuary. Ugly modern exterior, but grand rooms, a pool and pleasant grounds.

La Fuente, C/Vendederas 4, **t 95 350 46 29, *www.lfhoteles.com* (€€–€). Located in a historic building dating from the early 20th century with arches and wrought-iron balconies. There's a good restaurant.

*Logasasanti, C/Doctor Fleming 5, **t** 95 350 05 00, *www.logasanti.com* (€€–€). Respectable, central and comfortable, in a modern building.

Restaurante Madrid-Seville, Plaza del Sol 4, **t** 95 350 05 94 (€€). Patronized by the king and queen of Spain, and so called for its position on the old road. It's a favourite with the hunting fraternity, as well as the royals. Fresh fish is brought in daily and game features heavily on the menu.

Las Perolas, C/Serpiente 6, **t** 95 350 67 26 (€). An excellent local restaurant serving tasty local dishes, including game, washed down with local wine.

If you have the desire to stay up by the shrine at **Nuestra Virgen de la Cabeza** there are a few options, all of which have restaurants attached.

*La Mirada, **t** 95 354 91 11 (€€). Has a good view of the shrine, plus a pool, restaurant and campsite.

Complejo Turístico Los Pinos, **t** 95 345 90 79, *www.lospinos.es* (€). Comfortable rooms, a pool and a restaurant (€€) on the road up to the sanctuary.

*Pensión Virgen de la Cabeza, Carretera del Santuario de le Virgen de la Cabeza, km.0, **t** 95 312 21 65 (€). The cheapest adequate option.

Bailén ✉ 23710

***Cuatro Caminos, C/Seville 92, **t** 95 367 02 19, *www.hotelcuatro caminos.com* (€€). Part of the Husa chain. Central; plain, well-equipped rooms, wi-fi and a good restaurant.

***Bailén, Ctra A4, km 296, **t** 95 367 01 00, *hotelbailen@terra.es* (€€). Just outside Bailén in an old *parador* with pleasant gardens, air-conditioning and a swimming pool. It also houses a restaurant and tapas bar.

Baños de la Encina ✉ 23710

***Hospedería Rural Palacio Guzmanes, C/Trinidad 4, **t** 95 361 30 75, *www.palacioguzmanes.com* (€€€). A lovely rural hotel in a restored 18th-century palace, with just nine charming rooms, a pool and wonderful home-cooked food.

***Hotel Baños, C/Cerro de la Llaná s/n, **t** 95 361 40 68, *www.hotelbanos. com* (€€). Comfortable rooms with beautiful views over the Sierra. Hiking and other activities can be arranged. Houses the town's best restaurant.

Postá La Cestería, C/Conquista 25, **t** 697 953 318 (€€). A charming accommodation choice where you can either rent a room or the whole house; located just beneath the castle in the historic part of town.

Mesón del Duque, **t** 95 361 30 26 (€). At the top of town, opposite the Ermita Jesús del Llano. The name belies its simple, reasonable cooking. *Closed Wed.*

La Carolina ✉ 23200

****Perdiz, Ctra A4, km 268, **t** 95 366 03 00, *www.nh-hoteles.es* (€€€–€€). A classic stopover for travellers between Andalucía and northern Spain with an appealing, coaching-inn ambience. It's got wi-fi, and a good restaurant (€€).

***Orellana Perdiz/Orellana Perdiz II**, Ctra A4, km 265, **t** 95 366 12 51, *www.orellanaperdiz.com* (€€). A choice of two hotels, the three-star located around 3km away from the original Orellana Perdiz, refurbished in 2005 and part of a large tourist complex near the Sierra Morena Mountains. Organized activities include horseback treks to the deserted former mining villages, like Torreón del Águila.

Gran Parada, Avda Lindez Vilches 9, **t** 95 366 02 75 (€). A family-owned hotel. Rooms have shower or full bath; situated 10mins walk from the centre.

La Toja, Avda Juan Carlos 1, **t** 95 366 10 18 (€€–€). Set back from the main street, this large, open-plan restaurant serves good, reasonably priced local fare (such as game in season).

Linares ✉ 23700

***Aníbal**, C/Cid Campeador 11, **t** 95 365 04 00, *www.rlhoteles.com* (€€). The jumbo hotel 2mins from the main *plaza*, with spacious rooms, and an attractive grill restaurant with terrace.

***Victoria**, C/Cervantes 7–9, **t** 95 369 25 00, *www.victoriahotel.org* (€€). Located right in town, opposite the theatre, this good-value hotel has recently benefited from a revamp with plenty of shiny marble in the public areas and comfortable large, if rather frilly, rooms. Wi-fi.

****Cervantes**, C/Cervantes 23, **t** 95 369 05 00, *www.hotelcervantes.info* (€€). Despite the old-fashioned building, the rooms here are painted in bold modern colours, set round a pretty patio. It's next to the bullring and is always packed out during the summer festival held in late August. Excellent local restaurant.

****Baviera**, C/Virgen 25, **t** 95 360 71 15 (€). A pleasant little *pensión*, with rooms painted in pretty pastel colours and good facilities, including Internet access, satellite TV and parking. Located in the centre of town.

Mesón Campero, C/ Pozo Ancho 5, **t** 95 369 56 22 (€€). Excellent grilled meats and other traditional dishes make this popular with locals. *Closed Mon eve, Sun and Easter.*

Baeza

10

Córdoba and Jaén | From Córdoba to Úbeda: Baeza

Campo de Baeza, soñaré contigo cuando no te vea

(Fields of Baeza, I will dream of you when I can no longer see you)

Antonio Machado
(1875–1939)

Sometimes history offers its recompense. The 13th-century Reconquista was especially brutal here; nearly the entire population fled, many of them moving to Granada, where they settled the Albaicín. The 16th century, however, when the wool trade was booming in this corner of Andalucía, was good to Baeza, leaving it a distinguished little town of neatly clipped trees and tan stone buildings, with a beautiful ensemble of monuments in styles from Romanesque to Renaissance. It seems a happy place, serene and quiet as the olive groves that surround it.

The prettiest corner of the town is **Plaza del Pópulo**. It is enclosed by decorative pointed arches and Renaissance buildings, and contains a fountain with four half-effaced lions; the fountain was patched together with the help of pieces taken from the Roman remains at Castulo, and the centrepiece, the lady on the pedestal, is traditionally considered to be Imilce, the wife of Hannibal.

Palacio de Jabalquinto
open Thurs–Tues 10–2 and 4–6

Heading north on the Cuesta de San Felipe, which can be reached by the steps leading off the Plaza del Pópulo, you pass the 15th-century **Palacio de Jabalquinto**, with an eccentric façade covered with coats of arms and pyramidal stone studs (a Spanish fancy of that age; you can see others like it in Guadalajara and Salamanca).

Getting to Baeza

Come to Baeza by **train** at your own risk. The nearest station, officially named Linares-Baeza, **t** 95 365 02 02, is far off in the open countryside, 13km away. A bus to Baeza usually meets the train, but if you turn up at night or on a Sunday you may be left stranded at the station.

Baeza's **bus station, t** 95 74 04 68, is a little way from the centre on Paseo Arco del Agua. Baeza is a stop on the Úbeda–Córdoba bus route, with 10–12 buses a day running to Jaén (45mins); five to Granada (2hrs); two to Cazorla and one to Málaga (4–5hrs).

Antigua Universidad
indoor patio open Thurs–Tues 10–1 and 4–6; classroom open by appt only, t 95 374 01 50

The *palacio* was built in the 15th century by the Benavides family, and is now a seminary. Its patio is open to the public and boasts a beautiful two-tiered arcade around a central fountain, as well as a fine carved Baroque staircase. Adjoining the *palacio*, the 16th-century Antigua Universidad was a renowned centre of learning for three hundred years, until its charter was withdrawn during the reign of Fernando VII. It has since been used as a school; its indoor patio is open to the public. The school has found latter-day fame through Antonio Machado, the *sevillano* poet who taught there (1913–19). His most famous work of prose, *Sentencias, donaires, apuntes y recuerdos* (1936), draws on his experiences in Baeza. Machado's classroom has been preserved.

Santa Iglesia
Pza Santa María; open summer 10.30–1 and 5–7; winter 10.30–1 and 4–6

A right turn at the next corner leads to the 16th-century Santa Iglesia cathedral on Plaza S. María, a work of Andrés de Vandelvira. This replaced a 13th-century Gothic church (the chancel and portal survive), which in turn took the place of a mosque; a colonnade from this sits in the cloister. Drop a coin in the box marked *custodia* in one of the side chapels; this will reveal, with a noisy dose of mechanical *duende*, a rich, ornate revolving 18th-century silver tabernacle. The fountain in front of the cathedral, the **Fuente de Santa María**, with a little triumphal arch at its centre (1564), is Baeza's landmark and symbol. Behind it is the Isabelline Gothic **Casas Consistoriales**, formerly the town hall, while opposite stands the 16th-century seminary of **San Felipe Neri**, its walls adorned with student graffiti in bull's blood. It is curiously reminiscent of the rowing eights' hieroglyphics which cover the quadrangle walls of the sportier Oxbridge colleges.

The **Plaza de la Constitución**, at the bottom of the hill, is Baeza's main, albeit quiet, thoroughfare, an elegant rectangle lined with terrace cafés and bars. Two buildings are of note: **La Alhóndiga**, the 16th-century, porticoed corn exchange and, almost opposite, the **Casa Consistorial**, the 18th-century town hall. In Plaza Cardenal Benavides, the façade of the **Ayuntamiento** (1599) is a classic example of Andalucian Plateresque, and one of the last. From here it's a short walk to the 16th-century **Convento de San Francisco**, which now houses a restaurant (Vandelvira). At the end of the Paseo, the inelegant but lively **Plaza de España** marks the northern boundary of historic Baeza and is home to yet more bars.

Where to Stay and Eat in Baeza

ⓘ Baeza ›

Plaza del Pópulo (also called Plaza de los Leones), t 95 374 04 44, www.baeza.net; open April–Sept Mon–Fri 9–7, Sat 10–1 and 5–7; Oct–Mar Mon–Fri 9–6, Sat 10–1 and 4–6

Baeza ✉ 23440

****Hotel Palacio de los Salcedo, C/San Pablo 18, t 95 374 72 00, *www.palaciodelossalcedo.com* (€€€). Baeza's most luxurious hotel: sumptuous rooms in a beautifully restored Renaissance *palacio*. It also runs the much-lauded **Vandelvira** restaurant (*see* below).

****Hotel Puerta de la Luna, C/Canónigo Melgares Raya, t 95 374 70 19, *www.hotelpuertadelaluna.com* (€€€). A romantic, stylish little hotel tucked down a narrow passage in the heart of the old town. Lovely rooms, charming staff, a pool, gym and spa.

***La Casona del Arco, C/Sacramento 3, t 95 374 72 08, *www.lacasonadelarco.com* (€€€). Opened in 2006, this superb hotel is in a gracious 18th-century mansion with tasteful décor: antiques and parquet floors. Facilities include a pool and gardens. There are considerable reductions midweek.

⭐ Hospedería Fuentenueva ›

***Hospedería Fuentenueva, Pso Arca del Agua s/n, t 95 374 31 00, *www.fuentenueva.com* (€€). Elegant hotel in a striking Renaissance building which once did service as a women's prison, now a charming option. Extras include a fine restaurant and a pool.

***Hotel Palacete Santa Ana, C/Santa Ana Vieja 9, t 95 374 16 57, *www.palacetesantana.com* (€€). A lavishly restored noble palace – the closest thing you'll get to stepping back into the 18th century. Just 10 rooms, all of them different and stuffed full of original mirrors, paintings and sculptures. Live flamenco at weekends.

***Hacienda La Laguna, Ctra Baeza–Jaén, km 8, Puente del Obispo, t 95 377 10 05, *www.ehlaguna.com* (€€). A delightful rural hotel in an old *cortijo*, with two pools, two restaurants, an olive oil museum and lots of amenities for kids and adults.

**Comercio, C/San Pablo 21, t 95 374 01 00 (€). A comfortable 10-room lodging where Machado stayed, and perhaps even penned a few poems.

Hostal El Patio, C/Conde Romanones 13, t 95 374 02 00 (€). Renaissance mansion set around an atmospheric if dilapidated courtyard.

Juanito, Pso Arca del Agua s/n, t 95 374 00 40, *www.juanitobaeza.com* (€€€). Reputed to be one of the region's top restaurants, within a roadside hotel (€€) on the outskirts of Baeza. Quality can vary, however.

La Gondola, Portaes Carbonerías 13, t 95 374 29 84 (€€). Back from the main *paseo*, with an emphasis on grilled meats. A tasty speciality is *patatas baezanas* (sautéed potatoes with mushrooms).

Sali, C/Cardenal Benavides 15, t 95 374 13 65 (€€). Fish and shellfish, and game dishes like partridge in brine; one of the best tapas bars in the city. *Closed Wed*.

Vandelvira, C/San Francisco 14, t 95 374 75 19 (€€). An elegant restaurant inside the San Francisco convent, with tables filling the arched quadrangle. For more intimacy, dine upstairs. Delicious, innovative cuisine. *Closed Sun eve and Mon*.

Úbeda

✪ Úbeda

Even with Baeza for an introduction, the presence of this nearly perfect little city comes as a surprise. If the 16th century did well by Baeza, it was a golden age here, leaving Úbeda a 'town built for gentlemen' as the Spanish used to say, endowed with one of the finest collections of Renaissance architecture in all of Spain. Two men can be credited: Andrés de Vandelvira, an Andalucian architect who created most of Úbeda's best buildings, and Francisco de los Cobos, imperial secretary to Charles V, who paid for them. Cobos is a forgotten hero of Spanish history. While Charles was off

Getting to and around Úbeda and the Sierra de Cazorla

Úbeda's **bus station**, C/San José 6, **t** 95 375 21 57, is at the western end of town, and various lines connect the city directly to Madrid, Valencia and Barcelona, at least once daily. There are more frequent buses to Baeza (30mins), Córdoba (2½hrs), Jaén (1½hrs) Granada (2½hrs), and Sevilla. Cazorla and other villages can easily be reached from Úbeda, but the Sierra de Cazorla is poorly served by public transport and you will need a **car** to explore villages such as Hornos and Segura de la Sierra.

---

campaigning in Germany, Cobos had the job of running Castile. By the most delicate management, he kept the kingdom afloat while meeting Charles's ever more exorbitant demands for money and men. He could postpone the inevitable disaster, but not prevent it. Like most public officials in the Spanish 'Age of Rapacity', though, he also managed to salt away a few hundred thousand ducats for himself, and he spent most of them embellishing his home town.

Like Baeza, Úbeda is a peaceful and happy place; it wears its Renaissance heritage gracefully, and is always glad to have visitors. Tourism is less of a novelty here than it was even a couple of years ago, but it's still easy to understand the Spanish expression '*irse por los cerros de Úbeda*' ('take the Úbeda hill routes'). It equates to getting off the subject or wasting time, and arose many years ago after Úbeda gradually lost traffic to more commercial routes.

Úbeda today leaves no doubt about its political colours. In the **Plaza de Andalucía**, joining the old and new districts, there is an old metal statue of a Fascist Civil War general named Sero glaring down from his pedestal. The townspeople have put so many bullets into it that it looks like a Swiss cheese. They've left it here as a joke. The **Torre de Reloj**, in the *plaza*, is a 14th-century defensive tower now adorned with a clock. The plaque near the base, under a painting of the Virgin, records a visit from Charles V. From here, Calle Real takes you into the heart of the old town (at the time of writing, the streets were being dug up and replaced with traditional cobbles, so be prepared to clamber over piles of rubble and workmen's tools). Nearly every corner has at least one lovely palace or church on it. Two of the best can be seen on this street: the early 17th-century **Palacio de Condé Guadiana** has an ornate tower and distinctive windows cut out of the corners of the building, a common conceit in Úbeda's palaces. Two blocks down, the Palacio Vela de los Cobos is in the same style, with a loggia on the top storey. Northeast of here, on C/Cervantes, lies a small **museum** with the tiny monastic cell where San Juan de la Cruz died of cancer and ulceration of the flesh in 1591. Friar John is one of Spain's most illustrious poets and mystics.

Palacio Vela de los Cobos
private, but if the affable owner is home, he might let you in

San Juan de la Cruz Museum
in the Oratorio de San Jan de la Cruz; open Tues–Sun 11–1 and 5–7; adm

Plaza Vázquez de Molina

This is the only place in Andalucía where you can look around and *not* regret the passing of the Moors, for it is one of the few truly beautiful things in all this great region that was not built either by the Moors or under their influence. The Renaissance buildings around the Palacio de las Cadenas make a wonderful ensemble, and the austere landscaping, old cobbles and plain six-sided fountain create the same effect of contemplative serendipity as any chamber of the Alhambra. Buildings on the plaza include: the church of **Santa María de los Reales Alcázares**; a Renaissance façade on an older building with a fine Gothic cloister around the back; the *parador*; two sedate palaces from the 16th century, one of which, the Palacio del Marqués de Mancera, can be visited; and Vandelvira's **Sacra Capilla del Salvador**, begun in 1540, the finest of Úbeda's churches, where Francisco de los Cobos is buried. West of the *plaza*, at C/Narvaez 11, the latest Úbeda sight is the **Casa Museo Art Andalusí**, a traditional palace with antiques and art on show which also stages flamenco shows on Saturdays at 10pm.

Palacio del Marqués de Mancera
open daily 10am–11am, visits to the patio only

Sacra Capilla del Salvador
open Mon–Sat 10–2 and 5–7.30, Sun 10.45–2 and 4.30–7.30; adm

Casa Museo Art Andalusí
t 61 907 61 32; open 10.30–2.30 and 4–8.30; adm

All the sculpture on the façades of Úbeda is first-class, especially the west front of the Salvador. This is a monument of the time when Spain was in the mainstream of Renaissance ideas, and humanist classicism was still respectable. Note the mythological subjects on the west front and inside the church, and be sure to look under the arch of the main door. Instead of Biblical scenes, it has carved panels of the ancient gods representing the five planets; Phoebus and Diana with the sun and moon; and Hercules, Aeolus, Vulcan and Neptune to represent the four elements. The interior, with its great dome, is worth a look despite a thorough sacking in 1936 (the sacristan lives on the first door on the left of Calle Francisco Cobos, on the north side of the church).

Behind El Salvador, the **Hospital de los Honrados** has a delightful open patio – but only because the other half of the building was never completed. South of the *plaza*, the end of town is only a few blocks away, encompassed by a street called the **Redonda de Miradores**, a quiet spot favoured by small children and goats, with remnants of Úbeda's town wall. It's worth the walk to see the exceptional views out over the Sierra de Cazorla.

Úbeda's Pottery

Traditional dark green pottery, fired in kilns over wood and olive stones, is literally Úbeda's trademark. You'll see it all over town – try to pick up some authentic pieces before they become available at home. Tito, on the Plaza del Ayuntamiento, is a class establishment that produces and fires pieces on the premises. The designs are exquisite and are packed and shipped all over the world.

Highly recommended is a visit to the potters' quarter around the lovely cobbled Calle Valencia, a 15-minute stroll from the Plaza del Ayuntamiento. Heading northeast to the Plaza 1 de Mayo, cross the square diagonally and leave again by the northeast corner, along the Calle Losal to the Puerta de Losal, a 13th-century *mudéjar* gate. Continue downhill along the Calle de Merced, passing the Plaza Olleros on your left, and you come to Calle Valencia. Nearly every house is a potter's workshop; all are open to the public and you will soon find your own favourite. Ours is at No.36, where Juan José Almarza runs his family business, handed down through several generations. Juan spent two years in Edinburgh and is possibly the only potter in the province of Jaén with a Scottish accent.

Palacio de las Cadenas
interpretation centre open Tues–Sat 10–2 and 5–8, Sun 10–2

The home of Francisco de los Cobos's nephew, another royal counsellor, was the great **Palacio de las Cadenas**, now serving as Úbeda's *ayuntamiento*, on a quiet plaza at the end of Calle Real. The side facing the plaza is simple and dignified but the main façade, facing the Plaza Vázquez de Molina, is a stately Renaissance creation, the work of Vandelvira.

Beyond Plaza Vázquez de Molina

San Pablo
open Mon–Wed 11–12 and 5–8, Thurs–Sat 11–1 and 5–8, Sun 11–1.30

Northeast of El Salvador, along **Calle Horno Contado**, there are a few more fine palaces. At the top of the street, on Plaza 1 de Mayo, is the 13th-century **San Pablo** church, much renovated in the 16th century; inside is an elegant chapel of 1536, the Capilla del Camarero Vago. On the same square is the elegant town hall, dating from the 16th century. North from here along C/Cervantes is the **Casa de Mudéjar**, with a pretty courtyard containing the town's small **archaeological museum**. Further north, **San Nicolás de Bari** was originally a synagogue, though nothing now bears witness to this. It was confiscated in 1492, which has left it with one Gothic door and the other by Vandelvira, who oversaw the reconstruction.

Archaeological Museum
open Tues 3–8, Wed–Sat 9–8, Sun 9–3

San Nicolás de Bari
open daily 8.30am–9.30am

Trinity Church
open Tues–Sun 7.20pm–8.30pm

Take the road west from here, C/Condesa, and you will pass yet more fine palaces, Casa del Caballerizo Ortega, Palacio de los Bussianos, on C/Trinidad, and near it **Trinity Church**. On the western outskirts of town, near the bus station on Calle Nueva, is Vandelvira's most remarkable building, the **Hospital de Santiago**. This huge edifice has been called the 'Escorial of Andalucía'. It has the same plan as San Nicolás de Bari, a grid of quadrangles with a church inside. Oddly, both were begun at about the same time, though this one seems to have been started a year earlier, in 1568. Both are supreme examples of the *estilo desornamentado*. Now a cultural centre, it's used for exhibitions.

Hospital de Santiago
open Mon–Fri 8–3 and 3.30–10, Sat and Sun 11–3 and 6–9.30

Where to Stay and Eat in Úbeda

ⓘ **Úbeda >**
Palacio Marqués de Contadero, C/Baja del Marqués 4 (off Plaza del Ayuntamiento),
t 95 375 08 97, www.ubedainteresa.com;
open Mon–Sat 9–3

⊛ **Rosaleda de Don Pedro >>**

Úbeda ✉ 23400

****Parador de Úbeda, Pza de Vázquez de Molina s/n, t 95 375 03 45, *www.parador.es* (€€€€€). In a 16th-century palace with a glassed-in courtyard, one of the loveliest and most popular of the chain. All the beamed ceilings and fireplaces have been preserved and the restaurant is the best in town, featuring local specialities. Ask to see the ancient wine cellar.

****Álvar Fáñez, C/Juan Pasquau 5 (just off the Plaza San Pedro), t 95 379 60 43, *www.alvarfanez.com* (€€€€). Another handsomely converted ducal palace, with 11 tastefully decorated (albeit slightly austere) rooms, and a lovely *terraza* with views over the rooftops to the olive groves and the hills. There is also a café serving excellent tapas and a good restaurant in the *bodega*. Organizes cultural and environmental excursions.

***Rosaleda de Don Pedro, C/Obispo Toral 2, t 95 279 61 11, *www.rosaledadonpedro.com* (€€€). The city's latest hotel is very tastefully furnished with a combination of traditional and contemporary décor with terracotta tiles, stone-clad walls, custom-made beds and wrought iron furniture on the terrace. There is a pool and elegant restaurant.

Palacio de la Rambla, Plaza del Marqués 1, **t 95 375 01 96 (€€€). Romantic choice in the historic heart of the town, set in an ivy-clad Renaissance mansion that lets out beautiful double rooms (ask for room 106) surrounding a courtyard.

***María de Molina, Plaza del Ayuntamiento, s/n, **t** 95 379 53 56, *www.hotel-maria-de-molina.com* (€€€–€€). Probably has the edge over the others in terms of position. The patio has been modernized, but the 20 rooms have some original furniture and paintings. Also has a good restaurant, and five apartments close by.

La Paz, C/Andalucía 1, **t 95 375 21 40, *www.hotel-la-paz.com* (€). Family-run and clean with good amenities and rooms set around a pretty garden.

Sevilla, Avda Ramón y Cajal 9, **t 95 375 06 12 (€). By the Hospital de Santiago. Very good rates here.

*Pensión Victoria, C/Alaminos 5, **t** 95 375 29 52 (€). A simple *pensión* in a plain building by the bullring, but it's friendly. All rooms are en suite.

El Marqués, Pza Marqués de la Rambla 2, **t** 95 375 72 55 (€€). Popular restaurant with a big reputation and a popular terrace on the square.

Mesón Navarro, Plaza del Ayuntamiento, **t** 95 379 06 38 (€€). This place is hard to beat for atmosphere, located right on the *plaza* with a restaurant fronted by a generally crammed tapas bar. If you opt for the restaurant out back, try one of the traditional dishes, like partridge salad.

El Porche, Redono de Santiago 5, **t** 95 375 72 87 (€€). An elegant restaurant near the Hospital de Santiago with a terrace for al fresco dining and a fireplace for chillier evenings.

El Gallo Rojo, C/Manuel Barraca 16, **t** 95 375 20 38 (€€). A lively place in the evening with excellent tapas and a restaurant; full of characters by day.

El Seco, C/Corazón de Jesús 8, **t** 95 379 14 52 (€€). Tasty cooking: game in season and hearty stews. *Lunch only Mon–Thurs and Sun, also open eves Fri–Sat. Closed July.*

Nightlife in Úbeda

The **nightlife** scene is suprisingly lively in Úbeda. There are plenty of buzzy *terrazas* along **Avda del Cristo Rey** in summer. **Danzatoria**, C/Picasso 1, **t** 95 379 25 90, is a slick, designer club with an outpost in Barcelona.

Around Úbeda: The Sierra de Cazorla

Sierra de Cazorla

If you go east out of Úbeda, you'll be entering a zone few visitors ever reach. Your first stop might be the village of **Torreperogil**, where the Misericordia growers' co-operative in the Calle España produces first-class red and white wines, such as their *tinto El Torreño*, at a modest price. The **Sierra de Cazorla**, a jumble of ragged peaks, pine forests and olive-covered lowlands, offers some memorable mountain scenery, especially around **Cazorla**, a lovely white village of narrow alleys hung at alarming angles down the hillsides, with a strangely alpine feel to it. Cazorla's landmarks are a ruined Renaissance church (again, by Vandelvira) half-open to the sky, and its castle. But there's an even better castle, possibly built by the Templars; keep heading up the mountain to the hamlet of **La Iruela**. The castle is a romantic ruin even by Spanish standards, with a tower on a dizzying height behind. Beyond is the pass into the Sierra, the wild territory of hiking, hunting and fishing.

All of this area is poorly served by public transport and you will need a car to explore far-flung villages such as **Hornos** and **Segura de la Sierra**, both topped with Moorish castles. The latter is a pretty little town, untouched by tourism, with a number of monuments including some Moorish baths and a pretty Renaissance fountain. The road heads north to **Siles**, surrounded by embattlements and a lookout tower, before leaving the park via **Torres de Albánchez**, with more Moorish castle remains.

The mountain ranges of Cazorla and Segura make up one of Andalucía's most beautiful natural parks. The **Cazorla Natural Park** covers over half a million acres, and teems with wild boar, deer, mountain goat, buck and mouflon, while rainbow trout do their best to outwit anglers. The park abounds with mountain streams and is the source of the mighty Guadalquivir, nothing more than a trickle over a couple of stones at this point. Visitors interested in flora and fauna will find the area one of the richest in Europe, with a variety of small birdlife that's hard to match, as well as larger species such as eagles, ospreys and vultures.

Where to Stay and Eat in the Sierra de Cazorla

(i) **Cazorla >**
Pso del Santo Cristo 17, t 95 371 01 02, www. turismoencazorla.com, open daily 10–2

(i) **Segura de la Sierra (Natural Park information)**
Carretera del Tranco, km 51, t 95 371 30 17, www.ayto-cazorla.es

⭐ **Riogazas >**

Cazorla ✉ 23470

★★★Parador de Cazorla, El Sacejo (26km from Cazorla), t 95 372 70 75, *www.parador.es* (€€€). In the heart of the natural park, a mountain chalet with 33 rooms and a pool set right on the cliff edge. The restaurant is one of the best in the area.

Hotel Ciudad de Cazorla, Plaza de la Corredera 9 (right on the main square), t 95 372 17 00, *www.hotel ciudaddecazorla.com* (€€). Modern, well equipped and central, with plain rooms but a pool and restaurant.

Molino La Fárraga, Camino de la Hoz s/n, t 95 372 12 49, *www.molinola farraga.com* (€€). A charming B&B in an old windmill; pool and garden.

★★★La Finca Mercedes, Ctra de la Sierra, La Iruela, t 95 372 10 87, *www. lafincamercedes.com* (€€). Comfortable rooms, some with tremendous views; pool and super restaurant.

★★Riogazas, Ctra de Iruela al Chorro, t 95 312 40 35, *www.riogazas.com* (€€–€). For a real treat, take the (drive-able) dirt road 1.5km into the Natural Park to find this wonderful little rural inn. Charming staff, a restaurant, two pools (one for kids), breathtaking mountain scenery and utter tranquillity. *Open weekends only in winter.*

★Mirasierra, Santiago de la Espada, Ctra Cazorla–Pantana del Tranco, km 20, t 95 371 30 44 (€€–€). In a beautiful setting 20km north of Cazorla, on the road to the dam and reservoir at El Tranco; restaurant, pool.

★★Hotel Guadalquivir, C/Nueva 6, t 95 372 02 68, *www.hguadalquivir. com* (€). Friendly, family-run option near the centre.

Pensión Betis, Plaza Corredera 19, t 95 372 05 40 (€). An old-fashioned *pension* with washbasins in the rooms, but shared bathrooms. Rooms are plain but spotlessly clean.

There are a few rural hotels near Segura where you can get away from it all:

Hospedería Morceguillinas, Ctra Cortijos Nuevos–Beas, km 3, Cortijos Nuevos (near Segura de la Sierra), t 95 312 61 52 (€). Comfortable rural hotel in another pretty setting.

Hotel de Montaña Los Parrales, Carretera del Tranco, km 78, t 95 312 61 70, *www.turismoencazorla.com/ parrales.html*. A delightful friendly stone-clad rural hotel with comfortable rooms with magnificent views, plus a pool and barbecue area. A wide range of tours can be organized.

El Mesoncillo, in La Platera (a few km from Hornos), t 64 681 02 52, *www. elmesoncillo.com* (€). Self-catering cottages with great views, log fires and lots of chunky wooden furniture.

Jaén

In the middle of the vast tracts of olive groves upon which its precarious economy depends is Jaén, the most provincial of all the Andalucian capitals. Jaén lacks the Renaissance charms of Úbeda or Baeza, but it is a decent, modern town, not quite as unattractive as many guidebooks claim, and easily explored on foot in one day, along pleasant pedestrian walkways. Jaén was the first capital of the kingdom of Granada and the old Arab quarter is a part of the town that is well worth a visit. Its weaving, narrow, paved lanes are at the foot of the hill crowned by the 13th-century Moorish castle of **Santa Catalina**, built by ibn-Nasr. Towering above the town, it's an ideal place to take in views of the countryside and mountains. The city's pride is its monumental **cathedral** on Plaza Santa María, begun in 1548 by Andrés de Vandelvira. His work inside has suffered many changes, and the façade isn't his at all; not begun until 1667, Eufrasio López de Rojas's design was the first genuine attempt at Baroque in Andalucía, decorated with extravagant statuary by Pedro Roldán. There's a small **museum** inside, with a dull collection of local art and some rather more striking religious statuary.

Adjacent to the cathedral is the **Iglesia del Sagrario**, with a neoclassical interior designed by Ventura Rodríguez. On Calle Martínez Molina, west of the cathedral, the **Palacio de Villardompardo** has been beautifully restored to hold the extensive and engaging **Museum of Arts and Popular Customs**, and the smaller and less interesting **Museo de Arte Naif**. The real attraction is the **Baños Árabes** – 11th-century Moorish baths, complete with cold rooms, hot rooms and a tepidarium, discovered underneath.

Jaén has a number of other churches, convents, monasteries and fine palaces worth seeking out. Near the cathedral, on Calle Pescadería, is the 17th-century **Palacio de los Vilches**, and in the Plaza de San Francisco is the beautiful **Palacio Provincial**, where the regional *ayuntamiento* is based. Dating from the 19th century, the building has a fine central patio. Of the monasteries, perhaps the finest is that of **Santo Domingo**, in the street of the same name, which began life as a 14th-century monastery, before becoming the town's university and then the headquarters of the Inquisition; it now houses Jaén's historical archive. The façade is by Vandelvira. A few streets down is another monastery, **Santa Clara**, the town's oldest; inside is an odd figure of Christ made out of bamboo, Latin American in origin. Opposite stands the church of **San Bartolomé**, which has a fine *mudéjar* ceiling and the wonderful *Cristo de la Expiración*, by Martínez Montañés. The town's oldest church is **La Magdalena**, at the top of town on C/Molino Condesa. It dates from the 16th century and is built over an old mosque; the former minaret is now its bell tower. The exterior is Gothic; inside there are

Santa Catalina
t 95 312 07 33; open summer 10.30–1.30; winter 10–2; closed Wed; adm

Cathedral
open summer Mon–Sat 8.30–1 and 5–8, Sun 8.30–1; winter Mon–Sat 8.30–1 and 4–7, Sun 9–1; museum open Tues–Sat 10–1 and 4–7; adm

Palacio de Villardompardo
t 95 323 62 92; open Tues–Fri 9–8, Sat and Sun 9.30–2.30; adm, free to EU citizens

La Magdalena
open 9–12.30 and 5–8

Getting to and from Jaén

Jaén has few **train** services. There is one direct train daily to Sevilla (2hrs 50mins) via Córdoba (1hr 25mins) and about 4 services a day to Madrid (4hrs 15mins). The RENFE **station** is on the Paseo de la Estación, the main street, at the northern edge of town, by the Plaza de la Concordia.

Buses are the best bet – Jaén is a real transport hub. The **bus station** is on the Avenida de Madrid, near the tourist office. Buses run to Úbeda via Baeza, Granada, Málaga, Córdoba and Almería.

paintings, including *La Magdalena*, by Mateo de Medina. The area in which it stands was once the old Roman part of town.

Jaén's modern quarters can be a bit dreary, and peculiar at the same time. The centre, **Plaza de las Batallas**, has an extremely silly winged statue atop a pedestal, commemorating past victories over the Moors. Nearby, on the broad Plaza de la Estación, there is a good, but rather old-fashioned, archaeological collection in the **Museo Provincial** that includes one of the finest collections of Iberian artefacts in Spain.

If you're on the way to Granada, a possible detour is to **Alcalá La Real**, with an unusual town square and the picturesque **Castillo de la Mota** on top of a hill. The **Castillo de Solera**, in the tiny village of **Solera** just east of Huelma, is an even finer sight; the castle seems to grow out of its narrow crag. Like Cazorla, the views are breathtaking but it will be some trouble to get up to them on foot.

Museo Provincial
t 95 325 06 00; open Tues 3–8, Wed–Sat 9–8, Sun 9–3; adm, free to EU citizens

Where to Stay in Jaén

ⓘ **Jaén >**
C/Maestra 13, a small street near the cathedral, t 95 324 26 24/95 319 04 55, www.promojaen.es (for information on the whole province); open summer Mon–Fri 10–8, Sat, Sun and hols 10–1; winter Mon–Fri 10–7, Sat, Sun and hols 10–1

Jaén ✉ 23000

****Parador Castillo de Santa Catalina, in the castle overlooking Jaén, t 95 323 00 00, www.parador.es (€€€€). Charles de Gaulle spent time here working on his memoirs. A spectacular medieval castle with solid walls, it's one of the most characterful *paradores*. Excellent restaurant.

***Infanta Cristina, Avda de Madrid s/n, t 95 326 30 40, www.hotelinfanta cristina.com (€€€€). A large modern hotel on the outskirts of town, with spacious rooms, a pool and a restaurant known for local specialities.

***Xauen, Plaza de Deán Mazas 3 (near Plaza Constitución), t 95 324 07 89, www.hotelxauenjaen.com (€€). Central, modern, with good facilities for the price, and spacious rooms.

*Hostal Renfe, Pso de la Estación s/n, t 95 327 47 04 (€). Right next to the station; clean, bright and good value.

*La Española, Bernardo López 9, t 95 323 02 54 (€). A good choice near the cathedral, filled with plants and ceramics. Rooms with or without bath for a rock-bottom price.

Eating Out in Jaén

Casa Antonio, C/Fermín Palma 3, t 95 327 02 62 (€€€–€€). One of Jaén's most elegant restaurants, serving sophisticated Andalucían cuisine prepared with fresh, seasonal ingredients. For a treat, go for the *menú del degustación* at €45.

For less formal dining, there are numerous excellent tapas bars in the streets around the cathedral. In particular: C/Maestra and Arco del Consuelo, and Plaza de la Constitución and along the narrow alley, Calle Nueva, which leads off it. What nightlife there is centres around the streets at the bottom end of Pso de la Estación, bordered by C/Andalucía and the train station.

Café Zeluan, Plaza San Francisco. This Art Deco café is a good spot to linger over breakfast.

Huelva, Cádiz and Gibraltar

Everyone has heard of the Costa del Sol, but there is a good deal more to Andalucía, from the empty spaces of Huelva to the empty spaces of Almería. Stretching from Portugal to the Straits of Gibraltar, the Costa de la Luz, Andalucía's Atlantic coast, may not be all that scenic, but it has plenty of long, golden beaches that haven't yet become too crowded.

The piquant, sea-washed town of Cádiz is its major attraction. After Cádiz comes a glass of sherry in Jerez de la Frontera. Here the mountains begin to close in, with their white villages. Back on the coast, there is a clutch of growing resorts including windsurf city Tarifa; then Algeciras, a port town with the promise of a side-trip to Morocco, or to Ceuta, a tiny remnant of Spain's colonial empire in Africa. Finally we stop for meat and two veg in Gibraltar.

11

Don't miss

⭐ Europe's greatest wetland wildlife reserve
Parque Nacional del Coto Doñana p.191

⭐ An exuberant city and carnival
Cádiz p.192

⭐ Sherry, flamenco and horses
Jerez de la Frontera p.204

⭐ Extraordinary flora and fauna
Zahara and the Sierra de Grazalema p.210

⭐ A life undeground
Gibraltar's tunnels and caves p.234

See map overleaf

Huelva, Cádiz and Gibraltar

p.130

pp.238–9

50 km
10 miles

N

CÓRDOBA

Encinasola
Cumbres Mayores
Arroyomolinos de León
Cala
Rosal de la Frontera
N433
Aroche
Santa Olalla del Cala
Cortegana
Alájar
Aracena
Santa Bárbara de Casa
Sierra de Aracena
Zufre
Sierra Morena
Parque Natural de la Sierra de Hornachuelos

Cabezas Rubias
Minas de Río Tinto
Nerva
Puebla de Guzmán
Calañas
Zalamea la Real
A431
Alosno
HUELVA
Villanueva de los Castillejos
Río Odiel
Valverde del Camino
Coto Nacional de la Pata del Caballo
A66
Sanlúcar de Guadiana
San Bartolomé de las Torres
Beas
Carmona
Río Guadiana
Gibraleón
Canal del Bajo Guadalquivir
A364
N431
Trigueros
A472
Niebla
E1/A49
SEVILLA
Lepe
Bollullos par del Condado
A92
A Real de Santo Antonio
HUELVA
Palos de la Frontera
Almonte
SEVILLA
Punta Umbría
Los Cabezudos
Marismas del Guadalquivir
Utrera
Mazagón
El Rocío
A483
Río Guadalquivir
Torre de la Higuera
Parque Nacional del Coto Doñana
Matalascañas

ATLANTIC

Sanlúcar de Barrameda
Bonanza
Bornos
Villamartín
Olvera
Chipiona
Zahara de la Sierra
Setenil
Playa de Regla
Jerez de la Frontera
A382
Arcos de la Frontera
Ronda
Rota
Ubrique
El Puerto de Santa María
CÁDIZ
Cortes de la Frontera
MÁLAGA
Castillo de San Sebastián
Puerto Real
CÁDIZ
Reserva Nacional de Cortes de la Frontera
San Fernando
Medina Sidonia
Alcalá de los Gazules
El Colmenar
Parque Natural de los Alcornocales
Sierra Bermeja

OCEAN

Chiclana de la Frontera
Jimena de la Frontera
Embalse de Barbate
Castellar de la Frontera
Conil de la Frontera
Vejer de la Frontera
Sotogrande
Cabo de Trafalgar
Barbate
San Roque
La Línea de la Concepción
Zahara de los Atunes
Algeciras
Gibraltar
Tarifa
STRAITS OF GIBRALTAR
Costa de la Luz
Tenerife (Islas Canarias)
Málaga & Génova

Don't miss

Getting to and around Huelva Province

By train: The **railway station** in Huelva is on the Avenida de Italia, 5mins from the centre; there is a daily Talgo to Sevilla and Madrid, plus three local trains a day from Sevilla. You will have to change at Sevilla for Granada, Málaga, Almería, Cádiz, Jerez, Córdoba and other points in Andalucía. There are also regular trains to Ayamonte, on the Portuguese border.

By bus: Huelva's main **bus station** is on Avda Doctor Rubio s/n, **t** 95 924 56 14. There are services to Sevilla, Granada, Cádiz and Algeciras, and other destinations within the province: Ayamonte, Isla Cristina, Punta Umbria, Mazagón and Matalascañas on the coast, less frequently to Nerva and the mountain villages to the north. The nearest airport is Sevilla.

Huelva Province

Huelva

A Huelva una vez y nunca vuelvas.

(One trip to Huelva and you don't go back.)

This Andalucian saying does seem a little unkind, but the provincial capital is full of factories and freshly laid cement; from the outskirts it looks like some dilapidated Slovak town. Hit the centre, however, and, small as it is, it boasts an incongruously large number of fur shops and amusement arcades. Huelvans are an isolated bunch, flanked and maybe intimidated by the presence of haughty Sevilla on one side and the expanse of Portugal on the other. They are nonetheless friendly and welcoming, and fervent in their desire to play a more important role in the future of Spain.

The town's tourist brochure, in a unique and disarmingly modest display of candour, states that Huelva 'has no particular historic interest'. The town was severely damaged by the earthquake of 1755, explaining the near-absence of anything older than that; exceptions include the 16th-century Baroque church of **San Pedro** and the interesting Museo Provincial on Alameda Sundheim 13.

Museo Provincial
open Tues 3–8, Wed–Sat 9–8, Sun 9–3; closed Mon

The town's **theatre** is an Art Deco aberration that resembles an Italian ice-cream parlour, but the real curiosity of Huelva is the **Barrio Reina Victoria**, a neighbourhood constructed by and for the employees of the English Río Tinto mining company in the 19th century. The company houses, now in a state of disrepair, sport gable ends and chimney pots in true English suburban style. (You may still see the Río Tinto Company mentioned in the business pages. In the 1900s they were running one of the biggest copper mines in the world here; when the deposits gave out, they opened a new one in Zambia.) Just out of town is a 36m (118ft)

Chocos and Choqueros

Huelvan cuisine is based on fish and sausages – white, horseshoe-shaped, smoke-cured salami and blood sausage. The Huelva hills are home to the Iberian pig, which has a justifiably high reputation for the quality of its pork; the local ham is a fine aromatic meat. Huelvans are also known as *choqueros*, because of their love for *chocos*, small cuttlefish; but just as popular is *mojama*, an expensive, salty fish delicacy of raw wind-dried tuna. Although Condado de Huelva is near to Jerez, it is still within Huelva province and provides decent white table wine and *finos* such as Condado Pálido and Condado Viejo.

ⓘ Huelva ›
*Plaza de la Monjas,
t 95 925 12 18, www.
ayuntamientohuelva.es,
www.diphuelva.es; open
Mon–Fri 9–7, Sat 10–2;
closed Sun*

⭐ El Portichuelo
››

Where to Stay in Huelva

Huelva ✉ 21000

****NHLuz Huelva**, Alameda
Sundheim 26, **t** 95 925 00 11, *www.
nh-hoteles.com* (€€€). Modern,
anonymous, but central and
luxurious.

***Tartessos**, Avda Martín Alonso
Pinzón 13, **t** 95 928 27 11, *www.hotel-
tartessos.com* (€€€). Another giant:
comfortable and central with a good
restaurant and piano bar.

****Los Condes**, Alameda Sundheim 14,
t 95 928 24 00, *www.hotelloscondes.
com* (€€). Modern, central, comfortable and good value.

****Virgen de la Cinta**, Av Manuel Siurot
7, **t** 95 954 12 60, *www.hotelvirgen
delacinta.com* (€€). A delightful,
modest hotel in an attractive building
on the outskirts of town.

****Costa de la Luz**, C/José María Amo
8, **t** 95 925 64 22 (€€–€). In a good spot
bang in the centre of town, a few
minutes' walk from the theatre,
though the décor is a little dated.

Eating Out in Huelva

Huelva packs some surprises in the
culinary department; its markets keep
the restaurants well supplied with
gleaming fresh seafood, and Huelvans
like to eat out.

Farqueo, Muelle de Levante, Glorieta
de las Canoas, Puerto de Huelva,
t 95 925 26 90 (€€). Right on the port,
with a sophisticated menu of
contemporary Andalucian cuisine and
beautiful harbour views. It also has an
elegant bar with terrace.

El Portichuelo, Avda Martín Alonso
Pinzón, **t** 95 924 57 68 (€€). A local
favourite, serving up excellent local
grilled meat (*carnes a la brasa*) and a
hugely popular tapas bar.

Las Candelas, Ctra Punta Umbría (at
the Aljaraque crossing 6km out of
town), **t** 95 931 83 01 (€€). A classic,
serving perfect seafood at affordable
prices. *Closed Sun*.

Azabache, C/Vázquez López 22, **t** 95
925 75 28 (€). Traditional bar and
restaurant serving a wonderful range
of tapas, accompanied by excellent
wines from all over Spain.

statue of Columbus, sculpted by Gertrude Whitney and presented
to Spain by the USA in 1929.

The town also boasts an 18th-century cathedral, **La Merced**, off
Paseo de la Independencia, and next door the University of Huelva,
in an old hospital. Columbus-philes might also wish to trek up to
the top of town to visit the 15th-century **Santuario de Nuestra
Señora de la Cinta**, off Avda de la Cinta. Columbus prayed at this
chapel before his epic voyage to the New World, an event
commemorated in traditional *azulejo* tiles by Daniel Zuloaga.

Around Huelva

Twenty-seven kilometres east of Huelva on the A472 you may
visit the once-important town of **Niebla**, a drowsy warren of
twisting streets half-forgotten behind its crumbling Romano-
Moorish walls. There's a Roman bridge and some interesting old
churches and Moorish buildings. Santa María de la Granada is a
church/mosque which came about in the same way as Córdoba's
Mezquita – by fusing the two religious buildings together.

Huelva province is making great attempts to cash in on its
Columbus legacy and has organized a tourist itinerary to the

Santa María de
la Granada
*a key is available
from the town hall*

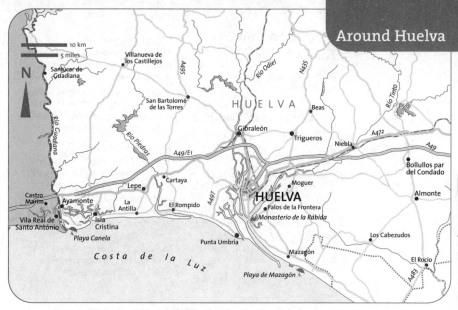

Lugares del Descubrimiento ('Places of Discovery', information and map from most tourist offices), which takes in the key spots associated with the great explorer, who set out on his first voyage to the New World from **Palos de la Frontera**, 5km southeast of Huelva. The town today is a rather uninspiring place, but it does have a number of key monuments associated with Columbus, including the church of **San Jorge Mártir**, where Columbus heard Mass before setting sail, and the fountain, **La Fontanilla**, which supplied water for the journey. Just beyond is a small park built to mark the quincentenary of Columbus's departure. Along C/Colón, at No.24, there is a small museum dedicated to Martín Alonso Pinzón, captain of the *Pinta* on Columbus's first voyage to America.

A few kilometres on from Palos, along a road lined with ceramics depicting each of the 50 states of the USA, and set in a forest of pines, lies the Monasterio de Santa María de la Rábida, where Columbus planned his epic journey. The rooms he used are maintained much as they were then, and can be viewed on a 45-minute tour, which also takes in an alabaster Virgin from the 14th century, the *mudéjar* cloisters and frescoes painted by Daniel Vázquez Díaz. The Muelle de las Carabelas, between the monastery and the river, features three full-size models of the ships that made the voyage, together with replicas of 15th-century quayside bars.

North of Palos lies **Moguer**, a pretty whitewashed village where *La Niña* was built before the river silted up and, along with Palos, where most of the crew were recruited for the voyage, including Juan and Pedro Alonso Niño, the captain and pilot of *La Niña*. Moguer was also home to Nobel Prize-winning poet Juan Ramón

Museo Pinzón
t 959 35 01 99, open Tues–Sun 10–2 and 5–7

Monasterio de Santa María de la Rábida
visits hourly by guided tour only, July and Aug Tues–Sun 10–1 and 4.45–8; Sept–June Tues–Sun 10–1 and 4–6.15; closed Mon; adm

Muelle de las Carabelas
open April–Sept Tues–Fri 10–2 and 5–9, Sat–Sun 11–8; Oct–Mar Tues–Sun 10–7; adm

ⓘ **La Rábida** >>
Paraje de la Rábida,
t *95 953 21 58*

ⓘ **Moguer** >>
C/Castillo s/n, **t** *95 937 18 98, www. aytomoguer.es*

Festivals around Huelva

Moguer: Fiesta de Virgen de Monte-mayor; the streets fill with horses.

Where to Stay and Eat around Huelva

Palos de la Frontera ✉ 21400

Hotel La Pinta, C/Rábida 75, **t 95 935 05 11 (€€). The best place to stay in the centre, with plenty of facilities and a very nice restaurant.

Hostal La Niña, C/Juan de la Cosa 37, **t 95 953 03 60 (€). Cheaper, but slightly out of town, which means that it can offer parking.

La Rábida ✉ 21810

Hotel Hacienda Santa María, on the road to Palos, **t 95 953 00 01 (€). Good on amenities but thin on character.

Restaurante Hostería La Rábida, **t** 95 935 03 12 (€€–€). Excellent restaurant in the monastery, serving solid traditional cuisine at reasonable prices.

Moguer ✉ 21400

Pensión Platero, C/Aceña 4, **t** 95 937 21 59 (€). The best basic place to stay in town, in a pretty *andaluz* house.

Hostal Pedro Alonso Niño, C/Pedro Alonso Niño 13, **t** 95 937 23 92 (€). A basic modern place to stay, with a small patio.

La Parrala, Plaza de las Monjas 22, **t** 95 937 04 52 (€€). The top place for a meal, on an attractive plaza.

Museo Jiménez
t *95 937 21 48; open Mon–Sat 10.15–1 and 5.15–7, Sun 10–1; adm, guided visits in Spanish only; closed for restoration in 2008 and exhibits temporarily on display at C/Ribera 2*

Santa Clara
t *95 937 01 07; open 11–1 and 5–7, Sun and Mon 11–1; adm*

Jiménez; his house, in the street of the same name, is now a **museum**, a Baroque building full of his notepads, books and documents. He is buried with his wife, Zenobia, in an atmospheric 19th-century **cemetery** on the eastern edge of town. You can also visit the 14th-century convent of **Santa Clara**, where Columbus spent the night in prayer after his return from the Indies in 1493. It's now a sacred art museum with a pair of exquisite *mudéjar* cloisters. The 18th-century **Iglesia de Santa María de Granada** has a bell tower similar in design to the Giralda, while nearby, on Plaza del Cabildo, is the beautiful **town hall**, described by Michael Jacobs in his book *Andalucía* as 'the finest neoclassical building in the whole of Huelva province'.

West of Huelva

Boats
river ferry information **t** *95 947 06 17; for* **cruises** *up the Guadiana, call* **t** *95 947 16 30*

Coming from Huelva by bus to **Ayamonte**, you'll be deposited next to the pretty square behind the harbour filled with small boats, which you can eye from the comfort of one of the *azulejo* benches. (If you're on your way to Portugal, walk through the square and follow the signs for the **Muelle de Portugal**, where a flat-bottomed **boat** will be waiting to take you and 40 cars across the narrow stretch of the Guadiana river to the Portuguese town of Vila Real de Santo António. Most people now take the striking contemporary bridge which passes by the Portuguese border town of Castro Marim.) The back streets of Ayamonte are not without character and there are plenty of little cafés where you can sit and muse, or bring your diary up to date. The town's major monument is the church of **Las Angustias**, a Baroque-*mudéjar* pile, dedicated to the town's patron saint: her fiestas are celebrated at the start of September. Just across the water, the beaches of **Isla Canela** and **Punta del Moral** are more popular with Spaniards than with foreigners. Both lie just a few kilometres from the town centre through a small natural park, the **Marismas de Isla Cristina**. This fragile ecosystem is under threat from burgeoning development on all sides, perhaps most acutely in Punta del Moral where a number of huge hotel complexes are under construction. Isla Canela is more restrained, a sleepy collection of restaurants, bars and apartments dominated by the vast faux-Moorish Riu Canela hotel. If you find yourself here around Easter, **Isla Cristina**'s Holy Week processions rival even those of Sevilla – it would be worth planning a visit for these alone. The working port is one of the most important in Spain: the catch ends up on Madrileños lunch tables via the early morning trains; get up early (5am) to see the boats come in.

Heading back east to Huelva, along the N431, you'll pass the sleepy town of **Lepe**, for some reason the butt of Andalucian jokes. Rather sportingly, every May the Leperos hold a festival of humour – and even if they mind the abuse, they're laughing all the way to the bank, for the ever-abundant strawberry, orange and asparagus crops in this area have made the town very wealthy. (Those silver lakes you see along the road are actually tinted plastic sheets protecting the strawberries.) This stretch of road between Huelva and Ayamonte has no real attraction – orange groves interspersed with derelict buildings, scrapyards and mud flats. South of Lepe on the coast are two spots worth a visit – **La Antilla**, with its fine white sandy beach (EU Blue Flag), and **El Rompido**, a pleasant seaside place that is rapidly being developed for tourism. The main development is taking place a few kilometres further on, at **El Portil**, a bland and ugly place. Further east, the peninsula of **Punta Umbría** is one of the main tourist resorts of the area; its long sandy beaches offer all types of water sports.

Where to Stay and Eat West of Huelva

(i) **Ayamonte >**

C/Huelva 27, **t** 95 932 07 37; open summer Mon–Fri 10–2 and 5–9; winter Mon–Fri 9.30–1.30 and 5–7

Ayamonte ✉ 21400

****Parador de Ayamonte, El Castillito, **t** 95 932 07 00, *www.parador.es* (€€€). Not on the beach but this has the benefit of a large pool and is located on the edge of the Guadiana river, with views over the sea. Although it occupies the site of a long-gone Moorish castle, the *parador* was built more recently, in 1966.

***Don Diego, C/Ramón y Cajal s/n, **t** 95 947 02 50, *www.hoteldondiego ayamonte.com* (€€€). A decent option in the town centre, a 1960s-style hotel with pink exterior and red bathrooms.

*Marqués de Ayamonte, C/Trajano 12, **t** 95 932 01 25 (€). A good budget hotel just off Plaza de Ribera in the centre.

There's a line of fine little restaurants along the *plaza*, on the Paseo de la Ribera.

Casa Luciano, C/Palma 1, **t** 95 947 10 71 (€€). Excellent seafood, fish stews and a good-value lunch *menú* at €15. *Closed Sun*.

Casa Barbieri, Paseo de la Ribera 12, **t** 95 947 01 37 (€€). Dine out on the terrace on traditional rice and seafood.

Mesones Juan Macías, Paseo de la Ribera 2, **t** 95 947 16 95 (€€). Great freshly caught seafood and fish. Try the local clams (*chirlas*).

Mesón la Casona, C/Lusitania 2, **t** 95 932 10 25 (€). A simple place that does a good *menú* for around €10 with seafood featuring heavily; there is a patio inside. Tasty tapas are available at the bar, too.

Passage Café, Plaza de la Laguna 11, **t** 95 947 10 81 (€). A good place to start the evening, this café hosts changing art exhibitions.

Isla Canela ✉ 21400

In July and August prices at these large hotels are high, but out of season they plummet dramatically.

****Playa Canela, Avda la Mojarra, Punta del Moral (7km from Ayamonte), **t** 95 947 95 45, *www.hotelesplaya.com* (€€€€). A huge, luxury beachside complex with pool, golf and every imaginable facility.

****Riu Atlántico, Punta del Moral s/n, **t** 95 962 10 00, *www.riu.com* (€€€). Luxuriously appointed two- to four-storey complex by the estuary, with a shuttle bus to Ayamonte on weekdays. Large pool.

Espuma del Mar, Pso de los Gavilanes s/n, **t** 95 947 72 85 (€). Serves simple, fresh seafood, with outside tables.

Bombadill, **t** 616 212 688 (€). A *chiringuito* actually on the beach in Isla Canela, serving delicious grilled sardines plus more elaborate dishes.

Isla Cristina ✉ 21410

*****Isla Cristina Palace, Avda Parque 148, **t** 95 934 44 99, *www.islacristinapalace.com* (€€€€). A vast, modern complex on the beach offering every five-star luxury including pools, gym and spa.

****Los Geranios, Avda de la Playa s/n, **t** 95 933 18 00, *www.hotellosgeraneoslaplata.com* (€€€€). 100 metres from the sea in an old-fashioned building, this was the first hotel here. The recently refurbished rooms have flowery fabrics and baths/showers.

Paraíso Playa, Avda de la Playa s/n, **t 95 933 18 73, *www.hotelparaisoplaya.com* (€€€). Provides all kinds of amenities, including a pool. Prices drop dramatically out of season.

Casa Rufino, Ctra de la Playa, **t** 95 933 08 10 (€€). The best food here. Try the *tonteo* (eight different kinds of fish, each with an appropriate sauce). *Closed eves except during* Semana Santa *and in summer*.

Acosta, Plaza del Caudillo 13, **t** 95 933 14 20 (€). A local favourite for fresh fish and Andalucían stews. *Closed Mon in winter*.

La Antilla ✉ 21449

La Antilla has a limited number of places to stay, all of which are booked up over summer.

***Hotel Valsequillo, Ctra Lepe-La Antilla, km 1.7, **t** 95 938 05 91, *www.hotelvalsequillo.net* (€€€). A modern hotel built in traditional style just outside Lepe, with a seawater pool, tennis court and restaurant.

Lepe Mar, C/Delfin 12, La Antilla, **t 95 948 10 01 (€€). The friendliest hotel on the seafront, in classic Spanish 1960s style, with parking, café and bars.

Hostal Azul, Avda de la Playa 15, La Antilla, **t 95 948 07 00 (€€). Central, modern, not far from the beach.

Hotel La Antilla, Plaza de la Parada 1, La Antilla, **t 95 948 00 56 (€). One of several places around the bus stop, with a sun terrace and parking.

El Rompido ✉ 21459

Large-scale tourism is seriously taking off here. Places to eat are along the main street in the lower part of the village, beside the beach.

*****El Rompido Golf Hotel, Ctra Cartaya-El Rompido, **t** 95 902 43 20, *www.sethotels.com* (€€€€). Large, modern luxury hotel with plenty of sports facilites including an 18-hole golf course.

****Hotel Fuerte El Rompido, Ctra H4111, km 8, **t** 95 939 99 29, *www.fuertehoteles.com* (€€€) This hotel is part of the prestigious Fuerte chain and is a self-proclaimed 'eco hotel' while sporting every luxury, with extras including free ferry trips to stretches of nearby unspoiled beach.

***Nuevo Portil Golf**, Urb Nuevo Portil, **t** 959 528240, *www.ac-hotels. com* (€€€). In between El Rompido and Punta Umbría, this handsome colonial style hotel is surrounded by an 18-hole golf course.

*****La Galera**, Urb. Los Pinos, **t** 95 939 91 76 (€). A simple seafront hotel, also out of town.

La Ola, Plaza del Mar 1, **t** 95 939 94 70 (€€–€). One of several reasonably priced fish restaurants by the beach.

(i) **Punta Umbría** >
*Avda Ciudad de Huelva s/n, **t** 95 949 51 60, www.puntaumbria.es*

Punta Umbría ✉ 21100

The choice is wider at Punta Umbría. All these little resorts have cheaper hotels within reasonable distance of the beaches. In the busy season, phone ahead.

****Hotel Barceló Punta Umbria**, Avenida Océano, **t** 95 949 54 00, *www.barcelo.com* (€€€€). The most luxurious hotel here, overlooking the beach with quasi-Moorish style architecture and every facility, including wi-fi, bar and restaurant and pool.

Hotel Ayamontino, Avda Andalucía 35, **t 95 531 14 50 (€€€–€€). Part of the reliable Husa chain, with little charm but just 250m from the beach.

Youth hostel, Avenida del Océano 13, **t** 95 931 16 50, *www.interjoven.com* (€). For those on a very tight budget.

El Paraíso, Ctra de Huelva–Punta Umbría, km 11, **t** 95 931 27 56 (€€). Generally regarded by locals as one of the best seafood restaurants in the region. Two dining rooms, one beachy, the other quite elegant.

Bar Antonio, Combes Punzones 10, **t** 95 931 41 32 (€). A small eatery by the market.

La Esperanza, Plaza Pérez Pastor 3, **t** 95 931 10 45 (€). Long popular, with satisfying, well-cooked dishes at reasonable prices.

The Sierra de Aracena

If you have a car you can comfortably explore the little-visited mountain villages in the Sierra de Aracena north of Huelva. The N435 from Huelva or the N433 from Seville pass through beautiful forests of holm oaks and cork trees to the heart of this area.

Aracena

Aracena makes a good base from which to explore the Sierra. Just 70km from the Portuguese border, the town became part of Spain in the 13th century and fell under the control of the Knights Templars. They built the **Iglesia de Nuestra Señora del Mayor Dolor**, which stands in the grounds of the Moorish castle above town. This fine medieval church has a *mudéjar* tower, once the minaret of the mosque that stood here before. Beneath it lies the region's major draw, the Gruta de las Maravillas, a series of cavernous natural chambers with underground lakes. Local legend has it that the caves, which rival Nerja's for their extraordinary beauty, were discovered by a shepherd late in the 19th century.

Gruta de las Maravillas
t 95 912 82 55; open 10–1.30 and 3–6; adm, tours hourly Mon–Fri, every 30mins Sat and Sun

The town has a number of other churches, including the **Ermita de Santa Catalina**, which was once a synagogue, and the unfinished **Iglesia de la Asunción**, which you pass on the way up to the ruins of a Moorish **castle**, once occupied by the Templars. The Ermita forms the focus for the town's main fiesta, the pilgrimage to the Sanctuary of the Virgin, which is held on 8 September and involves brotherhoods from neighbouring villages dressing up in

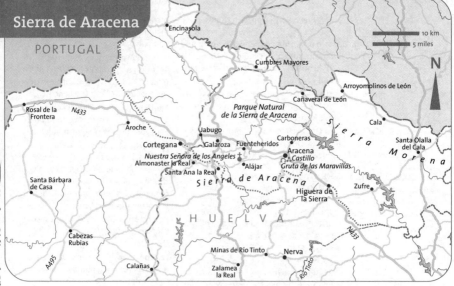

traditional costume and racing on horseback to the top of the hill. Another **hermitage** nearby is also worth visiting, with its 13th-century Gothic carvings and wonderful views over the mining lands of Río Tinto, excavated as early as Phoenician and Roman times, and bought by a British company in the late 19th century.

Around Aracena: Into the Sierra

Twelve kilometres from Aracena, to the west on the twisting A470, is the pretty village of **Alájar**, worth a stop for its natural caves, the **Sillita del Rey** and the **Salón de los Machos**, which form part of the **Peña de Arias Montano**, a spot long revered for its mystical qualities and named after Benito Arias Montano, an adviser to Philip II who came here to meditate and study the Bible. The king is said to have joined him at one point (hence 'del Rey').

South of here, **Minas de Río Tinto** is a small, shabby mining town set in an area scarred by open mines and lakes, once owned by the Río Tinto Mining Company and now gradually sliding into the history books. The town itself is worth a stop for just two things: the mining museum and the former British colony of **Bella Vista**. Now signposted as 'El Barrio Inglés' at the lower end of town, Bella Vista is a collection of Edwardian-gabled houses like the ones in Huelva, only set round an English-style village lawn, straight out of the Surrey countryside. It was built for the Río Tinto bosses, presumably to alleviate homesickness. The Museo Minero, in the old mining hospital on Plaza del Museo at the top of town, is a painstaking account of the mining practices that have taken place in this area since Roman times. There are recreations of mines from ancient times, plus exhibitions of Roman coins, a collection of

Museo Minero
*t 95 959 00 25;
open daily 10.30–3
and 4–7; adm*

semiprecious stones and some fascinating photos of miners through several generations. There are also some accounts ledgers and a hospital ledger detailing grim accidents suffered by miners. The centrepiece is two British-built locomotives and a sumptuous carriage, the Maharajah's Carriage, built for (but never used by) Queen Victoria for a trip to India. The museum runs a **tourist train** (pulled by Spain's oldest steam engine on Sundays, and a diesel engine on other days) which puffs along the 19th-century tracks laid by the Río Tinto mining company between April and October). It also organizes trips to the opencast mines, including the **Corte Atalaya**, the largest in Europe. You would probably be better off stopping at the *mirador*, signposted just before the village, where you can view the entire weird landscape yourself.

At El Chorro, a waterfall near the town of **Santa Ana La Real**, the road forks north to **Jabugo**, one of the most famous centres in Spain for *jamón* production, and west to **Almonaster la Real**, a pretty village with Roman origins and later Arabic influence – '*al*' derives from the Arabic *al-munia*, meaning fortress. Its chief feature is the 10th-century mosque, one of a handful of rural mosques in Andalucía. Its lines follow those of the Mezquita in Córdoba, perfect Moorish arches supported by slim columns. There is a fountain in the corner, and you can climb up the minaret which looks across the bullring to a parkland of blue and green oak-covered hills. The town itself has a number of medieval buildings and contains some fine examples of *mudéjar* and Gothic architecture, as well as the 14th-century church of **San Martín** and the **Puerta del Perdón**, in Manueline style.

The road from here to **Cortegana** passes right through pig territory, so drive slowly and look out for herds sheltering from the sweltering heat under the oaks. Cortegana is topped by a restored medieval castle and contains a fine *mudéjar* church, the **Iglesia del Divino Salvador**, a national monument dating from the 16th century. From here you might be best heading back east to Jabugo. If you do decide to press on, the N433 will take you past fields full of mean-looking *toros bravos* (fighting bulls): stop to take snaps by all means, but don't venture into the fields for a closer look.

In **Aroche**, further west, the white houses bask in the sun under the remains of an Almoravid fortress with 10 towers, containing a bullring. The town is just outside the Picos de Aroche National Park and about 25km from the border. There's a small municipal **archaeological museum** and the tiny **Museo del Rosario** – yes, a rosary bead museum with more than 1,300 rosaries donated by, among others, J. F. Kennedy, Franco, Mother Teresa and Nixon. The pilgrimage of San Mamés, a horseback procession, takes place on the third weekend in August (information from the town hall in Plaza Juan Carlos).

The **Picos de Aroche National Park** might not have the drama or arresting beauty of the Serranía de Ronda or the Sierra de Grazalema, but it is equally as pretty in its own way, with tiny villages nestling among forests of oak and pine, home to herds of black pigs and *toros bravos*, with vultures, eagles and kestrels soaring overhead. The last bears were killed just a few years ago, but in the remoter parts of the park wolves are still said to prowl, and there are even a few recorded Iberian lynx still in existence.

The main road back towards Huelva passes through the charming little village of **Galaroza**, surrounded by willow and ash forest, and crossed by a pretty stream. Continuing east will take you to **Fuenteheridos**, another picturesque village with a number of water-inspired sights, including the **Fuente de Doce Caños**, a 12-spring fountain in the main square, with a Baroque wooden sculpture.

To the southeast of Aracena, the N433 passes **Higuera de la Sierra**, dominated by a pretty Baroque church. Its Epiphany festival is the oldest in Spain. Four kilometres on lies the turning for the spectacular clifftop village of **Zufre** (along the A461), with a number of important monuments including a church built over a mosque, with a retable by Alonso Cano. The crumbling town walls date from the 12th century. Forests of gall and holm oak separate Zufre from **Santa Olalla del Cala**, dominated by a 13th-century Moorish castle. The church below is built over a synagogue, the anchor inside a reminder of the time when Santa Olalla served as the base for the marine infantry during the Napoleonic wars. Two kilometres north is the turn-off for **Cala**, with a 14th-century church, and the Cerro del Bujo viewpoint at **Arroymolinos de León**.

The Northern Border: Aracena to Encinasola

A quiet route heads north from Aracena via **Carboneras** to the borders of Extremadura. This is prime pig-spotting territory and, in summer, the landscape is reminiscent of the African bush, with parched reservoirs and scrubby brown hills. The road ends up at **Cañaveral de León**, allegedly famous for its gazpacho but not much else. You are best off continuing towards **Cumbres Mayores**, the largest of three villages with Cumbres (heights) in their name, all three famous for their sausages. In Cumbres Mayores there is a

Castle
enquire at the ayuntamiento for the keys

magnificent 13th-century **castle** built by Don Sancho IV 'El Bravo' during a war with Portugal. It has nine sides and eight turrets and was declared a national monument in 1895 by Alfonso XIII.

Next door is the church of **San Miguel**, which is the start of a waymarked hour-long walking tour. From here you could press on another 23km to **Encinasola**, which lies at the crossroads to Extremadura and Portugal and has a number of monuments, including a 10th-century Muslim fortress.

(i) Jabugo >>
C/Carratera 9,
t 95 912 11 32

(i) Aracena >
Plaza San Pedro s/n,
t 95 912 82 06; open
Mon–Sat 10–2.30
and 4–6.30
Natural Park*: visitor's*
centre, Edificio Cabildo
Viejo, Plaza Alta s/n,
t 95 912 88 25

(★) Finca
Buen Vino >

Where to Stay and Eat in the Sierra de Aracena

Aracena ✉ 21200

*Finca Buen Vino, Los Marines, Huelva, **t** 95 912 40 34, *www.fincabuenvino. com* (€€€€–€€€). A grand guesthouse up in the Sierra Morena (6km from Aracena), run by a locally well-known English family. Lunch is served beside the pool; dinner is taken with the family. There are also charming self-catering cottages for rent. Book early.

***Finca Valbono, Ctra de Carboneras 1, **t** 95 912 76 18, *www.fincavalbono. com* (€€€). A much better bet than staying in the town's lacklustre hotels; very friendly, sparkling clean and in the heart of the hills, with a pool and restaurant, and riding stables. Also has self-catering apartments.

***Posada de Valdezufre, C/Santa Marina 1, **t** 95 946 33 22 (€€€). A lovely rural hotel set in forest 7km from Aracena, with elegant rooms, a pool and a good restaurant.

Posada de Valdezufre, C/Santa Marina 1, Valdezufre, **t** 95 946 33 22, *www. valdezufre.com* (€€€). Just outside Aracena on the edge of the Aroche natural park, this delightful former 19th-century farmhouse is surrounded by olive groves. Rooms are home-like and comfortable and lunch and dinner are available on request.

Sierra de Aracena, Gran Vía 21, **t 95 912 61 75, *www.hsierraaracena.es* (€€). A modern place.

Restaurante Casas, C/Pozo de la Nieve 39–41, **t** 95 912 80 44 (€€). At the entrance to the caves in Aracena, styled after a traditional *venta*, serving Sierra pork every which way you can think of.

Manzano, Plaza del Marqués de Aracena, **t** 95 912 63 37 (€). This is the place for tapas in Aracena, over-looking the the square with a vast choice, including delicious seasonal wild mushrooms. *Closed Tues.*

Alájar ✉ 21290

***La Posada, Médico Emilio González 2, **t** 95 912 57 12, *http://laposadade alajar.com* (€€). A lovely historic inn run by a charming Anglo-Spanish couple; great facilities for the price.

Jabugo ✉ 21290

*La Aurora, C/Barco 9, **t** 95 912 11 46 (€). A small, friendly *pensión*, offering rooms with bath.

Mesón Cinco Jotas, Ctra de San Juan del Puerto s/n, **t** 95 912 10 71 (€€). Here they smoke their own hams and export them to every corner of Spain, and beyond. It is now part of a chain covering all of Spain.

Bodega Jamón, Ctra de San Juan del Puerto s/n, **t** 95 912 15 96 (€). Next door to Mesón Cinco Jotas, serving much the same fare but at a cheaper price and with a lovely shaded patio attached.

Almonaster la Real ✉ 21290

Hotel Casa García, Avda de San Martín 2, **t** 95 914 31 09, *www.hotelcasagarcia. com* (€€). At the entrance to the village. An upmarket place with a delightful courtyard, serving regional pork dishes and fish at a reasonable price. Rooms are plain, though.

*La Cruz, Plaza del Llano 8, **t** 95 914 31 35 (€). A basic but more than adequate *hostal* off a tiny square, with a restaurant.

Cortegana ✉ 21230

***La Posada de Cortegana, Ctra El Repilado-La Corte, km 2.5, **t** 95 950 33 01, *www.posadadecortegana.es* (€€). An old inn tucked away in the hills, with accommodation in wooden cabins surrounded by gardens. Pool, restaurant, horse-riding and bike hire.

Cervantes, Cervantes 27, **t** 95 913 15 92 (€). Very basic rooms, no bath.

Restaurante El Aceitón, Avda de Portugal s/n, **t** 95 913 13 56 (€). Come here for good dining on regional dishes. *Closed Tues.*

Aroche ✉ 21240

Picos de Aroche, Aroche, **t** 95 914 01 44, *www.picosdearoche.com* (€€). Six apartments with attractive traditional Andalusian-style accommodation with beams and wrought-iron bedheads. There are magnificent views of the historic town centre. Check the website for directions.

Finca Montefrio, Camino del Aroche, **t** 95 950 32 51, *www.fincamontefrio. com*. This working organic farm in wooded hills has four self-catering cottages sleeping 4–8 people; pool. Minimum one-week stay, €700.

Rosal de la Frontera ✉ 21250

El Mirador de la Frontera, Avda de Sevilla 60, t 95 914 14 08 (€€). Cheap and very basic.

Pensión Frontera, Avda de Portugal 109, t 95 914 10 28 (€€–€). This central place is the best the town has to offer; some rooms with bath.

Galaroza ✉ 21290

**Galaroza Sierra, Ctra Sevilla-Lisboa, km 103, t 95 912 32 37, *www.hotel galaroza.com* (€€). Good-value rooms or bungalows with view in a wonderful location in the heart of the Sierra de Aracena y Picos de Aroche Park.

Hostal Toribio, C/Iglesia 1, Galaroza, t 95 912 30 73, *www.hostaltoribio.com* (€€). Central, with pleasant tiles rooms and a restaurant.

Hostal Venecia, Ctra Sevilla-Lisboa 14, t 95 912 30 98 (€€). Roadside hotel with a decent restaurant (€).

Fuenteheridos ✉ 21292

***Villa Turística, Ctra Sevilla-Lisboa, km 97, t 95 912 52 02, *www.fp-hoteles. com* (€€€). A slightly soulless tourist complex, but upmarket with a restaurant. Also has furnished apartments.

Hostal Carballo, La Fuente 16, t 95 912 51 08, *www.hostalcarballo.com* (€). The budget option in town; just six delightful clean rooms. The friendly owners can arrange Sierra trips.

El Barrio, C/Esperanza Bermúdez s/n (on the road leading up from the main square), t 95 912 50 33 (€€). Tapas and main meals, including chestnut stew in season.

El Ricco, C/Esperanza Bermúdez s/n (€). The attractive *bodega* next door.

Zufre ✉ 21210

La Posada, C/Barrancos 5, t 95 919 81 10 (€). A simple *pensión* in the town centre; the only place to stay.

Casa Pepa, C/Portales 10, t 95 919 82 93 (€). Brick-lined restaurant serving tasty local dishes.

Cumbres Mayores ✉ 21380

Mayma, Pso Andalucía, t 95 971 05 92 (€). Has clean, cool rooms with bath; situated in the main square.

Togahilo, Antonio Machado 47, t 95 971 00 06 (€). On the way out of town, with extremely basic rooms with bath.

Eating options are limited to the *pensiones*, or you could try the **Pata Chica**, C/Machado 1, t 95 971 04 32 (€).

The Coast South of Huelva

El Rocío and its Pilgrimage

Twenty-three kilometres south of Huelva, along the coastal route, is **Mazagón**, a family resort surrounded by pine trees and lovely beaches. From here it's a straight shot to **Torre de la Higuera**, and the big hotel developments around the endless **Matalascañas Beach**, the most international of Huelva's resorts.

This is the dead end of the coastal highway; the only place you can go is the tiny inland village of **El Rocío**, which would not even be on the map were it not for the annual *romería* at Pentecost, the biggest and perhaps the oldest in Spain (*see* box, opposite page).

Las Marismas del Guadalquivir

Add the water of the broad Guadalquivir to this flat coastal plain, and the result is southern Europe's greatest marshland wildlife reserve. Las Marismas is another world, a bit of the Everglades in a country better known for hot dry mountains. Hundreds of species of migratory birds pass through in the spring and autumn – storks

The *Romería* at El Rocío

El Rocío is empty the rest of the year, but at Pentecost its population swells to hundreds of thousands. Three great processions (featuring the traditional covered wagons) begin in the Triana district of Sevilla, Sanlúcar de Barrameda and Huelva, and are managed by the religious confraternity, the *hermandades*.

No one knows exactly how long the *romería* of El Rocío has been going on; processions in honour of the Virgin Mary are often descendants of ancient pagan festivals. In its modern version, it is traced to the 1400s, when a shepherd from the nearby village of Villamanrique found an image of the Virgin in a hollow tree. Miracles followed, and a chapel was built to house the image. The Lady has acquired many names over the centuries: first *Nuestra Señora de las Rocinas*, then *Virgen del Rocío*, 'Virgin of the Dew'; today she is commonly called the White Dove, *La Paloma Blanca*. Every year pilgrims bring their families for a few days of music and merrymaking in the fields; it is traditional to arrive in a horse- or ox-drawn covered wagon, decorated with flowers and streamers – the wagons are to hold all the food and drink, for this pilgrimage is as serious a party as the April Fair in Sevilla. Campfires burn all night, and the atmosphere is pure electricity.

among them – but Las Marismas has a fantastically varied population of its own: rare golden eagles, snowy egrets, flamingos, griffin vultures, tortoises, red deer, foxes and European lynx. All these fauna have been responsible for keeping the area undisturbed; for centuries it was an aristocratic hunting preserve, belonging to King Alfonso X, then to the Dukes of Medina Sidonia, and finally to William Garvey, one of the sherry barons of Jerez. Much of the territory around the park is still held in private hunting preserves.

As in the Everglades, wildlife congregates around 'islands' among the wetlands; here they're called *corrales*, built of patches of dune anchored by surrounding shrubs and stands of low pines. Also like the Everglades, Las Marismas is threatened by development from growing resorts such as Matalascañas. This has become Spain's top environmental concern, and so the government has limited coastal development, setting aside a large slice of the area as the **Parque Nacional del Coto Doñana**.

⭐ Parque Nacional del Coto Doñana

Doñana was closed to visitors in 1998, after a chemical factory spilt thousands of tons of toxic mud into the Río Guadalquivir, and hence the park, causing an ecological disaster. The clean-up operation was lengthy and arduous, but €100 million was recently invested in a massive regeneration project called 'Doñana 2005', which has finally reversed much of the damage caused by the 1998 disaster. The **Centro de Recepción de Acebuche**, about halfway between El Rocío and Matalascañas, runs Land Rover tours around the park. It also upkeeps a number of hides to observe the wildlife, and there are some signposted walks from the visitors' centre. Keep in mind that the 'wetlands' are largely dry in the summer. Whenever you come, bring mosquito repellent and watch out for quicksand. At **La Rocina** is the next **visitors' centre**, reached by going north along the A483, with another 6km away in the **Palacio del Acebrón**. Both have signposted walks in the vicinity.

Centro de Recepción de Acebuche
t 95 944 87 11,
www. parquenaciona ldonana.com

La Rocina visitors' centre
t 95 944 23 40

Where to Stay and Eat on the Huelva Coast

ⓘ Mazagón >
Edificio Mancomunidad
Moguer–Palos, t 95 937
63 00 (same building as
the police station)

ⓘ El Rocío >>
Avda de la Canaliega s/n,
t 95 944 38 08; open
Mon–Fri 10–2

ⓘ Matalascañas >
Urbanización Playa
de Matalascañas,
t 95 943 00 86

Mazagón ✉ 21130

****Parador Mazagón**, Ctra Huelva–Matalascañas s/n, t 95 953 63 00, www.parador.es (€€€). In an attractive pine-tree setting, looking down on to Mazagón beach, this modern *parador* is the most comfortable option hereabouts, with pleasant gardens, pool and air-conditioned rooms.

Mazagón has a number of restaurants and cafés around Avenida Fuente Piña. There's not much to distinguish between them but at least they're lively.

El Remo, Avda Conquistadores 123, t 95 953 61 38 (€€€–€€). A good *chiringuito* restaurant, with a *terraza*, specializing in sardines and fresh local fish. *Closed Sun eve*.

Matalascañas ✉ 21760

There are a number of resort hotels at Matalascañas, predictably packed during the high season.

**Doñana Blues, Sector I, Parcela 129, t 95 944 98 17, www.donanablues.com (€€€). A pleasant alternative to the anonymous resort hotels, this is a pretty, chalet-style complex with flower-filled gardens and a pool. It's close to the beach.

Casa Miguel, Avenida Las Adelfas, t 95 944 84 72 (€€–€). A comfortable *hostal* with good-sized rooms and a bustling downstairs restaurant, usually packed with locals.

Tamarindos, Avda de las Adelfas 31, t 95 943 01 19 (€). Clean *pensión*, near the beach and the town centre; all rooms come with bath. Prices almost double between June and September.

You'll find plenty of restaurants, particularly along the Paseo Marítimo, but none is outstanding.

Bajo Guía, Paseo Marítimo, t 95 944 00 37 (€€). An elegant seafood restaurant with picture windows overlooking the sea. The menu includes a tasty paella.

Taberna Tío Paco, Pza de las Begonias, t 95 944 81 94 (€€–€). Atmospheric little tavern, with plenty of delicious tapas at the bar. *Closed Wed*.

El Rocío ✉ 21750

If you are planning to attend the pilgrimage, you'll need to book accommodation months in advance.

**Toruño, Plaza Acebuchal 22, t 95 944 23 23, www.toruno.com (€€€–€€). In a good spot near the town centre; again, prices quadruple when the pilgrimage is in flow.

Donana-Rural, C/Santolalla 222, www.donana-rural.com (€€). A whitewashed *casa rural* offering simple but stylish self-catering accommodation near the sanctuary.

Cristina, C/Real 32, t 95 944 24 13 (€). Run by Cristina, this appears to be the only hotel which doesn't take undue advantage of pilgrims.

Cádiz

⭐ Cádiz

If Cádiz were a tiny village, the government would immediately declare it a national monument and put up a sign. It's a big, busy seaport, though, and the tourist industry has only recently begun to wake up to its charms. Yet Cádiz is one of the most distinctive Spanish cities, worth spending a few days in even if there are few 'sights'. The city is a small peninsula, resembling a sturdy galleon patiently waiting to put to sea, packed tightly and pounded by the rough Atlantic breakers on all sides. It comes in colours – a hundred shades of off-white – bleached and faded by sun and spray into a soft patina, broken only by the golden dome of a rambling Baroque cathedral that would be a civic misfortune anywhere else, but seems inexplicably beautiful here.

Getting to and around Cádiz

By Ferry

Cádiz isn't the big passenger port it used to be, but you can still take the weekly ferries to Tenerife – Las Palmas – and Arrecife in the Canary Islands. They run a little more frequently in summer. There's also a regular ferry ride from the port to El Puerto de Santa María. **Tickets**: Acciona-Trasmediterránea office, Avda Ramón de Carranza 26, **t** 95 622 74 21/**t** 902 45 46 45, *www.trasmediterranea.com*.

By Train

You can go directly only to Jerez (20 daily, stopping at El Puerto de Santa María), Sevilla (8 daily) and Madrid. The **station** is just a few blocks from the Plaza San Juan de Dios, in Plaza de Sevilla, **t** 95 625 43 01.

By Bus

Los Amarillos, Avda Ramón de Carranza 31 (by the port), **t** 90 221 03 17, *www.losamarillos.es*, takes the route west to Rota and Sanlúcar de Barrameda, plus services to Córdoba; **Comes**, Plaza de Hispanidad 1, **t** 95 219 92 08, goes east to Tarifa and Algeciras. It also has buses to Ronda, Málaga, Granada, Sevilla and Córdoba. **Secorbus**, from Plaza Elio s/n, **t** 902 22 92 92, *www.secorbus.es*, goes to Madrid.

City bus no.1, from in front of the bus station, will take you from the Plaza de España to Cádiz's suburban beaches and to new Cádiz.

History

Cádiz modestly claims to be the oldest city in western Europe. It's hard to argue; the Phoenician city of Gadir has a documented foundation date of 1100 BC and, while other cities have traces of older settlements, it would be difficult to find another city west of Greece with a continuous urban life of at least 3,000 years. Gadir served as the port for shipping Spanish copper and tin, and was undoubtedly the base for the now-forgotten Phoenician trade routes with west Africa and England – and possibly even for explorations to America. Cádiz, however, prefers to consider Hercules its founder, and he appears on the arms of the city between his famous pillars.

Under Roman rule, Gades, as it was now called, was a favoured city, especially under Julius Caesar, who held his first public office here. Scant remains of the Roman theatre were discovered in 1980. Jazirat Qadis, as it was known to the the Moors, never was an important centre. Alfonso X conquered it for Castile in 1262, and began its cathedral. The city remained out of the spotlight until the 16th century, when the American trade and Spain's growth as a naval power made it a major port once again. Two of Columbus's four trips to the New World started from here. Sir Francis Drake visited in 1587 and, as every schoolchild knows, 'singed the King of Spain's beard'. Later British admirals followed the custom for the next two centuries, calling every now and then for a fish supper and an afternoon's sacking, notably in 1596, when under the Earl of Essex half the town was burned down; when the British were away, Barbary pirates took their place, and the city had to beat off their raids several times in the 1500s. The years after 1720, when Cádiz controlled the American market, shaped its present character. Street names like Calle Conde O'Reilly (an Irish-born royal governor who did a lot for Cádiz) and a statue of one José MacPherson y Hemas testify to the contacts the city enjoyed with the outside world, and it became the most liberal corner of Spain.

The Napoleonic Wars brought the pesky Brits back to plague the city again in 1797 and 1800. Its shining hour came in 1812, when the first Spanish constitution was declared here, and the city became the capital of free Spain. Understandably, Cádiz suffered after the restoration of the old absolutist government in 1823, when the constitution was abolished.

Worse troubles were to come; the loss of most of Spain's colonies in America was a heavy blow, and the city declined further when its port became too outdated to handle modern ships. That was remedied in time to give the city of the constitution one further indignity – it was here that Franco ferried his Moroccan army into Spain in 1936, leading to the fall of most of Andalucía.

Central Cádiz

Walking around Cádiz

The approach to Cádiz is a dismal one, through marshes and saltpans cluttered with power lines and industrial junk. After this, you must pass through a long, narrow strip of land full of modern suburbs before arriving at the **Puerta de Tierra**, entrance to the old city on the peninsula. Almost everything about warfare in the 18th century had a certain decorum to it, and Cádiz's gates and formidable land walls (1757), all well preserved, are among the most aesthetically pleasing structures in town.

You can walk around Cádiz in about an hour, past parks like the **Alameda Apodaca**, and forts of the 18th century. It's a great city for exploring. The old city is a maze of lanes bathed in soft lamplight after dusk, when the numerous cafés fill up with young, exuberant *gaditanos*. A walk through the myriad cobbled streets, past solid doors carved from the trees of South American forests, and balconies spilling over with flowers, will take you back to the time when mighty Cádiz bustled with industry as the gateway to the Americas. Keep an eye out for the little **plaques** – marking the birthplaces of, among others, Manuel de Falla, and Miranda, the first president of Venezuela – and reminders of what an important role this small city has often played. Note the houses, too, in a style unique to Cádiz, with roof terraces and Moorish-looking turrets.

Plaza San Juan de Dios and Around

From the Puerta de Tierra, the Cuesta de las Calesas leads down to the port and rail station, then around the corner to **Plaza San Juan de Dios**, the lively, palm-shaded centre of Cádiz, flanked at the end by the enormous *ayuntamiento*, with most of the restaurants and hotels on the surrounding streets. Two blocks away is the

Cádiz cathedral
t 95 628 61 54; open Tues and Thurs 10–1.30 and 4.30–7, Wed and Fri 10–1.30 and 4.30–6.15, Sat 10–12.30pm; adm; includes admission to Museo Catedralicio; crypt open Mon–Fri 10–1

cathedral, on a small plaza. Thorough restoration of this ungainly bulk has not destroyed its ingratiating charm. It was begun in 1722, at the height of Cádiz's prosperity. Funds soon started running short, sadly enough; if original architect Vicente Acero had had his way, he might have made this as fanciful a work as his cathedral in Guadix. Neglected for centuries, the crumbling stonework was corroding in Cádiz's salty air, before the damage was undone by a lengthy and expensive restoration project, now complete. Of the paintings within, Zurbarán's *Santa Úrsula* stands out. The composer Manuel de Falla, author of *Noches en los Jardines de España* (*Nights in the Gardens of Spain*), has his tomb in the cathedral **crypt**. The **Museo Catedralicio** has a lot of ecclesiastical gold and silverware, paintings by Murillo, Zurbarán and Alejo Fernández, and painted panels and an ivory crucifix by Alonso Cano. You can climb the cathedral tower, the **Torre de Poniente**, which has a separate entrance, for astounding views across the spires, watchtowers and huddled rooftops of the old city.

Torre de Poniente
open daily mid-June–mid-Sept 10–8; mid-Sept–mid-June 10–6; adm

Iglesia de Santa Cruz
open Sat–Thurs 9.30–1 and 6.30–9, Fri 9.30–1

Just behind the cathedral on Plaza Frey Félix is the simple Iglesia de Santa Cruz, the 'old cathedral'. Begun in the 13th century on the remnants of a mosque, it was virtually destroyed when the Duke of Essex and his armies sacked the city in 1596. Most of what you see was rebuilt or added in the 17th century, including the theatrical Baroque retable behind the main altar.

A couple of blocks east of the cathedral, on Campo del Sur, is the Teatro Romano, a restored Roman theatre built by a *gaditano*, Lucio Cornelio Balbo, and dating from the 1st century BC. Excavations have revealed the stands and a large section of an interior gallery. The idea was to extend the city into the area that today comprises the *barrios* of **Santa María** and **El Pópulo**. The theatre backs onto the latter, an atmospheric maze of streets and old *palacios* that have changed remarkably little since medieval times, and are now crammed full of tiny bars and dilapidated blocks of flats.

Teatro Romano
open Tues–Sun 10–2

West of the Cathedral to Plaza de Falla

Continuing westwards, **Plaza Topete** was named after a *tophet*, the Phoenician temple dedicated to that nasty habit of theirs – sacrificing first-born babies; the remains of one were found here (lately, some historians have begun to doubt that the Phoenicians and Carthaginians were really so brutish; they suspect that the children buried here died natural deaths, and that the stories about child sacrifice were only propaganda spread by the Greeks). Now, this area is Cádiz's almost excessively colourful **market district**, spread around a wonderful, dilapidated old market building around which countless little tapas bars are clustered.

San Felipe Neri
open Mon–Sat 10–1.30; adm

A few blocks west, the little church of San Felipe Neri on Calle Sacramento is an unprepossessing shrine to the beginnings of Spanish liberty. On 29 March 1812 an assembly of refugees from Napoleon's occupation of the rest of Spain gathered here, set up the Cortes and wrote a constitution declaring Spain an independent republic, guaranteeing full political and religious freedom. Though their constitution, and their revolution, proved stillborn, it was a notable beginning for Spain's struggle towards democracy. Big marble plaques, sent as tributes, cover the church's façade. Inside is a beautiful *Immaculate Conception* by Murillo.

Museo de las Cortes de Cádiz
t 95 622 17 88; open June–Sept Tues–Fri 9–1 and 5–7, Sat–Sun 9–1; Oct–May Tues–Fri 9–1 and 4–7, Sat–Sun 9–1; closed Mon and hols

Around the corner at C/Santa Inés 9, Cádiz's very good municipal museum, the Museo de las Cortes de Cádiz, has a huge Romantic-era mural depicting the 1812 event. In front of it, in the main hall, is the museum's star exhibit, a 15m (50ft) scale model of Cádiz, made entirely of mahogany and ivory by an unknown obsessive in 1779. Nearly every building is detailed – Cádiz hasn't changed much. Among a collection of portraits of Spanish heroes is the Duke of Wellington, who in Spain was called the Duke of Ciudad Rodrigo. The best picture, also from that era, shows Hercules about to give

Cádiz Virtual Sieglo XVIII
open same times as museum; adm

Torre Tavira
t 95 621 29 10; open 16 Sept–14 June 10–8; 15 June–15 Sept 10–6; adm

Gran Teatro Falla
t 95 622 08 94 for performance details; tickets through telentrada, t 90 210 12 12

Napoleon a good bashing. An audiovisual exhibition, **Cádiz Virtual Sieglo XVIII**, offers a virtual tour of the city as it was 200 years ago.

It's a short walk from here to C/Marqués del Real Tesoro and the **Torre Tavira**, the highest tower in the city, which is grafted onto an 18th-century mansion, and has an entertaining *cámera oscura* giving wonderful views of the city – including glimpses of secret watchtowers and spires that can't be spotted from street level. Walking back down Sacramento leads to the Plaza de Falla and the huge neo-*mudéjar* **Gran Teatro Falla**, named after the composer, who was born in a house in the Plaza de Mina.

Plaza de Mina and Around

Museo de Cádiz
open Wed–Sat 9–8.30, Tues 2.30–8.30, Sun 9.30–2.30; adm; call the museum on t 95 621 22 81 for information on Tía Norica shows

On this lovely square, in the northwestern corner of the peninsula, you'll find the **Museo de Cádiz**. The archaeology section contains a remarkable alabaster Phoenician sarcophagus, Phoenician jewellery, Roman pottery and Greek ceramics; among the statues there's a dumb-looking Emperor Trajan with a big Roman nose. But best in the museum are the paintings: some Murillos and a whole section of works by Zurbarán, including *Four Evangelists* and *John the Baptist*. On the top floor are unaffectedly charming puppets and stage sets from a Cádiz genre of marionette show called *Tía Norica*, still performed in these parts.

Oratorio de la Santa Cueva
open Tues–Fri 10–2 and 4.30–7.30, Sat and Sun 10–1; adm

Around the corner, on Calle Rosario, the 18th-century **Oratorio de la Santa Cueva** has emerged from an immaculate restoration to provide a gleaming, frilly backdrop for three Goya frescoes (the only ones in Andalucía): the *Miracle of the Loaves and Fishes*, the *Parable of the Wedding Guest* and the *Last Supper*, completed after he was stricken with the illness that left him completely deaf.

Cádiz Beaches

The old town beach, **Playa de la Caleta**, may not be large nor particularly clean, but it is lovely at dusk when the brightly painted fishing boats are pulled up on to the shore. Set against a backdrop of great architecture, including the florid turn-of-the-century domes of the old *balneario* (spa), it's a sheltered crescent of sand,

Castillo de Santa Catalina
open daily 10.30–6, until 8 in summer

sandwiched between the **Castillo de Santa Catalina** and the **Castillo de San Sebastián**, the latter at the end of a long zigzag pier. You can visit the former.

Playa de Santa María del Mar starts just outside the old town and becomes **Playa de la Victoria**, a long stretch of sand packed in season and flanked by bars, restaurants and kiosks.

Goat Cuisine

One of Cádiz's most well-known dishes is *berza* – a cabbage-based stew. Goat's cheese is called Cádiz cheese here, produced in the mountains where it is semi-cured and develops a yellow colour. Cheese from Grazalema is made only in the spring and must be consumed within two months. For dessert, try an almond pastry (*torta de almendra*) from the local convents.

(i) **Cádiz >**
*Regional: Avda Ramón
de Carranza s/n,
t 95 625 86 46,
www.andalucia.org;
open Mon and Sat 9–2,
Tues–Fri 9–7*

***Town:** Plaza de San
Juan de Dios 11,
t 95 624 10 01; open
Sat and Sun 5–8*

(★) **El Faro >>**

(★) **Hospedería Las
Cortes de Cádiz >**

Where to Stay in Cádiz

Cádiz ✉ 11000

There will be no problem finding cheaper rooms – lots of sailors pass through here. Some of the cheapest places are near the Plaza San Juan de Dios in the old town. Otherwise look for the *camas* signs.

On the other side of the Puerta de Tierra, in the new part of Cádiz, there's just as much choice. The Paseo Marítimo is lively, so don't feel you're missing out if you stay here.

****Playa Victoria**, Glorieta Ingeniero La Cierva 4, **t** 95 620 51 00, *www. palafoxhoteles.com* (€€€€). Probably the most upmarket place in town, this is a huge glitzy place right on the beach, with all the facilities you would expect, including a swimming pool. However it lacks the atmosphere of being in the old town.

***Regio**, C/Ana de Viya 11, **t** 95 627 93 31, *www.hotelregiocadiz.com* (€€€). In new Cádiz, within easy strolling distance of Playa de la Victoria; plain, spotless rooms and a cafeteria.

****Meliá La Caleta**, Avda Amílcar Barca 47, **t** 95 627 94 11, *www.solmelia. es* (€€€–€€). Almost all the amenities (no pool) plus direct access to the main beach, but out of the old town.

****Parador Hotel Atlántico**, Avda Duque de Nájera 9, **t** 95 622 69 05, *www.parador.es* (€€€–€€). Another good *parador* within a modern building and endowed with some wonderful views over the Atlantic; it has a large outdoor pool. The suites at the front of the building are especially nice, and don't cost much more.

***Francia y París**, Plaza San Francisco 2, **t** 95 622 23 48, *www.hotelfrancia. com* (€€€–€€). A quiet, old-fashioned but well-run hotel around the corner from Plaza de Mina.

***Hospedería Las Cortes de Cádiz**, C/San Francisco 9, **t** 95 621 26 68, *www.hotellascortes.com* (€€). An immaculate hotel in the old town, with pretty rooms and good services including a gym. There are wonderful views from the *mirador* in the tower.

***Pensión Bahía**, C/Plocia 5, off Plaza San Juan de Dios, **t** 95 625 90 61, *hostelbahia@terra.es* (€€). Well-

equipped rooms, all with air conditioning, TV and small balconies.

***Hostal Centro Sol**, C/Manzanares 7, **t** 95 628 31 03, *www.hostalcentrosol. com* (€€). A neat little *hostal* in a renovated neoclassical building in the old city, offering comfortable rooms set around a tiled patio.

Hostal Fantoni, C/Flamenco 5, **t** 95 628 27 04, *www.hostalfantoni.net* (€€). Full of tiles and cool marble with a breezy roof terrace. Rooms available with or without bath.

Pensión España, Marqués de Cádiz 9, **t** 95 628 55 00 (€€). Offers reasonable doubles, with bath available; right in the centre of the old town.

Pensión Colón, Marqués de Cádiz 6, **t** 95 628 53 51 (€€–€). Well situated in the old town opposite a good delicatessen; some rooms with bath.

Eating Out in Cádiz

Dedicated foodies should look out for a useful little booklet called *Cádiz's Gastronomic Guide* (€1.50), available from the tourist office, with descriptions of local specialities, recipes, lists of tapas bars and restaurants, and a guide to the various food festivals in the Cádiz region. Also, it's worth noting that many of the finest restaurants have tapas bars, including El Faro, El Balandro and El Sardinero.

El Faro, C/San Félix 15, **t** 95 622 58 58 (€€€–€€). Generally regarded as the best restaurant in town. It is now part of a small group including Ventorillo del Chato (*see* below) and El Faro del Puerto (*see* p.203). Come here to explore the amazingly wide range of seafood fished from this part of the Atlantic – things that we don't even have names for in English such as *mojarras* and *urtas*. There are also more recognizable varieties as well as a selection of meat dishes.

El Balandro, Alameda Apodaca 22, **t** 95 622 09 92 (€€). By the walls of the park known as Alameda Apodaca, with an upstairs dining room that looks over to Puerto de Santa María. It serves a characteristic mix of seafood and Spanish specialities.

Ventorillo del Chato, Via Augusta Julia, Cortadura, **t** 95 625 00 25 (€€). This rustic place on the road to San Fernando claims to have been around for more than 200 years and is still going strong. *Closed Sun*.

Arte Serrano, Pso Marítimo 2, t 95 622 72 58 (€€). In newer Cádiz, along the Paseo Marítimo, there's a wide choice of restaurants, nearly all with terraces or outside seating. This one specializes in meats from the Sierra and has a delicious range of tapas.

Casa Grimaldi, Plaza Libertad 9 (in the market district), t 95 622 83 16 (€€). Offers a good range of delicious fresh fish and seafood from the Bay at very reasonable prices. Great tapas.

⭐ El Sardinero >

El Sardinero, Plaza San Juan de Dios 4, t 95 626 33 37 (€€). One of the oldest restaurants in the city, with a variety of Basque and *andaluz* dishes. Outside tables available.

Achuri, C/Plocia 15, t 95 625 36 13 (€€). Just off Plaza de San Juan de Dios. Another old restaurant, popular with the locals, and specializing in Basque and Andalucían dishes.

El Ajibe, C/Plocia 25, t 95 626 66 56 (€). Housed in an evocative historic house, complete with namesake well (*ajibe*), the tapas are first-rate here, as well as the more substantial meat and seafood dishes.

Cigüeña, C/Plocia 2, t 95 625 01 79 (€). A charming spot, filled with works by local artists; a choice of imaginative cuisine.

Tapas and *Freidurías*

Bahía, Avda Ramón de Carranza 29, t 95 628 11 66. A classic, close to the port; try the famous spare ribs (*costillas de cerdo*).

Cervecería Aurelio, C/Zorilla 1, t 95 622 10 31. Shellfish and other local tapas.

Freiduría Cervecería Las Flores, Plaza de Topete 4, t 95 622 61 12. Fried fish

was invented in Cádiz, and nothing beats digging into a paper cone (*cartucho* or *papelón*) filled with freshly caught battered fish. Here, you can swig beer on the terrace, and sample the fried shrimps or cuttlefish.

Piccola, C/San José 4, t 95 622 50 99. A tiny bar serving up excellent tapas including spicy *pulpo a la gallega*. You can even finish up with an ice cream.

La Terraza, Plaza Catedral 3, t 95 628 26 05. Delicious *pescaíto frito* and a terrace out on the square.

Nightlife in Cádiz

The town buzzes with bars; the best area to find a bit of *marcha* outside summertime is around the university buildings, particularly Plaza San Francisco and Plaza España and the streets off and between them, including C/San Francisco and C/Rosario. Over the summer months the nightlife shifts to the beach area in the new part of town. The area along the Pso Marítimo by Playa de la Victoria is particularly lively. There is also a substantial gay scene in Cádiz; for information call **COLEGA**, t 95 622 62 62, *www.colegaweb.net*.

Barabass, C/Muñoz Arenillas 4, *www.barabasscadiz.com*. Trendy disco-bar: chill-out and lounge music gives way to house as the night wears on.

Café Poniente, C/Beato Diego de Cádiz 18. This gay café-bar has drag shows every Thurs.

Bar Zapata, Plaza Candelaria 1. An atmospheric, typically Andaluz old bar, with good tapas. It makes the perfect spot to start the night.

Taberna La Manzanilla, C/Feduchy 18, off C/Rosario. A wonderful old place serving all varieties of sherry, with a good range of tapas.

Cádiz Province

Like those to the east, the beaches around Cádiz are popular mostly with Spaniards and are more crowded, at least in summer. Just the same, the beaches are lovely and huge, and the towns behind them relatively unspoiled; there may be few better places in Spain to baste yourself, with plenty of opportunities for exploring *bodegas*.

Sanlúcar de Barrameda and Rota

Nuestra Señora de la O
open Mon–Fri and Sat 10–1, Sun 10–12; closed Thurs

Palace of the Dukes of Medina Sidonia
www.fcmedinasidonia. com; guided tours Sun at 11 and 1, call to book a place on t 95 636 01 61; in July and Aug tours must be booked 15 days in advance

Montpensier Palace
open 8–2.30

Town hall
open Fri–Wed, guided visits at 10.30, 11.30, 12.30 and 1.30; closed Thurs

Antonio Barbadillo
t 95 638 55 00, www. barbadillo.com; tours Mon–Sat 12–1; adm

La Guita
www.laguita.com; book English tours, held daily, in advance on t 95 631 95 64; free; closed Aug

Hidalgo La Gitana
t 95 638 53 04, www.vinicola-hidalgo.es; tours Mon–Fri at 12.30; adm

Motor boat
t 95 636 38 13, www. visitasdonana.com; open Mon–Sat 9–7

César Florido
t 95 637 12 85, www. bodegasflorido.com; large groups only in summer

Mellodo Martín
t 96 637 01 97

Sanlúcar de Barrameda makes *manzanilla*, most ethereal of sherries. It is known as the port that launched Magellan on his way around the world, and Columbus on his second voyage to the Indies and third to America, and for its annual horse races on the beach; Sanlúcar is also the birthplace of the artist-writer Francisco Pacheco, Velázquez's teacher. The town has a certain crumbling colonial charm and an exceptionally pretty main square, **Plaza de Cabildo**. Off nearby **Plaza Roque**, where a plaque commemorates Pacheco, is the town's market, one of the biggest in Andalucía and a delight to stroll around to soak up the myriad smells and sounds. From here C/Bretones leads up to the church of Nuestra Señora de la O, with its fine *mudéjar* portal and 16th-century coffered ceiling. Beside the church you will find the Palace of the Dukes of Medina Sidonia, who owned the town. The building dates from the 16th century and has an extensive private archive including copious notes on the Armada. Nearby is the 19th-century Montpensier Palace, with its extensive library and paintings by Murillo, El Greco, Rubens and Goya. To the west, along C/Caballeros, lies the **Palacio de Orléans y Borbóns** (Palace of Orleans and Bourbon), which was built by the Duke of Montpensier in the 19th century and is now the town hall. Go back east past the church and you will come across the ruins of the 15th-century Moorish castle, which is being converted into a cultural centre with shops and restaurants. Below here lies C/Ancha, the scene of much merriment on 15 August (*see* 'Fiestas', opposite).

The town has a number of sherry houses which you can visit, although you usually need to book tours in advance. The biggest is Antonio Barbadillo, C/Sevilla 1, which makes the bulk of the *manzanilla*; try also La Guita, C/Misericordia, another delicious make, and Hidalgo La Gitana, C/Banda de la Playa 42, one of the oldest *bodegas*.

Although its beaches are not major-league, Sanlúcar has always been a popular summer destination with Spanish holidaymakers for its excellent cheap seafood. The **Bajo de Guía** is a particularly charming fishing district, and from here you can take the motor boat over to Coto Doñana (*see* p.191) for a four-hour trip up the river, including two stops and two guided walks.

If you have an afternoon to spare, amuse yourself by visiting the public fish auction in **Bonanza**, 4km away. **Chipiona** is a family resort, full of small *pensiones* and *hostales*, with a good beach at Playa de Regla near the lighthouse, and a couple of *bodegas*; try César Florido, Padre Lerchundi 35–37, or Mellodo Martín, Ctra Chipiona-Nola 3. Next, on the edge of the bay of Cádiz, comes **Rota**, a bigger, flashier resort with the best and longest beach on the coast; the town is pretty, though it's a bit overbuilt. It's also full of

Americans from the largest naval base in the region, just outside town. This was the key base Franco gave up in the 1953 deal with President Eisenhower; in the 1980s, when Spain was debating its future role in NATO, the Americans made it unpleasantly clear that the base was not a subject for negotiation, although in the 1986 NATO referendum this region turned out the highest 'yes' vote in Spain. Lately, numbers at the base have fallen by about a third.

El Puerto de Santa María and Puerto Sherry

Across the bay from Cádiz lies **El Puerto de Santa María**, the traditional port of the sherry houses in Jerez, which has quite a number of *bodegas* of its own – **Osborne**, C/Fermín Caballero s/n, and **Terry**, C/Toneleros s/n, among other famous names. It's one of the prettiest towns on the whole of the Costa de la Luz, a maze of narrow streets crammed with low whitewashed houses and Baroque mansions meandering down to the port.

El Puerto itself isn't a big resort, but it's a typical town of Cádiz province, with bright, bustling streets, excellent restaurants and some good beaches. The town has some interesting churches, some mansions of the Anglo-Spanish sherry aristocracy, and the fine, restored 13th-century *mudéjar* **Castillo de San Marcos**. To get a taste of what the town was like in the glory days of the 18th century, visit the **Casa de los Leones**, C/La Placilla 2, where there's a permanent exhibition on the Baroque era. The century-old **bullring** ranks with those of Sevilla and Ronda in prestige.

Puerto Sherry is a modern marina, built in the late 1980s, and a pleasant place to spend an afternoon or evening. It has yet to reach its full potential (or occupancy) so it's a little lacking in character.

Osborne
*t 95 686 90 00,
www.osborne.es;
adm for tours*

Terry
*t 95 685 77 00;
adm for tours*

**Castillo de
San Marcos**
*t 95 685 17 51; open
July–Sept Tues–Sun
10–2; Oct–June Tues,
Thurs and Sat 11–2; adm*

Casa de los Leones
open 10–2 and 6–8

Bullring
*open Tues–Sun 11–1.30
and 6–7.30, except
when there's a bullfight*

Fiestas in Sanlúcar and Rota

The most famous fiesta involves **horse racing** along the beach at Sanlúcar in August. It's a beautiful sight that has its origins in the middle of the 19th century when the Spanish aristocracy stayed here. The town sends a few brotherhoods to El Rocío in May; at the end of that month is the *Feria de la Manzanilla*, which sees horseriding, bullfights, Andalucian dress and vast quantities of sherry; **15 August** sees C/Ancha covered with a pretty carpet of faux-flowers (in fact sawdust). A flamenco festival takes place in July, *Noches de Bajo de Guía*; and in mid-October there's a *Feria de Tapas*, where you can sample the town's wonderful food.

ⓘ **Sanlúcar de
Barrameda >>**
*Calzada del Ejército s/n,
t 95 636 61 10, www.
aytosanlucar.org; open
Mon–Fri 10–2 and 5–7,
Sat, Sun and hols
10–1.30 and 4–6.30*

Where to Stay in Sanlúcar and Rota

It's no problem finding a place to stay in the coastal resorts, especially in the high season; little old ladies meet the buses to drag you off to their *hostales*. The resorts around Cádiz are seasonal and many close during the winter.

Sanlúcar ✉ 11540

***Tartaneros**, Tartaneros 8, **t** 95 636 20 44 (€€€). A good option set in a neoclassical *palacio*.

****Hotel Posada de Palacio**, C/Caballero 11, **t** 95 636 48 40, *www.posadadel palacio.com* (€€€). A charming, family-run hotel in another converted *palacio*, with antique-filled rooms around a pretty patio.

(i) **El Puerto de Santa María >>**
C/Luna 22, t 95 654 24 13, www.elpuertosm. es; open daily 10–2 and 6–8

(i) **Chipiona >**
Plaza Andalucía s/n, t 95 637 28 28, www.chipiona.org; open Mon–Fri 10–2 and 5–7, Sat–Sun 11–1

(★) **Hotel Bodega Real >>**

(i) **Rota >**
C/Luna 2 (in the palace), t 95 684 61 74, www.turismorota.com; open daily 9–2 and 5–7

******Los Helechos**, Plaza de Madre de Dios 9, t 95 636 13 49, *www.hotellos helechos.com* (€€). In the old part of town and built around two court-yards, this is the most delightful hotel in Sanlúcar.

Hostal La Blanca Paloma, Plaza San Roque 9, t 95 636 36 44 (€). An old-fashioned *hostal*, the only place here suitable for those on a tight budget.

Chipiona ✉ 11550

***Playa de Regla, Pso Costa de la Luz, t 95 637 27 69, *www.hotelplaya.com* (€€€). A charming hotel in an early 20th-century family home with traditional Andalucian architecture and a roof terrace. Situated across from the beachfront.

***Al Sur, Avda Sevilla 101, t 95 637 03 00, *www.hotelalsur.com* (€€€–€€). With a swimming pool and garden.

***Brasilia, Avda del Faro 12, t 95 637 10 54 (€€€–€€). In its own grounds, with a decent-sized pool and pleasant restaurant.

La Española, C/Isaac Peral 4–6, t 95 637 37 71, *www.hotellaespanola.com* (€€). A pleasant hotel with good-sized rooms, some with ocean views.

San Miguel, Avenida de la Regla 79, t 95 637 29 76 (€€–€). A cheap but pretty option, and near the beach.

Hostal El Faro, Avda del Faro 25, t 95 637 41 54 (€). Simple, old-fashioned rooms in a delightful early 20th-century villa by the lighthouse.

Pinar de Chipiona, t 95 637 23 21 (€). A campsite 3km outside of Chipiona, towards Rota.

Rota ✉ 11520

****Duque de Nájera, C/Gravina 2, t 95 684 60 20, *www.hotelduquede najera.com* (€€€€€–€€€€). In the centre, with pool, minibar, satellite TV, sauna and gym.

****Playa de la Luz, on the beach at Arroyo Hondo, t 95 681 05 00, *www.hotelplayadelaluz.com* (€€€€). A sports-orientated modern resort hotel; pool and gardens.

***Caribe, Avda de la Marina 60, t 95 681 07 00, *www.hotel-caribe.com* (€€€–€€). A cheaper option in the centre, with pool, TV and terrace.

Sixto, Plaza Barroso 6, t 95 684 63 10 (€€€–€€). The latest hotel to open in

town, with a good restaurant and attractive beamed rooms with traditional wooden furniture and wrought-iron bedheads.

Camping Punta Candor, t 95 681 33 03 (€). A campsite just out of the town.

El Puerto de Santa María/ Puerto Sherry ✉ 11500

*****Hotel Duques de Medinaceli, Plaza de los Jazmines, t 95 686 07 77, *www.jale.com/dmedinaceli* (€€€€€). A plush hotel in an 18th-century palace, set in spectacular gardens with its own pool. Excellent restaurant.

****Hotel Monasterio San Miguel, C/Virgen de los Milagros, t 95 654 04 40, *www.jale.com/monasterio* (€€€€€–€€€€). This 16th-century former monastery is a lovely place to stay, with tranquil cloisters, religious artefacts and a swimming pool. The beautiful restaurant, **Las Bóvedas**, is excellent (*see* p.204).

****Hotel Bodega Real, C/Albareda 4, t 95 605 91 85, *www.hotelbodegareal. com* (€€€€€–€€€€). A new hotel (opened 2005) in a historic *bodega*, set around an elegant courtyard, with gym, spa and outdoor Jacuzzis.

****Puerto Sherry, Avda Libertad s/n, t 95 687 20 00, *www.puertosherry.com* (€€€€). In the marina area, with two pools, one heated, and a yacht club.

****Tryp Caballo Blanco, Avda de Madrid 1, t 95 656 25 41 (€€€€–€€€). In a picturesque spot, this hotel is not too pricey and also worth a try; facilities include a swimming pool, a café with terrace and parking.

***Los Cántaros, Curva 6, t 95 654 02 40, *www.hotelloscantaros.com* (€€€). Pitchers (*cántaros*) were once made here, but now it's an elegant, modern hotel in the town centre near the action; with parking and restaurant.

***Puertobahía, Avda de La Paz 38, Urbanización Valdelagrana, t 95 656 27 21, *www.hotelpuertobahia.com* (€€€). A big, modern resort hotel on the beach.

***Santa María, Avda de la Bajamar s/n, t 95 687 32 11, *www.hotelsanta maria.es* (€€€). A modern hotel behind the façade of an 17th-century palace; rooftop pool.

**Hotel Casa del Regidor, C/Ribera del Río, t 95 687 73 33, *www.hotelcasadel*

regidor.com (€€). In an 18th-century mansion, with bright rooms around a lovely patio. Prices plummet in low season.

Costa Luz, C/Niño del Matadero 2, t 95 605 47 01, *www.hostalcostaluz.com* (€€). An attractive hotel near the Plaza de Toros with a roof terrace and modern comfortable rooms. English–Spanish-owned.

Hostal Loreto, C/Ganado 17, t 95 654 24 10 (€). A good budget option, in a converted 18th-century mansion with lots of knick-knacks. Some of the rooms are huge.

Eating Out in Sanlúcar and Rota

Many of the restaurants in this area – informal cafés where you can pick out the fish you like – are open only during the summer.

Sanlúcar ✉ 11500

⭐ Casa Bigote >

Casa Bigote, Bajo de Guía, t 95 636 26 96 (€€). Famous throughout Andalucía for its delicious appetizers, classic dishes of the region, and the best seafood in all its varieties; the crayfish are a must, and you can try the local *manzanilla* with the day's catch. You may need more than one visit, as the tapas selection (at very good prices) in the bar is extensive and excellent. Get there early for a table. *Closed Sun and Nov.*

Mirador de Doñana, Bajo de Guía, t 95 636 42 05 (€€). Casa Bigote's main rival, this is another popular bar and restaurant, with a panoramic view across to the bird reserve. Try *cigalas* (crayfish), *angulas* (baby eels) and *nido de rapé a la Sanluqueña*, a nest of straw potato chips, deep-fried with monkfish. *Closed mid-Jan to mid-Feb.*

Casa Balbino, Plaza Cabildo 11 (€). One of the best tapas bars in Sanlúcar, with bulls' heads and faded posters; varied tapas, inevitably fish-dominated, all washed down by chilled *manzanilla*. It's full most of the time but it is worth hanging around for a table as this is infinitely superior to others in the square.

Bar La Concha, Plaza Bartolomé Pérez 8, t 95 681 27 04 (€). Another old-fashioned tapas bar, full of locals sipping *manzanilla*.

Chipiona ✉ 11550

Chipiona is full of reasonably priced seafood restaurants where you can try the town's sweet moscatel wine or the dry *manzanilla* from Sanlúcar.

El Gato, C/Pez Espada 9–11, t 95 637 07 87 (€€). One of the best restaurants in Chipiona, serving up *sopa de mariscos* (shellfish soup) and other delicious fish dishes.

Paco, Puerto Deportivo de Chipiona, t 95 637 46 64 (€€). A simple but wonderful seafood restaurant, run by a charming couple, with fabulously fresh fish which you can watch arriving from the boats.

Aurora, C/Miguel de Cervantes 5 (€). One of the best-loved tapas bars in town, with a wide array of local favourites.

Rota ✉ 11520

Bar El Fresquito, C/Mina 38, Rota, t 95 681 64 14 (€). In Rota, the cuisine is heavily influenced by the presence of the naval base – pizza and Chinese restaurants alongside the usual seafood. There are, however, a number of good tapas bars like this one.

El Puerto de Santa María ✉ 11500

The town's speciality is *urta*, like a sea bream, and there is a fiesta in mid-August to celebrate this tasty fish. Apart from the excellent *bodegas* and simple beach cafés, El Puerto has some deservedly popular restaurants.

La Goleta del Puerto, Ctra de Fuentebravía, km 0.75, t 95 685 42 32 (€€€). The most successful restaurant, with simple but well-prepared seafood dishes, especially the fish cooked in salt, the *tosta de salmón* and the *porgy* in brandy. *Closed Mon except in July and Aug.*

El Faro del Puerto, Ctra de Fuentebravía, km 0.5, t 95 687 09 52, *www.elfarodelpuerto.com* (€€€). The other El Faro (the original is in Cádiz), also with an excellent reputation for its regional cuisine, serving some of the finest seafood in the province. *Closed Sun, except Aug.*

Las Bóvedas, C/Larga 27, **t** 95 654 04 40 (€€€). In the former monastery of San Miguel, one of the most charming and romantic restaurants you'll find in town, with exquisite seafood and an array of *andaluz* specialities.

Casa Flores, C/Ribera del Río, **t** 95 654 35 12 (€€). *Urta* cooked in sherry and all kinds of beautifully prepared fish and shellfish in a charming traditional restaurant. It has a lovely tapas bar, too, hung with hams and dim lamps.

Romerijo, Ribera del Marisco 1, **t** 95 654 12 54, *www.romerijo.com* (€). The liveliest place to dine, where you can eat the freshest of fish and seafood at the tables outside or enjoy a takeaway wrapped in a paper cone. Everyone throws discarded shells into the red buckets on each table and munches their way through one of the five kinds of prawn on offer. A kilogram of shellfish is enough for four people.

Jerez de la Frontera

ⓘ Jerez de la Frontera

The name is synonymous with wine – by the English corruption of 'Jerez' into 'sherry' – but besides the *finos*, *amontillados*, *olorosos* and other varieties of that noble sauce, Jerez also ships out much of Spain's equally good brandy. Most of the well-known companies, whose advertising is plastered all over Spain, have their headquarters here, and they're quite accustomed to taking visitors – especially English ones – through the *bodegas*. Don't be shy. Most are open to visitors between 9am and 1pm on Mondays to Fridays, though not in August, or when they're busy with the *vendimia* (harvest) in September. Admission prices are around €3 upwards and usually include tasting sessions. Many are located out of town as land prices in the centre rise. However, booking is strongly advised – numbers are restricted on guided tours and many people who fail to reserve places are turned away.

González Byass
t 95 635 70 16,
www.gonzalesbyass.es

One of the most interesting *bodegas* to visit is that belonging to **González Byass**, C/Manuel María González 12. The tour includes a visit to the old sawdust-strewn *bodega* that has held the sherry *soleras* for two centuries; the casks have been signed by many famous visitors over the years, from Orson Welles to the Hollywood swimming star Esther Williams. You ends with a *degustación*. The tour also includes a video of the production process, with cellarmen demonstrating their skill at pouring sherry from distances of a metre or more into the small *copitas* (in order to aerate the wine). **John Harvey**, C/Arcos 54, is another *bodega* well worth a visit – watch out for the alligator at the end of the tour. Others include **Sandeman**, C/Pizarro 10, and **Williams and Humbert**, Ctra A4, km 641.7.

John Harvey
t 95 634 60 04,
www.jerezharveys.com

Sandeman
t 95 615 17 00,
www.sandeman.com

Williams and Humbert
t 95 635 34 06, www. williams-humbert.com

The *Semana Santa* festival in Jerez is more intimate than Sevilla's, but in its way just as splendid. The nightly processions escorting the saint and Madonna images create a city-wide pageant. Late in the night, returning home through the back streets, they are serenaded by impromptu solo voices; for the finest singers, the whole procession halts in appreciation.

Getting to and around Jerez de la Frontera

Cádiz is the base for visiting Jerez and the coasts. The **Amarillo** company provides regular **buses** from Cádiz to all the coastal towns, and at least five daily to Jerez. Infrequent buses connect Jerez with Rota, Sanlúcar and El Puerto. Almost all the Sevilla–Cádiz buses stop in Jerez and El Puerto, as do the **trains**. There are frequent bus connections for Arcos de la Frontera and Ronda and one bus a day to Córdoba and Granada. Jerez's stations for buses and trains are together on the eastern edge of town. **Bus station, t** 95 633 96 66; **train station t** 95 634 23 19.

There's a regular **ferry** service from El Puerto to Cádiz – more fun than the bus. Parking can be hard to find if you're in a car but it is sometimes best to be based in Jerez for the surrounding area to avoid the queues on the roads into Cádiz.

Business is not as good as it was, for sherry sales are falling worldwide, but Jerez is growing. It's an extremely attractive town, at least in the centre, and it has a few lovely buildings for you to squint at after you've done the rounds of the *bodegas*. Two in particular are worth a look: the **Ayuntamiento** in Plaza de la Asunción, a fine example of Renaissance architecture dating from the 16th century, and **Palacio Domecq**, at the start of the Alameda, an 18th-century palace built by the sherry clan.

Jerez's landmark is **La Colegiata** (also called San Salvador), the town's cathedral, a curious pseudo-Gothic church with a separate bell tower and Baroque staircase; though begun in the 13th century, its façade, largely the work of Vicente Acero, was not completed until 1750. Works inside include a *Madonna* by Zurbarán and sculptures by Juan de Mesa. Nearby, on the central Plaza de los Reyes Católicos, **San Miguel** (begun in 1482), which is open for Mass only, changes the scene to Isabelline Gothic – a fine example of that style, with a florid retable inside.

Alcázar
open May–15 Sept Mon–Sat 10–8, Sun 9–3; 16 Sept–April Mon–Sat 10–6; adm

There is a Moorish **Alcázar** at the end of Calle Pérez Galdós, with a tower and some remains of the baths, a *cámera oscura* with wonderful views of the city, an art gallery and a well-preserved mosque. A pair of museums occupy **La Atalaya**, at C/Cervantes 3, including **El Misterio de Jerez**, with a flashy multimedia presentation on sherry, and **El Palacio de Tiempo**, with more than 300 timepieces from around the world.

El Misterio de Jerez
open Tues–Sat; shows at 10, 12 and 7, Sun 10 and 12; call to confirm times, t 902 18 21 00

Museo Arqueológico
open Tues–Fri 10–2 and 4–7, Sat–Sun and hols 10–2.30; adm

The excellent **archaeology museum**, opposite San Mateo on Plaza del Mercado, contains a number of Greek and Roman artefacts in a very pretty restored 18th-century mansion. One of the highlights is a menacing Greek warrior's helmet, discovered in the river, and dating back to the 7th century BC. The top floor is devoted to Arabic ceramics and other finds from the Alcázar.

Outside town, on the road to Medina Sidonia, is the **Cartuja de la Defensión**, a 15th-century monastery with the best Baroque façade (added in 1667) in Andalucía – a sort of giant retable with sculptures by Alonso Cano and others. This is still a working monastery, and you'll need special permission to go inside. There is little reason to; what was the main attraction, a great altarpiece by

Cartuja gardens and patio
t 95 615 64 65; open Mon–Fri 9.30–11.15 and 12.45–6.30; book visits in advance

Yeguada de la Cartuja
t 95 616 28 09, www. yeguadacartuja.com; adm; book in advance

Museo de Etiquetas de Vino
t 95 631 96 50

Museo Taurino
t 95 632 30 00; usually open Mon–Sat 10–2

Museo de Traje Corto
t 95 634 61 74; book visits in advance

Zoo and botanical garden
t 95 615 31 64, www. zoobotanicojerez.com

Real Escuela Andaluz del Arte Ecuestre
t 95 631 96 35, www. realescuela.org

Centro Andaluz de Flamenco
t 95 634 92 65, http://caf.cica.es; open Mon–Fri 9–2; closed for two weeks in Aug

Zurbarán, is scattered to the four winds – you can see panels in the museums of Sevilla and Cádiz. The church is currently closed for restoration work, but do, however, visit the **gardens and patio**. Nearby is the **Yeguada de la Cartuja**, a centre for the breeding of the beautiful Jerezano horses, which you can see being put through their paces at 11am on Saturdays throughout the year.

Jerez also boasts a clutch of quirky little museums, devoted to things as diverse as wine labels (**Museo de Etiquetas de Vino**, in the Garvey *bodega* at Ctra A4), bullfighting (**Museo Taurino**, C/Pozo del Olivar), and costumes (**Museo de Traje Corto**, C/Bizcocheros 3). There is also a **zoo and botanical garden**, out of town on the curiously named C/Taxdirt.

Horses and Flamenco

While in Jerez, look out for exhibitions scheduled at the **Real Escuela Andaluz del Arte Ecuestre**, Avda Duque de Abrantes. Jerez's snooty wine aristocracy takes horsemanship very seriously; they have some of the finest horses you're likely to see anywhere, and they know how to use them. You can see them tarted up like Tío Pepe bottles at the annual **Horse Fair** during the first half of May. The origin of this fair can be traced back to the 13th century, and its events include jumping, classical riding, harness riding and Andalucian country riding. Being an Andalucian fair, it is provides a good excuse for attending the *corrida*, drinking plenty of sherry and, of course, joining in the flamenco extravaganza.

There are also a number of events during the *fiestas de otoño* in September and October, including sherry-tasting and horse racing in the main square. Every Thursday (and on Tuesday from March to October) there is a spectacular '**horse ballet**' at 12 noon. The show runs for about 1½ hours with a short interval (there's a bar which serves sherry), and afterwards you are free to wander through the stables to meet the stars of the show. Additionally, there are tours between 11am and 1pm weekdays except Thursdays. Check with the tourist information for details of any special shows and wear something warm during the winter months.

One of Jerez's attractions is its contrasts – as well as being home to the wealthiest Spaniards, it also has a large Gypsy population who live in the warren of streets stretching up from the cathedral to the **Barrio Santiago**. Here you can find the **Centro Andaluz de Flamenco**, Palacio Pemartín, Plaza de San Juan 1, housed in one of the most beautiful buildings of the old part of the city; the centre hosts different shows and activities throughout the year – concerts, exhibitions, seminars and video shows – in an effort to promote and prolong the art. You might also be able to locate a show which hasn't been put on solely for tourists (*see* 'Nightlife'

Santiago church
visits at time of Mass,
or call ahead,
t 95 618 08 39

p.208). There's also a spectactular flamenco festival held at the end of February or early March, and Friday nights are flamenco nights throughout the city in August. The area's main sight is the 15th-century church of **Santiago**, a wonderfully preserved Gothic pile.

Where to Stay in Jerez de la Frontera

(i) **Jerez de la Frontera >**
C/Paul, Edif. Xeritium,
t 95 635 98 63, and
Alameda Cristina, by
the Claustros de Santo
Domingo, t 95 632 47 47,
www.turismojerez.com

Jerez ✉ 11400

In Jerez, there are many unremarkable hotels. For atmosphere, stay close to the centre of town, convenient for the fair and the Spanish Riding School.

*****Hotel Prestige Palmera Plaza**, C/Pizarro 1, t 95 603 15 00, *www.palmeraplaza.com* (€€€€€). A modern hotel within a converted *bodega* surrounded by gardens. It has plush rooms and even plusher suites. There's a swimming pool and elegant restaurant too.

****Jerez**, Avda Alcalde Álvaro Domecq 35, t 95 633 06 00, *www.jerezhotel.com* (€€€€). Modern, but a classic in the city, with a swimming pool and tennis courts and luscious tropical gardens.

****Bellas Artes**, C/Piaza Arroyo 45, t 95 634 84 30, *www.hotelbellasartes.com* (€€€€–€€€). In a beautifully converted *palacio*, with delightfully quirky, if rather small, rooms and lovely views from the roof terrace.

****Royal Sherry Park**, Avda Alcalde Álvaro Domecq 11, t 95 631 76 14, *www.sherryparkhotel.com* (€€€€€–€€€). A modern place set in a park a little closer to town, with a pool and a restaurant, **El Ábaco**.

***Doña Blanca**, C/Bodegas 11, t 95 634 87 61, *www.hoteldonablanca.com* (€€€). The most pleasant three-star place in town, in the heart of Jerez; with its own car park.

***Serit**, C/Higueras 7, t 95 634 07 00, *www.hostalserit.com* (€€€). Central, plain and modern, but with comfortable rooms, a leafy courtyard and car parking.

*Trujillo**, C/Medina 36, t 95 634 24 38, *www.hoteltrujillo.com* (€€€–€€). A decent little hotel in an old town house.

*Las Palomas**, C/Higueras 17, t 95 634 37 73 (€). Very good value, although placed just out of the centre. It has a pleasant tiled patio, traditional tiles and a roof terrace.

*San Andrés I and II**, C/Morenos 12 and 14, t 95 634 09 83, *www.hotelsanandres.es* (€). A *hostal* and a hotel on the same street: both offer simple rooms (no private baths in the *hostal*) set around flower-filled patios, but the hotel has a touch more charm.

Eating Out in Jerez de la Frontera

Even in a region of Spain known for the late hours it keeps, Jerez seems to go a step further. It's not at all unusual here to sit down to lunch at 3.30pm. Don't even think about dinner until after 10pm.

El Bosque, Avda Álvaro Domecq 26, t 95 630 70 30 (€€€). Beautifully sited in woods near the Parque de González Montoria, yet only a short distance from town; formal, elegant, well-known but slightly dull. The seafood is good; try *langostinos de Sanlúcar*, tortillas of baby shrimps or strawberry gazpacho. *Closed Sun*.

Gaitán, Gaitán 3, t 95 616 80 21 (€€). One of the favourite dining places in town, a couple of streets behind the tourist office, Gaitán is a tiny place with a big reputation. Try the bull's tail *a la jerezana*. *Closed Sun eve*.

La Mesa Redonda, C/Manuel de la Quintana 3, t 95 634 00 69 (€€). This beautifully decorated restaurant has antique furniture and paintings, giving the impression of an old aristocratic Jerez home. Serves excellent game and seasonal specialities, and takes its food seriously. Reservations essential. *Closed Sun and Aug*.

Tendido 6, C/Circo 10, t 95 634 48 35 (€€). Closer to town, by the bullring, this place was originally a wine shop; these days the main room is decorated on a *feria* theme, with bullfighting memorabilia on the walls. Here the emphasis is on robust helpings of traditional food. *Closed Sun.*

La Parra Vieja, C/San Miguel 9, t 95 633 53 90 (€€). A traditional old restaurant and tapas bar where you can try fish or meat *a la parilla* – grilled over charcoal.

Bar Juanito, Pescadería Vieja 8–10, t 95 633 48 38 (€). The best among a clutch of tiny tapas bars on Pescadería Vieja, a passage off the Plaza del Arenal. Try the *alcachofas en salsa* or the *costillas en adobo* (marinaded grilled pork chops). It is a crush at lunchtime; arrive early if you want a table (*opens in the evening at 8pm*).

La Cañita, C/Porvera 11 (€). Superb tapas bar which specializes in delicious *montaditos* (tiny open sandwiches) with all kinds of toppings, including vegetarian.

La Taberna Marinera, Plaza Rafael Rivero 2, t 95 633 44 27 (€). One of a number of good tapas bars in Plaza Rivero, just behind the Alameda Cristina. It's small inside but during summer everyone spills out onto the square.

Nightlife in Jerez de la Frontera

Jerez has a great nightlife, but it's spread out all over the city. A good place to start for early evening *copas* is Plaza Canterbury, opposite the Williams and Humbert *bodega*, near the bullring on C/Paul. Around this are a number of bars, clubs and discos, and you'll find a bit more further north on Avda de Méjico.

Jerez is justly famous for **flamenco** and, unlike in Sevilla where many *tablaos* will be overpriced and catering for busloads of tourists, here you will find the real thing; but you've got to look for it (and don't expect it to happen just because it's advertised). Visit the Centro Andaluz de Flamenco (*see* p.206) for information on what's on. Here is a selection of venues, mostly situated in the Gypsy quarter:

Bar Arco de Santiago, C/Barreras 3, t 95 630 30 81.

El Lagá de Tío Parilla, Plaza del Mercado, t 95 633 83 34. Flamenco shows Mon–Sat.

Centro Cultural Flamenco, C/Salas 12, t 95 634 74 72.

Arcos de la Frontera and the *Pueblos Blancos*

Starting from Jerez, **Arcos de la Frontera** is the first of the *pueblos blancos* (white towns) you come to and one of the most spectacular, hanging on a steep rock with wonderful views over the valley of the Guadalete from the *mirador* near the Plaza del Ayuntamiento. The narrow streets twist and turn like an oriental maze, an inheritance from its Moorish past. Follow the long street up to the castle and you'll be rewarded with panoramic views in all directions. The older sections of town under the castle contain some ancient palaces and the Isabelline-Gothic **Santa María de la Asunción**, next to which is a rectangular esplanade hanging over the cliff above the Guadalete. Way below stretches the river and its fertile valley.

Arcos's history is full of feud and conflict. Its name is derived from the Roman Arx-Arcis, meaning 'fortress on high'. The town was an important centre for the Moors, a seemingly impregnable eyrie that was the capital of its own kingdom in the age of the *taifas*,

Getting to Arcos de la Frontera

Arcos de la Frontera has regular **bus** connections from Jerez, Cádiz and Ronda, and less frequent connections from Sevilla (two daily).

ruled by the Berber king, Bem Jazrum, who built the now privately owned *castillo* in the 11th century. Alfonso the Wise was smart enough to capture the town in 1264, dismantling the beautiful Moorish mosque in typical Spanish style and replacing it with the

Santa María de la Asunción
open Mon–Fri 10–1 and 4–7, Sat 10–1.30; adm

church of **Santa María de la Asunción**, which squats on the northern side of the Plaza del Cabildo, the old town's car park. The church's southern Plateresque façade is impressive, as are the 14th-century *mudéjar* wall paintings inside and the gilt altarpieces by Andrés Benítez. The crucifixes on the walls cover bits of saint, entombed in the superstructure in an attempt to make the church

San Pedro
open Mon–Fri 10–1 and 4–7, Sat 10–1.30; adm

holier than its arch-rival – the 18th-century church of **San Pedro**, perched on the clifftop to the east. A feud between them in the 18th century became so intense that the churches turned to the Vatican for adjudication. Santa María still proudly displays the papal decree which declares it the winner – it hangs on the wall next to the glass case containing the grey and withered, yet undecomposed, body of an obscure St Felix. St Peter's parishioners were so disgusted that they refused to pronounce the name of their rival, and addressed their prayers to 'St Peter, Mother of God' or 'The Divine Shepherdess', rather than to 'Mary, Mother of God'.

San Pedro may have lost the holiness competition but it nonetheless contains the town's most important religious art: the two paintings *San Ignacio* and *La Dolorosa* by Velázquez's teacher, Pacheco. They hang on either side of the 16th-century retable, the oldest in the province.

Convent of San Augustín
open Wed–Mon 10.30–12.30 and 4–6.30

The town's most venerated relic, a 17th-century *Jesús Nazareno* (*Christ Carrying the Cross*) by Jacomi Verdi, lies hidden within yet another holy shrine, the 16th-century **Convent of San Augustín** at the eastern end of the town. It is also possible to see the beautiful and ornate retable in the church of the **Convent of Mercedarias Descalzas** on Calle Maldonado, which only opens once a week, for Sunday Mass at 9am. At other times the convent and the nuns remain ensconced behind heavy iron bars, and communication with the outside world is carried out through a rotating grille, through which the sisters pass handmade sweets.

Arcos has one of the region's most colourful Easter parades. Fighting bulls are let loose in the streets, and those who choose not to be chased by them can watch the procession of priests in purple twist their way through the incense-filled streets carrying heavy gilt images of Christ covered in flowers and lit by tall candles. There's also a flamenco festival around the beginning of August.

East into the Sierra de Grazalema

Further east, **Grazalema** is another lovely village, full of flowers and surrounded by pine woods. It is considered by many to be the archetypal Sierra town, and its peaceful beauty is in perfect accord with its surroundings. Grazalema has been famous for hand-woven blankets since Moorish times, and they are still made here on big old wooden looms. The town's heyday was from the end of the 18th century to the middle of the 19th, when a resurgence in the demand for blankets swelled the population to more than 9,000, compared with today's 2,224. The **Iglesia de la Encarnación**, beside the hotel on the Plaza Pequeña, is the oldest church in the town, with *mudéjar* designs dating from the 17th century, though it suffered badly during both the War of Independence and the Civil War. Flanking the far end of the main square, **Plaza de España**, is the 18th-century **Nuestra Señora de la Aurora**, unusual for its octagonal plan. The roads leading off the *plaza* are especially pretty, lined with little shops and bars, and leading to **Plaza de los Asomaderos**, a viewing area which doubles as a market on Tuesdays. C/Juan de la Rosa continues up to the top of town, and the 18th-century chapel of **San José**, originally a Carmelite convent. Beside the chapel is a camp site office which can provide you with details of walks and horse-trekking.

⭐ **Sierra de Grazalema**
for activities, including riding, climbing or simply walking, contact **Horizon**, *C/Corrales Terceros 29, www. horzonaventura.com*

The **Sierra de Grazalema** is one of the most stunning and eco-logically important parks in Spain. Consisting mainly of limestone formed in the Jurassic and Triassic ages, the park is a microclimate with the highest average rainfall in Spain; many pre-Ice Age species of plants and trees have survived, including the Spanish fir, or *pinsapo*. This rare tree grows only above 1,000m (3,200ft), and elsewhere it can only be found in the nearby reserve of Las Nieves

Around the Sierra de Grazalema

and in the Urals. Animal life includes golden eagles, common vultures, mountain goats and, in the high peaks, ibex. There are wonderful walks and activities such as potholing, caving, hang-gliding and horse riding. It is bounded by some of the prettiest *pueblos blancos* in Andalucía. Nearby **Zahara** ('flower' in Arabic) is a quiet town perfumed by orange groves, at the foot of a hill crowned by a medieval castle, which the Christians captured from the Moors towards the end of the 15th century. Despite the fact that the centre has been classified as a national monument, on closer inspection there is not much more to the town save the views. Zahara is another good base for walks into the deep mountain gorges of the national park, including the stunning **Garganta Verde**, which leads to a little monastery.

Algodonales has nothing more to it than a long square topped by the pretty church of **Santa Ana**, a few cafés and a couple of places to stay, though it has a stunning setting in the shadow of a stony outcrop. You would do better stopping at **Olvera**, once a famous bandits' hide-out, and now a beautiful place poised high on a hilltop with a memorable silhouette – its 12th-century castle and 17th-century church, **La Encarnación**, sticking up bravely over the gleaming spiral of whitewashed houses.

To the south is **Benaocaz**, which has a small museum of local archaeological finds. Nearby **Ubrique** hangs over the Río Majaceite; though a growing industrial town, best known for its leatherwork, it still manages to retain some of its medieval charm.

Halfway between Olvera and Ronda is **Setenil**, a peculiar village with some of its streets lining the walls of a gorge. The houses are tucked under the overhanging rock, and their front doors overlook a stream. The village's proper name is Setenil de las Bodegas – it was once a wine-producing centre, until all its vines were killed off by the phylloxera in the 1890s, initiating a period of poverty and decay from which the place has only lately been recovering.

Fiestas in Arcos de la Frontera and the *Pueblos Blancos*

Arcos: Easter parades; August flamenco festival (*see* p.209).

Grazalema: Last Sun of May: *Romería de San Isidro Labrador*, a celebration of the sun and the earth. Third week of July: *Fiestas del Carmen*, culminating in the *Lunes del Toro*, a traditional local festival. Third week of Aug: *Las Fiestas Mayores/Feria de Grazalema*. Sept 8: *El Virgen de los Ángeles*, the town's patron saint.

Zahara: Feb/Mar: *Carnaval*; June: *Romería de Arroymolinos*; *Fiestas de Agosto*.

Setenil: Holy Week celebrations.

Where to Stay and Eat in Arcos and the *Pueblos Blancos*

Arcos de la Frontera ✉ 11630

***Parador de Arcos de la Frontera, Plaza de Cabildo s/n, **t** 95 670 05 00, *www.parador.es* (€€€€). A lovely place, and quite popular, so book ahead.

ⓘ **Arcos de la Frontera >>**
Plaza de Cabildo s/n,
t *95 670 22 64, www.*
ayuntamientoarcos.org;
open Mon–Sat 10–2
and 3.30–7.30

Request a room with a view, and, even if you don't stay, sit over a coffee in the café – a picture window looks out over the entire plain.

La Casa Grande, C/Maldonado 10, **t 95 670 39 30, *www.lacasagrande.net* (€€€). Utterly charming, in a converted *palacio*, the former home of a well-known dancer, with home-made marmalade for breakfast. Wonderful views from the roof terrace.

Cortijo Faín, Ctra de Algar, km 3, **t 95 670 41 31 (€€€). A charmingly restored 17th-century country house, with pool and lovely gardens.

***Peña de Arcos, C/Muñoz Vázquez 42, **t** 95 670 45 32 (€€). A tastefully designed building with all the amenities, but down in the new town.

***Los Olivos, C/San Miguel 2, **t** 95 670 08 11 (€€). Bright, modern, central and very reasonably priced, around a central courtyard.

Marqués de Torresoto, C/Marqués de Torresoto 4, **t 95 670 07 17 (€€). Simple rooms in an aristocratic 17th-century mansion, wonderfully situated in the historic quarter of Arcos near the Ayuntamiento.

El Convento >

El Convento, C/Maldonado 2, **t 95 670 23 33, *www.webdearcos.com/ elconvento* (€€). Another wonderful choice, in part of an old convent and full of character, with fabulous views from the terrace and an excellent restaurant (*see* below).

*Hotel La Fonda, C/Corredara 83, **t** 95 670 00 57 (€€–€). A simple old place, set in a historic building with café. The nicest rooms have little balconies.

*Hostal San Marcos, C/Marqués de Torresoto 6, **t** 95 670 07 21 (€). A very good budget option in the heart of town; clean, new and with a lively café-bar.

Grazalema >>
Plaza de España 11,
t *95 613 22 25,*
www.grazalema.es;
open Tues–Sun 10–2
and 5–7, closed Mon

El Convento, Marqués de Torresoto 7, **t** 95 670 32 22 (€€). Perhaps the top restaurant in town, offering typical cuisine of the Sierras, such as rabbit and partridge, in a 16th-century nobleman's house with a beautiful traditional *andaluz* patio.

Mesón de la Molinera, Urb. Santiscal, Lago de Arcos, **t** 95 670 80 02, *www. hotelmesondalamolinera.com* (€€). On the shores of the lake, 4km from town, this hotel-restaurant specializes

in delicious regional meat and game dishes; fabulous views of the town.

Parador de Turismo, Plaza del Cabildo, **t** 95 670 05 00 (€€). A fine restaurant, with a terrace with remarkable views over the whitewashed old town.

Taberna José de la Viuda, Plaza Rafael Perez del Alamo 13, **t** 95 670 12 09 (€). Although this lively bar is located in the new town, it is heaving with old-fashioned Andalucian atmosphere. The tapas are excellent and the background music stays firmly in flamenco mode.

Peña Flamenca, Plaza de la Caridad, **t** 95 670 12 51. Arcos is not renowned for its late-night activities, but there are a couple of flamenco bars, including this place, with shows most Saturdays, and a flamenco festival in July and August.

There are several bars along C/Sevilla for a late-night *copa*: try **La Cabaña**. The discos are mainly around Avda Duque de Arcos, where there are outdoor clubs in summer. The Arcos Festival, held in early September, features some big-name international bands and DJs.

El Bosque ✉ 11670

Las Truchas, Avda de la Diputación s/n, **t 95 671 60 61 (€€). Just outside El Bosque, which is a delightful little village set among forests (providing shady relief from the sun-blasted landscapes of the rest of this area) and the Río Majaceíte, which is stuffed full of trout. There is a pool and excellent restaurant specializing in – you guessed it – fresh trout *a la serranía*. There are lots of walking routes possible from this spot.

Grazalema ✉ 11610

****Hotel Puerta de la Villa, Plaza Pequeña 8, **t** 95 613 23 76, *www. grazalemahotel.com* (€€€€–€€€). This is the best place to stay and eat here. Light, spacious rooms with outstanding views and all the mod cons. The hotel is just off the main square and is an excellent base for exploring the surrounding countryside. Has a tiny pool, gym, sauna and a top restaurant, **La Garrocha** (*see* below).

ⓘ Zahara >>
www.zaharadela
sierra.es

ⓘ Ubrique
Avda Solís Pascual 19-A,
t 95 646 49 00,
www.ubrique.es; open
Tues–Sat 10–2 and
4.30–7.30, Sun 10–2;
closed Mon

ⓘ Algondoles >>
www.algondoles.org

ⓘ Setenil >>
www.setenil.com

Hotel Villa Turística de Grazalema, C/Olivar s/n, t 95 613 21 36 (€€). One of the comfortable, government-run self-catering places, which you will pass on the approach into town. Includes apartments with Jacuzzi.

**La Casa de las Piedras, C/las Piedras 32, t 95 613 20 14 (€). A sweet little *pensión* with very plain rooms in a whitewashed street just above the main square. They also rent apartments and have a lively restaurant.

La Garrocha, Plaza Pequeña 8, t 95 613 24 06 (€€€). Tasty *andaluz* dishes of fresh fish, meat and vegetables, prepared in an innovative way; attached to Hotel Puerta de la Villa (*see* above).

El Torreón, C/Agua 44, t 95 613 23 13 (€€). One of the best options in this area, a beautiful, traditional restaurant with local trout, steak and chicken featuring on the reasonably priced menu.

Cádiz El Chico, Plaza de España 8, t 95 613 20 27 (€€). On the main square, offering a *menú* of local dishes and a good wine list.

Elsewhere, most of the food and drink options can be found in the streets leading off Plaza de España, particularly **C/Agua** and around the delightful palm-shaded **Plaza Andalucía**. Grazalema has a surprising number of bars for such a small place, most of them to be found on C/Agua.

Villaluenga del Rosario
✉ 11611

Hotel La Posada, C/Torre, t 95 612 61 19 (€€). You might like to base yourself at this whitewashed inn to explore nearby prehistoric sites. The village

itself is a tiny place seemingly cut out of the limestone. The hotel has an excellent restaurant, well known for its game dishes.

Zahara ✉ 11192

**Arco de la Villa, Camino Nazarí s/n, Zahara de la Sierra, t 95 612 32 30, *www.tugasa.com/index2.htm* (€€). A fantastic location built into the cliff edge above the town and below the ruined castle. Rooms are modern with spectacular views.

**Hostal Marqués de Zahara, C/San Juan 3, Zahara de la Sierra, t 95 612 30 61, *www.marquesdezahara.com* (€). A pleasant place, with characterful rooms round a courtyard off the main square.

Zahara has a handful of eating possibilities. All the hotels have restaurants; there is a great tapas bar, **El Mirador**, on the main square.

Algodonales, Olvera and Setenil ✉ 11192

**Sierra y Cal, Avda Nuestra Señora de los Remedios 4, Olvera, t 95 613 05 42, *www.tugasa.com/sierraycal.htm* (€€). A comfortable hotel with 22 rooms, some with a separate sitting area. Facilities include a pool, bar and restaurant. Good value.

**El Almendral, Ctra Setenil–Pto del Monte, Setenil t 95 613 40 29, *www.tugasa.com/elalmendral.htm* (€€). A rare place to stay in Setenil, in a whitewashed villa with a swimming pool, and large rooms with balconies.

**Hostal Alameda, Avda Constitución 12, Algodonales, t 95 613 72 29 (€). A basic place but with lovely views over the square and the hills behind the town.

From Cádiz to Algeciras

The green, hilly countryside of this region looks a lot like the parts of Morocco just across the straits. The hills force the main road away from the sea, leaving a few villages with fine beaches. These make good places to take time out from your overactive holiday; the problem is, they're hard to reach unless you have a car.

Beyond the marshland around Cádiz, you'll see the turn-off for **Sancti Petri**, a small village with a ruined castle on an island off the beach and a little fishing harbour where the trawlers are now

Getting around between Cádiz and Algeciras

By Train

Trains go to Ronda and Granada from Algeciras, and from there to all points in eastern Andalucía; there are two daily services to Madrid and points north. The **train station** is across from the bus station.

By Bus

Buses to Algeciras from the **Comes** station in Cádiz are frequent enough, but services to coastal resorts like Conil, Barbate and Zahara are less so (two per day). The Comes **bus station** in Algeciras is at C/San Bernardo, **t** 95 665 34 56. Buses run by **Portillo** and **Alsina Graells** (for the Costa del Sol, Málaga, Granada and Sevilla) leave from Avda Virgen del Carmen 15.

By Boat

FRS, t 95 668 18 30, *www.frs.es*, runs ferries from Tarifa to Algeciras, and from Tarifa to Tangier. It also offers guided one- or two-day trips to Tangier. **Acciona-Trasmediterránea, t** 902 454 645, *www. trasmediterranea.es*, has services to Ceuta and Tangier.

outnumbered by yachts. The village is being swallowed up by the neighbouring soulless tourist resort of Novo Sancti Petri, where the admittedly glorious long sandy beaches are lined with endless banal new developments. Next along the coast is **Conil**, with a tiny harbour and what remains of the town's fishing fleet. It's a very popular resort for Spanish families, thanks to its vast, shallow bay. It is always crammed in August, when you'll have virtually no chance of finding anywhere to stay, but you can count on some pretty lively nightlife, especially along the Paseo Marítimo.

Twenty-three kilometres inland along the A390 is **Medina Sidonia**. This is one of the prettiest whitewashed towns, far less visited than Vejer (*see* below). It is set on top of a hill in the middle of rolling fields; on a clear day you can see the mountains of the Serranía de Ronda. Its origins stretch back to Roman and Phoenician times but its modern history dates from 1440, when it was handed over to Don Juan de Guzmán, who became the first Duke of Medina Sidonia. The town saw royal patronage for many years, although today it has a slightly dusty and neglected feel. There are a few monuments that stand out, including the 16th-century church of **Santa María la Coronada** in Plaza Iglesia Mayor, where the tourist office is housed. It has a huge carved retable inside stretching from floor to ceiling. Climb the hill and you will reach the ruins of the Moorish **castle**. The town also has three well-preserved Moorish gates, Puertas de Belén and del Sol, and the 10th-century **Arco de la Pastora**, perhaps the best preserved. The 17th-century **Ayuntamiento**, in fine Renaissance style, is in the Plaza de España, in the lower part of town.

The main attraction back on the coastal road is **Vejer de la Frontera**, whitest of the 'white villages' of Andalucía, strangely moulded around its hilltop site like a Greek island town. The village was probably a Carthaginian citadel before becoming the Roman

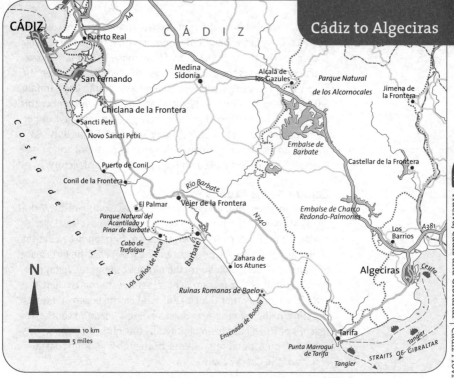

town of Besipo. Now it couldn't be more Moorish in its feel: a Moorish castle dominates the village and the 13th-century Gothic church, built over the site of a mosque, lies deep within the town's sparkling clean, narrow whitewashed streets. In the upper part of town you can see the original Moorish gates. Even the locals seem close to their Muslim past: until fairly recently women in Vejer wore the *cobija*, a piece of dark cloth like a Muslim hijab that covers the face, leaving only the eyes exposed. There's a long, sandy beach 9km away at **El Palmar** and, nearby, a Roman aqueduct in the beautiful village of **Santa Lucía**.

From Vejer the A393 goes down to the modern town of **Barbate**, whose income comes not from tourists but tuna. Twice a year large shoals of them pass here, to be slaughtered in a bloody ambush similar to the *mattanza* off the coast of Sicily. It's a small, scrubby working town, full of canning factories and cheap apartment blocks, but the fish restaurants and tapas bars along the Paseo Marítimo are all excellent.

Just inland from Barbate, not far from Vejer de la Frontera, is **NMAC** – look for signs for Montenmedio, on the main road N340, km 42.5. NMAC is a striking and original contemporary art centre with a twist: the landscape itself has become a 'gallery' for a collection of permanent site-specific sculptures and installations.

NMAC

t 95 645 51 34, www. fundacionnmac.com; open Tues–Sun 10–1.30 and 5.30–8.30; adm

A small road leads west out of Barbate to the resort of **Los Caños de Meca**, busy in the height of summer with tourists from Sevilla and Cádiz. The trendy, hippy crowd have moved on to Tarifa now, and in recent years the Germans have adopted the place as their haven. Half an hour's walk west of here takes you to **Cape Trafalgar**, where Nelson breathed his last in 1805. Spaniards remember this well; it was mostly their ships that were getting smashed, under incompetent French leadership. Every Spaniard did his duty, though, and with their unflappable sense of personal honour the Spanish have always looked on Trafalgar as a sort of victory.

Zahara de los Atunes

Ten kilometres south of here is another developing resort, Zahara de los Atunes ('of the tunas'). This is one of the most unspoilt coastlines in southern Spain, with miles of fine sandy beach that in spring and autumn will be all yours. The town was the birthplace of Francisco Rivera, or Paquirri, the famous bullfighter. Today it is fairly tranquil, with a few small hotels and restaurants. There's little to see or do other than laze around on the beach and watch the sun sinking into the sea whilst sipping a beer. The southern reaches of town have been blighted by unsightly modern *urbanizaciones*, but it remains one of the most alluring coastal resorts of the Costa de la Luz.

Tarifa

Tarifa, at the tip of Spain and of Europe, looks either exotic and evocative, or merely dusty and dreary, depending on the hour of the day and the mood you're in. You might even think you've arrived in Africa, it's so bleached by sun and salt. The town is one of the top destinations in Europe for wind- and kite-surfing; the *levante* and *poniente* winds are relentless in their attack on this coast and the associated young crowd has fomented a lively bar scene. Tarifa has also become a very popular spot for whale-watching tours: several companies run them.

Whale-watching
Whale Watch España:
t 95 662 70 13, www.
whalewatchtarifa.net
*Foundation for
Information and
Research on Marine
Mammals (FIRMM):* t 95
662 70 08/619 459 441

Baelo Claudio
t 95 668 85 30; open
Tues–Sat June–Sept
10–8; Mar–May and Oct
10–7; Nov–Feb 10–6;
Sun and hols all year
10–2; adm, free to
EU citizens

The town has a 10th-century Moorish **castle**, much rebuilt, and the site of the legend of Guzmán el Bueno. In 1292, this Spanish knight was defending Tarifa against a force of Moors. Among them was the renegade Infante Don Juan, brother of King Sancho IV, who had Guzmán's young son as a prisoner, and threatened to kill him if Guzmán did not surrender. Guzmán's response was to toss him a dagger. His son was killed, but Tarifa did not fall. Fascist propaganda recycled this legend for the 1936 siege of the Alcázar in Toledo, with the Republicans in the villain's role.

Outside Tarifa, along the beaches west of town, are the ruins of a Roman town, Baelo Claudio. Baelo Claudio was founded in the 2nd century BC, and became important for the production of *garum*, a fish sauce that was one of the prized condiments of the Roman kitchen; preserved in jars, it was shipped from Andalucía all over the Empire. The town rose to prominence in the 1st century AD, when it was made a self-governing municipality under Emperor Claudius. Its decline began in the second half of the 2nd century due to an earthquake, and it was abandoned by the 7th century. What remains is all that makes up a Roman town: a court, temples, basilica, roads – and the fish factory. The magnificent beach, with its sand dune cascading down the western end, is rarely crowded.

Algeciras

Ask at the tourist office what there is to see and you'll be told, 'Nothing. Nobody ever stays here.' Once you've seen the town you'll understand why: it's a dump. Nevertheless, Algeciras has an interesting history, and an attractive setting opposite the Rock of Gibraltar – if you can see through the pollution.

The city played a significant role in the colonization of the eastern Mediterranean, becoming an important port in the Roman era. From AD 713 on, it was occupied by the Moors, and its name derives from the Arabic *Al-Jazira al-Khadra* (Green Island). Today, apart from its importance as a port with regular connections to Ceuta, Tangier and the Canary Islands, Algeciras is a sizeable industrial centre. Its only recent claim to fame is its illustrious son Paco de Lucía, Spain's greatest guitarist; there's a small monument to him at the quay.

The bustling, seedy port area has little attraction for the visitor, although the small bazaars in the side streets, selling Moroccan leather goods, may whet your appetite for a trip across the straits – you can see Morocco's jagged, surreal peaks all along the coastal highway. It is also the centre of one of the busiest drug-smuggling routes in the world, and every stevedore and cab driver will be whispering little propositions in your ear if you look the type.

Inland, lying in a pleasantly wooded area, is **Los Barrios**, settled by refugees when Gibraltar was lost to the British; archaeological finds indicate that it was inhabited from earliest times. The parish church of **San Isidro** dates from the 18th century. There are two fairly decent beaches nearby – **Guadarranque** and **Palmones**.

The A7/E15 *autovia* heads north towards **San Roque**, with exceptional views over the bay of Algeciras and Gibraltar. Here are the ruins of **Carteya**, the first Roman settlement in the south of the peninsula. The 18th-century parish church of **Santa María Coronada** was built above the ancient hermitage of San Roque, and is worth a visit. This pretty little town is a relief after the more sordid quarters of Algeciras, and a bonus is the nearby clean beaches of **Puente Mayorga**, **Los Portichuelos** and **Carteya**.

Parque Natural de Los Alcornocales

ⓘ **Parque Natural de Los Alcornocales** *Park information offices: just outside Algeciras by the El Pelayo beach on the N340,* t *95 667 91 61; Alcalá de los Gazules,* t *95 642 05 29; Cortes de la Frontera,* t *952 15 45 99; all have guides to walking routes of varying difficulty in the park*

This natural park spreads out above Algeciras and Tarifa, reaching as far as **El Bosque**. Despite the presence of the recently built Algeciras–Jerez dual carriageway which slices through the park, it remains a quiet, sparsely populated region, scattered with villages and lovely white towns like Jimena de la Frontera and Alcalá de los Gazules. The name of the park refers to the cork oak, or *alcornoque*, which is spread right across the area, forming its largest forest in Europe. The park is an important spot for migratory birds coming over the Straits from Africa in spring and returning in autumn. March to May is the best time to spot species such as sea eagles and short-toed eagles as well as one of the largest groups of spotted vultures in Europe. Animals such as deer, mongoose and boar are also indigenous, as are trees including rhododendron, ash and hazel. It's a delight to explore on foot or by mountain bike, staying in one of the mountain villages, or on a leisurely day's drive from Algeciras or Tarifa.

The route north from Algeciras via Los Barrios, once a winding country road and now a highway, has changed dramatically since it was described by Laurie Lee in his book *A Rose for Winter*. But the landscape has changed little, and the road curves through former bandit country before arriving at the village of **Alcalá de los Gazules**, which Lee described as 'a terraced town of bright white houses hung with red flowers and roofed with gold'. Despite the new road, the village hasn't changed much in 70 years and there is not a great deal to see other than the church of **San Jorge** in the Plaza Alta, which has wonderful views over the surrounding countryside. The church is usually closed but if you ask at the *turismo* in the Casa Consistorial, or at Bar Luna opposite, someone should be able to rustle up the key. Inside there are a couple of curiosities: an odd-shaped choir stall adjusted from four seats to three for Inquisition purposes and an effigy of *San Cristóbal*, heavily scratched by superstitious townsfolk. There's also one of a pair of paintings of *San Esteban*; the other resides in the Vatican.

Southwest along the CA3331 is **Jimena de la Frontera**, topped by an impressive Moorish castle, once owned by the Dukes of Medina Sidonia. Just outside the castle wall lie the ruins of the **Church of the Misericordia**, and a few kilometres away are some prehistoric **caves** with ancient wall paintings.

There is another 13th-century Moorish castle at **Castellar de la Frontera**, entirely circled by the castle walls, from where, on a clear day, you can see right across to Africa. During the 1970s, owing to its primitive state, the old town was abandoned by its entire population, all of whom moved to Nuevo Castellar along the main road. It has been gradually repopulated though, mainly by Germans, who sit uneasily with the original populace down the road.

Where to Stay and Eat from Cádiz to Algeciras

(i) Conil >
C/Carretera s/n,
t 95 644 05 01, www.
conildelafrontera.es;
open Mon–Sat
9.30–1.30

(★) Fuerte Conil >

(i) Vejer de la
Frontera >>
Avda de los Remedios 2,
t 95 645 17 36; open
Mon–Fri 9–2 and 5–9,
Sat–Sun 11–2 and 6–9

(i) Barbate
C/Vázquez Mella 2,
t 95 643 39 62;
open Mon–Fri 8–3

(i) Medina
Sidonia >
Plaza Iglesia Mayor s/n,
t 95 641 24 04,
www.turismomedina
sidonia.com

Conil ✉ 11140

The town boasts some of the best beaches along the coast and one of the finest hotels.

★★★Flamenco, Fuente del Gallo s/n, **t** 95 644 07 11, *www.hipotels.com* (€€€€). Slightly out of town, but with many facilities including indoor and outdoor pool, direct beach access, tennis, golf and spa.

★★★★Fuerte Conil, Playa Fontanilla s/n, **t** 95 644 33 44, *www.fuertehoteles.com* (€€€). Faux-Moorish, in soft colours, stylish and subtly luxurious, and set in its own grounds with the rooms ranged round a huge outdoor pool. There is also an indoor pool, tennis courts, a gym and a diving school. The restaurant and bar are excellent, with everything at a reasonable price. Winner of Spain's first environmental award for hotels.

★★★Hotel Diufain, Cañada del Rosal s/n, **t** 95 644 25 51, *www.hoteldiufain. com* (€€). Built in a *hacienda* style on the top of a hill overlooking the town; small rooms but a big pool and a café.

Venta Melchor, Ctra Cádiz-Málaga, km 18, **t** 95 644 50 07 (€€). The best seafood place, though it's out of town. Family-run and dating from 1950, they still serve the freshest seafood from the area as well as delicious home-made *postres*.

El Rincón de Villa, Plaza de España 6, **t** 95 644 10 53 (€). A small restaurant and bar in town with a particularly good range of seafood tapas.

Plaza Santa Catalina and the streets off it, particularly **C/Ancha** and **C/José Tomás Borrego**, are where the night action takes place. There are more disco-bars on or around **Plaza Goya**. The nightlife hums in summer, but there's little open the rest of the year.

Medina Sidonia ✉ 11170

★★★Hotel Medina Sidonia, Pza Llanete de Herederos 1, **t** 95 641 23 17 (€€). Charming little hotel in an 18th-century *palacio* in the historic centre.

★Venta el Molino, Avda Al-Andalus s/n, **t** 95 641 03 00 (€). Slightly out of the centre; basic but friendly.

Pensión Napoleón, C/San Juan 21, **t** 95 641 01 83 (€). In a good location near the centre; the cheapest option.

La Duquesa, Ctra Medina–Benalup, km 3, **t** 95 641 08 36, *www.duquesa.com* (€€). Set in a converted farmhouse in the middle of bull-breeding territory, this restaurant offers superb local cooking including *rabo de toro*.

Cádiz, Plaza Espana 13, **t** 95 641 02 50 (€€–€). Has a lovely shaded patio and serves some good local dishes including partridge, rabbit and stew.

Vejer de la Frontera ✉ 11150

Casa Cinco, C/Sancho IV el Bravo 5, **t** 95 645 50 29, *www.hotelcasacinco. com* (€€€). Just five stylish little rooms, each individually decorated in a chic mix of antique and contemporary furnishings. Two-night minimum.

Aquí Vejer, C/Badillo 1–3, **t** 95 645 07 90, *www.aquivejer.com* (€€€). Evocative hotel with a Moorish-inspired décor, with courtyard and terrace, and just two beautifully decorated guest rooms.

★★★Convento de San Francisco, La Plazuela s/n, **t** 95 645 10 01 (€€). A delightful place; a restored former convent with tastefully designed rooms, lots of original furniture and an excellent restaurant, **El Refectorio**.

Trafalgar, Plaza de España 31, **t** 95 644 76 38 (€€). A traditional restaurant serving up imaginative *andaluz* cuisine. They make their own ice creams and sorbets, too. *Closed Mon during Oct–Mar.*

Zahara de los Atunes/ Los Caños de Meca ✉ 11393

★★★Doña Lola, Plaza Thomson 1, Zahara, **t** 95 643 90 09 (€€€€). One of the prettiest hotels in town, with rooms set around a patio and overlooking a large pool.

★★★★Melía Atlanterra, Bahía de la Plata, **t** 95 643 90 00, *www.solmelia.es* (€€€€–€€€). The big resort complex at the Bahía de la Plata; set around a lagoon-shaped pool, it offers a variety of sports and recreational activities. *Closed Nov–April.*

★★Hacienda Cabo de Plata, Ctra de Atlanterra, km 4, **t** 95 643 94 56 (€€€€– €€€). A whitewashed, 19th-century *cortjio* set around a series of

(i) **Tarifa >>**

northern end of Paseo Alameda, outside the western wall of the old town, t 95 668 09 93, www.tarifaweb.com; open summer Mon–Fri 10.30–2 and 6–8; winter Mon–Fri 10.30–2 and 5–7

(★) **Banti Tarifa >>**

lovely flower-filled patios; 14 antique-filled rooms and oodles of charm.

****Antonio II**, Urb. Atlanterra 1, t 95 643 93 46, *www.antoniohoteles.com* (€€€). A large modern hotel, with lovely views along the coast, light airy rooms and a large pool area; excellent value just out of season.

***Hotel Pozo del Duque**, Ctra Atlanterra 32, Zahara, t 95 643 90 97, *www.pozodelduque.com* (€€€). Spacious rooms with a terrace and sea view, a pool, and on the beach.

****Gran Sol**, on the beach at the end of C/Sánchez Rodríguez, t 95 643 93 58, *www.gransolhotel.com* (€€€). In Zahara itself, with air-conditioned rooms with TV, a terrace restaurant with superb views, and a pool.

****Antonio I**, just in front of Antonio II (*see* above, €€). The cheaper option, on the beach, with a good restaurant.

****Hotel Nicolás**, C/María Luisa 15, Zahara, t 95 643 92 74, *hotel-nicolas@terra.es* (€€). Friendly, old-fashioned little hotel in the village, with a classic café-bar downstairs.

Camping Bahía de la Plata, t 95 643 90 40 (€). A campsite at the south end of Zahara, with bungalows also.

Antonio, Ctra Atlanterra, km 1, t 95 643 95 42 (€€). Tourists flock to this restaurant on the beach for its high-quality fish and seafood; it has the same owners as the Antonio I and Antonio II hotels (*see* above).

Mesón Los Estribos, C/Fuerte 3, Zahara, t 95 612 31 45 (€€). A contemplative location opposite the main church and a menu of superbly prepared local dishes, including lamb stew and partridge. *Closed Mon.*

Bar Marisquería Porfirio, Plaza Tamarón, t 95 643 91 30 (€€). Serves excellent seafood in season.

Casa Juanito, C/Sagasta 7, t 95 643 92 11 (€€). One of the most popular local restaurants – getting a table can be difficult. Excellent seafood; try the locally caught tuna. *Closed Jan.*

Trafalgar, Los Caños de Meca, t 95 644 76 38 (€). Set back from the seafront with a pleasant terrace; the menu concentrates on international fare. *Closed in winter.*

Patio la Plazuela, Plaza Tamarón, Los Caños de Meca, t 95 643 90 09 (€).

Vegetarians won't be disappointed with the sumptuous pizza baked on the spot in Italian ovens.

Pericayo, C/Ilustre Fregona (parallel with main street), t 95 643 93 15 (€). Serves sangría and tasty tapas.

Tarifa ✉ 11380

As in Conil, rooms are surprisingly and unnecessarily expensive in the 'recently discovered' resort.

***Punta Sur**, Ctra Cádiz–Málaga, km 77, t 95 668 43 26, *www.hotelpuntasur.com* (€€€€). In a pretty spot by the Playa de los Lances, between Tarifa and Punta Palomas to the west of town, this is a relaxed and stylish place. Two pools, a gym, tennis courts and horse-riding. *Closed Nov–Mar.*

Arte-Vida, Ctra N340, km 79.3, t 95 668 52 46, *www.hotelartevidatarifa.com* (€€€€). Another trendy place for the 'boho-chic' crowd, this has stylish rooms set around a pool just back from a popular windsurfing beach, and a sleek blue and white restaurant and cocktail bar with wicker furniture.

***Escondite del Viento**, Comendador 1, t 95 668 1901, *www.elesconditedelviento.com* (€€€). One of the latest hotels on the Tarifa scene, located in the old town in a 200-year-old house. There are just six rooms with plenty of colour, light and glass; the whole place has a cutting-edge design look that somehow works well.

Molino El Mastral, Carretera Nuestra Señora Virgen de la Luz, km 2.3, t 95 679 193 503, *www.mastral.com* (€€€). Set amidst the beautiful natural park of Los Alcornocales, yet just 600 metres from the Tarifa beaches, this former water mill has 2- and 3-bedroom apartments that are simple and rustic, with terraces. The owners also run a riding school.

****Banti Tarifa**, N340, km82.7, t 95 668 15 09, *www.bantitarifa.com* (€€). Opened in 2007, this stylish place has just six rooms each distinctly decorated (hot pink and vibrant yellow), plus an excellent restaurant serving soul-cum-Asian-influenced food with regular live music.

Hostal Alameda, C/Santísima Trinidad 7, t 95 668 11 81 (€€). In the centre of town; some of its pleasant rooms have sea views.

*Hostal Las Margaritas, C/Antonio Maura 13, **t** 95 668 00 30, *www.lasmargaritas.info* (€€). On the edge of the old town, with pleasant rooms with small terraces for a good price.

Bar Restaurante Morilla, C/Sancho IV 2, **t** 95 668 17 57 (€). Classic *andaluz* restaurant and tapas bar with a terrace, serving good local seafood and other dishes.

Those seeking nightlife should wander around the old town, where the crowds congregate in the numerous bars from about 11pm; try **Café-Bar Almedina**, C/Almedina 3, which does good tapas and cocktails in a red-painted, cushion-strewn cavern, before heading down to the beachfront disco, **El Balneario**.

Algeciras ✉ 11200

****Reina Cristina, Pso de la Conferencia, **t** 95 660 26 22, *www.reina cristina.com* (€€€). The hotel of the town's bygone elegance, scene of the Algeciras Conference of 1906 (which carved up Morocco) and a hotbed of spies during the Second World War. W. B. Yeats spent a winter here.

****Octavio, C/San Bernardo 1, **t** 95 665 27 00, *www.husa.es* (€€€). Borders the bus station and is within a few metres of the train station. Mod cons, including satellite TV, but no pool.

***Alborán, C/Álamo s/n, Colonia San Miguel, **t** 95 663 28 70, *www.hotelesalboran.com* (€€€). A wonderful building in classical Andalucian style, on the outskirts of town. It's very atmospheric and keenly priced, with an indoor patio and porticoed terrace.

***Al Mar, Avda de la Marina 2, **t** 95 665 46 61, *www.eh.etursa.es* (€€€). Right on the seafront, above the busy arcades filled with cafés and ticket offices, looking out over the port area.

Hotel Marina Victoria, next to Al Mar at Avda de la Marina 7, **t 95 665 01 11 (€€–€). A less salubrious option, but with good views over to the Rock.

Versailles, C/Montero Ríos 12, **t 95 665 42 11 (€). One of a cluster of convenient little *hostales* in the back streets behind the Avda de la Marina.

There are lots of restaurants; look in the streets off **Plaza Alta**, particularly **C/Alfonso XI**.

El Copo, Trasmayo 2 (near Los Barrios), **t** 95 667 77 10 (€€€). A good place to splash out. The restaurant is draped with fishermen's nets and takes pride in its enormous tanks of lobsters, sea urchins, spider crabs and mussels; seafood is supremely fresh. Try to take a look upstairs at the bullfighters' room and the room with a painted panorama of views from Palmones several hundred years ago. *Booking essential. Closed Sun eve and Mon.*

Mesón El Copo, Trasmayo 2, **t** 95 667 77 10 (€€). An elegant seafood restaurant with several dining rooms, including one decked out like a ship's cabin. *Closed Sun.*

Almazara, C/Alfonso IX 9, **t** 95 665 74 77 (€€). One of the best local restaurants, serving tapas at the bar and steaks and fish in the tiny restaurant.

Casa Montes, C/San Juan 16, **t** 95 665 42 07 (€€). Popular place with working people, where *urta* surfaces again, along with roast kid and poultry.

Casa Maria, C/Emilio Castelar 53, **t** 95 665 47 02 (€€–€). This restaurant is carnivore heaven, with a meat-laden menu; seafood also available.

Pazo de Edelmiro, Plaza Miguel Martín 1, **t** 95 666 63 55 (€). Workers' favourite; very reasonable Galician dishes.

Alcalá de los Gazules ✉ 11180

Hostal Pizarro, Pso de la Playa 9, **t** 95 642 01 03 (€). A basic *hostal* with clean, albeit small and plain rooms.

San Jorge, Pso de la Playa s/n, **t** 95 641 32 55 (€€). Good restaurant and bar. *Closed Wed.*

Jimena de la Frontera ✉ 11330

Hostal El Anon, C/Consuelo 36, **t** 95 664 01 13, *www.andalucia.com/jimena/hostalanon* (€€). A delightful American-owned place with a series of pretty courtyards around which are ranged the rather basic rooms. There is a good restaurant and bar and even a pool on the roof with lovely views.

Los Arcos, Avda Reina de los Ángeles 8, **t 95 664 12 12 (€€–€). A more basic option, with gardens, but no pool.

The best place to eat here is the **El Anon** restaurant, but you could also try **La Parra**, C/Sevilla 18, or the **Venta El Vaquero**, Ctra Algeciras-Ronda, on the outskirts of town.

ⓘ **Algeciras >**
Avda Juan de la Cierva s/n, by the port, **t** 95 657 26 36

ⓘ **San Roque**
Plaza de Andalucia (corner of C/Felipe), **t** 95 669 40 05, *www.sanroque.es/turismo*

An Excursion to North Africa

The main reason for making the crossing to Morocco is to take a look at the limited attractions of Tangier. Unfortunately, the real treasures are all far to the south, in Fez, Marrakech and the kasbahs of the Drâa and Ziz valleys. But even an international city like Tangier will give you the chance to explore a fascinating society – and perhaps see a little reflection of the lost culture of al-Andalus. On the other hand, you could shop at Ceuta, one of Spain's last two *presidios* on the North African coast.

Hotels, restaurants and everything else will be almost half as expensive as in Spain. The food has an international reputation; national dishes like couscous and *harira* can be superb but seldom are. Don't judge Morocco by Ceuta, Tangier and Tetuan, and don't even judge these places by first impressions. A little side-trip to Morocco may not be an epiphany, but think how much you'll regret it if you pass up the chance.

Ceuta

Every time the Spanish make self-righteous noises about getting Gibraltar back, someone reminds them about their two colonial leftovers on the North African coast, Melilla (*see* p.260) and Ceuta. Ceuta has a mainly Spanish population; that is why it was excluded from the 1955 withdrawal from the Spanish-Moroccan protectorate. They are the stumbling block, and some way will have to be found to accommodate them before a transfer of sovereignty.

Ceuta is a pleasant enough town, but there's little reason to go there, perhaps only the impressive 16th-century walls and moat. The **Museo de Ceuta** has rather dull exhibits on local history, and

Museo de Ceuta
*open summer Mon–Fri
10–1 and 7–9;
winter Mon–Fri 5–8,
Sat 10–2; adm*

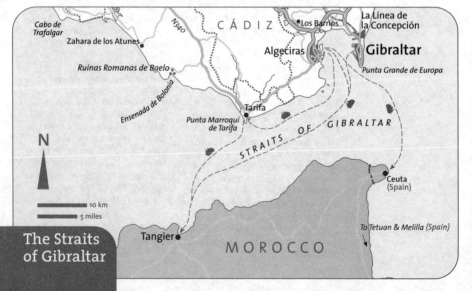

The Straits
of Gibraltar

Getting to North Africa

Algeciras's *raison d'être* is its port, and there's no trouble getting a **ferry** either to Ceuta (with at least 10 crossings a day in summer) or to Tangier (6 crossings in summer). A **jetfoil** (*www.buquebus.es*, **t** 902 41 42 42) runs at least five times daily except Sunday. There's also a summer **hydrofoil** service from Tarifa to Tangier and to Gibraltar. Ceuta is 1½hrs away by ferry, 30 mins by hydrofoil, and Tangier is 2½hrs away, or 1hr on a the jetfoil. There is a full list of ferry times on the official website, *www.ayto-algeciras.es*.

Among other companies, **FRS Maroc, t** 95 668 13 30, runs a guided one- or two-day tour.

There are plenty of official **Acciona-Trasmediterránea** agents at the port, as well as unofficial **ticket booths** along the N340, as far away as Estepona. The latter all look extremely dodgy, though they sell legitimate tickets. To avoid hefty commissions, buy directly from the Acciona-Trasmediterránea office at the port (Recinto del Puerto s/n, **t** 902 46 45 45). You'll need your passport.

If you're travelling from **Ceuta to Tangier**, you'll have to take a **cab** or city **bus** (the one marked '*frontera*') to the border; after some border confusion, wait for the infrequent bus or negotiate (be prepared to bargain hard) a **taxi** trip (taxis are usually shared and take up to six people) to Tetuan, 42km away. There's no train from Tetuan to Tangier, but buses run regularly from the central bus station. They'll take you right to Tangier's port.

Museo de La Legión

open Mon–Sat 11–1.30 and 3–6

the **Museo de La Legión** is devoted to Spain's Foreign Legion (a band of cut-throats who became notorious during the Civil War under a one-armed, one-eyed commander named José Millán Astray; their slogan: 'Long live Death'). The **Parque Marítimo del Mediterráneo** is a massive watery theme park, with plenty of pools, a vast lake, botanic gardens, shops and restaurants. Like Andorra, Ceuta is a big, duty-free supermarket. You can easily cross into Morocco from here, though it's better to take the ferry to Tangier.

Tetuan and Tangier

Aside from its polluted river and contraband appeal, **Tetuan** is a decent town, full of gleaming white, Spanish architecture; it has a famous market in its *medina*, a historical museum, and is a good place to purchase Moroccan crafts.

On the way into **Tangier**, note how the old **Plaza de Toros** has been turned into flats. Once in the square outside the port entrance, you may take your chances with the inexpensive hotels in the surrounding streets, or take a cab to fancier spots in the Europeanized districts. Tangier may not be as romantic as you expect; or you may find it more so. It is certainly exotic in parts. The wares in the markets of the *medina* are interesting, but the quarter itself is down-at-heel. Non-Muslims may not enter mosques in Morocco, but in the old **governor's palace** are two museums of archaeology and Moroccan art.

Moroccan Practicalities

Money

Wait until you get to Morocco to change money. Spanish travel agents often change money at a dishonestly low rate, and the rates at the border crossings aren't much better. The currency is the **dirham**, lately about 16 to the pound, 8 to the dollar, and 11 to the euro.

Dealers and Dealing

This corner of Morocco, being the fullest of tourists, is also full of English-speaking hustlers, particularly

ⓘ **Tangier**
29 Boulevard Pasteur,
t (039) 994 86 61,
www.tourism-in-
morocco.com

ⓘ **Tetuan**
30 Avenue
Mohammed V,
t (9) 96 19 15

ⓘ **Ceuta >**
Calle Edrissis, Edif.
Baluarte de los
Mallorquines s/n, t 856
200 560, www.ceuta.es

around bus stations, pushing tours and drugs. There's been a crackdown on hustlers in Tetuan which means things aren't quite as hectic. Beyond that, you'll need your wits to bargain with merchants, taxi drivers and even hotel-keepers. Also, crime is a problem after dark in Tetuan and Tangier.

Where to Stay and Eat in Northern Morocco

Ceuta ✉ 51001
There are only a few hotels.
★★★★**Parador La Muralla**, Plaza de Nuestra Señora de África 15, **t** 95 651 49 40 (€€€€). Offers the most comfort and luxury, with a pool and gardens.

★★★★**Ulises**, C/Camoens 5, **t** 95 651 45 40, *www.hotelulises.com* (€€). Well priced, with a pool and restaurant.
Al Andalus, Ctra Sanamaro-Pinogordo s/n, **t** 95 651 39 21 (€€). A romantic restaurant with sea views and Moroccan specialities.
El Portalón, C/Agustina de Aragón 2, **t** 95 651 75 00 (€). Tapas and seafood in a rustic little tavern with a terrace in the old heart of Ceuta.
Club Nautica, C/Edrissis, **t** 95 651 44 00 (€). Despite its rather clinical atmosphere, the setting is lovely, overlooking the yacht harbour. The fish and seafood are excellent value.
El Rincón de Nacho, C/Padilla 4, **t** 95 651 57 84 (€). Tasty local seafood and home-made desserts.

Gibraltar

At first sight it looks like a sphinx, crouching at the water's edge, her hindquarters resting in Europe, her head gazing over the sea and her forepaws stretching in front of her to form the most southerly part of our continent.

Alexandre
Dumas, 1846

In under two hours, you can experience the ultimate culture shock: sailing from the smoky souks of Tangier to Algeciras, Spain, with time for *churros* and chocolate before the bus takes you off to a mysterious enclave of red phone booths, Bisto, warm beer and policemen in silly hats.

The Spanish bus will really take you only as far as **La Línea** (*see* p.240) ('the Line', after Gibraltar's old land walls), a town that has built up dramatically over the last three decades. Hotel prices in Gibraltar are high by Spanish standards, and if you are on a budget you might be best staying in La Línea. It's then only a short walk through the neutral zone into Gibraltar, where you'll be confronted immediately with one of the Rock's curiosities: as you enter British territory you find yourself looking down the noses of 737s and Tridents. Where else does a busy street cross an airport runway? The airport, built on landfill at right angles to the narrow peninsula, symbolizes British determination to hold on during the years Franco was putting the squeeze on Gibraltar, and also points up the enclave's biggest problem – lack of space.

Seven million visitors come to Gibraltar each year, many just to shop at Europe's last true duty-free zone. British residents living on Spanish soil cross in droves to stock up with life's comforts – baked beans and Christmas crackers, Cheddar cheese and headache pills, pickled onions and liver salts. Smugglers are even known to drive into Gibraltar with an empty tank, fill up with cheap petrol, only to recross the border, siphon off the petrol for resale, and return to Gibraltar. This often adds to the border queues, which can vary from a couple of vehicles to a four-hour tailback, depending on

Getting to Gibraltar

By Air

There are at least three daily flights from London (Heathrow and Gatwick); twice-weekly flights from Manchester and regular flights from Casablanca and Tangier (20mins). **Monarch Airlines** also has flights to Gibraltar from the UK, while **Iberia** runs a daily flight from Madrid.

By Sea

There are usually at least three ferries a week making the crossing from Gibraltar to Tangier and from Tangier to Gibraltar. The fares are expensive, like everything else in Gibraltar. **FRS, t** 95 668 18 30, *www.frs.es* (office in Tarifa), runs a high-speed crossing (80mins) but the ferry journey usually takes 2–2½hrs. You'd be slightly better off doing it from Algeciras. **Bland Line** also also runs a ferry service, call for details, **t** 77 050.

Information: Book tickets and get information from **Turner & Co,** 5/67 Irish Town, **t** 78305, *turner@gibnynex.gi*, or **TourAfrica, t** 77 666.

Getting around Gibraltar

Gibraltar's tiny **buses** serve the frontier, which is only 800m from the town centre; from there it's a short walk to La Línea's **bus station**, with connections along the coast to Algeciras and the string of resorts along the Costa del Sol.

You can take a **taxi tour** of the Rock, taking in all the sights and lasting 1½ hours. The charge is £8 per person, minimum four passengers, plus additional costs per passenger to include compulsory admission to the Nature Reserve. **Information**: John L. López, **t** 72 726, *www.gibraltar-rock-tours.com*; **Gibraltar Taxi Association**, Feetham House, 19 Waterport Wharf, **t** 70 052 (24hr service **t** 70 027 or **t** 70 077).

But unless you're really pressed for time it's more fun (and cheaper) to take the **cable car** and walk. Gibraltar's taxis also serve the frontier, although it's only a ½-mile walk from the town centre.

If you are coming by **car**, try to leave it in La Línea, as there are frequently long delays while customs check the day-trippers' stash of goodies in both directions.

---

how thorough Customs decide to be. Other, more discreet visitors come over to take advantage of the no-questions-asked, tax-free offshore investments in Gibraltar's booming financial sector. Needless to say, this gets up the nose of the Spanish taxman. The other gripe is the political status of the Rock itself. Spain clamours for it like the little boy who kicked his ball into next door's garden, while Britain plays the grouchy old bachelor who says, 'I'm keeping it' (although Britain has changed the tune to: 'I'm keeping some bits for defence no matter what and, as for the rest, let's ask the ball.')

You'll soon find that Gibraltar has a unique mixture of people – mostly Genoese (who have been around for centuries), along with Maltese, Indians, Spaniards, Jews and Moroccans, all as British as Trafalgar Square. With English as their official language, most Gibraltarians are, however, bilingual. For many Gibraltarians, a local mixture of Spanish and English called *Llanito* is used in everyday situations and particularly in moments of high emotion; English is generally reserved for more formal situations.

History

Some 50,000 years ago, when Spain was a cooler, more forested place, **Neanderthal man** was minding his own business in the caves around Gibraltar, long before Palaeo-Spaniards found the rest of Andalucía of any interest. The Rock's location, where the continents of Europe and Africa rub noses and the Atlantic Ocean and Mediterranean Sea meet, is one of the world's most important crossroads; as a consequence it has been fought over for centuries. **Calpe**, as the Greeks knew it, was, of course, one of the Pillars of Hercules, beyond which the jealous **Phoenicians** would permit no other nation's ships to trade. The other, less dramatic pillar is Mount Abyla in Morocco, visible across the Straits on clear days.

The Phoenicians may have been the first people to pass through the Straits into the Atlantic, where they traded down the African coast and probably travelled as far north as Britain. They used the Rock solely as a naval base and never entertained the thought of settling there, preferring the more hospitable land near the Bay. Similarly, under **Roman** rule from 190 BC onwards, there was no permanent settlement. Six hundred years later the **Vandal** tribes surged through the Iberian peninsula on their way to North Africa, followed by the **Visigoths**, who remained as the most powerful local force until the late 7th century AD.

711–1462: Muslim Ascendancy

By the early 8th century the **Moors** were poised to invade the Iberian Peninsula, under the new and forceful banner of Islam. Having swept westward through North Africa from Arabia, converting the subjugated population by coercion, the Moors landed a small expeditionary force at what is now Tarifa in 710. The following year, **Tariq ibn-Ziyad** led a determined Berber army of 7,000 men to the Rock that came to bear his name – **Jebel Tariq** (Tariq's Mountain). As the Moors moved further north, Gibraltar remained a vital camp, but it was not until 1160 that any sort of permanent settlement was established.

Throughout the Moorish occupation of Andalucía, Gibraltar faced a number of sieges at the hands of Moorish caliphs fighting amongst themselves over its control and Christian Spaniards trying to win it back. **Guzmán el Bueno** seized it for Castile in 1309, and in the centuries that followed it was one of the major battle-grounds of the Mediterranean. It was not until 1462 that the Rock was finally wrested from the Moorish grasp by Enrico IV, King of Castile. (The day of liberation was 29 August, the feast day of St Bernard, the patron saint of Gibraltar.)

1462–1704: The Key of Spain

In 1469 a royal decree proclaimed the son of the Duke of Messina as the rightful owner. Queen Isabel granted the Rock a coat of arms, still used today, with the inscription 'Seal of the Noble City of Gibraltar, the Key of Spain'. During this time of Spanish occupation the town was divided into three districts: **Villavieja** (the old town),

Barcina ('wicker basket' – one was used to display the remains of the captured Count of Niebla) and **Turba**, which can be translated as 'mob'; but these names have now disappeared. This was a fairly tranquil period by Gibraltarian standards, until one fine day in 1540 when, as the townsfolk were going about their daily business, a fleet of 16 galleys, manned by 2,000 men, took them by surprise. These were the hordes of the Turkish admiral **Barbarossa**, who operated out of North African bases, raiding ships for goods and slaves; tempted by legends of dazzling booty, the pirates had decided to break with tradition and sack Gibraltar.

The horror stands out in Gibraltar's chequered history – a day of slaughter, rape and looting. Some were lucky enough to escape the carnage in the safety of the castle, but most were either killed or taken into slavery. The pirates headed straight for the Shrine of Our Lady of Europa at Europa Point and the Franciscan convent in the town (both well stocked with gold, jewels and precious coins) and stripped them bare, before making off across the Bay for further pillaging. Overconfidence proved to be their undoing, for the Christian fleet anchored in Tarifa had time to sail along the coast and cut off their escape route. A bloody battle ensued, and what was left of Barbarossa's mob fled back to the sanctuary of its North African ports with just 75 captives in tow. But Gibraltar was left in ruins. From this time on, the Rock was heavily fortified and became an important naval base for Spain's explorations to the Americas, but life was far from peaceful, as a pirate of a different ilk, Sir Francis Drake, would drop in occasionally.

The beginning of the 18th century brought the **War of the Spanish Succession**, with Britain on the side of the Habsburgs against the French. Admiral Sir George Rooke, commanding the Anglo-Dutch fleet, tried to take Toulon and Barcelona and, having failed on both counts, took Gibraltar instead. At the time (1704), Gibraltar was held by forces loyal to the French claimant to the Spanish throne. Rooke offered the inhabitants two choices – to pack their bags and leave, or swear allegiance to the Habsburg claimant. Most opted for the former, probably hoping that the tide of war would change.

1704 to the Present: British Colonial Rule

With Gibraltar in British hands, the grateful Habsburgs handed it over 'in perpetuity' as a reward, under the 1713 **Treaty of Utrecht**. It was a crucial acquisition; Britain's imperial expansion across the Mediterranean would have been inconceivable without it. Peace did not last long, however, and the Spanish laid siege to the Rock with the aid of French forces in 1727. Destruction was again suffered by the townsfolk, and the area around what is today Casemates Square was completely flattened.

From this point we can trace the mixed heritage of the present population, for after the disappearance of the original Spanish inhabitants it became necessary to import a workforce from around the Mediterranean, especially Genoa. This force helped strengthen the city's defences; Ragged Staff Wharf was constructed, new barracks were built and a number of Spanish churches were turned into accommodation for the troops. New batteries were put up – Montague, Orange and King's Bastion, Devil's Tongue on the Old Mole, Grand Battery north of Grand Casemates with the adjacent Couvreport and King's Lines above, Willis's, Catalan and Green's Lodge Batteries on the Upper Rock, and the Advance Batteries at Europa Point.

The preparations proved justified. In 1779 a combined Spanish and French force began the **Great Siege**, the worst siege ever experienced by the Rock. Yet both fortifications and people endured under the command of Lord Heathfield, and the phrase 'safe as the Rock of Gibraltar' came into common use as a result. Tunnels and galleries were painstakingly dug in 1782 to allow the gun batteries to take up positions near the top of the Rock, so they could fire down on the enemy entrenched on the peninsula below. The tunnelling continued after the Great Siege, opening up what is known as St George's Hall, a large chamber under 'the Notch'.

After a decade of uneasy peace the Gibraltarians were once again in the thick of things – this time at the outbreak of the **Napoleonic Wars** between Britain and France, in 1799. For once, Spain was an ally, and it can even be assumed that the people of the Rock actively welcomed the hostilities. Business, at least, perked up remarkably – repairing ships, supplying the Royal Navy with food and ammunition, and auctioning off the contents of ships captured by the British fleet. On 21 October 1805, Nelson and his 27 'Wild Geese' triumphed at **Trafalgar**, an event still celebrated in Gibraltar. The admiral's body was borne back to Rosia Bay preserved in a cask of brandy (whence the naval term 'Nelson's Blood'), where he was repacked in sherry for the journey back to London. Ten years later, in 1815, the end of the war heralded the start of a long period of peace and prosperity for Gibraltar, by which time the population was firmly established in occupations that relied not only on the military presence but also on external trade. 1814 saw the appointment of Sir George Don, a man of considerable calibre, as lieutenant governor. By this time the population had swelled to 10,000, and was badly in need of an efficient civil administration. Sir George embarked on an ambitious programme of improvements: hospitals were built, public gardens laid out, opportunities created for business and trade.

In the **20th century**, in both World Wars Gibraltar provided a safe harbour where the Allies could repair ships and replenish stocks. In the **Second World War** many of the civilians were evacuated to safer spots, notably the UK, Madeira, Jamaica and Morocco. (Those who ended up in Morocco were forced to move on again when the Vichy government made it clear they were not welcome.) The airstrip was built at this time, on the cricket and football pitches. The miles of tunnels under the Rock were developed further, and used for food storage, hospitals and military headquarters. The invasion of North Africa, Operation Torch, was spearheaded through Gibraltar, where Eisenhower and his advisers completed much of the planning.

By the time the war ended, the Gibraltarians had developed an even deeper sense of identity, partly through being separated from their homeland. In 1950 the Duke of Edinburgh inaugurated the first elected **Legislative Council**, and in 1964 Gibraltar was granted **domestic autonomy**, with the UK retaining responsibility for foreign affairs and defence. When a referendum on joining Spain was held in 1967, Gibraltarians voted it down by 99.6 per cent. The dissenters were tagged *Las Palomas* (the pigeons), and some of these subsequently flew to Spanish climes. The vote led to the introduction of a new constitution the following year, which entrenched the British promise never to surrender the sovereignty of Gibraltar against the wishes of her people. As a consequence,

The 'Expansion' of Gibraltar

Space is at a premium in Gibraltar. Most of the prime parts were owned by the Ministry of Defence (MOD) until 1990, when the British military presence was reduced and the three services amalgamated under one command. To give an indication of the severity of the cuts, in 1983 MOD spending was equal to 78 per cent of Gibraltar's GDP; by 2000, it had dropped to less than 5 per cent. This retrenchment released a certain amount of land and housing for civilian use and prompted successive governments to look elsewhere for income. Even the newly freed-up space wasn't enough to accommodate the level of growth planned by the socialist GSLP government when it took office in the late 1980s. They began an ambitious programme of land reclamation which continues today and was responsible for Europort, the large complex of commercial offices south of North Mole, which is now the heavily promoted financial heart of Gibraltar. The Rock's banking deposits increased from £1 billion in 1990 to £3 billion in 1996 and they continue to rise.

Gibraltar is also involved in a number of renovation projects. Main Street was pedestrianized and the barracks in Casemates Square are now full of boutiques, bars and restaurants. All the hotels have been made over, thanks to a £5 million loan from the last administration. There is a spanking new coach park and cruise terminal to deal with the 300 liners which dock here annually. And the next project is to spruce up the border to present visitors with a good first impression. The reclamation programme has also seen an extension of the industrial zone to the old dockyard region, and the development of Queensway Quays into a smart residential and dining area.

The third phase of Gibraltar's expansion caters for tourism and recreation on the Mediterranean side, and is well under way, with a new long seafront promenade linking the three beaches and plans to create a 60,000 square-metre resort and leisure centre. Such programmes for housing, industrial and commercial enterprise, and tourism are part of a government strategy to create a strong economy underpinned by foreign investment. Geographically, economically and politically, there is no reason why Gibraltar should not flourish as a kind of Monaco of the Southern Mediterranean.

Franco closed the border. This served only to strengthen the population's resolve, and to deepen the rift with Spain.

Far from being dismayed at the closure of the frontier, many older Gibraltarians were actually disappointed when it was reopened in 1985, feeling that they had lost their safe little haven, their isolated 'English village'. They now face the future with some trepidation, although for most Gibraltarians the main threat to the status quo at the moment is none other than the British government. Eager to reach an agreement with Spain, an important EU partner, then-prime minister Tony Blair announced in June 2002 that **shared sovereignty** seemed to be the only way forward. This caused uproar and cries of 'treason' in Gibraltar, and a referendum was called by Gibraltar's chief minister, Peter Caruana: once again, 99 per cent of Gibraltarians voted against the plan. More recently, however, the relationship between the two traditional foes has relaxed a smidgen, with the introduction of daily flights from the Spanish mainland to Gibraltar in November 2006, operated by Iberia airlines.

The Town

...a cosy smell of provincial groceries. I'd forgotten how much the atmosphere of home depended on white bread, soap and soup squares.

Laurie Lee, *As I Walked Out One Midsummer Morning*

Gibraltar is still much more than just a perfect replica of an English seaside town. The town itself is long and narrow, strung out along **Main Street**, which has most of the shops and pubs. The harbour is never more than a couple of blocks away, and the old gates, bastions and walls are fun to explore.

The short tunnel at **Landport Gate** will probably be your entry point if on foot; dating from the 18th century, it was for a long time the only entrance by land. It leads to **Casemates Square**, one-time parade ground and site of public executions. **Grand Casemates** itself, part of the town's defences and barracks, used to provide seedy accommodation for Gibraltar's 2,000-strong Moroccan labour force, but now bustles with new shops and restaurants. **King's Bastion** is now used as an electricity generating station, but probably started out as an Arab gate, added to by the Spanish in 1575 and further extended in the 18th century by the British under General Boyd. It played an important defensive role at the time of the Great Siege, and it was from this spot that General Elliott commanded during the fierce fighting in 1782. **Ragged Staff Wharf** takes its name not from the sartorial deficiency of its troops, but either from the flagstaff that marked safe passage into the harbour or from an emblem on the arms of the House of Burgundy, to which Charles V belonged.

Gibraltar Museum
open Mon–Fri 10–6, Sat 10–2; closed Sun; adm; last admission 30mins before closing time

Near the centre of town, off Line Wall Road, the small, excellent **Gibraltar Museum**, at 18–20 Bomb House Lane, offers a film and a thorough schooling in its complicated history. It also contains a replica of the female skull found in Forbes Quarry in 1848, a find that predates the Neanderthal skull found in Germany by eight years. Other exhibits include a painstakingly detailed room-sized model of the Rock as it was in the mid-1800s, and archaeological finds from Gibraltar's caves; an Egyptian mummy found floating in the Bay by local fishermen, dating from 750 BC and probably from Thebes; a natural history collection; and a gallery devoted to Gibraltar artists such as Gustavo Bacarisas, Mania and Olimpia Reyes. The museum is built over the remains of Europe's oldest Moorish baths, with Roman and Visigothic capitals on its columns.

In Library Street, the handsome **Garrison Library** (1804) was created in part to alleviate boredom among the officers; its well-preserved Georgian interior houses 35,000 books, including many rare ones, as well as extensive archives on Gibraltar's history. Nearby are the offices of *The Chronicle*, which was the first paper to report Nelson's victory off Trafalgar. The **Supreme Court** looks diagonally across the street to the 16th-century former Franciscan convent, now the **Governor's Residence**, where the changing of the guard takes place. If it's bucketing down, an occurrence frequent in winter months, you can watch these serious proceedings from the warmth and comfort of the Angry Friar, the pub on the corner.

Changing of the Guard
check with tourist office for times

Gibraltar shines as an example of religious tolerance. In Engineer Lane the **Great Synagogue**, rebuilt in 1768, is only one of several attended by Gibraltar's 700-strong Jewish community; the Flemish Synagogue, at 65 Line Wall Road, offers guided visits. The cathedral of **St Mary the Crowned** (between Main Street and Cannon Lane) stands on the site of the chief mosque of Gibraltar, of which some remains can still be seen. The airy Anglican **Cathedral of the Holy Trinity** (off Main Street, near the museum) was consecrated in 1838, and has walls designed to withstand the reverberations from

Flemish Synagogue
call for details of guided tours, t 76 477

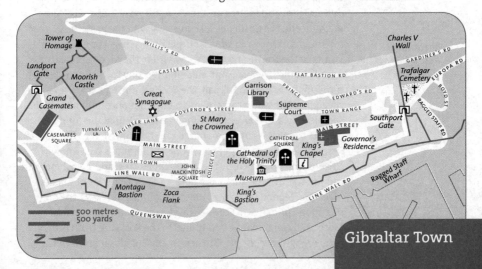

Gibraltar Town

bombardments. The nearby **King's Chapel**, part of the Franciscan convent, was one of the few buildings left standing at the end of the Great Siege. Legend has it that the chapel is haunted by the 'grey nun', Alitea de Lucerna, whose family forced her into taking vows because they disapproved of her lover. He, however, managed to sneak into the convent, dressed as a Franciscan friar, and the two continued their relationship until, inevitably, they were discovered. The lover drowned as they tried to escape.

Southport Gate, at the top of Main Street, was built in 1552, during the reign of Charles V, and has additions from the 19th century; the wall stretching east from the gate is **Charles V's Wall**, which ends just short of the water catchments at **Philip II's Arch**. Beyond the gate you can wander through the small, shady **Trafalgar Cemetery**, which in fact has the remains of only two sailors from the Battle of Trafalgar, and where sad little inscriptions tell of children killed by disease, and of young men who met their bloody end at sea. The **Alameda Gardens**, a few yards away, are more cheerful; you can stop in to see the exotic flora, cacti, fountains and waterfalls before taking the cable car up the Rock. The gardens now contain a **Wildlife Park**, a refuge for unwanted pets and animals confiscated from container ships.

Alameda Gardens
open 8am–sunset, free

Wildlife Park
www.gibraltar.gi/ alameda; open winter daily 10–4; summer daily 10–6; adm

The Rock

Everywhere you go, it looms overhead. The Rock is an enormous chunk of primordial limestone, forced up from the sea when Africa collided with Europe seven million years ago. The famous silhouette, surprisingly, does not hang over the seaward edge, but faces backwards towards La Línea. The most thrilling way to get to the top is by cable car from the Alameda Gardens, but a cab will do, too. From 500 metres up, the views from the upper Rock are magnificent: the Costa del Sol curves away to the east; the mountains of Morocco sit in a purple haze across the narrow Straits to the south; and way below, where the Mediterranean opens out into the wide and wild Atlantic, tiny toy-like craft plough through the waters in full sail. The Rock's entire eastern face is covered by the water catchment system that once supplied all of Gibraltar's water – an engineering marvel to equal the tunnels.

Cable car
t 72 735, www.gibcablecar.com; every 15mins 9.30–6, last cable car down at 5.45; adm; closed Sun from Nov–Mar

Apart from views of a panoramic variety, admission to the Nature Reserve (*see* p.234) will get you a look at Gibraltar's best-known citizens. The **Apes' Den**, by the upper cable-car station, is where you can see some of the Rock's 140 Barbary apes, a species of tailless macaque. Legend has it that these gregarious monkeys, the only free-range primates in Europe, travel to and from their native Morocco by an underground tunnel in the Rock; the truth is they were brought over in the 18th century by British sailors as pets.

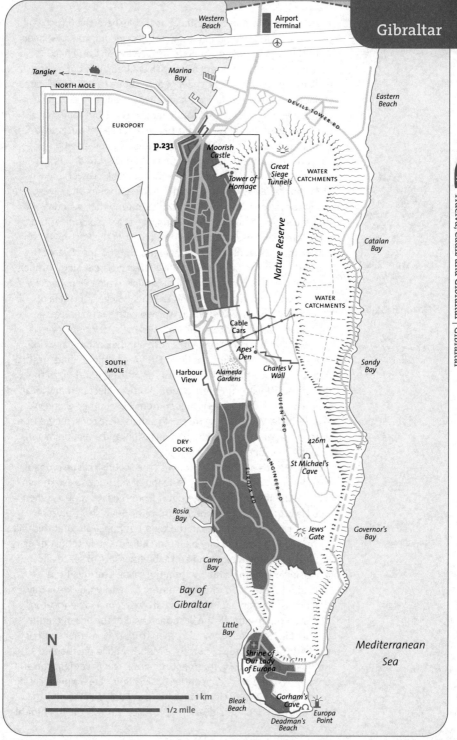

Western
Beach

Airport
Terminal

Tangier

NORTH MOLE

Marina
Bay

Eastern
Beach

EUROPORT

DEVILS TOWER RD

p.231

Moorish
Castle

Tower of
Homage

Great
Siege
Tunnels

WATER
CATCHMENTS

Nature Reserve

Catalan
Bay

WATER
CATCHMENTS

Cable
Cars

SOUTH
MOLE

Apes'
Den

Sandy
Bay

Harbour
View

Alameda
Gardens

Charles V
Wall

QUEEN'S RD

DRY
DOCKS

EUROPA RD

ENGINEER RD

426m

St Michael's
Cave

Rosia
Bay

Jews'
Gate

Governor's
Bay

Camp
Bay

Bay of
Gibraltar

Little
Bay

Mediterranean
Sea

N

Shrine of
Our Lady
of Europa

Gorham's
Cave

Europa
Point

1 km

1/2 mile

Bleak
Beach

Deadman's
Beach

There is an old saying that, as long as they're here, the British will never leave. Understandably, they're well cared for, and have been since the days of their great benefactor, Winston Churchill.

Nearby are the remains of a **Moorish wall**, and it is but a short walk to the beautiful **St Michael's Cave**, a huge cavern of delicate stalactites with *son et lumière* shows twice daily. In the 19th century wealthy merchants would rent the cave out for extravagant parties; it was also a favourite venue for illegal duels, away from the censorious eye of the authorities. It's now used for concerts (not to be missed!) and fashion shows, but do bring a waterproof hat if you attend one – the roof leaks. **Lower St Michael's Cave** was accidentally discovered when the caves were being converted into a military hospital during the Second World War. It contains a huge underground lake that is seldom visited.

The surprisingly lush upper, northern part of the Rock has been turned into a **Nature Reserve**, where most of the apes live. At the top end of the Rock are the **Upper Galleries**, or **Great Siege Tunnels**, an extensive section of the original tunnels, which were hacked and blown out of the rock during the Great Siege – the idea of Sergeant Major Ince, who was rewarded with a farm and a racehorse. Open to visitors, the Galleries have vertiginous views and wax dummies of 18th-century British soldiers hard at work digging and blowing up Spaniards. Others contain soldiers' grafitti. A radar dome confirms that the Brits are still here, although the rest of the Ministry of Defence command – subject of many local James Bondish rumours – is hidden from view in the Second World War Tunnels. More than 33 miles of tunnels were constructed from 1940 in preparation for a potential invasion, and a section has recently been opened to the public .

From here it's a short walk down to the **Moorish castle** probably founded in the 8th century by Tariq ibn-Ziyad, but its best-known feature, the **Tower of Homage**, dates from the 14th century when Abd Hassan recaptured Gibraltar from the Spanish. At present Gibraltar's prison is housed in the keep, but hopes are that this will be moved to a new military building. Unfortunately, some rather short-sighted town planning and Gibraltar's lack of space allowed a housing estate to be built within the castle's fortifications.

Heading south down the promontory from town, by **Rosia Bay**, don't miss the Napier of Magdala Battery's remarkable 100-ton **Victorian super-gun**; it's the best preserved of the dozen manufactured in 1870, and required 35 men to work it. Further south is the **Shrine of Our Lady of Europa**, a Moorish building adopted as a Catholic chapel in 1462; fragments of a Moorish pavement can still be seen. A flame was kept continuously alight here – a predecessor to the present **Trinity Lighthouse** (1841) at **Europa Point** – it's the only one ever built outside of the UK. Also nearby is the **Ibrahim-al-**

✪ **Lower St Michael's Cave**
tours by appointment only; call t 55 066 or contact the tourist office

Nature Reserve
open Mon–Sat 9.30–7; adm

✪ **Upper Galleries**
tickets from Princess Caroline's Battery, t 45 957; adm; Second World War tunnels accessible by guided visit only

Ibrahim Mosque, a gift from King Fahd of Saudi Arabia used by the thousands of Moroccans working on the Rock. **Gorham's Cave**, by the shore near Europa Point, was almost certainly inhabited by Neanderthals. Digs have uncovered important finds, largely of the animal-remains variety. From here Africa is only 11 miles away.

If you want to sit on a beach, Gibraltar has a few, but they're all on the more sheltered, Mediterranean side – accessible by bus (No.4). **Catalan Bay** and **Sandy Bay** are both a little built-up and crowded, and slated for even greater development in the near future. **Eastern Beach** (dubbed 'Margate' in the 19th century) is better, though unfortunately it's next to the airport.

The Bay and Straits of Gibraltar are home to whales and the playground of schools of dolphins, which on a good day will put on a show for the bipeds on the shore or on a **dolphin safari** – various companies offer trips. The tourist office plans to promote bird-watching during the two great annual migrations over the Straits.

ⓘ **Gibraltar >**
Gibraltar Information Bureau, Duke of Kent House, Cathedral Square, t 74 950, www.gibraltar.gi

Local information bureaux: Grand Casemates Square, t 74 982; open Mon–Fri 10–6, Sat 10–2; plus booths within the airport terminal, the customs building at the frontier, and at Waterport coach park

Gibraltar Practicalities

Currency
The Protectorate has its own currency, the **Gibraltar pound** (which is tied in value to sterling), as well as its own **stamps** – don't be stuck with any currency when you leave, as it's hard to get rid of anywhere else, especially in Britain! These days, most shops and restaurants in Gibraltar are perfectly happy to take euros, sterling or Gibraltarian money.

Telephones
The international calling code is **t** (350), both internationally and, now, from Spain.

Shopping in Gibraltar
Although expats on the *costas* flock across the border to shop at the enormous Morrison's for British groceries, the real bargains are to be had in the top range of VAT-free luxury goods. Here is a selection – but shop around for the best bargains.
Antiques: Benzaquan, 295 Main Street; **Sanguinetti**, 288 Main Street.
Cuban cigars: La Casa del Habano, 37 Main Street; **S. M. Seruya**, 165 Main St.
Electronics: Marquez, 72 Main Street.
Fashion: García, 192 Main St (Daks, Burberry, etc.); **Marble Arc**, 10 Main St.

Jewellery: The Red House, 66 Main Street; **The Jewel Box**, 148 Main Street, 8 Queensway Quay.
Perfume: S. M. Seruya, several locations including 59, 107, 151 and 187 Main St.
Porcelain: Omni, 182 Main Street.

Activities in Gibraltar
Many companies offer **guided tours** of Gibraltar and its sights: **Bland Travel**, Cloister Building, Irish Town, **t** 77 012, *www.blands.gi*, runs Gibraltar tours as well as excursions into Andalucía. A number of companies offer tours for dolphin viewing. For sports enthusiasts the waters are ideal for activities ranging from **windsurfing** to **scuba-diving**. In Marina Bay you can charter **yachts** or **cabin cruisers**.

Where to Stay in Gibraltar
****Caleta Hotel**, Sir Herbert Miles Road, on Catalan Bay, **t** 76 501, *www.caletahotel.com* (€€€€). If you need a beach, this resort hotel is very modern and tastefullly upgraded. There are rooms with balconies, a pool, restaurants and a bar.
Bristol, 8–10 Cathedral Square, **t** 76 800, *www.bristolhotel.gi* (€€€). In the heart of town, with a swimming pool, and TV in all rooms.

Continental, 1 Engineer Lane, **t** 76 900 (€€€). Just off Main Street and not quite as comfortable, with a fast-food restaurant on the ground floor.

Queen's Hotel, 1 Boyd Street, PO Box 99, **t** 74 000, *www.queenshotel.gi* (€€). Rather characterless but newly refurbished, this is located near the gardens, and there are good views of the Rock and bay.

Cannon Hotel, 9 Cannon Lane (just off Main Street), **t** 51 711, *www.cannon hotel.gi* (€€–€). Pretty, central, with patio, bar and restaurant.

(★) Gauchos >>

Eating Out in Gibraltar

Food in Gibraltar is no longer restricted to authentic pub grub and fish 'n' chips (although both are still available). For the best restaurants on the Rock, head for Queensway Quay or Marina Quay, where you will find a good selection of fish, Italian and even tapas restaurants. There are around 360 pubs in Gibraltar, many serving food in one form or another.

International Casino Club, 7 Europa Road, **t** 76 666 (€€€). The restaurant in the casino club is popular among the locals, and you won't find a better place for five-star service – a perfect place to watch the sun go down on the Atlantic, if not on the Empire.

Rock Hotel, 3 Europa Road, **t** 73 000, *www.rockhotelgibraltar.com* (€€€). Arguably the most pleasant place for lunch, with colonial-style décor. The steaks are flown in fresh from the UK daily.

Bianca's, 6–7 Admiral's Walk, **t** 73 379 (€€). Come here to sit out and watch the yachts or plane-spot while eating reasonably priced fish, meat and pizza. There's a children's menu and it's popular with families.

Casa Pepe, Unit 18, Queensway Quay, **t** 46 967 (€€). Probably Gibraltar's best tapas bar, specializing in paella, *jamón ibérico* and fresh fish dishes in taberna-style surroundings. *Closed Wed*.

(★) Da Paolo >

Da Paolo, The Tower, Admiral's Walk, **t** 76 799 (€€). Our favourite place to eat in Gibraltar, with well-prepared fish specialities, a good Spanish wine list and a fine view.

Maharaja, 5 Tuckey's Lane, **t** 75 233 (€€). One of a few Indian restaurants; this one has the simplest furnishings.

El Patio, 11 Casemates Square, **t** 70 822 (€€). A pleasant spot, decorated with old photos of the Rock; Basque cuisine and Mediterranean fish specialities. *Closed Sat lunch and Sun*.

Raffles, Queensway Quay, **t** 40 362 (€€). An extensive choice of tasty English and Spanish dishes at reasonable prices.

Gauchos, Waterport Casemates, **t** 59 700 (€€). Opened in 2007, this excellent restaurant located within the atmospheric 200-year-old Casemates has a mainly meaty menu with massive portions. There are four vegetarian options as well.

Yvey's Restaurant, 1Y and Z Casemates Square, **t** 41 611 (€€). In a courtyard off Casemates Square, this appealing restaurant has a selection of light snacks and more elaborate meals. Live jazz at weekends.

Cheers Brasserie, G1 Cornwall Centre, **t** 79 699 (€). Fills up with tourists at lunch time and is a popular meeting place, with a large terrace.

The Clipper, 78B Irish Town, **t** 79 791 (€). A gastro-pub which is popular with Gibraltarians and visitors alike for its roast beef and lasagne.

Solly's Salt Beef Parlour & Deli, 8 Canon Lane, **t** 78 511 (€). Perhaps the last thing you'd expect in Gibraltar, this New York-style café and deli offers great sandwiches and a wonderful deli counter, along with more substantial – and kosher – fare from the Carvery.

Nightlife in Gibraltar

Corks, 79 Irish Town, **t** 75 566. Try this wine bar for a change from the numerous pubs; also serves food and has occasional live music.

Casino, 7 Europa Road, **t** 76 666. Gibraltar's late nightlife happens here – dress well and take lots of cash.

There are a handful of clubs in Gibraltar: try the **Tunnel**, Casemates Square, **t** 44 878, or the **Midnight Club**, 1 Reclamation Road, **t** 41 458.

Málaga and the Costa del Sol

After a few decades of brash holiday intensity, this unlikely strip of land, all concrete and garish signboards, is beginning to develop a personality of its own. Any hype you hear or read about the Costa, anything that employs flowery prose and superlatives, is utter nonsense; on the other hand, it has become almost fashionable to mock the Costa for its brash turismo exuberance, and that is uncalled for. The Costa does attract people who don't want much more from their holiday (or retirement) than good weather, like-minded companions and places to play. Their presence, in such large numbers and from so many nations, has created a unique international community of everyday folks. It's easy to forget you're in Spain, but if you ever get homesick you can always take a break from Andalucía and have a noisy good time by the beach.

12

Don't miss

⭐ Hanging out with the smart set
Marbella p.245

⭐ A dramatic Serranía backdrop
Ronda p.263

⭐ Baroque and Platersque architecture
Antequera p.269

⭐ A glut of Picasso
Museo Picasso and Casa Natal Picasso, Málaga pp.259–60

⭐ Unspoiled whitewashed villages
The Axarquía p.274

See map overleaf

Málaga Province

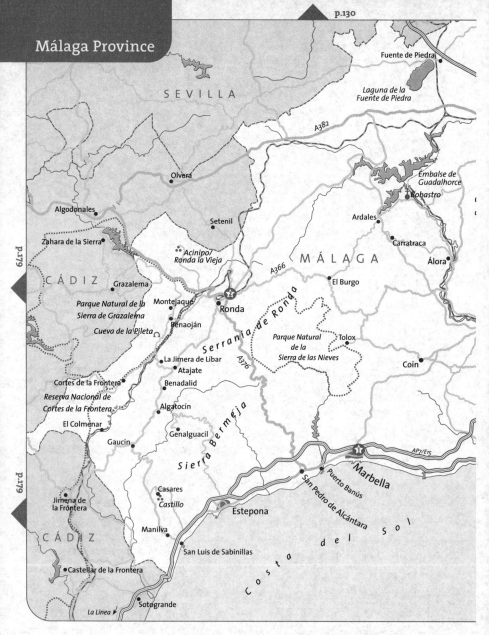

p.179

p.179

At first glance, it doesn't seem the speculators and developers could have picked a more unlikely place to conjure up the Mediterranean's biggest holiday playground. The stretch of coast between Gibraltar and Málaga is devoid of beautiful scenery, and its long beaches come in a uniformly dismal shade of grey. Spain's low prices are one explanation, and the greatest number of guaranteed sunny days in Europe another. The reason it happened

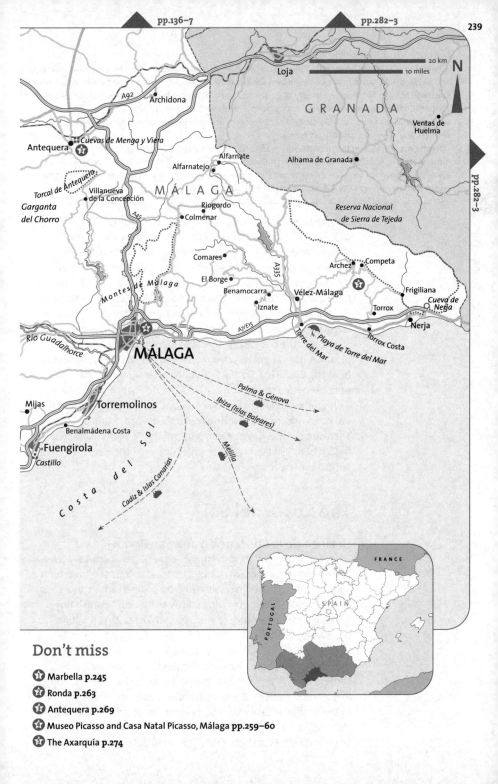

20 km
10 miles

N

GRANADA

Loja

Ventas de
Huelma

Archidona

A92

Antequera

Cuevas de Menga y Viera

Alfarnate

Alhama de Granada

Torcal de Antequera

Alfarnatejo

MÁLAGA

Garganta
del Chorro

Villanueva
de la Concepción

Riogordo

Reserva Nacional
de Sierra de Tejeda

Colmenar

Comares

A335

Archez   Competa

Montes de Málaga

El Borge

Benamocarra

Vélez-Málaga

Frigiliana

Iznate

Torrox

Cueva de
Nerja

A7/E15

Torrox Costa

Nerja

Río Guadalhorce

MÁLAGA

Torre del Mar

Playa de Torre del Mar

Palma & Génova

Mijas

Torremolinos

Ibiza (Islas Baleares)

Costa del Sol

Benalmádena Costa

Melilla

Fuengirola

Castillo

Cadiz & Islas Canarias

FRANCE

PORTUGAL

SPAIN

Don't miss

⓵ Marbella **p.245**

⓶ Ronda **p.263**

⓷ Antequera **p.269**

⓸ Museo Picasso and Casa Natal Picasso, Málaga **pp.259–60**

⓹ The Axarquía **p.274**

Málaga Virgen and Moorish Tarts

Two grapes, muscatel and Pedro Ximénez, define Málaga province wines and sherries. All are sweet and enjoyed with gusto in bars, and the best known are the Málaga Virgen. Fish and seafood dominate cuisine in Málaga but there are plenty of gazpachos, particularly *ajo blanco con uvas* – a creamy white soup made from almonds and garlic with grapes. Prawns and mussels are plump and, served simply with lemon, are divine. Virtually every tapas bar serves anchovies called *boquerones*; in Málaga *fritura mixta* is one of Spain's culinary art forms.

Nearly every village in the province has its own dessert, usually influenced by the Moors. Try the almond tarts in Ardales, the honey-coated pancakes in Archidona and the mixture of syrup of white roses, oil and eggs called *tocino de cielo* in Vélez. There again, you can always replace pudding with a sweet Málaga dessert wine – delicious sipped with dry biscuits.

here, though, is breathtakingly simple – cheap land. Fifty years ago, all this coast had was fantastically poor fishing villages and malaria, and it was one of the forgotten backwaters of Spain.

The *urbanizaciones* of the Costa begin right after the rock of Gibraltar, stretching eastwards along the main resorts of Estepona, Marbella, Fuengirola and Torremolinos. Málaga comes next, a busy city not without charm, and after it the only section of this coastline with any pretensions to scenery, around Nerja. This chapter also covers the two beautiful inland mountain areas of Málaga province, not yet entirely overrun by the tourist and expat hordes from the Costa: the Serranía de Ronda around Ronda and Antequera, and the more isolated Sierra de Tejada east of Málaga.

Altogether, these coasts have only one real purpose as far as the visitor is concerned – planting yourself on a beach and dozing off. There are the inevitable attractions (mini-golf, seafood dinners, funfairs, English beer on tap, nightclubs), but little else. Pack a potent sunscreen and have fun.

The Costa del Sol

La Línea de la Concepción and San Roque

Though it marks the westernmost edge of the Costa, **La Línea** (as it is commonly known) is not a resort at all, but the town on the Spanish side of the border with Gibraltar, named after Gibraltar's old land walls. Given its unique status as the only Spanish town to border British territory, La Línea has almost taken on a split personality. Whilst retaining its Spanish essence, it takes in its stride the daily invasion of day-trippers and smugglers (of tobacco especially), who have descended on the town since the barrier came down in 1985. Not that the people of La Línea are unhappy about the situation – the open frontier means they can scoot over in their coffee breaks to buy up tax-free goods and off-the-peg clothing, hoping that Spanish customs aren't too rigorous in their searches on the way back. There is little to detain you in La Línea –

Getting to and around La Línea

Two **bus** companies serve La Línea: **Transportes Comes** runs the service to Algeciras (every 30mins) and points west; and the **Portillo** company serves the Costa del Sol, Málaga, Granada and Madrid. The **bus station**, **t** 95 617 00 93, is on the Plaza de España, just off La Línea's central square. From here it's a 6min walk to the border with Gibraltar.

The nearest **railway station**, 12km away at San Roque-La Línea, has services to Ronda and Algeciras, with connections to other destinations in Andalucía.

only the 19th-century church of **La Inmaculada**, with its Baroque-style altar; and the **Cruz Herrera Museum**, in a modern building just off the main square, Plaza de la Constitución.

San Roque, just 8km away, is infinitely more attractive, perched on a hilltop and with a typically *andaluz* maze of steep, narrow streets lined with whitewashed houses sprouting flowers from the balconies. It was founded by Gibraltarians, who rejected a British offer to remain on the Rock when it was captured in 1704 and established their own colony while they waited for Spanish rule to be restored. They didn't get their home back, and suffered a second British invasion instead: this time from affluent 20th-century second-homers who built a ring of luxurious villa developments. San Roque doesn't have much in the way of sights, but you can gaze out at Gibraltar from the *mirador* (half-hidden behind the smoke billowing from the San Roque oil refinery on the outskirts of La Línea), and take a look at the local curiosity in the town hall: the *Pendón de Gibraltar*, a pennant reputedly embroidered by Juana la Loca, the supposedly mad daughter of Queen Isabel.

Where to Stay and Eat in La Línea

(i) **La Línea >**
*Avda del Ejército (on the corner with C/20 de Abril), **t** 95 676 99 50; open Tues–Fri 9–7, Sat 10–2, Mon 9–3*

La Línea ✉ 11300

The only reason to stay in La Línea is that it is cheaper than staying in Gibraltar (although more expensive than surrounding villages). The hotels here are mostly as dull as the town. Eating out is cheaper than in Gibraltar, particularly if you like fish.

***AC Hotel La Línea, Los Caireles 2, **t** 95 617 55 66, *www.ac-hoteles.com* (€€). Has a first-class view of the Rock and the Bay of Algeciras. The bullfighter El Cordobés used to stay here; now it's part of a massive chain.

***Mediterráneo, Paseo Marítimo s/n, **t** 95 617 56 66, *www.citymar.com* (€€). A modern hotel overlooking the bay.

Pensión Florida, C/Sol 37, **t 95 617 13 00 (€). Well placed, though recommended only if you are on a budget.

*La Campana, C/Carboneros 3 (just off the main plaza), **t** 95 617 30 59 (€). This *pensión* is the best bargain in town; there's a good little restaurant downstairs with a cheap *menú del día*.

La Marina, Paseo Marítimo, **t** 95 617 15 31 (€€). The speciality at this well-reputed seafood restaurant is a favourite of the southern coast: grilled sardines on a spit (*sardinas al espeto*).

Restaurante El Barque, Avda Príncipe de Asturias (Parque Reina Sofia), **t** 95 617 03 62 (€€). With views of the Rock; seafood, paellas and good tapas.

Mesón La Jerezana, C/Granada 61, **t** 95 676 86 04 (€). Serves simple, inexpensive *raciones*.

Moltobella, C/López de Ayala 23, **t** 96 617 08 89 (€). A better class of pizza and pasta; all made from scratch with real Italiano flavour and flair.

Asado Patagonia, Isabel La Católica 43, **t** 95 617 80 21. Specializing in Argentinian steaks.

Sotogrande to Marbella

Thirty years ago, Gibraltarians who had money bought villas in Algeciras or San Roque. Nowadays they prefer **Sotogrande**, a relatively old-established British enclave 10 minutes along the Costa from Gibraltar, where middle- and upper-middle-class Brits who don't go to Tuscany for their holidays have established a comfortable, manicured and totally un-Spanish colony. Apart from some big houses and a couple of polo fields, this glorified *urbanización* isn't nearly as interesting as the rather forbidding barriers at the entrance would suggest. The more recently created **Puerto Sotogrande**, situated some 10km further east along the coast, is an up-and-coming marina complex with an array of restaurants, shops and apartments. It could be worth a stop for lunch here if you want to break the drive along the Costa.

The next town of any note you will come to is unprepossessing **Manilva**, where there are the ruins of a Roman spa. The old spring still pours out strange, sulphurous water, and the locals still drop in to bathe. **San Luis de Sabinillas**, Manilva's coastal extension, is making valiant attempts to transform itself into a resort, with hotels, a golf course and a marina. There is an 18th-century fort, and of course a number of built-up beaches. Historically, Manilva was linked with **Casares**, up in the Sierra Bermeja, a typical white Andalucian village on a steep hill under the ruins of its castle. The village, which was granted independence in 1796, has several monuments, a restored house belonging to Blas Infante's uncle, and a collection of Roman ruins.

Estepona, the first of the big resort towns east of Gibraltar, is also the quietest. Unfortunately the big developers have moved in, concrete blocks are sprouting up all over the place and the town is losing its former appeal. The biggest attraction appears to be a nudist beach and club, Costa Natura (incidentally, the oldest in Spain of any size), although a touch of its past fishing-village simplicity has returned, now that the bypass diverts the horrendous traffic that used to slice through the centre of town. The **Paseo Marítimo** has been completely refurbished since the great cut in traffic and makes for a very pleasant evening stroll, where you can stop in at any of the cafés and bars that line its length. The old town remains a pleasant, quiet place, with narrow streets and some very pretty squares including **Las Flores**, bursting with palms and flowers and fringed by some good bars and restaurants, and **Plaza del Reloj**, named after the 15th-century clock tower, all that remains of a church built by Henry IV of Castile. It has a modern bullring, a covered market on C/Castillo and a marina, the **Puerto Deportivo**, where you can grab a beer and a bite to eat while you study the classy yachts. And, for a glimpse of how it all once was along this coast, get down to the port (**Puerto Pesquero**), at the far

Getting around between Sotogrande and Marbella

By Bus or Train

The **Portillo** bus company has the franchise for this stretch of coast; and with the growth of tourism its service has become almost like a city bus-line, stopping every few hundred yards in the developed areas between Algeciras and Málaga. Be sure to check how long your bus will take to arrive if you're planning an intercity journey, and change to an express service if necessary.

There's never too long a wait in either direction. San Pedro is where the buses branch off for Ronda, an easy destination from any town on the coast. You can also go directly to Sevilla or Madrid from the **bus station** in Marbella, Avda del Trapiche, t 95 276 44 00.

At Fuengirola you can pick up a **suburban train**, which runs a regular service to Málaga. It stops at Torremolinos and most other points in between (including the airport).

By Car

The N340 connects all the towns and villages along the coast, and becomes the A7 motorway in sections. This is toll-free but often crammed. The parallel AP7/E15 toll motorway is fast and usually empty.

---

west side of town, to watch the fishing boats come in from about 6am. On the way out of town towards Cádiz are a number of towers – lookout points dating back to Roman times and refurbished by the Moors as a defence against pirates.

San Pedro de Alcántara, along the coast, is a little fancier, though still pleasingly unsophisticated to look at. Most of the town is some way from the beaches (though walkable). From here the only good road through the mountains (the A376) takes you to Ronda and surrounding villages – the best excursion you can make.

Sports and Activities between Sotogrande and Marbella

ⓘ **Casares**
C/Carreras 51,
t 95 289 55 11

Escuela de Arte Ecuestre, Rio Padrón Alto, Ctra 340, km 159, t 95 280 80 77, *www.escuela-ecuestre.com*. Traditional *andaluz*-style horse-riding school.

Estepona Golf, t 95 293 76 05, *www.esteponagolf.com*.

Happy Divers Club, Hotel Atalaya Park, Ctra N340, km 169, t 95 288 90 00, *www.happy-divers-marbella.com*. Scuba-diving centre offering a number of courses and excursions; also has a branch at the marina.

Where to Stay and Eat between Sotogrande and Marbella

Manilva ✉ 29691

****Duquesa Golf and Country**, t 95 289 12 11, *www.laduquesahotel.com*

(€€€€€–€€€€). This is the place to stay – located in the marina area, and with all the facilities you would expect. Check the website for deals.

Manilva Park Hotel, Ctra del Peñoncillo 17, t 95 289 37 30, *www.manilvapark.com* (€€€). A luxury hotel with sparkling interior of dazzling white complemented by earth colours, plus private terraces, gym, spa, wi-fi, two pools and free shuttle to beach and marina.

***Hotel Doña Luisa**, Paseo Marítimo, in Sabinillas, t 95 289 22 50, *www.hoteldluisa.com* (€€). A comfortable little hotel on the seafront: most rooms have balconies with sea views.

Hostal Sibajas, Plaza San Luis de Sabinillas, t 95 289 02 59 (€). A basic option in town.

Manilva has a surprising number of decent restaurants, most near Castillo de la Duquesa.

Hachomar, C/San José 4, t 95 289 01 24 (€€). Specializes in seafood.

(i) **Estepona** >
Avda San Lorenzo 1,
t 95 280 20 02,
www.estepona.es

Roman Oasis, Camino Sabinallas-Casares, **t** 95 289 23 80 (€). Barbecued meats with a children's play area, making it a family favourite.

Estepona ✉ 29680

The main road to Estepona from Marbella has some of the finest hotels along the Costa del Sol, most of which have their own beach and extensive facilities, but be warned: this sort of splendour does not come cheap. Look online for deals. The town has a dearth of quality hotels, though there are a number of two-star places.

*****Las Dunas Beach Hotel and Spa**, Ctra 340, km 163, **t** 95 279 43 45, *www.las-dunas.com* (€€€€€). One of the 'Leading Hotels of the World', and with prices to match (over €600 for a double in high season), complete with health spa plus all the treatments, restaurants, bars, live music, vast pool.

*****Gran Hotel Playabella**, Ctra 340, km 163, **t** 95 288 08 68, *www.hotelesplaya.com* (€€€€€). A modern resort hotel set in tropical gardens, with sleek, stylish rooms with sea views. Sailing, tennis, three outdoor pools and tennis courts, plus 40 golf courses almost on the doorstep.

*****Kempinski Hotel**, Ctra 340, km 159, **t** 95 280 95 00, *www.kempinski-spain.com* (€€€€€). Faux-Moorish, with a private beach, health and beauty centre and a number of quality restaurants.

****Atalaya Park**, Ctra 340, km 169, **t** 95 288 90 00, *www.atalaya-park.es* (€€€€). The biggest along this stretch. If you are a sports fan then this is the one to go for: nine tennis courts, a football pitch, athletics track, basketball, volleyball and one of the best golf courses on the Costa.

***Albero Lodge**, Urb. Finca La Cancelada, C/Támesis 16, **t** 95 288 07 00, *www.alberolodge.com* (€€€). A boutique hotel with each room named after a city with matching décor, like exotic Fez with its rich tapestry of colours or more stream-lined New York. Located within strolling distance of the beach.

***Hotel Diana Park**, Ctra 340, km 168.5, **t** 95 288 76 59, *www.hoteldianapark.com* (€€€–€€). Back from the beaches (although there's a free shuttle service in summer), this is one of the best deals on this stretch of coast. Pool, tennis and golf course.

****Aguamarina**, Avda San Lorenzo 32, **t** 95 280 61 55, *www.hotelaguamarina.com* (€€€–€€). Just down from the *turismo*, with air-conditioning, spacious doubles, many with balconies, all with bath; near the beach.

****Hotel Mediterráneo**, Avda de España 68, **t** 95 279 38 93 (€€–€). A good-value hotel on the seafront: good views from many of the bright, attractively furnished rooms.

There are plenty of inexpensive *hostales* both in the town and on the beach.

****La Malagueña**, C/Castillo 1, **t** 95 280 00 11, *www.hlmestepona.com* (€). A good budget choice, with bright rooms on a pretty square close to the beach.

***El Pilar**, Plaza de las Flores 22, **t** 95 280 00 18 (€). Overlooking Estepona's prettiest square; rooms with or without bathrooms.

There are lots of restaurants in and around Estepona, some of them very good indeed. Fish, of course, is the town's speciality, particularly *fritura malagueña* and *espetos de sardinas*.

Alcaría de Ramos, Urb. El Paraíso, Ctra. N340, km 167, **t** 95 288 61 78 (€€€). The owner, José Ramos, is a recent winner of Spain's National Gastronomy Prize so you can expect exciting, innovative dishes that change according to what is in season.

Típico Andaluz, **t** 95 280 18 02, and **Bodega Sabor Andaluz**, **t** 95 279 10 30 (€€). A pair of restaurants at the far end of C/Caridad (Nos.55 and 57), offering wonderful *embutidos* such as *jamón ibérico* and *queso manchego*.

La Casa de Mi Abuela, C/Caridad 54, **t** 95 279 19 67 (€€). A selection of grills, including Argentinian-style *churrasco*.

La Escollera, **t** 95 280 63 54 (€€). A traditional local favourite in the fishing port, with a terrace.

Taberna Marinera, **t** 95 279 63 26 (€€). One of many restaurants at the marina specializing in fish.

Mesón Genaro, C/Lozano 15 (€). Offers very reasonably priced tapas, such as *chorizo*, *morcillo* and *pulpo*.

(i) **San Pedro de Alcántara** >
Avda Marqués del Duero 69, t 95 278 52 52

San Pedro de Alcántara
✉ 29670

***Cortijo Blanco**, Avda Jose Luís Carrillo Benítez, **t** 95 278 09 00 (€€€). Near El Pueblo Andaluz (*see* below), and of a similar quality, but with extra facilities such as parking and a crèche. It also allows pets.

***El Pueblo Andaluz**, Avda Luís Carrillo Benítez, **t** 95 278 05 97 (€€). A pretty place near the beach built around an old Andalucian home with a pool, restaurant and garden. Minimum 4 days' stay.

***Don Catalina**, Avenue Oriental 14, **t** 95 285 31 20, *www.hoteldonacatalina. com* (€€). One of the latest hotels to open here, in a modern Andalucian-style building. The rooms have terracotta tiles coupled with a pastel and white colour scheme.

There is a wide variety of bars and restaurants in San Pedro itself, on the 'Ronda Road' as you leave towards the Sierras, and in Nueva Andalucía, a vast area of beautiful countryside between San Pedro and Marbella with high-quality residential development.

Caruso, C/Andalucía, **t** 95 278 22 93 (€€€–€€). Elegant Italian restaurant acclaimed for its superb pasta dishes. The atmosphere is romantic with a dress-for-dinner feel. *Closed Sun.*

Alfredo, Avda Andalucía, Local 8, **t** 95 278 61 65 (€€). A choice selection of fresh grilled fish and meats; the lively atmosphere buzzes.

Méson El Coto, Ctra Ronda (El Madroñal), **t** 95 278 66 88 (€€). A handsome Andalucian house with magnificent views over sea and mountains and a top-class kitchen specializing in delicious grills and seasonal game. It is 6km above town on the road to Ronda, so you'll need a car or taxi.

(★) **Ogilvy & Mailer** >

Ogilvy & Mailer, t 95 281 53 98 (€€). On a charming site by Los Naranjos Country Club (in Nueva Andalucía), serving some of the finest and most innovative Mediterranean food on the coast, with well-selected wines. Very memorable and reasonable for such quality. *Closed Sun.*

Entertainment and Nightlife between Sotogrande and Marbella

For a place supposedly in the shadow of its wild sister up the road in Marbella, **Estepona** has a lot to offer, especially at the weekends. Since C/Real was pedestrianized, the town centre has exploded with clubs and bars. To discover what's on, check the local publications *Essential Marbella*, *Costa de Sol News* and a weekly English edition of Málaga's newspaper *Sur*, free every Friday (also online at *www.elsurinenglish.com*).

La Jerezana, C/Extremadura. A shrine to legendary flamenco star Camarón de la Isla, who died of a heroin over-dose. There are pictures of him all over the walls; if you hang around long enough you may be treated to some impromptu hand-clapping and guitar.

Bar 97, C/Caridad 97. One of a number of good bars along this street, many with an emphasis on food.

Delfi, Mar Playa Pinillos, N-340, km 158. Caribbean beats and seafood tapas.

There are a few discos in town, including the trendy **Melodie Cool** (C/Real, just behind the seafront) and Niágara (Avda Juan Carlos I), but for later-night action head to the **marina** where there are a number of other discos, including **Chico Diez** and **Mambo**. In summer, there's the massive outdoor disco **El Campo**, and several *chiringuitos* on the beaches also double as bars.

Marbella

(★) **Marbella**

Marbella finds herself more or less in the middle of the stretch of coast said to be the fastest-growing area in Europe, so it is not without its growing pains. Until recently, zoning laws were permissive to the point of being totally ineffective and developers,

Getting to and around Marbella

Marbella is well connected by **bus**, with frequent Portillo services trundling into town (if you are coming from Estepona or San Pedro de Alcántara) or into the new **bus station** north of the town on C/Trapiche.

If you are **driving**, the N340 connects all the towns and villages along the coast, which becomes the A7 motorway in sections. This is toll free but often crammed. The parallel AP7/E15 toll motorway is fast and usually empty.

eager to make a quick profit, threw up one unattractive building after another. But for every ugly development there is a stunningly beautiful one, carefully preserving Andalucian tradition and delightfully landscaped with trees, lawns and flowering shrubs. So, despite her limited charm for the 'serious' traveller, Marbella continues to thrive, and the fun-loving teenager she was is now turning into a respectable matron. Wild parties, eccentric ways and a live-for-today attitude have given way to serious business, fuelled by the property boom on the Costa del Sol in the 1980s.

Marbella is the smartest, most expensive and complex resort in Spain. When you arrive, you might find yourself asking why – its appeal is not obvious. When you get to know it, this in itself becomes one of Marbella's greatest attractions. The place has been much maligned and, it's true, overdeveloped, but the old quarter of town, with the pretty orange-blossom-scented **Plaza de los Naranjos** as its centrepiece, is still a delight, as whitewashed and charming as Andalucía at its most typical, and without being too cutesy or tripperish – at least out of season. The self-contained *urbanizaciones* around Marbella and the continuing expansion of Puerto Banús have actually done the old town a favour, reducing the number of chi-chi shops and 'returning' Marbella to the Spanish whose home it is. If you are ever in doubt as to whether Spaniards actually live here, come in May when Marbella's *feria* is in full swing – it's an event you're unlikely to forget.

Nonetheless, for the earnest tourist there is not a great deal of point in spending time in the town. You'll pay high prices without getting in on the action, which takes place in a score of private clubs, private villas and private yachts. There are a couple of attractions worth a visit: in the heart of the old town, the Museo del Grabado on C/Hospital Bazán is housed in an immaculately restored 16th-century hospital and has an extensive collection of etchings by Dalí, Miró and Picasso among others. Dedicated fans of the bonsai tree can make a pilgrimage to the Museo del Bonsái in the Parque del Arroyo de la Represa.

Museo del Grabado
*t 95 276 57 41;
open Tues–Sat 10–2
and 7–9; adm*

Museo del Bonsái
*open 10.30–1.30
and 5–8.30 in July and
Aug; 10.30–1.30 and
4.30–7.30 during the
rest of the year; adm*

Two kilometres south of Marbella is the **mosque**, financed by the late King Abdulaziz al-Saud, who also built himself a palace (in the style of the White House) next to it.

Few foreigners actually live in old Marbella itself; self-styled artists and flashy bachelors take studios in Puerto Banús, English and Scandinavian golfers head for 'Golf Valley' in Nueva Andalucía, and well-heeled, well-dressed French, Italians and Germans heave-ho at the Marbella Club and Puente Romano, both situated a few miles west of town. **Puerto Banús** is the brilliantly designed, ancient-looking (but modern) development 6km to the west, with a marina full of gin palaces; don't pass up the chance of spending an afternoon or evening in one of the many waterside cafés here, ogling all the yachts and some of the people. It also has one of the biggest El Corte Inglés stores in Spain, almost every designer clothes shop you can imagine, a huge cinema and numerous swanky restaurants.

Where to Stay in Marbella

ⓘ **Marbella >**
Glorieta de la Fontanilla, *Paseo Marítimo*, **t** 95 277 14 42; open summer Mon–Fri 9.30–9.30, Sat 10–4; winter Mon–Fri 9.30–8.30, Sat 10–2; there's also an office on **Plaza Los Naranjos**, **t** 95 282 35 50

ⓘ **Puerto Banús**
Avenida del Mar, **t** 95 281 24 45

Marbella ✉ 29600

There are fewer hotels than you might imagine in the Marbella area, where villa life is very much the form. Don't count on finding a room at any price during the season; package tours have taken over here just as they have in the resorts to the east, and most places are booked solid.

Luxury (€€€€€)

*****Meliá Don Pepe, Avda José Meliá, **t** 95 277 03 00, *www.solmelia. com*. One of the resort's several luxury, family-orientated hotels, facing out over the sea. It has a large sports complex, including an 18-hole golf course, 11 tennis courts, five squash courts, a riding school, a heated swimming pool, gym and sauna.

*****Puente Romano, Ctra Cádiz, km 178, **t** 95 282 09 00, *www.puente romano.com*. One of the most beautiful, if not the most expensive, hotels. Its name comes from the genuine Roman bridge incorporated into its lovely surroundings.

****Marbella Club Hotel, Boulevard Príncipe Alfonso de Hohenlohe, **t** 95 282 22 11, *www.marbellaclub.com*. Alfonso de Hohenlohe's jet-set retreat, which put Marbella on the map in the late 1950s, is still going strong and is the most sophisticated hotel in town. With golf course and spa.

****Los Monteros, Ctra Cádiz, km 187 (6km east of Marbella), **t** 95 277 17 00, *www.monteros.com*. One of the oldest hotels in these parts, and for many the best-loved. Its beach club is the height of restrained luxury and room prices include green fees at the hotel's own Río Real golf course.

Very Expensive–Expensive (€€€€–€€€)

The Town House, C/Alderete 7, **t** 95 290 17 91, *www.townhouse.nu*. In one of old town Marbella´s loveliest squares, this former family house has been exquisitely transformed into a boutique hotel. The rooms are luxurious, with a combination of antiques and modern fittings.

***San Cristóbal, Avda Ramón y Cajal 3, **t** 95 277 12 50, *www.hotelsan cristobal.com*. Central and located conveniently close to the beach, this modern hotel offers comfortable rooms and a pair of good, modestly priced restaurants.

Moderate (€€)

***Las Chapas, Ctra Cádiz, km 192, **t** 95 105 53 00, *www.hotellaschapas.com*. A nearly self-sufficient holiday complex with opportunities for tennis, golf and water sports; situated 900m from the beach on the coastal highway, 11km to the east of Marbella.

Hotel Central, C/San Ramón 15, **t 95 290 24 42, *www.hotelcentralmarbella. com*. A charming small hotel just 100m from the beach, with comfortably furnished rooms; friendly service.

Moderate–Inexpensive (€€–€)

Surprisingly, there is a wide selection of *hostales* in the €50 range, most of them in the old town, around Calle Peral and Calle San Francisco.

Hostal Enriqueta, Los Caballeros 18, **t 95 282 75 52. Particularly well placed, near the Plaza Los Naranjos, with rooms set around a patio.

Hostel Paco, C/Peral 16, **t 95 277 12 00. An adequate two-star option. *Open April–mid-Oct.*

Hostal de Pilar, C/Mesconcillo 4 (off C/Peral), **t** 95 282 99 36. A good little cheapie, full of young budget travellers. Lively bar, pool table and roof terrace.

Albergue Juvenil Marbella, C/Trapiche 2, **t** 95 277 14 91. A youth hostel with rooms for 2–6 and a pool.

Eating Out in Marbella

Expensive (€€€)

Finca Besaya, Río Verde Alto, **t** 95 286 13 82. This restaurant has long been a fixture on the Marbella scene, thanks to the charm of former owner Francis Butler. Now under new ownership, the restaurant remains romantic and welcoming, with a terrace overlooking the avocado trees and several rooms littered with antiques and warmed by open fires during the winter. Creative, international cuisine including heavenly desserts. There's also a DJ playing chill-out music, and lounging areas with *chaises longues* and cushions. Booking essential (if only to ask for directions). *Open eves only.*

Goizeko & Dalli's, Avda Buchinger s/n, **t** 95 276 90 30. An ultra-luxurious restaurant from Marbella's most celebrated restaurateurs, this offers spectacular Basque cuisine in a lavish setting. Everything – the food, the wine, the service, the surroundings – is exquisite, but don't expect much change from €100 per head.

La Hacienda, Ctra Cádiz, km 193, Urbanización Las Chapas, **t** 95 283 12 67. This elegant and romantic establishment east of Marbella prides itself on its super-fresh ingredients; try the hake in wine sauce, river crab and mushroom salad, fresh pasta, home-made ice cream. Dining out on the terrace, among the statues and stone arches, will set you back around €60. *Closed Mon and Tues, Sept–June and 14 Nov–21 Dec.*

La Meridiana, Camino de la Cruz s/n (just behind the mosque), **t** 95 277 61 90. Marbella's most expensive and glamorous restaurant, offering international cuisine and designer dishes such as salad of monkfish marinated in dill, or braised veal sweetbreads with grapefruit. *Open eves only in summer.*

El Portalón, Ctra de Cádiz 178, **t** 95 286 10 75. Opposite the Marbella Club. One of the most exclusive and talked-about restaurants on the Costa del Sol. The freshest local produce is used in the creative, contemporary cuisine with a Basque flavour. And if you've had enough of seafood, it's got the perfect antidote with excellent roast meats. *Closed Sun.*

Santiago, Pso Marítimo 5, **t** 95 277 00 78. Try this long-established place for the best paella in Marbella, suckling pig, or white beans with clams – some of the best Spanish cooking on the coast. One room is dedicated to the late Camilo José Cela, Nobel prize-winning novelist, who visited often.

Villa Tiberio, Ctra Cádiz, km 178.5, **t** 95 277 17 99. A well-appointed restaurant in an elegant villa, with soft music and luxurious surroundings. Your Italian host will kiss you (if you're female) on both cheeks, even though he's never met you before. Good *antipasto* dishes include the *bresaola con aguacate* (thinly sliced cured beef with avocado), and delicious pasta. Main courses are good, too, though less adventurous. *Closed Sun.*

Moderate (€€)

El Pozo Viejo, Plaza Altamirano 3, **t** 95 282 25 57. Enjoys a prime position on this pretty plaza in Marbella's old town. The menu includes a tasty *bacalao a la malagueña* (casserole of cod) with peppers, pumpkin and white wine.

La Comedia, Plaza de la Victoria, **t** 95 277 64 78. Swedish-run restaurant with an imaginative menu with starters like blue mussel *carpaccio* topped with grilled scallops and truffles followed by avocado and salmon spring rolls with mango and Marie rose sauce and tandoori sweet curried chicken.

Buenaventura, Plaza de la Iglesia de la Encarnación 5, **t** 95 285 80 69. A charming restaurant in the old town, where you can dine on the flower-filled patio on delicious, creative Andalucian cuisine.

La Pesquera, Plaza de la Victoria s/n, t 95 277 80 54. One of the oldest *marisquerías* in Marbella, serving some of the best-value seafood meals in the area.

La Relojera, Puerto Pesquero, t 95 277 14 47. Sit on the roof terrace overlooking the fishing port and watch the trawlers head out to sea while dining on tasty barbecued fish.

 Zozoï >

Zozoï, Plaza Altamarino, t 95 285 88 68. This stylish restaurant in Marbella's Casco Viejo has a terrace out on the pretty square and an even more sought-after private courtyard. The Mediterranean cuisine is prepared with the freshest local produce and a dash of Gallic flair.

Aquavit, Plaza del Puerto, Puerto Banús, t 95 281 91 27. A sunny, snazzily decorated restaurant serving fusion food like sushi nori rolls and fresh rocket salad followed by potato and anchovy gratin with a shot of chilled aquavit. *Dinner only*.

Messina La Mairena, C/Madrid, La Mairena, t 95 285 20 50. A romantic restaurant in the mountains serving international and Mediterranean cuisine, including roast shoulder of lamb, smoked trout mousse salad, Mexican chilli and duck with fresh couscous and mint. *Closed Mon*.

Inexpensive (€)

The tapas bars of Marbella are excellent, both in the old town and in the streets behind the Alameda, such as Calle Carlos Mackintosh. Plenty of inexpensive places, mostly seafood, can be found in the area around Calle Aduar. Many of the inexpensive beach restaurants that run the length of the coast, known as *chiringuitos*, are open year-round. You won't go far wrong anywhere with a plate of grilled sardines, but some places are inevitably better than others.

Balcón de la Virgen, C/Remedios 2, t 95 277 60 92. Charming little restaurant set in a 17th-century house in the old town. Good *cazuelas* (stews) and desserts.

Ceuta, C/Buitrago 1, t 95 277 00 59. Crammed with taurine memorabilia, this likeable little place has good

tapas and more substantial offerings in the small dining room.

Freiduría Miraflores, Avda del Mercado 22, t 95 282 68 02. You'll be lucky to get a seat at this Marbellan favourite; excellent fish.

El Estrecho, C/San Lázaro 12, t 95 277 00 44. A characterful tapas bar tucked down a side street near the lovely Plaza de los Naranjos.

Bar Bartolo, C/San Lázaro s/n, t 95 282 69 50. Another great old-fashioned bar where you can enjoy *raciones* and tapas at reasonable prices, washed down with beer on tap or sangria.

Entertainment and Nightlife in Marbella

Most of the action will be found in **Puerto Banús**, with its numerous late bars, discos and piano bars. The best bars in **Marbella**'s old town are concentrated on and around the **Plaza de los Naranjos**, and slightly off to the west at **Plaza de los Olivos**.

Nikki Beach, the beach by Hotel Don Carlos. A summer beach party, hosted by the famous Miami nightspot. White loungers, candles and excellent music on the beach.

La Notte, Camino de la Cruz, t 95 277 61 90. A classic on the Golden Mile, this flashy, ultra-luxurious club attracts a moneyed crowd.

Pangea Sky Lounge. A restaurant, bar and club, popular with TV celebs and football stars. Bring your Ferrari, or at least a fat wallet.

Sinatra's, Puerto Banús, at the main entrance to the port. The classic hangout: perfect for yacht-watching.

Salduba Bar. Next door to Sinatra's and slightly less crowded.

In **Marbella** itself action can be found in the streets leading up from the **Paseo Marítimo** and around the **Puerto Deportivo**. **Calle Peral** has lots of hip bars; try **Alaska**, **Moloko** or **El Invernadero**. A good place to start the evening on this street is the relaxed Arab-style tea room **La Tetería**.

Olivia Valere, Ctra de Istán, km 0.8. Restaurant, club and piano bar for the very glamorous and the very wealthy, with faux-Moorish décor inspired by the Alhambra.

Fuengirola

You should really come on a package tour if you find Fuengirola and Torremolinos to your taste. That's what these places are for, and you would get a better deal. If you're just passing and want to rest in anonymity by the beach, however, there are possibilities.

Fifty years ago, Fuengirola was a typical whitewashed Spanish fishing village. It's still white, but hardly typical, and even less Spanish. With the miles of speculative *urbanizaciones* that surround it, it would be easy to be unkind to Fuengirola except that everyone there seems to be having such a good time. The town, and its adjacent community of **Los Boliches**, may be the only place in Spain where you'll see a sign in a shop window reading '*Se habla español*'; the laid-back international community appreciates a good joke. The shops of the old village have been transformed into pubs, English bookshops, travel agencies and Swiss, Chinese, Belgian, Italian, Moroccan and even Spanish restaurants, but there's something genuine in the atmosphere of this casual European village – now grown into a fair-sized city. The Spaniards live mostly in town, picnicking and sunbathing on their flat roofs or balconies; the foreigners drive in from the *urbanizaciones* for pub-hopping or to shop in the vast hypermarkets. But today the centre is becoming ever more determinedly multinational and multilingual, while upwardly mobile Spaniards are buying their way into the *urbanizaciones*. Fuengirola is becoming quite interesting; the best place to observe this curious community is at the Tuesday market.

Unlike other resorts on the Costa, there are some things to see – the Moorish **Castillo de Sohail** above town, a **bullring**, even the brand new façade of a **Roman temple**. In Roman times there were important marble quarries in the mountains near here, and off the coast divers recently discovered a wreck with these stones, bound for somewhere else; they've been salvaged and assembled on a spot near the beach.

Mijas

Visitors from Fuengirola totally overwhelm the village of Mijas, 3km up in the hills above town, but at dusk it returns to the hands of the foreign residents, who count for 90 per cent of the village's population. To escape the coastal sprawl, visitors come up here by the coachload to find *real* Spain and a typical Andalucian village, which it obviously is not, nor has it been for 30 years. Yet it's still pretty enough, with sea views from its promenade, a votive shrine to the Virgin, pine woods, dozens of souvenir shops and 'officially licensed *burro* taxis'. The whitewashed **bullring** sees its fair share of action, but the **museum of miniature curiosities** is hard to take, even as a joke.

Where to Stay in Fuengirola and Mijas

(i) **Fuengirola** >
*Avda Jesús Santos
Rein 6, in an old railway
station, t 95 246 74 57,
www.fuengirola.org;
open Mon–Fri 9.30–1.30
and 4–8, Sat 10–1*

(i) **Mijas**
*Plaza Virgen de la Peña,
t 95 258 94 34,
www.mijas.es*

(★) **Restaurante
Pueblo Lopez** >>

Fuengirola ✉ 29640

★★★★★Byblos Andaluz, Urbanización Mijas Golf, **t** 95 247 30 50, *www. byblos-andaluz.com* (€€€€€). This haven of peace and tranquillity with thalassotherapy centre and spa is only 5km from the centre of Fuengirola, with every imaginable luxury.

★★★★Las Palmeras, Paseo Marítimo s/n, **t** 95 247 27 00 (€€€€). A massive, modern beachfront hotel with all the trimmings from a pool to tennis courts. Prices drop by more than half out of season.

★★Más Playa, Urbanización Torreblanca del Sol, **t** 95 247 53 00 (€€€). Next door to Cendrillón, both places on the beach, popular with families.

Hotel Las Rampas, Jacinto Benavente s/n, **t** 95 247 07 35, *www.hotellas rampas.com* (€€€). Right in the heart of town, surrounded by shops, cafés and bars, yet just a couple of blocks from the beach. Rooms are large and comfortable. Pool.

Villa de Laredo, Paseo Marítimo 42, **t** 95 247 76 89, *www.hotelvillade laredo.com* (€€). Located on the promenade, this hotel is well priced given the location and facilities, which include terraces with sea views and an excellent restaurant.

Hostal Italia, C/de la Cruz 1, **t** 95 247 41 93 (€€). Just off the main square and within a short stroll of the beach, this *hostal* has sparkling rooms and a roof terrace for catching the rays.

Eating Out in Fuengirola and Mijas

Dining in Fuengirola is an experience; you can choose from Indonesian to Belgian without going broke. There are plenty of choices along **Calle del Hambre**, which means 'hungry street', and **Calle Moncayo**, known as 'fish alley'.

El Higuerón, Ctra Benalmádena-Mijas, km 3, **t** 95 211 91 63 (€€€). A romantic and elegant restaurant with spectacular coastal views, serving traditional Asturian as well as *andaluz* dishes.

El Mirlo Blanco, Plaza de la Constitución, Mijas, **t** 95 248 57 00 (€€). In a whitewashed house, with a vine-covered terrace, serving Basque specialities with the emphasis firmly on seafood. *Closed Tues eve in winter*.

Bistro, C/Palangreros 30, **t** 95 247 77 01 (€€). An unpretentious, reliably good restaurant in the attractive older part of town. Scrubbed pine interior and an international and Spanish menu; popular with foreign residents.

Guy Massey, Rotonda de la Luna, **t** 95 258 51 20 (€€). Celebrated UK chef has opened this French-Mediterranean restaurant with an eclectic menu that includes dishes like salmon and goat's cheese salad and roast duck. Music and dancing at weekends. *Dinner only*.

La Alcazaba, Plaza de la Constitucíon, Mijas, **t** 95 259 02 53 (€€). Prime position with panoramic windows and a view that stretches to Morocco on a clear day. Traditional Spanish menu includes paella and the best *ajo blanco* (almond and garlic soup) on the coast.

Valparaíso, Ctra de Mijas, km 4, **t** 95 248 59 96 (€€). Outside Fuengirola on the road to Mijas, this is one of the most popular in the area, with bars, terrace, and a varied menu. It's a favourite haunt of local expats. *Closed lunchtimes and Sun except July–Oct*.

Mesón La Salina, Avda de les Salines 28, Fuengirola, **t** 95 247 18 06 (€€–€). With a flower-filled terrace in summer, and a fireplace in winter, this has grilled meats and a good range of tapas. *Closed Wed*.

Restaurante Pueblo Lopez, C/Mijas 9, Pueblo Lopez, **t** 95 247 19 29 (€). A delightful Swedish-owned restaurant with seating in a pretty cobbled square. There's a reasonable daily menu with a choice of meat or fish as main course which can be substituted by a vegetarian option. *Dinner only*.

Miercoles, C/Marbella, **t** 95 266 41 36 (€). Lovely old building transformed into a tasteful tapas bar and restaurant just off the church square; innovative Mediterranean cuisine.

Alleycats, Pasaje Jimenez Martinéz s/n, Benalmádena Pueblo, **t** 610 223 328 (€). A fashionable new bar and tapas lounge located in between Fuengirola and Mijas, serving traditional Spanish and innovative international tapas created by renowned professional chef (and native New Yorker) Michael Stone.

Entertainment and Nightlife in Fuengirola

Fuengirola might not rock like Torremolinos and Marbella, but it does have its fair share of drinking establishments and *discotecas*. In the centre, these are concentrated in and around the streets of **Plaza Constitución**, and include the inevitable slew of 'authentic' Irish pubs and English bars. Off the Paseo Marítimo, **C/Martínez Catena** is the place to be, with bars, discos and numerous restaurants.

Torremolinos

All sources agree about Torremolinos, the 'fishing village' immortalized in James Michener's *The Drifters*. The oldest and biggest resort town on the Costa, it has become a ghastly, hyperactive, unsightly holiday inferno. In other words, it has character. Torremolinos isn't at all interested in our opinion, though, or in yours either; it's doing quite well with its endless screaming blocks of bars, shopping centres and concrete hotels. For those who want to spend their holiday in the fast lane, in a raucous, international, entirely synthetic environment, this is the place.

Part of Torremolinos' character arises from its status as capital of what the newspapers used to call the 'Costa del Crime'. Literally thousands of bank-heisters, con men and embezzlers, mostly from Britain, once added to the local colour, courtesy of Spain's traditional unwillingness to conclude extradition treaties with other nations. Now that an agreement with Britain has been reached, the crooks have had to move along as their visas ran out. There are still plenty of other types left – smooth operators of uncertain nationality, religious cult agents, hedonists of all shapes and sizes, and other European detritus. They're only the surface, though; the most noticeable segment of an enormous permanent and transient population is made up of gawking sun-seekers from every corner of Europe. In summer, Torremolinos swells dramatically to become the third largest city in Andalucía, when the 36,000 residents are joined by some quarter of a million tourists.

To escape the horde, step down to one of the beach cafés, popular day and night; if your luck is in, you'll be treated to some of the local street performers sharing their talents: an *anís*-soaked troubadour mangling an aria, cigarette dangling from his lower lip, or a transvestite flamenco dancer, whirling between the passing cars, his grim-looking mother handing round the hat. This is all received with good humour by the Spaniards, even if some of the tourists look a bit nonplussed.

In recent years the city has made attempts to cloak itself in green; in among the concrete blocks there are now a surprising number of leafy spaces. The tree-lined **Paseo Marítimo** – a 6km stretch leading to the Puerto Marina at **Benalmádena** – makes a pleasant stroll. The **marina** is Torre's answer to Marbella's Puerto Banús, another spot for sophisticated dining and yacht-gazing. Benalmádena itself was where Fernando and Isabel chose to defend this stretch of the coast, and it claims an ancient history going back as far as the Phoenicians. There's the **Castillo del Bil Bil** – of Moorish origins and now used to stage concerts – a **bullring**, and the **Museo Arqueológico** at Avenida Juan Peralta 49, which has one of Europe's best collections of Pre-Columbian artefacts.

Museo Arqueológico
t 95 244 85 93; open Mon–Fri 10–2 and 4–7

ⓘ **Torremolinos >**
Plaza Pablo Picasso, t 95 237 95 12, www.ayto-torremolinos.org

ⓘ **La Carihuela**
Borbollón Bajo, t 95 237 29 56

ⓘ **Bajondillo/ Playamar**
Plaza de las Comunidades Autónomas, t 95 237 19 09

ⓘ **Benalmádena**
Avda Antonio Machado 14, t 95 244 24 94, www.benalmadena.com

Where to Stay in Torremolinos

Torremolinos ✉ 29620

In Torremolinos and Benalmádena Costa, the possibilities are endless, though these, too, will probably be packed with package tours.

Very Expensive–Expensive (€€€€–€€€)

There are a number of swanky four-star hotels in Torremolinos, all offering much the same – swimming pool, air-conditioned rooms and dull food.

****Royal Al-Andalus**, C/Al-Andalus 3, t 95 238 12 00, *www.royalpremier hoteles.com*. Just off the main road towards Benalmádena and set in its own grounds, complete with huge pool and sea-facing rooms.

****Cervantes**, Las Mercedes s/n, t 95 238 40 33, *www.hotasa.es*. Just a few yards from the heart of the action, this hotel is surprisingly reasonable (except in August) and offers all the creature comforts you would expect, with two pools (one indoor, one out), big rooms with balconies, a disco, a café and a very good restaurant.

****Pez Espada**, C/Salvador Allende 11, t 95 238 03 00, *www.medplaya.com*. The hotel that started it all off – built in 1959, it was the first luxury hotel to appear in the city, and it put Torre on the map. Fading now, but still of a high standard and in a good spot just out of the centre and near the beach.

***La Luna Blanca**, Pasaje Cerillo 2, t 95 205 37 11, *www.la-luna-blanca.com*. A Japanese-owned hotel, with immaculate rooms (European or Japanese style), a Japanese restaurant and gardens that are right by the beach.

Moderate (€€)

****Adriano**, Avda de los Manantiales 1, t 95 205 08 38, *www.hoteladriano.info*. In the heart of town – albeit slightly noisy – but this is Torre and you're not here to get away from it all. All rooms come with bath, air-conditioning, phone and TV.

****Picasso**, C/María Barrabino, t 95 238 76 00. Overlooking the main square, this is very reasonably priced; rooms have balconies. Popular with Spanish holidaymakers.

Red Parrot, Avenida Los Manantiales 4, t 95 237 54 45, *www.theredparrot.net*. In the centre of town, this English owned hotel offers comfortable rooms with balconies and a downstairs English pub and restaurant.

Guadalupe, C/Peligro 15, Bajondillo, t 95 238 19 37. This *pensión* is near the beach and away from the mayhem.

Miami, C/Aladino 14, La Carihuela, t 95 238 52 55. Perhaps Torremolinos's last secret. The house was built as a holiday villa by Picasso's cousin Manolo Blasco, and is quite charming despite its shabbiness.

Inexpensive (€)

Budget places are few and far between here, and most are some way out of town. Some of the good bargains can be found out towards La Carihuela, along **Avda Carlota Alessandri**.

*Flor Blanco**, Pasaje de la Carihuela 4, t 95 238 20 71. Delightfully situated just off the Carihuela beach in the former fishing village, this low-rise hotel has small seaview rooms.

Hotel Micaela, C/Bajondillo 4, t 95 238 33 10. Clean and has rooms with bath; just down from C/San Miguel.

Eating Out in Torremolinos

Expensive (€€€)

La Cónsula/Escuela de Hostelería de Málaga, Finca La Cónsula, Churriana, **t** 95 262 25 62, *www.laconsula.com*. In a beautiful colonial-style house where Hemingway used to stay, this is an interesting dining experience. The hotel school's students prepare delectable lunches featuring innovative *andaluz* recipes. *Must book*.

Frutos, Ctra Cádiz, km 235, **t** 95 238 14 50. A popular restaurant on the main carretera (next to Los Álamos petrol station), with high-quality food at reasonable prices; generous portions: leg of lamb, suckling pig, Málaga fried fish and delicious desserts.

Mar de Alborán, Hotel Alay, Avda de Alay 5, Benalmádena Costa, **t** 95 244 64 27. Highly recommended for excellent Basque and Andalucian cuisine; the food, prepared by chef Álvaro Arriaga, gets better and better. *Closed Sun eve and Mon*.

Moderate (€€)

Casa Guaquín, C/Carmen 37, **t** 95 238 45 30. Local seafood specialities and great tapas on the seafront. *Closed Mon*.

Figón de Montemar, Avenida Pez Espada 101, **t** 95 237 26 88. A traditional restaurant lined with bottles, serving tasty local specialities out on the terrace. *Closed Sun*.

La Jábega, Paseo Marítimo, La Carihuela, **t** 95 238 63 75. A good place on the beach, with fish, and a wide variety of starters and shellfish.

Med, Las Mercedes 12, Balcón de San Miguel, **t** 95 205 88 30. Exquisite contemporary Mediterranean cuisine in a stylish restaurant with spectacular views.

Los Pinos del Coto, Cañada de Ceuta s/n, Churriana, **t** 95 243 58 00, *www.lospinosdelcoto.com*. To escape the bedlam of Torre, head up into the hills to this rambling, ranch-type restaurant; it's a 10min drive. The spacious, attractive interior has a log fire, and the terrace offers wonderful views over the coast; lots of meat dishes. *Closed Mon and Tues*.

Mesón Gallego Antoxo, C/Hoyo 5, **t** 95 238 45 33. A short walk from the Torremolinos bus station, this is a typical Spanish restaurant with a beautiful interior and charming little courtyard. A wide choice of fish, many dishes cooked to Galician recipes.

Inexpensive (€)

Casa Juan, C/de San Ginés 20, **t** 95 237 35 12. Run by Guaquín's cousin (*see* Casa Gauquín), with similar fare at affordable prices.

Bodega Quitapenas, Cuesta del Tajo. On the central steps down to the beach. Sit outside this *bodega* for a cheap *apéritif*.

La Chacha, Avda Palma de Mallorca, 3, **t** 95 238 49 10. Real old-style *comedor* where you can choose from *gambas* and *pulpo* as you sit at the bar.

La Lonja, C/Mar 12, **t** 95 237 58 86. Overlooking the port; deliciously fresh seafood tapas.

El Vietnam del Sur, Pso del Colorado, Urbanización Playamar, Bloque 9, **t** 95 238 67 37. If you've never had the Vietnamese variations on Chinese cuisine that are so popular in France, try this place – the food is delicious and affordable. *Closed lunch, plus Jan and Feb*.

Entertainment and Nightlife in Torremolinos

Torremolinos was once a byword for hedonistic fun, but the party is beginning to move on. There are a few discos in town, but the best action is to be found 3km down the road at Puerto Marina in Benalmádena. Torre is currently awash with English theme bars on **Calle San Miguel** and **Plaza de la Independencia** – take your pick, if that's your thing.

In town there are loads of enormous clubs along the **Avenida Palma de Mallorca**: **The Palladium**, one of the biggest gay clubs, in the style of a Roman baths; **Voltage**, for hard-core home-grown techno; or **Fun Beach**, supposedly the biggest club in Spain, with seven different dance floors and six bars.

⭐ La Cónsula >

Málaga

Much-maligned Málaga, capital of the Costa del Sol and also of a certain amount of sleaze in southern Spain, is making a determined effort to improve its reputation and attract more tourists. In the past, a brief visit to its shops was often the only reason tourists spent any time here at all, between the airport and the beach, but the opening of the Museo Picasso has enticed a flood of culture-hungry visitors from all over Europe. With its newly spruced-up boulevards and *paseos*, smart new shops and terrace cafés, Málaga is successfully shrugging off its former reputation for seediness.

To miss Málaga means to miss the most Spanish of cities, certainly on the Costa del Sol. Whatever you may think of the place, it is alive and real: ungainly cranes and elegant palm trees compete for dominance of the skyline; police helicopters roar over the Plaza de la Constitución as pretty Spanish girls toss their skirts and stamp their heels to flamenco music, for a private audience in a public square; elegant old Spanish ladies, scented with Maja soap, sit and reminisce, and dark-eyed tattooed Gypsy boys flash their double-edged smiles to lure you into a shoeshine. From its tattered billboards and walls splashed with political slogans to its public gardens overflowing with exotic fauna, Málaga is a jamboree of colours, aromas and sounds.

Admittedly Málaga cannot compete with Sevilla or Granada for sheer wealth of cultural distractions, but the Malagueños are proud of their fun-loving metropolis. To experience a real local *juerga* (spree), treat yourself to an afternoon ramble through her famous tapas bars, where you will encounter more Spaniards in one afternoon than in a week in Torremolinos. Unfortunately, the old quarters of Málaga have been treated ruthlessly by town planners, and **El Perchel**, once the heart of Málaga's flamenco district, has lost a lot of its charm. The Avenida de Andalucía cuts through this old district and then becomes the Alameda Principal and the Paseo del Parque. The essence of Málaga is within this limited area, from the elegant Avenida de Andalucía to the seedy, teeming neo-Moorish market on the Calle Atarazanas.

You may find it difficult to decide whether you love or loathe this city – will you notice the two snarling drivers impatient for the green light, or the two old gentlemen sipping sherry in the doorway of a cool, dark *bodega*, hung with *serrano* hams and lined with wine casks?

The Heart of Málaga

As the **Avenida de Andalucía**, the main road from the west, crosses the dry rocky bed of the Guadalmedina river, it becomes the **Alameda Principal**, a majestic 19th-century boulevard. North of

San Pablo

HILERA

MÁRMOLES

COMPOSITOR LEHMBERG RUIZ

AVENIDA DE ANDALUCÍA

AVENIDA DE LA AURORA

ARMENGUAL DE LA MOTA

ESQUILACHE

PUENTE

Santo Domingo

PASILLO DE GUIMBARDA

PASILLO SANTA ISABEL

PASILLO AGUJERO

MARQUÉS

PASILLOS DE SANTO DOMINGO

PUENTE SANTO DOMINGO

PLAZA DE ARRIOLA

PLAZA ARRIOLA

Central Market

PASEO DE LOS TILOS

RENFE Train Station

EL PERCHEL

Centro de Arte Contemporáneo

Málaga Centro Train Station

CUARTO ESLAVA

CALLE CUARTELES

Río Guadalmedina

PUENTE TETUÁN

CALLE ATARAZANA

PANADEROS

PASTORA

ALAMEDA PRINCIPAL

AVENIDA DE HEREDIA

CASAS DE CAMPOS

AVENIDA TOMÁS DE HEREDIA

CALLE CÓRDOBA

ALAMEDA DE COLÓN

PUENTE DEL CARMEN

AVENIDA MANUEL AGUSTÍN HEREDIA

N

Puerto Pesquero (Fishing Port)

500 metres
500 yards

Getting to and around Málaga

As it is the main port of entry to the Costa del Sol and southern Andalucía, you'll probably pass through Málaga either coming or going.

By Air

Málaga's often frenetic **airport**, currently being expanded, connects the city to Madrid, Valencia, Almería, Sevilla, Melilla and Tangier, besides being the charter-flight gateway to the Costa del Sol.

The easiest way to get into the city, or to Torremolinos or Fuengirola, is the **suburban railway line**, connected to the airport via a pedestrian flyover. These trains (get off at Málaga Centro for the city centre) run every 30mins between around 7am and 11.30pm. **Taxis** cost about €15 to Málaga or Torremolinos. The **airport bus** runs to the city centre from the arrivals hall at Terminal 1 and the departures hall of Terminal 2 approximately every 30mins from 7am to 11.30pm (€1.10). **Airport information**, t 95 204 88 04.

By Train

Five or more daily high-speed trains go to Madrid (4hrs 10mins), plus four normal trains (7½hrs), two trains to Valencia and Barcelona, and there are direct connections to Sevilla (2½ hrs) and Córdoba. For all other destinations in Andalucía, change at the almost inescapable Bobadilla Junction. The spanking new **train station** is off Calle Cuarteles on the Explanada de la Estación.
Information: RENFE, t 90 224 02 02.

By Bus

The **main bus station** is by the train station at Paseo de los Tilos, south of the Avenida de Andalucía, t 95 235 00 61. Connections for local destinations run hourly; for provincial destinations, generally every 1–2 hours. Most long-distance services (Madrid, Barcelona, Murcia, etc.) are run by **Alsa**, t 90 242 22 42.

Portillo, t 90 214 31 44, operates buses to Sevilla, Ronda, Algeciras and towns and villages in the interior; **Bacoma**, t 95 223 84 96, to Álora and Ronda; **Los Amarillos**, t 95 231 59 78, to Antequera, Carratraca; **Alsina Graells**, t 95 231 04 00, to Granada, Nerja and Almería, and also Alicante and Barcelona.

There's a **smaller bus station** – little more than a string of bus shelters – along Avenida Manuel Agustín Heredia (close to Plaza de la Marina). Buses for Torremolinos, Fuengirola and other resorts leave from here, but most pass through the main bus station.

---

the Alameda is the **Plaza de la Constitución**, in the heart of the commercial centre, and the **Pasaje Chinitas**, an atmospheric complex of alleyways with bars and old-fashioned shops; look for the plaque on a corner marking the original site of the Café Chinitas, where bullfighters and flamenco singers would gather in the old days, the spirit of which was captured by García Lorca.

The Alameda continues into the **Paseo del Parque**, a tree-lined promenade that runs along the port area, and leads to the city's **bullring**, built in 1874 with a capacity of 14,000, and very much in use today. Nearby is the **English cemetery**. William Mark, the 19th-century consul, so loved Málaga that he described it as a 'second paradise', and encouraged his fellow countrymen to join him here. In 1830 he founded this cemetery, allowing a decent burial to Protestants. Hans Christian Andersen declared he could 'well understand how a splenetic Englishman might take his own life in order to be buried in this place'. Its sea views, however, have long since been blocked by buildings.

High above the oldest part of Málaga is the Moorish **Alcazaba** (entrance on Plaza de la Duana, off C/Alcazabilla). Under the Moors, Málaga was the most important port of al-Andalus, and from

English cemetery
*open Mon–Fri 10–12,
Sat–Sun 12–1*

Alcazaba
*open April–Oct Tues–Sat
9.30–8; Nov–Mar
8.30–7; adm*

contemporary references it seems also to have been one of its most beautiful cities. King Fernando thoroughly ruined it in the conquest of 1487, and after the expulsion of the Moors in 1568 little remained of its ancient distinction. Little, too, remains of the Alcazaba, except a few Moorish gates, but the site has been restored to a lovely series of terraced gardens, full of fountains and birdsong. At the top there's a small, virtually empty **museum**, in plain open-air galleries set around patios, which hint at the form of the old palace and are sparsely decorated with fragments of elaborate plasterwork salvaged from the ruins. The top of the Alcazaba also affords fine views over Málaga, beautifully framed by horseshoe arches.

The half-ruined **Roman theatre** next to the main entrance on the lower slopes of the hill is still being excavated, but works have advanced sufficiently for it to be used occasionally for outdoor concerts in the summer (check with the tourist office). Behind the Alcazaba you can make the long dusty walk to the **Gibralfaro**, the ruined Moorish castle that dominates the city, or pick up a shuttle bus. Just below the Alcazaba, overlooking the Paseo del Parque, note the chunky Art Nouveau **Ayuntamiento**, one of the more unusual buildings in Málaga.

On the opposite side of the Alcazaba is the **Museo Picasso**, C/San Agustín 8, in a restored 16th-century palace set around a patio dotted with orange trees. Picasso was a native of Málaga, although once he left it at the age of 14 he never returned. The gallery contains more than 200 of his works, making it one of the largest collections in Europe, and spans all genres and periods. Galleries I and II are dedicated to portraits, including an intense depiction of Picasso's tortured friend Casagemas, who committed suicide in Paris in 1901. The sketches in Gallery III illustrate Picasso's experimentation with space and form during the early years in Paris, and, in Gallery IV, the airy, abstract figures of *Three Women Dancing on a Grey Background* (1930) and *Woman Sunbathing* (1932) reflect Picasso's inter-war flirtation with Surrealism. The latter was a portrait of his latest muse and lover, Marie-Thérèse Walter, who appears again in a series of paintings in Gallery V (upstairs). Here, she gazes out coolly from the *Portrait of a Woman with a Green-Collar Dress* (1938), in marked contrast to Picasso's charged and passionate depictions of Dora Maar, with whom he lived from 1936. Galleries VI and VII contain lovely, nostalgia-filled sketches of Picasso's villa 'La Californie' in Cannes, portraits of Françoise Gilot, Picasso's companion for more than a decade, and colourful ceramics, like the playful *Pitcher in the Form of a Bird* (1947) and a tiny Pan-like figure with goat. The old goat himself got married again in 1961, to Jacqueline Roque – captured in the slim, silvery *Bust of a Woman* (1961) in Gallery IX. The magisterial later

Gibralfaro

open 9.30–9; adm; shuttle bus from outside the Alcazaba ticket office

⭐ **Museo Picasso**

t 96 560 27 31, www. museopicassomalaga. org; open Tues–Thurs 10–8, Fri–Sat 10–9; adm; tickets can be purchased in advance by calling t 90 124 62 46

12

Málaga and the Costa del Sol | Málaga

paintings and ceramics are displayed in Galleries X–XII, and include *Lunar Face* (1955–6), the joyful *Bather* (1971) and the monumental *Seated Woman with Playing Child* (1960).

⭐ Casa Natal Picasso
t 95 206 02 15;
open Mon–Sat 10–8,
Sun 10–2; adm

The artist's birthplace, **Casa Natal Picasso**, which incorporates the Picasso Foundation, is just around the corner on Plaza de la Merced, and has acquired a substantial collection of works by *malagueño* artists, along with a small but interesting collection of ceramics, illustrated books and graphics by the man himself. There are temporary exhibitions on the ground floor, plus a gift shop with posters and all kinds of knick-knacks stamped with a Picasso design, and three galleries on the first floor dedicated to his work.

Cathedral
open Mon–Fri 9–6.45,
Sat 9–5.45; closed
Sun; adm

Málaga's **cathedral** is a few blocks away on Calle Molina Larios. Known as *La Manquita* (the one-armed lady), it's an ugly, unfinished 16th-century work, immense and mouldering, its only interesting feature the faded, gaudy façade of the sacristy, left over from the earlier Isabelline Gothic church that once stood here.

Centro de Arte Contemporaneo
t 95 212 00 55,
www.cacmalaga.org;
open summer Tues–Sun
10–2 and 5–9; winter
Tues–Sun 10–8

Museo de Artes Populares
open Mon–Fri 10–1.30
and 4–7, Sat 10–1.30;
closed Sun; adm

Further west and close to the garden-filled river bed, the **Centro de Arte Contemporaneo** (C/Alemania s/n), in a striking angular Rationalist building from the 1930s, houses works from Spanish and international artists including Eduardo Chillida, Susana Solano and Miquel Barceló. It also hosts usually excellent temporary exhibitions. Nearby, the **Museo de Artes Populares**, Pasillo de Santa Isabel 10, occupies a restored 17th-century inn with a collection of often charming household bric-a-brac and local costumes.

Jardines de la Finca de la Concepción
open 10–dusk; adm

The **Jardines de la Finca de la Concepción**, an old farm 5km north of Málaga (just off the CN-331), has been transformed into Spain's second most important botanical gardens. They were founded in the mid-19th century by Jorge Loring and Amalia Heredia, who encouraged ships' captains to bring them plants from around the world. The gardens passed on to the Echevarría family, who eventually could no longer afford their upkeep, and by the time Málaga city council bought them in 1990 they had grown into a virtual jungle. After a good deal of pruning, they were reopened in 1994 and now display a variety of plants from around the world, including a 700-year-old Canary Islands Dragon Tree.

For some reason the tourist industry has neglected the areas east of the city. There are a few resorts strung out along the coastal highway, notably **Torre del Mar**, but they are all grim-looking places: little bits of Málaga that escaped to the beach. Nearby are some scanty remains of **Mainake**, a Greco-Phoenician settlement.

Melilla

Nobody ever goes to Melilla, the more obscure of Spain's two remaining *presidios* on the North African coast. It's a long boat ride from Málaga, or a slightly shorter one from Almería, and onward destinations are severely limited. Morocco's big towns are far away, though you may consider Melilla a quieter, less exasperating way to slip into Morocco than Tangier or Tetuán (*see* p.223), with their hustlers and aggravations. The town itself is prettier than Ceuta, hiding behind stern-looking fortifications over the water's edge, a mile-long beach spreading awkwardly from the walls.

Where to Stay in Málaga

ⓘ Málaga >

Main office: Avda Cervantes 1, t 95 260 44 10; open Mon–Sat 8–8

Provincial information office: Pasaje Chinitas 4, t 95 221 34 45

Airport: t 95 224 37 84; open Mon–Sat 9–2

Booth at the main bus station, t 95 235 00 61

★ Larios >

ⓘ Melilla

C/Fortuny 21, t 95 267 54 44, www.melilla.es

Málaga ✉ 29000

★★★★Larios, Marqués de Larios 2, t 95 222 22 00, *www.hotel-larios.com* (€€€€€). Well appointed and very comfortable (cheaper at weekends), with a fabulous roof terrace.

★★★★Parador de Málaga Golf, Apartado de Correos 324, t 95 238 12 55, *www.parador.es* (€€€€€–€€€€). A modern resort hotel, just beyond the airport on the way to Torremolinos, with a heavy emphasis on golf. Also has a swimming pool.

★★★★Cortijo la Reina, Ctra Málaga–Colmenar, km 548.5, t 95 101 40 00, *www.hotelcortijolareina.com* (€€€€). A beautiful, rural hotel in the mountains 4km from the city, with elegant gardens and every four-star luxury.

★★★★AC Málaga Palacio, Avda Cortina del Muelle 1, t 95 221 51 85, *www.ac-hotels.com* (€€€€). Part of the ultra-modern AC chain, with an excellent location at the top of the Alameda, and sweeping views over the port.

★★★★Parador de Gibralfaro, Castillo de Gibralfaro s/n, 29016, t 95 222 19 02, *www.parador.es* (€€€€). A modern, stone-built *parador* next to the Moorish castle above the city, with a swimming pool; offers the best view of Málaga, and is one of the nicest places to stay, following a facelift. A great terrace for lunch outside.

★★★Hotel Don Curro, C/Sancha de Lara 7, t 95 222 72 00, *www.hoteldoncurro.com* (€€€). Just behind the Alameda and a few hundred yards from the cathedral. Bar, restaurant and – er – bingo hall attached.

★★★Hotel del Pintor, C/Álamos 27, t 95 206 09 80, *www.hoteldelpintor.com* (€€€). A sleek new hotel with original paintings by local artist and owner Pepe Bornoy. Contemporary décor and utterly charming service.

★★★Humaina, Parque Natural Montes de Málaga, Carretera del Colmenar, t 95 264 1025, *www.hotelhumaina.es* (€€€–€€). 16km north of the city surrounded by a thickly forested park; the rooms are painted a sunny yellow and plenty of activities are available including riding, bird-watching and walks. There's an excellent restaurant.

★★Hotel Carlos V, C/Císter 10, t 95 221 41 20, *carlosv@spa.es* (€€). Convenient location, and well-equipped rooms for a modest price. The garage is a plus.

★★★Las Acacias, Paseo Acacias 5, t 95 229 75 60 (€€–€). The most charming budget option, this pretty *hostal* is set in a lovely 19th-century villa close to the beach 6km from the city centre.

★Alameda, C/Casas de Campos 3, t 95 222 20 99 (€€–€). A central hotel with reasonable if unexceptional rooms with or without bathrooms.

★Castillo, C/Don Fernando 40, t 95 284 30 90, *www.castillahotel.com* (€€–€). A modern hotel, but in an elegant building right in the historic centre. The rooms are bright and comfortable and the downstairs restaurant serves good traditional food.

Eating Out in Málaga

Adolfo, Paseo Marítimo Ruiz Picasso 12, t 95 260 19 14 (€€€). A smart restaurant in a perfect location on the Malagueta beach; excellent grilled meats as well as seafood.

Café de Paris, C/Vélez-Málaga 8, t 95 222 50 43 (€€€). Perhaps the best place in Málaga to try truly innovative Mediterranean cuisine, accompanied by an excellent wine list.

La Mensula, C/Trinidad Grund 28, t 95 222 13 14 (€€€–€€). Fronted by a traditional tapas bar, hung with hams. The dining room is elegant yet rustically cosy with beams, arches and a barrel vault ceiling. Menu includes stone-cooked steak. *Closed Sun.*

Antonio Martín, Playa de la Malagueta, t 95 222 21 13 (€€). Locals flock to the many beachfront restaurants in Paseo Marítimo and the El Palo district east of town, on Sunday especially. This place is a favourite, with fish and rice dishes.

El Cabra, C/Copo 21, Pso El Pedregal, t 95 229 50 70 (€€). One of the best known restaurants, with a pricier range of seafood and a terrace.

Casa Pedro, C/Quitapenas 57, El Palo, t 95 229 00 13 (€€). You may well be deafened by the din as you tuck into skewered sardines or Sierra-style monkfish. *Closed Mon eve.*

Mesón Astorga, C/Gerona 11, t 95 234 25 63 (€€). A really atmospheric *malagueño* restaurant that's on the up and up – a good place to enjoy a long, late lunch.

Mesón El Chinitas, C/Moreno Monroy 4–6, t 95 221 09 72 (€€). A local legend, with bullfighting and flamenco memorabilia. There's a pricey, smart restaurant, and very good tapas at the bar. A lovely terrace, too.

Antigua Casa de Guardia, Alameda 18, t 95 221 46 80 (€). For sherry, shrimps and a marvellous atmosphere, choose a drink from one of the 20 or so barrels lining the bar.

⭐ **El Vegetariano de la Alcazabilla** >

El Vegetariano de la Alcazabilla, Pozo del Rey 5, t 95 221 48 58 (€). Excellent vegetarian restaurant with a daily set menu and plenty of choice including pasta, vegetable turnovers and salads. Plus a reasonable wine list and delicious desserts and cakes.

Media Luna, C/Marques 6, t 95 222 59 47 (€). Tucked down a side street off Plaza de la Constitución, this earthy local bar and restaurant is Moroccan owned and has delicious couscous.

⭐ **Bar Lo Güeno** >

Bar Lo Güeno, Marín García 9 (€). Head here for tapas – it's literally a hole in the wall serving imaginative *raciones* and a decent choice of wines.

Café Cosmopolita, C/Marqués de Larios (€). Start your day with breakfast at this café, where tables spill onto the pavement and surround the wooden horseshoe bar inside. Service is outrageously slow but at least this allows you to relax over a paper from the kiosk next door, or watch the shoeshine boys at work.

Orellana, C/Moreno Monroy 5, t 95 222 30 12 (€). One of the city's oldest and most classic tapas bars (they still offer a free *tapa* – or 'lid' – with your first glass of sherry).

Mesón la Aldea, C/Esparteros 5, t 95 222 76 89 (€). A great tapas restaurant, with a speciality of the house you won't find anywhere else in Málaga: *carne al curry.*

Rincón del Tillo, C/Esparteros, t 95 222 31 35 (€). A more upmarket *taberna* opposite Mesón la Aldea. *Closed Sun.*

La Tetería, C/San Agustín 9. Málaga is also, slowly, discovering its Moorish roots, and a number of Moroccan-style tea rooms have opened. This one serves various couscous dishes, cakes and mint tea.

Nightlife in Málaga

Málaga has a buzzing summer club scene. On Friday or Saturday nights, it's hard to move between Plaza de la Constitución and Plaza de Siglo. Some of the best bars are to be found around **Plaza de Uncibay**, **C/Granada** and **Plaza de la Merced**. A few bars and disco-bars can also be found down by the bullring. In summer, the action moves out to the city beaches, particularly **Pedragalejo** and **El Palo**.

Bar Pimpi, C/Granada. A good place to start your nocturnal wanderings – a small doorway leads into a courtyard with rooms off every angle – cellars, patios, balconies – full of beautiful Malagueños.

El Cantor de Jazz, C/Lazcano 7. Smoky, sophisticated jazz joint, with live acts on Thursdays.

Gibralfaro Bar, Pasaje de Chinitas. Anything can happen in this appealingly scruffy bar; you might be treated to some impromptu flamenco. Tapas and a terrace.

Liceo, C/Beatas 21. A lively disco-bar, popular with students.

Onda Passadena, C/Gómez Pallete 9. Live music (everything from flamenco to pop), a mini dance floor, cheap drinks and a friendly young crowd.

Terraza Larios, C/Marqués de Larios 2. Sleek cocktail bar (open spring and summer only) at the Hotel Larios; has a terrace with gorgeous city views.

The Serranía de Ronda

The Serranía de Ronda is a region of difficult topography, and it made life difficult for most would-be conquerors. A band of southern Celts gave the Romans fits in these mountains; various Christian chieftains held out for centuries against the Moors; and to return the favour the Moors kept Castile at bay here until 1485, just seven years before the conquest of Granada.

Ronda

 Ronda

Ronda, the only city in the Serranía, is a beautiful place, blessed with a perfect postcard shot of its lofty bridge over the steep gorge that divides the old and new towns. Because of its proximity to the Costa del Sol, it has lately become the only really tourist-ridden corner of the interior. The town's monuments are few; what Fernando the Catholic didn't wreck in 1485, the French finished off in 1809. Ronda saw plenty of trouble in the Civil War, with hundreds of bodies tossed into the gorge (the exact numbers, and who was doing the tossing, depend on who is telling the story).

Don't be discouraged from a visit; the views from the top of the city alone are worth the trip. One of the best places from which to enjoy them is the **Alameda del Tajo**, a park on the edge of the **Mercadillo**, as the new town is called. At its northern end is the 16th-century Carmelite **Convento de la Merced** on the *plaza* of the same name, where the nuns will sell you sweets (down the Pasaje de Letrán). Next to it, Ronda has one of Spain's oldest and most picturesque bullrings. The 1785 **Plaza de Toros**, the 'cathedral of bullfighting', stages only about three *corridas* a year – including *La Goyesca* at the beginning of September, in traditional 18th-century costume – but it still has great prestige: the art of bullfighting was developed here. There's also a small **bullfighting museum**, at Virgen de la Paz 15, which has a selection of pictures, costumes and photos, including those of Orson Welles, who wished his ashes to be scattered in the bullring, and Ernest Hemingway, who mentions the bullring in *Death in the Afternoon*.

Bullfighting museum
open daily 10–8; adm

Ronda's other landmark, the **Puente Nuevo**, was built at the second try in 1740 – the first one immediately collapsed. The bridge's two thick piers descend almost 92m (300ft) to the bottom of the narrow gorge; you can find out more about its construction in the **Centro de Interpretación**, in a former tavern built into one of the piers, which is dull but offers vertiginous views into the gorge.

Centro de Interpretación
open Mon–Fri 10–7, Sat–Sun 10–3; adm

The main square, **Plaza de Socorro**, is where most of the town comes out before dinner. It is flanked by a church, **Nuestra Señora del Socorro**, and a number of bars and restaurants both on and off the side streets.

Getting to and around the Serranía de Ronda

By Bus

Without a car in this region, you'll be depending on buses, run by **Amarillos**, **t** 95 218 70 61, or **Portillo**, **t** 95 287 22 62. From Ronda you can go directly to Jerez, Cádiz, Málaga, Sevilla and most of the towns along the Costa del Sol. Ronda has connections to villages in the hinterlands – usually only once a day, so if you're day-tripping, make sure there's a return.

Ronda's **bus station** is in the new town, on the Plaza de Concepción, Glorieta Redondo 2, **t** 95 287 26 57.

By Train

Ronda has trains, too; no direct trains to Málaga (the bus is the best bet), but at least three a day for Algeciras, with connections at Bobadilla Junction for Madrid and for the other cities of Andalucía. Some trains stop at Gaucín and Setenil. The **station** is on the edge of town at Avda Alférez Provisional s/n, **t** 90 224 02 02.

By Car

When you are travelling by car, be warned that some streets of the Serranía towns and villages are very narrow, and difficult for a large vehicle to negotiate.

Museo Lara
open daily 10–8; adm; flamenco performances summer Thurs–Sat at 10pm

Museo Peinado
open Mon–Sat 10–2 and 5–8, Sun 10–2; adm

Casa del Gigante
open Mon–Fri 10–7, Sat–Sun 10–3; adm

Palacio de Mondragón
open Mon–Fri 10–6, Sat–Sun 10–3; adm

Santa María La Mayor
open daily 10–7; adm

Casa Juan Bosco
open 9–5.30; adm

Museo del Bandolero
open daily summer 10–7; winter 10–6; adm

Casa del Rey Moro
open daily 10–8; adm

Crossing the bridge into the **Ciudad** (old town), continue up C/Armiñán to find the Museo Lara, with a fascinating collection of archaeological bits and bobs, pistols, paintings, clocks and old cameras housed in the sumptuous 18th-century Casa Palacio de los Condes de la Conquista. It also hosts flamenco performances.

West along C/Moctezuma, another lavish palace contains the Museo Peinado, dedicated to Rondeño artist Joaquín Peinado. Opposite, the Casa del Gigante contains the sparse remnants of a lavish town house built under the Nasrids, with fragments of lavish plaster work and scorched artesonado ceilings. It gets its name, the 'Giant's House', from a strange, amorphous statue discovered in the walls. The Palacio de Mondragón, in Plaza Mondragón, is one of Ronda's most beautiful palaces, where Fernando and Isabel bedded down on their visits; now it's the town's museum with local finds and some well-preserved patios and woodwork. Just east of here is the town's main church, Santa María La Mayor, still retaining the mihrab and minaret of the mosque it replaced, and with an interior apparently inspired by Granada's cathedral and the ruins of the Alcázar, blown up by the French. Also in the old town is the Casa Juan Bosco, C/Tenorio 20, a 19th-century mansion that is now a college, with beautiful gardens and fountains, while the Museo del Bandolero, C/Armiñán 59, up from the Arab walls, offers a look at the region's past of banditry.

A steep cobbled street heads downwards to a clutch of 18th-century palaces: the **Palacio de Salvatierra**, a Renaissance mansion still used as a private house, and the Casa del Rey Moro, built over Moorish foundations. From the garden of the Casa del Rey Moro there is a stairway – 365 steps, cut out of the rock, called *La Mina* – that takes you down to the bottom of the gorge: best stay in the charming little garden, as the reward for the clamber down the dank, dark steps is only a close-up view of the smelly, stagnant river. Further down from the Casa del Rey Moro you reach the **Puente Viejo**, the old Moorish bridge, and, a little further along, the well-preserved remains of a Moorish bath. Inside you can make out the individual pools and changing rooms and see the graceful arches, reminiscent of a mini-Mezquita. Beyond this, the city walls start; you can walk along the walls, with views out over the *vega*.

Moorish bath
*t 656 950 937 (mobile);
open Mon–Fri 10–7,
Sat–Sun 10–3; adm*

Across the Puente Viejo, to the north, is the Gothic-*mudéjar* **Convento de San Francisco**, founded by Fernando and Isabel in 1485. It has an arch with florid decoration and sports the coat of arms of the Franciscan monks. From here, a pleasant walk back up to town runs via the **Jardines Ciudad de Cuenca**, a series of tiered viewing platforms on the side of the gorge.

For wonderful views of the town, head out of Ronda on the C/Torrejores towards Algeciras and take a right towards the Iglesia de la Virgen de la Cabeza, which is about 2km away. The building dates from the 9th century and is built into the rock. Come towards sunset when the dying rays illuminate the rock. There are some excellent walking trails around Ronda – including one to the chapel of Virgen de la Cabeza – described in leaflets available from the tourist office, or online at *www.turismoronda.org*.

Iglesia de la Virgen de la Cabeza
open Mon–Sat 10.30–2; adm

Where to Stay in Ronda

(i) **Ronda >**
*Plaza de España 1,
t 95 287 12 72; open
Mon–Fri 10–2 and 4–7,
Sat 10–3; also Paseo de
Blas Infante (by the
bullring), t 95 218 71 19;
open Mon–Fri 9.30–
7.30, Sat–Sun 10–2
and 3–6.30*

Ronda ✉ 29400

Ronda has a wide choice in all ranges. There are dozens of small *hostales* and *camas* over bars – most of them quite agreeable – on the side streets of **C/Jerez** in the Mercadillo.

La Fuente de la Higuera, Partido de los Frontones, t 95 211 43 55, *www.hotel lafuente.com* (€€€€€–€€€€). A sensitively converted mill is now a stylish hotel surrounded by olive groves and mountain. The rooms are decorated with real flair and there's a library and bar; dinner on request.

****Hotel Molino del Arco**, Partido de los Frontones s/n, t 95 211 40 17, *www.hotelmolinodelarco.com* (€€€€). An exquisite, luxurious hotel 8km from Ronda, with rooms and suites painted in tranquil shades of white and cream. There's a pool and excellent restaurant.

****Reina Victoria**, Avda Fleming, t 95 287 12 40 (€€€€). A fine and handsome old hotel, which can no longer afford to rest on its laurels. Built by the British around the turn of the century as a retreat for the military in Gibraltar, and now run by the Husa chain, the hotel has lovely views over the cliffs. The German poet Rainer Maria Rilke stayed here for a season in 1912, and wrote some of his best-known works; his room 208 is preserved as a museum.

****Hotel Maestranza**, C/Virgen de la Paz 24, t 95 218 70 72, *www.hotel maestranza.com* (€€€€). This former residence of Pedro Romero, the legendary bullfighter, is one of the best options in town. It is in an excellent position just yards from the bullring and the heart of town, and with all the four-star comforts you would expect, including the use of a country club with pool and tennis courts. It also has a good restaurant, **Sol y Sombra**.

****Parador de Ronda**, Pza de España, t 95 287 75 00, *www.parador.es* (€€€€). This newish *parador* preserves the façade of the old town hall, but is painfully modern inside. It is the flagship of the *parador* chain; comfort and service are excellent, and the views from the duplex suites are matchless. The restaurant has an excellent-value menu.

***Polo**, C/Mariano Soubirón 8, **t** 95 287 24 47, *www.hotelpolo.net* (€€€). A busy little place in the centre of town, with pretty blue and white rooms at a modest price that makes it popular with tour groups.

Ancinipo, C/José Aparicio 7, **t** 95 216 10 01, *www.hotelacinipo.com* (€€€). This central hotel has a striking interior of exposed stone panels, steel and glass fittings, mosaic-tile bathrooms, dramatic murals and paintings. The restaurant attracts a loyal following with dishes like oxtail stew.

(★) Hotel San Gabriel >

***Hotel San Gabriel**, C/Marqués de Moctezuma 19, **t** 95 219 03 92, *www.hotelsangabriel.com* (€€€). Probably the loveliest hotel in town in terms of décor, service, atmosphere and value; a private house from 1736 before its conversion to a hotel in 1998. Wood panelling and old prints line the walls, plus there's billiards, a café and a lovely, shaded patio. Bedrooms are individually designed.

Alavera de los Baños, C/San Miguel s/n, **t** 95 287 91 43, *www.andalucia.com/alavera* (€€€). A beautiful little whitewashed hotel with beamed ceilings and gardens. Slightly inconvenient in that it's at the bottom of town, next to the Moorish baths; but it is in a pretty setting and has a pool, restaurant and rooms with *terrazas* to watch the sunrise over the hills.

Hotel Don Miguel, C/Villanueva 4 and 8, **t** 95 287 77 22, *www.dmiguel.com* (€€€). Very good value for such a great spot on the cliff edge and opposite the *parador*. Excellent restaurant.

Enfrente Arte, C/Real 42, **t** 95 287 47 33, *www.enfrentearte.com* (€€€). A stylish Belgian-owned guesthouse, in an old inn surrounded by tropical gardens. Filled with quirky art. The price includes a lavish breakfast and use of the sauna and outdoor pool.

Hostal El Tajo, C/Cruz Verde 5, **t** 95 287 40 40 (€€). A simple, modest *hostal* with recently refurbished rooms, all with TV and air-conditioning.

Royal, C/Virgen de la Paz 42, **t 95 287 11 41 (€€). Modern and charmless, but in a good spot near the bullring.

Hostal Virgen del Rocío, C/Nueva 18, **t** 95 287 74 25 (€€–€). A friendly, central little place, with a restaurant.

Eating Out in Ronda

Quite a few really inferior tourist restaurants have been opening in conspicuous places to take advantage of day-trippers from the Costa.

Tragabuches, C/Jose Aparicio 1, **t** 95 219 02 91 (€€€). This is a *cuatro tenedores* place, Spain's top award for a restaurant, so you know you are in for a treat. The food is traditional *andaluz* cuisine combined with some unexpected flavours. The warm chocolate soufflé and ice-cream pud is out of this world. You can buy a cookbook with the best recipes. Superb wine list. *Closed Mon.*

Duquesa de Parcent, C/Tenorio 12, **t** 95 219 07 63 (€€€–€€). The place you can see from the bridge, with three tiered terraces perched above the gorge. This 19th-century house has been sumptuously renovated inside, and features grilled pork and lamb and fish in salt crust as the house specials. Ideal for an early evening drink as you watch the sun set over the mountains.

Casa Santa Pola, C/Santo Domingo 3, **t** 95 287 92 08 (€€). Set in a 9th-century Moorish mosque, with a terrace by the river, and great décor inside; the food is traditional *andaluz* and Rondan – roast meats and fresh fish. Flamenco show on Fridays and Saturdays (phone for details).

Doña Pepa, Plaza del Socorro 10 (overlooking the square), **t** 95 287 47 77, *restopepa@ronda.net* (€€). A good bet around the Mercadillo, with quail sautéed in garlic, and partridge.

Don Miguel, Villanueva 4, **t** 95 287 10 90 (€€). At the hotel of the same name. Some of the best meals Ronda can offer, by the gorge next to the famous bridge.

Escudero, Chalet del Tajo, Paseo de Blas Infante 1, **t** 90 243 45 45 (€€). This has a lovely garden setting and serves traditional dishes such as roasts and grills. It has probably the best view in town, just behind the bullring. Good-value lunch menu.

Pedro Romero, Virgen de la Paz 18, **t** 95 287 11 10 (€€). Opposite the bullring and decorated with bullfighting paraphernalia; the food here is similarly traditional, with oxtail and stewed partridge on the menu, as well as the more unusual house dessert of fig ice cream topped with chocolate sauce.

La Farola, Plaza de Carmen Abela s/n, **t** 95 287 91 52 (€). A friendly, family-run bar serving a great range of tapas, and some home-cooked dishes.

Tréz, C/Los Remedios 27, **t** 95 287 72 07 (€). Mellow, friendly vegetarian café, with wooden tables and ochre walls. Good sandwiches, juices and cakes.

Nightlife in Ronda

Ronda doesn't really rock, but there are one or two late-night bars dotted around.

Café las Bridas, C/Los Remedios 16/18. One of several bars on this busy street. This has a flamenco flavour – but also serves Guinness on tap.

El Choque Ideal, C/Espiritu Santo 9. A trendy café-bar which also functions as a fashion store and art gallery.

Around Ronda

Besides the opportunities for walks in and around the valleys under Ronda, an interesting excursion can be made to an area of curiosities 15–20km west of town. The hills around the hamlet of **Montejaque** are full of caves. Two of them, the **Cueva del Gato** and **Cueva del Hundidero**, both full of stalactites and odd formations, are connected. A little stream, the Gaduares, disappears into one cave and comes out in the other. Five kilometres south, past the village of **Benaoján**, the Cueva de la Pileta has some 25,000-year-old art – simple drawings in black of animals and magic symbols.

Cueva de la Pileta www.cuevadelapileta. org, **t** 95 216 72 42; open mid-April–Oct daily 10–1 and 4–6; Nov–mid-April daily 4–5 only; adm

Twelve kilometres west of Ronda, off the road to Grazalema, are the Roman ruins of Acinipo known locally as **Ronda la Vieja**, with a theatre and stage building like Mérida's. If you have a car or even a bicycle, take the 40km 'scenic route' along the spectacular MA549, which leaves Ronda to the southwest. From Benaoján the road wends down towards **Cortes de la Frontera**, a village founded by the Phoenicians, with a wonderful main square surrounded by old mansions adorned with the previous owners' coats of arms. It's worth making a brief detour (along the MA508) to **Jimera de Líbar**, which has an ancient castle of Moorish and Roman origins. From Jimera you can strike out on a number of walking routes.

Walking routes information from the ayuntamiento, **t** 95 218 00 04

From Cortes the MA512 twists and turns via the tiny village of **El Colmenar**. You'll pass by the villages of **Atajate**, **Benadalid** and **Algatocín** before reaching the ancient village of **Gaucín**. This agreeable but undistinguished place has become a magnet for a certain kind of American and English expat, including a number of artists, who came here in the 1970s and '80s looking for the 'real' Spain. From their balconies, they have remarkable views of Gibraltar and the African coast over the peaks of the Serranía.

On the way back to Ronda, stop in at the tiny village of **Genalguacil**, east along the MA536 after Algatocín. The village has been turned into an open-air art museum, with sculptures of wood, ceramics, iron and pottery brightening up the streets and squares, and there's an annual art festival in early August.

The scenery of the Serranía is justly famous; mountains and ravines sprinkled with tiny white villages nestling under crags, hair-raising mountain passes and a wilderness where vultures, golden eagles and ibex can be spotted. Much of it has been turned into nature reserves: to the east lies the **Reserva Nacional de Serranía de Ronda**, to the southwest the **Reserva Nacional de Cortes de la Frontera**, and to the northwest the **Parque Natural Sierra de Grazalema** (*see* pp.210–13). There are many walking routes and plenty of outdoor activities such as rock climbing, potholing and horse riding to detain you, as well as natural sights: caves, gorges, lakes and rivers. There are also some wonderful restaurants and hotels tucked away in the hills and villages.

Ronda to Málaga

A far more relaxing and scenic route to Málaga than the hectic N340 takes you inland along the twisting and turning A366: all stone outcrops and dark hills. The road passes by a little-known nature reserve, the **Sierra de las Nieves**, which has a huge pine forest dating back to prehistoric times, as well as a number of birds including goshawks, sparrowhawks and falcons.

The first place of any note is **El Burgo**, a typical white town nestling in a valley. From here you can take a number of walks or stop for a bite to eat. The road passes the northern limit of the reserve before dropping down towards the dusty town of **Coín** and then east to Málaga or west to Marbella.

Where to Stay and Eat around Ronda

Benarrabá ✉ 29490

**Hotel Banú Rabbah, C/Sierra Bermeja s/n, t 95 215 02 88, *www.hbenarraba.es* (€€). Has a huge swimming pool which you can spot from the main road, attached to a very reasonably priced and comfortable hotel on the edge of the pine forest, with a nice restaurant.

Benaoján ✉ 29370

***Molino del Santo, Bda Estación, t 95 216 71 51, *www.molinodelsanto.com* (€€€€). A British couple run this converted water mill beside a mountain stream, close to the Pileta caves and with a spring-fed swimming pool. The kitchen serves up local ingredients. It's friendly and intimate and offers details on excursions, including local hikes.

Casitas de la Sierra, C/Estrecha 3, Montejaque, t 95 216 73 92, *www.casitasdelasierra.com* (€€). Furnished village houses with all mod cons; a cheaper and more rustic option.

Gaucín ✉ 29400

**Hotel Casablanca, C/Teodoro de Molina 12, t 95 215 10 19, *www.casablanca-gaucin.com* (€€€€€). An exquisite boutique hotel with just eight delightful rooms in magnificent gardens with magnolia, palm and Jacaranda trees overlooking the roof and mountains. Pool, restaurant.

La Fructuosa, C/Convento 67, t 95 215 10 72, *www.lafructuosa.com* (€€€). This rural hotel has beautifully decorated rooms, some with Jacuzzi, and a charming self-catering cottage. The excellent restaurant, a highly recommended place for a romantic dinner or a lazy lunch, is *open to non-guests on Saturdays only*.

El Pilar, Ctra Ronda-Algeciras, opposite filling station, t 95 215 13 47 (€). A real workman's *comedor*, but with a nobleman's view from the terrace on a sunny day. Offers an excellent-value lunch with wine.

Genalguacil ✉ 29492

Centro de Iniciativas Turísticas, t 95 227 62 29, *www.ruralandalus.es*. Genalguacil has no hotels, but it does have a wealth of *casas rurales*. Contact this central reservation office for details. There are also a number of *casas rurales* in Jimera de Líbar.

Benalauría ✉ 29491

Mesón La Molienda, C/Moraleda 59, t 95 215 25 48, *www.molienda.com* (€€). A restaurant with rooms, set in an old olive mill; specializes in mountain dishes with a Moorish influence. Magnificent views across the Serranía.

El Burgo ✉ 29420

La Casa Grande, C/Mesones 1, t 95 216 02 32, *www.hotel-lacasagrande.com* (€€). Spotlessly clean and done out in an old style with beams and brickwork and a wonderful shaded patio.

Antequera and Around

Antequera

⚑ Antequera

Known in Roman times as Antiquaria, this was the first of the Granadan border fortresses to fall to the Reconquista, in 1410, although subsequently it was retaken by the Moors and lost again. The centre of a leather-tanning industry, set below an outcrop overlooking the vega, Antequera is one of the architectural showpieces of the entire region, with an impressive ensemble of 16th–18th-century buildings.

It is topped by the ruined **Alcazaba**, where you can stroll around the gardens and admire beautiful views over the spires and rooftops. The **Nájera Palace** houses the **Municipal Museum**, with many religious works including a *St Francis* by Alonso Cano and a Roman bronze of a young boy, known as 'Ephebus of Antequera'.

Up the Cuesta Zapateros is the 16th-century **Arco de los Gigantes**, meant as a sort of triumphal arch for the seldom-victorious Philip II; next to it, the ruins of a Moorish **fortress** offer views over the town to one of the main landmarks of the area: **La Peña de los Enamorados** (Lovers' Rock), halfway between the town and Archidona. It looks like the head of a sleeping giant and is known colloquially as 'Franco's nose', but it got its name from the legend of a Moorish girl who fell in love with a Christian boy; realizing they could never be together in life, they threw themselves from the rock. Nearby is the Plateresque church of **Santa María La Mayor**, attached to which is an art restoration centre. Next to the church are some recently discovered Roman baths (*termas romanas*), still glittering in places with faded mosaics. To the east of the square lies **La Iglesia del Carmen**, which has one of Andalucía's finest Baroque altars. At the **Museo Convento de Las Descalzas** on the Plaza de las Descalzas, you can visit the museum of religious art, or pick up some sweet treats from the cloistered nuns.

Municipal Museum
open Tues 10–1.30, Wed–Fri 10–1.30 and 8.30–10.30, Sat 10–1.30, Sun and hols |11–1.30; adm

Santa María La Mayor
open Tues 10.30–2, Wed–Fri 10.30–2 and 8.30–10.30, Sat 10.30–2, Sun 11.30–2

La Iglesia del Carmen
open Mon 11–2, Tues–Fri and Sun 10–2, Sat 10–2 and 4–7; adm

Museo Convento de Las Descalzas
t 95 284 19 59; open Tues–Fri 10.30–1.30 and 6–7.30, Sat 10–12; adm

Getting to and around Antequera

Antequera is on the **rail** line from Algeciras to Granada, and there are easy connections to all points from nearby Bobadilla Junction. The **station** is on Avenida de la Estación, **t** 90 224 02 02.

Lots of **buses** go to Málaga and Sevilla, fewer to Granada and Córdoba, as well as to Olvera, Osuna and other villages. The **bus station**, **t** 95 284 19 57, is at Campillo Alto s/n, at the top of town, near the *parador*.

To the west of the Alcazaba, on the Plaza de Portichuelo, **Capilla de la Virgen de Socorro** stakes a claim as one of the prettiest churches in Antequera, with a combination of architectural styles ranging from Baroque to *mudéjar*.

North and West of Antequera

Heading northwest out of Antequera into the gentler hills flanking the southern slopes of the Guadalquivir valley, you'll be on your way to Sevilla via Estepa and Osuna (*see* p.132). If you're going that way, turn off the N334 at Fuente de Piedra and you'll come to the **Laguna de Fuente de Piedra**, one of Europe's largest breeding grounds for flamingos from March to September.

Mollina, a tiny village at the top of Málaga province, has a history dating back to Neolithic times, while its name comes from Norman times when it was known as Mollis, or 'drizzle', as in olive oil. There are some 40 caves at **La Sierra de la Camorra**, about 6km north of the village, and a 17th-century church, **Nuestra Señora de la Oliva**. Roman monuments include the 2nd-century **Mausoleo de la Capuchina**, and the 3rd-century **Castellum de Santillon**, in the park 3km from town.

East of Antequera

The Romans may have given Antequera its name, 'old town', and there was probably a settlement here some centuries before the arrival of the Phoenicians. Another possibility is that the name is related to *anta*, the local word for dolmen. Just out of town are the Neolithic monuments known as the **Cuevas de Menga**, the 'first real architecture in Spain'. They are hardly as impressive as the *talayots* and *taulas* of the island of Menorca, but there's nothing like them elsewhere on mainland Spain. Le Corbusier came here in the 1950s, as he said, 'to pay homage to my predecessors'. There are

Menga and Viera dolmens
open Tues–Sat 9–6, Sun 10–2.30

three, dating from anything between 4500 BC and 2500 BC. The two largest, the **Menga and Viera dolmens**, are covered chambers about 21m (70ft) long, roughly elliptical and lined with huge, flat stones; other monoliths support the roof-like pillars. Nearby at

El Romeral dolmen
open Tues–Sat 9–6, Sun 10–2.30

El Romeral, under a mound and in the grounds of a sugar factory, the third of these temples has two chambers with domed ceilings. Originally the mound would have been about 100 metres in diameter, as big as Newgrange in Ireland. All three have figures and symbols etched around the walls.

Fifteen kilometres east of Antequera on the N342 is **Archidona**. The town overlooks acres of olive trees, but its main feature is the unique, octagonal Plaza Mayor, the **Ochavada**. Built between 1780 and 1786 by Francisco Astorga and Antonio González, it is one of the loveliest *plazas* in Andalucía, and was built using stones from El Torcal (*see* below).

In nearby **Loja** is the 16th-century church of **San Gabriel**, which has a cupola attributed to Diego de Siloé. The town's other main sites, which can be seen on the approach from Antequera, are the hilltop ruins of its Moorish **castle** and, just below, the **Santuario de la Virgen de Gracia**, a simple brick building built over a mosque. Inside is a font, a gift from Queen Isabel. The views across the *vega* to the **Peña de los Enamorados** and the olive-tree clad slopes are impressive.

Santuario de la Virgen de Gracia
open May–Aug daily 7–2 and 5–10; Feb–April and Sept–Oct daily 8–2 and 4–8; Nov–Jan daily 9–2 and 3–7

South of Antequera

The sierras between Antequera and Málaga contain some of the remote villages of the region and offer some spectacular scenery – almond trees, cacti, olive groves and mountains that drop steeply away to the silver ribbon of a stream down below. A spectacular natural park has been laid out around the rock formations at **El Torcal**, a tall but hikeable mountain with unusual red limestone crags. The nearest town is **Villanueva de la Concepción**, 14km south of Antequera (access to the park is off the A6311, which links the two towns). From Villanueva, take the MA424 and travel south for about 17km. You will be rewarded with **Almogía**, presenting a dramatic spectacle overlooking a high ridge. From 15 to 18 August this place comes to life with dancing in the streets in celebration of San Roque and San Sebastián. The best views are from the ruined tower.

El Torcal
*info centre at Torcal Alto, **t** 95 203 13 89*

The A343 south from Antequera will take you to the town of **Álora**. Originally a Roman settlement and one of the last towns to be held by the Moors, it is mainly of interest now as the point where you should turn northeast towards one of Andalucía's natural wonders. **El Chorro Gorge**, in the deep rugged canyon of the Río Guadalhorce, has sheer walls of limestone tossed about at crazy angles. It used to be possible to circumnavigate it on a concrete catwalk called El Camino del Rey, built in 1920 for Alfonso XIII, and poorly maintained ever since, but this has been permanently closed, after several terrible accidents. El Chorro has a train station on the Antequera–Málaga line, and you can get an excellent view of the gorge from the train.

If you have time to explore this region, seek out the church of **Bobastro**, a 9th-century basilica cut out of bare rock; it supposedly contains the tomb of ibn-Hafsun, the Christian emir who founded a short-lived independent state in the mountains around 880.

Some remains of the city and fortress he built can be seen on the heights nearby. The lakes were created as part of a large-scale hydroelectric scheme, but their shores, surrounded by gentle hills, make an ideal place to have a lazy picnic.

From Bobastro follow the road to **Carratraca**, a spa town from Greek and Roman times, though its heyday was in the 19th and early 20th centuries. Visitors to the spa on C/Baños 1 included Byron, Dumas, Rilke and Napoléon III's Spanish wife, the Empress Eugénie, who gadded about everywhere else in Europe and lived to the age of 94. Now the town is famous for its Passion play. As part of their *Semana Santa* celebrations, 140 of the villagers perform *El Paso* in the **bullring**.

From here the road winds its way back to Álora.

Carratraca spa
t 95 245 90 64

Where to Stay and Eat in and around Antequera

ⓘ **Antequera >**
Plaza San Sebastián 7,
t 95 270 25 05,
www.antequera.es;
open 10–2 and 5–8

Antequera ✉ 29200

****Hotel Conde de Pinofiel, t 95 284 24 64, *www.hotelcondepinofiel.com* (€€€). A beautiful Baroque town house which has retained many of its original lavish details, with elegant rooms set around a patio.

****Hotel Golf Antequera, Urbanización Santa Catalina s/n, **t** 95 270 45 31, *www.hotelantequera. com* (€€€). A modern complex with gym, golf, tennis, pool and restaurant.

***Parador de Antequera, Pso García del Olmo s/n, **t** 95 284 02 61, *www. parador.es* (€€€). A plain, modern building but with the most comforts in Antequera, including a pool; reasonably priced.

***Hotel Las Villas de Antikaria, Ctra de Córdoba 3, **t** 95 284 48 99, *www.hotellasvillas.com* (€€). A modern place near the bus station, lacking much character but with an excellent restaurant and bike hire. No pool.

***Hotel Mesón Papabellotas, C/Encarnación 5, **t** 95 270 50 45 (€€). Excellently sited in the heart of the old town, the hotel is a converted whitewashed town house.

Hotel Castilla, C/Infante de Fernando 40, **t 95 284 30 90 (€€–€). In a completely new building, but in the heart of the old town, with air-conditioning, bath and satellite TV.

Pension Madrona, C/Calzada 25, **t 95 284 00 14 (€). Clean and basic; does good *churros* and breakfasts.

*Hotel Nuevo Infante, C/Infante de Fernando 5, **t** 95 270 00 86 (€). Small apartments in the centre, equipped with kitchens.

El Angelote, C/Encarnación (corner of Coso Viejo), **t** 95 270 34 65 (€€). An excellent restaurant in the old town near the Palacio de la Nájera, serving Antequerana dishes.

Ca Serío de San Benito, Ctra Málaga-Córdoba, km 108, **t** 95 211 11 03 (€€). One of the finest restaurants in the area, in an elegant *cortijo*. Good Andalucian cuisine and service. *Closed Mon.*

Restaurante Plaza de Toros, Paseo María Cristina s/n, **t** 95 270 84 46 62 (€€). Unusually located inside the bullring; come for the location rather than the rather average food.

Nightlife is centred up and down the **Calle Alameda**, which has a number of tapas bars and pubs.

ⓘ **Archidona >>**
Plaza Ochavada 2,
t 95 271 64 79;
open Mon–Fri 10–1.30,
Sat 11–2

Archidona ✉ 29200

*****La Bobadilla, Finca La Bobadilla, A92, km 175, **t** 95 832 18 61, *www.la-bobadilla.com* (€€€€€). Turn off the road at the sign for Villanueva de Tapia, halfway to Loja. Replicates a typical Andalucian *pueblo*, complete with Moorish touches, set in oak forest and almond groves. Excellent sports facilities and three restaurants.

**Hotel Escua, Ctra Jérez-Cartagena, km 176, t 95 271 70 21, *www. hotelescua.com* (€€–€). On the outskirts of town, this agreeable hotel offers attractive, welcoming rooms. The restaurant is equally good.

*Las Palomas, Ctra Jerez–Granada, km 177, t 95 271 43 26 (€). The best bet if you are on a budget.

El Central, C/Nueva 49, t 95 271 48 11 (€). This is the best restaurant in town, just up from the square. It serves seafood, tapas and regional wines. Try the speciality, *porra*, a kind of thick gazpacho.

Villanueva de la Concepción ✉ 29230

***Posada del Torcal, Partido de Jeva, t 95 203 11 77, *www.eltorcal.com* (€€€€€–€€€€). A beautiful white retreat amid almond groves, with just 10 elegant bedrooms, fine views and a refined restaurant. Pool and tennis; massage can be arranged. The company also lets luxury villas in the area.

Álora ✉ 29200

Cortijo Jacaranda, Apdo de Correos 279, t 679 091 689, *www.cortijo jacaranda.com* (€€€). An English-run rural hotel in a former farm with a choice of accommodation; all with private terraces and superb views. Children welcome and activities organized.

Casa Rural Domingo, Arroyo Cansino 4, t 95 211 97 44, *www.casarural domingo.com* (€€€–€€). Located high above Álora, this Belgian-run delightful rural accommodation has stunning views, and a choice of artistically decorated rooms or self-

catering bungalows with terraces. There's also a pool.

*Durán, C/La Parra 9, t 95 249 66 42 (€). A reasonable, basic place to stay in the centre of Álora.

El Chorro ✉ 29552

La Garganta, t 95 249 51 19 (€€). The best option if you want to stay near the gorge; offers excellent apartments with kitchen and lounge areas, great views, a rooftop pool and a good restaurant attached.

Carratraca ✉ 29200

*****Carratraca Hotel & Spa, C/Antonio Riobo 11, t 95 248 95 42 (€€€€€). The Ritz-Carlton chain has recently taken over the romantic former El Principe Hotel and transformed it into a luxury spa hotel. Call for details as it had not yet reopened at time of going to press.

Guadal Arte, C/Baños 3, t 95 245 83 40 (€). Delicious *malagueño* recipes with a hint of Morocco in some dishes. Save room for the home-made desserts, and enjoy the fabulous views from the terrace.

Venta los Conejitos, Ctra de Carratraca–Álora, km 5, t 95 249 69 42, *www.restaurante-losconejitos.com* (€). One of many roadside *ventas* around the Serranía, this is bigger and fancier than most, with good-value local cooking.

Ardales ✉ 29550

***La Posada del Conde, Pantano del Chorro 16 & 18, t 95 211 24 11, *www.laposadadelconde.com* (€€). A lovely hotel wonderfully situated on the reservoir; large doubles with balconies and a good restaurant.

The Coast East of Málaga

Vélez-Málaga and the Axarquía

Torre del Mar, the first resort east of Málaga, is a carbon copy of any of the Costa del Sol towns, with grey sand beaches and the usual concrete monstrosities lining the seafront, and, if anything, lacking the party atmosphere of the others. The town has attempted a bit of prettification with a long, tree-lined promenade, and there are some lovely views to the Sierra de Tejeda.

Getting to and around the Coast East of Málaga

The Portillo and Alsina Graells **buses** from Málaga or Motril serve Nerja, Almuñécar and Salobreña, and connections can be made from these towns to the interior villages. Note that long-distance buses along the coast do not usually stop at these towns. Almuñécar's buses set off from Avda Juan Carlos I, **t** 95 863 01 40.

From Torre del Mar you can make a short detour inland to **Vélez-Málaga**, lying in a fertile valley at the foot of the Axarquía mountain area. The new town holds no particular charm, but the old part tells of its Moorish past; the castle, **La Fortaleza** (of which a restored tower remains, set in pretty gardens), was one of the last Moorish outposts to fall to Christian forces during the campaigns of Isabel and Fernando. Below the castle, the church of **Nuestra Señora de la Encarnación** has had a chequered career – first as a Visigothic church, then a mosque, then a church again when the town was recaptured by Christian forces in 1487. In town there are a number of sites, none particularly outstanding: the **Hospital de San Juan de Dios**, C/Confrade, founded by Fernando and Isabel, used as a theatre in the 17th century, and now an old people's home; the 15th-century **Convento de San Francisco**, on Plaza de San Francisco, and a Baroque church with a *mudéjar* courtyard.

Just to the west of Vélez is **Benamocarra**. Although not as dramatically placed as towns further inland, it is mercifully free of tourist buses and retains much of its character. The main church, **Iglesia Santa Ana**, dates from 1505 and was restored in 1949; its tower and main nave, which is octagonal, are in *mudéjar* style. Close by is **Iznate**, which has several monuments, including the castle of Omar ibn-Hafsun, the rebel Andalucian leader, and a *mudéjar* church. Iznate is most famous for its riotous grape festival, the *Fiesta de la Uva Moscatel*, held on 5 August, where you can join the locals in a food and drink blowout from eight till late, with music and prizes.

⭐ **The Axarquía** A less-explored region than the Serranía de Ronda, but no less beautiful, is the **Axarquía**, a collection of tiny whitewashed villages surrounding Vélez-Málaga on the slopes of the **Sierra de Tejeda**, a natural park. To really explore, you will need your own car, as public transport links are scarce. Some towns, such as Frigiliana (*see* p.276) and Torrox (*see* p.275), both of which are a short drive from the coast, have suffered much the same fate that befell Mijas, above Torremolinos, and are consequently overrun with tourists all day, although tranquillity returns when the tour buses leave.

Press on into the hills, however, and you will find little gems like Cómpeta and Almáchar – famous for sweet wines and flower displays respectively (*see* p.275) – and **Comares**, perched atop one of the highest peaks. It's known as the 'Balcón de Axarquía', with views from the platform in the main square across the valley and towards the coast. The town was of strategic importance during Moorish times and was one of the bases of Omar-ibn Hafsun; there are the ruins of a Moorish **castle** at its highest point, and the **cemetery** has the best view of all.

West of Vélez, **Almáchar** is an exquisite little village of tumbling houses and winding streets, best explored on foot. Leave your car at the top of town near what was the old bus shelter and head down C/Eugenia Ríos. In spring and summer, the town is a riot of colours, with flowers spilling from every balcony, patio and window box (look for the plaques dotted about town commemorating individual streets for their displays). The **Iglesia San Mateo**, Plaza de España, is worth a peek, as are the small gardens at the bottom of the C/Forfe where, legend has it, a Moor hid some treasure that has never been found.

Nearby **El Borge** is smaller and not as immediately pretty, but it does have a lovely church, **Nuestra Señora de Rosario**, which has a *mudéjar* ceiling, two octagonal towers and a small crypt.

From Comares you could press on to **Colmenar**, a dusty town on the borders of Málaga province and a centre for honey production; or head back east to **Alfarnate**, which claims the oldest inn in Andalucía, the 13th-century **Venta de Alfarnate**, which doubles as a museum about the various *bandoleros* who frequented the place.

Another Axarquía route, perhaps less dramatic and a great deal shorter, begins on the coast east of Vélez and winds through **Salares** and **Sedella**, two of the prettiest villages in the area. Both have churches built on Moorish foundations, **Santa Ana** and **San Andrés** respectively, the former still bearing an old Moorish minaret.

Continue on to **Competa**, a truly lovely old village known principally for its sweet wines; the grapes are sun-dried to sweeten and fortify them. Its big wine fiesta is held on 15 August in the main square. As has happened with many Andalucian villages near the coast, northern invaders have discovered its charm, Brits and Danes particularly. Beyond Competa begin the wilds of the **Reserva Nacional de Sierra de Tejeda**; you'll have to leave your car to explore it, though, and strong comfortable shoes are recommended. To get back to the coast, take the MA137 through beautiful vine-clad slopes to **Torrox**, another Nordic enclave with a history dating back to 2000 BC, and continue down to **Torrox-Costa**, an expanding resort 8km from Nerja.

Alhama de Granada

For a further detour into the mountains, you can tackle the 50km drive along the A335 from Vélez over the Sierra to Alhama de Granada. The road snakes its way up through olive trees, trickling streams and rocky gulches; but pay close attention – there are some helter-skelter turns. Alhama balances precariously on a rocky lip and looks down to the deep grass-banked gorge, through which the Alhama runs. Up here you're away from it all. 'Oh, for my Alhama' was the lament of Boabdil el Chico, who had to abandon this beauty spot to the Christians in 1482. The town's 17th–18th-century church of **El Carmen** has a terrace from which you can enjoy the panorama.

No prizes for guessing the town's other attractions – the remains of a Moorish **castle**, in the main square, and a 15th-century parish **church**, a gift to the town from Fernando and Isabel. The Catholic Kings' Granada architects, Enrique de Egas and Diego de Siloé, both worked on it. Alhama has been famous since Roman times for its spa waters; ask at the modern spa, the Hotel Balneario, to see the Roman and Moorish baths beneath.

Nerja

As you approach this town, the scenery becomes impressive as the mountains loom closer to the sea. Sitting at the base of the Sierra de Tejeda, Nerja itself is pleasant and quiet for a Costa resort. In Moorish times the town was a major producer of silk and sugar, an industry that fell into rapid decline after the Moors' departure. An earthquake in 1884 partially destroyed Nerja, and from then to the early 1960s it had to eke a living out of fishing and farming. Its attractions are the **Balcón de Europa**, a promenade with a fountain overlooking the sea, and a series of secluded beaches under the cliffs – the best are a good walk away on either side of the town.

Cueva de Nerja
www.cuevadenerja.es;
open daily summer
10–2 and 4–8; winter
10–2 and 4–6.30; adm

A few kilometres east, the **Cueva de Nerja** is one of Spain's fabled grottoes, full of Gaudíesque formations and needle-thin stalactites – one, they claim, is the longest in the world. The caves were discovered in 1959, just in time for the tourist boom, and they have been fitted out with lights and music. The caves were popular with Cro-Magnon man, and there are some Palaeolithic artworks in evidence. Occasionally, this perfect setting is used for ballets and concerts.

A scenic 7km drive north of Nerja on the MA105 finds pretty **Frigiliana**, a pristine whitewashed village of neat houses and cobbled streets. There are splendid views down to the eastern coast, especially from the ruins of the Moorish fort. One of the last battles between Christians and Moriscos in 1569 took place just outside the village; the story of the battle is retold on ceramic plates around the village's old quarter. To find out more, contact local resident **Dave Riordan** who offers fascinating guided tours.

Dave Riordan
t 95 253 42 40,
david@frigiliana.com

Almuñécar

The coastal road east of Nerja, bobbing in and out of the hills and cliffs, is the best part of the Costa, where avocado pears and sugar cane keep the farming community busy; however, the next resort, **Almuñécar**, is a nest of dreary high-rises around a beleaguered former fishing village. Even so, this has a lot to offer. Laurie Lee immortalized it in *As I Walked Out One Midsummer Morning*, describing his experiences just prior to the outbreak of the Civil War, and in *A Rose For Winter*, when he returned some 20 years later. Although the hotel where he stayed, 'a white, square crumbling hotel where I had previously worked as a porter and a minstrel', is long gone and replaced by an apartment block, a plaque in the square in front mentions his books. Lee carefully disguised Almuñécar as 'Castillo' owing to its strong resistance against Franco's forces, so there is no mention of individual bars or restaurants. He did, however, speak of the castle in ruins, a fairly accurate description today. Lee aficionados may also like to visit the pretty **Ayuntamiento**, on Plaza de la Constitución (where the peasants raised flags before the town was overcome by Fascists), and **Iglesia de la Encarnación**, Plaza Nueva, which the locals set alight during the uprising.

Museo Arqueológico
open Tues–Sat 10.30–1.30 and 6–9, Sun 10.30–1.30; adm

For an idea of the ancient history of the town, visit the **Cueva de los Siete Palacios**, where the town's archaeological museum is based. Almuñecar was founded by the Phoenicians as Sexi, which can be confusing for the first-time visitor: the *ayuntamiento* has taken to putting up signs declaring certain areas 'Sexi'. The museum has artefacts from this period through to the Romans and the Moors, as well as an Egyptian vase fired between 1700 and 1600 BC for Pharoah Apophis I, and inscribed with the oldest written text found in Iberia.

Castillo
open Tues–Sat 10.30–1.30 and 6–9, Sun 10.30–1.30; adm

Parque Ornitológico
open summer 11–2 and 6–9; winter 10–2 and 4–6; adm

At the Castillo you can pick among the ruins and enjoy the views, or visit the **municipal museum** in a neoclassical pavilion. Below it lies the **Parque Ornitológico**, which holds 1,500 birds from all over the world, and a cactus garden. Despite its being the Granadinos' favourite resort, Almuñécar's numerous beaches are pretty dire, consisting of black sand and pebbles, while the nudist stretch is disconcertingly called **El Muerto**, 'the dead man'. Outside town are the remains of a Roman aqueduct. The prettiest place for a swim is the perfectly curved bay of **La Herradura** on the town's western outskirts, with a couple of restaurants on the beach.

Salobreña and Motril

Salobreña is nicer than Almuñécar, though relentless development has taken its toll here too. The village's dramatic setting, slung down a steep, lone peak overlooking the sea, is the most stunning on the coast, and helps to insulate it a little from the tourist industry. The beaches – filling up with endless *urbanizaciones* – are about 2km away. From here the next town is

Motril, set back from the sea, with little to attract visitors; it's the centre of the coastal sugar-cane production, thanks to the gin family of Larios. The land between the town and the beaches is now one long *urbanización*.

⭐ El Molino de los Abuelos >>

Tourist Information on the Coast East of Málaga

The tourist offices have a map with general information about the Axarquía and a number of routes to follow.

Sports and Activities on the Coast East of Málaga

La Herradura, effectively a suburb of Almuñécar but far less developed, mainly consists of beachfront restaurants, a windsurfing school and a diving centre – **Centro de Buceo**, Puerto Deportivo del Este, **t** 95 882 70 83, *www.buceolaherradura.com*. In summer the clear water teems with fish.

Where to Stay and Eat on the Coast East of Málaga

ⓘ Torre del Mar >

Paseo de Larios s/n,
t 95 254 11 04

Torre del Mar ✉ 29740

****Hotel Husa Mainake, C/Copo s/n, **t** 95 254 72 46, *www.hotelhusa mainake.com* (€€€). The best hotel in the area, 100m from the beach. It has all the amenities, including a pool on the roof.

Miraya, C/Patrón Veneno 6, **t 95 254 59 69, *www.hotelmiraya.com* (€€€–€€). Virtually on the beach; friendly, with clean, bright rooms, all en suite, and a café.

*Hostal Generalife, C/Patrón Veneno 22, **t** 95 254 33 09 (€). A reasonably priced beachside option.

Vélez-Málaga ✉ 29700

Hotel Dila, Avenida Vivar Téllez 3, **t 95 250 39 00 (€€–€). Basic rooms with baths.

Comares ✉ 29195

El Molino de los Abuelos, Plaza 2, **t** 95 250 93 09, *info@molino-abuelos.com* (€€). Splendid setting, in a converted olive-pressing mill, with four rooms and two apartments; the ones to go for are the front-facing double or the suite, which look right out across the valley. The restaurant below serves reasonably priced local dishes.

Mirador de la Axarquía, C/Encinillas, **t** 95 250 92 09 (€€). On the approach to the village, the pine-clad motel style rooms are good value here, and the downstairs restaurant and bar serves excellent meals; try the *revuelta* (scrambled eggs) with asparagus and prawns while contemplating the magnificent mountainous views stretching down to the coast.

Sedella ✉ 29215

Casa Pintá, just outside Sedella, **t** 95 250 89 55 (€). The best place to stay in the area is this dramatically located hotel; it's friendly and very reasonable, with an excellent restaurant and a pool that looks out across the sierras.

Competa ✉ 29754

***Hotel Balcon de Competa, C/San Antonio 75, **t** 95 255 35 35, *www.hotel-competa.com* (€€). Has fantastic views, a restaurant, café and pool. Also offers activities such as horse riding, safaris, hiking and golf. For self-catering stays, ask about the apartment.

Posada La Plaza, Canillas de Albaida (3km from Competa), **t** 95 255 48 07, *www.posada-laplaza.eu* (€€–€). A 16th-century building in the lovely white village of Canillas de Albaida, this has a handful of traditionally decorated rooms. There's a good little restaurant. Dutch-owned.

Árchez ✉ 29753

Posada-Mesón Mudéjar, C/Álamo 6, **t** 95 255 31 06, *www.posadameson mudejar.com* (€). A delightful restored

17th-century building converted into a hotel; all five rooms have bath, phone and air-conditioning, plus there is a restaurant serving local dishes.

Canillas de Aceituno ✉ 29716

Hostal Canillas, t 95 251 81 02 (€). This village, apparently untouched by tourism, has this one little place to stay above a shop on a quiet street. Also has apartments to let.

Torrox-Costa ✉ 29793

**Cortijo Amaya, El Morche, t 95 253 02 45, *www.cortijoamaya.com* (€€). Close to the beach and in a lovely garden with a swimming pool and tennis court. The *cortijo* is a restored farmhouse, with big rooms and a good restaurant; rooms can also be hired on a reduced weekly rate.

Nerja ✉ 29780

****Parador de Nerja, Playa de Burriana, C/Almuñécar 8, t 95 252 00 50, nerja@parador.es (€€€€). A luxurious place; modern and newly renovated, but with a bland exterior.

****Balcón de Europa, Paseo Balcón de Europa 1, t 95 252 08 00, *www. hotelbalconeuropa.com* (€€€). Though not as luxurious as the *parador*, the beautiful location on the 'balcony of Europe' in the town centre and the reasonable rates make the difference. Both hotels have lifts down to the beaches under Nerja's cliffs.

***Plaza Cavana, Plaza Cavana, t 95 252 40 00, *www.hotelplazacavana.com* (€€€–€€). Very close to the Balcón de Europa, with air-conditioning and two swimming pools, plus sauna.

**Puerta del Mar, C/Gómez s/n, t 95 252 73 04 (€€€–€€). A modest hotel, but with a good beachside location not far from the Balcón de Europa.

Hostal Miguel, C/Almirante Ferrandíz 31, t 95 252 15 23, *www.hostalmiguel. com* (€). A charming English-run option: central and friendly, with fridges in the rooms and a pretty roof terrace for breakfast.

Udo Heimer, Pueblo Andaluz 27, t 95 252 00 32 (€€€–€€). For a special dinner: a tranquil, elegant restaurant serving contemporary Spanish cuisine on the terrace. *Closed lunch, plus Wed and Jan.*

El Candil, Plaza Balcón de Europa, t 95 252 07 97 (€€). Has a good selection of Spanish dishes in a lovely setting, in a square just off the Balcón.

Casa Luque, Plaza de Cavana 2, t 95 252 10 04 (€€). One of the finest restaurants in Nerja, with superb views. *Closed Sun lunch, Wed, and mid-Jan–mid-Feb.*

Frigiliana ✉ 29788

***Los Caracoles, Ctra Frigiliana-Torrox, t 95 203 06 80, *www.hotellos caracoles. com* (€€€€€). An attractive and very unusual hotel, offering snail-shaped (*caracol* means snail) bunga-lows in the mountains. The Moorish-themed restaurant is excellent. Prices halve in low season.

La Posada Morisca, t 95 253 41 51, *www.laposadamorisca.com* (€€€). A delightful rural hotel in the hills about 2km from Frigiliana, with just a dozen rooms, a garden, pool and excellent restaurant.

*Las Chinas, Pza Capitán Cortés 14, t 95 253 30 73 (€). At present, the only inexpensive hotel in the town centre itself; clean and hospitably run by Miguel and Puri.

Frigiliana is full of restaurants; some of the best include:

El Tangay, Avda Andalucía, t 95 253 30 49 (€). A locals' favourite.

La Bodeguilla, C/Chorruelo 7, t 95 253 41 16 (€). Serves typical Spanish mountain food.

Almuñécar ✉ 18690

There are plenty of hotels to be found in Almuñécar in the old town, with cheaper ones around the **Plaza de la Rosa**.

***Hotel Helios, Paseo San Cristóbal, t 95 863 44 59, *www.heliosalmunecar. com* (€€€). Probably the best value of the many beachside hotels; indoor and outdoor pools and a wide range of sports facilities.

**Casablanca, Plaza San Cristóbal 4, t 95 863 55 75 (€€). A family-run pseudo-Moorish affair, this has rooms looking out to sea or to the castle and the sierras.

*Hotel La Tartana, C/San Nicolás de la Herradura, *www.hotellatartana.com*, t 95 864 05 35 (€€). One of very few

(i) Frigiliana >>
Plaza del Ingenio s/n, t 95 253 42 61, www. frigiliana.com; open Mon–Fri 9–8, Sat and Sun 10–1.30 and 4–8

(i) Nerja >
C/Puerta del Mar 2, t 95 252 15 31, www.nerja.org; open Mon–Fri 10–2 and 5–7, Sat 10–1

(i) Almuñécar >>
Avda de Europa (in the small Moorish palace), t 95 863 11 25, www. almunecar.info; open Mon–Sat 10–2 and 5–8

(i) La Herradura
Avenida Prieto Moreno (by the market), t 95 864 04 25, www.almunecar.info/ herradura

accommodation options in the pretty little bay of La Herradura. Basic, spotless rooms and charming service.

*Hotel Playa San Cristóbal, Plaza San Cristóbal, **t** 95 863 36 12 (€). Has sea-facing rooms and balconies.

Bodega Francisco, C/Real 15, **t** 95 263 01 68 (€). A wonderful watering hole serving tapas and the usual *andaluz* staples.

(i) Salobreña >

*Plaza de Goya s/n, **t** 95 861 03 14, www. ayto-salobrena.org; open Mon–Fri 9.30–1.30 and 4.30–7, Sat 9.30–1.30*

Salobreña ✉ 18680

Casa de los Bates, A7-E15, km 329.5, **t** 95 834 94 95, *www.casadelosbates. com* (€€€€). An aesthetically restored late 19th-century mansion surrounded by lush gardens with a pool. The rooms are charmingly furnished with antiques and floral fabrics. Located between Salobreña and Motril.

***Salobreña, outside the town on the coastal highway, **t** 95 861 02 61, *www.hotelsalobrena.com* (€). Near the beach with pool and garden. The restaurant does barbecues in summer; lovely views.

*Mari Tere, Ctra Antigua de la Playa 7, **t** 95 882 84 89 (€). A *hostal* near the beach with doubles and bath, and a restaurant.

Camping El Peñón, **t** 95 861 02 07 (€). A campsite near the beach. *Closed Nov–Mar.*

Mesón de la Villa, Plaza F. Ramírez de Madrid, **t** 95 861 24 14 (€€). Salobreña's best restaurant; local fish dishes. *Closed Wed.*

There are also a number of good *chiringuitos* along the beach during the summer season.

Granada
and Almería

Everyone who comes to Andalucía stops to see the Alhambra in Granada, but there is infinitely more to this magical though somewhat introverted city. Not content with having the biggest collection of wonders from Moorish al-Andalus, Granada also possesses the greatest monuments of the Reconquista.

Even Granada's setting is a land of excess, where Spain's tallest mountain, Mulhacén in the Sierra Nevada, stands only 40km from the sea – you can ski and swim on the same day. The peaks provide the backdrop for the Alhambra, while their southern face overlooks the hidden villages of the Alpujarras, the last redoubt of the Moors in Spain.

To the east, the province of Almería is another world – perfect for the filming of Sergio Leone's spaghetti westerns and complete with its own 'Mini Hollywood' at Tabernas.

13

Don't miss

⭐ A refined and gracious palace
Alhambra p.289

⭐ The elegant Gothic memorial of Fernando and Isabel
Capilla Real p.300

⭐ White mountain villages
Las Alpujarras p.306

⭐ Home of the spaghetti western
Mini Hollywood p.318

⭐ An exotic white-washed town
Mojácar p.320

See map overleaf

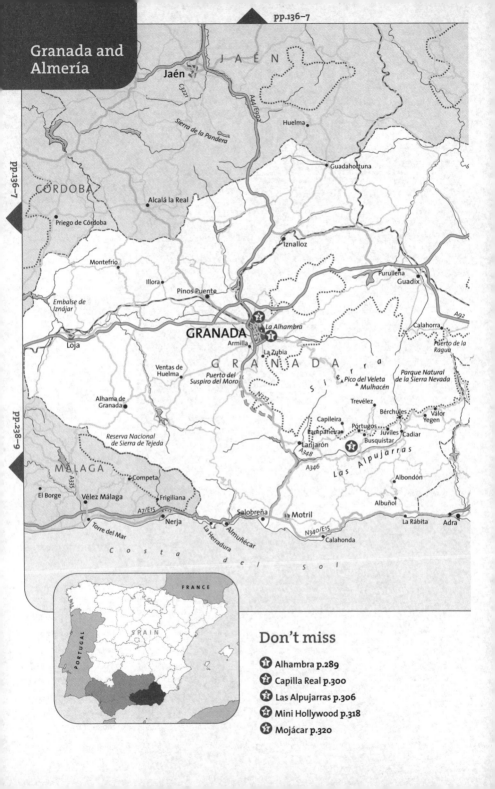

Granada and Almería

J A É N

Jaén

C321

A44/E902

Sierra de la Pandera

Huelma

Guadahortuna

CÓRDOBA

Alcalá la Real

Priego de Córdoba

Iznalloz

Purullena

Guadix

Montefrío

Illora

Pinos Puente

Embalse de
Iznájar

Calahorra

A92

Puerto de la
Ragua

Loja

GRANADA

Armilla

La Alhambra

La Zubia

G R A N A D A

S
i
e
r
r
a

Pico del Veleta
Mulhacén

Parque Natural
de la Sierra Nevada

Ventas de
Huelma

Puerto del
Suspiro del Moro

N323

Trevélez

Bérchules

Válor
Yegen

Alhama de
Granada

Capileira

Pampaneira

Pórtugos

Juviles

Cadiar

Reserva Nacional
de Sierra de Tejeda

Lanjarón

A348

Busquístar

Las Alpujarras

Albondón

MÁLAGA

A335

Competa

A346

Albuñol

El Borge

Vélez Málaga

Frigiliana

A7/E15

Nerja

Salobreña

Motril

La Rábita

Adra

Torre del Mar

Almuñécar

La Herradura

N340/E15

Calahonda

C o s t a   d e l   S o l

FRANCE

PORTUGAL

SPAIN

Don't miss

⭐ Alhambra p.289

⭐ Capilla Real p.300

⭐ Las Alpujarras p.306

⭐ Mini Hollywood p.318

⭐ Mojácar p.320

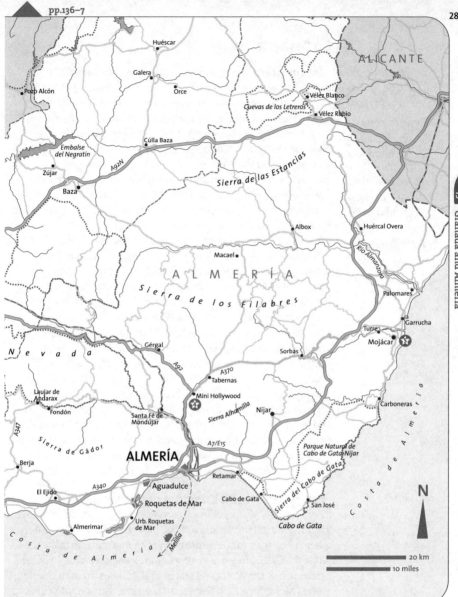

Beyond the Sierra Nevada the landscapes merge into the arid expanses typical of southeastern Spain. Out in the dry and lonely eastern reaches of Granada's province, the main attraction is the bizarre cave-city of Guadix.

After Mini Hollywood, the highlights of Almería province are the city of Almería itself, the pristine beaches and small villages of the Cabo de Gata natural park, and the exotic, whitewashed coastal resort of Mojácar.

Granada

*Dale limosna
mujer, que no hay
en la vida nada
Como la pena de
ser ciego y en
Granada.*

*(Give him alms,
woman, for there
is nothing in life
so cruel as being
blind in Granada.)*

Francisco de Icaza

The city where Fernando and Isabel chose to be buried is still a capital of romance, a city where 'Nights in the Gardens of Spain' is not merely a fantasy, but something encouraged by the tourist office. Upon arrival, pick up a copy of Washington Irving's *Tales of the Alhambra*. Every bookshop in town can sell you one in just about any language. It was Irving who put Granada on the map, and established the Alhambra as the necessary romantic pilgrimage of Spain. Granada, in fact, might seem a disappointment without Irving: the modern city underneath the Alhambra is a stolid, unmagical place, with little to show for the 500 years since the Catholic Kings put an end to its ancient glory.

As the Moors were expelled, the Spanish Crown replaced them with Castilians and Galicians from up north, and even today *granadinos* are thought of as a bit foreign by other Andalucíans. Their Granada has never been a happy place. Particularly in the last hundred years it has been full of political troubles. Around the turn of the 20th century even the Holy Week processions had to be called off for a few years because of disruptions from the leftists, and at the start of the Civil War the reactionaries who always controlled Granada conducted one of the first big massacres of Republicans. One of their victims was Federico García Lorca (*see* also p.302), the *granadino* who, in the decades since his death, has come to be recognized as one of the greatest Spanish dramatists and poets since the 'Golden Age'. If Irving's fairy tales aren't to your taste, consider Lorca, for whom Granada and its sweet melancholy are recurring themes. He wrote that he remembered Granada 'as one should remember a sweetheart who has died'.

History: the Nasrid Kingdom of Qarnatah

First Iberian *Elibyrge*, then Roman *Illiberis*, the town did not make a name for itself until the era of the *taifas* in the early 11th century, when it emerged as the centre of a very minor state. In the 1230s, while the Castilians were seizing Córdoba and preparing to polish off the rest of the Almoravid states of al-Andalus, an Arab chieftain named Mohammed ibn-Yusuf ibn-Nasr established himself around Jaén. When that town fell to the Castilians in 1235, he moved his capital to the town the Moors called *Qarnatah*. Ibn Nasr (or Mohammed I, as he is generally known) and his descendants in the Nasrid dynasty at first enjoyed great success extending their domains. By 1300 this last Moorish state of Spain extended from Gibraltar to Almería, but this accomplishment came entirely at the expense of other Moors. Mohammed and his successors were in fact vassals of the kings of Castile, and aided them in campaigns more often than they fought them.

Getting to and away from Granada

By Air

There are two flights a day from Madrid (*Mon–Sat*), two a day from Barcelona (*Mon–Fri*) and three flights a week from the Balearics and Canaries. There are also flights from the UK (*see* **Planning Your Trip**). The airport is 17km west of Granada, near Santa Fé. There is a regular daily bus link between the airport and the city centre (**t** 95 849 01 64); two services on Sundays. **Information**: **t** 95 824 52 23, *www.aena.es*.

By Train

Granada has connections to Guadix and Almería (four daily), to Algeciras via Bobadilla Junction (three daily); Sevilla and Córdoba (four daily); and two daily to Madrid and Barcelona; three daily to Alicante; and one a day to Valencia. The **station** is at the northern end of town, about a mile from the centre, on Avenida de Andalucía. **Information t** 90 224 02 02, *www.renfe.es*.

By Bus

All buses arrive at and leave from the main **bus station**, on the outskirts of town on the Carretera de Jaén. **Information t** 95 818 54 80; **sales t** 90 233 04 00. Bus no.3 runs between the bus station and the city centre.

Getting around Granada

By Bus

Bus nos.30 and 32 from the Plaza Nueva take you to the Alhambra. Bus 32 also makes a loop to the Albaicín; no.34 goes to Sacromonte.

By Car

Parking is a problem, so if you plan to stay overnight make sure that your hotel has parking facilities and check whether there is a charge or not – it can cost as much as the accommodation in some places. Traffic police are vigilant. Fines of up to €120 are payable on the spot if you are a tourist. The old centre is only open to local traffic or for hotel access during certain hours of the day.

Qarnatah at this time is said to have had a population of some 200,000 – almost as many as it has now – and both its arts and industries were strengthened by refugees from the fallen towns of al-Andalus. Thousands came from Córdoba, especially, and the Albaicín quarter was largely settled by the former inhabitants of Baeza. Although a significant Jewish population remained, there were very few Christians. In the comparatively peaceful 14th century, Granada's conservative, introspective civilization reached its height, with the last flowering of Arabic-Andaluz lyric poetry and the architecture and decorative arts of the Alhambra.

This state of affairs lasted until the coming of the Catholic Kings. Isabel's religious fanaticism made the completion of the Reconquista the supreme goal of her reign; she sent Fernando out in 1484 to do the job, which he accomplished in eight years by a breathtakingly brilliant combination of force and diplomacy. Qarnatah at the time was suffering the usual curse of al-Andalus states – disunity founded on the egotism of princes. In this fatal feud, the main actors were Abu al-Hasan Ali (Mulay Hassan in Irving's tales), king of Qarnatah, his brother El Zagal ('the valiant') and the king's rebellious son, Abu abd-Allah, better known to

Granada

PLAZA HAZA GRANDE

Moorish walls (ruins)

SACROMONTE

CARRETERA DE MURCIA

PLAZA CRUZ DE PIEDRA

SAN LUÍS

CUESTA DEL CHAPIZ

City University

CALLEJÓN DE LEBRIJA

PLAZA CASTILLAS

San Salvador

PANADEROS

CUESTA ALJIBE DE TRILLO

PLAZA CARNICEROS

ALBAICÍN

PLAZA SAN NICOLÁS

NUEVO SAN NICOLÁS

La Cartuja

CARGA SAN CRISTÓBAL

Moorish walls (ruins)

CUESTA MARÍA DE LA MIEL

CARDENAL PARRADO

REAL DE CARTUJA

Monasterio de Santa Isabel la Real

TIÑA

PLAZA SAN JOSÉ

AVENIDA DE MURCIA

HORNILLO DE CARTUJA

CUESTA ALHACABA

PLAZA SAN MIGUEL BAJO

SAN JOSÉ

PULIANAS

Hospital Real

AVENIDA HOSPICIO

ZENETE

QUIRÓS

PLAZA SAN ISIDRO

Puerta de Elvira

AVENIDA DE ANCHA DE CAPUCHINOS

PLAZA DEL TRIUNFO

CALLE DE ELVIRA

Bus Station

Jardines del Triunfo

GRAN VÍA DE COLÓN

MADRID

DOCTOR GUIRAO GEA

SANTA BARBARA

SAN JUAN DE DIOS

MANO DE HIERRO

PLAZA SAN AGUSTÍN

SAN JERÓNIMO

Basílica de San Juan de Dios

University

AVENIDA DE LA CONSTITUCIÓN

Bus Stand

San Jerónimo

MISERICORDIA

PLAZA LOBOS

AV. ANDALUCÍA

GRAN CAPITÁN

Train Station

CARRIL DEL PICÓN

AVENIDA FUENTE NUEVA

PLAZA GRAN CAPITÁN

OBISPO

MELCHOR ALMAGRO

MARTÍNEZ ROSA

PLAZA ALBERT EINSTEIN

CALLE PEDRO ANTONIO DE ALARCÓN

CAMINO RONDA

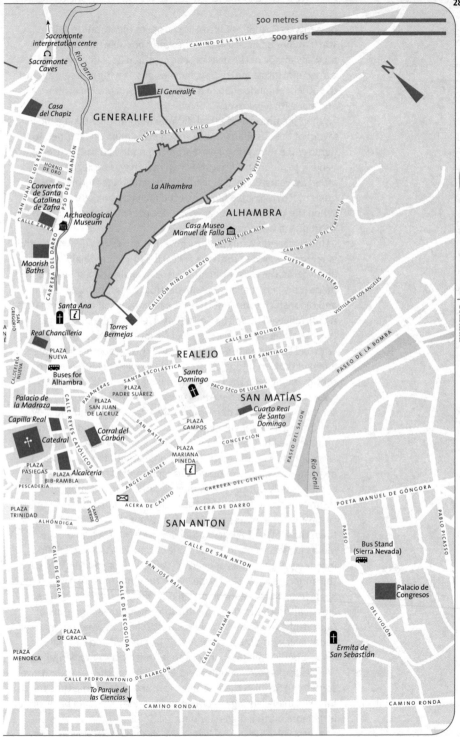

500 metres
500 yards

Sacromonte
interpretation centre

Sacromonte
Caves

Río Darro

Casa
del Chapiz

CAMINO DE LA SILLA

GENERALIFE

El Generalife

CUESTA DEL REY CHICO

La Alhambra

CAMINO VIEJO

ALHAMBRA

HORNO
DE ORO

SAN JUAN DE LOS REYES

Convento
de Santa Catalina
de Zafra

Archaeological
Museum

Casa Museo
Manuel de Falla

ANTEQUERUELA ALTA

CALLE ZAFRA

PSO DEL P. MANJÓN

CARRERA DEL DARRO

CAMINO NUEVO DEL CEMENTERIO

CUESTA DEL CAIDERO

Moorish
Baths

CALLEJÓN NIÑO DEL ROYO

VISTILLA DE LOS ANGELES

SAN GREGORIO

Santa Ana

Real Chancillería

CALDERERÍA NUEVA

Torres
Bermejas

REALEJO

CALLE DE MOLINOS

CALLE DE SANTIAGO

PASEO DE LA BOMBA

PLAZA
NUEVA

Buses for
Alhambra

PAVANERAS

SANTA ESCOLÁSTICA

PLAZA
PADRE SUÁREZ

Santo
Domingo

PACO SECO DE LUCENA

SAN MATÍAS

Palacio de
la Madraza

CALLE REYES CATÓLICOS

PLAZA
SAN JUAN
DE LA CRUZ

SAN MATÍAS

PLAZA
CAMPOS

Cuarto Real
de Santo
Domingo

CONCEPCIÓN

PASEO DEL SALÓN

Río Genil

Capilla Real

Catedral

Corral del
Carbón

PLAZA
MARIANA
PINEDA

PLAZA
PASIEGAS

PLAZA
BIB-RAMBLA

Alcaicería

ANGEL GAVINET

CARRERA DEL GENIL

PESCADERÍA

POETA MANUEL DE GÓNGORA

CAMPO VERDE

ACERA DE CASINO

ACERA DE DARRO

PLAZA
TRINIDAD

ALHÓNDIGA

SAN ANTON

PASEO

PABLO PICASSO

CALLE DE GRACIA

CALLE DE SAN ANTON

Bus Stand
(Sierra Nevada)

SAN JOSÉ BAJA

Palacio de
Congresos

CALLE DE RECOGIDAS

PLAZA
DE GRACIA

CALLE DE ALHAMAR

DEL VIOLÓN

PLAZA
MENORCA

Ermita de
San Sebastián

CALLE PEDRO ANTONIO DE ALARCÓN

To Parque de
las Ciencias

CAMINO RONDA

CAMINO RONDA

posterity as Boabdil el Chico. His seizure of the throne in 1482 started a period of civil war at the worst possible time. Fernando took advantage of the divisions; he captured Boabdil twice, and turned him into a tool of Castilian designs. Playing one side against the other, Fernando snatched away one Nasrid province after another with few losses.

When the unfortunate Boabdil, after renouncing his kingship in favour of the Castilians, finally changed his mind and decided to fight for the remnants of Qarnatah, Fernando had the excuse he needed to mount his final attack. Qarnatah was besieged and, after two years, Boabdil agreed to surrender under terms that guaranteed his people the use of their religion and customs. When the keys of the city were handed over on 2 January 1492, the Reconquista was complete.

Under a gentlemanly military governor, the Conde de Tendilla, the agreement was kept until the arrival in 1499 of Cardinal Ximénez de Cisneros, the most influential cleric in Spain and a man who made it his personal business to destroy the last vestiges of Islam and Moorish culture. That led to the famous revolt in Las Alpujarras (1568), followed by a rising in the city itself. Between 1609 and 1614, the last of the Muslims were expelled, including most of those who had converted to Christianity, and their property confiscated. It is said that, even today, there are old families in Morocco who sentimentally keep the keys to their long-lost homes in Granada.

Such a history does not easily wear away, even after so many centuries. The Castilians corrupted Qarnatah to *Granada*; just by coincidence that means 'pomegranate' in Spanish, and the pome-granate itself has come to be the symbol of the city. With its associations with the myth of Persephone, with the mysteries of death and loss, no symbol seemed more suitable for this capital of melancholy. But the pomegranate can also be a symbol of resurrection, and there are signs today that Granada is starting to cast aside some of its glum Castilian torpor. It's a much livelier town than it was 20 years ago, and most remarkably of all, the Moors are returning. In a new spirit of *convivencia*, the city's first mosque since 1492 has opened in the Albaicín, a spiritual home for the hundreds of Muslims who live in the city – most of them Spanish converts. Granada now has a whole constellation of new cross-cultural educational institutions, including an Institute of Arab Studies and a Euro-Arab business school; between them they count over 3,000 Muslim students. The political and cultural leaders behind all this point out that Andalucía's Arab heritage was also a distinctly Spanish one. By reviving it, they hope to revive something Spanish that has been lost, and at the same time to make Granada a bridge between two worlds that could badly use a little more mutual understanding.

A Sentimental Orientation

In spite of everything, more of the lost world of al-Andalus can be seen in Granada than even in Córdoba. Granada stands where the foothills of the Sierra Nevada meet the fertile Vega de Granada, the greenest and best stretch of farmland in Andalucia. Two of those hills extend into the city itself. One bears the **Alhambra**, the fortified palace of the Nasrid kings, and the other the **Albaicín**, the most evocative of the 'Moorish' neighbourhoods of Andalucian cities. Parts of old Qarnatah extended down into the plain, but they have been largely submerged within the new city.

How much you enjoy Granada will depend largely on how successful you are in ignoring the new districts, in particular three barbarically ugly streets that form the main automobile route through Granada: the **Gran Vía de Colón** chopped through the centre of town in the 19th century, the **Calle Reyes Católicos** and the **Acera del Darro**. The last two are paved over the course of the Río Darro, the stream that ran picturesquely through the city until the 1880s.

Before these streets were built, the centre of Granada was the **Plaza Nueva**, a square that is also partly built over the Darro. The handsome building that defines its character is the **Audiencia** (1584), built by Philip II for the royal officials and judges. **Santa Ana** church, across the *plaza*, was built in 1537 by Diego de Siloé, one of the architects of Granada's cathedral. From this *plaza* the ascent to the Alhambra begins, winding up a narrow street called the **Cuesta de Gomérez**, past guitar-makers' shops and Gypsies with vast displays of tourist trinkets, and ending abruptly at the **Puerta de las Granadas**, a monumental gateway erected by Charles V.

The Alhambra

⭐ **The Alhambra**
open Mar–Oct daily 8.30am–9pm, plus night visits Tues–Sat 10–11.30pm, ticket office open daily 8–7 plus Tues–Sat 9.30–10.30pm; Nov–Feb daily 8.30–6, plus night visits Fri and Sat 8–9.30pm, ticket office open daily 8–5 plus Fri and Sat 7.30–8.30pm; adm (discount with Granada City Pass, see 'Tourist Information', p.302); night visits only include entrance to the Nasrid Palaces; you are strongly advised to book your tickets in advance: at www.alhambratickets.com, at any branch of the BBVA bank, or by phone on t 902 224 460 (t +34 91 346 59 36 from outside Spain)

The grounds of the Alhambra begin at the Puerta de las Granadas with a bit of the unexpected. Instead of the walls and towers, there is a lovely grove of great elms, the **Alameda**, planted at the time the Duke of Wellington passed through during the Peninsular War. Take the path to the left – it's a stiff climb – and in a few minutes you'll arrive at the **Puerta de la Justicia**, the former entrance of the Alhambra. The orange tint of the fortress walls explains the name *al-hamra* (the red), and the unusual style of the carving on the gate is the first clue that here is something very different. The two devices, a hand and a key, carved on the inner and outer arches, are famous. According to one of Irving's tales, the hand will one day reach down and grasp the key; then the Alhambra will fall into ruins, the earth will open, and the hidden treasures of the Moors will be revealed. Follow the road uphill to the car park and visitor's centre, where you'll find the ticket office and entrance. There are three routes around the Alhambra complex, all marked on the map that comes with the ticket. You will be given a time slot for entrance to the Nasrid Palaces, which could well start an hour or two after your entrance to the complex and should give you time to explore the Alcazaba and perhaps the Generalife before visiting the Palaces.

The Alcazaba

Not much remains of the oldest part of the Alhambra, out on the tip of the promontory. This citadel probably dates back to the first of the Nasrid kings. Its walls and towers are still intact, but only the foundations of the buildings that once stood within it have survived. The **Torre de la Vela** at the tip of the promontory has the best views over Granada and the *vega*. Its big bell was rung in the old days to signal the daily opening and closing of the water gates of the *vega*'s irrigation system; the Moors also used the tower as a signal post for sending messages. The Albaicín (*see* pp.296–8), visible on the opposite hill, is a revelation; its rows of white, flat-roofed houses on the hillside, punctuated by palm trees and cypresses, provide one of Europe's most exotic urban landscapes.

In front of the Alcazaba is a broad square known as the **Puerta del Vino**, so called from a long-ago Spanish custom of doling out free wine from this spot to the inhabitants of the Alhambra.

Palacios Nazaries (Nasrid Palaces)

Note: You must enter the palace within the time slot on your ticket; once in, you may stay as long as you like

Words will not do, nor will exhaustive descriptions help, to communicate the experience of this greatest treasure of al-Andalus. This is what people come to Granada to see, and it is the surest, most accessible window into the refinement and subtlety of the culture of Moorish Spain – a building that can achieve in its handful of rooms what a work like Madrid's Royal Palace cannot even approach with its 2,800.

It probably never occurs to most visitors, but one of the most unusual features of this palace is its modesty. What you see is what the Nasrid kings saw; your imagination need add only a few carpets and tapestries, some well-crafted furniture of wood inlaid with ivory, wooden screens, and big round braziers of brass for heat or incense, to make the picture complete. Most of the actual building is wood and plaster, cheap and perishable, like a World's Fair pavilion; no good Muslim monarch would offend Allah's sense of propriety by pretending that these worldly splendours were anything more than the pleasures of a moment (much of the plaster, wood and all of the tiles are the products of careful restorations over the last 100 years). The Alhambra, in fact, is the only substantially intact medieval Muslim palace – anywhere.

Like so many old royal palaces (those of the Hittites, the Byzantines or the Ottoman Turks), this one is divided into three sections: one for everyday business of the palace and government; the next, more secluded, for the state rooms and official enter-tainments of the kings; and the third, where few outsiders ever reached, for the private apartments of the king and his household.

The Mexuar

Of the first, the small Mexuar, where the kings would hold their public audiences, survives near the present-day entrance to the palace complex. The adjacent **Patio del Mexuar**, though much restored, is one of the Alhambra's finest rooms. Nowhere is the

100 metres
100 yards

N

RÍO DARRO
CARRERA DEL DARRO

Generalife

Teatro

CUESTA DE LOS CHINOS

TORRE DEL AGUA

Ticket Gate & Visitor's Centre

TORRE DE LAS INFANTAS

TORRE DE LA CAUTIVA

Convento de San Francisco

TORRE DE SIETE SUELOS

TORRE DE LOS PICOS

TORRE DEL MIHRAB

TORRE DE LAS DAMAS

Jardines del Portal

Church of Santa María

TORRE DE LAS CABEZAS

PEINADOR DE LA REINA

12
11
10
8
9
6
7

5
4
3
1

14

13

2

Outer walls

PUERTA DEL VINO

TORRE DEL CUBO

PASEO DE LOS COCHES

PUERTA DE LA JUSTICIA

Alameda

Alcazaba

TORRE DE LA VELA

PUERTO DE LAS GRANADAS

C. DE GOMÉREZ

TORRES BERMEJAS

1 Nasrid Palaces
2 Patio del Mexuar
3 Patio de los Arrayanes
4 Sala de la Barca
5 Salón de Embajadores
6 Patio de los Leones
7 Sala de los Abencerrajes
8 Sala de las dos Hermanas

9   Sala de los Reyes
10 Sala de los Ajimeces
11 Patio de Lindaraja
12 Queen's Chamber
13 Palacio de Carlos V / Museo de Bellas Artes / Museo del Alhambra
14 Chapel and Crypt

meditative serenity of the palace more apparent (unless you arrive when the tour groups do) and the small central fountain provides an introduction to an important element of the architecture – water. Present everywhere, in pools, fountains and channels, water is as much a part of the design as the wood, tile and stone.

Patio de los Arrayanes (or Patio de Comares)

If you have trouble finding your way around, remember the elaborately decorated portals never really lead anywhere; the door you want will always be tucked unobtrusively to the side; here, as in Sevilla's Alcázar, the principle is to heighten the sense of surprise. The entrance to the grand Patio de los Arrayanes (Court of the Myrtles), with its long goldfish pond (where the moon is reflected perfectly on night visits) and lovely arcades, was the centre of the second, state section of the palace; directly off it, you pass through the **Sala de la Barca** (Hall of the Boat), so called after its hull-shaped wooden ceiling, and into the **Salón de Embajadores** (Hall of Ambassadors), where the kings presided over all important state business. The views and the decoration are some of the Alhambra's best, with a cedarwood ceiling and plaster panels (many were originally painted) carved with floral arabesques or Arabic calligraphy. These inscriptions, some Koranic scripture (often the phrase 'Allah alone conquers', the motto of the Nasrids), some eulogies of the kings, and some poetry, recur throughout the palace. The more conspicuous are in a flowing script developed by the Granadan artists; look closely and you will see others, in the angular Kufic script, forming frames for the floral designs.

In some of the chambers off the Patio de los Arrayanes, you can peek out over the domed roofs of the baths below. Opposite the Salón de Embajadores is a small entrance (often closed) into the dark, empty **crypt** of the Palace of Charles V.

Patio de los Leones

Another half-hidden doorway leads you into the third and most spectacular section, the king's residence, built around the Patio de los Leones (Court of the Lions). Here the plaster and stucco work is at its most ornate, the columns and arches at their most delicate, with little pretence of any structural purpose; balanced on their slender shafts, the façades of the court seem to hang in the air. As in much of Moorish architecture, the overripe arabesques of this patio conceal a subtle symbolism. The 'enclosed garden' that can stand for the attainment of truth, or paradise, or for the cosmos, is a recurring theme in Islamic mystical poetry. Here you may take the 12 endearingly preposterous lions who support the fountain in the centre as the months, or signs of the zodiac, and the four channels that flow out from the fountains as the four corners of the cosmos, the cardinal points, or, on a different level, the four rivers of paradise.

The rooms around the patio have exquisite decorations: to the right, from the entrance, the **Sala de los Abencerrajes**, named after the legend of the noble family that Boabdil supposedly had massacred at a banquet here during the civil wars just before the fall of Granada; to the left, the **Sala de las dos Hermanas** (Hall of the Two Sisters). Both of these have extravagant domed *muqarnas* ceilings. The latter chamber is also ornamented with a wooden window grille, another speciality of the Granadan artists; this is the only one surviving in the Alhambra. Adjacent to the Sala de las dos Hermanas is the **Sala de los Ajimeces**, so called for its doubled windows. The **Sala de los Reyes** (Hall of the Kings), opposite the court's entrance, is unique because of the paintings on its ceiling. The central panel may represent six of Granada's 14th-century kings; those on the side are scenes of a chivalric court. The artist is believed to have been a visiting Spanish Christian painter, possibly from Sevilla. From the Sala de las dos Hermanas, a passage leads through the Imperial chambers to the **Patio de Lindaraja** (or Mirador de Daraxa), with its fountain and flowers, Washington Irving's favourite spot in the Alhambra. Originally the inner garden of the palace, it was remodelled for the royal visits of Charles V and Philip V. Irving actually lived in the **Queen's Chamber**, decorated with frescoes of Charles V's expedition to Tunis – in 1829, apartments in the Alhambra could be had for the asking! Just off this chamber, at ground-floor level, is the beautiful **hammam**.

Follow the arrows out of the palace and into the outer gardens, the **Jardines del Partal**, a broad expanse of rose terraces and flowing water. The northern walls of the Alhambra border the gardens, including a number of well-preserved towers: from the west, the **Torre de las Damas**, entered by a small porch; the **Torre del Mihrab**, near which is a small mosque, now a chapel; the **Torre de los Picos**; the **Torre de la Cautiva** (Tower of the Imprisoned Lady), one of the most elaborately decorated; and the **Torre de las Infantas**, one of the last projects in the Alhambra (*c.* 1400).

Palacio de Carlos V

Anywhere else, this elegant Renaissance building would be an attraction in itself. Here it seems only pompous and oversized, and our appreciation of it is lessened by the mind-numbing thought of this emperor, with a good half of Europe to build palaces in, having to plop it down here – ruining much of the Alhambra in the process. Once Charles had smashed up the place he lost interest, and most of the palace, still unfinished today, was not built until 1616. The original architect, Pedro Machuca, had studied in Italy, and he took the opportunity to introduce into Spain the chilly,

Olympian High Renaissance style of Rome. At the entrances are intricately detailed sculptural **reliefs** showing scenes from Charles's campaigns and military 'triumphs' in the antique manner: armoured torsos on sticks amidst heaps of weapons. This is a very particular sort of Renaissance fancy, arrogant and weird, and wherever it appears around the Mediterranean it will usually be associated with the grisly reign of the man who dreamt of being Emperor of the World.

For all its Doric gravity, the patio was used almost from its completion for bullfights and mock tournaments. In 1922, Lorca and the painter Ignacio Zuloaga organized a famous festival of flamenco here, with performances in the courtyard that contributed greatly to the revival of flamenco as a serious art.

The Museums

Museo de Bellas Artes
currently closed for restoration

Museo de La Alhambra
open Tues–Sat 9–2; adm, free to EU citizens; free guided visits to the museum by volunteers, Tues–Sat 11–1

On the top floor of the palace is the Museo de Bellas Artes, a largely forgettable collection of religious paintings from Granada churches. Downstairs, the Museo de La Alhambra contains perhaps Spain's best collection of Moorish art, including some paintings, similar to those found in the Moorish palace's Sala de los Reyes. Also present are original *azulejo* tiles and plaster arabesques from the palace, and some exceedingly fine wooden panels and screens. There is a collection of ceramic ware with fanciful figurative decoration and some lovely astronomical instruments. One room contains four big copper balls stacked on a pole, a strangely compelling ornament that once stood atop a Granada minaret. These were a typical feature of Andalucían minarets; Granada's great mosque had a big one designed to be visible to travellers a day's journey from the city.

Behind Charles's palace a street leads into the remnants of the town that once filled much of the space within the Alhambra's walls, now reduced to a small collection of restaurants and souvenir stands. In Moorish times the Alhambra held a large permanent population, and even under the Spaniards it long retained the status of a separate municipality. At one end of the street, the church of **Santa María** (1581), by Juan de Herrera, occupies the site of the Alhambra's mosque; at the other, the first Christian building on the Alhambra, the **Convento de San Francisco** (1495), has been converted into a *parador*.

Around the Alhambra

The Generalife
same opening hours as the Alhambra; adm included in Alhambra ticket, or you can purchase a separate ticket which only includes the Generalife

The Generalife

The heavenly Generalife (*Djinat al-Arif*: high garden) was the summer palace of the Nasrid kings, built on the height the Moors called the Mountain of the Sun. Many of the trillions of visitors the Alhambra receives each year have never heard of it, and pass up a chance to see one of the finest gardens in Spain. To get there, it's about a five-minute walk from the Alhambra along a lovely avenue of tall cypresses.

The buildings here hold few surprises if you've just come from the Alhambra. They are older than most of the Nasrid palaces, begun around 1260. The gardens are built on terraces on several levels along the hillside, and the views over the Alhambra and Albaicín are transcendent. The centrepiece is the **Patio de la Alegría** (the 'Courtyard of Joy'), with a long pool with many water sprays that passes through beds of roses. A lower level, with a promenade on the hill's edge, is broken up into secluded bowers by cypress

Nights in the Gardens of Spain

The first proper garden in al-Andalus, according to legend, was planted by the first caliph himself, Abd ar-Rahman. This refugee from Damascus brought with him fond memories of the famous Rusafah gardens in that city, and he also brought seeds of the palm tree to plant. As caliph, he built an aqueduct to Córdoba, partly for the city and partly to supply his new Rusafah; his botanists sent away for more palms, and also introduced the peach and the pomegranate into Europe.

Following the caliph's example, the Arabs of the towns laid out recreational gardens everywhere, particularly along the river fronts. The widely travelled geographer al-Shaquindi wrote in the 11th century that the Guadalquivir around Córdoba was more beautiful than the Tigris or the Nile, lined with orchards, vines, pleasure gardens, groves of citrus trees and avenues of yews. Every city did its best to make a display, and each had its district of villas and gardens. Sevilla's was in Triana and on the river islands. Valencia too, which had another copy of the Rusafah, came to be famous for its gardens; poets called the city 'a maiden in the midst of flowers'.

All this gardening was only part of a truly remarkable passion for everything green. Andalucía's climate and soil made it a paradise for the thirsty Arabs and Berbers, and bringing southern Spain into the wider Islamic world made possible the introduction of new techniques, flowering plants and crops: rice, sugar, cotton, saffron, oranges (*naranja* in Spanish, from the Persian *nārang*), even bananas. In the 12,000 villages of the Guadalquivir valley, Moorish farmers were wizards; they learned how to graft almond branches on to apricot trees, and they refined irrigation and fertilizing to fine arts (one manuscript that survives from the time is a 'catalogue of dung'; pigs and ducks were considered very bad, while the horse was best for almost all fields). Sophisticated techniques of irrigation were practised throughout al-Andalus, and everywhere the rivers turned the wooden water wheels, or *norias* (another Persian word, *nā'urāh*); one in Toledo was almost 62m (200ft) tall. No expense was spared in bringing water where it was needed; near Moravilla remains can be seen of a mile-long subterranean aqueduct, 9m (30ft) in width. The farmers had other tricks, mostly lost to us; it was claimed they could store grain to last for a century, by spreading it between layers of pomegranate leaves and lime or oak ash.

Flowers were everywhere. On the slopes of Jabal al-Warad, the 'Mountain of the Rose' near Córdoba, vast fields of these were grown for rose water; other blooms widely planted for perfumes and other products included violet, jasmine, gillyflower, narcissus, gentian and tulip. And with all the flowers and gardens came poetry, one of the main preoccupations of life in al-Andalus for prince and peasant alike. When Caliph Abd ar-Rahman saw his palm tree growing, he wrote a lyric in its honour:

In the centre of the Rusafah I saw a palm tree growing,
born in the west, far from the palm's country.

I cried: 'Thou art like me, for wandering and peregrination,
and the long separation from family and friends.

May the clouds of morning water thee in thy exile.
May the life-giving rains that the poor implore never forsake thee.'

bushes cut into angular walls and gateways. Beautiful as it is, there is no evidence that the original Moorish gardens looked anything like this; everything here has been done in the last 200 years.

Back to Plaza Nueva

If you're walking back down from the Alhambra, you might consider another route into town, across the Alameda and down through the picturesque streets below the **Torres Bermejas**, an outwork of the Alhambra's fortifications built on foundations that date back to the Romans. The winding lanes and stairways around Calle del Aire and Calle Niño del Royo, one of the most beautiful quarters of Granada, will lead you back down near the Plaza Nueva.

Albaicín

Even more than the old quarters of Córdoba, this hillside area of whitewashed houses and tall cypresses has successfully preserved some of the atmosphere of al-Andalus. Its difficult site and former status as the district of Granada's poor explain the lack of change, but it is now becoming fashionable again.

From the Plaza Nueva, a narrow street called the **Carrera del Darro** leads up the valley of the Darro between the Alhambra and Albaicín hills; here the little stream has not been covered over, and you can get an idea of how the centre of Granada looked in centuries past. On the Alhambra side, old stone bridges lead up to a few half-forgotten streets hidden among the forested slopes; here you'll see some 17th-century Spanish houses with curious painted *esgrafiado* façades. Nearby, traces of a horseshoe arch can be seen where a Moorish wall once crossed the river; in the corner of Calle Bañuelo there are well-preserved **Moorish baths**.

Moorish baths
open Tues–Sat 10–2

Even more curious is the façade of the **Casa Castril** on the Darro, a flamboyant 16th-century mansion with a portal carved with a phoenix, winged scallop shells and other eccentric-looking devices that have been interpreted as elements in a complex mystical symbolism. Over the big corner window is an inscription reading 'Waiting for her from the heavens'. The house's owner, Bernardo de Zafra, was once a secretary to Fernando and Isabel, and he seems to have got into trouble with the Inquisition.

Casa Castril archaeological museum
t 95 822 56 40; open Tues 2.30–8.30, Wed–Sat 9–8.30, Sun 9–2; adm, free to EU citizens

Casa Castril has been restored as Granada's **archaeological museum** with a small collection of artefacts from the huge number of caves in Granada province, many inhabited since Palaeolithic times, and a few Iberian settlements. There is a Moorish room, with some lovely works of art, and finally, an even greater oddity than Casa Castril itself. Room 4 (upstairs) holds a collection of beautiful alabaster burial urns, made in Egypt, but found in a Phoenician-style necropolis near Almuñécar. Nothing else like them has ever been discovered in Spain, and the Egyptian hieroglyphic inscriptions on them are provocative in the extreme (translations given in Spanish), telling how the deceased travelled here in search of some mysterious primordial deity.

Farther up the Darro, there's a small park with a view up to the Alhambra; after that you'll have to do some climbing, but the higher you go the prettier the Albaicín is, and the better the views. Among the white houses and white walls are some of the oldest Christian churches in Granada. As in Córdoba, they are tidy and extremely plain, built to avoid alienating a recently converted population unused to religious imagery. **San Juan de los Reyes** (1520) on Calle Zafra and **San José** (1525) are the oldest; both retain the plain minarets of the mosques they replaced. Quite a few Moorish houses survive in the Albaicín, and some can be seen on **Calle Horno de Oro**, just off the Darro. On **Calle Daralhorra**, at the top of the Albaicín, are ruins of a Nasrid palace, largely destroyed to make way for Isabel's **Convento de Santa Isabel la Real** (1501). Here, running parallel to Cuesta de la Alhacaba, is a long-surviving stretch of **Moorish wall**. There are probably a few miles of walls left, visible around the hillsides over Granada; the location of the city made a very complex set of fortifications necessary. In this one, about halfway up, you may pass through **Puerta de las Pesas**, with its horseshoe arches. The heart of the Albaicín is here, around the pretty, animated **Plaza Larga**; only a few blocks away the **Mirador de San Nicolás**, in front of the church of that name, offers the most romantic view imaginable of the Alhambra with the snow-capped peaks of the Sierra Nevada behind it. Note the brick, barrel-vaulted fountain on the *mirador*, a typical Moorish survival; fountains like this can be seen throughout the Albaicín and most are still in use. Granada today has a small but growing Muslim community, including a substantial number of western converts, and a new **mosque**, the first built in Granada for 500 years, has emerged by the Mirador de San Nicolás. Once again, the evening call to prayer floats above the Albaicín, and the pretty gardens (which offer fabulous views across the Alhambra) are open to the public.

On your way back from the Albaicín you might consider taking a different route, down a maze of back streets to the **Puerta de Elvira**, one of the most picturesque corners of the neighbourhood.

Sacromonte

For something completely different, you might strike out beyond the Albaicín hill to the **Gypsy caves of Sacromonte**. Granada has had a substantial Gypsy population for several centuries now. Some have become settled and respectable; others live in trailers on vacant land around town. The most visible are those who prey on the tourists around the Alhambra and the Capilla Real, handing

Tortilla al Sacromonte

Regional dishes include cod rissole soup, chickpeas and onions, plus, of course, the famous *tortilla al Sacromonte*, made from a delightful concoction of brains, lamb's testicles, vegetables and eggs. The name originates from the Sacromonte Gypsies. Broad beans *granadine*, cooked with fresh artichokes, tomatoes, onions, garlic, breadcrumbs and a smattering of saffron and cumin, may seem less adventurous compared with *Sacromonte* but it's just as typical of Granada's dishes.

If you're in Las Alpujarras, try the fresh goats' cheese; and in Trevélez you'll be hard pushed to avoid its famous ham. But if you're west of Granada near Santa Fé, make a detour to sample its sumptuous *piononos* – *babas* with cream.

out carnations with a smile and then attempting to extort huge sums out of anyone dumb enough to take one (of course, they'll tell your fortune, too). The biggest part of the Gypsy community, however, still lives around Sacromonte in streets of some quite well-appointed cave homes, where they wait to lure you in for a little display of flamenco. The consensus of opinion has for long been that the music and dancing are usually indifferent, and the Gypsies' eventually successful attempts to shake out your last *centimo* can make it an unpleasantly unforgettable affair. Hotels sell tours for around €25. Nevertheless, if you care to match wits with the experts, proceed up the Cuesta del Chapiz from the Río Darro, turn right at the **Casa del Chapiz**, a big 16th-century palace housing a school of Arab studies, and keep going until some Gypsy child drags you home with him. The bad reputation has been keeping tourists away, so it's now much safer and friendlier as the Gypsies are worried about the loss of income. Serious flamenco fans will probably not fare better elsewhere in Granada except during the festivals, though there are some touristy flamenco nightspots – the **Reina Mora** by Mirador San Cristóbal is the best of them. On the third Sunday of each month, though, you can hear a **flamenco Mass** in the San Pedro church on the Carrera del Darro.

Centro del Interpretación de Sacromonte
C/Barranco de los Negros s/n, t 95 821 51 20, www.sacromonte granada.com; open summer Tues–Fri 10–2 and 5–9, Sat–Sun 11–9; winter Tues–Fri 10–2 and 4–7, Sat–Sun 11–7; adm

The **Centro de Interpretación del Sacromonte** is a museum and arts centre, set in a pair of display caves, where traditional crafts are carried out and frequent performances (including flamenco) are held in summer. It offers a fascinating glimpse into Gypsy life, explaining the history of the neighbourhood, recounting local legends, and illustrating traditional crafts and trades. There's a *mirador* with beautiful views and a herb garden where medicinal herbs are grown. For even better views, climb up beyond the stretch of old city walls to see the whole city unfold beneath you.

Central Granada

The old city wall swung in a broad arc from Puerta de Elvira to Puerta Real, now a small *plaza* full of traffic where Calle Reyes Católicos meets the Acera del Darro. Just a few blocks north of here, in a web of narrow pedestrian streets that make up modern

Granada's shopping district, is the pretty **Plaza de Bib-Rambla**, full of flower stands and toy shops, with an unusual fountain supported by leering giants at its centre. This was an important square in Moorish times, used for public gatherings and tournaments of arms. The narrow streets leading off to the east are known as the **Alcaicería**. This area was the Moorish silk exchange, but the buildings you see now, full of souvenir shops, are not original; the Alcaicería burned down in the 1840s and was rebuilt in more or less the same fashion with Moorish arches and columns.

The Cathedral

Cathedral
*Plaza de Pasiegas,
entrance on Gran Vía de
Colón,* **t** *95 822 29 59;
open Mon–Sat 10–1.30
and 4–8, Sun 4–8*

The best way to see Granada's cathedral is to approach it from Calle Marqués, just north of the Plaza Bib-Rambla. The unique façade, with its three tall, recessed arches, is a striking sight, designed by the painter Alonso Cano (1667). On the central arch, the big plaque bearing the words '*Ave María*' commemorates the exploit of the Spanish captain who sneaked into the city one night in 1490 and nailed up this message up on the door of the great mosque this cathedral has replaced. The other conspicuous feature is the name 'José Antonio Primo de Rivera' carved on the façade. Son of the 1920s dictator, Miguel Primo de Rivera, José Antonio was a mystic Fascist who founded the Falangist Party. His thugs provoked many of the disorders that started the Civil War, and at the beginning of the conflict he was captured by the loyalists and executed. Afterwards his followers treated him as a sort of holy martyr, and chiselled his name on every cathedral in Spain. That you can still see it here says a lot about Granada today.

The rest of the cathedral isn't up to the standard of its façade, and there is little reason to go in and explore its cavernous interior or dreary museum. Work was begun in 1521, after the Spaniards broke their promise not to harm the Great Mosque. As in many Spanish cathedrals, the failure of this one stems from artistic indecision. Two very talented architects were in charge: Enrique de Egas, who wanted it Gothic, like his adjacent Capilla Real, and (five years later) Diego de Siloé, who decided Renaissance would look much nicer. A score of other architects got their fingers in the pie before its completion in 1703. Some features of the interior are: the grandiose **Capilla Mayor**, with statues of the apostles, and of Fernando and Isabel, by Alonso de Mena, and enormous heads of Adam and Eve by Alonso Cano, whose sculptures and paintings can be seen all over the cathedral; the **Retablo de Jesús Nazareno** in the right aisle, with paintings by Cano and Ribera, and a *St Francis* by El Greco; the Gothic **portal** (now closed), leading into the Capilla Real, by de Egas. At the foot of the bell tower is a **museum**; its only memorable work is a subject typical of the degenerate art of the 1700s – a painted wooden head of John the Baptist.

Capilla Real

Leaving the cathedral and turning left, you pass the outsized **sacristy**, begun in 1705 and incorporated in the cathedral façade. Turn down Calle de los Oficios, a narrow lane paved in charming patterns of coloured pebbles – a Granada speciality; on the left, you can pay your respects to *Los Reyes Católicos*, in the **Capilla Real**. The royal couple had already built a mausoleum in Toledo, but after the capture of Granada they decided to plant themselves here. Even in the shadow of the bulky cathedral, Enrique de Egas's **chapel** (1507) reveals itself as the outstanding work of the Isabelline Gothic style, with its delicate roofline of traceries and pinnacles. Charles V thought it not monumental enough for his grandparents, and only the distraction of his wars kept him from wrecking it in favour of some elephantine replacement.

㉒ Capilla Real
C/de los Oficios;
open Mon–Sat 10.30–1
and 4–7, Sun 11–1
and 4–7; adm

Inside, the Catholic Kings are buried in a pair of Carrara marble sarcophagi, decorated with their recumbent figures, elegantly carved though not necessarily flattering to either of them. The little staircase behind them leads down to the **crypt**, where you can peek in at their plain lead coffins and those of their unfortunate daughter, Juana the Mad, and her husband, Philip the Handsome, whose effigies lie next to the older couple above. Juana was Charles V's mother, and the rightful heir to the Spanish throne. There is considerable doubt as to whether she was mad at all; when Charles arrived from Flanders in 1517, he forced her to sign papers of abdication, and then locked her up in a windowless cell for the last 40 years of her life. The interior of the chapel is sumptuously decorated – it should be, considering the huge proportion of the crown revenues that were expended on it. The iron *reja* by Master Bartolomé de Jaén and the retable are especially fine; the latter is largely the work of a French artist, Philippe de Bourgogne. In the chapel's sacristy you can see some of Isabel's personal art collection – works by Van der Weyden, Memling, Pedro Berruguete, Botticelli (attributed), Perugino and others, mostly in need of some restoration – as well as her crown and sceptre, her illuminated missal, some captured Moorish banners, and Fernando's sword.

Across the narrow street from the Capilla Real, an endearingly garish, painted Baroque façade hides **La Madraza**, a domed hall of the Moorish *madrasa* (Islamic seminary) and one of the best Moorish works surviving in Granada. It has now become the university shop, and you can visit the small patio to admire its delicate arches and the creamy, sculpted *muqarna* ceiling. The Christians converted it into a town hall, whence its other name.

Across Calle Reyes Católicos

Even though this part of the city centre is as old as the Albaicín, most of it was rebuilt after 1492, and its age doesn't show. The only

Moorish building remaining is also the only example left in Spain of a *khan* or *caravanserai*, the type of merchants' hotel common throughout the Muslim world. The 14th-century **Corral del Carbón**, just off Reyes Católicos, takes its name from the time, a century ago, when it was used as a coal warehouse. Under the Spaniards it also served time as a theatre; its interior courtyard with balconies lends itself admirably to the purpose, being about the same size and shape as a Spanish theatre of the classical age, like the one in Almagro (La Mancha). Today it is once again used for outdoor performances and houses a small government handicrafts outlet.

The neighbourhood of quiet streets and squares behind it is the best part of Spanish Granada and worth a walk if you have the time. Here you'll see the *mudéjar* **Casa de los Tiros**, a restored mansion built in 1505 on Calle Pavaneras, with strange figures carved on its façade; it houses a small museum of traditional arts and customs. **Santo Domingo** (1512), the finest of Granada's early churches, is just a few blocks to the south. Fernando and Isabel endowed it, and their monograms figure prominently on the lovely façade. Just north of here is the Campo del Príncipe, another delightful square frequented by students and full of cafés.

Casa de los Tiros
open Tues 2.30–8, Wed–Sat 9–8, Sun 9–2.30; adm, free to EU citizens

From here various winding streets provide an alternative ascent to the Alhambra. This neighbourhood is bounded on the west by the Acera del Darro, the noisy heart of modern Granada, with most of the big hotels. It's a little discouraging but, as compensation, just a block away the city has adorned itself with a beautiful string of wide boulevards, a wonderful spot for a stroll. The **Carrera del Genil** usually has some sort of open-air market on it, and further down, the **Paseo del Salón** and **Paseo de la Bomba** are quieter and more park-like, joining the pretty banks of the Río Genil.

Parque de las Ciencias
t 95 813 19 00; open Tues–Sat 10–7, Sun and hols 10–3; adm

Out in a modern park in the southern suburbs 2km south is the city's most high-tech attraction: **Parque de las Ciencias**, which has an excellent, child-friendly museum with plenty of absorbing interactive activities and exhibits, a planetarium, and an IMAX theatre.

Northern Granada

From the little street on the north side of the cathedral, the Calle de la Cárcel, Calle San Jerónimo skirts the edge of Granada's markets and leads you towards the old **university district**. Even though much of the university has relocated to a new campus half a mile to the north, this is still one of the livelier spots of town, and the colleges themselves occupy some fine, well-restored Baroque structures. The long yellow College of Law is one of the best, occupying a building put up in 1769 for the Jesuits. Calle San Jerónimo ends at the Calle del Gran Capitán, where the landmark is the basilica of **San Juan de Dios**, with a Baroque façade and a big green and white tiled dome. **San Jerónimo**, a block west, is another of the oldest and largest Granada churches (1520); it contains the tomb of Gonzalo de Córdoba, the 'Gran Capitán' who won so many victories in Italy for the Catholic Kings. Here you're not far from the Puerta de Elvira, in an area where old Granada fades into anonymous suburbs to the north. The big park at the end of the Gran Vía is the **Jardines del Triunfo**, with coloured, illuminated fountains the city hardly ever turns on. Behind them is the Renaissance **Hospital Real** (1504–22), designed by Enrique de Egas.

North of here, your senses will be assaulted by the gaudiest Baroque chapel in Spain, in the **Cartuja**, or Carthusian monastery, on Calle Real de Cartuja. Gonzalo de Córdoba endowed this Charterhouse, though little of the original works remain. The 18th-century chapel and its sacristy, in the richest marble, gold and silver, and painted plaster, oozes with twisted spiral columns, rosettes and curlicues. Often described as a Christian attempt to upstage the Alhambra, the inspiration more likely comes from the Aztecs, via the extravagant Mexican Baroque.

Cartuja
Paseo de Cartuja,
t 95 816 19 32; open
April–Oct Mon–Sat 10–1
and 4–8; Nov–Mar
Mon–Sat 10–1 and
3.30–6, Sun 10–12; adm

Outside the City: Lorca

Outside Spain, Federico García Lorca is popularly regarded as Spain's greatest modern dramatist and poet. The Spanish literati would acknowledge others from the generation of 1925 and from the previous generation of 1898 to have at least equal stature – the Galician dramatist and poet Ramón del Valle-Inclán springs to mind. But Lorca's murder enhanced his reputation outside Spain. Under Franco, any mention of him was forbidden (understandably so, since it was Franco's men who shot him). Today the *granadinos* are coming to terms with Lorca, and seem determined to make up for the past. Lorca fans pay their respects at two country houses, now museums, where he spent many of his early years: the **Huerta de San Vicente**, on the outskirts at Virgen Blanca, and the **Museo-Casa Natal Lorca** at Fuente Vaqueros, the village where he was born, 17km to the west near the Córdoba road.

**Huerta de
San Vicente**
t 95 825 84 66, www.
huertadesanvicente.com;
guided visits July–Aug
Tues–Sun 10–2.30; April–
June and Sept Tues–Sun
10–12.30 and 5–7.30;
Oct–Mar Tues–Sun 10–
12.30 and 4–6.30; adm

**Museo-Casa
Natal Lorca**
t 95 851 64 53, www.
museogarcialorca.org;
visits Tues–Sun April–
Sept 10–1 and 5–7; Oct–
Mar 10–1 and 4–6; adm

ⓘ **Granada >**
C/Santa Ana 4, t 95
822 10 22; Pza Mariana
Pineda 10, t 95 824
71 28, www.turismode
granada.org
Municipal office,
Avda Virgen Blanca s/n,
t 90 240 50 45; open
Mon–Sat 9.30–7
Alhambra office, *Avda*
del Generalife s/n,
t 95 822 95 75

Tourist Information in Granada

The tourist offices issue a *Bono Turístico* (City Pass, €22–24.50), which includes a tour on the city sightseeing bus; discounts on main sights and in restaurants and shops; plus nine free bus rides; visit *www.granadatur.com*, or call **t** 90 210 09 05.

Where to Stay in Granada

Granada ✉ 18000
The centre, around the Acera del Darro, is full of hotels, and there are lots of *hostales* around the Gran Vía – but the less you see of these areas, the better. Fortunately, you can choose from a wide range near the Alhambra and in the older parts of town.

Luxury (€€€€€)

*****Palacio de Santa Paula**, Gran Vía de Colón 31, **t** 95 880 57 40, *www.ac-hotels.com*. The city's first five-star hotel, in a converted convent, with opulent rooms and suites set around a vast cloister.

*****Parador Nacional San Francisco**, **t** 95 822 14 40, *granada@parador.es*. Right in the Alhambra, this is perhaps the most famous of all *paradores*, in a convent where Queen Isabel was interred. It is beautiful, very expensive and small; book well in advance – a year ahead, perhaps, is recommended.

★ Casa del Aljarife >>

***Hotel Plaza Nueva**, Plaza Nueva 2, **t** 95 821 52 73, *www.hotelplazanueva.com*. An immaculate hotel right on the square, with views of the Alhambra. Rates leap in high season.

Very Expensive (€€€€)

****Alhambra Palace**, Pza Arquitecto García de Paredes 1, **t** 95 822 14 68, *www.h-alhambrapalace.es* A grand neo-Moorish hotel at the back of the Alhambra. Most of the comfortable rooms have fabulous city views.

***Casa Morisca**, Cuesta de la Victoria 9, **t** 95 822 11 00, *www.hotelcasamorisca.com*. A beautiful converted 15th-century house just below the Alhambra, with a patio garden and coolly stylish rooms.

★ Casa de los Migueletes >

Casa de los Migueletes, C/Benalúa 11, **t** 95 821 07 00, *www.casamigueletes.com*. One of Granada's latest boutique hotels; this beautifully restored 17th-century mansion in the Albaicín has simply furnished, elegant rooms with beams and lashings of white linen, plus patios, galleries and views.

***El Ladrón de Agua**, C/del Darro 13, **t** 95 821 50 40, *www.ladrondeagua.com*. An exquisite 16th-century *palacio* in the heart of the Albaicín has been converted to contain this enchanting hotel, with fabulous Alhambra views. There's a restaurant for guests only. Prices vary according to the room; some are in the *expensive* category.

★ Britz >>

Expensive (€€€)

***Palacio de Santa Inés**, Cuesta de Santa Inés 9, **t** 95 822 23 62, *www.palaciosantaines.com*. A 16th-century palace in the Albaicín with murals in the patio attributed to Alejandro Mayner, Raphael's disciple. Some rooms have priceless views of the Alhambra. Parking.

***Los Ángeles**, Cuesta Escoriaza 17, **t** 95 822 14 24. Below the Alhambra, with swimming pool and a/c.

***Hotel Navas**, C/Navas 24, **t** 95 822 59 59, *www.hotelesporcel.com*. In an excellent spot; quiet rooms, air-conditioning; good restaurant.

*Hotel América**, Real de la Alhambra 53, **t** 95 822 74 71. Right beside the *parador* but up to a third of the price, with simple, pretty rooms and a delightful garden and patio.

Casa del Aljarife, Placeta de la Cruz Verde 2, **t** 95 822 24 25, *www.casadelaljarife.com*. 17th-century Moorish house with refurbished rooms. One of a handful of hotels in the Albaicín and one of the most delightful places to stay, with Alhambra views. Only four rooms, so book in advance.

Moderate (€€)

The residential area around the Campo del Principe hides some possibilities.

Hotel Maciá Plaza, Plaza Nueva 4, **t** 95 822 75 36, *www.maciahoteles.com*. A good bet if you want a few more mod cons than the *hostales* and *pensiones* in this area.

Cuevas El Abanico, Verea de Enmedio 89, **t** 95 822 61 99, *www.el-abanico.com*. Your very own Sacromonte cave – each sleeps 1–5 people and has its own kitchen area. Two nights min.

Pensión La Ninfa, C/Cocheras de San Cecilio 9, **t** 95 822 26 61. A very quirky hotel covered in ceramic plates, jars and other bits and bobs, overlooking the lively Campo del Principe. Simple restaurant across the square.

Inexpensive (€)

For cheap *hostales*, the first place to look is the Cuesta de Gomérez, the street leading up to the Alhambra from Plaza Nueva. Failing this, try around Plaza del Carmen.

Britz, Cuesta de Gomérez 1, **t 95 822 36 52. Bright and cheerful; rooms with or without bathrooms.

Lisboa, Pza del Carmen 27, **t** 95 822 14 13. Adequate, if uninspiring.

*Hotel Niza**, C/Navas 16, **t** 95 822 54 30, *www.hniza.com*. Good value but in a noisy location, between a number of bars.

*Posada Doña Lupe, C/Alhambra s/n, t 95 822 14 73, *www.donalupegranada.com*. An excellent budget choice near the Alhambra, popular with students and backpackers. There's even a rooftop pool (*summer only*).

Landázuri, Cuesta de Gomérez 24, t 95 822 14 06. With a restaurant and a small roof terrace. Parking (€10).

Hostal Suecia, C/Molinos (Huerta Los Ángeles), t 95 822 50 44. A delightful budget option: clean, quiet, in its own grounds, with parking and views of the palace.

Viena, Cuesta de Gomérez, t 95 822 18 59, *www.hostalviena.com*. One of three good Austrian-run budget options around Cuesta de Gomérez; all are clean and functional.

Off Calle San Juan de Dios, in the university area, there are dozens of small *hostales* that are used to accommodating students:

Hostal Venecia, Cuesta de Gomérez 2, t 95 822 39 87. Lovely *hostal* with lots of character and friendly owners.

*San Joaquín, C/Mano de Hierro 17, t 95 828 28 79. Has a pretty patio.

Eating Out in Granada

Granada isn't known for its cuisine. There are too many touristy places around the Plaza Nueva, with very little to distinguish between them. Below are some better finds.

Expensive (€€€€)

El Huerto de Juan Ranas, Callejón de Atarazana 8, t 95 828 69 25. Magical, romantic restaurant in the Albaicín with views of the Alhambra from the terrace.

Moderate (€€€)

Chikito, Pza de Campillo 9, t 95 822 33 64. Popular with *granadinos*, serving classic Granada dishes in an intimate atmosphere. Built on the site of another of Lorca's erstwhile haunts. Great tapas bar, too.

Cunini, Plaza de Pescadería 14, t 95 825 07 77. The *granadinos* trust dining out at this place, where the menu depends on availability. *Closed Sun eve and Mon.*

Sevilla, Oficios 12, t 95 822 12 23. Dating from 1930, there are four dining rooms and an outdoor terrace, plus a popular tapas bar. Local dishes like *sopa sevillana* (shellfish soup).

Mirador de Morayma, C/Pianista García Carrillo 2, Albaicín, t 95 822 82 90. In a charming 16th-century house with views over the Alhambra from the top-floor dining room. *Closed Sun eve.*

Tragaluz, C/Nevot 26, t 95 822 29 24. Enjoy delicious Moorish cuisine, like houmous and tagines, in a fashionable setting. *Closed Mon.*

Mesón Antonio, Ecce Homo 6, t 95 822 95 99. No better in Granada for agreeable dining in an intimate family-run restaurant. *Closed Sun, and July–Aug.*

Tendido 1, Avda Doctor Olóriz 25, t 95 827 23 02. Huge, atmospheric restaurant underneath the bullring. Tapas and fixed-price menus.

Inexpensive (€€)

La Entriaya (Casa Rafa), C/Pagés 15, t 95 828 53 11. A tiny bar with a *comedor* tucked away at the back: off the tourist track, at the top of the Albaicín. Home-cooked dishes, tapas and *raciones*. The lunch *menú* is €8.

El Ladrillo, C/Panaderos del Albaicín s/n, t 95 828 61 23. This friendly restaurant In the Albaicín has a pretty patio and serves up delicious soups, grilled meat and fish.

Tapas Bars

Granada rivals Sevilla for its tapas and has a fine tradition of serving up mini-meals for the price of a drink. Areas worth exploring are the roads off the top end of Gran Vía and the Plaza Nueva, particularly *calles* Almireceros, Joaquín Costa, Elvira and Cetti Meriém. Near the cathedral, Plaza Bib-Rambla and C/Pescadería are particularly good.

Leading up into the Albaicín are a number of Moroccan-style tea bars, or *teterías*, where you can sip expensive mint tea in Alhambra-style décor. Try in particular *calles* Calderias Vieja and Nueva, and Carcel Alta.

El Bañuelo Tetería, C/Bañuelos. One of the most charming *teterías* in Granada, with quiet, cushioned nooks

(★) El Huerto de Juan Ranas >

and silver teapots, Arabic cakes and views of the Alhambra.

Bar Casa Julio, C/Hermosa s/n. This tiny locals' bar is tucked down a narrow passage. You don't choose tapas – they come free with your drink, but they're always good.

⭐ Castañeda >

Castañeda, C/Elvira 5. Great *andaluz* bar with tiles and huge barrels; generous and reasonably priced tapas.

La Cava, Plaza del Realejo 5. Tiny wood-panelled wine shop; good selection of wines and a few tapas.

La Fragua, C/Panaderos 14. At the top of the Albaicín, this is a simple but popular local haunt with a young, hippyish crowd.

Bar Gracia, C/Gracia 21. Creative tapas and *raciones* to the accompaniment of flamenco.

Bodega La Mancha, C/Joaquín Costa s/n. Another classic *andaluz* bar with *vermut* from the barrel; good range of wines, tapas, *raciones* and *bocadillos* (filled baguettes).

Las Tinajas, C/Martínez Campos 17. A classy, old-fashioned tapas bar.

Entertainment and Nightlife in Granada

Flamenco

Granada is one of the best places in Andalucía to catch flamenco. Though there are more touristy shows on offer in the caves of Sacromonte (the tourist office has a list), there are also some more spontaneous venues, but take care up here at night. Most can be found along the Camino del Sacromonte. Try to get recommendations from locals on who's performing while you are in town; **Festival Discos**, C/San Sebastián 10 (just off Plaza Bib-Rambla), is a music shop with a friendly owner who is usually happy to make a few recommendations.

Bars and Nightclubs

Granada's nightlife is centred in the streets around the Plaza Nueva and in the new part of town, along C/Pedro Antonio de Alarcón (where there are plenty of bars full of local teenagers).

El Camborio, Camino del Sacromonte, 47, Sacromonte. One of several discos popular with locals in Sacromonte.

Bar Candela, C/Sta Escolástica 11. A small, bohemian bar with a great atmosphere.

Eshavira, Postigo de la Cuna 2 (off C/Elvira), t 95 829 41 25. An old Moorish-style house with regular live performances of flamenco, jazz and world music (*Thurs and Sun, Sept–June only*).

Cervecería La Riviera, C/Cetti Meriém 7. This young bar is a good place to start the night.

Bar Makeba, Placeta Sillería 7. A tiny, packed, central bar, with great African and Latin music, good cocktails and dancing later on.

Granada Province

From everywhere in Granada, the mountains peer over the tops of buildings. Until the 20th century they were associated with the so-called icemen, who made the gruelling journey to the peaks and back again with chunks of ice to sell in town. Today, Spain's loftiest peaks are rather more accessible.

The Sierra Nevada and Las Alpujarras

Dress warmly. As the name implies, the Sierra Nevada is snow-capped nearly all year, and even in late July and August it's as chilly and windy as you would expect it to be, some 3,300m (10,825ft) above sea level. These mountains, a geological curiosity of sorts, are

Getting to the Sierra Nevada and Las Alpujarras

Sierra Nevada

There are two or three buses a day from the main bus station in Granada, to the main square of the ski resort, **Pradollano**. Buses are operated by **Autocares Bonal**, **t** 95 827 31 00. Some 20km before you reach Veleta, you'll enter the Pradollano ski area; from here there are cable cars up to the peak itself.

Las Alpujarras

Some years ago it was still possible to penetrate the white villages of Las Alpujarras by bus over the top of the Sierra Nevada. However, the high road past Mulhacén has been closed to all motorized traffic, even in high summer. If you still wish to take this incredibly scenic route you can walk, cycle or go by horse, in the summer months. **Alsina Graells**, **t** 95 818 54 80, operates infrequent bus services from Granada's main bus station to Las Alpujarras, but to explore this region properly you'll need your own transport.

just an oversized chunk of the Penibetic System, the chain that stretches from Arcos de la Frontera almost to Murcia. Their highest peak, **Mulhacén** (3,481m/11,420ft), is less than 40km from the coast. From Granada you can see nearly all of the Sierra: a jagged snowy wall without any really distinctive peaks. The highest expanses are barren and frosty, but on a clear day they offer a view to Morocco. Mulhacén and especially its sister peak **Veleta** (3,392m/11,125ft) can be climbed without too much exertion.

Up until quite recently, the area was fairly inaccessible and the facilities – certainly compared with Alpine standards – pretty basic. But the place has come on in leaps and bounds in recent years – so much so that it was deemed good enough to host the 1995 World Skiing Championships (which were postponed until 1996, owing to a lack of snow). The Sierra Nevada cannot compete in terms of scale and variety with Alpine resorts but there are more than enough pistes to detain you for a long weekend.

 Las Alpujarras

Once, you could cross the Sierra Nevada by a narrow, twisting road into **Las Alpujarras**, a string of white villages along the valley of the Río Guadalfeo, between the Sierra Nevada and the little Contraviesa chain along the sea coast. Now you have to head south from Granada to reach them, but on the way you'll pass the spot called **Suspiro de Moro**, where poor Boabdil sighed as he took his last look back over Granada (now, sadly, just a signpost on the motorway). His mother was less than sympathetic – 'You weep like a woman for what you were incapable of defending like a man,' she told him. It gave Salman Rushdie the title for his novel *The Moor's Last Sigh*. The last 33km of this route, where the road joins the Guadalfeo valley down to Motril, is one of the most scenic stretches in Spain.

In Moorish times this was a densely populated region, full of vines and orchards. Much of its population was made up of refugees from the Reconquista, coming mainly from Sevilla. Under the conditions for Granada's surrender in 1492, the region was granted as a fief to Boabdil el Chico; with forced Christianization

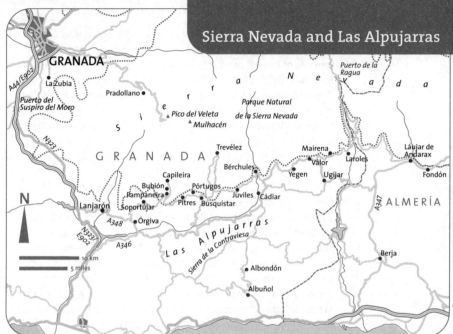

GRANADA

La Zubia
Pradollano
Puerto del
Suspiro del Moro
Pico del Veleta
Mulhacén
Parque Natural
de la Sierra Nevada
Puerto de la
Ragua

GRANADA

Trevélez
Mairena
Laujar de
Andarax
Válor
Laroles
Capileira
Bérchules
Yegen
Ugíjar
Fondón
Bubión
Pórtugos
Rampanéira
Juviles
Cádiar
Lanjarón
Pitres
Busquístar
Soportújar
Órgiva
ALMERÍA

Las Alpujarras
Sierra de la Contraviesa

Berja

Albondón
Albuñol

10 km
5 miles

and the resulting revolts, however, the population was exiled and replaced by settlers from the north.

Though often described as one of the most inaccessible corners of Spain, this region has attracted growing numbers of visitors since Gerald Brenan wrote *South from Granada* and, more recently, Chris Stewart wrote *Driving Over Lemons* and its two sequels, an account of setting up home in one of the remoter corners of this region. The roads wind past stepped fields, cascades of water, high pastures and sudden drops, and when the almond trees are in blossom it is at its most appealing. Unlike the other Andalucían villages with their red-tiled roofs, the *pueblos* of Las Alpujarras are flat-roofed. Though you won't be the only visitors to Las Alpujarras, the region is hardly spoiled; and with the villages relatively close to each other, and plenty of wild country on either side, it's a great spot for hiking or just finding some peace and quiet.

Lanjarón, the principal tourist centre in the region, has been attracting visitors to its spas since Roman times and now markets its bottled water all across Spain. It's not particularly attractive, just a strip of road lined with functional-looking spas. There are eight springs in all, each offering a different blend of natural minerals, while shops along the main street offer complementary remedies for whatever ails you. The ruined Moorish castle on the hill saw the Moors' last stand against the imperial troops on 8 March 1500. Well and truly Catholic today, Lanjarón's *Semana Santa* celebrations are the most famous in the province.

Órgiva was made the regional capital by Isabel II in 1839 and it remains the biggest town of Las Alpujarras today. There are few remains of its Moorish past; the castle of the Counts of Sástago may look the part but it dates from the 17th century. The Renaissance church has a carving by Martínez Montañés and there is an old olive mill just outside the town (*see* p.310). Órgiva springs to life on Thursdays, when everyone congregates for the weekly market. The town has become a magnet for New Age travellers and you can't fail to notice them or their beaten-up transit vans passing through the streets.

From here you'll have a choice of keeping to the main road for Ugíjar or heading north through the highest and loveliest part of the region, with typical white villages climbing the hillsides under terraced fields. **Soportújar**, the first, has one of Las Alpujarras' surviving primeval oak groves behind it. Next comes **Pampaneira**, a pretty little town of cobbled streets. In the Plaza de la Libertad there's a **museum** dedicated to the customs and costumes of Las Alpujarras and a locally run office for the **Parque Natural de la Sierra Nevada**. All sorts of activities are on offer here, such as horse rides, skiing, hang-gliding, nature walks and caving expeditions. They also sell good maps of the park.

Tibetan Monastery of Clear Light
Camino Forestal, www.oseling.com; open daily 3–6

If you'd prefer something more contemplative, the **Tibetan Monastery of Clear Light**, the birthplace of a reincarnated Spanish Tibetan *lama*, Osel, sits above the town on the sides of a gorge, complete with a visitor centre offering retreats and courses in Mahayana Buddhism. To get there, take the road marked *camino forestal*, on the right just before the turn-off for Pampaneira; it's about 7km along a dirt track.

Bubión is a Berber-style village in a spectacular setting with a textile mill and tourist shops. This and the next village, Capileira, are within sight of each other, on a short detour along the edge of the beautiful – and walkable – ravine called Barranco de Poqueira. **Capileira** is the last village on the mountain-pass route over Mulhacén and Veleta, and sees more tourists than most. Its treasure, in the church of **Nuestra Señora de la Cabeza**, is a statue of the Virgin donated to the village by Fernando and Isabel.

North from here a tremendously scenic road crosses the Sierra Nevada. Although it is permanently closed to motor vehicles, you can do it either on foot (about 5½ hours), by bike or on horseback. Alternatively, continue on the GR421 to **Pitres**, centre of a Hispano-Japanese joint venture that produces handcrafted ballet shoes, of all things. There is a ruined hilltop mosque, and the remains of a few other Moorish buildings.

The road carries on through the villages of **Pórtugos**, a pilgrimage centre for Our Lady of Sorrows, and **Busquístar**, before arriving in **Trevélez**, on the slopes of Mulhacén. Trevélez likes to claim it's the highest village in Europe. It's also famous in Andalucía for its snow-cured hams – Henry Ford and Rossini were fans – and a ham feast is held in their honour every August. Today, Trevélez is full of tour buses, and a string of ugly developments has removed most of its former charm. This is the main starting point for climbers heading for the summit of Mulhacén and the other peaks in the Sierra Nevada. While the countryside is spectacular, there's little besides tacky tourist shops to detain other visitors. From there, the road slopes back downwards to **Juviles** and **Bérchules**, one of the villages where the tradition of carpet-weaving has been maintained since Moorish times. From here you can go down to **Cádiar**, the 'navel' of Las Alpujarras, as Gerald Brenan described it, a nondescript place with an attractive main square. From there you could cut down to the coast via **Albondón** and **Albuñol** (both famous for rosé wines), finishing at **La Rabita**, in Almería.

The A7208 from Bérchules takes you to **Yegen**, some 10km further, which became famous as the long-time home of Gerald Brenan. His house is still in the village – ask for 'La Casa del Inglés'. After that come more intensively farmed areas on the lower slopes, with oranges, vineyards and almonds. You can either hit Ugíjar or detour to the seldom-visited villages of **Laroles** and **Mairena** on the slopes of **La Ragua**, one of the last high peaks of the Sierra Nevada. In 1569 Fernando de Córdoba y Válor rallied the last remaining Moors in the area to revolt against the Christians; **Válor** is the site of the Moors' last stand. The events are recreated in the annual 'Moors and Christians' festival in September.

The A337 will take you north over the mountains and towards Guadix (*see* p.312). Farther east, through countryside that rapidly changes from healthy green to dry brown, the road enters Almería province and the town of **Láujar de Andarax**. It was here that the deposed Boabdil planned on setting up his court to rule the Alpujarras after being expelled from Granada in 1492. But his plans were short-lived, and in less than a year the Christian kings had reneged on their promise and expelled him. His last view of Spain was from Adra before he set sail for Africa.

A few kilometres on, the village of **Fondón** is of particular interest; an Australian architect, Donald Grey, and his Spanish partner, José Antonio Garvayo, have set up a school to teach the traditional crafts of ironwork, carpentry, tile- and brick-making, so most of the buildings have been restored and Fondón is now a model village. The church tower was once a mosque's minaret.

The road from here passes through some nondescript villages before arriving in **Alhama de Almería**, a spa town since Moorish times. You can take the waters here or drop down to the coast and Almería.

Tourist Information in the Sierra Nevada and Alpujarras

For **skiing information**, contact the tourist office in Granada, or visit the excellent website *www.sierranevada ski.com*. The central reservation number for accommodation and ski packages is **t** 90 270 80 90.

Where to Stay and Eat in the Sierra Nevada and Alpujarras

Most of the ski hotels close from June to December. Among the modern hotels in the ski resort of Pradollano, none stands out; in skiing season accommodation at these places means a week's stay on half board for €500–1,000.

In Las Alpujarras, Lanjarón has most of the rooms; a score of good bargains in the €40–50 range are to be found on or near the main road into town, the Avenida Andalucía, and its continuation, the Avenida de la Alpujarra. It also has the majority of the upmarket accommodation. Elsewhere, you'll find acceptable rooms and food in Órgiva, Pampaneira, Capileira and Ugíjar. The area abounds in apartments, *casas rurales* and privately rented houses for longer stays. You can pick up lists of these from the tourism offices in the area, including **Rustic Blue**, **t** 95 876 33 81, *www. rusticblue.com*, and **Global Spirit**, Ctra de la Sierra s/n, **t** 97 132 51 11, *www. global-spirit.com*, both in Bubión.

(★) **Casa Rocio >>**

(i) **Lanjarón >**
Avda de Madrid,
t *95 877 02 02;*
opening times vary

(i) **Pampaneira >>**
Parque Natural de la
Sierra Nevada, Plaza de
la Libertad s/n, **t** *95 876*
31 27; open summer
Tues–Sat 10–2 and 4–7,
winter 10–2 and 3–6;
Mon and Sun 10–3

Lanjarón ✉ 18420

***Miramar, Avda Andalucía 10, **t** 95 877 01 61, *www.elhotelmiramar. com* (€€€). Lanjarón's plushest hotel, with pretty terraces and a pool.

***Alcadima, C/Francisco Tarrega 3, **t** 95 877 08 09, *www.alcadima.com* (€€). In one of the best spots in town, with rooms set round a pool/dining area with views to the castle and across the valley. They also let apartments for longer stays.

***Nuevo Palas, Avda de Alpujarra 24, **t** 95 877 00 86, *www.hotelnuevopalas. com* (€€). A traditional hotel: comfort-

able rooms with views, a tiny pool, gym, games room and restaurant.

*España, Avda Andalucía 44, **t** 95 877 01 87, *h.espana@turinet.net* (€€). Excellent value for what it offers, which includes a pool, gardens and plenty of old-fashioned charm.

Alcadima, C/Francisco Tarrega 3, **t** 95 877 08 09, *www.alcadima.com* (€€). In the hotel of the same name; good value, with gardens, terraces, pool and tennis court.

El Rincón de Jamón, Pza Constitución 1, **t** 95 877 02 04. Come here to enjoy a *copa* of *vino* and a few slices of *jamón* from Trevélez, in spit-and-sawdust surroundings.

Órgiva ✉ 18400

***Taray, Ctra Talbate-Albuñol, km 18, **t** 95 878 45 25, *www.turgranada.com/ hoteltaray* (€€€–€€). On the road out of Órgiva, one of the best places to stay in this area: comfortable rooms in a *cortijo*-style hotel, set round a large pool, and with a bar and restaurant.

Casa Rocio, Ctra A348 Lanjarón-Almería, km 17.9, **t** 95 878 57 14, *www. casaruralrocio.com* (€€). This lovely old stone house (just outside Órgiva) has been converted into a *casa rural*.

El Molino, C/González Robles 16, **t** (mobile) 646 616 628, *www.casa ruralelmolino.com* (€€). Friendly little five-bedroom B&B in a converted mill, with wood-beamed ceilings and open fires, a patio garden, pool and outdoor Jacuzzi.

Ugíjar ✉ 18480

Hostal Vidaña, Ctra de Almería, **t** 95 876 70 10 (€). Serves up huge portions of mountain fare, such as partridge, goat and rabbit; also provides basic accommodation.

Aben-Humeya, Los Bolos, Válor, **t** 95 885 18 10 (€). Excellent *alpujarraneña* cuisine in this tiny village north of Ugíjar. The wine list features a lot of locally produced organic wines.

Pampaneira ✉ 18411

*Hostal Ruta de Mulhacén, Avda Alpujarra 6, **t** 95 876 30 10, *www.rutadelmulhacen.com* (€). On the main road as you go through the town, this is simple but comfortable; traditional prints on the beds.

⭐ Alcazaba de Busquístar >>

*Hostal Pampaneira, José Antonio 1, t 95 876 30 02 (€). Slightly cheaper and a bit more basic.

Guillermo, C/Pampaneira, km 46, t 95 876 30 23 (€). Pleasant, good-value bar and restaurant with a terrace affording superb views.

Bubión ✉ 18412

Hostal Las Terrazas, Plaza del Sol s/n, t 95 876 30 34, *www.terrazas alpujarra.com* (€). A perfectly acceptable budget option with simple en-suite rooms in the *hostal*. The owners also run good-value apartments (€€), with log fires and *terrazas*. Breathtaking views across the valley.

Villa Turística de Bubión, Barrio Alto s/n, t 95 876 39 09, *www.villabubion.com* (€€). Self-catering apartments with the advantages of a hotel. Prices depend on apartment size.

La Artesa, C/Carretera 2, t 95 876 30 82 (€€). The best restaurant, serving hearty, well-priced fare.

Teide, C/Carretera s/n, t 95 876 30 84 (€€). Another good restaurant, with a shady terrace.

Capileira ✉ 18143

***Finca Los Llanos, Ctra de Sierra Nevada, t 95 876 30 71, *www.hotel fincalosllanos.com* (€€€). A hotel with a huge pool; its restaurant is known for its aubergines in honey.

Mesón Poqueira, Doctor Castilla 6, t 95 876 30 48 (€). Rooms with a view, and a good restaurant.

Panjuila, Ctra de Sierra s/n, t 95 876 30 61 (on the road just outside the village). If you're here on a Thursday then track down this café-restaurant to see some flamenco.

Pitres ✉ 18414

**Posada San Roque, C/Cruz,1, t 95 885 75 28 (€€). Simple whitewashed hotel, with airy rooms, beamed ceilings and a good little restaurant.

Sierra y Mar, La Taha, t 95 876 61 71, *www.sierraymar.com* (€). Pretty rooms in a simple stone house surrounded by gardens. Charming hosts, use of kitchen, and an unforgettable view.

Pórtugos ✉ 18415

**Nuevo Malagueño, Ctra Órgiva–Trevélez, t 95 876 60 98 (€€). Offers good rooms and views.

Busquístar ✉ 18416

***Alcazaba de Busquístar, Ctra Órgiva–Láujar, km 37, t 95 885 86 87, *www.alcazabadebusquistar.com* (€€€). One of the most luxurious options, a modern hotel in traditional Alpujarras style. Rustically decorated apartments and studios, all with log fires, kitchen, phone and satellite TV. There is a heated indoor pool, squash court, excellent restaurant, three cafés and a games room.

Trevélez ✉ 18417

La Fragua II, Posadas s/n, t 95 885 86 28; ***La Fragua I, C/San Antonio 4 (in the Barrio del Medio), t 95 885 85 73 (both €). The original, La Fragua I, has the most atmosphere, with warm rooms and a good restaurant (€€€), which concentrates on Alpujarras specialities.

Hostal Mulhacén, Ctra Ugíjar, t 95 885 85 87 (€). Well situated for hill walks and the annual all-night pilgrimage up Spain's highest mountain at midnight on 4 August. Beside the river, where locals swim in summer.

Casa Julio, Haza de la Iglesia s/n, t 95 885 87 08 (€€). Cosy bar-restaurant, with a beamed dining room and a terrace; regional specialities.

Cadiar ✉ 18440

**Alquería de Morayma, C/Alquería de Morayma, t 95 834 32 21 (€€). Recreated *cortijo* with individual and charmingly decorated apartments for 2–6 people, pool and good restaurant. The best place to stay in town.

Yegen ✉ 18460

El Rincón de Yegen, Camino de las Eras, t 95 885 12 70 (€€). Probably the best place to stay, just east of the village with a pool and a good restaurant. It also offers *casas rurales* to let.

La Fuente, in the main square, t 95 885 10 67 (€). A bar with rooms, just round the corner from Gerald Brenan's house. Also lets apartments.

Láujar de Andarax ✉ 04470

**Almirez, Ctra Láujar-Órgiva, km 1.6, t 95 051 35 14, *www.hotelalmirez.com* (€). Modern, family-run hotel in a rural setting, with a pool and a restaurant.

Alhama de Almería ✉ 04400

**San Nicolás, C/Baños s/n, t 95 064 13 61 (€€€–€€). On the site of the original Moorish baths, offering comfortable rooms.

Pradollano and Monachil (Sol y Nieve) ✉ 18196

Most of what you'll need for **skiing** can be found here: ski hire shops rent out the boots and skis for about €30–40. What is reputed to be the biggest covered car park in Spain has space for almost 3,000 cars.

Ski passes cost €27–35 a day, depending on the season. Seasoned alpine skiers will not be hugely challenged by the slopes, but there are plenty of wide gentle pistes for beginners. There is plenty for two or three days, and the views from the top of Veleta, across to Morocco on clear days, are unsurpassable.

All hotels listed below are open year-round unless stated. Prices mostly drop by half in summer.

Hotel Rumaykiyya, Urb Solynieve, Monachil, t 95 848 14 00 (€€€€€). A luxurious hotel with spacious, well-equipped rooms and a spa with massage available for those aching post-piste muscles.

****Meliá Sierra Nevada, C/Pradollano s/n, t 95 848 03 00, *www.solmelia.es* (€€€€). Huge block back from the square; similar luxuries as above, at a slightly higher price.

****Kenia Nevada, C/Virgen de las Nieves 6, t 95 848 09 11, *www. kenianevada.com* (€€€€). Alpine-style, with a Jacuzzi, pool, gym and sauna. A five-day ski package here for two costs around €700 in the high season.

***Ziryab, Plaza de Andalucia, t 95 848 05 12, *hziryab@cetursa.es* (€€€€–€€€). On the main square, with big, comfortable rooms and chunky wooden furniture.

**El Ciervo, t 95 848 04 09 (€€€). Large *pensión. Open Dec–April.*

Albergue Universitario, Peñones de San Francisco, t 95 848 01 22 (€€–€). Cheaper accommodation like this can be had in this village at the end of the bus route.

Most restaurants are only open in the season, and are a little pretentious – but that's ski resorts for you.

Restaurante Nevasol, next to the Veleta cable-car station (€€–€). Come up here by cable car to enjoy the view on the way, as well as from the restaurant terrace.

Around the Sierra Nevada

It's a better road entering Granada from the west than when you are leaving it to the east. Between the city and Murcia are some of the bleakest landscapes in Spain. The first village you pass through is **Purullena**, long famous for its pretty ceramic ware; the entire stretch of highway through it is lined with stands and displays.

The poverty of this region has long forced many of its inhabitants to live in caves, and nowhere more so than in **Guadix**. Several thousand of this city's population, most of them Gypsies, have homes – complete with whitewashed façades, chimneys and television aerials – built into the hillsides. The cave dwellings have their advantages: they're warmer in the winter and cooler in summer than most Andalucian homes, relatively spacious and well ventilated – and all you need is a pick and shovel to create a new room. If you care to venture around the caves, largely concentrated in the **Barrio de Santiago**, beware of being lured into someone's home and charged an exorbitant fee. For a better understanding of troglodyte culture head to the **Cave Museum**, at Plaza del Beato Poveda s/n.

Cave Museum
*t 95 866 08 08;
open Mon–Sat 10–2
and 4–6, Sun 10–2; adm*

The centre of Guadix is dominated by a Moorish **Alcazaba**, largely rebuilt in the 16th century; near the arcaded central **Plaza Mayor** stands the huge **cathedral**, begun by Diego de Siloé, builder of Granada's cathedral, and given its magnificent façade in the 1700s by Andalucía's great rococo eccentric, Vicente Acero. The ornate church and the imposing castle, appearing together out of the eroded hills, make a striking sight. Come for market day if you can: the entire city centre erupts, and entertainment is provided by the colourful stallholders vying for the attention of the crowd.

Forty-six kilometres northeast on the A92N lies **Baza**, important in Moorish times as a centre of silk production, in Roman times when it was known as Basti and was capital of the area, and in prehistoric times as a centre for ancient Iberian tribes. Today it is an unassuming market town, worth an afternoon's wander. It too has a cave quarter, though not as extensive as in Guadix, and a ruined **Alcazaba**. More rewarding though are the **Moorish baths** – some of the oldest in Spain, dating from at least the 10th century – which are still privately owned but can be visited (check with the *turismo*). But Baza is most famous for its *Dama de Baza*, an Iberian sculpture of a goddess dating from the 3rd or 4th century BC, unearthed nearby but now residing in Madrid; a copy can be seen

Museo Arqueológico
t 95 870 35 55; open 10–2 and 4–6.30; adm

in the local archaeological museum in Plaza Mayor. There are a couple of other buildings worth seeking out, including the 16th-century cathedral of **Santa María** and the **Palacio de los Enriquez**, just off the main square, which dates from the 15th or 16th century and has many interesting Moorish-influenced designs. The town is bounded by a **natural park** which has many ancient settlements including cave dwellings found on nearby **Mount Jabalcón**, accessible from the village of **Zújar**.

From Baza the main highway heads into Almería towards Vélez-Rubio and Vélez-Blanco (*see* p.320).

Alternatively you could make a detour to **Huéscar**, some 37km from Baza along the A92N then north along the A330 at Cúllar Baza. Huéscar has a stormy past. It constantly fell in and out of Moorish and Christian hands through the Middle Ages, suffering terribly in the Moorish uprising of the 16th century. As a result most of its buildings have been replaced with ugly modern blocks. However, seek out its church, **Santa María de la Encarnación**; both Diego de Siloé and Vandelvira had a hand in its construction.

Near the village of **Galera**, about 7km to the south, are some hilltop caves which form part of the ancient Iberian settlement of Tútugi (5th to 6th century BC). **Orce**, to the east, is built round an old Alcazaba, which has been largely reconstructed. There's not much else to distract you in these parts. If you're heading for Almería and the coast (N324), you'll pass near **La Calahorra**, which has a spectacular Renaissance castle, and **Gérgal**.

Where to Stay and Eat around the Sierra Nevada

ⓘ Guadix ›
*Avda Mariana Pineda
s/n, t 95 866 26 65,
www.guadix.es;
open Mon–Fri 8–3*

Guadix ✉ 18500

Cuevas de Pedro Antonio Alarcón, Camino de San Torcuato s/n, t 95 866 49 86, *www.cuevaspedroantonio.com* (€€). For something completely different, try a night in a cave: the hotel comprises a series of luxuriously appointed caves complete with a pool and a decent restaurant.

***Comercio, C/Mira de Amezcua 3, t 95 866 05 00, *www.hotelcomercio. com* (€€). The best place to stay, in a refurbished mansion which has seen better days, with all mod cons.

**Mulhacén, Avda Buenos Aires 41, t 95 866 07 50, *www.hotelmulhacen.*

com (€€). An acceptable alternative, near the train station, with a café.

***Carmen, Avda Mariana Pineda 61, t 95 866 15 00, *www.hotelcarmen guadix.com* (€). Has a TV and phone in each spacious, comfortable room. Plus restaurant and café.

Baza ✉ 18800

**Robemar, Ctra de Murcia 175, t 95 886 07 04, *www.hoteltobemar.com* (€€–€). The best place to stay, out of the centre, but it does boast a pool.

Pensión Anabel, C/María de Luna 3, t 95 886 09 98 (€). All rooms are en suite with TV; café attached.

Galera ✉ 18840

Casas Cuevas, C/Iglesia 1, t 95 873 90 68, *www.casas-cueva.es* (€€). Another charming, comfortable cave hotel.

Almería Province

On the coast at Adra you enter the province of Almería, Europe's sunniest, driest and hottest corner. What they call winter here lasts from the end of November to March; scores of films (famously *Lawrence of Arabia*) have been shot here, taking advantage of the light and scenery. Until the 1970s the **Costa de Almería**, difficult of access and bereft of utilities, was untouched by tourism. Now, charter flights arrive from northern Europe, but compared with the region further west, it's pleasantly underwhelming.

Almería

Almería has been a genial, dusty little port since its founding by the Phoenicians, though for a short time in the 11th century, after the fall of the caliphate, it dominated this end of al-Andalus, rivalling Córdoba and Sevilla. The upper city, with its narrow streets, tiny pastel houses and whitewashed cave dwellings hugging the looming walls of the **Alcazaba**, has retained a fine Moorish feel to this day. Built by Caliph Abd ar-Rahman II in the 10th century, the Alcazaba was the most powerful Moorish fortress in Spain; today its great curtain walls and towers defend mostly market- and flower-gardens – nothing remains of the once-splendid palace.

Alcazaba
*open May–Sept daily
10–2 and 5–8; Oct–April
daily 9.30–1.30 and
3.30–7; adm, free to
EU citizens*

The main complex is divided into three distinct sections. The first and largest is reached through the **Puerta de la Justicia**, which opens out on to a large space consisting mainly of flowerbeds. It is hard to imagine that this once contained the military barracks as

Getting to and around Almería Province

By Air

Almería's **airport** is 8km from the city on the road to Níjar, **t** 95 033 31 11, *www.aena.es*. There are scheduled flights from London, Dublin and various UK cities, and plenty of charter flights to choose from in summer. There are also regular connections with Madrid, Barcelona and Melilla. Bus no.20 leaves for the airport from C/Gregorio Marañon every 40mins Mon–Fri, and every 1hr 20mins Sat–Sun, **t** 95 062 47 35.

By Boat

Acciona-Trasmediterránea, **t** 90 245 46 45, *www.trasmediterranea.com*, runs car ferries from Almería to Melilla on the North African coast, and Al Hoceima and Nador in Morocco. Book early to be sure of a place. **Ferri-Maroc**, **t** 95 027 48 00, runs services at least twice daily to Nador.

By Train

Almería's RENFE station is a block from the bus station, on Ctra Ronda, easy walking distance from the centre, **t** 90 224 02 02. There are daily regional and high-speed trains to Madrid, Barcelona and Valencia, one daily to Córdoba and two daily to Sevilla.

By Bus

The bus station, on the Plaza Barcelona, **t** 95 021 11 35, has a daily service to the major cities of the Levante up to Barcelona; also to Madrid, Granada, Sevilla, Cádiz, Málaga and Algeciras. There are two buses daily to Adra; hourly connections to Aguadulce and Roquetas; five buses daily to Berja; at least three to Cabo de Gata, four to Mojácar, two each to Níjar and Tabernas and connections to Jaén and Guadix.

---

the first line of defence. The views from here, across the entire town to the sparkling sea, are extraordinary. The second level is where the Moorish baths and palaces, the private residences and leaders' homes once stood, now an ugly open space resembling an archaeological dig – a few taped-off ruins and scratched-out signs the only indication of the glory that once stood here. The third level was added by the Catholic Kings and bears a coat of arms on the **Torre de Homenaje**. Look to the west of here and you will see **Barrio de La Chanca**, the poorest part of the city, where you can make out front doors leading into former cave dwellings. The main structure is joined to the northern hills by the **wall of Jayrán**, which rises up towards a high cross. This can be visited on the same ticket.

Parque de Rescate de la Fauna Sahariana
t 95 028 10 45

Between the two is the **Parque de Rescate de la Fauna Sahariana** (Centre for the Rescue of Animals of the Sahara) where gazelles and other African animals are cared for: before going up, get permission from the centre's headquarters off the Avda de Federico García Lorca (C/General Segura 1) – they'll give you a permit to wander among the cages and enclosures of a variety of endangered animals, in an environment that must feel like home.

Cathedral
open Mon–Fri 10–5, Sat 10–1; adm

Almería's **cathedral**, begun in 1524 on the site of a mosque destroyed by an earthquake, was built to defend against marauding Berber pirates; its four mighty towers once held cannons. On the eastern wall you can make out the *indalo*, symbol of Almería, which was originally found in a cave some 4,000 years BC. On the front is another inscription, 'José Antonio Primo de Rivera' – rather bizarre considering Almería was a Republican stronghold and one of the last cities to fall to Franco. Inside there are a two paintings worth seeing, an *Annunciation* by Cano and an *Immaculate Conception* by Murillo, as well as a red and black marble altar; otherwise it's a huge and barren vault. Prettier, and boasting a fine carving of *St James* (Santiago) *Matamoros* ('Matamoros' means 'the Moor-slayer') and a minaret-like tower, is **Santiago El Viejo**, just off the Puerta de Purchena near the top of the Paseo de Almería. It's a bit unusual to find a pilgrimage church, complete with St James's cockleshells, so far off the main routes.

Almería's small archaeological museum has been closed for some time and is in no danger of reopening, but it contains remains from the remarkable Neolithic culture of Los Millares, which flourished here about 3500–3000 BC. Neolithic fans will have to go to **Los Millares** itself, in stark, barren mountains about 25km north on the N324 at **Santa Fé de Mondújar**. Five thousand years ago this was rich farmland, and the people who lived here had the leisure to create one of the most advanced prehistoric civilizations in Spain. The burial mounds here are almost true temples, with interior passages and surrounding concentric stone circles, broken by concave semicircular entrances. Five millennia of erosion have made these difficult to discern, and you'll have an even harder time distinguishing the remains of the walled town that once stood nearby. Located just north of the train station, the **Centro de Arte** on Plaza Barcelona, housed in a dramatic neo-*mudéjar* building, has an interesting permanent collection of Spanish contemporary art, as well as temporary exhibitions.

Los Millares
open Wed–Sun 9–2; always ring ahead, t 677 903 404, informacion. camillares.al.ccul@junt adeandalucia.es

Centro de Arte
t 95 026 64 80; open Mon–Fri 11–2 and 6–9, Sat–Sun 11–2

Where to Stay in Almería

(i) **Almería** >
Parque de Nicolás Salmerón at Martínez Campos, t 95 027 43 55, almeria@andalucia. org; open Mon–Fri 9–7, Sat and Sun 10–2; municipal tourist office, Avda Marqués de la Ensenada 1, t 95 859 76 00

Almería ✉ 04000

****Gran Hotel Almería, Avenida Reina Regente 8, t 95 023 80 11, *www. granhotelalmeria.com* (€€€€). When on location in Almería, Hollywood denizens have traditionally checked in here. Rooms are plush, with air-conditioning, and among the diversions are a pool and bingo hall.

***Costasol, Paseo de Almería 58, t 95 023 40 11, *www.hotel.costasol.com* (€€). The city's other quality choice, located right where all the action is and with all three-star amenities.

Torreluz Hotel Complex, Plaza de las Flores 1, t 95 023 43 99, *www. amtorreluz.com* (€€). Two-, three- and four-star accommodation, all in the same pretty square. Includes a good restaurant, the **Asador Torreluz**, t 95 023 45 45.

**HR Perla, Plaza del Carmen 7, t 95 023 88 77, *www.githoteles.com* (€€). Solid, much modernized, with parking and a café.

**Congress, Plaza de las Flores 5, t 95 023 49 99 (€€). One of the newest hotels in town, with well-appointed rooms in an excellent central location in the centre of the old town.

**Baños Sierra de Alhamilla, t 95 031 74 13 (€€–€). Seven km from Almería at Pechina, look out for this prettily restored 18th-century palace next to the thermal springs.

*Sevilla, C/Granada 25, t 95 023 00 09 (€). The best in the range, well placed off the Puerta Purchena. All en suite.

Almería also has plenty of *hostales* near the **Puerta de Purchena**, **Plaza San Sebastián** and the streets around.

*Maribel, Avda F G Lorca 153, t 95 023 51 73 (€). Within easy walking distance of the bus and train stations; simple but adequate rooms.

Nixar, C/Antonio Vico 24, **t** 95 023 72 55 (€). Near the Alcazaba; basic; café attached.

Eating Out in Almería

Valentín, C/Tenor Iribarne 19, **t** 95 026 44 75 (€€). An elegant restaurant specializing in exquisitely prepared seafood and fish dishes.

El Bello Rincón, Ctra Nacional 340, km 436, **t** 95 023 84 27 (€€). Wonderfully fresh seafood and sea views. *Closed Mon, July and Aug.*

Bodegon La Gruta, **t** 95 023 93 35 (€€). Beside the Bello Rincón in a natural grotto, a decent restaurant serving mainly meat dishes and grills. *Closed Sun and Nov.*

Merendero la Playa, Playa del Alquián, **t** 95 052 01 71 (€€–€). On the beach at Perdigal, this family favourite offers great tapas and more substantial seafood dishes.

Tapas Bars

The city has a large number of tapas bars and restaurants, many of which are on a map available from the tourist office. Here is a selection to the west of Paseo de Almería:

El Barril, Parque Nicolás Salmerón 7. With a breezy terrace, and cinema-inspired décor, this offers all the standards.

La Bodeguilla, C/Trajano 16. One of the oldest and most atmospheric bars in town, this is tiny and always packed.

Bodeguilla Ramón, C/Padre Alfonso Torres 4. Atmospheric place with bullfight pictures.

Cafeteria Granada, C/Granada 26. Offers a wide range of tapas, *raciones*, *platos*, *dulces*, as well as Internet access; younger crowd.

Casa Puga, C/Jovellanos 7. A family-run place, ancient, noisy and with a vast wine list.

There are also a number of tapas bars to the east of the Paseo:

El Quinto Toro, C/Juan Leal 6. Offers good tapas in an atmospheric setting.

La Tahona, C/Reyes Católicos 30. Has a big bar downstairs and a restaurant upstairs. Its faux-French bistro style is quite appealing, and there is a huge range of nibbles on offer.

Entertainment and Nightlife in Almería

There are plenty of possibilities in the maze of streets to the west of the **Paseo de Almería**, between Puerta de Purchena and Plaza San Pedro and the streets off it. Plunge into these and you will stumble across numerous bars and discos (try the **Pub Zaguán**, C/San Leonardo s/n, for live music and theatre acts, the lively **Yelamos**, C/Real 41, or **La Clásica**, C/Poeta Villaespesa 4, which keeps on going when everything else shuts and is a classic for the *ultima copa*). However, stick to the lit streets and note that the further west you go, the seedier it becomes.

Around Almería

West of the provincial capital, near the border with Granada, is **Adra**, which was an ancient Phoenician town, and the last spot in Spain surrendered by the Moors at the moment Boabdil sailed from here to Africa. Though it's still basically a fishing and agricultural village, it has spawned **Almerimar**, a large new development of mostly villas and flats, with a new marina and one of Spain's best golf courses. From here you can dip into the eastern Alpujarras to the pretty 'city' of **Berja**, with its palatial country homes; this area supplies most of northern Europe's Christmas grapes. The bland, overbuilt resorts at **Roquetas de Mar** (more golfing) and **Aguadulce** (oldest and biggest course on the Almería coast) are easily reached from Almería by bus.

Inland from these resorts is an encroaching sea of plastic – not coastal development, but agricultural plastic, allowing a good percentage of Europe's winter vegetables to grow on the otherwise barren land. The boom town of **El Ejido** – centre of 'plastic culture' (*plasticultura*) – has grown in the past two decades from a relatively small village to the second biggest town after the region's capital, boasting a population of more than 50,000. A small few of these inhabitants are new *plasticultura* millionaires, those who realized the potential of this once worthless land, exploiting the cheap labour of immigrants and itinerant workers. Shocking working conditions in the torpid air beneath hectares of plastic tents are causing uneasiness among the locals, with strikes and riots in recent years. Meanwhile the region's meagre water supply continues to be drained dry. The only relief from the encroaching plastic is a couple of salt lakes near **Roquetas**, a good spot for birdwatching.

Almería Inland

East of Almería the road goes through the **Alhamilla** – one of the driest, most rugged and lunar of the Spanish *sierras* – and on into **Tabernas**, Europe's only desert. The A92 motorway passes by the dusty town of **Benahadux**, where you could take the A348 into the Almerían Alpujarras, and on through Rioja into an ever more arid and desolate landscape. About 24km from Almería the motorway forks – east towards Sorbas (*see* below) and west towards the small village of **Gérgal**, above which a joint German-Hispano **observatory** was constructed in the late 1970s: they claim you can see the stars more clearly here than anywhere in Europe. It's actually a series of observatories, built on the highest peak of the Sierra, at an altitude of over 2,780m (9,000ft). The Spanish handled the infrastructure; the Germans built the telescopes. You can visit the site any time by following the signs just beyond Gérgal to Calar Alto, along a hair-raising 26km road.

More interesting sights lie to the east: just beyond the fork, off the N340A (on some maps marked as the A370), lies Mini Hollywood, the town built by Sergio Leone for such classics as Clint Eastwood's first vehicle, *A Fistful of Dollars*, and subsequent spaghetti westerns including *For A Few Dollars More* and *The Good, The Bad and The Ugly*. When Leone completed the trilogy the extras from those films decided to buy the place and run it as a tourist attraction rather then let it vanish into the desert, maintaining it and re-enacting various scenes from the films, with shoot-outs and mock hangings twice a day. Today it is run and owned by a hotel group (hence the astronomical admission prices – probably the highest for any attraction in Andalucía – but worth it for fans!).

⭐ Mini
Hollywood
t 95 036 52 36; open summer 10–9; winter 10–7; adm exp

The area around the town itself is the setting for, most famously, *Lawrence of Arabia* and *Cleopatra*, and more recently *Indiana Jones and the Last Crusade* and *Conan the Barbarian*, among countless others. The reason Sergio Leone, David Lean and Steven Spielberg chose this particular spot is its extraordinarily clear light and stark landscape: here the sun shines for 3,000 hours a year and just a few millimetres of rain fall. Sadly, this paucity of rain and relentless sunshine does little good for the animals living in the **zoo** attached to the town. There are some wonderful creatures here – black panthers, Siberian tigers, jaguars, lions and hippos, all living in cramped, searing conditions in cells surrounded by electric fences. Closer to Tabernas is **Texas Hollywood**, a film studio with attached theme park, where some of above-mentioned movies were actually shot.

Texas Hollywood
www.texashollywood. com, **t** *96 016 54 58*

The main road east winds through the northern flanks of the sierra, passing first through **Tabernas**, a dusty, uninviting place, and then through a lush *huerta* of country estates before rising into a perfectly desolate region, where even in springtime green is a foreign colour.

Sorbas, with its hanging houses, is most impressive seen from the highway, but if you do care to stop there are a couple of buildings worth looking out for: two privately owned mansions on the main square, Plaza de la Constitución, belonging to the Dukes of Alba and Valoig, who own much of the land round here. A walk to the edge of town affords some great views across this bizarre landscape and precarious housing. The surrounding area forms part of the **Parque Natural de Karst En Yesos**, which has a series of caves that can be visited on a guided tour organized by the *turismo*.

Between Tabernas and Sorbas a turn-off south along the AL102 will take you to the white village of **Níjar**. The road winds along for about 20km through some wonderful terrain, blasted and weirdly beautiful. As you begin to descend you will catch glimpses of the valley, now a sea of plastic. Níjar was recently a charming oasis in an arid setting where potters actively carried on a craft introduced by the Phoenicians, but the craftsmen and their cheap tapestries now attract coachloads of tourists, who swamp the town most days. Federico García Lorca's play *Blood Wedding* was based on incidents that occurred here around the turn of the last century. From Níjar it is a short drive to the coast.

The Almería Coast

The coastal road struggles out to the **Cabo de Gata**, a natural park with pretty beaches, a solitary lighthouse and crystal-clear waters, popular with divers. The area has two main resorts, the little town of Cabo de Gata itself and San José, beyond the lighthouse. Cabo de Gata and its extension, **La Almadraba de Monteleva**, have some fine beaches but little else to detain you.

To get to **San José** you could walk, but it will take at least half an hour; to drive you have to double back on yourself – the road past the lighthouse is closed to traffic. San José is set round a small, dirty beach, used by its inhabitants as a dog toilet and general rubbish tip. Fortunately, better beaches lie either side; one of the loveliest is **Los Genoveses**, a delightful walk through scrub and cacti over the top of town.

The town itself is charming, though how long it will stay that way is unclear: the landscape is scarred with building sites and cranes. There are two diving schools, a number of good restaurants, a pretty harbour and some reasonably priced places to stay, especially out of season when prices plummet. From here you can walk or drive to numerous secluded beaches and delightful little villages including **Los Escullos**, **La Isleta de Moro** and **Las Negras**, a straggle of white houses along a pristine beach. One particularly pleasant drive is northeast along the small coastal road which rises through spectacular landscape after La Isleta, before dropping into the pretty valley of **Rodalquilar**. To reach one of the loveliest places in the park, take the unpaved but driveable road to **Agua Amarga**, a delightful town with a white-sand beach and translucent waters protected by eroded cliffs. The park ends just north of here, before **Carboneras**, an ugly town made worse by a huge cement factory. Despite this it is being developed for tourism and marks the southern point of a stretch of development which is going the way of the Costa del Sol.

Mojácar

⭐ Mojácar

Isolated amid the rugged mountains, on a hill 2km from the beach, trendy Mojácar has often been compared to a pile of sugar cubes. No town in Spain wears such a Moorish face, its little flat-roofed white houses stacked almost on top of one another. Before the equally white hotels were added to the scene a couple of decades ago, the women covered their faces with their veils when passing a stranger; a plaque by the fountain tells how the towns-people valiantly defended themselves against the army of the Catholic Kings.

Most unusually, the old women in the village used to paint a symbol known as the *indalo* (a stick figure with outstretched arms, holding up an arc) on their doors as a charm against the evil eye and thunderbolts. No one knows when this practice originated, though in the nearby caves of **Vélez-Blanco** Neolithic drawings of *indalos* dating from 3000 BC have led anthropologists to believe that this a rare case of a prehistoric symbol being handed down in one place for thousands of years. It is now the official symbol of

Almería. Before the onslaught of tourism this was a grindingly poor place, with a population reduced to just 300, post-Civil War. Today it has been heavily prettified with whitewashed houses and trinket stalls on every corner – better this, though, than the excesses of the beachfront. The coast road north to **Garrucha** is now an almost continuous stream of *urbanizaciones*; to the south it's bars, discos and English-run pubs. There's nothing but empty space as far as the Andalucía-Murcia border (and well beyond it, for that matter). The nondescript village of **Palomares** occupied all the world's headlines for a while in 1966, when an American B-52 crashed nearby and littered the countryside and sea with live hydrogen bombs.

Where to Stay and Eat around Almería

Adra ✉ 04770

★★★★Mirador de Adra, C/Fábricas 84, **t** 95 060 40 00, *www.solmelia.com* (€€€€€). Occupies a fine, secluded position some way away from the town, with views out to sea, plus two swimming pools, one indoor and one outdoor.

Roquetas de Mar ✉ 04740

This village has a vast number of top-end hotels to choose from, all offering more or less the same things – swimming pools (indoor and out), tennis, quality restaurants, but little character.

★★★★Sabinal, Avda Gaviotas, **t** 95 033 36 00, *www.hesperia.com* (€€€). Enormous, modern hotel with two swimming pools and gold nearby.

★★★★Mediterráneo Park Hotel, Pez Espada s/n, **t** 95 033 32 50, *www.mediterraneo-park.com* (€€). This probably represents the best value, offering all the facilities at roughly half the price of the other four-stars.

Hostal El Faro, Avda Sabinal 190, **t** 95 032 10 15, *www.hostalelfaro.es* (€). The budget option.

Aguadulce ✉ 04720

★★★★Meliá Almerimar, **t** 95 049 70 07, *www.solmelia.com* (€€€€). Even plusher than the likes of Playadulce (*see* below), with more facilities including a covered pool; the best deals are on their website.

★★★★Playadulce, Avda El Palmeral, **t** 95 034 12 74, *www.hotelesplaya. com* (€€€€–€€€). Two pools, a café, restaurant and tennis.

★★★★Portomagno, Pso Marítimo s/n, **t** 95 034 22 16 (€€€). Better placed and a little cheaper.

Hostal Juan de Austria II, Avda de Carlos III 150, **t** 95 034 01 63, *www. hostaljuandeaustria.com* (€€). A comfortable budget choice with parking and satellite TV for all guests.

Níjar ✉ 04700

★★Venta del Pobre, C/Venta del Pobre, **t** 95 038 51 92 (€). Has en suite rooms with air-conditioning, but it's just off the motorway.

Asensio, C/El Parque 2, **t** 95 036 03 65 (€). One of several basic *pensiones* in town.

San José ✉ 04118

In San José you have a choice between either four-star luxury hotels or simple *hostales*; rather bizarrely there is nothing much in between. For further options head up the coastline to Los Escullos, La Isleta, La Negra and Agua Amarga, where there are moderate options.

★★★★Don Ignacio, Pso Marítimo s/n, **t** 95 061 10 80, *www.servimar.net* (€€€€). A huge, modern luxury hotel and the only place right on the beach. Comfortable rooms with sea views and a small pool. Very good value out of season (mid-Sept–May), but overpriced in season. Restaurant and bar attached.

ⓘ **Sorbas**
C/Terraplén 9,
t 95 036 44 76

ⓘ **Tabernas**
Ctra Nacional 340, km 364, **t** *95 052 50 30*

ⓘ **San José >>**
C/Correos s/n,
t 95 038 02 99, www. cabodegata-nijar.es

ⓘ **Mojácar** >>
*C/Glorieta s/n, t 95 061
50 25, www.mojacar.es*

ⓘ **Carboneras**
*Ayuntamiento, Plaza del
Castillo 1, t 95 013 60 52;
open summer only*

⭐ **Tito's** >>

***El Sotillo, Ctra San Jose-Níjar, **t** 95 061 11 00, *www.cortijoelsotillo.com* (€€€€–€€€). The best place in town, a *finca*-style hotel set in its own grounds at the entrance to the village, with large reception areas, pool table, swimming pool, big bedrooms and a good restaurant. Horse-riding on offer.

Hotel Atalaya, C/Correo s/n, **t 95 038 00 85, *www.atalayadelsur.com* (€€€). This well-designed place is perhaps the next best option; all rooms have little *terrazas* looking out onto a very pretty courtyard. Good-sized bedrooms with bath.

Agades, **t** 95 038 03 90 (€€–€). Located slightly out of town on the main road, but has the advantage of a pool, its own grounds, a café and airy rooms, some with *terrazas* and views.

Hostal Sol Bahía, C/Correo s/n, **t** 95 038 03 07 (€€–€). Simple but clean and bang in the centre of town, 100 yards from the beach; a few rooms with balconies.

In San José there are two eating-out areas: the road into town or the harbour; the latter, with sea views is preferable.

La Gallineta, Ctra AL 202, Níjar-San José, El Pozo de los Frailes (4km from San José), **t** 95 038 05 01 (€€€–€€). One of the smartest options in the region, in a small village in the heart of the natural park, with impeccable seafood dishes, a fine wine list and a beautiful garden terrace.

La Cueva, on the harbour, **t** 95 038 01 54 (€€€–€€). Slightly overpriced but with deliciously fresh fish, good house wines and decent meats; with a beautiful sea view over the *terraza*. Probably has the edge over the other options.

Taberna del Puerto, **t** 95 038 00 42 (€€). The prettiest place to dine in San José, with a small terrace overlooking the boats in the port and friendly service.

Mojácar ✉ 04638

****Parador Reyes Católicos, just over the road from the beach, **t** 95 047 82 50, *www.parador.es* (€€€). Probably the best option, a modern *parador* with a pool in season, tennis and air-conditioned rooms.

***El Moresco, Avda D'Encamp, **t** 95 047 80 25 (€€€). Open all year, with a rooftop pool, as well as fine views.

Virgen del Mar, on the beach, **t 95 047 22 22, *www.hotelvirgendelmar.com* (€€€). On the beach, but no pool.

***Indalo, Pso del Mediterráneo 1, **t** 95 047 80 01 (€€€–€€). A modern hotel with pool, tennis and sea views.

Mamabel's, C/Embajadores 3, **t** 95 047 24 48, *www.mamabels.com* (€€€–€€). A delightful whitewashed beach house owned by Belgian poet Jean-Marie Raths. Ask for Room No.1 if it's available. Dinner is prepared here as well.

Tito's, Mojácar Playa, **t** 95 061 50 30 (€€). A long-time favourite beach bar and restaurant run by a bohemian Calfornian, with an eclectic menu, including Thai and Mexican choices, and occasional live music during the summer months.

Casa Adelina, Avda Almería 9, Turre (3km from Mojácar), **t** 95 047 91 53 (€€). Try typical regional favourites like *gurullos* (a kind of local pasta), and tasty seafood.

Turre ✉ 04638

Finca Listonero, Cortijo Grande, **t** 95 047 90 94, *www.fincalistonero.com* (€€€). A restored farmhouse on an estate in the Turre mountains, just outside Mojácar.

Garrucha ✉ 04630

El Almejero, Explanada del Puerto, **t** 95 046 04 05 (€€). North of Mojácar, this restaurant serves super-fresh seafood, with a view of the fishing port where the catch is landed.

Language

Castellano, as Spanish is properly called, was the first modern language to have a grammar written for it. When a copy was presented to Queen Isabel in 1492, she asked what it was for. 'Your majesty', replied a perceptive bishop, 'language is the perfect instrument of empire'. In centuries to come, this concise, flexible and expressive language would prove just that: an instrument that would contribute more to Spanish unity than any laws or institutions, while spreading itself over much of the New World.

Among other European languages, Spanish is closest to Portuguese and Italian – and of course, Catalan and Gallego. Spanish, however, may have the simplest grammar of any Romance language, and if you know a little of any one of these, you will find much of the vocabulary looks familiar. It's quite easy to pick up a working knowledge of Spanish; but Spaniards speak colloquially and fast, and in Andalucía they leave out half the consonants and add some strange sounds all of their own. Expressing yourself may prove a little easier than understanding the replies. Spaniards will appreciate your efforts, and when they correct you, they aren't being snooty; they simply feel it's their duty to help you learn. Note that the Spaniards increasingly use the familiar *tú* instead of *usted* when addressing complete strangers.

For food and drink vocabulary, *see* 'Spanish Menu Reader', pp.68–70.

Pronunciation

Pronunciation is phonetic but somewhat difficult for English speakers.

Vowels

a short *a* as in 'pat'
e short *e* as in 'set'
i as *e* in 'be'
o between long *o* of 'note' and short *o* of 'hot'

u silent after *q* and in gue- and gui-; otherwise long *u* as in 'flute'
ü *w* sound, as in 'dwell'
y at end of word or meaning *and*, as **i**

Diphthongs

ai, ay as *i* in 'side'
au as *ou* in 'sound'
ei, ey as *ey* in 'they'
oi, oy as *oy* in 'boy'

Consonants

c before the vowels *i* and *e*, it's a *castellano* tradition to pronounce it as *th*; many Spaniards and all Latin Americans pronounce it in this case as an *s*
ch like *ch* in 'church'
d often becomes *th*, or is almost silent, at end of word
g before *i* or *e*, pronounced as **j** (see below)
h silent
j the *ch* in 'loch' – a guttural, throat-clearing *h*
ll *y* or *ly* as in 'million'
ñ *ny* as in 'canyon' (the ~ is called a tilde)
q *k*
r usually rolled, which takes practice
v often pronounced as *b*
z *th*, but *s* in parts of Andalucía

Stress

If the word ends in a vowel, an *n* or an *s*, the stress falls on the penultimate syllable, otherwise it falls on the last syllable; exceptions to the rule are marked with an accent.

If all this seems difficult, remember that English pronunciation is even more difficult for Spaniards; if your Spanish friends giggle at your pronunciation, get them to try to say *squirrel*.

Practise on some Spanish place names:

Madrid ma-DREED
León lay-OHN
Sevilla se-BEE-ah
Cáceres CAH-ther-es

Cuenca KWAYN-ka
Jaén ha-AIN
Sigüenza sig-WAYN-thah
Trujillo troo-HEE-oh
Jerez her-ETH
Badajoz ba-da-HOTH
Málaga MAHL-ah-gah
Alcázar ahl-CATH-ar
Valladolid ba-yah-dol-EED
Arévalo ahr-EH-bah-lo

Useful Words and Phrases

yes *sí*
no *no*
I don't know *No sé*
I don't understand Spanish *No entiendo español*
Do you speak English? *¿Habla usted inglés?*
Does someone here speak English? *¿Hay alguien que hable inglés?*
Speak slowly *Hable despacio*
Can you help me? *¿Puede usted ayudarme?*
Help! *¡Socorro!*
please *por favor*
thank you (very much) *(muchas) gracias*
you're welcome *de nada*
It doesn't matter *No importa/Es igual*
all right *está bien*
OK *vale*
excuse me *perdóneme*
Be careful! *¡Tenga cuidado!*
maybe *quizá(s)*
nothing *nada*
It is urgent! *¡Es urgente!*
How do you do? *¿Cómo está usted?*
   or more familiarly *¿Cómo estás?, ¿Qué tal?*
Well, and you? *¿Bien, y usted?*
   or more familiarly *¿Bien, y tú?*
What is your name? *¿Cómo se llama?*
   or more familiarly *¿Cómo te llamas?*
My name is ... *Me llamo ...*
My number is ... *Mi nombre es ...* (this also means 'My name is')
Hello *¡Hola!*
Goodbye *Adiós*
Good morning *Buenos días*
Good afternoon *Buenas tardes*
Good evening *Buenas noches*
What is that? *¿Qué es eso?*
What ...? *¿Qué ...?*
Who ...? *¿Quién ...?*
Where ...? *¿Dónde ...?*

When ...? *¿Cuándo ...?*
Why ...? *¿Por qué ...?*
How ...? *¿Cómo ...?*
How much? *¿Cuánto/Cuánta?*
How many? *¿Cuántos/Cuántas?*
I am lost *Me he perdido*
I am hungry/thirsty *Tengo hambre/sed*
I am sorry *Lo siento*
I am tired (man/woman) *Estoy cansado/a*
I am sleepy *Tengo sueño*
I am ill *No me siento bien*
Leave me alone *Déjeme en paz*
good *bueno/buena*
bad *malo/mala*
slow *despacio*
fast *rápido/rápida*
big *grande*
small *pequeño/pequeña*
hot *caliente*
cold *frío/fría*
toilet/toilets *servicios/aseos*
men *señores/hombres/caballeros*
women *señoras/damas*

Numbers

one *uno/una*
two/three/four *dos/tres/cuatro*
five/six/seven *cinco/seis/siete*
eight/nine/ten *ocho/nueve/diez*
eleven/twelve *once/doce*
thirteen/fourteen *trece/catorce*
fifteen/sixteen *quince/dieciséis*
seventeen/eighteen *diecisiete/dieciocho*
nineteen *diecinueve*
twenty *veinte*
twenty-one *veintiuno*
thirty/thirty-one *treinta/treinta y uno*
forty/forty-one *cuarenta/cuarenta y uno*
fifty/sixty *cincuenta/sesenta*
seventy/eighty *setenta/ochenta*
ninety *noventa*
one hundred *cien*
one hundred and one *ciento-uno*
five hundred *quinientos*
one thousand *mil*
first/second *primero/segundo*
third/fourth/fifth *tercero/cuarto/quinto*
tenth *décimo*

Time

What time is it? *¿Qué hora es?*

Language | The Beach

It is two o'clock *Son las dos*
... half past two ... *las dos y media*
... a quarter past two ... *las dos y cuarto*
... a quarter to three ... *las tres menos cuarto*
noon/midnight *mediodía/medianoche*
month/week/day *mes/semana/día*
morning/afternoon *mañana/tarde*
evening *noche*
today *hoy*
yesterday *ayer*
tomorrow *mañana*
soon *pronto*
now *ahora*
later *después*
it is early/it is late *es temprano/es tarde*

Days

Monday *lunes*
Tuesday *martes*
Wednesday *miércoles*
Thursday *jueves*
Friday *viernes*
Saturday *sábado*
Sunday *domingo*

Months

January *enero*
February *febrero*
March *marzo*
April *abril*
May *mayo*
June *junio*
July *julio*
August *agosto*
September *septiembre*
October *octubre*
November *noviembre*
December *diciembre*

Colours

red/blue/green *rojo/azul/verde*
yellow *amarillo*
orange *de color naranja*
pink/brown *rosa/marrón*
purple *púrpura, morado*
black/grey/white *negro/gris/blanco*

Shopping and Sightseeing

I would like ... *Quisiera ... /Me gustaría ...*
Where is/are ...? *¿Dónde está/están ...?*

How much is it? *¿Cuánto vale eso?*
open/closed *abierto/cerrado*
cheap/expensive *barato/caro*
shop *tienda*
antique shop *anticuario*
bakery *panadería*
butcher's *carnicería*
department store *grandes almacenes*
clothing *ropa*
shoes *zapatos*
pharmacy *farmacia*
supermarket *supermercado*
jeweller's *joyería*
kiosk *kiosko*
market *mercado*
stationer's *papelería*
sweet shop/confectioner's *confitería*
winery *bodega*
tobacconist's *estanco*
newspaper (foreign) *periódico (extranjero)*
beach *playa*
sea *mar*
church *iglesia*
hospital *hospital*
police station *comisaría*
policeman *policía*
telephone *teléfono*
museum *museo*
theatre *teatro*
booking/box office *taquilla*
post office *correos*
postage stamp *sello*
bank *banco*
money *dinero*
Do you have any change? *¿Tiene cambio?*
wallet *cartera*
purse (for holding coins) *bolsa*

The Beach

sand *arena*
sea *mar*
wave *ola*
seaweed *alga*
dune *duna*
high/low tide *marea alta/baja*
cove *cala*
bay *bahía*
lifeguard *vigilante*
lifeboat *lancha de socorro*
swimsuit *traje de baño*
sunbathe *tomar el sol*
sun cream *crema bronceadora*

tan *bronceado*
sunburn *quemadura*
sunglasses *gafas de sol*
parasol *sombrilla*
hat *sombrero*
towel *toalla*

Accommodation

Where is the hotel? *¿Dónde está el hotel?*
Do you have a room? *¿Tiene usted una habitación?*
Can I look at the room? *¿Podría ver la habitación?*
How much is the room per day/week? *¿Cuánto cuesta la habitación por día/ semana?*
... with two beds *con dos camas*
... with double bed *con una cama grande*
... with a shower/bath *con ducha/baño*
... for one person/two people *para una persona/dos personas*
... for one night/ one week *una noche/ una semana*

Transport and Tickets

aeroplane *avión*
airport *aeropuerto*
bus/coach *autobús/autocar*
bus/railway station *estación de autobuses/ de ferrocarril*
bus stop *parada*
car/automobile *coche*
customs *aduana*
platform *andén*
port *puerto*
seat *asiento*
ship *buque/barco/embarcadero*
ticket *billete*
train *tren*
I want to go to... *Deseo ir a.../Quiero ir a...*
How can I get to...? *¿Cómo puedo llegar a...?*
Where is...? *¿Dónde está...?*
When is the next...? *¿Cuándo sale el próximo...?*
What time does it leave (arrive)? *¿Parte (llega) a qué hora?*
From where does it leave? *¿De dónde sale?*
Do you stop at... ? *¿Para en... ?*
How long does the trip take? *¿Cuánto tiempo dura el viaje?*

I want a (return/round-trip) ticket to... *Quiero un billete (de ida y vuelta) a...*
How much is the fare? *¿Cuánto cuesta el billete?*
Have a good trip! *¡Buen viaje!*

Driving

rent *alquiler*
car *coche*
motorbike/moped *moto/ciclomotor*
bicycle *bicicleta*
petrol (gasoline) *gasolina*
garage *garaje*
This doesn't work *Este no funciona*
road *carretera*
motorway *autopista*
Is the road good? *¿Es buena la carretera?*
breakdown *avería*
(international) driver's licence *carnet de conducir (internacional)*
driver *conductor, chófer*
speed *velocidad*
exit *salida*
entrance *entrada*
danger *peligro*
dangerous *peligroso*
no parking *estacionamento prohibido*
narrow *estrecho/a*
give way/yield *ceda el paso*
roadworks *obras*

Directions

here *aquí*
there *allí*
close *cerca*
far *lejos*
left *izquierda*
right *derecha*
straight on *todo recto*
forwards *adelante*
backwards *hacia atrás*
up *arriba*
down *abajo*
north (n./adj.) *norte/septentrional*
south (n./adj.) *sur/meridional*
east (n./adj.) *este/oriental*
west (n./adj.) *oeste/occidental*
corner *esquina*
square *plaza*
street *calle*

Glossary

ajaracas trellis-work brick design, often decorating *mudéjar* apses

ajimez in Moorish architecture, an arched double window

alameda tree-lined promenade

albarrani projecting fortification tower joined to a main wall by a bridge

alcazaba Moorish fortress

Almohads (Muwahhids) sect of Berber origin that founded a North African dynasty and ruled Spain from 1147 to 1243

Almoravids (Murabits) North African military-religious sect that created an empire and conquered al-Andalus in the 11th century

arabesque decoration in the form of scrolling or interlacing flowers and leaves

arrabal quarter of a Moorish city

artesonado *mudéjar*-style carved wooden ceilings, panels or screens

ayuntamiento city hall

azulejo painted glazed tiles, popular in *mudéjar* work and later architecture (from the Arabic *az-zulaiy*, a piece of terracotta)

banderillero bullfighter's assistant who plants *banderillas* (sharp darts) into the base of the bull's neck to weaken the animal

barrio city quarter or neighbourhood

bodega wine bar, cellar or warehouse

bóveda vault

capilla mayor seat of the high altar in a cathedral

carmen Carmelite convent, or *morisco* villas with pleasure gardens outside Granada

carretera main road

cartuja Carthusian monastery

castrum Roman military camp, or a town plan that copies its rectilinear layout

Churrigueresque florid Baroque style of the late 17th and early 18th centuries in the manner of José Churriguera (1665–1725), architect and sculptor

ciudadela citadel

converso a Jew who converted to Christianity

coro the walled-in choir of a Spanish cathedral

coro alto raised choir

corregidor chief magistrate

corrida de toros bullfight

cortijo Andalucían country house

cúpula cupola; dome or rounded vault forming a roof or ceiling

custodia tabernacle, where sacramental vessels are kept

diputación seat of provincial government

embalse reservoir

ermita hermitage

esgrafiado style of painting, or etching designs in stucco, on a façade

estilo desornamentado austere, heavy Renaissance style inaugurated by Philip II's architect, Juan de Herrera; sometimes described as Herreran

fandango traditional dance and song, greatly influenced by the Gypsies of Andalucía

feria major festival or market, often an occasion for bullfights

finca farm, country house or estate

fonda modest hotel, from the Arabic *funduq* or inn

fuero exemption or privilege of a town or region under medieval Spanish law

grandee select member of Spain's highest nobility

hammam Moorish bath

Herreran see *estilo desornamentado*

hidalgo literally 'son of somebody' – the lowest level of the nobility, just good enough for a coat of arms

humilladero Calvary, or Stations of the Cross along a road outside town

Isabelline Gothic late 15th-century style, roughly corresponding to English perpendicular

judería Jewish quarter

junta council, or specifically, the regional government

khan inn for merchants

Kufic angular style of Arabic calligraphy originating in the city of Kufa in Mesopotamia, often used as architectural ornamentation

lonja merchants' exchange

madrasa (or *madrassa*) Muslim theological school, usually located near a mosque

majolica type of porous pottery glazed with bright metallic oxides

mantilla silk or lace scarf or shawl, worn by women to cover their head and shoulders

maqsura elevated platform, usually with grills

matador the principal bullfighter, who finally kills the bull

medina walled centre of a Moorish city

mercado market

mezquita mosque

mihrab prayer niche facing Mecca, often elaborately decorated in a mosque

mirador scenic viewpoint or belvedere

monterías hunting scenes (in art)

Moriscos Muslims who submitted to Christianization to remain in al-Andalus after the Reconquista

moufflon wild, short-fleeced mountain sheep

Mozarábs Christians under Muslim rule in Moorish Spain

mudéjar Moorish-influenced architecture, characterized by decorative use of bricks and ceramics; Spain's 'national style' in 12th to 16th centuries

muqarnas hanging masonry effect created through multiple use of support elements

ogival pointed (arches)

parador state-owned hotel, often a converted historic building

paseo promenade, or an evening walk along a promenade

patio central courtyard of a house or public building

picador bullfighter on horseback, who goads and wounds the bull with a *pica* or short lance in the early stages of a bullfight in order to weaken the animal

Plateresque heavily ornamented 16th-century Gothic style

plaza town square

plaza de toros bullring

Plaza Mayor main square at the centre of many Spanish cities, often almost totally enclosed and arcaded

posada inn or lodging house

pronunciamiento military coup

pueblo village

puente bridge

puerta gate or portal

Reconquista the Christian Reconquest of Moorish Spain beginning in 718 and completed in 1492 by the Catholic Kings

reja iron grille, either decorative inside a church or covering the exterior window of a building

retablo retable (carved or painted altarpiece)

Los Reyes Católicos the Catholic Kings, Isabel and Fernando

romería pilgrimage, usually on a saint's feast day

sagrario the chapel where the Holy Sacrament is kept

sala capitular chapterhouse

sillería choir stall

souk open-air marketplace found in Muslim countries

stele stone slab marking a grave or displaying an inscription

taifa small Moorish kingdom; especially one of the so-called Party Kingdoms which sprang up in Spain following the 1031 fall of the caliph of Córdoba

taracea inlaid wood in geometric patterns

torero bullfighter, especially one on foot

torre tower

torre del homenaje the tallest tower of fortification, sometimes detached from the wall

vega cultivated plain or fertile river valley

Further Reading

General and Travel

Baird, David, *Inside Andalusia* (Mirador Publications, 1993). Background reading. Glossy, full of history and anecdote.

Borrow, George, *The Bible in Spain* (*Indy publish.com*, 2002). One of the best-known travel books about Spain, opinionated and amusing; first published in 1842.

Brenan, Gerald, *South from Granada* (Penguin, 1998). Spain before the Civil War.

Chetwode, Penelope, *Two Middle-Aged Ladies in Andalusia* (John Murray Travel Classics, 2002). A delightful bosom-heaving *burro*-back look at the region.

Elms, Robert, *Spain: A Portrait After the General* (Heinemann, 1992). Incisive, witty, honest look at the new Spain.

Ford, Richard, *Gatherings from Spain* (Pallas Athene, 2003). A boiled-down version of the all-time classic travel book *A Handbook for Travellers in Spain*, written in 1845.

Gibson, Ian, *Lorca's Granada* (Faber and Faber, 1992). The city's association with the poet.

Josephs, Allen, *White Wall of Spain* (University Press of Florida, 1990). Interesting collection of essays on Andalucían folklore.

Lee, Laurie, *As I Walked Out One Midsummer Morning* and *A Rose for Winter*. Adventures of the young Lee in Spain in 1936, and his return 20 years later.

Stewart, Chris, *Driving Over Lemons* (Sort of Books, UK, 1999), *A Parrot in the Pepper Tree* (2002). An Englishman setting up home in a farmhouse in Las Alpujarras, Granada.

History

Carr, Raymond (ed.), *Spain: A History* (OUP, 2000). The best concise history available.

Castro, Américo, *The Structure of Spanish History* (E. L. King, 1954). A remarkable interpretation of Spain's history, published in exile during the Franco years.

Cohen, J. M. (ed.), *The Four Voyages of Christopher Columbus* (Penguin Classics).

Elliott, J. H., *Imperial Spain 1469–1714* (Penguin, 2002). Elegantly written.

Gibson, Ian, *The Assassination of Federico García Lorca* (Penguin, 1983).

Mitchell, David, *The Spanish Civil War* (Harper Collins, 1983). Anecdotal; wonderful photos.

O'Callaghan, J. F., *History of Medieval Spain* (Cornell University, 1983).

Thomas, Hugh, *The Spanish Civil War* (Penguin, 2003). The best general work.

Watt, W. H. and Cachia, P., *A History of Islamic Spain* (Edinburgh University Press, 1996).

Art and Literature

Brenan, Gerald, *The Literature of the Spanish People* (Cambridge, 1976).

Burckhardt, Titus, *Moorish Culture in Spain* (Fons Vitae, 2001). The world of al-Andalus.

García Lorca, Federico. Any works by the great Andalucían playwright and poet, who was murdered by Fascists in Granada.

Goodwin, Godfrey, *Islamic Spain* (Chronicle, 1991). Covers all the significant Islamic buildings in Spain.

Hemingway, Ernest, *For Whom the Bell Tolls* (Vintage, 2000). Set in Civil War Andalucía.

Irving, Washington, *Tales of the Alhambra* and *The Conquest of Granada* (London, 1986).

Jiménez, Juan Ramón, *Platero and I* and *Pepita Jiménez*. Noble Prize-winning poet from Andalucía. The former evokes the people and landscape of Andalucía through conversations with the poet's donkey.

Rice, David Talbot, *Islamic Art* (Thames & Hudson, 1975). A renowned introduction to the whole of Islamic art and achitecture.

Index

Main page references are in **bold**. Page references to maps are in *italics*.

About the Updater

Mary McLean has updated several Cadogan guidebooks, including *Sicily, Northern Spain* and *Bilbao & the Basque Lands*, as well as the *Madrid* city guide. She has lived in Andalucía for 15 years, has travelled extensively throughout the province and continues to be enthralled with the history, culture, and sheer beauty of this fascinating corner of southern Spain.

8th edition published 2008

Cadogan Guides is an imprint of
New Holland Publishers (UK) Ltd
London • Cape Town • Sydney • Auckland

New Holland Publishers (UK) Ltd	80 McKenzie Street	Unit 1, 66 Gibbes Street	218 Lake Road
Garfield House	Cape Town 8001	Chatswood, NSW 2067	Northcote
86–88 Edgware Road	South Africa	Australia	Auckland
London W2 2EA			New Zealand

Cadogan@nhpub.co.uk
www.cadoganguides.com
t 44 (0)20 7724 7773

Distributed in the United States by Globe Pequot, Connecticut

Copyright © Dana Facaros and Michael Pauls 1991, 1994, 1996, 1999, 2001, 2003, 2006, 2008
© 2008 New Holland Publishers (UK) Ltd

Cover photographs: © Demetrio Carrasco/JAI/Corbis, © Susannah Sayler
Photo essay photographs © Susannah Sayler
Maps © Cadogan Guides, drawn by Maidenhead Cartographic Services Ltd
Cover and photo essay design: Sarah Rianhard-Gardner
Editor: Linda McQueen
Indexing: Isobel McLean

Printed in Italy by Legoprint
A catalogue record for this book is available from the British Library

ISBN: 978-1-86011-389-5

Andalucía touring atlas

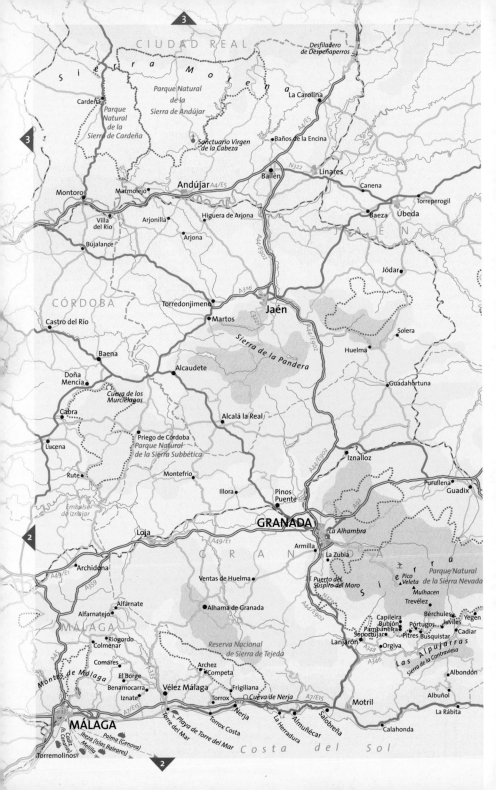

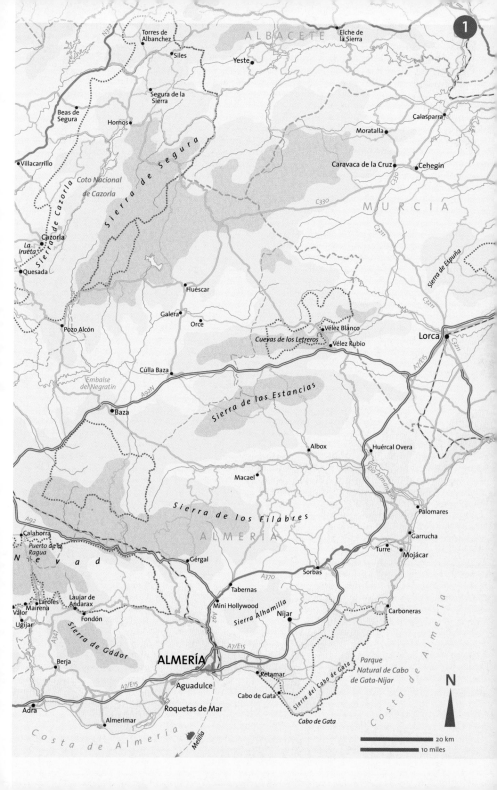

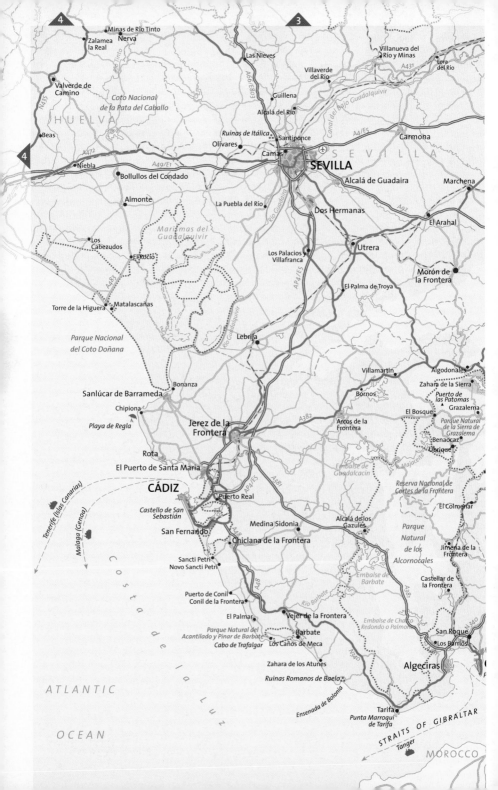

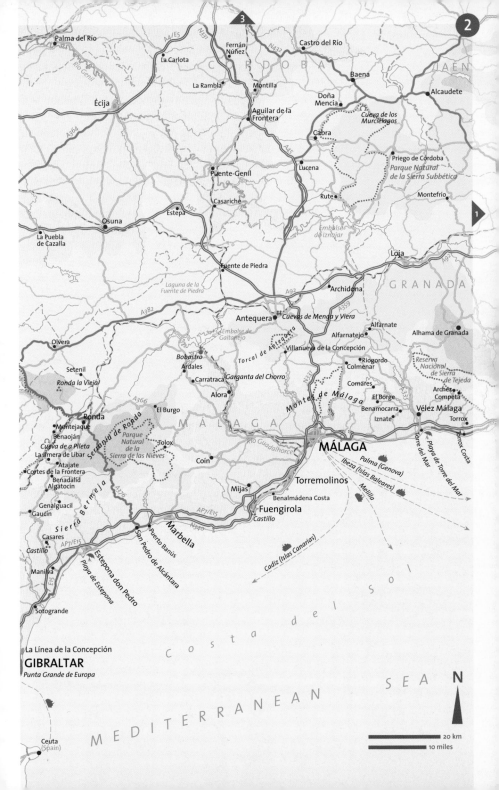

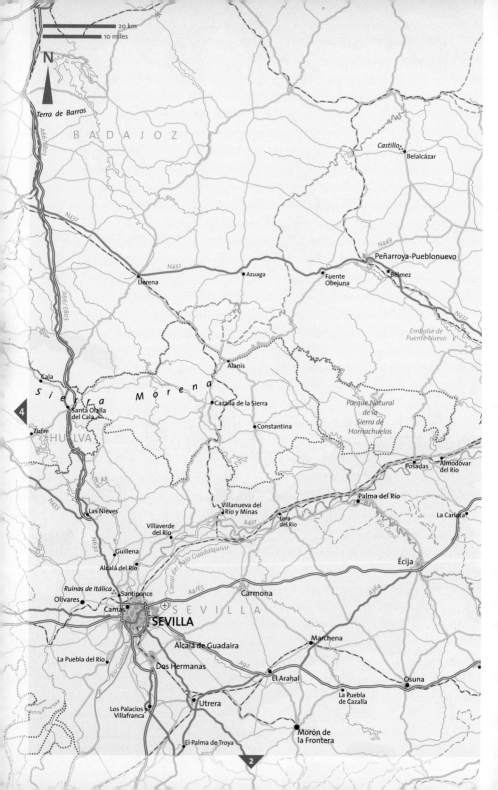

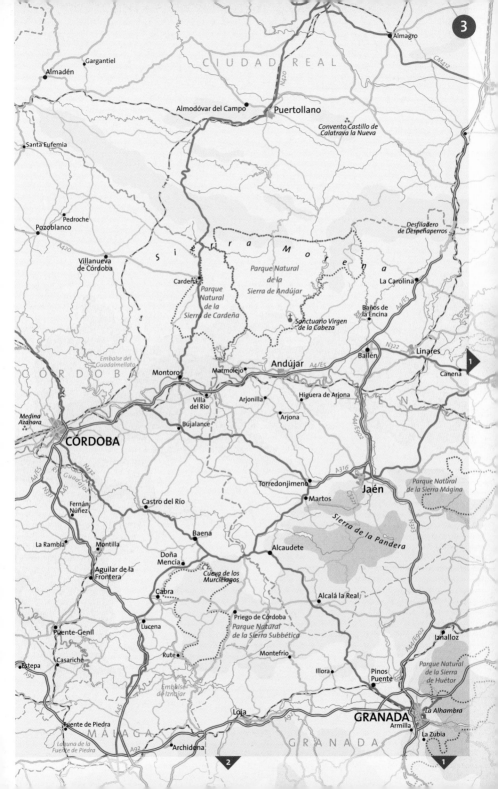